NEW PERSPECTIVES ON
Microsoft® Windows® 8

INTRODUCTORY

NEW PERSPECTIVES ON

Microsoft® Windows® 8

INTRODUCTORY

June Jamrich Parsons
Dan Oja
Lisa Ruffolo

Australia • Brazil • Japan • Korea • Mexico • Singapore • Spain • United Kingdom • United States

New Perspectives on Microsoft Windows 8, Introductory

Editor-in-Chief: Marie L. Lee

Executive Editor: Donna Gridley

Associate Acquisitions Editor: Amanda Lyons

Product Development Manager: Leigh Hefferon

Senior Product Manager: Kathy Finnegan

Product Manager: Julia Leroux-Lindsey

Associate Product Manager: Angela Lang

Editorial Assistant: Melissa Stehler

Director, Brand Manager: Jason Sakos

Brand Manager: Elinor Gregory

Director, Market Development Manager: Lisa Lyne

Market Development Managers: Gretchen Swann, Kristie Clark

Developmental Editor: Jane Pedicini

Senior Content Project Manager: Jennifer Goguen McGrail

Composition: GEX Publishing Services

Art Director: GEX Publishing Services

Text Designer: Althea Chen

Cover Art: ©Philip Meyer/Shutterstock

Copyeditor: Suzanne Huizenga

Proofreader: Kathy Orrino

Indexer: Alexandra Nickerson

© 2013 Course Technology, Cengage Learning

ALL RIGHTS RESERVED. No part of this work covered by the copyright herein may be reproduced, transmitted, stored or used in any form or by any means graphic, electronic, or mechanical, including but not limited to photocopying, recording, scanning, digitizing, taping, Web distribution, information networks, or information storage and retrieval systems, except as permitted under Section 107 or 108 of the 1976 United States Copyright Act, without the prior written permission of the publisher.

> For product information and technology assistance, contact us at
> **Cengage Learning Customer & Sales Support, 1-800-354-9706**
> For permission to use material from this text or product, submit all requests online at **www.cengage.com/permissions**
> Further permissions questions can be emailed to
> **permissionrequest@cengage.com**

Some of the product names and company names used in this book have been used for identification purposes only and may be trademarks or registered trademarks of their respective manufacturers and sellers.

Windows® is a registered trademark of Microsoft Corporation. © 2012 Microsoft. Microsoft and the Office logo are either registered trademarks or trademarks of Microsoft Corporation in the United States and/or other countries. Course Technology, Cengage Learning is an independent entity from the Microsoft Corporation, and not affiliated with Microsoft in any manner.

Disclaimer: Any fictional data related to persons or companies or URLs used throughout this book is intended for instructional purposes only. At the time this book was printed, any such data was fictional and not belonging to any real persons or companies.

Library of Congress Control Number: 2012920862

ISBN-13: 978-1-285-08088-8

ISBN-10: 1-285-08088-2

Course Technology
20 Channel Center Street
Boston, MA 02210
USA

Cengage Learning is a leading provider of customized learning solutions with office locations around the globe, including Singapore, the United Kingdom, Australia, Mexico, Brazil, and Japan. Locate your local office at:
international.cengage.com/global

Cengage Learning products are represented in Canada by Nelson Education, Ltd.

To learn more about Course Technology, visit **www.cengage.com/course technology**

To learn more about Cengage Learning, visit **www.cengage.com.**

Purchase any of our products at your local college store or at our preferred online store **www.cengagebrain.com**

ProSkills Icons © 2014 Cengage Learning.

Printed in the United States of America
1 2 3 4 5 6 7 8 9 16 15 14 13 12

Preface

The New Perspectives Series' critical-thinking, problem-solving approach is the ideal way to prepare students to transcend point-and-click skills and take advantage of all that Microsoft Windows 8 has to offer.

In developing the New Perspectives Series, our goal was to create books that give students the software concepts and practical skills they need to succeed beyond the classroom. We've updated our proven case-based pedagogy with more practical content to make learning skills more meaningful to students.

With the New Perspectives Series, students understand *why* they are learning *what* they are learning, and are fully prepared to apply their skills to real-life situations.

"This text introduces students to the new software in a very organized manner that is easy to follow. There are some very new concepts with Windows 8 that were explained and demonstrated in a way that students will understand."

—Stacy Hollins
St. Louis Community College

About This Book

This book provides coverage of the essential topics for the new Microsoft Windows 8 operating system, and includes the following features:

- Introduction to the basics of Microsoft Windows 8, offering hands-on instruction so that students can use the operating system with confidence and ease
- Guided tours of the innovative Windows 8 Start screen for people using a traditional mouse and keyboard and for people with a touchscreen computer
- Overview of the Windows 8 desktop, apps, and file system, teaching students how to start and turn off Windows, run applications, and organize files
- Exploration of the exciting advances in Windows 8, including Start screen tiles, the new Charms bar and Apps screen, and the updated File Explorer

New for this edition!

- Each tutorial has been updated with new case scenarios throughout, which provide a rich and realistic context for students to apply the concepts and skills presented.
- Some tutorials include a new Troubleshoot type of Case Problem, in which certain steps of the exercise require students to identify and correct errors—which are intentionally placed in the files students work with—to promote problem solving and critical thinking.

System Requirements

This book assumes a typical installation of Microsoft Windows 8 Pro. (Note that most tasks in this text can also be completed using the Windows 8 edition, the basic edition of the operating system.) The browser used for any steps that require a browser is Internet Explorer 10.

www.cengage.com/ct/newperspectives

> *"The clear step-by-step instructions, real-world data files, and helpful figures make New Perspectives texts excellent for courses taught in the classroom, the hybrid/blended format, or entirely online."*
> —Sylvia Amito'elau
> Coastline Community College

The New Perspectives Approach

Context
Each tutorial begins with a problem presented in a "real-world" case that is meaningful to students. The case sets the scene to help students understand what they will do in the tutorial.

Hands-on Approach
Each tutorial is divided into manageable sessions that combine reading and hands-on, step-by-step work. Colorful screenshots help guide students through the steps. **Trouble?** tips anticipate common mistakes or problems to help students stay on track and continue with the tutorial.

VISUAL OVERVIEW
Visual Overviews
Each session begins with a Visual Overview, a two-page spread that includes colorful, enlarged screenshots with numerous callouts and key term definitions, giving students a comprehensive preview of the topics covered in the session, as well as a handy study guide.

PROSKILLS
ProSkills Boxes and Exercises
ProSkills boxes provide guidance for how to use the software in real-world, professional situations, and related ProSkills exercises integrate the technology skills students learn with one or more of the following soft skills: decision-making, problem-solving, teamwork, verbal communication, and written communication.

KEY STEP
Key Steps
Important steps are highlighted in yellow with attached margin notes to help students pay close attention to completing the steps correctly and avoiding time-consuming rework.

INSIGHT
InSight Boxes
InSight boxes offer expert advice and best practices to help students achieve a deeper understanding of the concepts behind the software features and skills.

TIP
Margin Tips
Margin Tips provide helpful hints and shortcuts for more efficient use of the software. The Tips appear in the margin at key points throughout each tutorial, giving students extra information when and where they need it.

REVIEW
APPLY
Assessment
Retention is a key component to learning. At the end of each session, a series of Quick Check questions helps students test their understanding of the material before moving on. Engaging end-of-tutorial Review Assignments and Case Problems have always been a hallmark feature of the New Perspectives Series. Colorful bars and headings identify the type of exercise, making it easy to understand both the goal and level of challenge a particular assignment holds.

REFERENCE
TASK REFERENCE
GLOSSARY/INDEX
Reference
Within each tutorial, Reference boxes appear before a set of steps to provide a succinct summary and preview of how to perform a task. In addition, a complete Task Reference at the back of the book provides quick access to information on how to carry out common tasks. Finally, each book includes a combination Glossary/Index to promote easy reference of material.

www.cengage.com/ct/newperspectives

Our Complete System of Instruction

Coverage To Meet Your Needs
Whether you're looking for just a small amount of coverage or enough to fill a semester-long class, we can provide you with a textbook that meets your needs.
- Brief books typically cover the essential skills in just 2 to 4 tutorials.
- Introductory books build and expand on those skills and contain an average of 5 to 8 tutorials.
- Comprehensive books are great for a full-semester class, and contain 9 to 12+ tutorials.

So if the book you're holding does not provide the right amount of coverage for you, there's probably another offering available. Visit our Web site or contact your Cengage Learning sales representative to find out what else we offer.

CourseCasts – Learning on the Go. Always available…always relevant.
Want to keep up with the latest technology trends relevant to you? Visit http://coursecasts.course.com to find a library of weekly updated podcasts, CourseCasts, and download them to your mp3 player.

Ken Baldauf, host of CourseCasts, is a faculty member of the Florida State University Computer Science Department where he is responsible for teaching technology classes to thousands of FSU students each year. Ken is an expert in the latest technology trends; he gathers and sorts through the most pertinent news and information for CourseCasts so your students can spend their time enjoying technology, rather than trying to figure it out. Open or close your lecture with a discussion based on the latest CourseCast.

Visit us at http://coursecasts.course.com to learn on the go!

Instructor Resources
We offer more than just a book. We have all the tools you need to enhance your lectures, check students' work, and generate exams in a new, easier-to-use and completely revised package. This book's Instructor's Manual, ExamView testbank, PowerPoint presentations, data files, solution files, figure files, and a sample syllabus are all available on a single CD-ROM or for downloading at www.cengage.com.

www.cengage.com/ct/newperspectives

SAM: Skills Assessment Manager
Get your students workplace-ready with SAM, the premier proficiency-based assessment and training solution for Microsoft Office! SAM's active, hands-on environment helps students master computer skills and concepts that are essential to academic and career success.

Skill-based assessments, interactive trainings, business-centric projects, and comprehensive remediation engage students in mastering the latest Microsoft Office programs on their own, allowing instructors to spend class time teaching. SAM's efficient course setup and robust grading features provide faculty with consistency across sections. Fully interactive MindTap Readers integrate market-leading Cengage Learning content with SAM, creating a comprehensive online student learning environment.

Acknowledgments

I would like to thank the following reviewers for their contributions in the development of this text: Debi Griggs, Bellevue College; Clara Groeper, Illinois Central College; and Stacy Hollins, St. Louis Community College - Florissant Valley. Their valuable insights and excellent feedback helped to shape this text, ensuring it will meet the needs of instructors and students both in the classroom and beyond.

Many thanks also to everyone on the New Perspectives team for their guidance, insight, encouragement, and good humor, including Donna Gridley and Jennifer Goguen McGrail. Special thanks go to Julia Leroux-Lindsey, whose attention to detail and thoughtful solutions make this book more accessible, appealing, and instructive. Jane Pedicini deserves special mention for her wit and spirit, which made this project fun, and for her pursuit of clarity, which elevates this book into a superior teaching tool. I also appreciate the careful work of Susan Pedicini and Serge Palladino, Manuscript Quality Assurance testers. Additional thanks go to June Parsons and Dan Oja, on whose previous work this book is based.
– Lisa Ruffolo

www.cengage.com/ct/newperspectives

BRIEF CONTENTS

WINDOWS

Tutorial 1 Exploring the Basics of Microsoft Windows 8 .... WIN 1
Investigating the Windows 8 Operating System

Tutorial 2 Organizing Your Files .... WIN 45
Managing Files and Folders in Windows 8

Tutorial 3 Personalizing Your Windows Environment..................... WIN 97
Changing Desktop Settings

Tutorial 4 Working with the Internet and Email .... WIN 161
Communicating with Others

Tutorial 5 Protecting Your Computer .... WIN 221
Managing Computer Security

Tutorial 6 Searching for Information.................................. WIN 281
Finding Apps, Settings, Files, and Information

Appendix A Using Windows 8 with a Touchscreen Device .... WIN A1

Glossary/Index   **REF 1**

Task Reference   **REF 10**

TABLE OF CONTENTS

Preface v

Tutorial 1 Exploring the Basics of Microsoft Windows 8
Investigating the Windows 8 Operating System . . . . **WIN 1**

SESSION 1.1 . . . . **WIN 2**

Introducing Windows 8 . . . . WIN 4

Starting Windows 8 . . . . WIN 4

Touring the Start Screen . . . . WIN 6

    Interacting with the Start Screen . . . . WIN 6

Exploring the Desktop . . . . WIN 10

    Displaying Shortcut Menus . . . . WIN 12

    Returning to the Start Screen . . . . WIN 13

Starting Applications . . . . WIN 14

Running Multiple Applications . . . . WIN 18

    Switching Between Applications . . . . WIN 19

Manipulating Apps and Windows . . . . WIN 20

Using Tools in Desktop Applications. . . . . WIN 24

    Using the Ribbon . . . . WIN 24

    Using Dialog Boxes . . . . WIN 25

Closing Applications . . . . WIN 26

Session 1.1 Quick Check . . . . WIN 27

SESSION 1.2 . . . . **WIN 28**

Exploring Your Computer . . . . WIN 30

    Navigating with File Explorer . . . . WIN 30

    Changing the View . . . . WIN 31

    Using the Navigation Pane . . . . WIN 33

Getting Help . . . . WIN 34

    Viewing the Get Started Topics . . . . WIN 36

    Selecting a Topic from the Browse
    Help List . . . . WIN 36

    Searching the Help Pages. . . . . WIN 37

Turning Off Windows 8 . . . . WIN 38

Session 1.2 Quick Check . . . . WIN 40

Review Assignments . . . . WIN 41

Case Problems. . . . . WIN 42

Tutorial 2 Organizing Your Files
Managing Files and Folders in Windows 8 . . . . **WIN 45**

SESSION 2.1 . . . . **WIN 46**

Preparing to Manage Your Files . . . . WIN 48

    Understanding the Need for Organizing Files
    and Folders . . . . WIN 49

    Developing Strategies for Organizing Files
    and Folders . . . . WIN 50

Exploring Files and Folders . . . . WIN 51

    Using Libraries and Folders . . . . WIN 53

    Navigating to Your Data Files . . . . WIN 56

    Navigating with the Address Bar . . . . WIN 58

Using the Search Text Box to Find Files . . . . WIN 60

Managing Files and Folders . . . . WIN 61

    Creating Folders . . . . WIN 62

    Moving and Copying Files and Folders . . . . . WIN 63

    Selecting Files and Folders . . . . WIN 66

    Copying Files and Folders . . . . WIN 66

Session 2.1 Quick Check . . . . WIN 67

SESSION 2.2 . . . . WIN 68

Naming and Renaming Files . . . . WIN 70

Deleting Files and Folders. . . . . WIN 71

Working with New Files. WIN 72

    Creating a File. . . . . WIN 72

    Saving a File . . . . WIN 73

    Opening a File. . . . . WIN 75

Refining the Organization of Files. . . . . WIN 77

    Sorting and Filtering Files. . . . . WIN 77

    Grouping Files. . . . . WIN 80

Customizing a Folder Window . . . . WIN 81

    Changing the Layout of a Folder Window . . . WIN 82

    Customizing the File List. . . . . WIN 83

    Customizing the Navigation Pane. . . . . WIN 85

Working with Compressed Files . . . . WIN 86

Restoring Your Settings. . . . . WIN 88

Session 2.2 Quick Check . . . . WIN 89

Review Assignments . . . . WIN 90

Case Problems. . . . . WIN 91

ProSkills Exercise: Decision-Making . . . . WIN 95

Tutorial 3 Personalizing Your Windows Environment
Changing Desktop Settings . . . . **WIN 97**

SESSION 3.1 . . . . WIN 98

Personalizing the Start Screen. . . . . WIN 100

    Pinning Apps to the Start Screen . . . . WIN 101

    Pinning Folders to the Start Screen . . . . WIN 106

    Adding Custom Shortcuts to the Start
Screen . . . . WIN 107

Customizing Start Screen Tiles . . . . WIN 112

    Grouping Tiles. . . . . WIN 112

    Removing Tiles . . . . WIN 115

    Modifying Tiles . . . . WIN 116

Changing the Appearance of the
Start Screen .... WIN 118

    Changing the Start Screen Background .... WIN 119

    Changing the User Picture .... WIN 121

Session 3.1 Quick Check .... WIN 123

SESSION 3.2 .... **WIN 124**

Personalizing the Desktop .... WIN 126

    Adding Icons to the Desktop .... WIN 127

    Changing the Appearance of
    Desktop Icons .... WIN 128

Creating Desktop Shortcuts .... WIN 130

    Creating a Shortcut to a Drive .... WIN 130

Customizing the Desktop with the
Control Panel .... WIN 132

    Selecting Themes .... WIN 134

    Changing the Desktop Background .... WIN 136

    Changing Desktop Colors .... WIN 138

    Activating a Screen Saver .... WIN 140

    Saving Themes .... WIN 142

Managing the Desktop with Taskbar Tools.... WIN 142

Changing Display Settings .... WIN 146

    Changing the Screen Resolution .... WIN 146

    Changing the Size of Text and Objects .... WIN 147

Modifying the Taskbar .... WIN 148

    Pinning Desktop Apps to the Taskbar ..... WIN 149

    Setting Taskbar Properties .... WIN 151

Restoring Your Settings .... WIN 153

Session 3.2 Quick Check .... WIN 154

Review Assignments .... WIN 155

Case Problems .... WIN 156

Tutorial 4 Working with the Internet and Email
Communicating with Others .... **WIN 161**

SESSION 4.1 .... **WIN 162**

Exploring the Internet and the Web .... WIN 164

    Using Web Browsers .... WIN 165

Getting Started with Microsoft Internet
Explorer .... WIN 166

Opening a Page on the Web .... WIN 167

    Opening a Web Page Using a URL .... WIN 168

    Navigating with Links .... WIN 169

    Navigating with IE Windows 8 Tools ...... WIN 171

Managing Web Pages in IE Windows 8 ...... WIN 172

    Pinning Web Pages .... WIN 174

    Using the Internet Explorer Charms Bar .... WIN 175

    Using Flip Ahead .... WIN 177

Using Internet Explorer on the Desktop . . . . . . WIN 179

    Browsing Web Pages with IE Desktop . . . . . WIN 181

    Using the History List . . . . WIN 183

Using Favorites . . . . WIN 185

    Adding an Item to the Favorites List . . . . . . WIN 185

    Organizing the Favorites List . . . . WIN 186

    Adding Pages and Feeds to the
Favorites Bar . . . . WIN 187

    Pinning a Web Page to the Taskbar . . . . WIN 188

Finding and Using Accelerators . . . . WIN 190

Printing and Saving Web Pages . . . . WIN 191

Session 4.1 Quick Check . . . . WIN 193

SESSION 4.2 . . . . **WIN 194**

Getting Started with Mail . . . . WIN 196

    Examining How Email Works . . . . WIN 196

    Addressing Email . . . . WIN 197

Setting Up Mail . . . . WIN 197

Sending and Receiving Email Using Mail . . . . . WIN 199

    Creating and Sending Email Messages . . . . WIN 200

    Receiving and Reading Email Messages. . . . WIN 202

    Responding to Email Messages . . . . WIN 202

    Deleting Email Messages . . . . WIN 203

    Attaching a File to a Message . . . . WIN 204

Adding Information to the People App . . . . . . WIN 206

Managing Your Schedule with Calendar . . . . . . WIN 207

    Scheduling Appointments . . . . WIN 208

Restoring Your Settings. . . . . WIN 210

Session 4.2 Quick Check . . . . WIN 212

Review Assignments . . . . WIN 213

Case Problems. . . . . WIN 214

Tutorial 5 Protecting Your Computer
Managing Computer Security. . . . . **WIN 221**

SESSION 5.1 . . . . **WIN 222**

Using the Action Center . . . . WIN 224

    Managing Windows Firewall . . . . WIN 226

    Setting Up Windows Update . . . . WIN 230

    Protecting Your Computer from Malware . . WIN 232

Defending Against Spyware . . . . WIN 235

    Scanning Your Computer with
Windows Defender . . . . WIN 236

    Setting Windows Defender Options . . . . . . WIN 239

Defending Against Email Viruses . . . . WIN 240

Session 5.1 Quick Check . . . . WIN 241

SESSION 5.2. . . . . **WIN 242**

Managing Microsoft Internet Explorer
Security . . . . WIN 244

    Checking Web Sites with the
    SmartScreen Filter . . . . WIN 244

    Downloading Files Safely . . . . WIN 247

    Blocking Malware with Protected Mode
    and Security Zones . . . . WIN 249

    Blocking Pop-Up Windows . . . . WIN 251

    Managing Add-On Programs . . . . WIN 253

Selecting Internet Explorer Privacy Settings . . . WIN 254

    Protecting Your Privacy with InPrivate
    Browsing . . . . WIN 258

    Using Tracking Protection . . . . WIN 259

    Blocking ActiveX Controls . . . . WIN 261

Setting Up User Accounts . . . . WIN 262

    Selecting a User Name and Password . . . . . WIN 264

    Creating a Microsoft Account . . . . WIN 265

Controlling Access to Your Computer . . . . WIN 270

Startup and App Security Features . . . . WIN 271

Restoring Your Settings . . . . WIN 271

Session 5.2 Quick Check . . . . WIN 273

Review Assignments . . . . WIN 274

Case Problems . . . . WIN 276

Tutorial 6 Searching for Information
Finding Apps, Settings, Files, and Information . . . **WIN 281**

SESSION 6.1 . . . . **WIN 282**

Developing Search Strategies . . . . WIN 284

Searching for Apps . . . . WIN 285

Searching for Settings . . . . WIN 286

Searching for Files . . . . WIN 288

    Finding Files by Name and Contents . . . . . . WIN 289

    Searching by File Type . . . . WIN 291

    Filtering the Search Results by Size . . . . WIN 293

    Filtering Search Results by
    Date Modified . . . . WIN 294

    Examining the Search Results . . . . WIN 296

    Saving a Search . . . . WIN 297

Using Tags and Other Properties . . . . WIN 298

    Adding Tags to Files . . . . WIN 299

Session 6.1 Quick Check . . . . WIN 301

SESSION 6.2 . . . . **WIN 302**

Using Advanced Search Criteria . . . . WIN 304

    Combining Criteria When Searching
    File Contents . . . . WIN 305

    Combining Boolean Filters and
    File Properties . . . . WIN 308

Searching Within Windows 8 Apps . . . . WIN 308

Searching the Internet . . . . WIN 311

    Narrowing Your Search . . . . WIN 313

    Choosing Search Providers . . . . WIN 317

Restoring Your Settings . . . . WIN 320

Session 6.2 Quick Check . . . . WIN 321

Review Assignments . . . . WIN 322

Case Problems . . . . WIN 323

ProSkills Exercise: Problem Solving . . . . WIN 327

Appendix A Using Windows 8 with a Touchscreen Device

Mastering Touch Features in Microsoft Windows 8 . . **WIN A1**

Using Touch Gestures . . . . WIN A4

Navigating the Start Screen . . . . WIN A6

Using Windows 8 Apps . . . . WIN A10

Using a Touch Keyboard . . . . WIN A10

    Adjusting Touch Keyboard Settings . . . . WIN A13

Interacting with the Desktop . . . . WIN A14

GLOSSARY/INDEX . . . . **REF 1**

TASK REFERENCE . . . . **REF 10**

TUTORIAL 1

Exploring the Basics of Microsoft Windows 8

Investigating the Windows 8 Operating System

OBJECTIVES

Session 1.1
- Start Windows 8
- Explore the Start screen
- Start and close Windows 8 apps
- Run desktop applications, switch between them, and close them
- Identify and use the controls in windows and dialog boxes

Session 1.2
- Navigate your computer using File Explorer
- Change the view of the items in your computer
- Get help when you need it
- Turn off Windows 8

Case | Behind the Scenes

Behind the Scenes is a small but growing temporary employment agency in St. Louis, Missouri. The agency specializes in training and providing virtual assistants, high-quality support staff that work from home to perform office tasks and projects for clients. As the training manager at Behind the Scenes, Emma Garcia coordinates staff training sessions on a wide range of professional and computer skills.

Emma recently hired you as her assistant. She has asked you to lead the upcoming training sessions on the fundamentals of the Microsoft Windows 8 operating system. As you prepare for the sessions, she offers to help you identify the topics you should cover and the skills you should demonstrate while focusing on the new features in Windows 8.

In this tutorial, you will start Windows 8 and practice some fundamental computer skills. You'll tour the Start screen and the desktop, start applications, and then navigate a computer using File Explorer. Finally, you'll use the Windows 8 Help and Support system and turn off Windows 8.

STARTING DATA FILES

There are no starting Data Files needed for this tutorial.

Microsoft product screenshots used with permission from Microsoft Corporation.

Session 1.1 Visual Overview:

The four corners of the Start screen are **hot corners**; point to one to display objects for interacting with Windows.

The **desktop** is where you run applications designed for previous versions of Windows.

Calendar is an example of a **Windows 8 app**, which uses the full screen and includes touch-friendly controls.

A **tile** represents an application or other resource, such as a Web page.

The **Start screen** appears after you sign in to Windows; you use it to start apps.

Tutorial 1 Exploring the Basics of Microsoft Windows 8 | Windows WIN 3

Windows 8 Start Screen

The name you use to sign in to Windows appears next to the user icon.

The **user icon** identifies the current user and provides access to your account settings; you can personalize the Start screen by using a photo instead.

Scroll the Start screen to the right to display additional apps.

A **live tile** displays content that changes frequently.

An **app**, short for application, is a small program created for a specific purpose.

Click the Zoom button to reduce the size of the tiles and display more apps on the Start screen.

Introducing Windows 8

The **operating system** is software that manages and coordinates activities on the computer and helps the computer perform essential tasks, such as displaying information on the computer screen and saving data on disks. (The term *software* refers to the applications, or programs, that a computer uses to complete tasks.) Your computer uses the **Microsoft Windows 8** operating system—**Windows 8** for short. Windows is the name of the operating system, and 8 indicates the version you are using.

The most popular features of Windows 8 include its speed, flexibility, and design. Windows 8 runs software created specifically for Windows 8 and for earlier versions of Windows, such as Windows 7. In either case, you can use more than one application at a time and switch seamlessly from one application to another to perform your work effectively.

Windows 8 is designed to run on computers that use a touchscreen, such as tablets, and those that use a keyboard and mouse, such as a laptop or desktop computer. A **touchscreen** is a display that lets you touch areas of the screen to interact with software. To select an application button, for example, you touch the button on the tablet screen with your fingertip. However, you are not required to use a touchscreen with Windows 8. This book assumes that you are using a computer with a keyboard and pointing device, such as a mouse.

Starting Windows 8

TIP

If you have a Microsoft account, you can use the user name and password for that account to sign in to Windows 8.

Windows 8 starts automatically when you turn on your computer. After completing some necessary start-up tasks, Windows 8 displays a **lock screen**, which includes a picture, the date, and the time. You clear the lock screen to display the Welcome screen. Depending on how your computer is set up, the Welcome screen might list only your user name or it might list all the users for the computer. Before you start working with Windows 8, you might need to click your user name and type a password. A **user name** is a unique name that identifies you to Windows 8, and a **password** is a confidential series of characters that you must enter before you can work with Windows 8. If you installed Windows 8 yourself, you probably created a user name and password as you set up your computer. If not, the person who created your account assigned you at least a user name and possibly a password. After selecting your user name or entering a password, the Windows 8 Start screen appears (as shown in the Session 1.1 Visual Overview).

To begin preparing for your training session on Windows 8, Emma asks you to start Windows 8.

To start Windows 8:

1. Turn on your computer. After a moment, Windows 8 starts and the lock screen appears.

   Trouble? If you are asked to select an operating system, do not take action. Windows 8 should start automatically after a designated number of seconds. If it does not, ask your instructor or technical support person for help.

2. Press any key to clear the lock screen and display the Welcome screen.

   Trouble? If the Welcome screen does not appear, click the lock screen, hold down the mouse button, and then drag the picture up to display the Welcome screen.

3. If necessary, click your user name, type your password, and then press the **Enter** key.

Tutorial 1 Exploring the Basics of Microsoft Windows 8 | Windows   WIN 5

The Windows 8 Start screen appears, as shown in the Session 1.1 Visual Overview. Your screen might look different.

Trouble? If your user name does not appear on the Welcome screen, try pressing the Ctrl+Alt+Del keys to enter your name. If necessary, ask your instructor or technical support person for further assistance.

Trouble? If a blank screen or an animated design replaces the Start screen, your computer might be set to use a **screen saver**, a program that causes a monitor to go blank or to display an animated design after a specified amount of idle time. Press any key or move your mouse to restore the Start screen.

Trouble? If your computer is using a screen resolution other than 1366 x 768, the figures shown in this book might not match exactly what you see in Windows 8 as you work through the steps. Take the screen resolution difference into account as you compare your screen with the figures.

The screen that appears after you sign into Windows 8 is called the Start screen because you start working on your computer from this screen. The Start screen includes multicolored rectangles called tiles, which represent applications. Some tiles display an **icon**, a small picture that represents a resource available on your computer, such as an application or file. See Figure 1-1.

Figure 1-1 Tiles on the Start screen

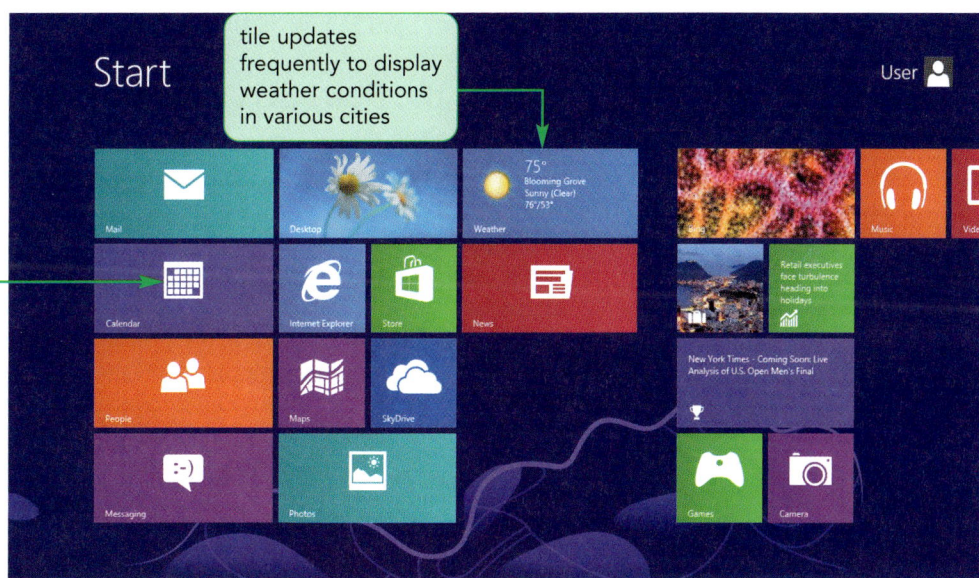

While some tiles display icons, others display pictures that preview the contents of the tile. For example, the Weather tile might display current weather conditions in cities around the world. A tile that displays updated content is called a live tile. The Weather tile is an example of a Windows 8 app. You can use this app to check the current and forecasted weather in various locations.

INSIGHT

The Windows 8 User Interface

The part of the operating system you use when you work with a computer is called the **user interface (UI)**. The UI includes everything that lets you interact with the computer, including the layout of the screen and the controls, such as icons and buttons, that the operating system provides so you can make selections and change settings. On the Start screen, the Windows 8 UI uses a design that emphasizes large, clear text rather than graphical icons to identify screen objects. When you use a Windows 8 app, such as Calendar, the focus is on the content, so the screen is not cluttered with tools and windows. The Windows 8 UI also uses animation and fluid motions to respond to your actions and selections, which make the system seem livelier than a collection of static objects. To take advantage of wide screens, multiple monitors, and touch devices, the Windows 8 UI is more horizontally oriented than previous versions of Windows. For example, you scroll right and left to access content currently out of view.

Touring the Start Screen

The first time you start a computer after installing Windows 8, the computer uses **default settings**, those preset by the operating system. The default Start screen you see after you first install Windows 8, for example, displays a number of tiles, including those for Internet Explorer (a program you use to access the Internet), Weather, and Photos. However, Microsoft designed Windows 8 so that you can easily change the appearance of the Start screen. You can, for example, move and add tiles and change their size.

Interacting with the Start Screen

If you are using a laptop or desktop computer, you use a **pointing device** to interact with the objects on the screen. Pointing devices come in many shapes and sizes. The most common one is called a **mouse**, so this book uses that term. If you are using a different pointing device, such as a trackball or touchpad, substitute that device whenever you see the term *mouse*. Some pointing devices are designed to ensure that your hand won't suffer fatigue while using them. Some are attached directly to your computer by a cable, whereas others work wirelessly like a TV remote control and provide access to your computer without being plugged into it.

You use a pointing device to move the pointer over locations and objects on the screen, or to **point** to them. The **pointer** is an on-screen object, often shaped like an arrow, though it changes shape depending on its location on the screen and the tasks you are performing. As you move the mouse on a surface, such as a table top, the pointer on the screen moves in a corresponding direction.

If your Start screen contains more tiles than Windows can fit on one screen, you can point to the right edge of the Start screen to scroll, which displays any tiles out of view. Emma suggests that during your class, you introduce Behind the Scenes employees to the Start screen by showing them how to use the pointer to scroll.

To use the pointer to scroll:

1. Use the mouse to point to the **right edge** of the Start screen. The screen scrolls to display additional tiles not shown on the main Start screen. See Figure 1-2.

TIP

Make sure you position the pointer on the very edge of the Start screen. You might also need to hold down the mouse button as you scroll.

Tutorial 1 Exploring the Basics of Microsoft Windows 8 | Windows **WIN 7**

Trouble? If a bar of buttons appears on the right side of the screen, you pointed to the upper-right or lower-right corner. Point to the right edge of the screen to scroll.

Trouble? If the screen does not scroll, your Start screen might not contain additional tiles. If there are more tiles, click the right arrow button ▶ on the scroll bar at the bottom of the screen to scroll to the right.

Figure 1-2 Scrolling the Start screen

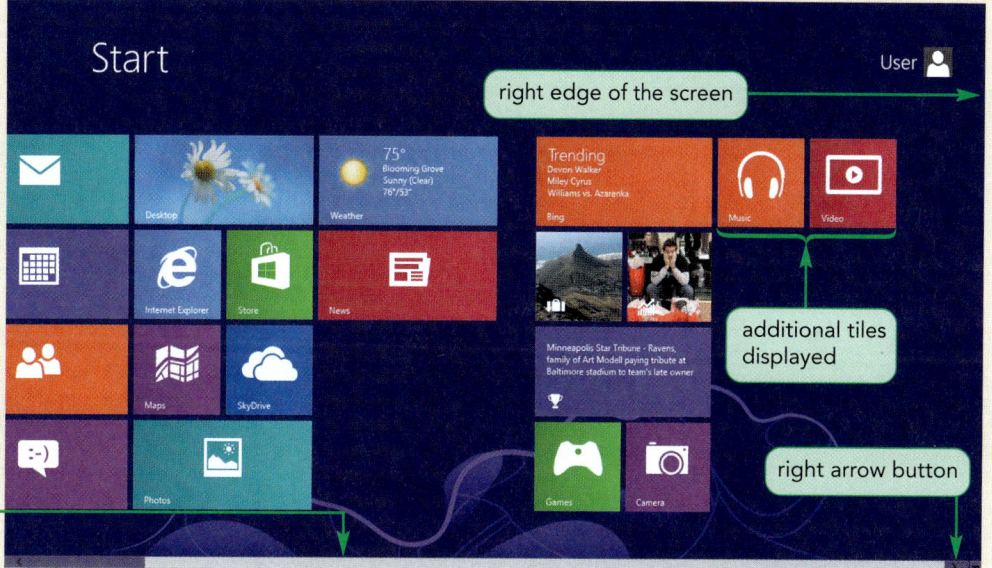

2. Point to the **left edge** of the Start screen to scroll back to the main Start screen (or click the left scroll arrow button ◀ on the scroll bar).

When you move the pointer, a scroll bar appears at the bottom of the screen indicating that the screen includes content currently out of view. (Some screens display both vertical and horizontal scroll bars.) You can drag the scroll bar or click the arrow buttons to scroll.

Clicking refers to pressing a mouse button and immediately releasing it. Clicking sends a signal to your computer that you want to perform an action with the object you click. In Windows 8, you perform most actions with the left mouse button. If you are told to click an on-screen object, position the pointer on that object and click the left mouse button, unless instructed otherwise.

Besides scrolling the Start screen to display additional tiles, you can zoom the Start screen to make the tiles smaller (to display more tiles) or larger (to display fewer tiles). You do so by clicking the Zoom button, which appears in the lower-right corner of the Start screen when you move the pointer.

To zoom the Start screen:

1. Move the pointer until the Zoom button ▬ appears in the lower-right corner of the Start screen. See Figure 1-3.

Figure 1-3 Displaying the Zoom button

2. Click the **Zoom** button ▬ to reduce the size of the tiles. See Figure 1-4.

Figure 1-4 Zooming the Start screen

tiles are smaller to display more of them on the Start screen

3. Click a blank spot on the Start screen to return the tiles to their original size.

When you moved the pointer to the Zoom button to click it, a bar appeared on the right edge of the Start screen. This is called the **Charms bar**, and it contains buttons, also called **charms**, for interacting with Windows 8. The Charms bar appears when you point to the upper-right or lower-right corner of the screen. These locations are two of the four hot corners Windows 8 provides for mouse users. When you point to the Charms bar, it appears with a black background, indicating it is the **active object**. You can interact with active objects by clicking them, for example. When you click the Search charm on the Charms bar, a menu opens. A **menu** is a list, or group, of commands, and a **menu command** is text that you can click to perform a task. The **Search menu** provides access to applications, documents, settings, and much more. Emma suggests you use the Search charm on the Charms bar to open the Search menu.

To open the Search menu:

1. Point to the upper-right corner of the screen to display the Charms bar.
2. Point to the **Charms bar** to display it with a black background, which means it is active. See Figure 1-5.

TIP

You can also press and hold down the Windows key and then press C to display the Charms bar.

Tutorial 1 Exploring the Basics of Microsoft Windows 8 | Windows   WIN 9

Figure 1-5   Active Charms bar

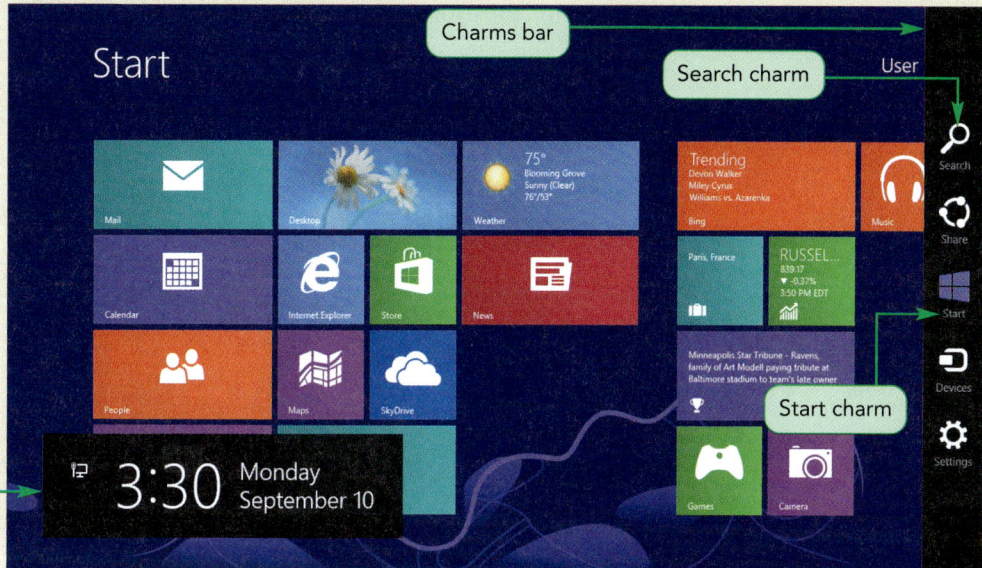

3. Click the **Search** charm on the Charms bar to display the Search menu, shown in Figure 1-6.

Figure 1-6   Search menu

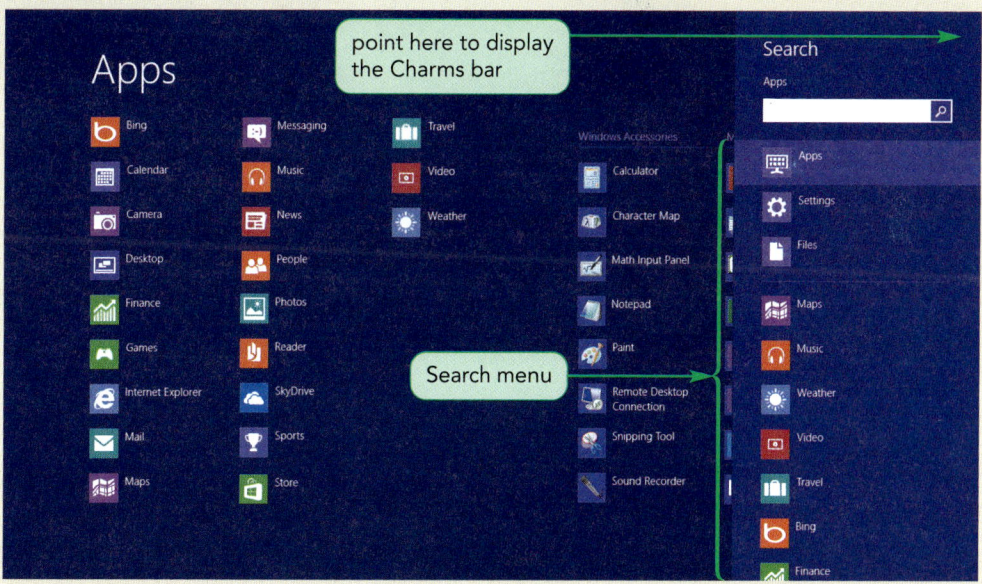

4. Point to the lower-right corner of the Start screen to display the Charms bar again, and then click the **Start** charm to return to the Start screen.

When you activate the Charms bar, a status box appears on the screen displaying the date and time. It might also display other status information, such as the strength of your network connection or battery level.

Although you can use the Search menu to find applications, settings, and files, the Start screen is designed to provide quick access to all the information, applications, and locations on your computer. For example, you can use the Start screen to display the desktop, which is your work area for using applications designed to run in previous versions of Windows.

Exploring the Desktop

In addition to the Start screen, Windows 8 includes the desktop where you can access tools for managing Windows and other programs. You also use the desktop to work with files and folders. A **file** is a collection of related information; typical types of files include text documents, spreadsheets, photos, and songs. A **folder** is a container that helps you organize the contents of your computer.

The Start screen includes a Desktop tile (shown in the Session 1.1 Visual Overview), which you click to display the Windows 8 desktop.

To display the desktop:

▶ 1. Click the **Desktop** tile on the Start screen to display the desktop, shown in Figure 1-7. Your desktop might contain additional or different items.

Figure 1-7   **Windows 8 desktop**

Most of the features you use on the Start screen are available on the desktop. For example, you can point to the upper-right hot corner to display the Charms bar. In addition, the desktop includes the features described in Figure 1-8.

| Figure 1-8 | Features of the Windows 8 desktop |

Feature	Description
Date/time control	Control that shows the current date and time, and lets you set the clock
Desktop graphic	Part of a Windows 8 theme, which is a set of desktop backgrounds, window colors, sounds, and screen savers
Notification area	Area containing icons that correspond to services running in the background, such as an Internet connection
Pinned programs	Programs you can start by clicking their button on the taskbar
Recycle Bin	Icon for a folder that holds items deleted from the hard drive until you remove them permanently
Taskbar	Strip that contains buttons to give you quick access to common tools and running programs

© 2014 Cengage Learning

On the Start screen or the desktop, you need to select an object before you can work with it. To **select** an object on the Start screen, you point to the object, such as a tile. To select an object on the desktop, you point to and then click the object. Windows 8 often indicates that the object is selected by highlighting it, typically by changing the object's color, putting a box around it, or making the object appear to be pushed in.

Clicking an object on the desktop usually selects it. To open a folder or start the application associated with an object, you double-click the object on the desktop. For example, you can double-click a folder icon to open the folder and see its contents. **Double-clicking** means clicking the left mouse button twice in quick succession.

Emma suggests that you have students practice double-clicking by opening the Recycle Bin. The Recycle Bin holds items deleted from the hard drive until you remove them permanently.

To view the contents of the Recycle Bin:

1. Point to the **Recycle Bin** icon, and then click the left mouse button twice quickly to double-click the icon. The Recycle Bin window opens, as shown in Figure 1-9.

Figure 1-9   **Contents of the Recycle Bin**

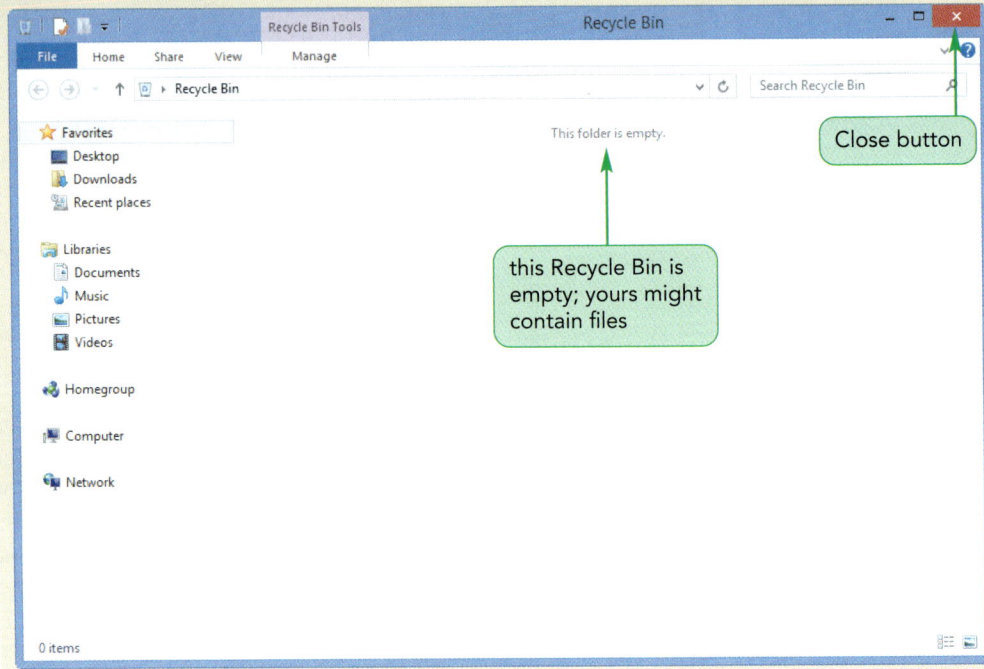

> **Trouble?** If the Recycle Bin window does not open and you see only the Recycle Bin name highlighted below the icon, you double-clicked too slowly. Double-click the icon again more quickly.
>
> Now you can close the Recycle Bin window.
>
> ▶ 2. Click the **Close** button ❌ in the upper-right corner of the Recycle Bin window.

You'll learn more about opening and closing windows later in this session.

Displaying Shortcut Menus

Your mouse most likely has more than one button. In addition to the left button, the mouse has a right button that you can use to perform certain actions in Windows 8. However, the term *clicking* refers to the left button; clicking an object with the right button is called **right-clicking**. (If your mouse has only one button, you right-click by pressing the right side of the button.)

In Windows 8, right-clicking usually selects an object and opens its **shortcut menu**, which lists actions you can take with that object. You can right-click practically any object—a tile on the Start screen, a desktop icon, the taskbar, and even the desktop itself—to view commands associated with that object. Emma suggests that when you're not sure what to do with an object in Windows 8, you should right-click it and examine its shortcut menu. Now you can right-click the Recycle Bin icon to open its shortcut menu.

To right-click an object on the desktop:

1. Point to the **Recycle Bin** icon on your desktop, and then right-click the icon to open its shortcut menu. This menu offers a list of actions you can take with the Recycle Bin icon. See Figure 1-10.

Figure 1-10 Recycle Bin shortcut menu

Trouble? If the shortcut menu does not open and you are using a trackball or a mouse with a wheel, make sure you click the button on the far right, not the one in the middle.

2. Click **Open** on the shortcut menu to open the Recycle Bin window again.
3. Click the **Close** button in the upper-right corner of the Recycle Bin window.

Now that you've explored the desktop, you can return to the Start screen and use it to start applications.

Returning to the Start Screen

You can use a few techniques to return to the Start screen. The easiest way is to use a **keyboard shortcut**, which means you press one or more keys on the keyboard to perform an action. Another way is to point to the lower-left hot corner to display a miniature image, or **thumbnail**, of the Start screen and then click. Recall that you can also click the Start charm on the Charms bar to display the Start screen.

Windows 8 provides many keyboard shortcuts for streamlining your work. The keyboard shortcut for displaying the Start screen is to press the Windows key. If you press the Windows key when the Start screen is displayed, you return to your previous location.

To return to the Start screen:

1. Press the **Windows** key to display the Start screen.
2. Press the **Windows** key again to display the desktop.
3. Point to the lower-left corner of the screen until a thumbnail of the Start screen appears, as in Figure 1-11.

Start screen thumbnail

4. Click the **thumbnail** to display the Start screen.

> **Trouble?** If the Start screen does not appear, point to the lower-left corner of the screen again, and without moving the pointer, click to display the Start screen.

Starting Applications

Computers can run two types of software: system software and applications. **System software** is the software that runs a computer, including the operating system. An **application** is the software you use most directly to perform tasks such as writing a screenplay or viewing a Web page. In general, a computer runs system software to perform computer tasks, and you run applications to carry out your work or personal tasks.

REFERENCE

Starting an Application

- Click the application's tile on the Start screen.

or

- On the Start screen or the Search menu, type the name of the application until the application appears in the search results on the Apps screen.
- Click the application in the search results.

Windows 8 runs two types of applications. Windows 8 apps are designed to use the Windows 8 interface and work with touchscreen devices. Windows 8 apps appear only on the Start screen. For example, the Calendar tile is for the Calendar Windows 8 app, which displays a full-screen calendar where you can schedule appointments and other events. You can also use Windows 8 to run **desktop applications**, which are programs developed for previous versions of Windows. For example, WordPad is a desktop application you use to create basic word-processing documents.

To start a Windows 8 app, you click its tile on the Start screen. Emma suggests that you demonstrate how to start the Calendar app.

To start the Calendar app:

▶ 1. Click the **Calendar** tile on the Start screen to start the Calendar app. See Figure 1-12.

> **Trouble?** If a Sign in with a Microsoft account screen appears and you have a Microsoft account, enter your email address and password, and then click the Sign In button.

Tutorial 1 Exploring the Basics of Microsoft Windows 8 | Windows   WIN 15

Figure 1-12   Calendar app

- your Calendar screen might differ
- Calendar is displayed as a full-screen app

2. Press the **Windows** key to redisplay the Start screen.
3. Point to the upper-left corner of the screen to display a thumbnail of the Calendar app, which is still running, as shown in Figure 1-13.

Figure 1-13   Thumbnail of the Calendar app

- thumbnail indicates the Calendar app is still running

You use the upper-left hot corner to display a thumbnail for each running app, even if it doesn't appear on the screen. The list of running apps is called the **Switch List** because you can click a thumbnail in the list to switch to that app. You can display the Switch List from the Start screen, while working with a Windows 8 app, or from the desktop.

Another way to start a desktop application or a Windows 8 app is to use the Search menu, which you displayed earlier, and the Apps screen. You use the Search menu to search for or select items, including applications. When you open the Search menu, it appears on top of the Apps screen, which lists all the applications installed on your computer. See Figure 1-14.

TIP

To display the Apps screen without the Search menu, right-click the Start screen and then click the All apps button in the lower-right corner of the screen.

Figure 1-14 Apps screen and Search menu

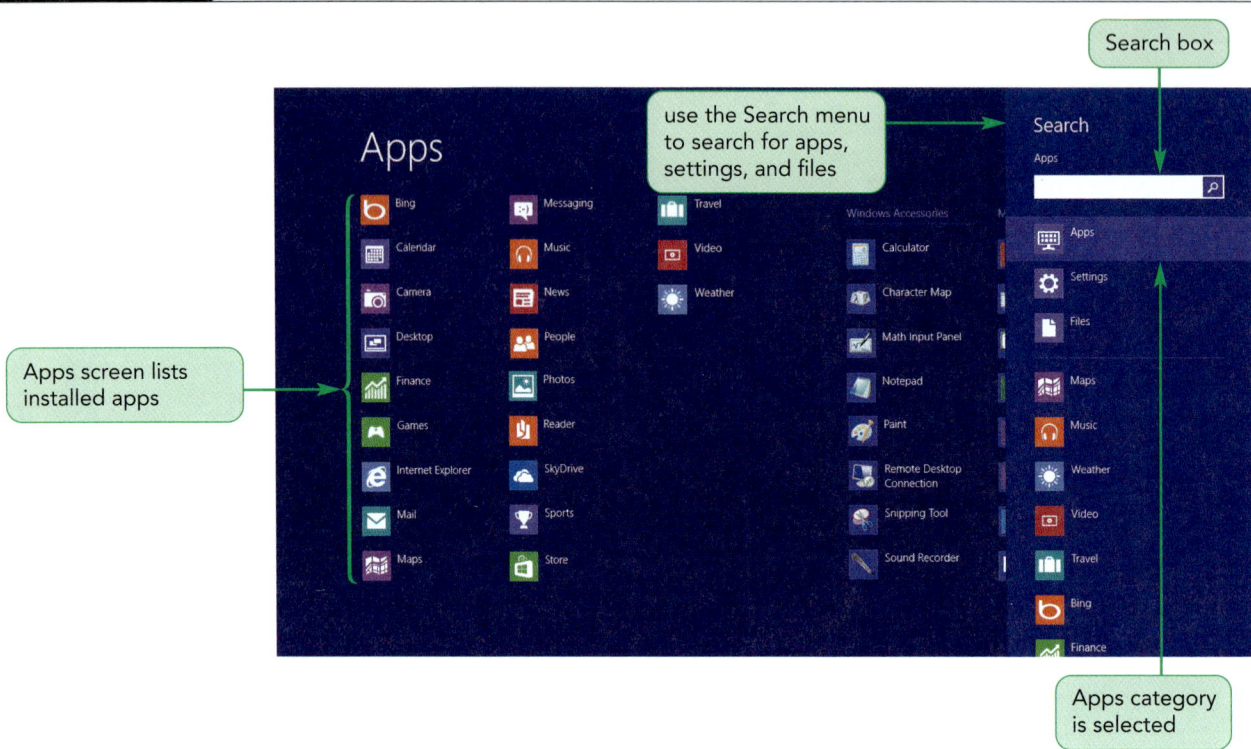

At the top of the Search menu is the **Search box**, which you use to quickly find anything stored on your computer including applications, documents, pictures, music, videos, and settings. Below the Search box, the Search menu lists three major categories of items you can search for: Apps, Settings, and Files. The Apps category is selected by default. To search for an application, start typing the name of the application. As you type, the Apps screen displays the search results: applications containing words beginning with that text in their names. For example, if you want to find and start Paint, a graphics editor provided with Windows 8, you could type *paint* in the Search box. Windows 8 searches your computer for applications whose names start with "paint" and displays them on the Apps screen, where you can click the Paint application to start it.

If you want to search for settings related to the text you entered, click Settings in the category list. For example, with "paint" displayed in the Search box, you could click Settings to display the Settings screen with system settings related to "paint," including one that lets you turn Windows features such as Paint on or off.

Searching for files works the same way: type the text related to the file you are looking for (for example, "paint") in the Search box and then click Files in the category list. The Files screen opens and displays files that contain "paint" in their filenames, contents, or file details, including files created in applications with "paint" in their names, such as a drawing created in Paint.

Below the category list in the Search menu are Windows 8 apps installed on your computer. These apps are also displayed on the Start screen.

Now that you've explored the Search menu, you're ready to use it to start an application. If you start typing on the Start screen, the Search menu opens and the text you typed appears in the Search box. Emma suggests you use this method to start WordPad, which Behind the Scenes employees can use to write and open text documents.

To start WordPad:

1. Type **wordp** to display the Search menu with "wordp" inserted in the Search box. The search results include the WordPad application. See Figure 1-15.

Figure 1-15   **WordPad in the search results**

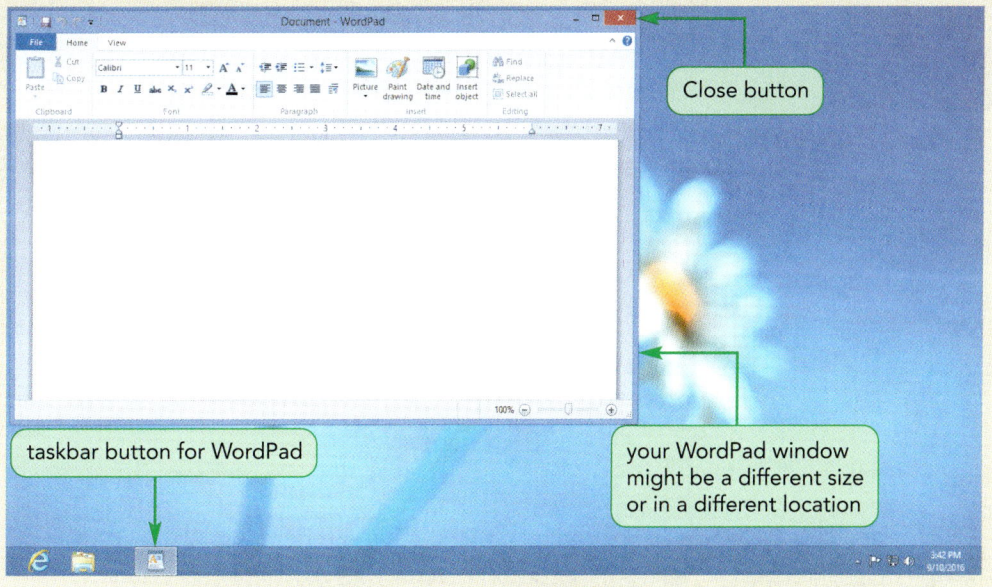

Trouble? If settings or files appear in the search results, click Apps in the category list, and then repeat Step 1 if necessary, making sure the search term is displayed in the Search box.

2. Click **WordPad** in the search results. The WordPad window opens on the desktop, as shown in Figure 1-16.

Figure 1-16   **WordPad window**

Unlike Windows 8 apps, which open as full-screen programs, a desktop application opens in a **window**, which is a rectangular work area that contains tools for performing tasks. When a window is open on the desktop, a button appears on the taskbar for that window. (Recall that the **taskbar** is a strip at the bottom of the desktop that gives you quick access to common tools and running desktop applications.) **Taskbar buttons** are buttons on the taskbar that you use to work with open programs easily. These buttons are especially useful if you have many windows open on the desktop. To quickly display a particular window, you can click its button on the taskbar.

Running Multiple Applications

One of the most useful features of Windows 8 is its ability to run multiple programs at the same time. This feature, known as **multitasking**, allows you to work on more than one task at a time and to switch quickly between projects.

Two applications are now running at the same time: WordPad and Calendar. If more than one application is open on the desktop, you can click a button on the taskbar to switch between the open applications. If one of the applications is a Windows 8 app, however, you use a hot corner to switch from one application to another. You can also use the Alt+Tab keyboard shortcut to switch between applications. To do so, you hold down the Alt key and then press the Tab key to display thumbnails of all running applications (both Windows 8 and desktop), press the Tab key again to select a thumbnail, and then release the Alt key to make that application active.

To demonstrate multitasking and switching between applications, Emma suggests that you start Paint, another desktop application. You use Paint to draw, color, and edit digital pictures. You start Paint from the Start screen.

To run WordPad and Paint on the desktop:

1. Press the **Windows** key to display the Start screen, and then type **paint**. The Search menu appears with "paint" in the Search box, and Paint appears in the search results.

2. Click **Paint** in the search results to start it. Now two applications are open on the desktop at the same time.

3. If the Paint window fills the entire screen, click the **Restore Down** button in the upper-right corner of the window to reduce the size of the window. See Figure 1-17.

Figure 1-17   Two applications open on the desktop

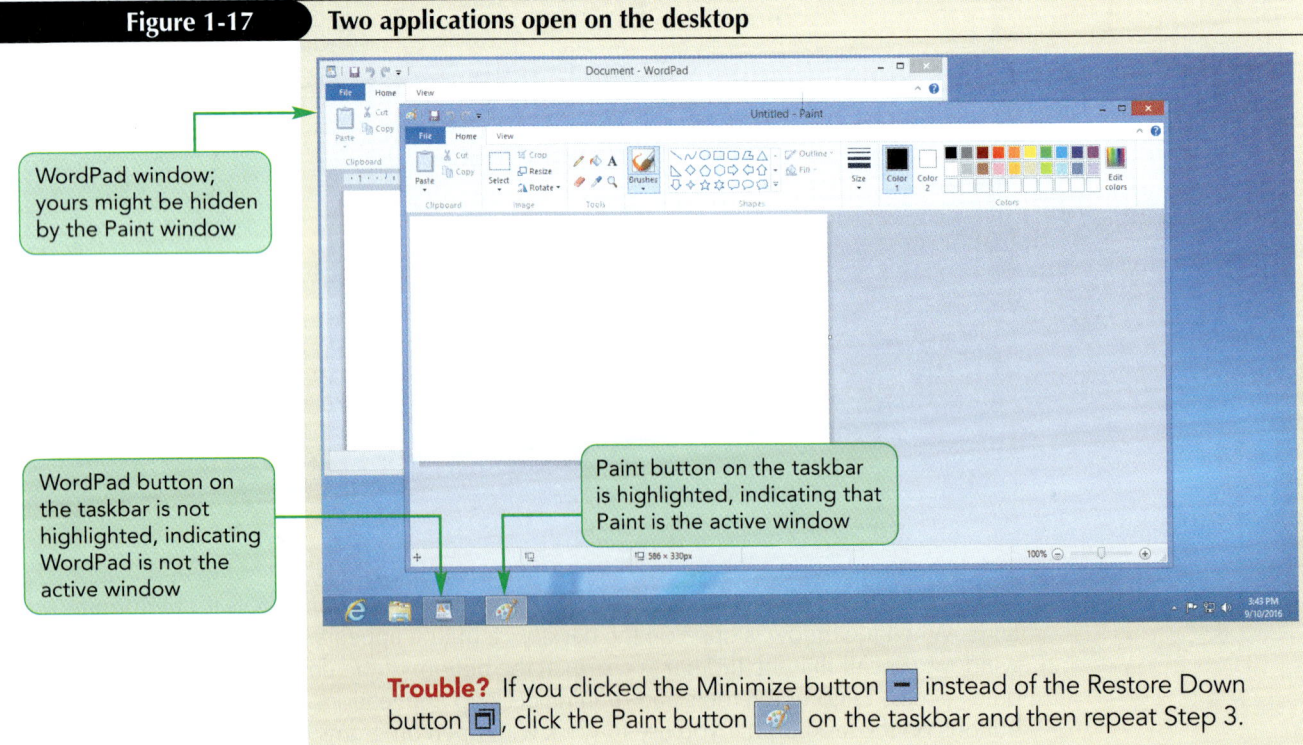

WordPad window; yours might be hidden by the Paint window

WordPad button on the taskbar is not highlighted, indicating WordPad is not the active window

Paint button on the taskbar is highlighted, indicating that Paint is the active window

Trouble? If you clicked the Minimize button instead of the Restore Down button, click the Paint button on the taskbar and then repeat Step 3.

On the desktop, the **active window** is the one you are currently working with—Windows 8 applies your next keystroke or command to the active window. Paint is the active window because it is the one you are currently using. If two or more windows overlap, the active window appears in front of the other windows. The button for the active window is highlighted on the taskbar. The WordPad button is still on the taskbar, indicating that WordPad is running even if you can't see its program window. The taskbar organizes all the open windows so you can quickly make one active by clicking its taskbar button.

Switching Between Applications

Because only one application is active at a time, you need to switch between applications if you want to work in one or the other. On the desktop, the easiest way to switch between applications is to use the taskbar buttons.

To switch between WordPad and Paint:

1. Click the **WordPad** button on the taskbar. The WordPad window moves to the front, and the WordPad button appears highlighted on the taskbar, indicating that WordPad is the active window.

2. Click the **Paint** button on the taskbar to switch to the Paint program. The Paint window is again the active window.

TIP
You can also click an inactive window to make it the active window.

Besides WordPad and Paint, the Calendar app is also open and running. Because Calendar is a Windows 8 app and not a desktop application, no Calendar button appears on the taskbar. When an app is open but not visible on the screen, it is said to be running in the **background**. To access a desktop application running in the background, you click its button on the taskbar. To access a Windows 8 app running in the background, you use the Switch List to display thumbnails of open apps.

To switch to the Calendar app:

1. Point to the upper-left hot corner of the desktop to display a thumbnail of the Calendar app in the Switch List.

2. Click the **Calendar** thumbnail to display the Calendar app.

The Switch List includes thumbnails for Windows 8 apps only, not desktop applications. Because Windows 8 treats the desktop as an app, the Switch List displays one thumbnail for the desktop. WordPad and Paint are now open and running on the desktop.

TIP
To display the Switch List as a bar, point to the upper-left hot corner and then move the pointer down along the left edge of the screen.

If two or more Windows 8 apps are running in the background, the Switch List appears as a bar with a black background on the left of the screen. In Figure 1-18, the Weather and Calendar apps are running in addition to the desktop, so the two apps appear in the Switch List.

Figure 1-18 Switch List displayed on the desktop

- thumbnail of the Calendar app in the Switch List
- thumbnail of the Start screen appears at the bottom of the Switch List
- if two or more Windows 8 apps are running in the background, the Switch List appears as a bar

Manipulating Apps and Windows

Windows 8 apps start and run as full-screen programs so you can focus on your task and the content of the app. Occasionally, you need to refer to information in one app while you are working in another app. For example, if you are creating your schedule for the week in Calendar, you might want to display the Maps app to find and record directions to an appointment. If you are using a high screen resolution (at least 1366 × 768), you can **snap** an app, which means you display an app on the left or right side of the screen and leave it open as you work in other apps.

To start the Maps app and snap the Calendar app:

1. Press the **Windows** key to display the Start screen.
2. Click the **Maps** tile to start the Maps app.
3. Point to the upper-left hot corner, and then drag the pointer down along the left edge of the screen to display the Switch List.
4. Right-click the **Calendar** thumbnail, and then click **Snap left** on the shortcut menu to snap the Calendar app to the left side of the screen while the Maps app is open on the right. See Figure 1-19.

Figure 1-19 Calendar app snapped on the left

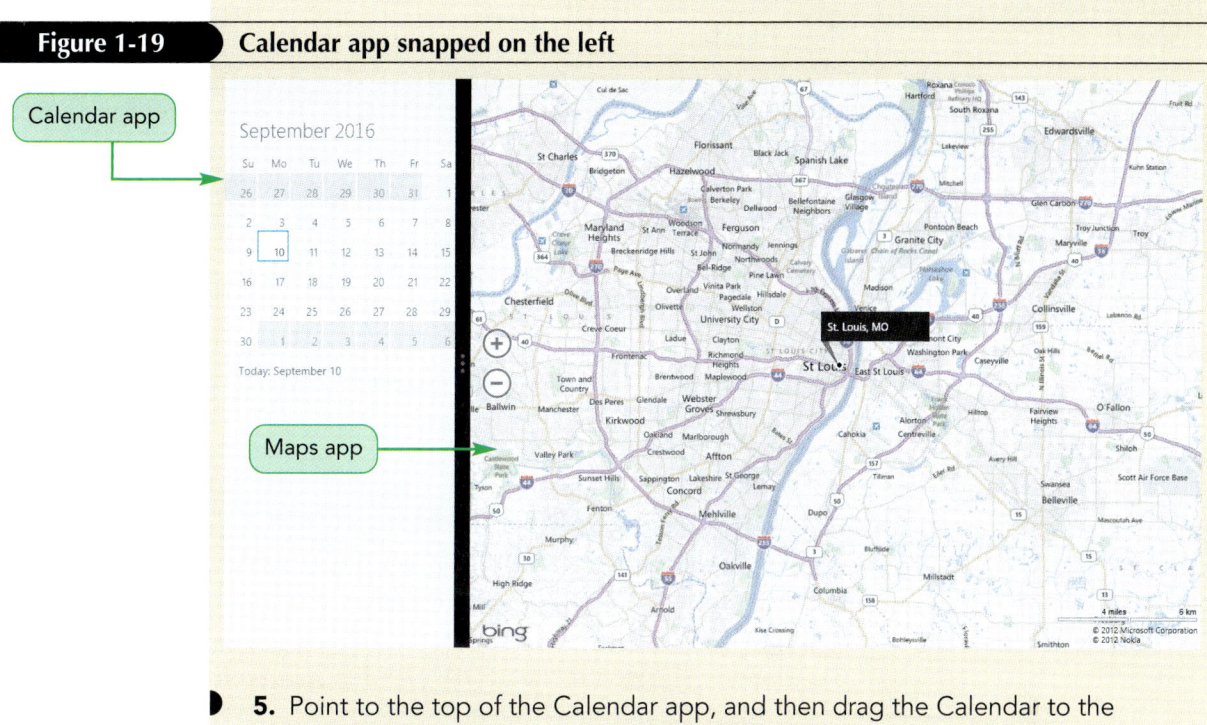

5. Point to the top of the Calendar app, and then drag the Calendar to the bottom of the screen to unsnap and close the app.

You can snap only Windows 8 apps. Because these apps usually appear in full-screen view, snapping lets you display more than one app at a time. In contrast, a desktop application appears in a window. Recall that a window is a rectangular area of the screen that contains an application, text, graphics, or data. You can open more than one window on the desktop and then manipulate the windows to display as much or as little information as you need. In most windows, three buttons appear on the right side of the title bar. See Figure 1-20. The first button is the Minimize button, which hides a window so that only its button is visible on the taskbar. Depending on the status of the window, the middle button either maximizes the window or restores it to a predefined size. The last button is the Close button, which closes the window.

Figure 1-20 Window buttons

WordPad and Paint are open on the desktop, so Emma encourages you to show employees how to use their window controls. First, you will return to the desktop and then close a window so you can focus on manipulating a single window.

To close Paint:

▶ 1. Press the **Windows** key to display the Start screen, and then click the **Desktop** tile to display the desktop, where the WordPad and Paint windows are open.

▶ 2. Click the **Close** button in the upper-right corner of the Paint window. Paint closes while the WordPad window remains open.

Trouble? If a dialog box opens with a message asking if you want to save changes, click the Don't Save button.

You can use the Minimize button when you want to temporarily hide a window but keep the program running.

To minimize the WordPad window:

▶ 1. Click the **Minimize** button on the WordPad title bar. The WordPad window shrinks so that only the WordPad button is visible.

Trouble? If the WordPad window closed, you accidentally clicked the Close button. Use the Search menu to start WordPad again, and then repeat Step 1. If you accidentally clicked the Maximize button or the Restore Down button, repeat Step 1.

You can redisplay a minimized window by clicking the window's button on the taskbar. When you redisplay a window, it becomes the active window.

To redisplay the WordPad window:

▶ 1. Click the **WordPad** button on the taskbar to redisplay the WordPad window.

The taskbar button provides another way to switch between a window's minimized and active states.

▶ 2. Click the **WordPad** button on the taskbar again to minimize the window.

▶ 3. Click the **WordPad** button once more to redisplay the window.

The Maximize button enlarges a window so that it fills the entire screen. Emma recommends that you work with maximized windows on the desktop when you want to concentrate on the work you are performing in a single program.

To maximize the WordPad window:

▶ 1. Click the **Maximize** button on the WordPad title bar.

Trouble? If the window is already maximized, it fills the entire screen, and the Maximize button doesn't appear. Instead, you see the Restore Down button. Skip this step.

TIP

You can also double-click a window's title bar to maximize the window. Double-click the title bar again to restore the window to its previous size.

The Restore Down button reduces the window so that it is smaller than the entire screen. This feature is useful if you want to see more than one window at a time. Also, because the window is smaller, you can move it to another location on the screen or change its dimensions.

To restore a window:

1. Click the **Restore Down** button on the WordPad title bar. After a window is restored, the Restore Down button changes to the Maximize button.

You can use the mouse to move a window to a new position on the screen. When you click an object and then press and hold down the mouse button while moving the mouse, you are **dragging** the object. You can move objects on the screen by dragging them to a new location. If you want to move a window, you drag the window by its title bar. You cannot move a maximized window.

To drag the restored WordPad window to a new location:

1. Position the mouse pointer on the WordPad title bar.
2. Press and hold down the left mouse button, and then move the mouse up or down a little to drag the window. The window moves as you move the mouse.
3. Position the window anywhere on the desktop, and then release the left mouse button. The WordPad window stays in the new location.
4. Drag the WordPad window near the upper-left corner of the desktop.

   Trouble? If the WordPad window becomes maximized when you drag it near the upper part of the desktop, click the Restore Down button before performing the next set of steps.

You can also use the mouse to change the size of a window. When you point to an edge or a corner of a window, the pointer changes to the resize pointer, which is a double-headed arrow, similar to . You can use the resize pointer to drag an edge or a corner of the window and change the size of the window.

To change the size of the WordPad window:

1. Position the pointer over the lower-right corner of the WordPad window. The pointer changes to . See Figure 1-21.

Figure 1-21 Preparing to resize a window

2. Press and hold down the mouse button, and then drag the corner down and to the right.
3. Release the mouse button. Now the window is larger.
4. Practice using the resize pointer to make the WordPad window larger or smaller.

You can also use the resize pointer to drag any of the other three corners of the window to change its size. To change a window's size in any one direction only, drag the left, right, top, or bottom window borders left, right, up, or down.

Using Tools in Desktop Applications

Desktop application windows contain **controls**, which are graphical or textual objects used for manipulating the window and for using the application. Many desktop applications organize controls in two places: ribbons and dialog boxes.

Emma mentions that the WordPad program displays the controls you are likely to see in most windows, including the ribbon, which might be unfamiliar to Behind the Scenes employees. She suggests that you identify the controls on the WordPad ribbon and in WordPad dialog boxes during your first training session.

Using the Ribbon

TIP
By default, the ribbon displays the Home tab when you start WordPad. To display the contents of the View tab, you click the View tab on the ribbon.

Many desktop applications use a **ribbon** to consolidate the application's features and commands. The ribbon is located at the top of a desktop application window, immediately below the title bar, and is organized into tabs. Each **tab** contains commands that perform a variety of related tasks. For example, the Home tab has commands for tasks you perform frequently, such as changing the appearance of a document. You use the commands on the View tab to change your view of the WordPad window.

To select a command and perform an action, you use a button or other type of control on the ribbon. Controls for related actions are organized on a tab in **groups**. For example, to enter bold text in a WordPad document, you click the Bold button in the Font group on the Home tab. If a button displays only an icon and not the button name, you can point to the button to display a **ScreenTip**, which is text that identifies the name or purpose of the button. Figure 1-22 shows examples of the types of controls on the ribbon.

Figure 1-22 Examples of ribbon controls

Figure 1-23 describes the types of ribbon controls.

Figure 1-23 Types of controls on the ribbon

Control	How to Use	Example
Button with arrow	Click the button to display a menu of related commands.	
Text box	Click the text box and type an entry, or click the arrow button to select an item from the list.	Calibri
Toggle button	Click the button to turn on or apply a setting, and then click the button again to turn off the setting. When a toggle button is turned on, it is highlighted.	**B**
Two-part button with arrow	If an arrow is displayed on a separate part of the button, click the arrow to display a menu of commands. Click the button itself to apply the current selection.	A▾

© 2014 Cengage Learning

Using Dialog Boxes

When you click some buttons on the ribbon, you open a **dialog box**, a special kind of window in which you enter or choose settings for how you want to perform a task. For example, you use the Print dialog box to enter or select settings for printing a document.

Besides using buttons on ribbon tabs, you can also open dialog boxes by selecting a command on the File tab. You click the File tab to display a list of commands such as Open, Save, and Print. To open a dialog box, such as the Print dialog box, you click the appropriate command, such as Print.

Dialog box controls include command buttons, tabs, option buttons, check boxes, and text boxes to collect information about how you want to perform a task. Emma says a good way to learn how dialog box controls work is to open a typical WordPad dialog box, such as the Print dialog box.

To work with a typical Windows 8 dialog box:

1. Click the **File** tab on the ribbon, and then click **Print** to open the Print dialog box. See Figure 1-24.

Figure 1-24 Print dialog box

2. Click the **Pages** option button. You use this control to print only specified pages, not the entire document.

TIP
You can also click an arrow button in the Number of copies text box to change the number of copies you want to print.

3. Double-click the **Number of copies** text box and then type **2**. You use this control to indicate how many copies of the document you want to print.

4. Click the **Cancel** button to close the Print dialog box.

If you were ready to print a document with the settings you specified, you would click the Print button instead of the Cancel button. To retain your selections while you perform other tasks in a dialog box, such as setting preferences or finding a printer, you can click the Apply button, complete the other tasks, and then click the Print button.

You're finished working with applications for now, so you should close all open windows.

Closing Applications

You should close an application when you are finished using it. Each application uses computer resources, such as memory, so Windows 8 works more efficiently when only the applications you need are open.

REFERENCE

Closing an Application

- To close a Windows 8 app, display the Switch List, right-click the app's thumbnail, and then click Close on the shortcut menu; or click the top edge of the app and then drag the app to the bottom edge of the screen.
- To close a desktop application, click its Close button on the title bar, or right-click its taskbar button and then click Close window on the shortcut menu.

Emma reminds you that you've already closed an open desktop application using its Close button. You can also close an application, whether active or inactive, by using the shortcut menu associated with the application button on the taskbar.

To close WordPad using the taskbar button shortcut menu:

▶ 1. Right-click the **WordPad** button on the taskbar. The shortcut menu for the WordPad taskbar button opens.

▶ 2. Click **Close window** on the shortcut menu. The WordPad window closes and its button no longer appears on the taskbar.

Trouble? If a message appears asking if you want to save changes, click the Don't Save button.

You've closed all the desktop applications, but the Maps app is still running. You can use the Switch List to close a Windows 8 app such as Maps from the desktop or the Start screen.

To close the Maps app:

▶ 1. Point to the upper-left hot corner to display the Switch List.

▶ 2. Right-click the **Maps** thumbnail, and then click **Close** on the shortcut menu. The Calendar app closes.

▶ 3. Press the **Windows** key to return to the Start screen.

PROSKILLS

Problem Solving: Working with Apps Efficiently

As you work on your computer throughout the day, you may end up with quite a few Windows 8 apps and desktop applications open and running at the same time. This can lead to two common problems that affect your productivity: Finding the information you need becomes more difficult as you switch between applications, and the performance of your computer can slow significantly.

To address both these issues, decide which applications need to be running, and then close what you don't need. Closing unnecessary applications allows you to focus on the information you need for the tasks at hand, and it frees up system resources, which makes your computer faster and more responsive and can solve performance problems.

REVIEW

Session 1.1 Quick Check

1. What does the operating system do for your computer?
2. The Start screen includes multicolored rectangles called _____, which represent _____.
3. What is a live tile?
4. When you're not sure what to do with an object in Windows 8, you can right-click the object and examine its _____.
5. Name two ways to display out-of-view tiles on the Start screen.
6. How can you display the Charms bar?
7. Explain the difference between the Start screen and the desktop.
8. To access a Windows 8 app running in the background, you use the _____, which displays thumbnails of open apps.

Session 1.2 Visual Overview:

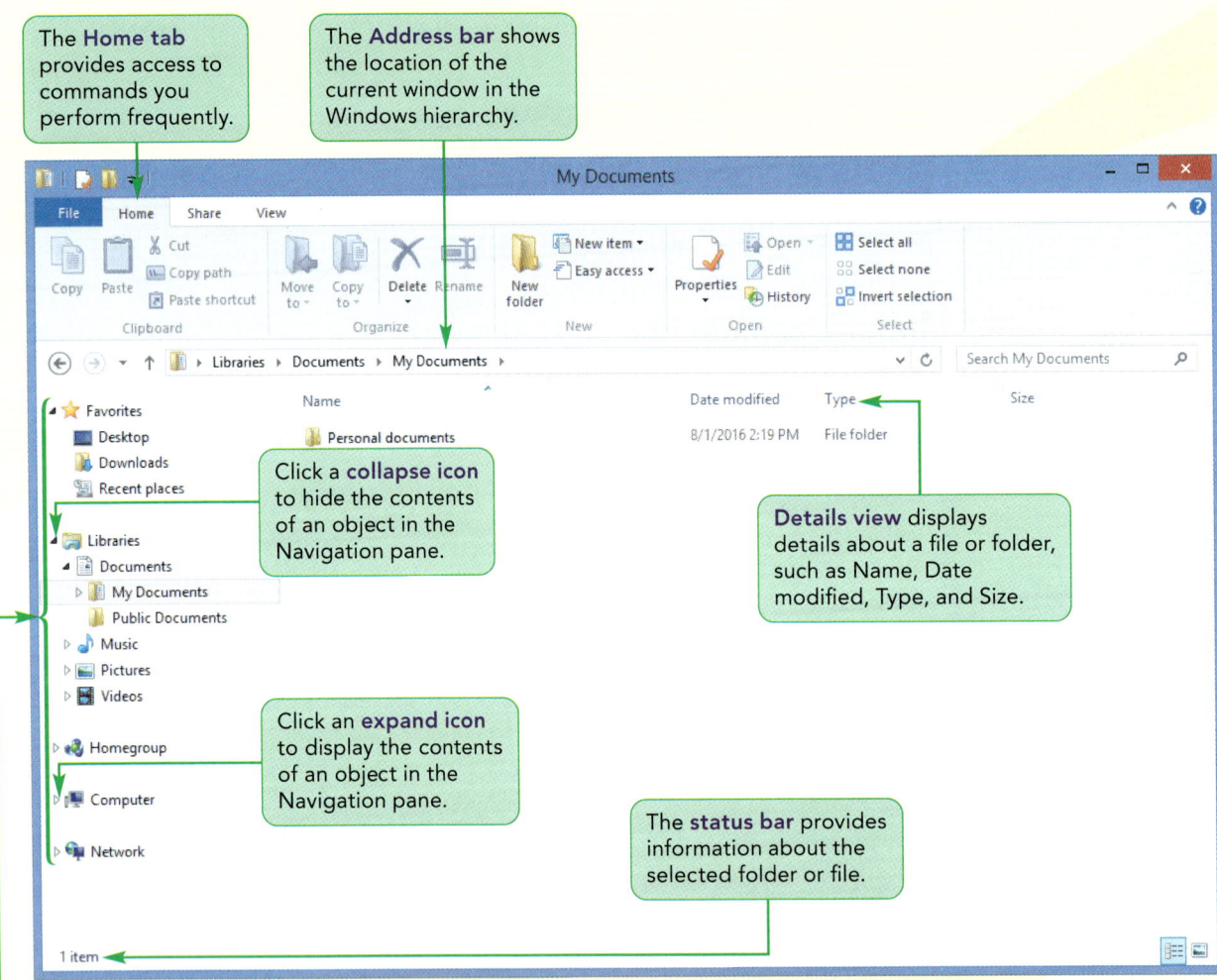

Tutorial 1 Exploring the Basics of Microsoft Windows 8 | Windows   WIN 29

Working in File Explorer

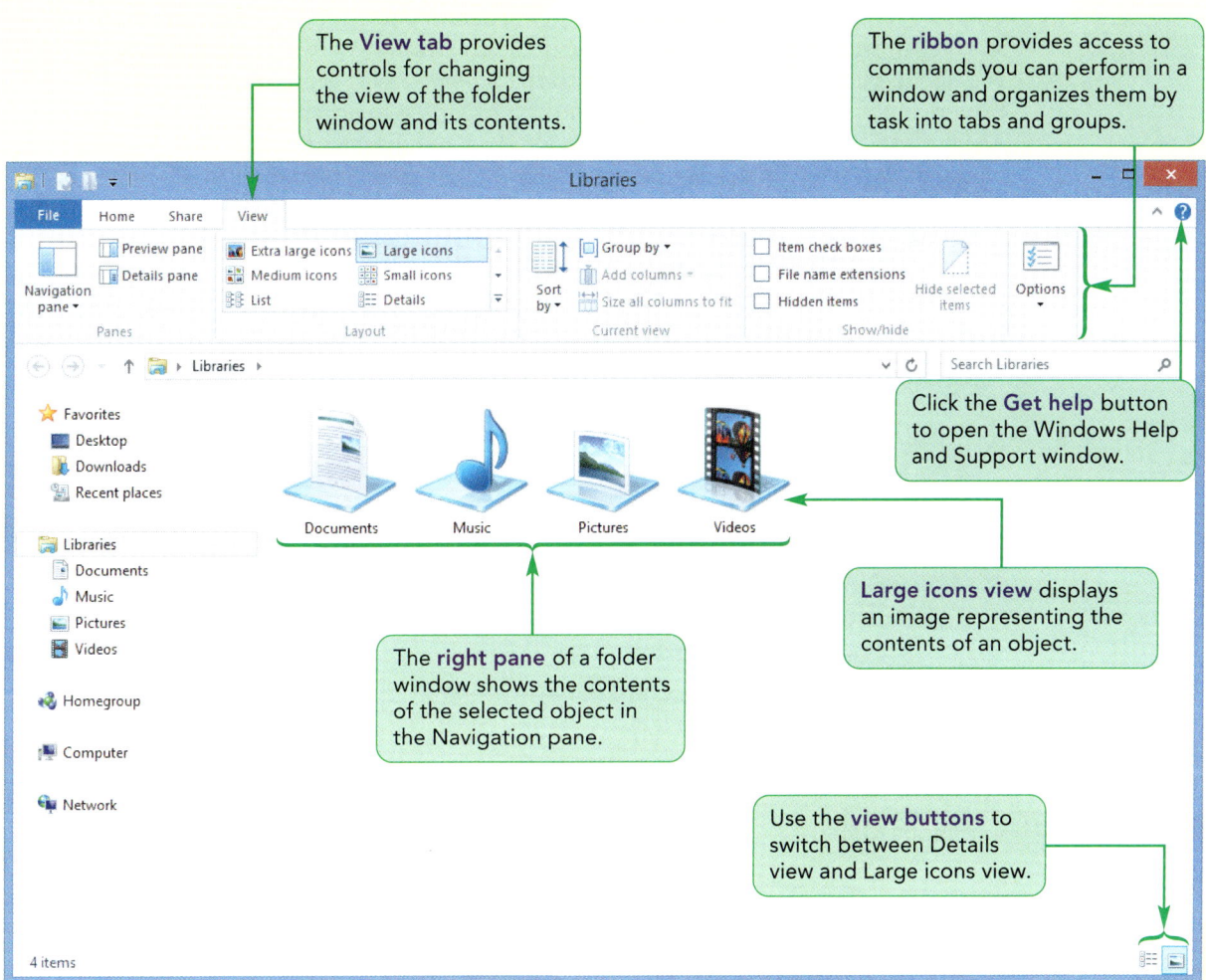

Exploring Your Computer

To discover the contents and resources on your computer, you explore, or navigate, it. **Navigating** means moving from one location to another on your computer, such as from one file or folder to another, or from one drive to another. In Windows 8, you use **File Explorer** (as shown in the Session 1.2 Visual Overview) to navigate, view, and work with the contents and resources on your computer.

Navigating with File Explorer

File Explorer is a window that is divided into two separate areas, called **panes**. The left side of the window is called the Navigation pane, which you use to access locations on your computer. The right pane displays the details of the location you navigated to, so you can work with your files, folders, or devices easily. At the top of the window is a ribbon with buttons that let you perform common tasks. When you first open File Explorer, the ribbon is collapsed, but you can expand it to access its tabs and controls. A status bar appears at the bottom of the window and displays the characteristics of an object you select in the File Explorer window. You use File Explorer to keep track of where your files are stored and to organize your files.

Emma Garcia, the director of Behind the Scenes, is helping you plan a training session for employees on the basics of Windows 8. She wants you to start this session by opening File Explorer and exploring the contents of your computer. She suggests exploring the libraries, which are convenient locations for storing your documents, music, pictures, and videos. A **library** is a central place to view and organize files and folders stored anywhere that your computer can access, such as those on your hard disk, removable drives, and network.

To explore the contents of your computer using File Explorer:

1. If you took a break after the previous session, make sure that your computer is on and Windows 8 is running. If necessary, press the **Windows** key to display the Start screen.
2. Click the **Desktop** tile on the Start screen to display the desktop.
3. Click the **File Explorer** button on the taskbar. A window opens showing the contents of the Windows libraries. See Figure 1-25.

Figure 1-25   Windows libraries

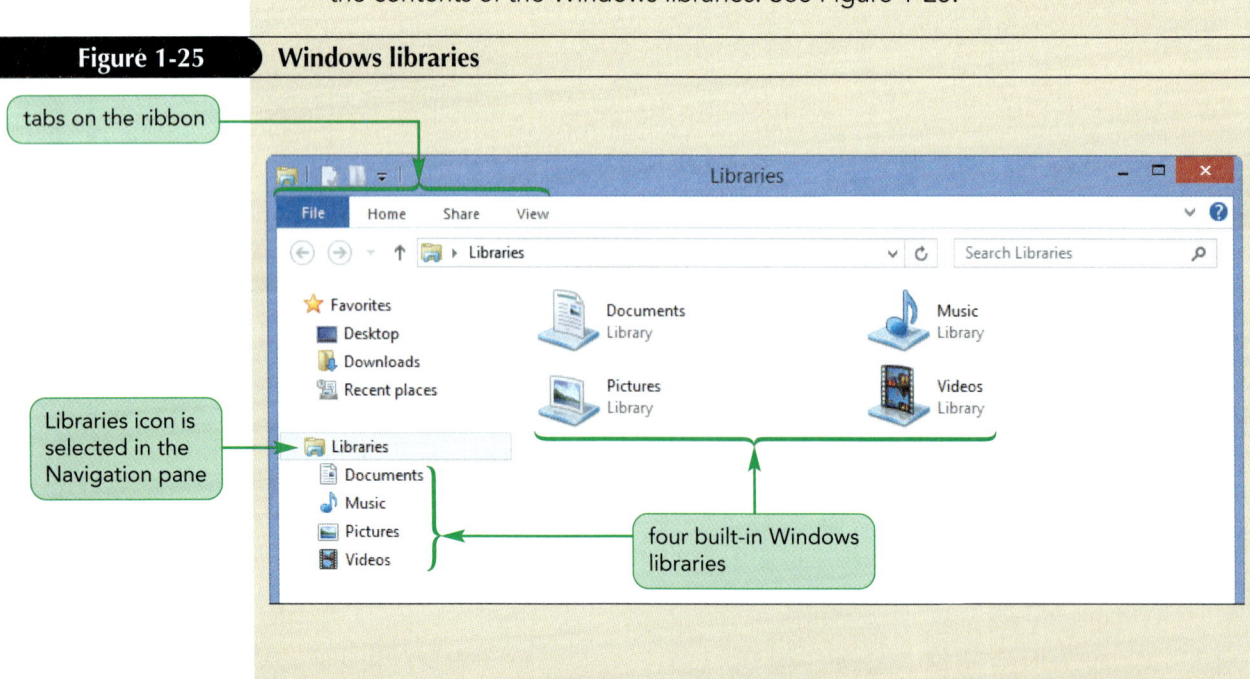

4. In the Navigation pane, click the **Pictures** library. The right pane of the window shows the contents of the Pictures library, which is designed for storing your photos and other picture files. See Figure 1-26. Your Pictures library might contain files and folders.

Figure 1-26   **Pictures library in File Explorer**

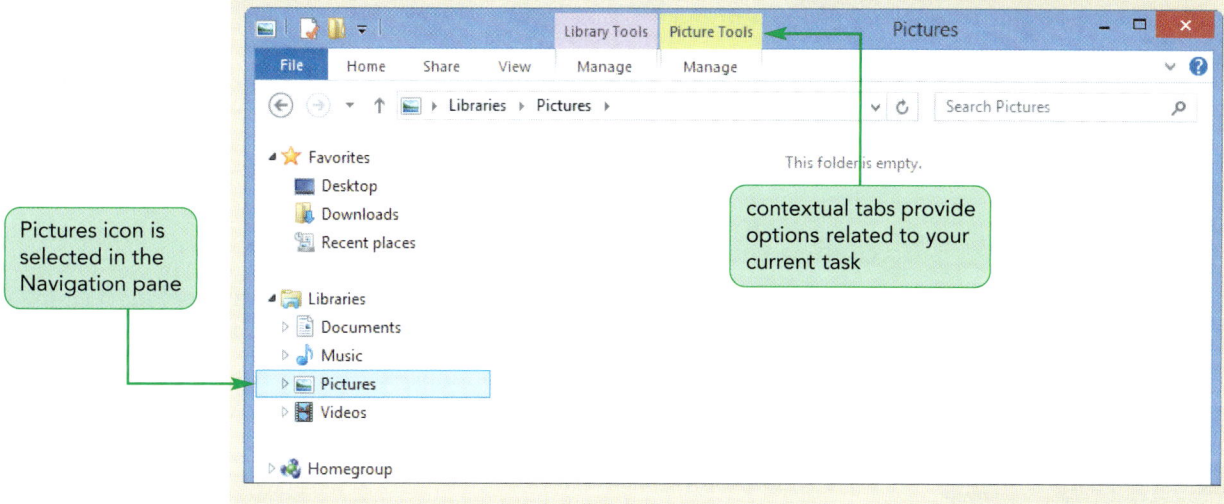

As you open folders and navigate with File Explorer, tabs might appear at the top of the window just above the standard ribbon tabs. For example, the Picture Tools Manage tab appears when you navigate to the Pictures library. This type of tab is called a **contextual tab**, and it contains options related to your current task. For example, the Picture Tools Manage tab contains options for working with pictures.

Emma mentions that you can change the appearance of most windows to suit your preferences. You'll change the view of the File Explorer window next so you can see more details about folders and files.

Changing the View

Windows 8 provides eight ways to view the contents of a folder: Extra large icons, Large icons, Medium icons, Small icons, List, Details, Tiles, and Content. The default view for any folder in the Pictures library is Large icons view, which provides a thumbnail image of the file contents. The default view for other types of folders is Details view, which displays a small icon instead of a thumbnail and lists details about each file. Although only Details view lists all file details, such as the date a photo was taken and its rating, you can see these details in any other view by pointing to a file to display a ScreenTip.

REFERENCE

Changing the Icon View

- In File Explorer, click a view button on the status bar.

or

- Click the View tab on the ribbon.
- In the Layout group, click the view option, or click the More button, if necessary, and then click a view option.

INSIGHT

Selecting a View

When you display files in Medium icons view or larger, the icon displays a preview of the file's content. The preview images are big and easy to see; however, the window shows fewer files with large icons. When you display files using smaller icons, the window can show more files, but the preview images are not as easy to see. The view you select depends on your preferences and needs.

To demonstrate switching from one view to another, Emma says you can display the Windows libraries in Details view. To do so, you'll use the Details view button on the status bar.

To change the view of the Libraries window:

1. In the Navigation pane, click the **Libraries** link to display the four built-in Windows libraries in Tiles view, which is the default for this window.

2. Click the **Details view** button on the status bar. The window shows the same four libraries, but with more details and smaller icons. See Figure 1-27.

Figure 1-27   Libraries window in Details view

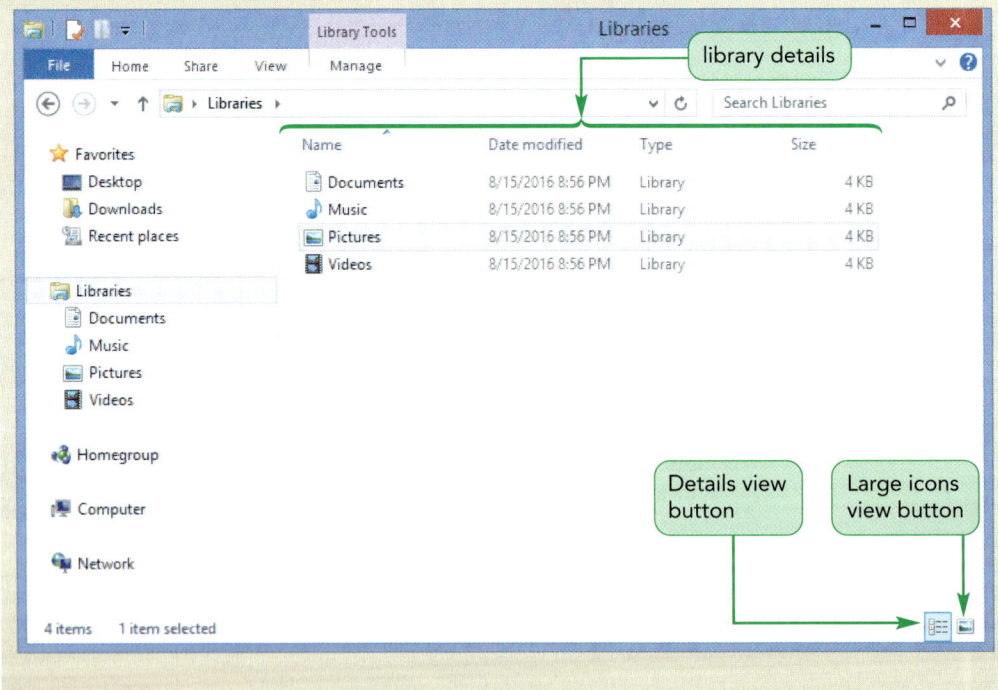

3. Click the **Large icons view** button on the status bar. The window shows the files with large icons and no file details.

Emma suggests that you now use File Explorer to navigate your computer.

Using the Navigation Pane

To navigate your computer, you use the Navigation pane on the left side of the File Explorer window. The Navigation pane organizes computer resources into five categories: Favorites (for locations you access frequently), Libraries (for the Windows default libraries), Homegroup (for your shared home network, if any), Computer (for the drives and devices on your computer), and Network (for network locations your computer can access).

When you move the pointer into the Navigation pane, triangles appear next to some icons. An open triangle, or expand icon, indicates that a folder contains other folders that are not currently displayed in the Navigation pane. Click the triangle to expand the folder and display its subfolders. (A **subfolder** is a folder contained in another folder.) A filled triangle, or collapse icon, indicates the folder is expanded, and its subfolders are listed below the folder name. You can click a folder in the Navigation pane to navigate directly to that folder and display its contents in the right pane.

Using the Navigation pane to explore your computer usually involves clicking expand icons to expand objects and find the folder you want, and then clicking that folder to display its contents in the right pane. To display a list of all the folders on a drive, expand the Computer icon in the Navigation pane, and then expand the icon for the drive, such as Local Disk (C:). The Navigation pane shows the hierarchy of folders on the drive, so you can use it to find and manage your files and folders.

INSIGHT

Identifying Storage Devices

Each storage device you can access on your computer is associated with a letter. The first hard drive is drive C. (If you add other hard drives, they are usually drives D, E, and so on.) If you have a CD or DVD drive or a USB flash drive plugged in to a USB port, it usually has the next available letter in the alphabetic sequence. If you can access hard drives located on other computers in a network, those drives sometimes (although not always) have letters associated with them as well. Naming conventions for network drives vary. For example, the network drive on a typical computer might have the drive letter Z.

Now you're ready to use the Navigation pane to find and open a folder people use often—the My Documents folder, which is a convenient place to store your documents and other work. The My Documents folder is stored in the Documents library by default.

To open the My Documents folder:

1. If necessary, click the **expand** icon ▷ next to Libraries in the Navigation pane to display the four built-in library folders for Documents, Music, Pictures, and Videos. (Your computer might include additional library folders.) Note that the expand icon ▷ changes to a collapse icon ◢.

   Trouble? If the expand icon ▷ does not appear next to Libraries in the Navigation pane, the Libraries folder is already expanded. Skip Step 1.

2. Click the **expand** icon ▷ next to Documents to display the folders in the Documents library. See Figure 1-28.

Figure 1-28 Folders in the Documents library

3. Click the **My Documents** folder to display its contents in the right pane. (Your My Documents folder might not contain any files or folders.)

The Address bar in File Explorer provides handy shortcuts for navigating to locations on your computer. For example, you can use the Back button to return to the last location you visited. You can use it now to return to the Sample Pictures folder.

To return to the Libraries window:

1. Click the **Back** button ⊛ on the Address bar to return to your last location: the Libraries window.
2. Click the **Close** button ✕ to close File Explorer.
3. Press the **Windows** key ⊞ to display the Start screen.

Getting Help

Windows 8 **Help and Support** provides on-screen information about the program you are using. Help for the Windows 8 operating system is available by displaying the Start screen, typing *help*, and then clicking Help and Support in the search results.

When you start Help for Windows 8, the Windows Help and Support window opens, which gives you access to Help files stored on your computer as well as Help information stored on the Microsoft Web site. If you are not connected to the Web, you have access to only the Help files stored on your computer.

Emma suggests that you start Windows 8 Help and Support, and then explore the information provided in the Windows Help and Support window.

To start Windows 8 Help and Support:

1. On the Start screen, type **help** to open the Search menu with "help" already entered in the Search box.

TIP

You can also start Windows 8 Help and Support from File Explorer by clicking the Get help button on the ribbon.

2. Click **Help and Support** in the search results on the Apps screen. The home page of Windows Help and Support opens on the desktop.

3. Click the **Maximize** button to maximize the Windows Help and Support window. See Figure 1-29. The contents of the home page differ depending on whether you are connected to the Internet.

   Trouble? If the Help and Support window does not display the page in the figure, click the Help home link near the top of the window to view the Help home page.

Figure 1-29   Windows Help and Support window

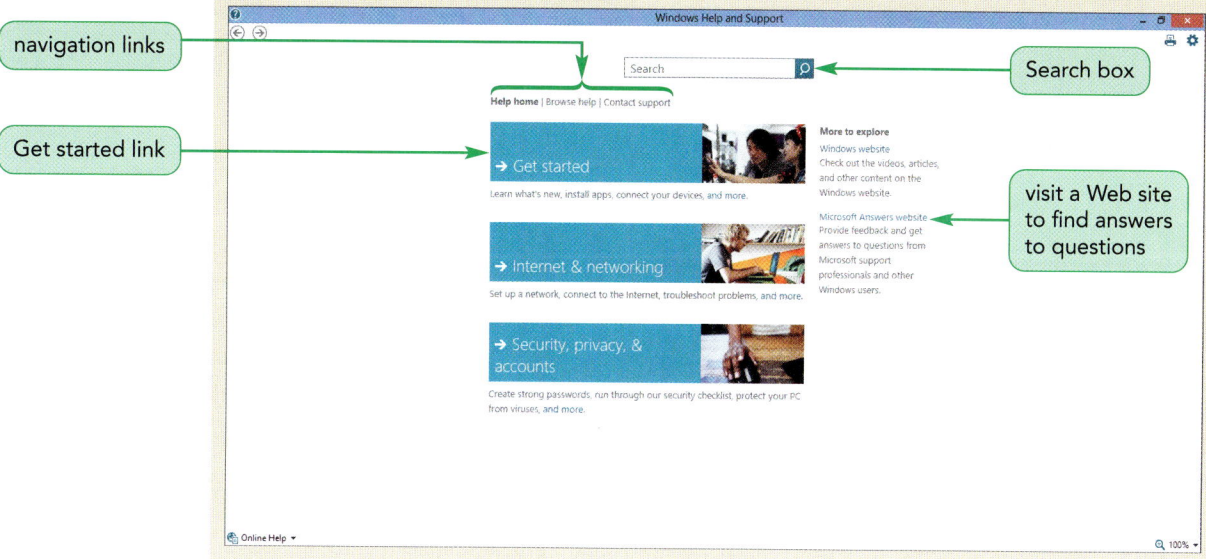

The Help home page in Windows Help and Support provides tools for finding answers and other information about Windows 8. For information about setting up your computer after installing Windows 8, click the Get started link. If you have an Internet connection, you can click the Internet & networking link to find information on setting up a network and connecting to the Internet. For help with maintaining security, privacy, and user accounts, click the Security, privacy, & accounts link. You can also connect to the Microsoft Web sites to get help. Click the Windows website link to visit the Windows pages on the Microsoft Web site. Click the Microsoft Answers website link to visit an interactive site where you can search for answers to specific questions about using Windows 8.

You can also use the other navigation links in the Windows Help and Support window to access Help topics. Click the Browse help link to display the most commonly explored Help topics, such as using files and folders. To list your options for contacting Microsoft support, click the Contact support link. These three navigation links are available on all pages in the Windows Help and Support window.

In addition to links providing access to pages in Windows Help and Support, the window contains two navigation buttons—the Back button and the Forward button. You use these buttons to navigate the pages you've already opened. Use the Back button to return to the previous page you viewed. By doing so, you activate the Forward button, which you can click to go to the next page of those you've opened. At the top of almost every Help page is the Search box, which you can use to quickly find Help content. Type any word or phrase in the Search box and press the Enter key, and Windows 8 lists all the Help pages that contain that word or phrase.

Viewing the Get Started Topics

Windows Help and Support includes instructions on the basics of using Windows 8. You can learn more about these basic topics by using the Get started link on the Windows Help and Support home page.

To view Get started topics:

1. Click the **Get started** link. A list of topics related to using Windows 8 appears in the Windows Help and Support window.
2. Click the topic **Mouse and keyboard: What's new**. An article explaining how to use the mouse and keyboard appears, including a video demonstrating these skills.
3. Scroll down to the bottom of the page and then click the **Get to know Windows 8** link. A page opens describing the new features in Windows 8.
4. Click the **Back** button to return to the previous page you visited, which is the Mouse and keyboard page, and then click the **Back** button to return to the Get started page.

You can access the full complement of Help pages by using the Browse help list.

Selecting a Topic from the Browse Help List

The Browse help list organizes the information in Windows Help and Support into topics and categories. You can click a link to display the titles of related categories. You can click a topic under a specific category to get help about a particular task or feature. For example, you can use the Browse help list to learn more about files, folders, and searching logically.

To find a Help topic using the Browse help list:

1. Click the **Browse help** link. A list of Windows Help topics appears in the Windows Help and Support window.
2. Click the topic **Files, folders, and search** to display a list of topics divided by categories all related to files, folders, and searching.
3. Under the Work with your files category, click the topic **How to work with files and folders**. The Windows Help and Support window displays information about that topic.
4. Scroll down to review the information on this page.
5. Click the **Top of page** link to return to the top of the page.

Another Help tool is the Search box, a popular way to find answers to your Windows 8 questions.

Searching the Help Pages

If you can't find the topic you need by clicking a link or browsing topics, or if you want to quickly find Help pages related to a particular topic, you can use the Search box. Emma provides a typical example. Suppose you want to know how to exit Windows 8, but you don't know if Windows refers to this as exiting, quitting, closing, or shutting down. You can search the Help pages to find just the right topic.

To search the Help pages for information on exiting Windows 8:

1. Click the **Help home** link to return to the home page.
2. Click the **Search** box. A blinking insertion point appears.
3. Type **shut down** and then press the **Enter** key. A list of Help pages containing the words "shut down" appears in the Windows Help and Support window. See Figure 1-30. (Your results might differ.)

Figure 1-30   Search Help results

- search term
- number of topics found
- How do I shut down (turn off) my PC? link
- Help pages containing the search term

4. Click the **How do I shut down (turn off) my PC?** link. The instructions appear in the Windows Help and Support window.

   Trouble? If a "Topic not found" message appears in the window instead of a Help topic, click the Back button, and then click a different link in the Windows Help and Support window.

   If this topic did not answer your question, you could click the Help home link and then click the Microsoft Answers website link. Doing so opens a Web page where you can search for answers to your questions.

5. Click the **Close** button on the title bar to close the Windows Help and Support window.

Now that you know how Windows 8 Help works, Emma reminds you to use it when you need to perform a new task or want a reminder about how to complete a procedure.

Turning Off Windows 8

> **TIP**
> Shutting down does not automatically save your work, so be sure to save your files before selecting the Shut down or Restart option.

When you're finished working in Windows 8, you should always turn it off properly. Doing so saves energy, preserves your data and settings, and makes sure your computer starts quickly the next time you use it.

You can turn off Windows 8 using the Power button on the Settings menu. (Use the Charms bar to display the Settings menu.) When you click the Power button, you can choose the Sleep, Shut down, or Restart option. If you choose the Sleep option, Windows saves your work and then turns down the power to your monitor and computer, a condition called **sleep**. A light on the outside of your computer case blinks or changes color to indicate that the computer is sleeping. Because Windows saves your work, you do not need to close your programs or files before your computer goes to sleep. To wake a computer, you typically press the hardware power button on your computer case. Some computer manufacturers might set the computer to wake when you press a key or move the mouse. After you wake a computer, the screen looks exactly as it did when you put your computer to sleep.

If you choose the Shut down option, your computer closes all open programs, including Windows itself, and then completely turns off your computer. Shutting down doesn't save your work, so you must save your files first.

If you select the Restart option, your computer shuts down and then immediately restarts, which you might need to do after installing new programs or hardware.

PROSKILLS

Decision Making: Sign out, Sleep, or Shut Down?

If you are using a computer on the job, your organization probably has a policy about what to do when you're finished working on the computer. If it does not, deciding on the best approach depends on who uses the computer and how long it will be idle. Keep the following guidelines in mind as you make your decision:

- Sign out—If another person might use your computer shortly, sign out of Windows to protect your data and prepare the computer for someone else to use. To sign out of Windows 8, click your user icon on the Start screen and then click Sign out.
- Sleep—By default, Windows 8 is set to sleep after 15–30 minutes of idle time, depending on whether you are using a mobile or desktop computer. If you will be away from the computer for more than 15 minutes but less than a day, you can generally let the computer go to sleep on its own.
- Shut down—If your computer is plugged in to a power outlet and you don't plan to use the computer for more than a day, such as over the weekend, you save wear and tear on your electronic components and conserve energy by turning the computer off. You should also turn off the computer when it is susceptible to electrical damage, such as during a lightning storm, and when you need to install new hardware or disconnect the computer from a power source. If your mobile computer is running on battery power only and you don't plan to use it for more than a few hours, you should also turn it off to save your battery charge.

Emma suggests that you compare putting your computer to sleep and shutting down Windows 8.

To turn off Windows 8:

▶ 1. Press the **Windows** key to display the Start screen.

▶ 2. Point to the upper-right hot corner on the Start screen to display the Charms bar.

3. Click the **Settings** charm on the Charms bar to display the Settings menu, shown in Figure 1-31.

Figure 1-31 | Settings menu

Power button

4. Click the **Power** button to display the power options.

5. Click **Sleep**. Windows 8 saves your work and then puts the computer to sleep. The light in the hardware power button changes color or blinks to indicate the computer is in a sleep state.

   Trouble? If a Sleep option does not appear when you click the Power button, your computer might be set to go to sleep only automatically. Click Shut down on the Power menu, and skip the remaining steps.

6. If the light in the hardware power button changes color or is now blinking, press the hardware power button to wake up the computer. If necessary, clear the lock screen and enter your password. Otherwise, move the mouse or press a key to wake the computer.

7. Display the Charms bar, and then click the **Settings** charm to display the Settings menu.

   Trouble? If you are instructed to sign out instead of shut down, click twice anywhere on the Start screen to close the Settings menu and Charms bar, click your user icon on the Start screen, and then click Sign out. Skip Step 8.

8. Click the **Power** button, and then click **Shut down**. Windows 8 turns off the computer.

   Trouble? If the Power button displays the Update and shut down option instead of Shut down, click Update and shut down.

In this session, you learned how to use File Explorer to navigate your computer. You also learned how to change the view of the contents of the File Explorer window. Finally, you learned how to get help when you need it and how to turn off Windows 8. With Emma's help, you should feel comfortable with the basics of Windows 8 and well prepared to demonstrate the fundamentals of using this operating system.

Session 1.2 Quick Check

REVIEW

1. _____ means moving from one location to another on your computer, such as from one file or folder to another.
2. The left pane in File Explorer is called the _____, which provides access to resources and locations on your computer.
3. What is the purpose of the Pictures library?
4. Describe the difference between Details view and Large icons view.
5. In the File Explorer window, what appears in the right pane when you click a folder icon in the Navigation pane?
6. Explain how to expand a folder or other objects in the Navigation pane.
7. How do you access Windows Help and Support in Windows 8?
8. What option(s) save(s) your work before turning off your computer?

Review Assignments

There are no Data Files needed for the Review Assignments.

The day before your first Windows 8 training session for Behind the Scenes employees, Emma Garcia offers to observe your tour of the operating system and help you fine-tune your lesson. You'll start working on the Start screen, with no applications open. Complete the following steps, recording your answers to any questions according to your instructor's preferences:

1. Start Windows 8 and sign in, if necessary.
2. Use the mouse to scroll the Start screen. How many full tiles appear on the screen when you scroll?
3. Zoom the Start screen to reduce the size of the tiles. How many tiles appear on the screen now?
4. Start the Calendar app.
5. Display the desktop. List the major parts of the desktop, including any icons.
6. Start WordPad. Identify each object on the taskbar (not including the notification area).
7. Start Paint and maximize the Paint window. How many buttons appear on the taskbar?
8. Switch to WordPad. How do you know that WordPad is the active program?
9. Close WordPad, and then restore the Paint window to its original size.
10. Open the Recycle Bin window. Record the number of items it contains, and then drag and resize the Recycle Bin window so that you can see both it and the Paint window.
11. Close the Paint window from the taskbar. What command did you use?
12. Display the Switch List. Which thumbnails are displayed in the Switch List?
13. Maximize the Recycle Bin window and then click the Home tab. Which buttons are active (not gray)? Use any button on the Home tab to open a dialog box. What dialog box did you open? What do you think this dialog box is used for? Click the Cancel button to close the dialog box, and then close the Recycle Bin window.
14. Change the view of the items displayed in the right pane of the File Explorer window. What view did you select and how did your selection change the appearance of the items? Close File Explorer.
15. Open Windows Help and Support. Use the Get started link to learn something new about Windows 8. What did you learn? How did you find this topic?
16. Browse Help topics to find information about customizing your computer. How many topics are listed in the Customize your PC category?
17. Use the Search box to find information about customizing your computer. How many topics are listed?
18. Close Help, and then return to the Start screen.
19. Turn off Windows 8 by using the Sleep command, shutting down, or signing out.
20. Submit your answers to the preceding questions to your instructor, either in printed or electronic form, as requested.

Case Problem 1

There are no Data Files needed for this Case Problem.

Up and Running   Up and Running is an independent firm located in major electronics stores throughout the Midwest. The firm installs software, repairs hardware, and provides training to customers of the electronics stores. Ken Mathias is the manager of a store in Red Wing, Minnesota. Ken hired you to work with customers in their homes or businesses. You are preparing for a visit to a customer who is new to Windows 8 and wants to determine the contents of his computer, including media apps and sample media files. Complete the following steps:

1. Start Windows 8 and sign in, if necessary.
2. Examine the tiles on the Start screen and use one to start an app that plays music or videos or displays photos. Which app did you start?
3. Start another media app. Which app did you start?
4. Search for apps installed on your computer related to media. What apps did you find?
5. Start one of the apps you found in Step 4. Which app did you start? Is it a Windows 8 app or a desktop application? How can you tell?
6. Start an app you could use to take photos. Which app did you start? Is it a Windows 8 app or a desktop application?
7. Use the Search menu to find settings related to media. How many settings did you find?
8. Close all open applications.
9. Start File Explorer, and then navigate to a folder that contains files. Which folder did you open? View the files in Details view, and then sort them by Size. Which file is the largest? (*Hint*: If there are no folders with files on your computer, display the contents of the Desktop.)
10. Change to Large icons view, and then point to a file to display a ScreenTip. What type of file did you select? What details are provided in the ScreenTip? Close File Explorer.
11. Open Windows Help and Support, and then find and read topics that describe two Windows features that make your PC more secure.
12. Close all open windows.
13. Submit your answers to the preceding questions to your instructor, either in printed or electronic form, as requested.

Case Problem 2

There are no Data Files needed for this Case Problem.

Austin Framing   After earning a degree in fine arts and working as a conservator of prints and paintings, Danielle Reid opened a store called Austin Framing in Austin, Texas. She specializes in archival framing to preserve manuscripts and fine prints. So that she can concentrate on building her business, Danielle hired you to help her perform office tasks. She asks you to start by teaching her the basics of using her computer, which runs Windows 8. She especially wants to know which applications are installed on her computer and what they do. Complete the following steps:

1. Write down the apps listed on the Start screen.
2. Start one of the apps and then describe what it does. Close the app.
3. **Explore**   Open the Search menu, display the items in the Apps category, if necessary, and then click the Apps screen to display all the applications installed on the computer. Examine the applications in the Windows Accessories list.
4. Use Windows Help and Support to research one of the applications you examined in the previous step, such as Calculator or Notepad. Describe the purpose of the application.

5. Use the Search box in Windows Help and Support to list all the Help topics related to the application you researched in the previous step. How many topics are displayed in the results? Select a topic and review the Help information.

Explore 6. Start the application you researched. If the application opened on the desktop, press the F1 key to display Help for the application. Click each link in the Help window to explore the Help topics. Compare these topics to the ones included in the Windows Help and Support window. Are they the same topics or different?

Explore 7. Use Windows Help and Support to search for Help topics about WordPad. If you are connected to the Internet, also find Help information about WordPad on the Microsoft Answers Web site. Compare the two search results.

8. Close all open windows.

9. Submit the results of the preceding steps to your instructor, either in printed or electronic form, as requested.

Case Problem 3

CHALLENGE

There are no Data Files needed for this Case Problem.

Thorpe Consulting Kara Thorpe recently started her own consulting firm in Santa Rosa, California, to help nonprofit organizations raise funds. Thorpe Consulting recommends fundraising strategies and helps clients earn grants for specific projects. Kara uses her Windows 8 laptop to create proposals, reports, and other documents and to communicate with clients. She uses File Explorer to work with files, but suspects she is not taking full advantage of its features. As Kara's new assistant, one of your responsibilities is to show her around the File Explorer window and demonstrate how to customize its appearance. Complete the following steps:

1. Start File Explorer. Click each tab on the ribbon to find out the kind of commands that are provided. Write down any commands that seem related to changing the appearance of the folder window.

2. In the Libraries window, switch to Large icons view, if necessary.

Explore 3. Change the view to Content view. (*Hint*: Click the View tab, and then click the More button in the Layout group.) Describe the differences between Large icons view and Content view.

4. Click the Pictures library, and then describe any changes in the ribbon.

5. Click the Music library, and then describe any changes in the ribbon.

Explore 6. Select a command on the View tab that displays a pane showing the details of the selected library. What command did you select?

Explore 7. Select a command on the View tab that closes the Navigation pane. What command did you select?

Explore 8. Click the Up one level button next to the Address bar. (*Hint*: Point to a button to display its name in a ScreenTip.) What happens when you click the Up one level button twice? How can you return to the Libraries window?

Explore 9. Close the pane showing the details of the selected library, and then redisplay the Navigation pane. (*Hint*: Perform Steps 6 and 7 again.)

10. Close File Explorer, and then open the Windows Help and Support window and search for information about changing folder options. Find instructions explaining how to show hidden files. Explain how to do so. (*Hint*: A hidden file is not listed in a window, though it is actually stored in that folder.)

11. Close all open windows.

12. Submit the results of the preceding steps to your instructor, either in printed or electronic form, as requested.

CREATE

Case Problem 4

There are no Data Files needed for this Case Problem.

Home Care Therapy After earning their certifications as physical and occupational therapists, Josh Cohen and Deborah Whiting decided to start a service called Home Care Therapy for people who need physical or occupational therapy in their homes. They have been using Windows 8 on laptops to schedule client appointments and track client progress, but recently purchased tablet computers to use when they are working with clients face to face. They hired you as a consultant to help them use and maintain their computers. Because Josh and Deborah learned to use Windows 8 on laptop computers, they anticipate that they might have trouble adapting to tablets. Josh asks you to help them troubleshoot by researching the skills and techniques they need to use Windows 8 on a tablet. Complete the following:

1. In Windows Help and Support, find information about how to perform the following tasks on a tablet computer:
   - Display the Charms bar.
   - Scroll the Start screen.
   - Zoom the Start screen.
   - Display the desktop.
   - Display app settings, such as Save and Edit.
2. Use the Windows website link to visit the Microsoft Web site to obtain more information about Windows 8 on a tablet computer. Watch a video that showcases Windows 8 touch features. Then, describe how you rearrange tiles on the Start screen.
3. Choose a topic that describes how to browse the Web, and then watch the related video. Explain what's new and different in Internet Explorer for touchscreen devices.
4. Choose a topic that describes how to connect to the cloud and then watch the related video. Explain what Microsoft means by connecting to the cloud.
5. Write one to two paragraphs for Josh and Deborah explaining the basics of using Windows 8 on a tablet with a touchscreen.
6. Submit the results of the preceding steps to your instructor, either in printed or electronic form, as requested.

TUTORIAL 2

Organizing Your Files

Managing Files and Folders in Windows 8

OBJECTIVES

Session 2.1
- Develop file management strategies
- Plan the organization of your files and folders
- Explore libraries, folders, and files
- Find files and folders quickly
- Create folders
- Copy and move files and folders

Session 2.2
- Name and delete files and folders
- Work with new files
- Sort and group files
- Set the appearance of a folder window
- Compress and extract files

Case | Savvy Traveler

After spending a summer traveling in Italy, Matt and Joanna Marino started Savvy Traveler, a travel company that organizes small tours in Europe. As sales manager, Matt is in charge of creating resources that describe the tours and destinations. He hired you to help him develop sales materials, especially using computer tools to track and select photos, illustrations, and text documents for brochures and Web pages. For your first task, Matt asks you to organize the files on his new computer. Although he has only a few files, he wants to use a logical organization to help him find his work as he stores more files and folders on the computer.

In this tutorial, you'll work with Matt to devise a strategy for managing files. You'll learn how Windows 8 organizes files and folders, and you'll examine Windows 8 file management tools. You'll create folders and organize files within them. You'll also use techniques to display the information you need in folder windows, and explore options for working with compressed files.

STARTING DATA FILES

Microsoft product screenshots used with permission from Microsoft Corporation.

Session 2.1 Visual Overview:

Files in a Folder Window

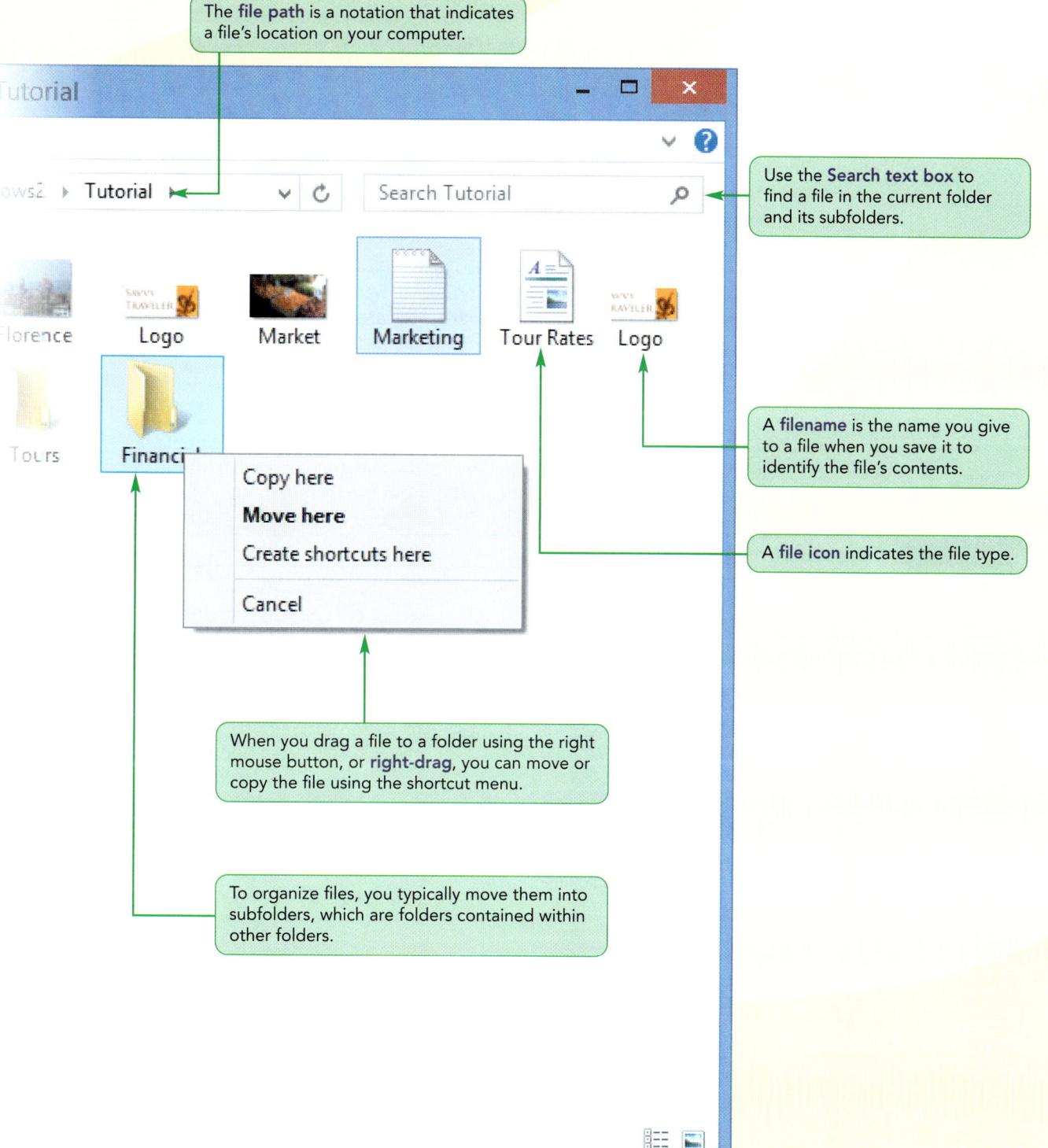

Preparing to Manage Your Files

Knowing how to save, locate, and organize computer files makes you more productive when you are working with a computer. After you create a file, you can open it and edit the file's contents, print the file, and save it again—usually using the same program you used to create it. You organize files by storing them in folders. You need to organize files and folders so that you can find them easily and work efficiently.

A file cabinet is a common metaphor for computer file organization. A computer is like a file cabinet that has two or more drawers—each drawer is a storage device, or **disk**. Each disk contains folders that hold documents, or files. To make it easy to retrieve files, you arrange them logically into folders. For example, one folder might contain financial data, another might contain your creative work, and another could contain information you're gathering for an upcoming vacation.

A computer can store folders and files on different types of disks, ranging from removable media—such as **USB flash drives** (also called flash drives, thumbnail drives, or simply USB drives) and digital video discs (DVDs)—to **hard disks**, or fixed disks, which are permanently stored on a computer. Hard disks are the most popular type of computer storage because they provide an economical way to store many gigabytes of data. (A **gigabyte**, or **GB**, is about 1 billion bytes, with each byte roughly equivalent to a character of data.)

To have your computer access a removable disk, you must insert the disk into a **drive**, which is a computer device that can retrieve and sometimes record data on a disk. See Figure 2-1. A computer's hard disk is already contained in a drive inside the computer, so you don't need to insert it each time you use the computer.

Figure 2-1   **Computer drives and disks**

© 2014 Cengage Learning

A computer distinguishes one drive from another by assigning each a drive letter. As you learned earlier, the hard disk in a computer is assigned to drive C. The remaining drives can have any other letters, but are usually assigned in the order that the drives were installed on the computer—so your USB drive might be drive D, drive E, or drive F.

Understanding the Need for Organizing Files and Folders

Windows 8 stores thousands of files in many folders on the hard disk of your computer. These are system files that Windows 8 needs to display the Start screen and desktop, use drives, and perform other operating system tasks. To keep the system stable and to find files quickly, Windows organizes the folders and files in a hierarchy, or **file system**. At the top of the hierarchy, Windows stores folders and important files that it needs when you turn on the computer. This location is called the **root directory** and is usually drive C (the hard disk). The term *root* refers to another popular metaphor for visualizing a file system—an upside-down tree, which reflects the file hierarchy that Windows uses. In Figure 2-2, the tree trunk corresponds to the root directory, the branches to the folders, and the leaves to the files.

Figure 2-2 **Windows file hierarchy**

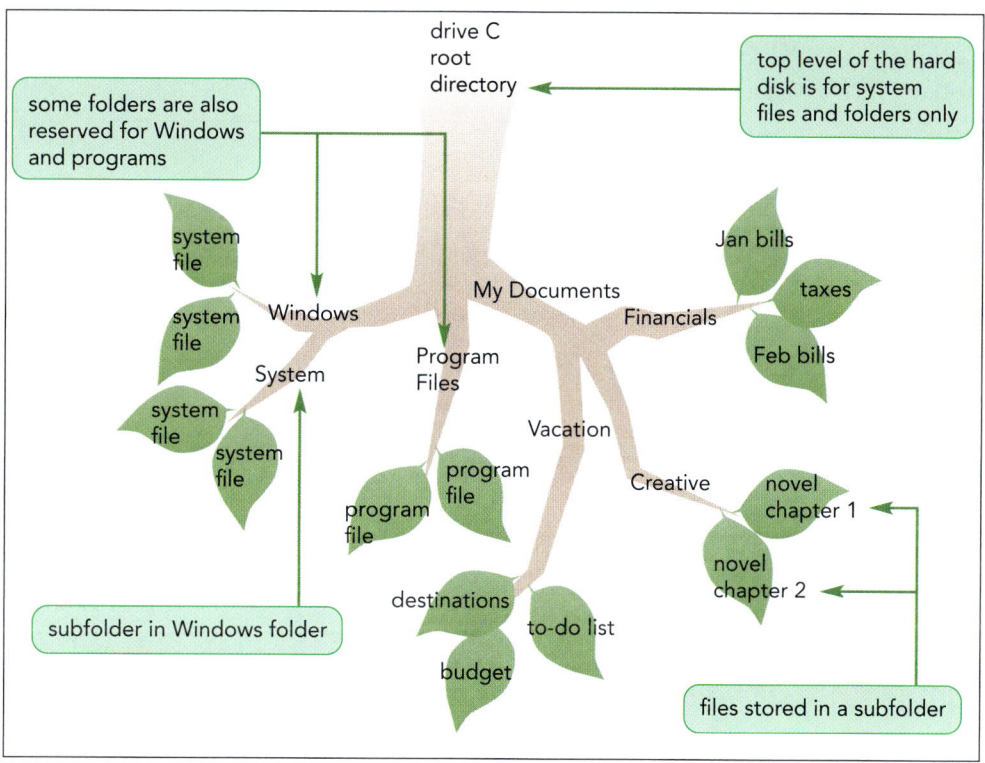

© 2014 Cengage Learning

Note that some folders contain other folders. An effectively organized computer contains a few folders in the root directory, and those folders contain other folders, also called subfolders.

The root directory, or top level, of the hard disk is for system files and folders only. You should not store your own work in the root directory because your files could interfere with Windows or a program. (If you are working in a computer lab, you might not be allowed to access the root directory.)

Do not delete or move any files or folders from the root directory of the hard disk; doing so could disrupt the system so that you can't run or start the computer. In fact, you should not reorganize or change any folder that contains installed software because Windows 8 expects to find the files for specific programs within certain folders. If you reorganize or change these folders, Windows 8 can't locate and start the programs stored in those folders. Likewise, you should not make changes to the folder (usually named Windows) that contains the Windows 8 operating system.

Developing Strategies for Organizing Files and Folders

The type of disk you use to store files determines how you organize those files. Figure 2-3 shows how you could organize your files on a hard disk if you were taking a full semester of business classes. To duplicate this organization, you would open the main folder for your documents, create four folders—one each for the Basic Accounting, Computer Concepts, Management Skills, and Professional Writing courses—and then store the writing assignments you complete in the Professional Writing folder.

Figure 2-3   Organizing folders and files on a hard disk

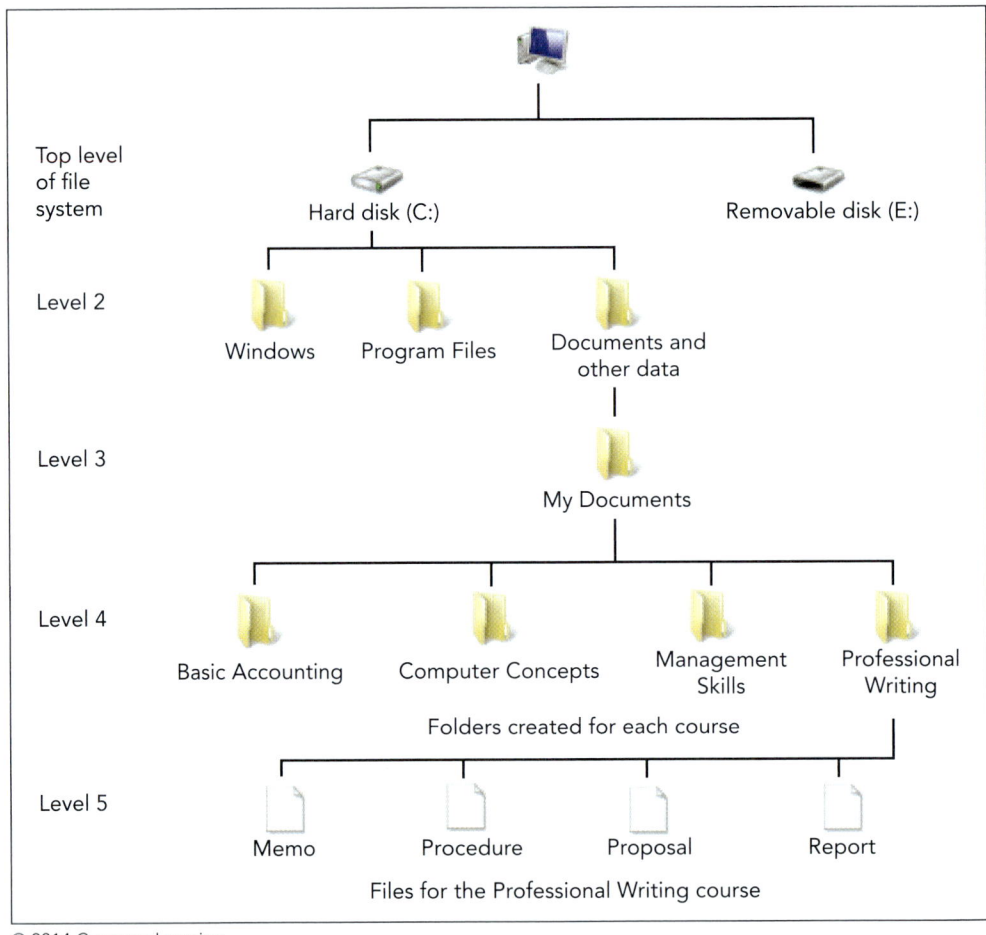

© 2014 Cengage Learning

If you store your files on removable media, such as a USB drive, you can use a simpler organization because you do not have to account for system files. In general, the larger the medium, the more levels of folders you should use because large media can store more files and, therefore, need better organization. For example, if you were organizing your files on a 12 GB USB drive, you could create folders in the top level of the USB drive for each general category of documents you store—one each for Courses, Creative, Financials, and Vacation. The Courses folder could then include one folder for each course (Basic Accounting, Computer Concepts, Management Skills, and Professional Writing), and each of those folders could contain the appropriate files.

If you have USB drives with a lower storage capacity, you might use one USB drive for your courses, another for creative work, and so on. If you need to create large documents for your courses, you can use one USB drive for each course.

PROSKILLS

Decision Making: Determining Where to Store Files

When you create and save files on your computer's hard disk, you should store them in subfolders. The top level of the hard disk is off-limits for your files because they could interfere with system files. If you are working on your own computer, store your files within the My Documents folder in the Documents library, which is where many programs save your files by default. When you use a computer on the job, your employer might assign a main folder to you for storing your work. In either case, if you simply store all your files in one folder, you will soon have trouble finding the files you want. Instead, you should create subfolders within a main folder to separate files in a way that makes sense for you.

Even if you store most of your files on removable media, such as USB drives, you still need to organize those files into folders and subfolders. Before you start creating folders, whether on a hard disk or removable disk, you need to plan the organization you will use. Following your plan increases your efficiency because you don't have to pause and decide which folder to use when you save your files. A file organization plan also makes you more productive in your computer work—the next time you need a particular file, you'll know where to find it.

Exploring Files and Folders

To explore the files and folders on your computer in Windows 8, you use File Explorer. This tool displays the contents of your computer, using icons to represent drives, folders, and files. When you start File Explorer, it opens to show the contents of the Windows default libraries, making it easy to find the files you work with often, such as documents and pictures. To display only the drives on your computer, you can use another Windows tool: the Computer window. You typically open this window to perform system tasks, such as viewing system information. Like File Explorer, the Computer window is a folder window that displays locations on your computer.

A **folder window** refers to any window that displays the contents of a folder. It is divided into two sections, called panes. The left pane is the Navigation pane, which contains icons and links to locations you use often. The right pane displays the contents of your folders and other locations. If you select a folder in the Navigation pane, the contents of that folder appear in the right pane. To display the hierarchy of the folders and other locations on your computer, you select the Computer icon in the Navigation pane, and then select the icon for a drive, such as Local Disk (C:) or Removable Disk (E:). You can then open and explore folders on that drive.

If the Navigation pane showed all the folders on your computer at once, it could be a very long list. Instead, you open drives and folders only when you want to see what they contain. If a folder contains undisplayed subfolders, an expand icon appears to the left of the folder icon. (The same is true for drives.) To view the folders contained in an object, you click the expand icon. A collapse icon then appears next to the folder icon; click the collapse icon to hide the folder's subfolders. To view the files contained in a folder, you click the folder icon, and the files appear in the right pane. See Figure 2-4.

Figure 2-4   Viewing files in a folder window

*Callouts on figure:*
- name of the selected folder in the Address bar
- click to collapse the folder
- selected folder
- click to expand the folder
- contents of the selected folder

Folder window shows: Professional Writing folder containing:

Name	Date modified	Type	Size
Memo	8/17/2016 5:11 PM	Text Document	1 KB
Procedure	8/17/2016 5:12 PM	Text Document	1 KB
Proposal	8/17/2016 5:12 PM	Text Document	2 KB
Report	8/17/2016 5:13 PM	Text Document	1 KB

Navigation pane shows: Favorites (Desktop, Downloads, Recent places); Libraries (Documents > My Documents > Basic Accounting, Computer Concepts, Management Skills, Professional Writing, Public Documents; Music; Pictures; Videos); Homegroup; Computer.

4 items   1 item selected 585 bytes

Using the Navigation pane helps you explore your computer and orients you to your current location. As you move, copy, delete, and perform other tasks with the folders in the right pane of a folder window, you can refer to the Navigation pane to see how your changes affect the overall organization.

In addition to using the Navigation pane, you can explore your computer from a folder window in other ways. Use the following navigation techniques in any folder window and many dialog boxes:

- Opening drives and folders in the right pane—To view the contents of a drive or folder, double-click the drive or folder icon in the right pane of the folder window. For example, to view the contents of the Professional Writing folder shown in Figure 2-5, you can double-click the Professional Writing folder in the right pane.

Figure 2-5 Viewing the contents of a folder

- Using the Address bar—You can use the Address bar to navigate to a different folder. The Address bar displays your current folder as a series of locations separated by arrow buttons. Click a folder name such as My Documents or an arrow button to navigate to a different location. You'll explore these controls later in the tutorial.
- Clicking the Back, Forward, Recent locations, and Up one level buttons—Use the Back, Forward, and Recent locations buttons to navigate to other folders you have already opened. After you use the Address bar to change folders, for example, you can use the Back button to return to the original folder. You can click the Recent locations button to navigate to a location you've visited recently. Use the Up one level button to navigate up to the folder containing the current folder. The ScreenTip for this button changes to reflect the folder to which you can navigate. For example, when you are working in the My Documents folder, the ScreenTip is Up to "Documents".
- Using the Search text box—To find a file or folder stored in the current folder or its subfolders, type a word or phrase in the Search text box. The search begins as soon as you start typing. Windows finds files based on text in the filename, text within the file, and other characteristics of the file, such as **tags** (descriptive words or phrases you add to your files) or the author. For example, if you're looking for a document named September Income, you can type *Sept* in the Search text box. Windows searches the current folder and its subfolders, and then displays any file whose filename contains a word starting with "Sept," including the September Income document.

Using Libraries and Folders

When you open File Explorer, it shows the contents of the Windows built-in libraries by default. A library displays similar types of files together, no matter where they are stored. In contrast, a folder stores files in a specific location, such as in the Professional Writing subfolder of the My Documents folder on the Local Disk (C:) drive. When you want to open the Report file stored in the Professional Writing folder, you must navigate to the Local Disk (C:) drive, then the My Documents folder, and finally the Professional Writing folder. A library makes it easier to access similar types of files. For example, you might store some music files in the My Music folder and others in a folder named Albums on your hard disk. You might also store music files in a Songs folder on a

USB drive. If the USB drive is connected to your computer, the Music library can display all the music files in the My Music, Albums, and Songs folders. You can then arrange the files to quickly find the ones you want to open and play.

Next, you'll navigate to the My Documents folder from the Documents library.

To open the My Documents folder from the Documents library:

1. Display the desktop, if necessary, and then click the **File Explorer** button on the taskbar. The File Explorer window opens, displaying the contents of the default libraries.

2. In the Libraries section of the Navigation pane, click the **expand** icon next to the Documents icon. The folders in the Documents library appear in the Navigation pane; see Figure 2-6. The contents of your computer will differ.

   Trouble? If your window displays icons in a view different from the one shown in the figure, you can still explore files and folders. The same is true for all figures in this session.

Figure 2-6   Viewing the contents of the Documents library

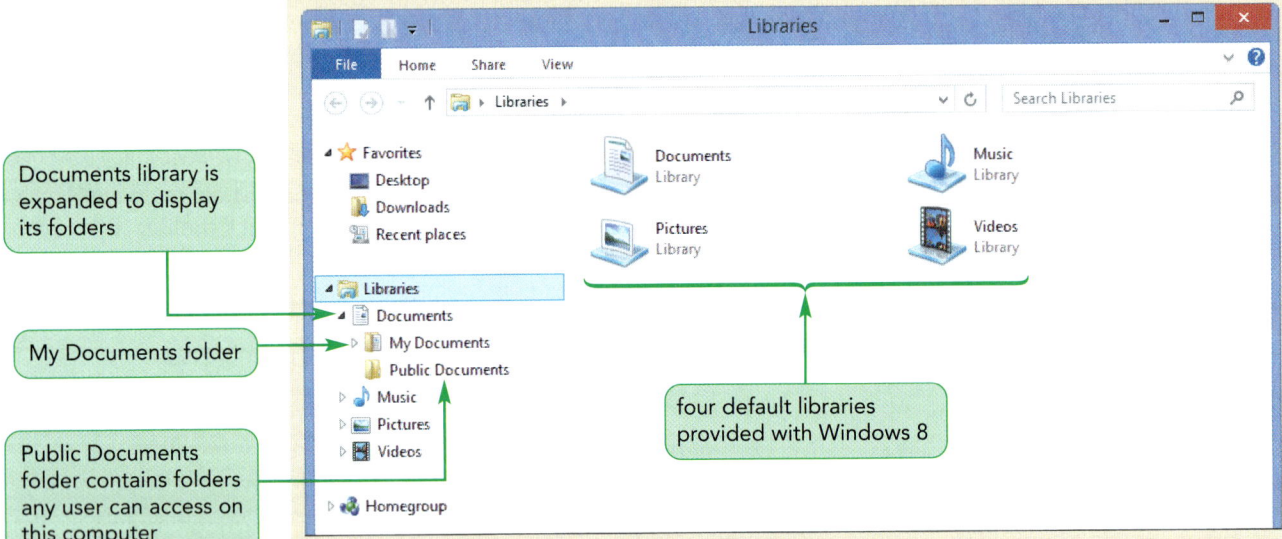

3. Click the **My Documents** folder in the Navigation pane to display its contents in the right pane.

You can think of the Documents library as containing links to folders and files that are physically stored in other locations. The My Documents folder is not stored in the Documents library—it is actually located in your personal folder, which is labeled with the name you use to sign in to the computer, such as Matt. The My Documents folder is designed to store your files—the memos, reports, spreadsheets, presentations, and other files that you create, edit, and manipulate in a program. Your personal folder contains other folders that most users open frequently, such as My Pictures found in the Pictures library and My Music found in the Music library. Although the My Pictures folder is designed to store graphics and the My Music folder is designed to store music files, you can store graphics, music, or any other type of file in the My Documents folder, especially if doing so makes it easier to find these files when you need them.

Tutorial 2 Organizing Your Files | Windows WIN 55

Now that you've shown Matt how to display the contents of the My Documents folder from the Documents library, you can show him how to navigate to the actual location of the My Documents folder using the hierarchy of folders on your computer.

To open the My Documents folder using the hierarchy of folders on your computer:

1. In the Navigation pane of the open folder window, click the **Desktop** icon. This icon represents resources you can access from the desktop. See Figure 2-7. Your desktop might have other icons.

Figure 2-7   Resources accessed from the desktop

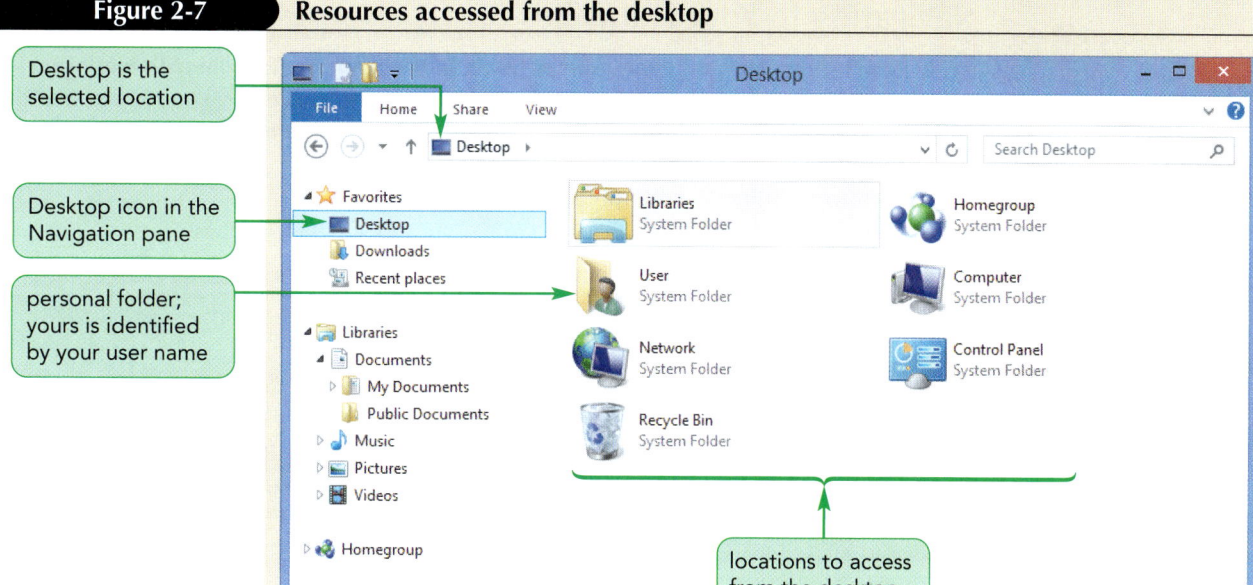

2. In the right pane, double-click your personal folder (the one with your user name). The personal folder shown in Figure 2-8 is named User. A list of folders stored in your personal folder appears in the right pane. Yours might appear in a different view.

Figure 2-8   Contents of your personal folder

> **TIP**
> When you are working in the Navigation pane, you only need to click a folder to open it, not double-click it.

3. In the right pane, double-click the **My Documents** folder. The Address bar shows the actual location of the My Documents folder on your computer—in your personal folder.

You've already mastered the basics of using a folder window to navigate your computer. If necessary, you click expand icons in the Navigation pane until you find the folder that you want. Then, you click the folder icon in the Navigation pane to view the folders and files it contains, which are displayed in the right pane. You can also double-click folders in the right pane to display their contents.

Navigating to Your Data Files

> **TIP**
> To display the file path in a folder window, click to the right of the text in the Address bar.

To navigate to the files you want, it helps to know the file path. The file path leads you through the folder and file organization to your file. For example, the Logo file is stored in the Tutorial subfolder of the Windows2 folder. If you are working on a USB drive, for example, the path to this file might be as follows:

E:\Windows2\Tutorial\Logo.png

This path has four parts, with each part separated by a backslash (\ ):

- E:—The drive name followed by a colon, which indicates a drive rather than a folder
- Windows2—The top-level folder on drive E
- Tutorial—A subfolder in the Windows2 folder
- Logo.png—The full filename, including file extension

In this example, drive E is the name for the USB drive. (If this file were stored on the primary hard disk, the drive name would be C.) If someone tells you to find the file E:\Windows2\Tutorial\Logo.png, you know you must navigate to your USB drive, open the Windows2 folder, and then open the Tutorial folder to find the Logo file.

You can keep track of your current location as you navigate between drives and folders using the Address bar, which displays the full file path in a folder window. You can use the open folder window to navigate to the Data Files you need for the rest of this tutorial. Before you perform the following steps, you need to know where you stored your Data Files, such as a USB drive. The following steps assume that drive is Removable Disk (E:), a USB drive. If necessary, substitute the appropriate drive on your system when you perform the steps.

To navigate to your Data Files:

1. Make sure your computer can access your Data Files for this tutorial. For example, if you are using a USB drive, insert the drive into the USB port.

   Trouble? If you don't have the starting Data Files, you need to get them before you can proceed. Your instructor will either give you the Data Files or ask you to obtain them from a specified location (such as a network drive). In either case, make a backup copy of your Data Files before you start using them so you will have the original files available in case you need to start over. If you have any questions about the Data Files, see your instructor or technical support person for assistance.

2. In the open folder window, click the **expand** icon ▷ next to the Computer icon to display the drives on your computer, if necessary.

3. Click the **expand** icon ▷ next to the drive containing your Data Files, such as Removable Disk (E:). A list appears below the drive name showing the folders on that drive.

4. If the list of folders does not include the Windows2 folder, continue clicking the **expand** icon ▷ to navigate to the folder that contains the Windows2 folder.

5. Click the **expand** icon ▷ next to the Windows2 folder to expand the folder, and then click the **Windows2** folder so that its contents appear in the Navigation pane and in the right pane of the folder window. The Windows2 folder contains the Case1, Case2, Case3, Review, and Tutorial folders, as shown in Figure 2-9. (Because Case Problem 4 does not require any files, the Windows2 folder does not include a Case4 folder.) The other folders on your system might vary.

Figure 2-9 Navigating to the Windows2 folder

- contents of the Windows2 folder; your Date modified information will differ
- selected Windows2 folder is expanded in the Navigation pane
- Tutorial folder
- your Data Files might be stored on a different drive

6. In the Navigation pane, click the **Tutorial** folder. The files it contains appear in the right pane. To preview the contents of the graphics, you can display the files as medium icons or larger.

TIP
If you change the view of one folder, other folders continue to display files in their specified view.

7. Click the **View** tab on the ribbon, and then click **Medium icons** in the Layout group. The files appear in Medium icons view in the folder window. See Figure 2-10.

Figure 2-10 Files in the Tutorial folder in Medium icons view

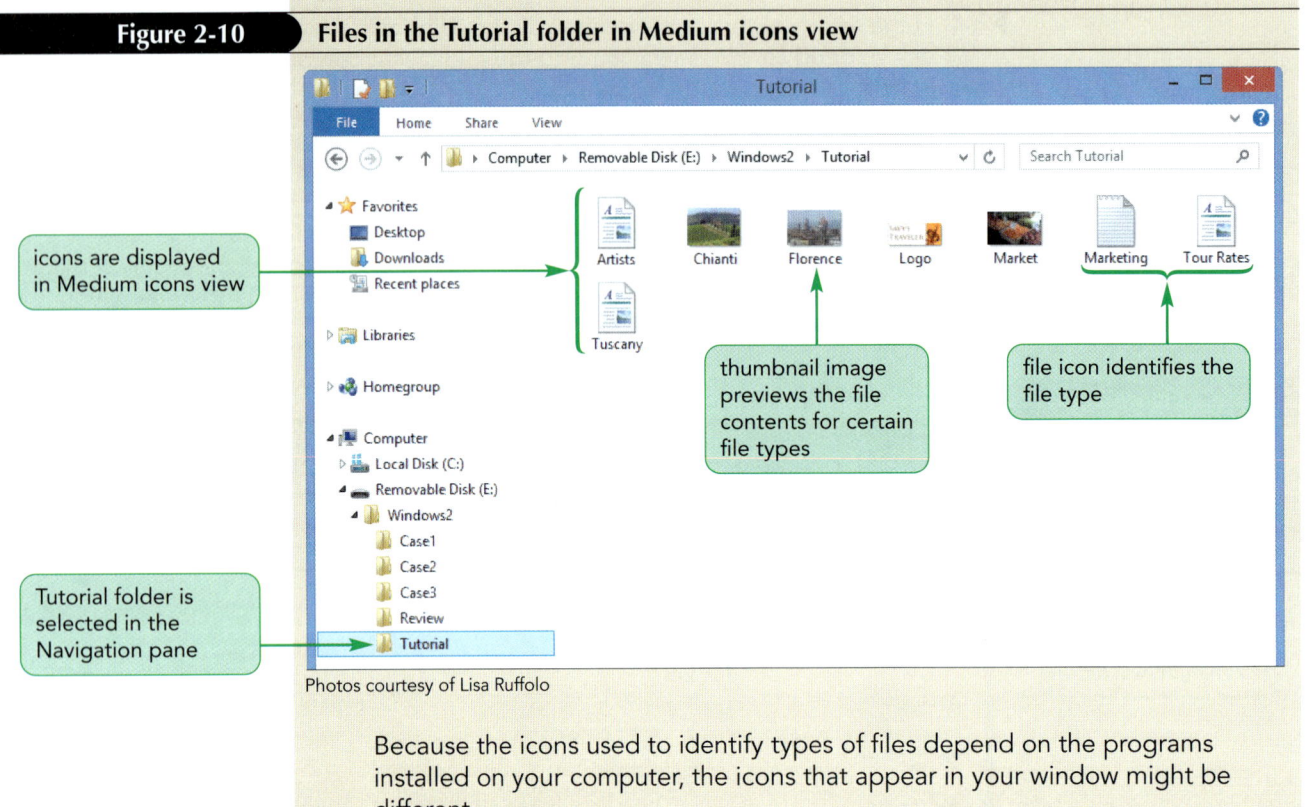

Photos courtesy of Lisa Ruffolo

Because the icons used to identify types of files depend on the programs installed on your computer, the icons that appear in your window might be different.

Matt wants to know how to use the Address bar effectively, so you offer to navigate with the Address bar to compare that technique to using the Navigation pane.

Navigating with the Address Bar

The Address bar, located at the top of every folder window, displays your current folder as a series of locations separated by arrow buttons. For example, in Figure 2-11, the Address bar shows the Windows2 and Tutorial folders separated by an arrow button, indicating that Tutorial is the current folder and it's stored in the Windows2 folder. Click the arrow button after the Windows2 folder to display a list of subfolders in the Windows2 folder. If a chevron button ≪ appears, you can click it to list the folders and drives containing the locations displayed in the Address bar. The first item in the Address bar is Computer, which contains Removable Disk (E:). Windows2 is contained in Removable Disk (E:), and the Tutorial folder is contained in the Windows2 folder.

Figure 2-11 Navigating with the Address bar

Photos courtesy of Lisa Ruffolo

To change your location, you can click or type a folder name in the Address bar. For example, you can click Windows2 to navigate to that folder. You can also type the path to the folder you want, or type the name of a standard, built-in Windows folder or library, such as the My Documents or Favorites folders or the Music or Pictures libraries.

After you navigate to a location by any method, you can click the Back, Forward, and Recent locations buttons to revisit folders you've already opened. For example, if you navigate first to drive E:, then to the Windows2 folder, and then to the Tutorial folder, you can click the Back button to open your previous location, the Windows2 folder. When you do, the Forward button becomes active. You can then click the Forward button to open the next location in your sequence, the Tutorial folder. To navigate to any recent location, click the Recent locations button, and then click a location in the list.

To navigate the hierarchy of folders and drives on your computer, recall that you can use another navigation button: the Up one level button. For example, if you are working in the Tutorial folder, you can click the Up one level button to navigate to the Windows2 folder. If you click the Up one level button again, you navigate to the root directory of your removable disk, such as Removable Disk (E:).

TIP

To navigate to any location you visited in a folder window, click the Previous Locations button in the Address bar, and then click the location you want to visit.

To navigate using the Address bar and navigation buttons:

1. In the folder window displaying the contents of your Tutorial folder, click the drive containing your Data Files, such as Removable Disk (E:), in the Address bar. The window displays the contents of the drive containing your Data Files.

   Trouble? If the drive containing your Data Files is not listed in the Address bar, click the chevron button « in the Address bar, and then click Removable Disk (E:).

   Trouble? If the drive letter of your removable disk is different, substitute the correct drive letter for drive E for the remaining steps.

> 2. Click the **arrow** button ▶ to the right of Computer on the Address bar, and then click the name of a hard disk, such as **Local Disk (C:)**.
>
>   **Trouble?** If the hard disk on your computer has a different name, click that name instead of Local Disk (C:).
>
> 3. Click the **Back** button ⬅ on the Address bar two times to return to the Tutorial folder.
>
> 4. Click the **Recent locations** button ▼ to display a list of locations you visited, and then click **Windows2**. The subfolders in your Windows2 folder appear in the right pane.

Leave the folder window open so that you can work with other file and folder tools.

Using the Search Text Box to Find Files

After you use a computer awhile, you're likely to have hundreds of files stored in various folders. If you know where you stored a file, it's easy to find it—you can use any navigation technique you like to navigate to that location and then scan the file list to find the file. Often, however, finding a file is more time consuming than that. You know that you stored a file somewhere in a standard folder such as My Documents or My Music, but finding the file might mean opening dozens of folders and scanning many long file lists. To save time, you can use the Search text box to quickly find your file.

The Search text box appears next to the Address bar in any folder window. To find a file in the current folder or any of its subfolders, you start typing text associated with the file. This search text can be part of the filename, text within the file, tags (keywords you associate with a file), or other file properties. By default, Windows searches for files by examining the names of the files displayed in the folder window and files in any subfolders. If it finds a file whose filename contains a word starting with the search text you specify, it displays that file in the folder window. For example, you can use the search text *travel* to find files named Savvy Traveler and Travel Agencies. If you are searching a hard drive, Windows also looks for files that contain a word starting with your search text. If it finds one, it displays that file in the folder window. For example, using *travel* as the search text also finds files containing words such as "traveled" and "travelogue." If you are searching a removable drive, Windows searches filenames only by default. However, you can change settings to specify that you want to search other properties, including the contents. The following steps assume you are searching a removable drive.

Matt asks you to find a digital photo of an Italian market on his computer. He knows he has at least one photo of a market. You can find this file by starting to type *market* in the Search text box.

> **TIP**
>
> The name of the Search text box reflects the location you are searching. If you select the My Documents folder in the left pane, for example, the Search text box name is *Search My Documents*.

> **To use the Search text box to find a file:**
>
> 1. In the folder window displaying the contents of your Windows2 folder, click the Search text box.
>
> 2. Type **m** and then pause. Windows 8 examines the files in the Windows2 folder and its subfolders, searching for a filename that includes a word starting with *m*. The files in the Windows2 folder that meet this criterion are displayed in the search results. You can continue typing to narrow the selection.
>
> 3. Type **ar** after the *m* so that the search text is now *mar*. Only two files have filenames that include a word beginning with *mar*. See Figure 2-12. The first three letters in each filename are highlighted. Your files might appear in a different view.

Trouble? If you are searching a hard drive, you will see additional files that contain words beginning with *mar*.

Figure 2-12 Searching for a file

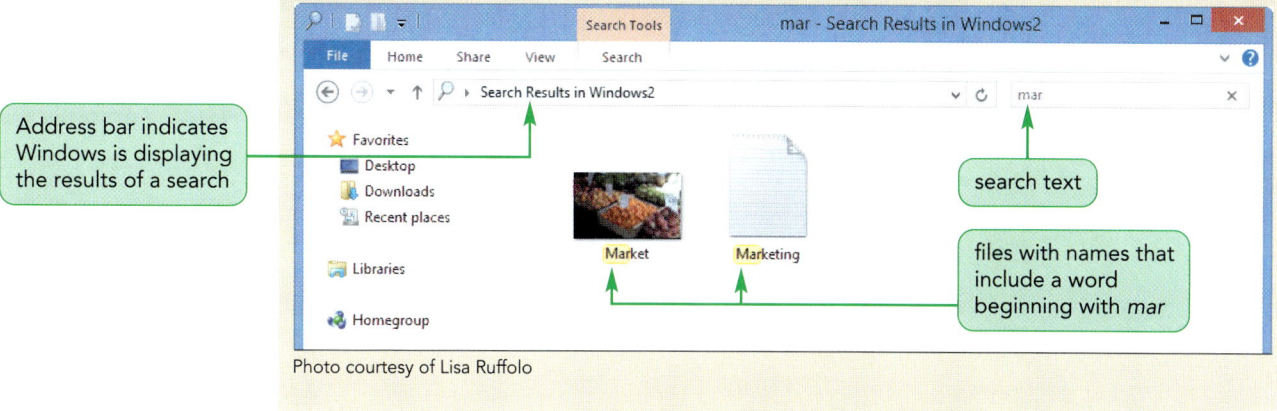

Photo courtesy of Lisa Ruffolo

Using the Search text box in a folder window, you found a photo of an Italian market for Matt—the Market image file.

Now that Matt is comfortable navigating a computer to find files, you're ready to show him how to manage his files and folders.

Managing Files and Folders

After you devise a plan for storing your files, you are ready to get organized by creating folders that will hold your files. You can do so using any folder window. In this tutorial, you create folders in the Tutorial folder, which is probably stored on a USB drive, not a hard drive. When you are working on your own computer, you usually create folders within the My Documents folder and other standard folders, such as My Music and My Pictures. However, Chianti, Florence, Logo, and Market are all graphics files that Matt uses for marketing and sales. The Artists and Tuscany files were created for Italian tour descriptions. The Marketing and Tour Rates files relate to business finances.

One way to organize these files is to create three folders—one for graphics, one for tours, and another for the financial files. When you create a folder, you give it a name, preferably one that describes its contents. A folder name can have up to 255 characters. Any character is allowed, except / \ : * ? " < > and |. Considering these conventions, you could create three folders as follows:

- Marketing Graphics folder—Chianti, Florence, Logo, and Market files
- Tours folder—Artists and Tuscany files
- Financial folder—Marketing and Tour Rates files

Before creating the folders, you show your plan to Matt. You point out that instead of creating a folder for the graphics files, he could store them in the Pictures library that Windows 8 provides for photos, clip art, drawings, and other graphics. However, Matt wants to keep these marketing graphics files separate from any other files. He also thinks storing them in a folder along with the Tours and Financial folders will make it easier to find his business files later.

INSIGHT

Guidelines for Creating Folders

Keep the following guidelines in mind as you create folders:
- Keep folder names short and familiar. Long folder names can be more difficult to display in their entirety in folder windows, so use names that are short but clear. Choose names that will be meaningful later, such as project names or course numbers.
- Develop standards for naming folders. Use a consistent naming scheme that is clear to you, such as one that uses a project name as the name of the main folder, and includes step numbers in each subfolder name (for example, 01 Plan, 02 Approvals, 03 First Draft, and so on).
- Create subfolders to organize files. If a file list in a folder window is so long that you must scroll the window, consider organizing those files into subfolders.

Matt asks you to create the three new folders. After that, you'll move his files to the appropriate folders.

Creating Folders

You've already seen folder icons in the windows you've examined. Now, you'll create folders within the Tutorial folder using the ribbon that appears in all folder windows.

REFERENCE

Creating a Folder in a Folder Window

- In the Navigation pane, click the drive, folder, or library in which you want to create a folder.
- Click the Home tab and then click the New folder button in the New group, or click the New folder button on the Quick Access toolbar.
- Type a name for the folder, and then press the Enter key.

or

- Right-click a drive, folder, or library in the Navigation pane or right-click a blank area in the folder window, point to New, and then click Folder.
- Type a name for the folder, and then press the Enter key.

Now you can create three folders in your Tutorial folder as you planned—the Marketing Graphics, Tours, and Financial folders. You create these folders in three ways: using the Home tab, shortcut menu, and Quick Access toolbar. (The Quick Access toolbar is a row of buttons on a program's title bar that gives you one-click access to frequently used commands, including creating a folder.)

To create folders:

1. Navigate to the **Tutorial** folder included with your Data Files.
2. Click the **Home** tab, and then click the **New folder** button in the New group. A folder icon with the label "New folder" appears in the right pane. See Figure 2-13.

Figure 2-13 Creating a subfolder in the Tutorial folder

- Quick Access toolbar
- type to replace the selected text with a different folder name

Photos courtesy of Lisa Ruffolo

Trouble? If the "New folder" name is not selected, right-click the new folder, click Rename, and then continue with Step 3.

Windows uses *New folder* as a placeholder, and selects the text so that you can replace it immediately by typing a new name. You do not need to press the Backspace or Delete key to delete the text.

3. Type **Marketing Graphics** as the folder name, and then press the **Enter** key. The new folder is now named Marketing Graphics and is the selected item in the right pane. To create a second folder, you can use a shortcut menu.

4. Right-click a blank area in the right pane, point to **New** on the shortcut menu, and then click **Folder**. A folder icon appears in the right pane with the New folder text selected.

5. Type **Tours** as the name of the new folder, and then press the **Enter** key.

6. Click the **New folder** button on the Quick Access toolbar, type **Financial**, and then press the **Enter** key to create and name the folder. The Tutorial folder now contains three new subfolders.

After creating three folders, you're ready to organize your files by moving them into the appropriate folders.

Moving and Copying Files and Folders

If you want to place a file into a folder from another location, you can either move the file or copy it. **Moving** a file removes it from its current location and places it in a new location that you specify. **Copying** also places the file in a new location that you specify, but does not remove it from its current location. Windows 8 provides several techniques for moving and copying files. The same principles apply to folders: You can move and copy folders using a variety of methods.

REFERENCE

Moving a File or Folder in a Folder Window

- Right-drag the file or folder you want to move to the destination folder.
- Release the mouse button, and then click Move here on the shortcut menu.

or

- Right-click the file or folder you want to move to the destination folder, and then click Cut on the shortcut menu. (You can also click the file or folder and then press the Ctrl+X keys.)
- Navigate to and right-click the destination folder, and then click Paste on the shortcut menu. (You can also click the destination folder and then press the Ctrl+V keys.)

Matt suggests that you move some files from the Tutorial folder to the appropriate subfolders. You'll start by moving the Marketing file to the Financial folder using the right-drag technique, which you will learn next.

To move a file using the right mouse button:

1. Point to the **Marketing** file in the right pane, and then press and hold the right mouse button.

2. With the right mouse button still pressed down, drag the **Marketing** file to the **Financial** folder. When the Move to Financial ScreenTip appears, release the button. A shortcut menu opens.

3. With the left mouse button, click **Move here** on the shortcut menu. The Marketing file is removed from the main Tutorial folder and stored in the Financial subfolder.

   Trouble? If you released the mouse button before you dragged the Marketing file all the way to the Financial folder and before seeing the Move to Financial ScreenTip, press the Esc key to close the shortcut menu, and then repeat Steps 1–3.

   Trouble? If you moved the Market file instead of the Marketing file, press the Ctrl+Z keys to undo the move, and then repeat Steps 1–3.

4. In the right pane, double-click the **Financial** folder. The Marketing file is in the Financial folder.

   Trouble? If the Marketing file does not appear in the Financial folder, you probably moved it to a different folder. Press the Ctrl+Z keys to undo the move, and then repeat Steps 1–4.

5. Click the **Back** button on the Address bar to return to the Tutorial folder.

The advantage of moving a file or folder by dragging with the right mouse button is that you can efficiently complete your work with one action. However, this right-drag technique requires polished mouse skills so that you can drag the file comfortably. When you drag to move files, be sure to verify the destination by waiting for the Move to ScreenTip. Otherwise, you might move the file to an unintended folder and have trouble finding the file later.

Another way to move files and folders is to use the **Clipboard**, a temporary storage area for files and information that you copy or move from one place and plan to use somewhere else. Although the Clipboard does not appear in a folder window, you can use it when working with files and folders. Select a file and use the Cut or Copy command to temporarily store the file on the Clipboard, and then use the Paste command to insert the file elsewhere. Although using the Clipboard takes more steps, some users find it easier than dragging with the right mouse button.

You'll move the Artists file to the Tours folder next by using the Clipboard.

To move files using the Clipboard:

1. Right-click the **Artists** file, and then click **Cut** on the shortcut menu. Although the file icon is still displayed in the folder window, Windows 8 removes the Artists file from the Tutorial folder and stores it on the Clipboard.

2. In the right pane, right-click the **Tours** folder, and then click **Paste** on the shortcut menu. Windows 8 pastes the Artists file from the Clipboard to the Tours folder. The Artists file icon no longer appears in the folder window.

3. In the Navigation pane, click the **expand** icon ▷ next to the Tutorial folder, if necessary, to display its contents, and then click the **Tours** folder to view its contents in the right pane. The Tours folder now contains the Artists file. See Figure 2-14.

Figure 2-14 Moving a file

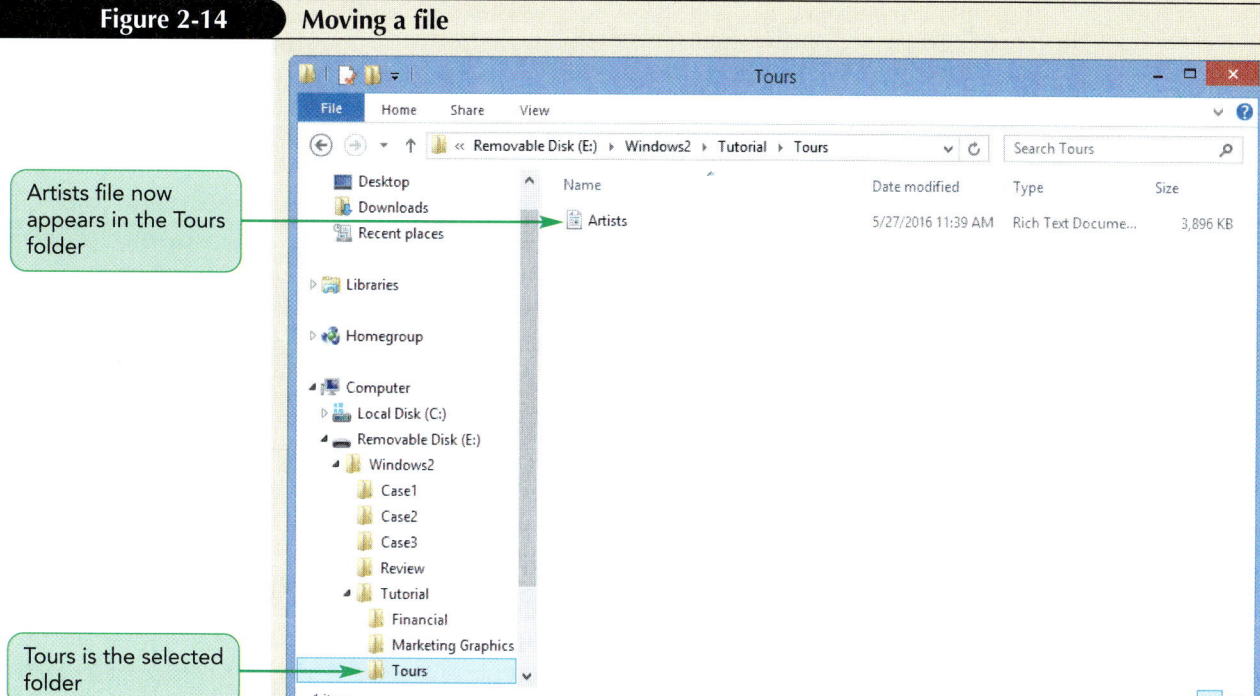

Artists file now appears in the Tours folder

Tours is the selected folder

Next, you'll move the Tuscany file from the Tutorial folder to the Tours folder.

4. Click the **Back** button ⬅ on the Address bar to return to the Tutorial folder, right-click the **Tuscany** file in the folder window, and then click **Cut** on the shortcut menu.

5. In the Navigation pane, right-click the **Tours** folder, and then click **Paste** on the shortcut menu. The files are moved into the Tours folder.

6. Click the **Forward** button ➡ on the Address bar to return to the Tours folder. The Tours folder now contains the Artists and Tuscany files.

One way to save steps when moving or copying multiple files or folders is to select all the files and folders you want to move or copy, and then work with them as a group. You'll show Matt how to do that next.

Selecting Files and Folders

You can select multiple files or folders using several techniques, so you can choose the most convenient method for your current task. First, you open the folder that contains the files or folders you want to select. Next, select the files or folders using any one of the following methods:

- To select files or folders that are listed together in a folder window, click the first item, hold down the Shift key, click the last item, and then release the Shift key.
- To select files or folders that are listed together in a folder window without using the keyboard, drag the pointer to create a selection box around all the items you want to include.
- To select files or folders that are not listed together, hold down the Ctrl key, click each item you want to select, and then release the Ctrl key.
- To select all of the files or folders, click the Select all button in the Select group on the Home tab.
- To clear the selection of an item in a selected group, hold down the Ctrl key, click each item you want to remove from the selection, and then release the Ctrl key.
- To clear the entire selection, click a blank area of the folder window.

Copying Files and Folders

When you copy a file or folder, you make a duplicate of the original item. You can copy files or folders using techniques similar to the ones you use when moving them.

REFERENCE

Copying a File or Folder in a Folder Window

- Right-drag the file or folder you want to copy to the destination folder.
- Release the mouse button, and then click Copy here on the shortcut menu.

or

- Right-click the file or folder you want to copy to the destination folder, and then click Copy on the shortcut menu. (You can also click the file or folder and then press the Ctrl+C keys.)
- Navigate to and right-click the destination folder, and then click Paste on the shortcut menu. (You can also click the destination folder and then press the Ctrl+V keys.)

You'll copy the four graphics files from the Tutorial folder to the Marketing Graphics folder now.

To copy files using the Clipboard:

1. Using any navigation technique you've learned, return to the Tutorial folder window.
2. Click the **Chianti** file, hold down the **Shift** key, click the **Market** file, and then release the **Shift** key. Four files are selected in the Tutorial folder window.
3. Right-click the selected files, and then click **Copy** on the shortcut menu. Windows copies the files to the Clipboard.
4. Right-click the **Marketing Graphics** folder, and then click **Paste** on the shortcut menu.
5. Double-click the **Marketing Graphics** folder to verify it contains the four files you copied, and then return to the Tutorial folder.

Now that you have copied files using the Copy and Paste commands, you can use the right-drag technique to copy the Tour Rates file to the Financial folder. As with moving files, you point to the file, hold down the right mouse button, and then drag the file to a new location. However, when you release the mouse button, you click Copy here (instead of Move here) on the shortcut menu to copy the file.

To copy a file:

1. Right-drag the **Tour Rates** file from the Tutorial folder to the Financial folder.
2. Release the mouse button, and then click **Copy here** on the shortcut menu.
3. Double-click the **Financial** folder to verify it contains the Marketing and Tour Rates files, and then return to the Tutorial folder.

When you move or copy a folder, you move or copy all the files contained in the folder.

You can use a third technique to copy or move a file or folder. You can drag the file or folder (using the left mouse button) to another location. Whether the file or folder is copied or moved depends on where you drag it. A ScreenTip appears when you drag a file to a new location—the ScreenTip indicates what happens when you release the mouse button. Figure 2-15 summarizes how to copy and move files and folders by dragging.

Figure 2-15 Dragging to move and copy files

Drag a File or Folder:	To:
Into a folder on the same drive	Move the file or folder to the destination folder
Into a folder on a different drive	Copy the file or folder to the destination folder

© 2014 Cengage Learning

Although the copy and move techniques listed are common ways to copy and move files and folders, be sure you can anticipate what happens when you drag a file or folder.

Session 2.1 Quick Check

REVIEW

1. You organize files by storing them in _____.
2. What is the purpose of the Address bar in a folder window?
3. A(n) _____ can have up to 255 characters of any kind, except / \ : * ? " < > and |.
4. Explain how to use a folder window to navigate to a file in the following location: E:\Courses\Computer Basics\Operating Systems.txt.
5. Describe how to find files using the Search text box.
6. One way to move files and folders is to use the _____, a temporary storage area for information that you cut or copied.
7. Explain one advantage and one disadvantage of moving a folder using the right-dragging method.
8. What happens if you click the first file in a folder window, hold down the Shift key, click the last file, and then release the Shift key?

Session 2.2 Visual Overview:

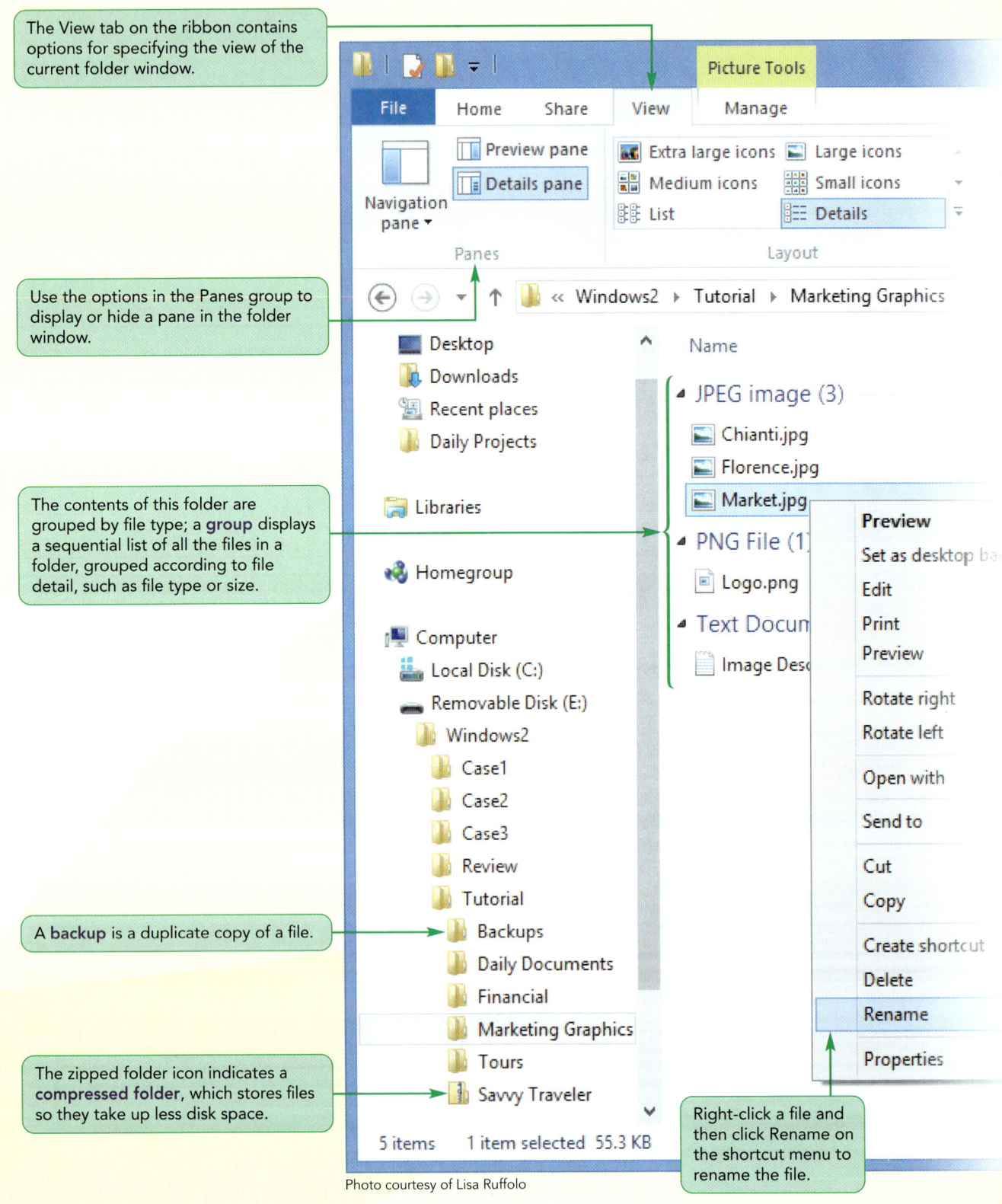

The View tab on the ribbon contains options for specifying the view of the current folder window.

Use the options in the Panes group to display or hide a pane in the folder window.

The contents of this folder are grouped by file type; a **group** displays a sequential list of all the files in a folder, grouped according to file detail, such as file type or size.

A **backup** is a duplicate copy of a file.

The zipped folder icon indicates a **compressed folder**, which stores files so they take up less disk space.

Right-click a file and then click Rename on the shortcut menu to rename the file.

Photo courtesy of Lisa Ruffolo

Customized Folder Window

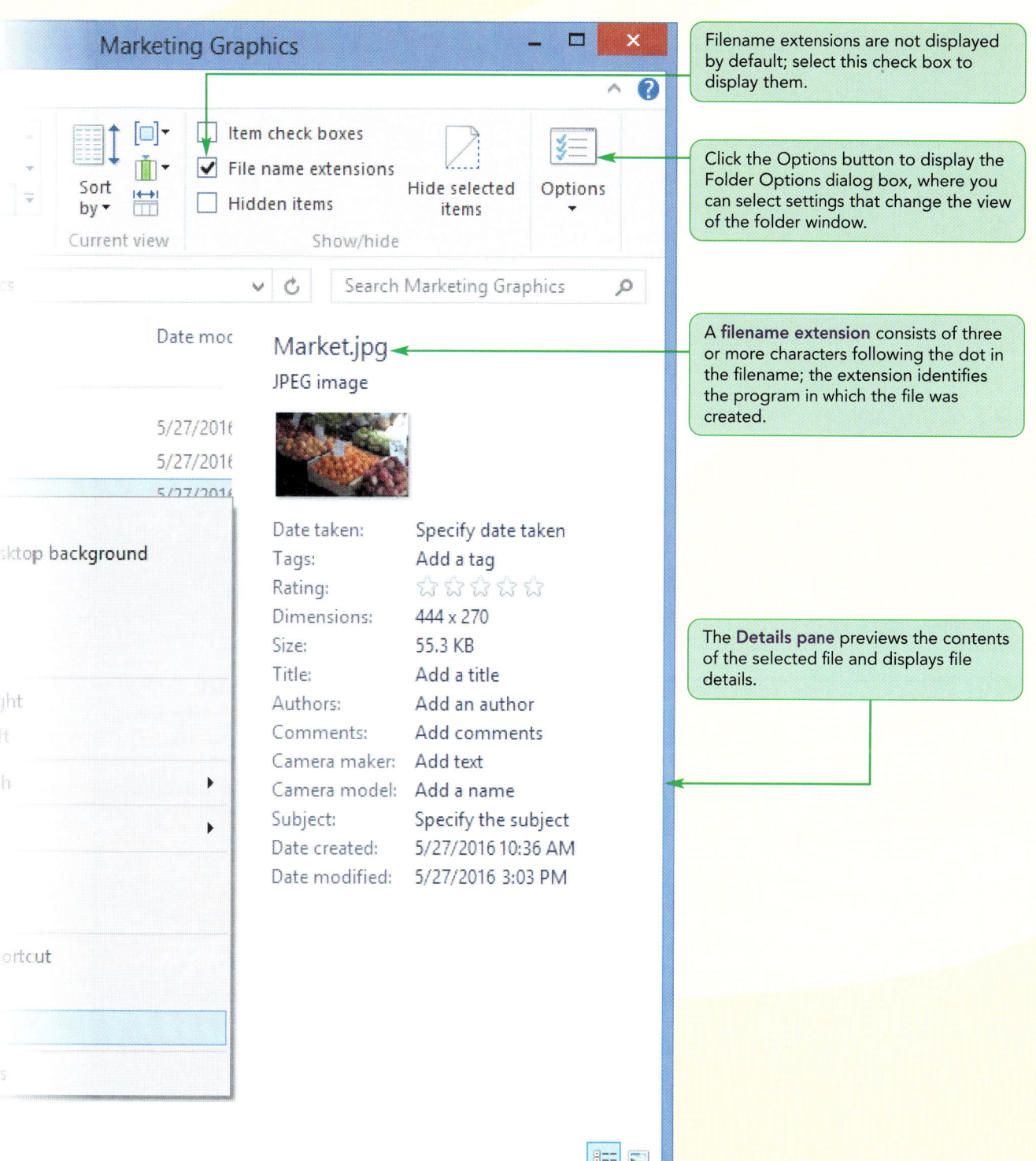

Filename extensions are not displayed by default; select this check box to display them.

Click the Options button to display the Folder Options dialog box, where you can select settings that change the view of the folder window.

A **filename extension** consists of three or more characters following the dot in the filename; the extension identifies the program in which the file was created.

The **Details pane** previews the contents of the selected file and displays file details.

Naming and Renaming Files

As you work with files, pay attention to filenames—they provide important information about the file, including its contents and purpose. A filename such as Italian Tours.docx has three parts:

- Main part of the filename—The name you provide when you create a file, and the name you associate with a file
- Dot—The period (.) that separates the main part of the filename from the filename extension
- Filename extension—Usually three or four characters that follow the dot in the filename

The main part of a filename can have up to 255 characters. This gives you plenty of room to name your file accurately enough so that you'll know the contents of the file just by looking at the filename. You can use spaces and certain punctuation symbols in your filenames. Like folder names, however, filenames cannot contain the symbols / \ : * ? " < > or | because these characters have special meanings in Windows 8.

A filename might display its filename extension. For example, in the filename Italian Tours.docx, the extension *docx* identifies the file as one created in Microsoft Word, a word-processing program. You might also have a file called Italian Tours.png—the .png extension identifies the file as one created in a graphics program such as Paint. Though the main parts of these filenames are identical, their extensions distinguish them as different files.

An extension also helps Windows identify what program should open the file. For example, the .txt extension in a file named Brochure.txt indicates that it is a text file and can be opened by programs associated with that extension, such as WordPad, Notepad, and Microsoft Word. You usually do not need to add extensions to your filenames because the program you use to create the file adds the extension automatically. However, although Windows 8 keeps track of extensions, by default, Windows 8 is not set to display them. (You will learn how to show filename extensions later in the tutorial.)

Be sure to give your files and folders meaningful names that will help you remember their purpose and contents. You can easily rename a file or folder by using the Rename command on the file's shortcut menu.

INSIGHT

Guidelines for Naming Files

The following are best practices for naming (or renaming) your files:
- Use common names. Avoid cryptic names that might make sense now but could cause confusion later, such as nonstandard abbreviations or imprecise names like Stuff08.
- Don't change the filename extension. Do not change the filename extension when renaming a file. If you do, Windows might not be able to find a program that can open it.
- Find a comfortable balance between too short and too long. Use filenames that are long enough to be meaningful, but short enough to be read easily on the screen.

Matt notes that the Artists file in the Tours folder could contain information about any artists. He recommends that you rename that file to give it a more descriptive filename. The Artists file was originally created to store text specifically about Florentine painters and sculptors, so you'll rename the file Florentine Artists.

To rename the Artists file:

1. If you took a break after the previous session, make sure that a folder window is open, and then navigate to the **Windows2** folder included with your Data Files. Click the **Tutorial** folder in the left pane and change to **Medium icons** view, if necessary.

2. Open the **Tours** folder to display its contents.

3. Right-click the **Artists** file, and then click **Rename** on the shortcut menu. The filename is highlighted and a box appears around it.

4. Type **Florentine Artists**, and then press the **Enter** key. The file now appears with the new name.

   Trouble? If you make a mistake while typing and you haven't pressed the Enter key yet, press the Backspace key until you delete the mistake and then complete Step 4. If you've already pressed the Enter key, repeat Steps 3 and 4 to rename the file again.

   Trouble? If your computer is set to display filename extensions, a message might appear asking if you are sure you want to change the filename extension. Click the No button, and then repeat Steps 3 and 4.

> **TIP**
> To rename a file, you can also click the file, pause, click it again to select the filename, and then type to enter a new filename.

All the files that originally appeared in the Tutorial folder are now stored in appropriate subfolders. You can streamline the organization of the Tutorial folder by deleting the duplicate files you no longer need.

Deleting Files and Folders

You should periodically delete files and folders you no longer need so that your main folders and disks don't get cluttered. In a folder window, you delete a file or folder by deleting its icon. When you delete a file from a hard disk, Windows 8 removes the file from the folder but stores the file contents in the Recycle Bin. The Recycle Bin is an area on your hard disk that holds deleted files until you remove them permanently. When you delete a folder from the hard disk, the folder and all of its files are stored in the Recycle Bin. If you change your mind and want to retrieve a deleted file or folder, you can double-click the Recycle Bin, right-click the file or folder you want to retrieve, and then click Restore. However, after you empty the Recycle Bin, you can no longer recover the files it contained.

> **TIP**
> In most cases, a file deleted from a USB drive does not go into the Recycle Bin. Instead, it is deleted when Windows 8 removes its icon, and the file cannot be recovered.

REFERENCE

Deleting a File or Folder

- Click the file or folder you want to delete. (If you want to delete more than one file or folder, select them first.)
- Press the Delete key, and then click the Yes button.

or

- Right-click the file or folder you want to delete. (If you want to delete more than one file or folder, select them first.)
- Click Delete on the shortcut menu, and then click the Yes button.

Because you copied the Chianti, Florence, Logo, Market, and Tour Rates files to the subfolders in the Tutorial folder, you can safely delete the original files. As is true for moving, copying, and renaming files and folders, you can delete a file or folder in many ways, including using a shortcut menu or selecting one or more files and then pressing the Delete key.

To delete files in the Tutorial folder:

1. Use any technique you've learned to navigate to and display the **Tutorial** folder.

2. Click **Chianti**, hold down the **Shift** key, click **Tour Rates**, and then release the **Shift** key. All files in the Tutorial folder are now selected. None of the subfolders should be selected.

3. Right-click the selected files, and then click **Delete** on the shortcut menu. Windows 8 might ask if you're sure you want to permanently delete these files.

4. If necessary, click the **Yes** button.

> Make sure you have copied the selected files to the Marketing Graphics and Financial folders before completing this step.

So far, you've worked with files in folder windows, but you haven't viewed any file contents. To view a file's contents, you open the file. When you double-click a file in a folder window, Windows 8 starts the associated program and opens the file. You'll have a chance to try these techniques in the next section.

Working with New Files

The most common way to add files to a drive or folder is to create new files when you use a program. For example, you can create a text document in a word-processing program, a drawing in a graphics program, or a movie file in a video-editing program. When you are finished with a file, you must save it if you want to use the file again. To work with the file, you open it in an appropriate program; you can usually tell which programs can open a file by examining the filename extension or file icon.

Before you continue working with Matt's files, you decide to create a task list to summarize your remaining tasks. You'll create the task list file, save it, close it, and then reopen it to add some items to the list.

Creating a File

You create a file by starting a program and then saving the file in a folder on your computer. Some programs create a file when you open the program. When you open WordPad, for example, it starts with a blank page. This represents an empty (and unsaved) file. You type and format the document to create it. When you are finished, you save your work using the Save As dialog box, where you can select a location for the file and enter a filename that identifies the contents. By default, most programs save files in a library such as Documents, Pictures, or Music, which makes it easy to find the files again later.

The task list you want to create is a simple text document, so you can create this file using Notepad, the basic text-editing program that Windows 8 provides.

To create a Notepad file:

1. Press the **Windows** key to display the Start screen.

2. Type **notep** to display the Search menu with "notep" inserted in the Search text box. The search results include the Notepad application.

▶ **3.** Click **Notepad** in the search results. The Notepad program window opens on the desktop. See Figure 2-16.

Figure 2-16 Creating a file

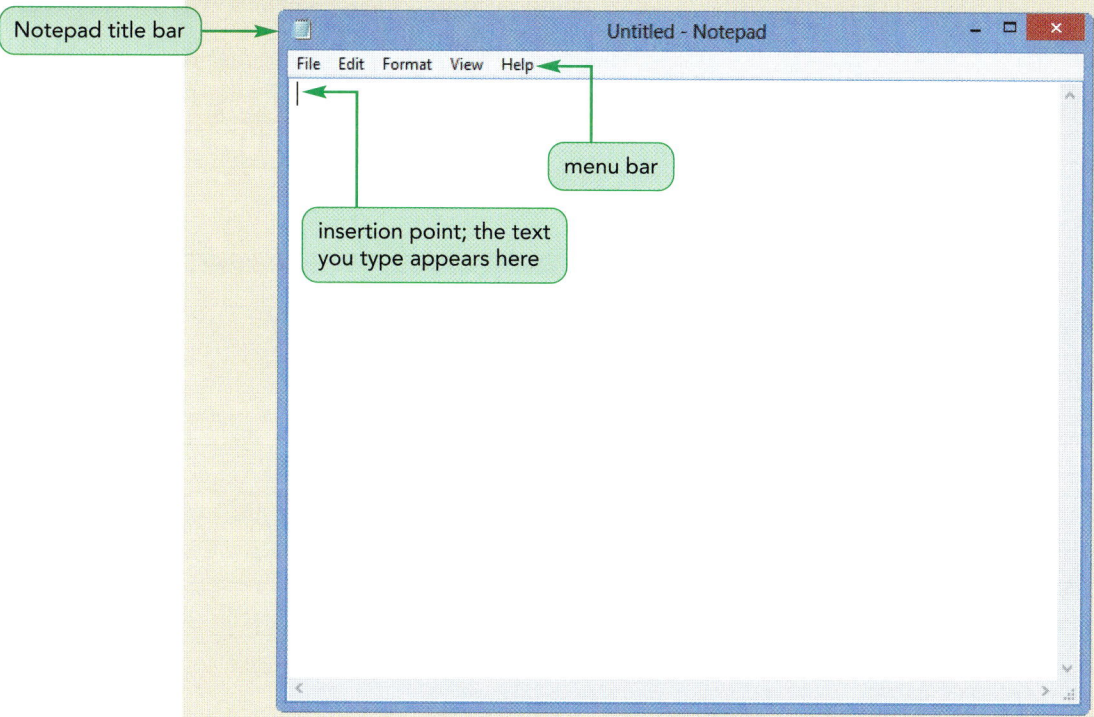

▶ **4.** Type the following text in the Notepad window, pressing the **Enter** key at the end of each line, including the last line:

To Do for Matt's Files

1. Organize files in a folder window.

2. Customize a folder window.

3. Show and hide filename extensions.

4. Compress and extract files.

The Notepad title bar indicates that the name of this file is "Untitled." To give it a more descriptive name, preserve the contents, and store the file where you can find it later, you must save the file.

Saving a File

TIP

After you create a file, avoid cluttering the desktop by saving the file in a subfolder on your computer, not on the desktop.

As you are creating a file, you should save it frequently so you don't lose your work. When you save a new file, you use the Save As dialog box to specify a filename and a location for the file. When you open a file you've already created, you can use the application's Save command to save the file with the same name and location. If you want to save the file with a different name or in a different location, however, you use the Save As dialog box again to specify the new name or location. You can create a folder for the new file at the same time you save the file.

The Save As dialog box can contain the same navigation tools found in a folder window, such as an Address bar, Search text box, Navigation pane, and right pane displaying folders and files. You might need to click the Browse Folders button to expand the Save As dialog box. (When the dialog box is expanded, this button changes to the Hide Folders button.) Then, you can specify the file location, for example, using the same navigation techniques and tools that are available in all folder windows.

In addition, the Save As dialog box always includes a File name text box where you specify a filename, a Save as type list where you select a file type, and other controls for saving a file. If the expanded Save As dialog box covers too much of your document or desktop, you can click the Hide Folders button to collapse the dialog box so it hides the Navigation pane, right pane, and toolbar. You can still navigate with the Back, Forward, Recent locations, and Up one level buttons; the Address bar; and the Search text box, and you can still use the controls for saving a file, but you conserve screen space.

> **INSIGHT**
>
> ### Saving Files on SkyDrive
>
> Some Windows 8 applications, such as Microsoft Office, include SkyDrive as a location for saving and opening files. SkyDrive is a Microsoft service that provides up to 7 GB of online storage space for your files by default. Because these files are stored online, they take up no storage space on your computer and are available from any computer with an Internet connection. To protect the privacy of your files, you can designate which SkyDrive users can access them: only you, you and some other users, or anyone. To use SkyDrive, you need a free Microsoft account. (You can sign up for a Microsoft account at https://signup.live.com. If you use Hotmail, Xbox LIVE, or have a Windows Phone, you already have a Microsoft account.)

Now that you've created a task list, you need to save it. A good name for this document is Task List. However, none of the folders you've already created for Matt seems appropriate for this file. It belongs in a separate folder with a name such as Daily Documents. You can create the Daily Documents folder at the same time you save the Task List file.

To save the Notepad file:

1. In the Notepad window, click **File** on the menu bar, and then click **Save As**. The Save As dialog box opens.

2. If the Navigation pane does not appear in the Save As dialog box, click the **Browse Folders** button. The Browse Folders button toggles to become the Hide Folders button, as shown in Figure 2-17.

| Figure 2-17 | Saving a new file |

By default, Notepad saves files in the Documents library on your hard drive. You want to create a subfolder in the Tutorial folder for this document.

▶ 3. In the Save As dialog box, use any technique you've learned to navigate to the **Windows2\Tutorial** folder provided with your Data Files.

▶ 4. Click the **New folder** button on the toolbar in the Save As dialog box. A new folder appears in the Tutorial folder, with the *New folder* name highlighted and ready for you to replace.

▶ 5. Type **Daily Documents** as the name of the new folder, and then press the **Enter** key.

▶ 6. Double-click the **Daily Documents** folder to open it. Now you are ready to specify a filename and save the task list file in the Daily Documents folder.

▶ 7. Click the **File name** text box to select the *.txt text, and then type **Task List**. Notepad will automatically provide a .txt extension to this filename, so you don't have to type it.

▶ 8. Click the **Save** button. Notepad saves the Task List file in the Daily Documents folder. The new filename now appears in the Notepad title bar.

▶ 9. Click the **Close** button ![x] to close Notepad.

Next, you can open the file to add another item to the task list.

Opening a File

If you want to open a file in a running application, you use the Open dialog box, which is a folder window with additional controls for opening a file, similar to the Save As dialog box. You use the application's Open command to access the Open dialog box, which you use to navigate to the file you want, select the file, and then open it. If the application you want to use is not running, you can open a file by double-clicking it

> **TIP**
> To open a file using the default program, right-click the file, point to Open with, click Choose default program, click a program, and then click the OK button.

in a folder window. The file usually opens in the application that you used to create or edit it. If it's a text file with a .txt extension, for example, it opens in a text editor, such as Notepad. If it's a text file with a .docx extension, it opens in Microsoft Word.

Not all documents work this way. Double-clicking a digital picture file usually opens a picture viewer app, which displays the picture. To edit the picture, you need to use a graphics editing application. When you need to specify an application to open a file, you can right-click the file, point to Open with on the shortcut menu, and then click the name of the app that you want to use.

To open and edit the Task List file:

1. In the right pane of the Tutorial folder window, double-click the **Daily Documents** folder.

2. Double-click the **Task List** file. Notepad starts and opens the Task List file.

   Trouble? If an application other than Notepad starts, such as WordPad, click the Close button to close the program, right-click the Task List file, point to Open with, and then click Notepad.

3. Press the **Ctrl+End** keys to move the insertion point to the end of the document, press the **Enter** key if necessary to start a new line, and then type **5. Review how to customize the Navigation pane.**

   Because you want to save this file using the same name and location, you can use the Save command on the File menu to save your work this time.

4. Click **File** on the menu bar, and then click **Save**. Notepad saves the Task List file without opening the Save As dialog box because you are using the same name and location as the last time you saved the file.

As long as Notepad is still open, you can create another simple text file that describes the graphics in the Marketing Graphics folder.

To create and save another file:

1. Click **File** on the menu bar, and then click **New** to open a new, blank document.

2. Type the following text in the Notepad window, pressing the **Enter** key at the end of each line:

   Marketing Graphics files:

   Chianti: Photo of the Chianti valley

   Florence: Photo of Florence

   Logo: Copy of the company logo for Web pages and ads

   Market: Photo of an Italian market

3. Click **File** on the menu bar, and then click **Save**. The Save As dialog box opens because this is the first time you are saving the file.

4. Navigate to the **Marketing Graphics** folder in the Tutorial folder.

5. Click in the **File name** text box, and then type **Image Descriptions**.

6. Click the **Save** button. Notepad saves the Image Descriptions file in the Marketing Graphics folder.

> **7.** Click the **Close** button [x] to close Notepad. (Because Notepad only allows one file to be opened at a time, the program closed the first file for you when you created the new file.)

Now that you've organized Matt's files and then created and saved new folders and files, you're ready to refine the organization of the files.

Refining the Organization of Files

To refine the organization of your files, you can fine-tune the arrangement of your files and folders in a folder window. Changing the order of files in a list can often help you find files and identify those that share common features, such as two versions of the same file. One way to change the view is to sort your files. **Sorting** files and folders means listing them in a particular order, such as alphabetically by name or type, or chronologically by their modification date. You can also **filter** the contents of a folder to display only files and folders with certain characteristics, such as all those you modified yesterday. In short, sorting reorganizes all of the files and folders in a list, while filtering displays only those files and folders that share a characteristic you specify. Both actions change your view of the files and folders, not the items themselves.

Windows 8 provides another way to change the view of your files and folders—grouping. When you group your files by type, for example, Windows separates the files into several groups, such as Microsoft Word documents in one group and photo files (or JPEG files) in another group.

PROSKILLS

Problem Solving: Preventing Lost File Problems

Many computer users, even very experienced ones, fall into the trap of saving or moving a file to a folder and then forgetting where it's stored. You can prevent these types of lost file problems by managing your files systematically. To manage files so you know where to find them later, start by formulating a logical plan for organizing your files. Some people sketch a simple diagram of the file structure to help them visualize where to store files. Next, create the folders you need to store the files, and then move and copy your existing files into those folders. As you create files using programs, save them in an appropriate folder and use folder names and filenames that help you identify their contents. If possible, use a similar organization scheme in all of your folders. For example, if you organized the files for one project into subfolders such as Phase 1, Phase 2, Phase 3, and Follow Up, use the same organization for each project. To make it easier to find files, especially in a long file list, you can sort, filter, and group the files in a way that seems logical to you. Performing these basic management tasks helps you keep track of your files so you can easily find information when you need it.

You want to show Matt how to change the view of his files by sorting, filtering, and grouping so he can choose one view that makes the most sense for him or his current task.

Sorting and Filtering Files

When you are working with a folder window in Details view, you can sort or filter the files using the column headings in the right pane of the window. To sort files by type, for example, click the Type column heading. You can sort files in ascending order

(A to Z, 0 to 9, or earliest to latest date) or descending order (Z to A, 9 to 0, or latest to earliest date). To switch the order, click the column heading again.

Sorting is often an effective way to find a file or folder in a relatively short file list. By default, Windows 8 sorts the contents of a folder in ascending alphabetic order by filename, with any subfolders listed before the files. A file named April Marketing appears at the top of the list, and a file named Winter Expenses appears at the end. You can change the sort criterion to list files according to any other file characteristic.

If you are working with a longer file list, filtering the list might help you find the file you want. To filter the contents of a folder, you click the arrow button to the right of a column heading, and then click one or more file properties such as a specific filename, created or modified date, author, or file type. Windows displays only files and folders with those properties. For example, if you want to list only music files by a particular artist, you can filter by that artist's name.

Details view always includes column headings corresponding to file details. To sort files in other views that do not display column headings, you can right-click a blank area of the folder window, point to Sort by on the shortcut menu, and then click a file detail such as Type. (You cannot filter files in views without column headings.)

> **TIP**
> To sort by a file detail that does not appear as a column heading, right-click any column heading and then select a file detail.

To sort and filter the files in the Marketing Graphics folder:

1. Navigate to the **Marketing Graphics** folder in the Tutorial folder.

2. If necessary, click the **View** tab, and then click **Details** in the Layout group to switch to Details view.

3. Click the **Type** column heading to sort the files in ascending order according to file type. A sort arrow ▲ appears at the top of the Type column heading. The sort arrow points up to indicate the column is sorted in ascending order.

   Trouble? If the Type column does not appear in your folder window, right-click any column heading and then click Type. Then complete Step 3.

4. Click the **Type** column heading again to reverse the sort order. The sort arrow now points down, indicating the column is sorted in descending order.

5. Right-click any column heading to display a list of file details. Details with a check mark are displayed in the folder window. If the Date modified column heading does not appear in your folder window, click **Date modified** to display this column. Otherwise, click a blank area of the window. Your folder window should now display only the Name, Date modified, Type, and Size columns.

   Trouble? If your folder window contains columns other than Name, Date modified, Type, and Size, right-click any column heading, and then click the name of the column you want to remove from the folder window. The content of the column is not erased; it is just no longer visible on-screen.

6. Click the **Date modified** column heading to sort the files in descending chronological order by the date they were modified. See Figure 2-18.

> **TIP**
> When you sort files by Date modified with the most recent files on top, you can quickly find the files you created or modified recently.

Tutorial 2 Organizing Your Files | Windows   WIN 79

| Figure 2-18 | Sorting files by date modified |

sort arrow points down, indicating the column is sorted in descending order

files are sorted so that the most recently modified files appear first

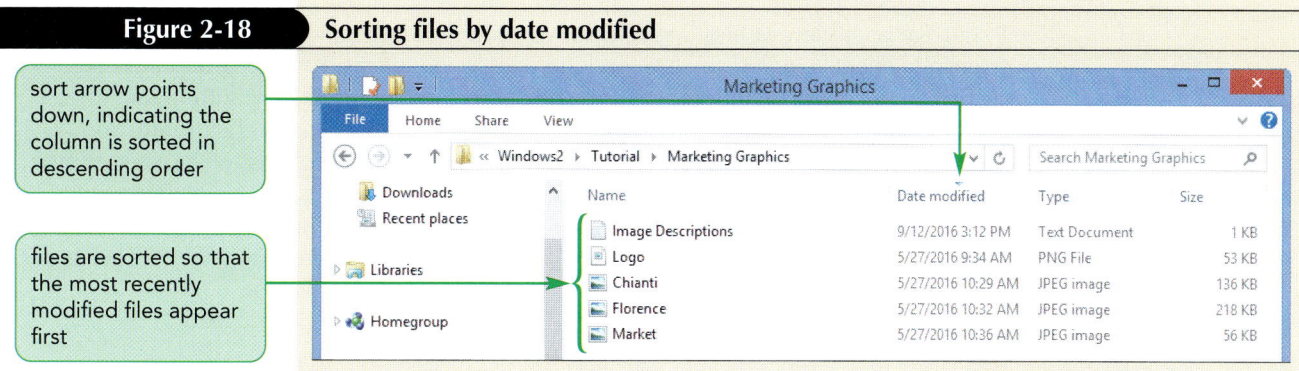

To compare sorting and filtering, you can filter the files by their modified date to display only the files you modified today.

7. Point to the **Date modified** column heading, and then click its **arrow** button to display a list of filtering options.

8. Click the **Today** check box to select today's date. The folder window displays only the Image Descriptions file. See Figure 2-19.

   Trouble? If you modified the Image Descriptions file on a different date, click that date on the calendar.

   Trouble? If you clicked Today rather than the check box, skip Step 9.

| Figure 2-19 | Filtering to display files modified today |

only files modified today appear in the filtered list

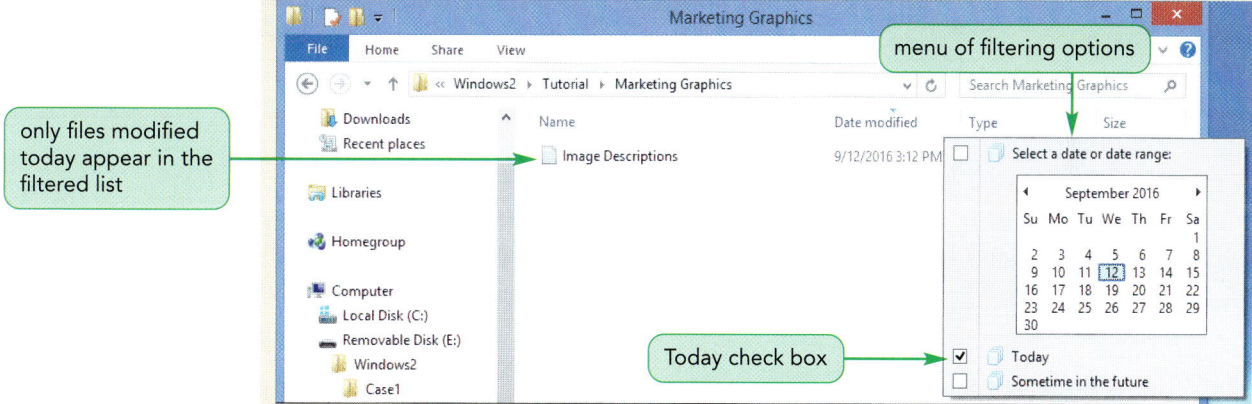

Note that you can filter by two or more properties by selecting the corresponding check boxes.

9. Click a blank area of the window to close the list. A check mark appears next to the Date modified column heading to indicate the file list is filtered by a Date modified detail.

Next, you can group the files in the Marketing Graphics folder and compare this view to the views displayed when you sorted and filtered the files.

Grouping Files

To change your view of files and folders, you can group them—a technique that is especially effective when you are working with long file lists. You can group files according to any file detail such as Type or Authors. To group files by author, for example, right-click a blank area of the window, point to Group by, click More, and then click Authors. Windows divides the folder window into sections, with one section listing files you wrote, for example, and another section for files your colleague wrote.

Before grouping files, you must remove any filters you are using in the folder window. If you don't, you'll rearrange only the files that appear in the filtered list. After removing the filter, you'll group the files in the Marketing Graphics folder by type.

To remove the filter and group the files in the Marketing Graphics folder:

1. In the Marketing Graphics folder window, click the **check mark** on the Date modified column heading, and then click the **Today** check box (or the **Select a date or date range** check box if you selected a date on the calendar earlier) to clear the check box. Click a blank area of the folder window. The complete list of Marketing Graphics files appears in the window.

TIP
You can click the triangle next to a group name to show or hide a group of files.

2. Click the **View** tab on the ribbon, click the **Group by** button in the Current view group, and then click **Type**. Windows arranges all the files in the Marketing Graphics folder into three groups, one for each file type. See Figure 2-20.

Figure 2-20 Grouping files

3. Click the **View** tab, click the **Group by** button in the Current view group, and then click **(None)** to ungroup the files.

4. If necessary, click the **Type** column heading to sort the files in ascending order again by type.

Now that Matt knows how to sort, filter, and group files in a folder window, he mentions that he might want to hide or show elements of the folder window itself, such as the Navigation pane. You'll show him how to customize the folder window elements next.

Customizing a Folder Window

As you learned earlier, you can change how you view your files and folders in a folder window, such as changing from large icons to a detailed list. You can make other changes to the layout of your folder windows. For example, you can hide the Navigation pane to devote more space to file lists. The View tab includes options you can use to fine-tune the layout of a folder window. You have already used some options in the Current view and Layout groups. Figure 2-21 summarizes all the options on the View tab.

Figure 2-21   View tab options

Group	Option	Description
Panes	Navigation pane	Show or hide the Navigation pane in this window only, and specify whether to expand the Navigation pane to the open folder, show all folders, or show favorites.
	Preview pane	Show or hide the Preview pane. When you select this option, you can preview the contents of a file without having to open a program.
	Details pane	Show or hide the Details pane. When you select this option, you display the most common properties associated with a selected file, such as the author of the file or its type.
Layout	View options	Select one of eight views for displaying the contents of the current folder: Extra large icons, Large icons, Medium icons, Small icons, List, Details, Tiles, Content.
Current View	Sort by	Select a file property to use for sorting, select ascending or descending sort order, and choose one or more columns to display in the current folder window.
	Group by	Group files by a file detail displayed in the current folder window.
	Add columns	Select a file detail to display as a column in the current folder window or choose a file detail not included in the list.
	Size all columns to fit	Change the width of all columns to fit the contents.
Show/Hide	Item check boxes	Show or hide check boxes next to files and folders; use the check boxes to select items.
	File name extensions	Show or hide the extensions for all files in the current folder window.
	Hidden items	Show or hide the files and folders marked as hidden.
	Hide selected items	Hide the selected files or folders.
	Options	Use the Folder Options dialog box to change settings for opening items, file and folder views, and searching.

© 2014 Cengage Learning

You'll show Matt how to change the layout of a folder window, and then how to customize the appearance of the folder contents. Finally, you'll demonstrate how to add items to the Navigation pane to suit the way he works.

Changing the Layout of a Folder Window

You can change the layout of a folder window by showing or hiding the Navigation pane and either the Preview pane or the Details pane. The Preview pane appears on the right side of a folder window and displays the contents of a picture file and some other types of files. The Details pane also appears on the right and provides information about a selected file, such as the author and file type. Only one of these panes can be open in a folder window. Neither pane appears by default. Figure 2-22 shows a folder window with the Navigation and Preview panes open.

| Figure 2-22 | Folder window displaying the Navigation and Preview panes |

Photo courtesy of Lisa Ruffolo

Matt wants to see if he likes having the Details pane in the folder window, so he asks you to display that pane. He is also curious about the Preview pane, so you'll open that for him first. The Marketing Graphics folder window should currently be open in Details view, with files sorted according to type.

To change the layout of a folder window:

1. Click the **Chianti** file to select it, click the **View** tab on the ribbon, and then click the **Preview pane** button in the Panes group to display the Preview pane.

2. Click the **View** tab, and then click the **Details pane** button in the Panes group to close the Preview pane and display the Details pane. See Figure 2-23. Your file details might vary.

Figure 2-23 | **Folder window displaying the Navigation and Details panes**

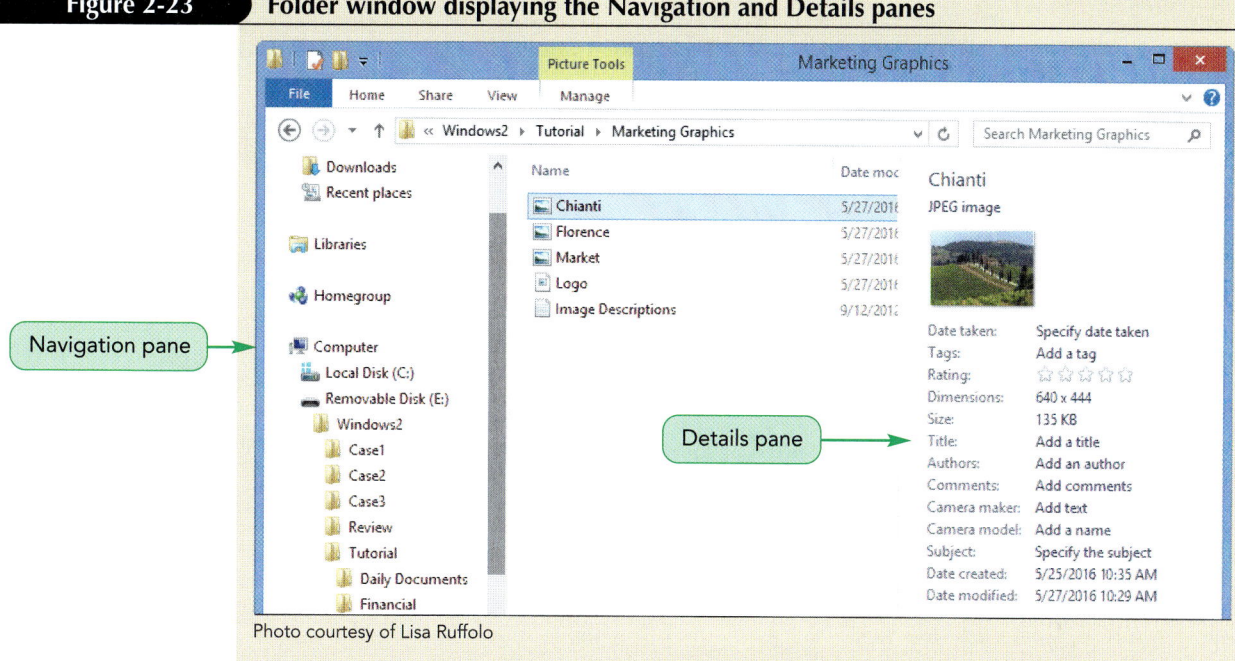

Photo courtesy of Lisa Ruffolo

You can also use options in the Show/hide group on the View tab to customize the file list.

Customizing the File List

TIP

Windows hides filename extensions only for file types it can identify. If it can't identify the file type, Windows always displays the extension.

Although Windows 8 refers to a filename extension to identify a file's type, filename extensions are not displayed by default in a folder window. Windows hides the extensions to make filenames easier to read, especially for long filenames. If you prefer to display filename extensions, you can show them in all the folder windows (as you do in the following steps).

Another type of file not displayed by default in a folder window is a **hidden file**. Windows hides many types of files, including temporary files it creates before you save a document. It hides these files so that you do not become confused by temporary filenames, which are similar to the names of the files you store on your computer. By default, Windows 8 also hides system files, which are files the operating system needs to work properly. You should keep these files hidden unless a reliable expert, such as a technical support professional, instructs you to display them. Keep in mind that hidden files still take up space on your disk.

You use the options in the Show/hide group on the View tab to show and hide filename extensions in all windows. To show and hide hidden files, you use the Folder Options dialog box.

To show filename extensions:

1. Click the **Expand the Ribbon** button to expand the ribbon.
2. On the View tab, click the **File name extensions** check box in the Show/hide group to insert a check mark so filename extensions appear in all windows. See Figure 2-24.

| Figure 2-24 | Folder window showing filename extensions |

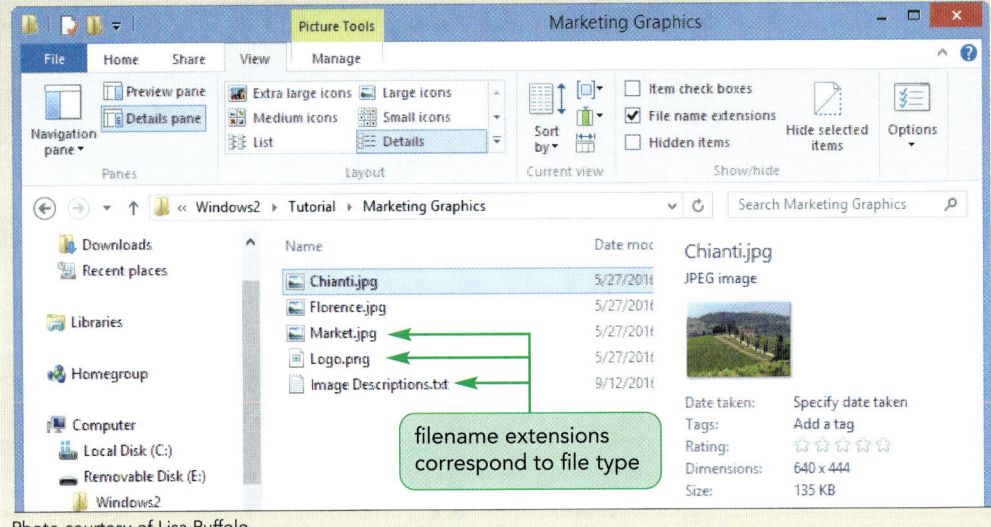

Photo courtesy of Lisa Ruffolo

> 3. Click the **Options** button to open the Folder Options dialog box.
>
> 4. Click the **View** tab in the Folder Options dialog box. See Figure 2-25. The settings selected on the View tab of your Folder Options dialog box might differ.

| Figure 2-25 | Folder Options dialog box |

> 5. Click the **Hide extensions for known file types** check box to insert a check mark, and then click the **OK** button to hide the filename extensions again.
>
> **Trouble?** If the Hide extensions for known file types check box already contains a check mark, just close the dialog box.

Next, you can customize the Navigation pane by changing its appearance and adding a folder to the Favorites list.

Customizing the Navigation Pane

You can customize the Navigation pane by adding, renaming, and removing items in the Favorites list. For example, if you use the Navigation pane to open a particular folder, you can drag that folder to the Favorites list to make it one of your favorite locations.

TIP

When you delete a folder link in the Favorites list, you remove only the link, not the folder itself.

To customize your Navigation pane, first, you'll add the Daily Documents folder as a link in the Favorites list so you can access the folder quickly. Then, you'll rename this link to distinguish it from the Documents library, which is also listed in the Navigation pane. When you rename an item in the Favorites list, you rename the link only—not the actual file or folder. Later, when you restore the settings on your computer, you'll delete this link.

To customize the Navigation pane:

1. Use any navigation method you've learned to display the folders in the Tutorial folder. Scroll to the top of the Navigation pane, if necessary.

2. Drag the **Daily Documents** folder from the Tutorial folder to the end of the Favorites list in the Navigation pane. When the Create link in Favorites ScreenTip appears, release the mouse button to insert a new link named Daily Documents in the Favorites list. See Figure 2-26.

Figure 2-26 Daily Documents folder as a link in the Favorites list

3. Right-click the **Daily Documents** link in the Favorites list, and then click **Rename** on the shortcut menu. The current name is selected.

4. Type **Daily Projects** as the new name of this link, and then press the **Enter** key. The link is renamed, but the Daily Documents folder in the Tutorial folder still has its original name. See Figure 2-27.

Figure 2-27 Daily Documents link renamed as Daily Projects

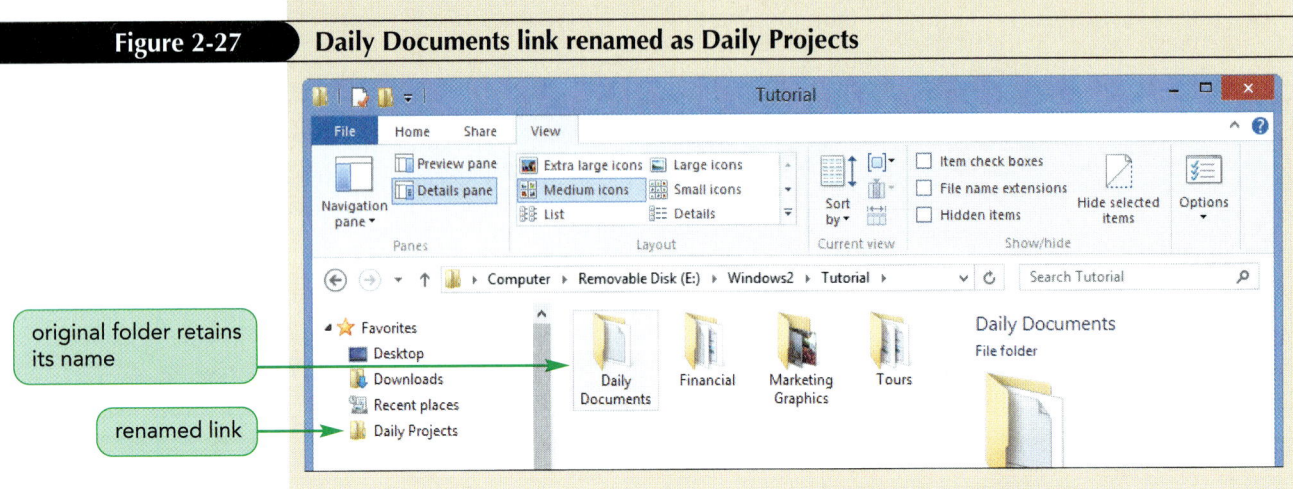

Now that you've refined your file organization and customized the folder window, you are ready to show Matt two final tasks—compressing and extracting files.

Working with Compressed Files

If you transfer files from one location to another, such as from your hard disk to a removable disk or vice versa, or from one computer to another via email, you can store the files in a compressed (zipped) folder so that they take up less disk space. You can then transfer the files more quickly. If you or your email contacts can send and receive files only up to a certain size, compressing large files might make them small enough to send and receive. When you create a compressed folder using Windows 8's compression tool, a zipper appears on the folder icon.

You compress a folder so that the files it contains use less space on the disk. Compare two folders—a folder named Photos that contains about 8.6 MB of files, and a compressed folder containing the same files, but requiring only 6.5 MB of disk space. In this case, the compressed files use about 25 percent less disk space than the uncompressed files.

You can create a compressed folder using the Zip button in the Send group on the Share tab of a folder window. Then you can compress additional files or folders by dragging them into the compressed folder. You can open a file directly from a compressed folder, although you cannot modify the file. To edit and save a compressed file, you must extract it first. When you **extract** a file, you create an uncompressed copy of the file in a folder you specify. The original file remains in the compressed folder.

If a different compression program, such as WinZip, has been installed on your computer, the Zip button might not be available on the Share tab. In this case, refer to your compression program's Help system for instructions on working with compressed files.

Matt suggests that you compress the files and folders in the Tutorial folder so that you can more quickly transfer them to another location.

TIP

Another way to compress files is to select the files, right-click the selection, point to Send to on the shortcut menu, and then click Compressed (zipped) folder.

To compress the folders and files in the Tutorial folder:

1. Select all the folders in the Tutorial folder, click the **Share** tab on the ribbon, and then click the **Zip** button in the Send group. After a few moments, a new compressed folder with a zipper icon appears in the Tutorial window with the filename selected.

Trouble? If the Zip button is not available on the Share tab, this means that a different compression program is probably installed on your computer. Read but do not perform the remaining steps.

2. Type **Savvy Traveler** and then press the **Enter** key to rename the compressed folder. See Figure 2-28.

Figure 2-28   Creating a compressed folder

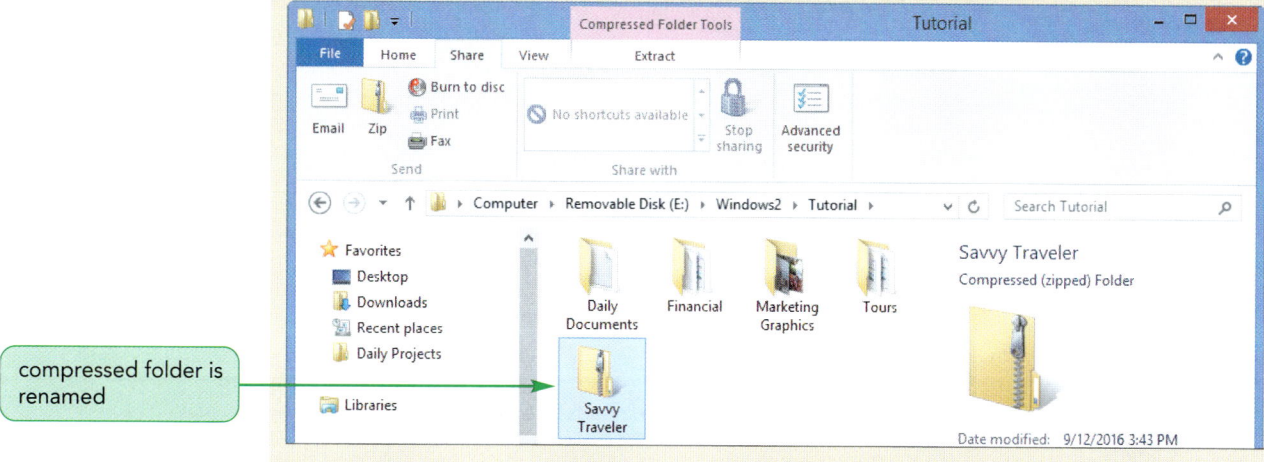

compressed folder is renamed

You open a compressed folder by double-clicking it. You can then move and copy files and folders from the opened compressed folder to other locations, although you cannot rename the files. More often, you extract all of the files in the compressed folder. Windows 8 then uncompresses and copies them to a location that you specify, preserving the files in their original folders as appropriate.

INSIGHT

Understanding Compressed File Types

Some types of files, such as JPEG picture files (those with a .jpg or .jpeg filename extension), are already highly compressed. If you compress JPEG pictures into a folder, the total size of the compressed folder is about the same as the collection of uncompressed pictures. However, if you are transferring the files from one computer to another, such as by email, it's still a good idea to store the compressed files in a zipped folder to keep them together.

To extract the compressed files:

1. Click the **Compressed Folder Tools Extract** tab on the ribbon, and then click the **Extract all** button. The Extract Compressed (Zipped) Folders Wizard starts and opens the Select a Destination and Extract Files dialog box.

2. Press the **End** key to deselect the path in the text box and move the insertion point to the end of the path, press the **Backspace** key as many times as necessary to delete the Savvy Traveler text, and then type **Backups**. The final three parts of the path in the text box should be \Windows2\Tutorial\Backups. See Figure 2-29.

Figure 2-29   Extracting files from a compressed folder

- your path might differ, but should end with Windows2\Tutorial\Backups
- check box should be selected

3. Make sure the Show extracted files when complete check box is checked, and then click the **Extract** button. Windows extracts the files and then opens the Backups folder, showing the Daily Documents, Financial, Marketing Graphics, and Tours folders.

4. Open each folder to make sure it contains the files you worked with in this tutorial.

5. Close the Backups folder window, and then click a blank area of the Tutorial folder window.

In this session, you renamed and deleted files according to your organization plan, and then created a file, saved it in a new folder, and opened and edited the file. Then you refined the organization of the files and folders, customized a folder window, and worked with compressed files. Before you end your Windows 8 session, you should restore your computer to its original settings.

Restoring Your Settings

If you are working in a computer lab or on a computer other than your own, complete the steps in this section to restore the original settings on the computer.

To restore your settings:

1. In the Tutorial folder window, click the **View** tab, and then click the **Details pane** button in the Panes group to hide the Details pane in the folder window.

2. Click the **Minimize the Ribbon** button to show only tab names on the ribbon.

> **3.** Right-click the **Daily Projects** link in the Favorites list in the Navigation pane, and then click **Remove**.
>
> **4.** Close all open windows.

REVIEW

Session 2.2 Quick Check

1. A filename _____ identifies the file's type and indicates the program that created the file.
2. When you delete a file from a hard disk, Windows removes the file from the folder but stores the file contents in the _____.
3. Explain one way to create a file.
4. Explain the difference between sorting and filtering files.
5. If you _____ files by author, Windows divides the folder window into sections, with each section listing files written by a different author.
6. To display the contents of pictures and some other types of files, you can customize folder windows to display the _____ or the Details pane.
7. When you _____ a file, you create an uncompressed copy of the file in a folder you specify.
8. Describe how to create a compressed folder.

Review Assignments

Data Files needed for the Review Assignments: Banner.png, Colosseum.jpg, Lectures.xlsx, Rome.jpg, Schedule.rtf, Tours.rtf

Matt has saved a few files from his old computer to a removable disk. He gives you these files in a single, unorganized folder, and asks you to organize them logically into subfolders. Before you do, devise a plan for managing the files, and then create the subfolders you need. Next, rename, copy, move, and delete files, and perform other management tasks to make it easy for Matt to work with these files and folders. Complete the following steps:

1. Use a folder window to navigate to and open the Windows2\Review folder provided with your Data Files. Examine the six files in this folder and consider the best way to organize the files.
2. In the Review folder, create three folders: **Business**, **Destinations**, and **Supplements**.
3. To organize the files into the correct folders:
    - Move the Banner and Schedule files from the Review folder to the Business folder.
    - Move the Colosseum, Rome, and Tours files to the Destinations folder.
    - Move the Lectures file to the Supplements folder.
4. Copy the Tours file in the Destinations folder to the Business folder.
5. Rename the Schedule file in the Business folder as **2016 Schedule**. Rename the Lectures file in the Supplements folder as **On-site Lectures**.
6. Return to the Review folder and use the Search text box to find a file whose filename begins with the text *ban*. Rename this file **Company Banner**.
7. Create a Notepad file that includes the following text:
   Traveler's Tips
   Make sure your passport is up to date.
   Store photocopies of important documents.
   Arrange all forms of transportation.
8. Save the Notepad file as **Tips** in the Supplements folder. Close the Notepad window.
9. Navigate to the Supplements folder, open the Tips file, and then add the following tip to the end of the document: **Prepare electronic tools for the trip.**
10. Save the Tips file with the same name and in the same location. Open a new document in Notepad, and then type the following text:
    Eating in Rome
    Avoid main tourist area restaurants.
    Pick up sandwiches and pizza by the slice.
11. Save the file as **Eating in Rome** in the Destinations folder. Close Notepad.
12. Navigate to the Destinations folder and then perform the following tasks:
    - Sort the files by Date modified. How many files appear in the folder window?
    - Filter the files by today's date (or the date you created the two text files). How many files appear in the folder window?
13. Remove the filter, and then group the files by type. How many types are displayed? How many files are displayed of each type?
14. Navigate to the Supplements folder, and then display filename extensions in the folder window. Group the files by size.
15. Change the layout of the folder window by displaying the Details pane, and then change the grouping to (None).
16. In the Review folder, add the Business folder to the Favorites list in the Navigation pane. Rename the link **Savvy Traveler**.

17. Click the Savvy Traveler link, click the Company Banner.png file, and then press the Print Screen key to capture an image of the folder window. (*Hint*: Depending on the type of computer you are using, the Print Screen key might be labeled differently, for example, PrtScn.) Start Paint, and then press the Ctrl+V keys to paste this image in a file. Save this file as **Review** in the Windows2\Review folder provided with your Data Files. Close Paint.
18. Restore your computer's settings by hiding the Details pane, hiding filename extensions in the folder window, and removing the Savvy Traveler link from the Favorites list in the Navigation pane.
19. Create a compressed (zipped) folder in the Review folder named **Rome** that contains all the files and folders in the Review folder.
20. Extract the contents of the Rome compressed folder to a new folder named **Rome Backups** in the Review folder. (*Hint*: The file path will end with \Windows2\Review\Rome Backups.)
21. Close all open windows.
22. Submit the results of the preceding steps to your instructor, either in printed or electronic form, as requested.

Case Problem 1

APPLY

See the Starting Data Files section at the beginning of this tutorial for the list of Data Files needed for this Case Problem.

Bay Shore Arts Center Casey Sullivan started the Bay Shore Arts Center in Monterey, California, to provide workshops and courses on art and photography. Attracting students from the San Francisco and San José areas, Casey's business has grown and she now holds classes five days a week. She recently started a course on fine art landscape photography, which has quickly become her most popular offering. Knowing you are multitalented, Casey hired you to help her design new classes and manage other parts of her growing business, including maintaining electronic business files and communications. Your first task is to organize the files on her new Windows 8 computer. Complete the following steps:

1. In the Windows2\Case1 folder provided with your Data Files, create three folders: **Classes**, **Landscapes**, and **Management**.
2. Move the Fall Classes, Spring Classes, Summer Classes, and Winter Classes files from the Case1 folder to the Classes folder.
3. Rename the four files in the Classes folder by deleting the word *Classes* from each name.
4. Move the four JPEG files from the Case1 folder to the Landscapes folder.
5. Copy the remaining two files to the Management folder. Also, copy the Workshops file to the Classes folder.
6. Delete the Instructors and Workshops files from the Case1 folder.
7. Open the Recycle Bin folder by double-clicking the Recycle Bin icon on the desktop, and then display the window in Details view. Sort the contents of the Recycle Bin by filename in descending order.
8. Filter the files by their deletion date to display only the files you deleted today. (*Hint*: If you deleted files from the Case1 folder on a different date, click that date on the calendar.) Do the Instructors and Workshops files appear in the Recycle Bin folder? Explain why or why not. Remove the filter, and then close the Recycle Bin window.
9. Make a copy of the Landscapes folder in the Case1 folder. The name of the duplicate folder appears as Landscapes—Copy. Rename the Landscapes—Copy folder as **California Photos**.
10. Search for the Workshops file and then copy it to the California Photos folder. Rename this file **California Workshops**.
11. Compress the graphics files in the California Photos folder in a new compressed folder named **Photos**, and then move the zipped Photos folder to the Case1 folder.
12. Close all open windows.
13. Submit the results of the preceding steps to your instructor, either in printed or electronic form, as requested.

Case Problem 2

See the Starting Data Files section at the beginning of this tutorial for the list of Data Files needed for this Case Problem.

Charlotte Area Business Incubator Antoine Jackson is the director of the Charlotte Area Business Incubator, a service run by the University of North Carolina in Charlotte to consult with new and struggling small businesses. You work as an intern at the business incubator and spend part of your time organizing client files. Antoine recently upgraded to Windows 8 and asks you to examine the folder structure and file system on his computer, and then begin organizing the files logically. Complete the following steps:

Explore 1. Open a folder window, click the Desktop icon in the Navigation pane, and then open and identify each folder that appears in the Desktop folder window.

2. Examine the files in the Windows2\Case2 folder provided with your Data Files. Display the Details pane in the folder window and then select each file to display its details. Based on the filenames and the descriptions displayed in the Details pane, create an organization plan for the files.

3. In the Windows2\Case2 folder, create the folders you need according to your plan.

4. Move the files from the Case2 folder to the subfolders you created. When you finish, the Case2 folder should contain at least two subfolders.

5. Rename the spreadsheet files in each subfolder as follows. (*Hint*: If Microsoft Excel is not installed on your computer, Windows displays the .xlsx filename extension as you rename the files.)
   - Budget01: **Web Site**
   - Budget02: **Marketing**
   - Budget03: **Event**
   - Report01: **Travel Expenses**
   - Report02: **Project**
   - Report03: **Balance Sheet**

6. Search for a file in the Case2 folder that contains *budget* in its filename.

7. Open the text document you found, and then add the following tip at the end of the file: **Revise the budget as the business changes throughout the year**. Save and close the file.

8. Open the folder window for one of the subfolders you created. Expand the ribbon in the folder window.

9. Change the view of the folder window to Content. Press the Print Screen key to capture an image of the folder window. (*Hint*: Depending on the type of computer you are using, the Print Screen key might be labeled differently, for example, PrtScn.) Start Paint, and then press the Ctrl+V keys to paste this image in a file. Save the image as **Content View** in the Windows2\Case2 folder provided with your Data Files. Close Paint.

Explore 10. In one of the Case2 subfolders, compress all Excel workbooks (that is, all XLSX files) in a new compressed folder named **Workbooks** in the Case2 folder. (*Hint*: After you create the compressed folder in a Case2 subfolder, move it to the Case2 folder.)

11. Restore your computer by hiding the Details pane and minimizing the ribbon in the folder window.

12. Close all open windows.

13. Submit the results of the preceding steps to your instructor, either in printed or electronic form, as requested.

Case Problem 3

Data Files needed for this Case Problem: Customer Satisfaction.pdf, Customer Service.pptx, Customers.accdb, Guidelines.docx, New Employees.pptx

Upcycle Products Wally Ping founded Upcycle Products to convert discarded products such as plastic containers and cardboard packaging into useful materials and consumer products. The company's most successful products include tote bags made from discarded soda bottles. Wally recently installed Windows 8 on the company's computers, and now finds that he cannot open some files with any installed program. You offer to help him identify the file types and organize the files. Complete the following:

1. Examine the files in the Windows2\Case3 folder provided with your Data Files. In the Case3 folder, create the subfolders you need to organize the files.
2. Use the View tab on the ribbon to display the filename extensions for all of these files. List the filename extensions not already discussed in this tutorial.
3. **Explore** Use your favorite search engine to find information about each file type you listed in Step 2. For example, search for PDF files to learn what type of program can open files with a .pdf extension.
4. Move the files from the Case3 folder to the subfolders you created.
5. Open the Guidelines file in WordPad, read the contents, and then close WordPad. Based on the contents of the Guidelines file, move it to a different folder, if necessary.
6. **Explore** Open the Guidelines file in its new location. Type your name at the beginning of the file, and then use the Save As dialog box to save the file as a different type, such as .rtf or .txt, but using the same location. (*Hint*: Click the Save as type arrow and then click a file type.) Close the application.
7. Double-click any other file in a Case3 subfolder and describe what happens.
8. **Explore** If an application did not start when you double-clicked the file in Step 8, right-click the file, and then click Open with. If you are connected to the Internet, look for an app in the Windows Store that might open this file. Go to the Windows Store and scroll through apps, looking for one that might open the file. Return to the desktop. Describe what you found.
9. Close all open windows.
10. Submit the results of the preceding steps to your instructor, either in printed or electronic form, as requested.

Case Problem 4

There are no Data Files needed for this Case Problem.

Fort Worth Professional Employment Doris Salazar owns Fort Worth Professional Employment, an employment agency in Fort Worth, Texas. The company works with employers and potential employees to fill positions and develop careers. Doris and her staff use Windows 8 laptop and tablet computers when they meet with employers and employees to record the details of positions and qualifications. You are working as a part-time trainer to teach the staff about using their computers efficiently. One common problem is losing files they have saved in a library subfolder. Doris asks you to prepare a lesson on troubleshooting this problem so the staff can avoid losing files in Windows 8. Complete the following:

⚙ **Troubleshoot** 1. Windows 8 provides a new feature called File History, which will be very helpful to the company employees. Use Windows Help and Support to find information on File History. What is the purpose of this feature?

⚙ **Troubleshoot** 2. Use Windows Help and Support to learn how to turn on File History. Explain how to do so.

⚙ **Troubleshoot** 3. Use Windows Help and Support to find topics about restoring (or recovering) files. Which Windows 8 tools let you restore (or recover) files?

⚙ **Troubleshoot** 4. Use Windows Help and Support to learn how to change File History settings. Explain the steps.

5. Submit the results of the preceding steps to your instructor, either in printed or electronic form, as requested.

Decision Making

Choosing the Most Efficient Organization for Your Computer Files

Decision making is choosing the best alternative from many possible alternatives. The alternative you select is your decision. When making a decision, you typically complete the following steps:

1. Gather information
2. Make predictions
3. Select the best alternative
4. Prepare an action plan
5. Perform tasks and monitor results
6. Verify the accuracy of the decision

If you are involved in making a complex decision that affects many people, you perform all six steps in the process. If you are making a simpler decision that does not affect many people, such as how to organize your computer files, you can condense the steps or perform only those that relate to your decision.

Gather Information and Select the Best Alternative

Start by gathering information to identify your alternatives. For example, when organizing your files, you could store most of your work on your computer hard disk or on removable media, such as a USB drive or an external hard drive. Ask questions that quantify information, or use numbers to compare the alternatives. For example, how much space do you need for your files? How often do you work with your files?

Also, ask questions that compare the qualities of the alternatives. For example, is one alternative easier to perform or maintain than another? Does each alternative make sense for the long term?

After testing each alternative by asking both types of questions, one alternative should emerge as the best choice for you. If one option does not seem like the best alternative, continue comparing alternatives by listing the pros and cons of each.

Prepare an Action Plan

After you make a decision, prepare an action plan by identifying the steps you need to perform to put the decision into practice. One way to do this is to work backward from your final goal. If you are determining how best to manage your computer files, your final goal might be a set of folders and files organized so that you can find any file quickly. Start by listing the tasks you need to perform to meet your goal. Be as specific as possible to avoid confusion later. For example, instead of listing "Create folders" as a task, identify each folder and subfolder by name and indicate which files or types of files each should contain.

Next, estimate how long each task will take, and assign the task to someone. For simple decisions, you assign most tasks to yourself. If you need to use outside resources, include those in the action plan. For example, if you decide to store your files on USB drives, include a step to purchase the drives you need. If someone else needs to approve your plan or any of its tasks, be sure to include that step in the action plan.

If appropriate, the action plan can also track your budget. For example, you could track expenses for a new hard disk or backup media.

Complete the Tasks and Monitor the Results

After you prepare an action plan and receive any necessary approvals, perform the tasks outlined in the plan. For example, create or rename the folders you identified in your action plan, and then move existing files into each folder. As you perform each step, mark its status as complete or pending, for example.

When you complete all the tasks in the action plan, monitor the results. For example, after reorganizing your files, did you meet your goal of being able to quickly find any file when you needed it? If so, continue to follow your plan as you add files and folders to your computer. If not, return to your plan and determine where you could improve it.

Organize Your Files

Even if you are familiar with some features of Windows 8 or regularly use your computer for certain tasks, such as accessing Web sites or exchanging email, take time to explore the basics of Windows 8 on your computer. Decide how you want to organize the files and folders you use for course work or for job-related projects on your own computer. Be sure to follow the guidelines you learned for developing an organization strategy, creating folders, naming files, and moving, copying, deleting, and compressing files. As you begin to work through this ProSkills exercise, you will record settings on your computer. To do so, you can capture and save images of the desktop and windows you open by pressing the Print Screen key to capture an image of the screen, and then saving the image in a WordPad or Paint file. You can print these images to use as references if you experience problems with your computer later or want to restore these settings. Complete the following tasks:

1. Start Windows 8 and sign in, if necessary.
2. To solve system problems that might appear later, capture an image or two of the Start screen. (*Hint*: Zoom in on the Start screen so most, if not all, tiles appear on one screen). Start WordPad or Paint, and copy the images into a file and save it in the My Pictures folder, so you can refer to it later. Then, capture and save images of the your current desktop and the File Explorer window with the Favorites, Libraries, and Computer expanded.
3. Use a program, such as WordPad or Notepad, to create a plan for organizing your files. List the types of files you work with on a regular basis, and then determine whether you want to store them on your hard disk or on removable media. Describe the folders and subfolders you will use to manage these files. (*Hint*: Remember where you save the file.)
4. In File Explorer, create one of your main folders and then create its subfolders. Locate the file you created and move it to one of the new folders. Navigate to that folder and then use the Address bar to display the contents of this folder. Capture and save an image of this window.
5. Change the view of a folder window using two different view options. Capture and save images of the folder window in each view.
6. Start a Windows 8 app, and then capture and save an image of the app. Start a second Windows 8 app, and then display the Switch List on the desktop. Capture and save the image of the screen with the Windows 8 apps running.
7. Use Windows Help and Support to find information about a feature or technique covered in this tutorial. Choose a topic that you want to know more about. Capture and save an image of the Windows Help and Support window displaying information about this topic.
8. Use a folder window to navigate to your files. Note which tools you prefer to use for navigating your computer.
9. Create any additional folders and subfolders you want to use for your files.
10. Move and copy files to the appropriate folders according to your plan, and rename and delete files as necessary.
11. Create a backup copy of your work files by creating a compressed file and then copying the compressed file to a removable medium, such as a USB flash drive.
12. Submit your finished plan to your instructor, either in printed or electronic form, as requested.

TUTORIAL 3

Personalizing Your Windows Environment

Changing Desktop Settings

OBJECTIVES

Session 3.1
- Personalize the Start screen
- Pin apps to the Start screen
- Create shortcuts on the Start screen
- Customize Start screen tiles
- Change the appearance of the Start screen

Session 3.2
- Personalize the desktop
- Create shortcuts on the desktop
- Customize the desktop using the Control Panel
- Change display settings
- Modify the taskbar

Case | Preserve Africa

Preserve Africa is a charitable organization in Washington, DC, that raises funds for wildlife preserves in African countries. Jodi Berman started the organization with Amanda Jameson about two years ago. Amanda now travels throughout the United States and Africa to meet with donors and representatives of wildlife preserves, and Jodi runs the operations in Washington, DC.

You have been working as the office manager for Preserve Africa for a few months, providing general assistance to Jodi, Amanda, and the staff. Jodi recently upgraded the office computers to Windows 8, and now she asks you to customize the organization's computers so that everyone can access frequently used applications, important files, and computer resources. She also wants the desktop to reflect the image of Preserve Africa. You will start by personalizing Jodi's computer so she can approve the changes. Later, she will apply the changes to the other office computers.

STARTING DATA FILES

Windows3 → Tutorial
Buffalo.jpg
Elephant.jpg
Leopard.jpg
Lion.jpg
Rhino.jpg

Review
Giraffe.jpg
Gorilla.jpg
Impala.jpg
Lemur.jpg
Zebra.jpg

Case1
America.jpg
France.jpg
Puerto Rico.jpg
Sea Cliff.jpg
Tokyo.jpg

Case2
Cabinet.jpg
Chairs.jpg
Chest.jpg
Drawer.jpg
Table.jpg

Case3
Aqua Green.jpg
Checkers.jpg
Festival.jpg
Lime Green.jpg
Red Stripe.jpg

Case4
(none)

Microsoft product screenshots used with permission from Microsoft Corporation.

Session 3.1 Visual Overview:

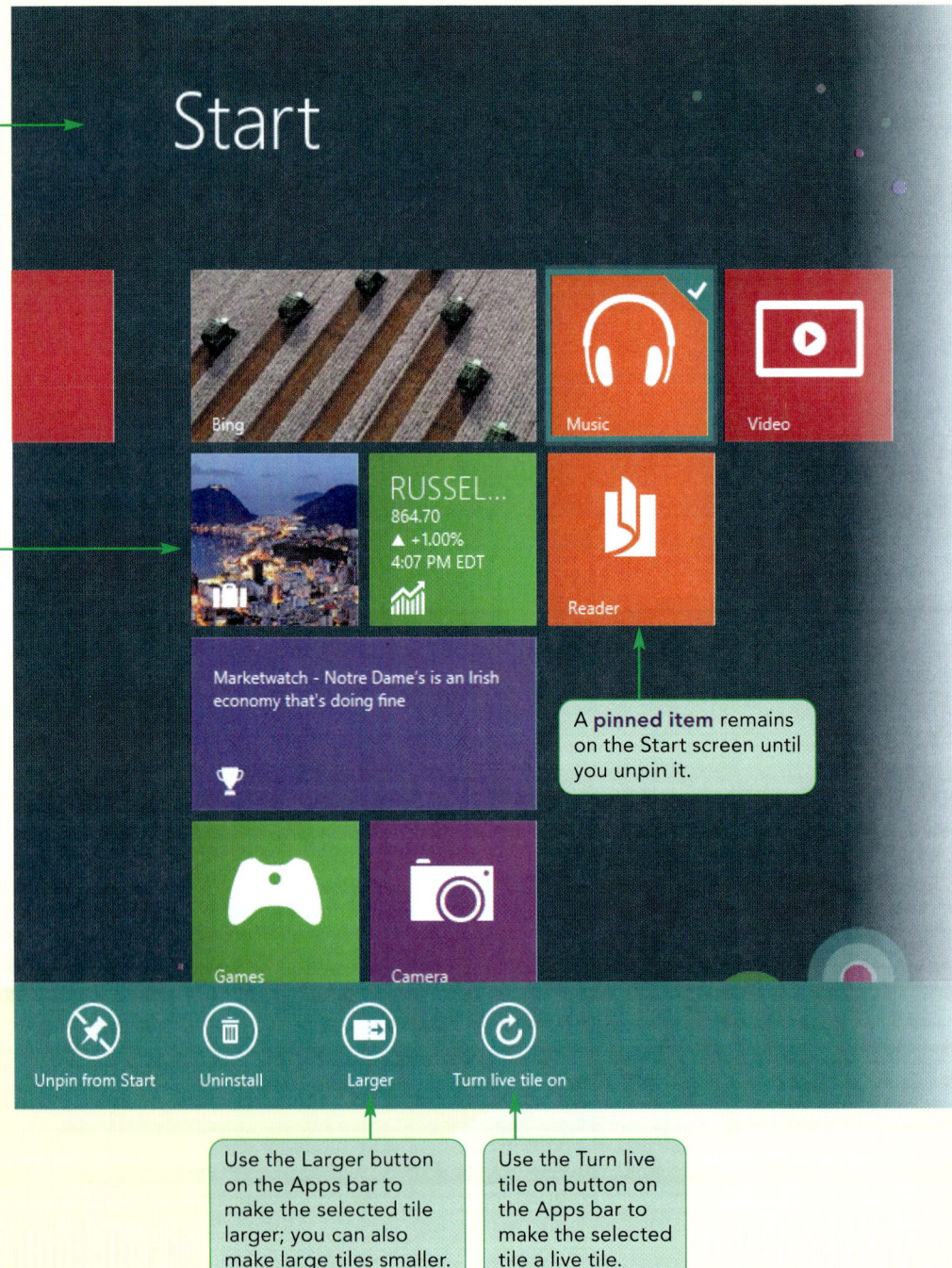

Change the appearance of the Start screen by changing the background design and selecting a different **color scheme**, a set of colors including a background color and coordinated accent color.

Many tiles have a live tile feature that you can turn on and off.

A **pinned item** remains on the Start screen until you unpin it.

Use the Larger button on the Apps bar to make the selected tile larger; you can also make large tiles smaller.

Use the Turn live tile on button on the Apps bar to make the selected tile a live tile.

Photo courtesy of Oliver Wright

Tutorial 3 Personalizing Your Windows Environment | Windows WIN 99

Personalized Start Screen

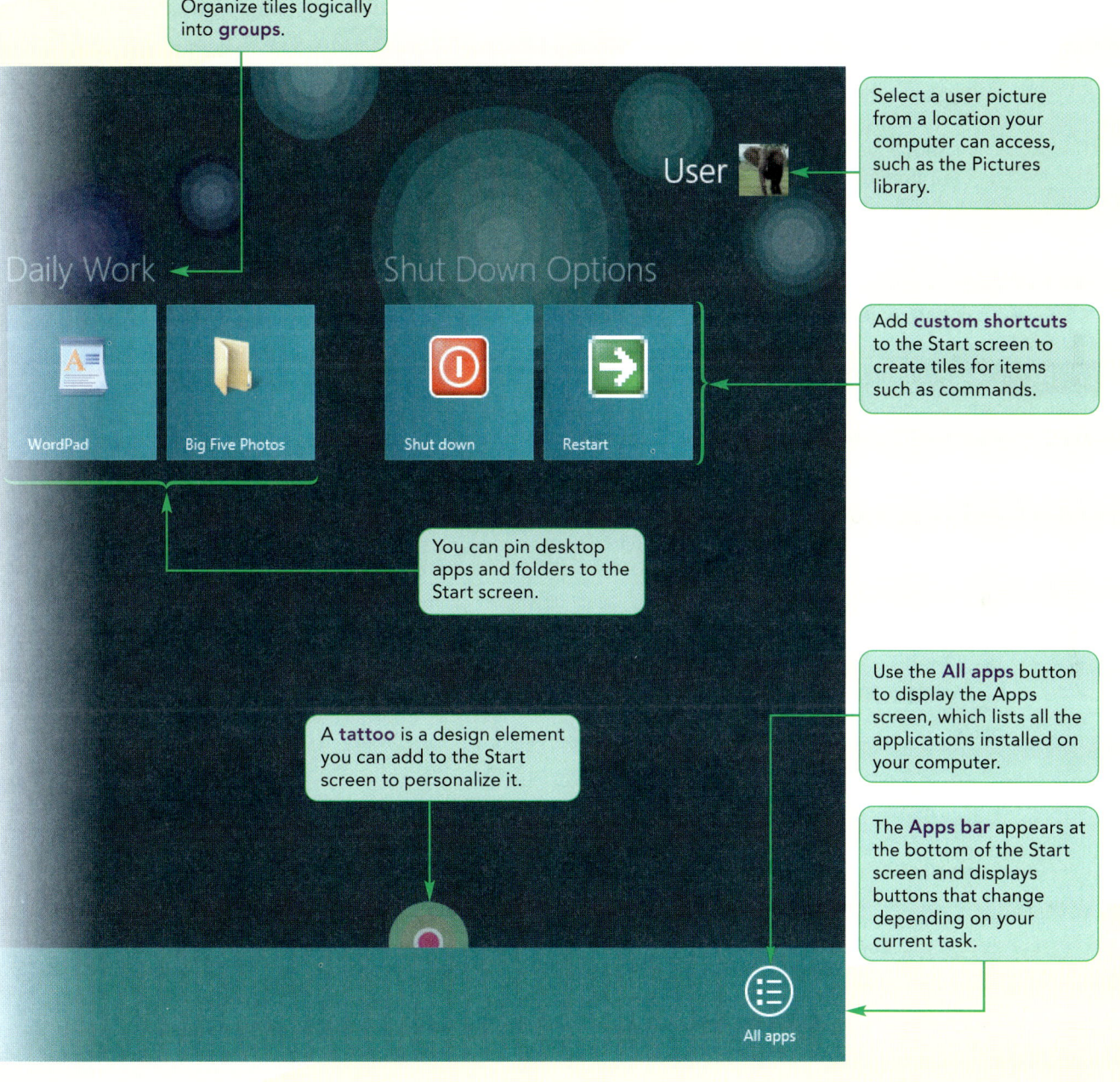

Personalizing the Start Screen

As you know, after you start Windows 8 and sign in, the Start screen appears, displaying tiles for the apps installed on your computer. When you first install Windows 8, the Start screen displays a collection of standard apps, including Calendar, Mail, Photos, and Weather. Because the Start screen is the gateway to your computer, it should display the apps you use most often, organized in a way that makes sense for how you work.

To personalize the Start screen, you can add tiles for apps you use often and remove tiles for the apps you don't use. Each tile is a **shortcut**, a quick way to perform an action such as starting an app. Instead of navigating to the Apps screen, which lists all of the apps and system tools on your computer, and then clicking an app, you can click a tile on the Start screen to start an app. Besides shortcuts for apps, you can add shortcuts for folders such as the My Documents folder and commands such as the Shut down command. When you add a shortcut to the Start screen, you are adding, or **pinning**, a tile to the Start screen. You can arrange the tiles on the Start screen into groups. For example, you might want to keep folders in one group, entertainment apps such as Music and Games in another group, and apps for keeping in touch with people, such as Mail, Messaging, and People, in a different group.

You can also change the appearance of the Start screen to make it more appealing and useful to you. Figure 3-1 summarizes the Start screen features you can personalize.

Figure 3-1 Customizable Start screen features

Feature	Description
Background	Change the color and design of the Start screen background.
Tile	Add tiles for apps (including desktop programs), folders, and commands, and then arrange them into groups. You can also remove tiles you don't use, change the size of a tile, and turn the live tile feature on or off.
User picture	Change the picture displayed next to your user name.

© 2014 Cengage Learning

PROSKILLS

Problem Solving: Adding Apps to Work Productively

In addition to the default apps that come with Windows 8, you can purchase and install apps using the Windows Store, a Microsoft Web site accessible from the Start screen. The Windows Store provides apps created by Microsoft and other developers. It organizes apps by categories, such as Social, Productivity, Tools, and Security. If you're looking for a specific app, you can use the Search menu to search for the app by name. Most of the default apps are designed for entertainment and connecting with your contacts. The Windows Store includes Windows 8 and desktop apps to help you work productively, such as dictionaries, eBook readers, antivirus software, and even the latest version of Microsoft Office. When you sign in to Windows 8, you are eligible to purchase, download, and install apps from the Windows Store. Microsoft and other developers frequently post new apps in the Windows Store, so you should visit the site occasionally to see whether new productivity apps are available. When you visit the site, look for an App updates link on the home page. You can click this link to update apps you've already installed.

Amanda is in Kenya this week visiting a wildlife organization. This gives Jodi time to work with you to customize her computer, starting with the tiles on her Start screen. You'll also show her how to change the Start screen background and change the user picture.

Pinning Apps to the Start Screen

The Start screen displays a tile for each app that Microsoft provides by default. If you download and install an app from the Windows Store, a tile automatically appears on the Start screen. You can also add a tile for any Windows 8 or desktop app installed on your computer. When you do, you are adding a pinned item, which is a shortcut you click to open the app. Tiles are called pinned items because they remain on the Start screen until you unpin them. When you unpin an item, Windows removes the tile from the Start screen, but it doesn't remove the app from your computer.

> **REFERENCE**
>
> ### Pinning an App to the Start Screen
> - Right-click the Start screen, and then click the All apps button on the Apps bar.
> - Right-click an app on the Apps screen, and then click the Pin to Start button on the Apps bar.

To pin an app to the Start screen, you must first display the app on the Apps screen. In previous tutorials, you accessed the Apps screen using the Charms bar; however, the Start screen provides a quicker way to display installed apps: the Apps bar. The buttons on the Apps bar change depending on your current task. When you display the Apps bar on the Start screen, it includes one button, the All apps button, for opening the Apps screen, where you can access all of the apps and system tools installed on your computer. When you right-click an app on the Apps screen, the Apps bar opens again, this time with buttons for performing tasks with the selected app, such as pinning the app to the Start screen and uninstalling the app from your computer.

Jodi mentions that she often receives reports and other documents as **PDF files**, which are files in the Portable Document Format. Reader is a Windows 8 app that lets you read and navigate PDF documents. Because Jodi thinks she will use Reader often, she wants to add a tile for the app to the Start screen. She also uses WordPad to create and edit text documents. In addition, she wants to open File Explorer directly from the Start screen so she can access files and folders quickly.

You'll show Jodi how to pin Reader, WordPad, and File Explorer to the Start screen so they appear as tiles. You are already familiar with WordPad and File Explorer, which are desktop apps, so you will pin Reader to the Start screen first. You'll start by using the Apps bar to display all of the apps installed on Jodi's computer, including Reader. Make sure your computer is turned on and displaying the Start screen before you perform the following steps.

To display the Apps screen and pin Reader to the Start screen:

1. Right-click a blank area of the Start screen to display the Apps bar. See Figure 3-2. The apps on your Start screen might differ.

| Figure 3-2 | Apps bar on the Start screen |

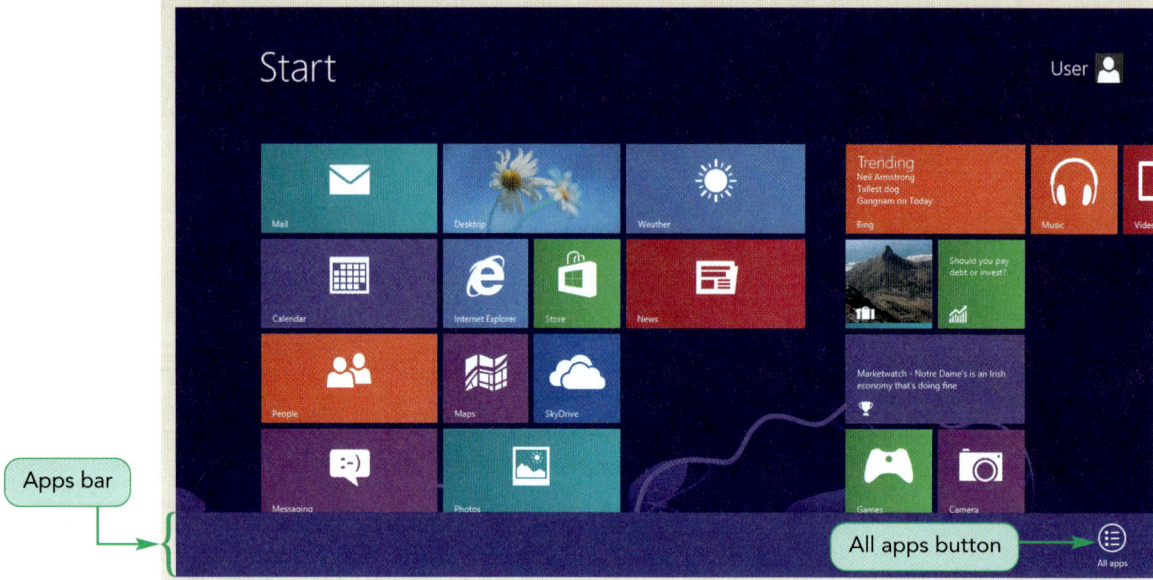

2. Click the **All apps** button to display the Apps screen, which organizes apps and system tools into categories, with Windows 8 apps listed on the left. See Figure 3-3. Your Apps screen might contain different apps.

| Figure 3-3 | Apps screen |

3. Right-click the **Reader** tile. The Apps bar opens again, and Reader tile appears highlighted with a check mark, indicating it is selected.

4. Click the **Pin to Start** button on the Apps bar to pin Reader to the Start screen.

5. Press the **Windows** key to display the Start screen, move your mouse to display the scroll bar, and then scroll to the right to display the Reader tile. See Figure 3-4.

Trouble? If the Reader tile appears in the main section of the Start screen, you do not need to scroll.

Figure 3-4 Reader tile on the Start screen

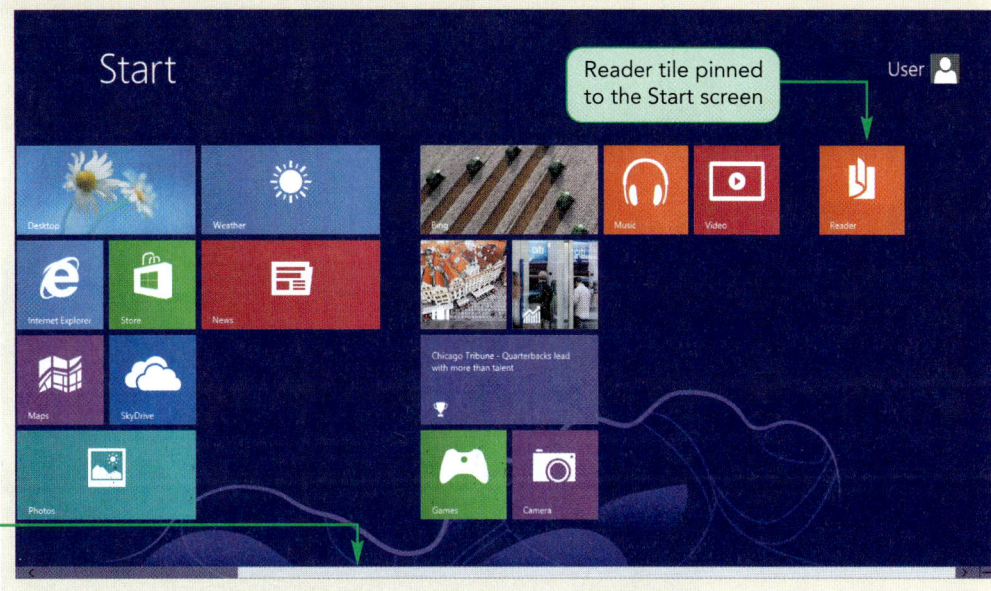

Next, you can add tiles for WordPad and File Explorer to the Start screen. Although both of these are desktop apps, you use the same technique to pin them to the Start screen as you do for Windows 8 apps. You can pin desktop apps to the Start screen and to the taskbar on the desktop. Where you pin a desktop app (the Start screen, taskbar, or both) depends on your personal preferences and where you do most of your computer work. If you routinely start and work with apps on the Start screen, and only occasionally work with a few desktop apps, pin those desktop apps to the Start screen. If you spend most of your time on the desktop working with desktop apps, include only the Desktop tile on the Start screen (where it appears by default) and pin the desktop apps you use often to the taskbar.

To pin any type of app to the Start screen, you open the Apps screen, which organizes apps and system tools into at least four categories: Windows 8 apps, Windows Accessories, Windows Ease of Access, and Windows System. Categories for other installed desktop apps appear after the Windows 8 apps in alphabetical order. Figure 3-5 describes these categories of apps.

Figure 3-5 Categories of apps

Category	Description
Windows 8 apps	Apps developed for the Windows 8 user interface, including the standard apps installed when you set up Windows and any apps downloaded and installed from the Windows Store
Windows Accessories	Desktop apps provided with Windows for performing basic tasks, including Paint, WordPad, Windows Media Player, and Calculator
Windows Ease of Access	Desktop apps that make the computer easier to use for people with vision, hearing, and mobility impairments
Windows System	Desktop tools for working with the operating system, files, and folders, including the Control Panel and File Explorer
Other desktop apps	Desktop apps installed on your computer, such as Microsoft Office

© 2014 Cengage Learning

Jodi thinks she will often use WordPad and File Explorer as soon as she signs in to Windows, so you'll pin these desktop apps to the Start screen.

To pin WordPad and File Explorer to the Start screen:

1. Right-click a blank area of the Start screen to display the Apps bar, and then click the **All apps** button to display the Apps screen.

2. Scroll the Apps screen to the right to display the Windows Accessories, Windows Ease of Access, and Windows System categories. See Figure 3-6. Your screen might include additional categories of apps.

Figure 3-6   **Scrolled Apps screen**

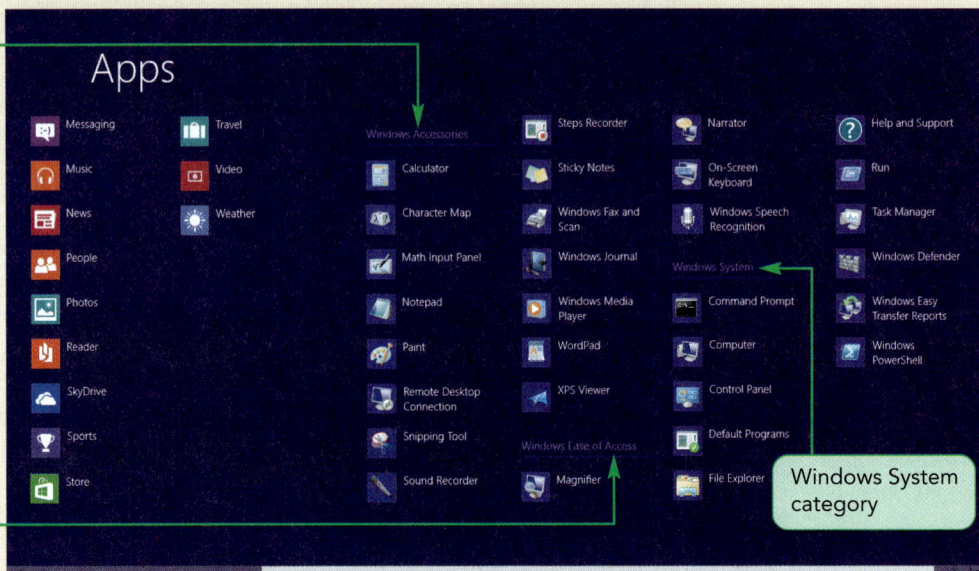

3. In the Windows Accessories category, right-click the **WordPad** app to highlight it with a check mark and to display the Apps bar, which contains buttons for working with desktop apps. See Figure 3-7.

Figure 3-7 Apps bar for desktop app

- WordPad is the selected desktop app
- Apps bar buttons for a desktop app
- Pin to Start button

▸ 4. Click the **Pin to Start** button on the Apps bar to pin WordPad to the Start screen.

▸ 5. In the Windows System category, right-click the **File Explorer** app, and then click the **Pin to Start** button on the Apps bar.

▸ 6. Press the **Windows** key to display the Start screen, and then scroll the Start screen to the right to display the WordPad and File Explorer tiles. See Figure 3-8.

Figure 3-8 WordPad and File Explorer tiles on the Start screen

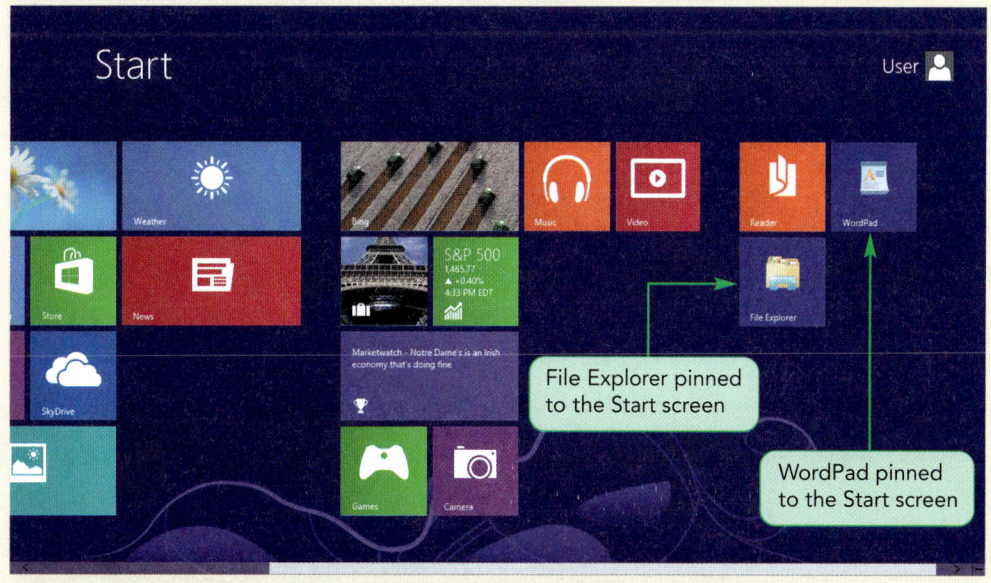

- File Explorer pinned to the Start screen
- WordPad pinned to the Start screen

You can test the three new tiles on the Start screen to make sure each opens the appropriate app.

To test the Reader, WordPad, and File Explorer tiles:

1. Click the **Reader** tile on the Start screen to start Reader. When the app starts, it might display a document explaining how to convert PDF files into Word documents or it might display a Browse button, which you can click to find a PDF file to open.

2. Drag the top of the Reader app screen down until it shrinks to a thumbnail, and then continue dragging it to the very bottom of the screen to close the app.

> **TIP**
> You can also press the Alt+F4 keys to close a Windows 8 app.

3. Scroll the Start screen to the right, if necessary, and then click the **WordPad** tile on the Start screen. The WordPad program window opens on the desktop.

4. Click the **Close** button ☒ to close WordPad.

5. Press the **Windows** key ⊞ to display the Start screen, scroll to the right, if necessary, and then click the **File Explorer** tile to open the File Explorer window on the desktop.

6. Click the **Close** button ☒ to close File Explorer, and then press the **Windows** key ⊞ to return to the Start screen.

Now that you've pinned apps to the Start screen, you can add tiles for other items, including folders and commands.

Pinning Folders to the Start Screen

If you often use a folder soon after you sign in to Windows, you can pin the folder to the Start screen, where it appears as a tile. Because pinned items remain on the Start screen until you unpin them, you should unpin them when you no longer need them so the Start screen doesn't become cluttered. You can pin folders located on the hard disk to the Start screen, but not folders on removable media such as a USB flash drive.

Jodi frequently uses photos of the so-called big five African animals: the buffalo, elephant, leopard, lion, and rhinoceros. She has image files of these animals stored on a removable disk. To provide Jodi with easy access to the photos, you will create a new folder for the photos on the hard disk, copy the image files to the new folder, and then pin the folder to the Start screen. You can create the new folder in the Public Pictures folder on the hard disk. Public Pictures is one of four public folders that are available to anyone using the computer. (Public Documents, Public Music, and Public Videos are the other public folders.) People often use the public folders to share files with other users. To locate the photos so you can copy them, you can use the new File Explorer tile on the Start screen to navigate to the folder containing the African animal photos on a removable disk.

To pin a folder to the Start screen:

1. Scroll the Start screen to the right, if necessary, and then click the **File Explorer** tile on the Start screen to open File Explorer on the desktop.

2. Use any technique you've learned to navigate to the **Tutorial** folder in the Windows3 folder provided with your Data Files.

3. Select the five image files (**Buffalo**, **Elephant**, **Leopard**, **Lion**, and **Rhino**) and then press the **Ctrl+C** keys to copy the files to the Clipboard.

4. In the Navigation pane, click the **expand** icon next to the Pictures link to display the folders in the Pictures library, and then click the **Public Pictures** folder to open the folder.

5. If necessary, click the **Expand the Ribbon** button on the ribbon, and then click the **New folder** button in the New group on the Home tab to create a folder.

6. Type **Big Five Photos** and then press the **Enter** key to name the folder.

7. Right-click the **Big Five Photos** folder and then click **Paste** on the shortcut menu to paste the five image files into the Big Five Photos folder.

8. Right-click the **Big Five Photos** folder and then click **Pin to Start** on the shortcut menu.

9. Press the **Windows** key to return to the Start screen, and then scroll to the right, if necessary, to display the tile for the Big Five Photos folder. See Figure 3-9.

Figure 3-9 Start screen with pinned folder

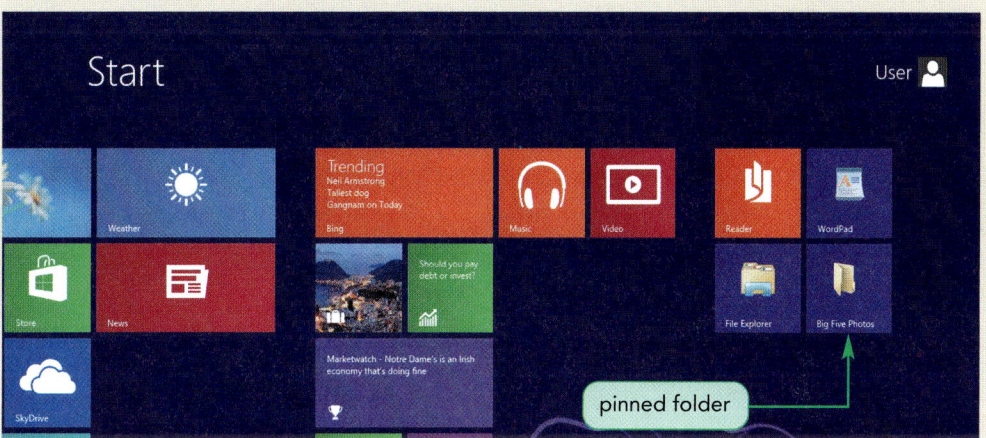

10. To test the new pinned item, click the **Big Five Photos** tile on the Start screen. The folder opens in File Explorer on the desktop.

11. Close all open windows, and then press the **Windows** key to return to the Start screen.

Jodi mentions that she would like a quicker way to shut down and restart the computer without having to display the Settings menu. To accommodate this request, you will add custom shortcuts to the Start screen to shut down or restart the computer in one step.

Adding Custom Shortcuts to the Start Screen

TIP

Windows uses the term *shortcut* to refer to items you click to open a related app, file, or folder, and to refer to the menu that appears when you right-click an item.

Recall that when you pin an app or folder to the Start screen, you are creating a shortcut to the item that Windows displays as a tile on the Start screen. So far, you have pinned three apps by working directly with each one: You located the app on the Apps screen, right-clicked it, and then selected an option for pinning the item to the Start screen. In some cases, however, you can't work directly with the item you want to pin. For example, although you can click the Power button on the Settings menu to display the Shut down, Sleep, and Restart commands, right-clicking one of these commands does not display a shortcut menu or the Apps bar with the Pin to Start option. Instead, you must use the Create Shortcut wizard to create a custom shortcut on the desktop, and then pin that shortcut to the Start screen. A **wizard** is a series of dialog boxes that guides you through the steps of performing a task. The **Create Shortcut wizard** guides you through the steps of creating a shortcut.

When you start the Create Shortcut wizard, the first dialog box displays a text box for entering the location of the item. Instead of entering the path to a file or folder, you can enter the name of a Windows command, such as shutdown. The shutdown command turns off the computer or restarts it. To specify which action you want the shutdown command to take, you include a switch after the command name, such as /s. A switch starts with a slash (/) followed by a letter or number. Use the /s switch for a complete shutdown and the /r switch to restart the computer.

After entering the command, you use the Create Shortcut wizard to provide a name for the shortcut, such as Shut down or Restart. The shortcut icon appears on the desktop or in the window where you created the shortcut. Shortcut icons on the desktop include a small arrow so you can distinguish them from regular icons. The small arrow is a reminder that the icon points to an item stored elsewhere on the computer. Although custom shortcuts each use the same generic icon, you can customize the shortcut by selecting a different icon with a more meaningful image. Finally, you can right-click the shortcut icon to display a menu that includes the Pin to Start command.

You'll start by creating two custom shortcuts on the desktop—one to shut down the computer and another to restart it. You will also customize the shortcut icons so they are easy to recognize. After that, you will pin the shortcuts to the Start screen.

To create custom shortcuts:

> **TIP**
> You can also press the Windows+D keys to display the desktop.

1. Click the **Desktop** tile on the Start screen to display the desktop.
2. Right-click a blank area of the desktop, point to **New** on the shortcut menu, and then click **Shortcut** to start the Create Shortcut wizard and open its first dialog box. See Figure 3-10.

Figure 3-10   First dialog box in the Create Shortcut wizard

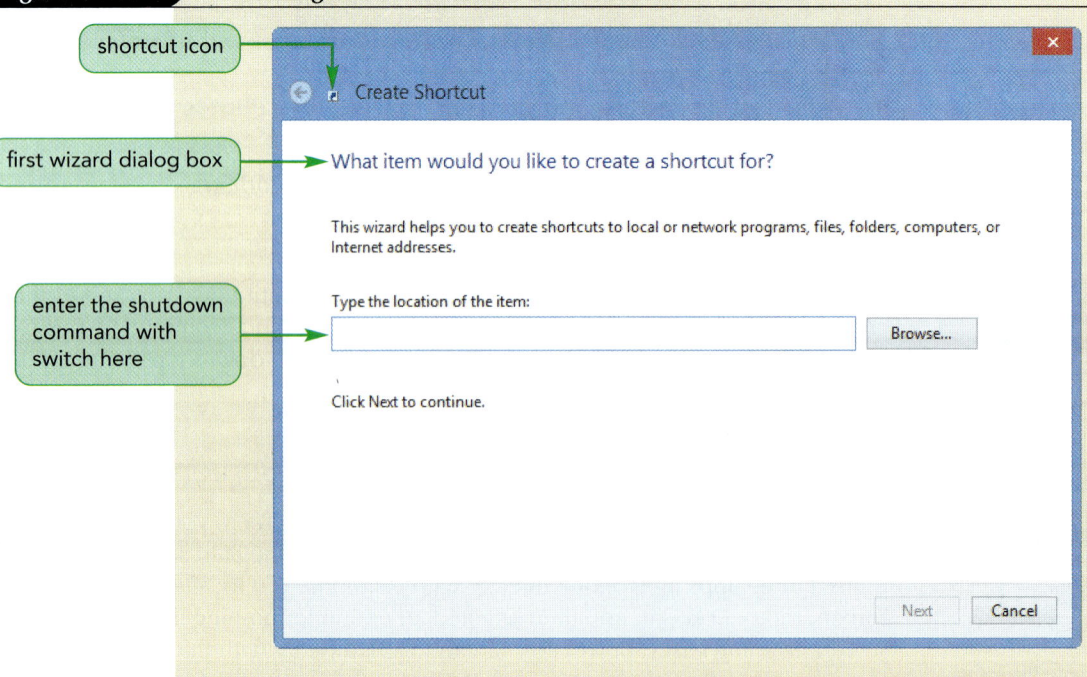

3. Type **shutdown /s** to enter the command for performing a complete shutdown, and then click the **Next** button to open the second dialog box in the wizard, where you name the shortcut.

4. Type **Shut down** to replace the command text with a more meaningful name for the shortcut, and then click the **Finish** button to display the Shut down shortcut icon on the desktop. Next, you can create another custom shortcut for the Restart command.

5. Right-click a blank area of the desktop, point to **New** on the shortcut menu, and then click **Shortcut** to start the Create Shortcut wizard again.

6. Type **shutdown /r** to enter the command for restarting the computer, and then click the **Next** button to open the second dialog box in the wizard.

7. Type **Restart** to enter a name for the shortcut, and then click the **Finish** button to display the Restart shortcut icon on the desktop. See Figure 3-11.

| Figure 3-11 | Shut down and Restart shortcut icons on the desktop |

generic icons for both shortcuts

shortcut arrow

Both shortcuts use the same icon, which would be confusing to anyone using the shortcuts. You can customize the icon for each shortcut to make them easier to distinguish. You do so by opening the Properties dialog box for each icon. A **property** is a characteristic of an object such as a file or shortcut.

To change the icons for the shortcuts:

1. Right-click the **Shut down** shortcut icon on the desktop, and then click **Properties** on the shortcut menu to open the Shut down Properties dialog box.

2. If necessary, click the **Shortcut** tab to display settings and options for working with shortcuts.

3. Click the **Change Icon** button to open a Change Icon dialog box with a message explaining that the shutdown command does not include any icons.

4. Click the **OK** button to acknowledge the message and to open the Change Icon dialog box containing images you can apply to the icon. See Figure 3-12.

Figure 3-12   Change Icon dialog box

select an icon for the Shut down shortcut

5. Click the image of a red power button in the fourth row, seventh column, and then click the **OK** button to close the Change Icon dialog box.

6. Click the **OK** button to close the Shut down Properties dialog box and display the Shut down shortcut with a new icon.

You'll use the same technique to customize the icon for the Restart shortcut.

7. Right-click the **Restart** shortcut icon on the desktop, and then click **Properties** on the shortcut menu.

8. On the Shortcut tab, click the **Change Icon** button, and then click the **OK** button to close the message dialog box and open the Change Icon dialog box containing images you can apply to the icon.

9. Scroll to the right, click the image of a green arrow ➔ in the top row and then click the **OK** button.

   Trouble? If an image of a green arrow does not appear in your Change Icon dialog box, click any other suitable image.

10. Click the **OK** button to close the Restart Properties dialog box and display the Restart shortcut with a new icon. See Figure 3-13.

Figure 3-13 Custom shortcut icons

Now that you've created custom icons for the Shut down and Restart shortcuts, you can pin these items to the Start screen.

To pin the custom shortcuts to the Start screen:

1. Right-click the **Shut down** shortcut icon on the desktop, and then click **Pin to Start** on the shortcut menu.

2. Right-click the **Restart** shortcut icon on the desktop, and then click **Pin to Start** on the shortcut menu.

3. Press the **Windows** key to display the Start screen, and then scroll to the right to display the tiles for shutting down and restarting the computer. See Figure 3-14.

Figure 3-14 Start screen with custom shortcuts

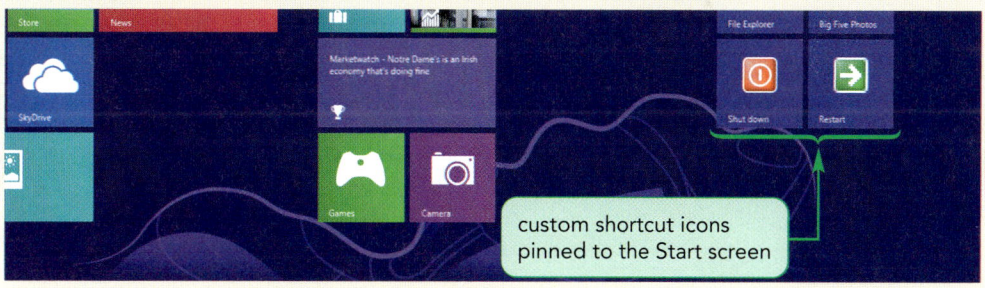

Now that the custom Shut down and Restart shortcuts are pinned to the Start screen, you can return to the desktop and delete the original shortcut icons. When you pinned the custom shortcuts to the Start screen, you created a copy of each shortcut, so deleting a custom shortcut on the desktop does not affect the pinned item. Likewise, unpinning a shortcut does not affect the shortcut icon on the desktop. In this case, Jodi is in the habit of returning to the Start screen when she finishes working on the desktop, so she only needs the Shut down and Restart shortcuts on the Start screen. You'll delete the shortcut icons on the desktop.

To delete the custom shortcuts on the desktop:

1. Scroll to the left, if necessary, and then click the **Desktop** tile to display the desktop.
2. Right-click the **Shut down** shortcut icon, and then click **Delete** on the shortcut menu.
3. Right-click the **Restart** shortcut icon, and then click **Delete** on the shortcut menu.

No shortcut icons remain on the desktop.

Customizing Start Screen Tiles

If you continue to pin items to the Start screen, you will eventually have an unmanageable number of tiles on the Start screen. One way to keep the tiles organized is to group them so that similar tiles appear together. When you group tiles, you can assign a name to the group, which helps you quickly find the tile you want. Another way to organize the tiles is to modify their appearance. For example, you can reduce the size of tiles to fit more on the Start screen and turn live tiles on or off. If you're not using a tile, you can remove it from the Start screen, which helps to keep the Start screen uncluttered. Removing a tile from the Start screen does not remove the app from your computer. You can still use the Apps screen to start and use the app.

Grouping Tiles

In addition to the standard tiles Windows displays on the Start screen, you added six other tiles for Windows Reader, File Explorer, WordPad, the Big Five Photos folder, the Shut down command, and the Restart command. All of these new tiles appear together in their own group. You can start organizing the tiles by moving the Reader tile into the main group of tiles for Windows 8 apps. Next, you can create a group for the File Explorer, WordPad, and Big Five Photos folder tiles. Jodi will use these tiles in her daily work. Finally, you can create a group for the Shut down and Restart tiles. They should remain separate from other tiles so Jodi does not click one and turn off the computer accidentally.

REFERENCE

Grouping Tiles on the Start Screen

- To create a group, drag a tile to the left or right until a vertical bar appears. Release the tile to add it to the new group.
- To move a tile into an existing group, drag the tile to the group.
- To change the position of a tile within a group, drag the tile to a new position.

Jodi asks you to organize the tiles on the Start screen into three groups: the Reader tile in the group of Windows 8 apps; the File Explorer, WordPad, and Big Five Photos tiles in a new group; and the Shut down and Restart tiles in another new group. The new tiles were added to a new group when you pinned them to the Start screen, so you only need to move the Reader tile and create a group for the Shut down and Restart tiles.

To group the tiles on the Start screen:

1. Press the **Windows** key to display the Start screen, and then scroll to the right to display the Reader tile.
2. Drag the **Reader** tile to the left to add it to the second group of tiles for Windows 8 apps. See Figure 3-15.

Figure 3-15 Moving the Reader tile

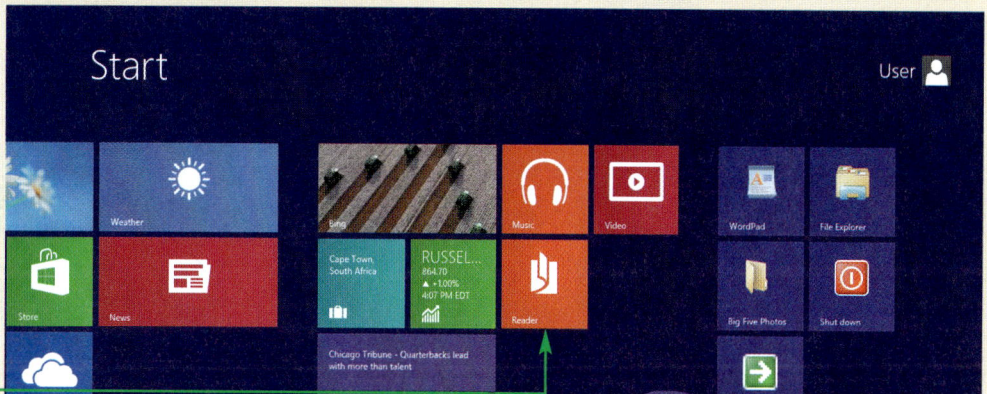

Reader tile moved to main group of Windows 8 tiles; your tile might appear in a different position

Trouble? If the Reader tile appears in a location different from the one shown in the figure, continue with the steps. Windows positions the tile in the most convenient spot in a Windows 8 apps group.

Next, you'll create a group for the Shut down and Restart files.

3. Drag the **Shut down** tile to the right until a vertical bar appears, as shown in Figure 3-16.

Figure 3-16 Creating a group on the Start screen

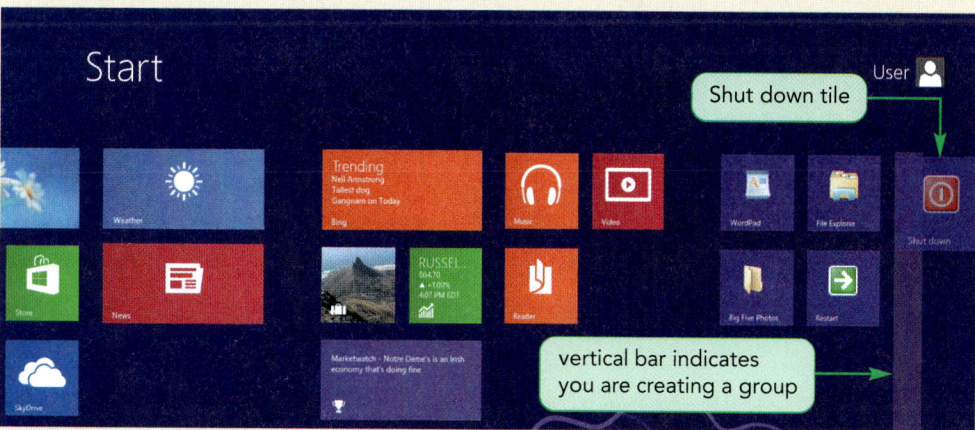

Shut down tile

vertical bar indicates you are creating a group

4. Release the Shut down tile to add it to the new group.
5. Drag the **Restart** tile just to the right of the Shut down tile to add it to the same group. Now the Start screen includes an additional group of tiles. See Figure 3-17.

Figure 3-17 Start screen with three groups of tiles

Trouble? If you drag the Restart tile too far to the right and accidentally create another group, drag the tile to the left of the Shut down tile.

After organizing tiles into groups, you can work with each group directly to name the group or move it to a different location on the Start screen. To do so, you must zoom the Start screen to display all of the tiles at once. Right-clicking a tile on the zoomed Start screen selects the group of tiles and displays the Apps bar.

To identify the new groups of tiles on Jodi's Start screen, you'll display a label above each new group. The group of Windows 8 apps doesn't need a label because those tiles obviously belong together.

To name the new groups of tiles:

1. Point to the lower-right corner of the Start screen until the Zoom button appears, and then click the **Zoom** button to zoom in and display all of the tiles.

2. Right-click the group containing the File Explorer tile to select the group.

3. Click the **Name group** button on the Apps bar to display a text box where you can enter a group name. See Figure 3-18.

TIP
You can also press the Ctrl+Plus (+) keys to zoom in and the Ctrl+Minus (-) keys to zoom out.

Figure 3-18　Naming a group of tiles

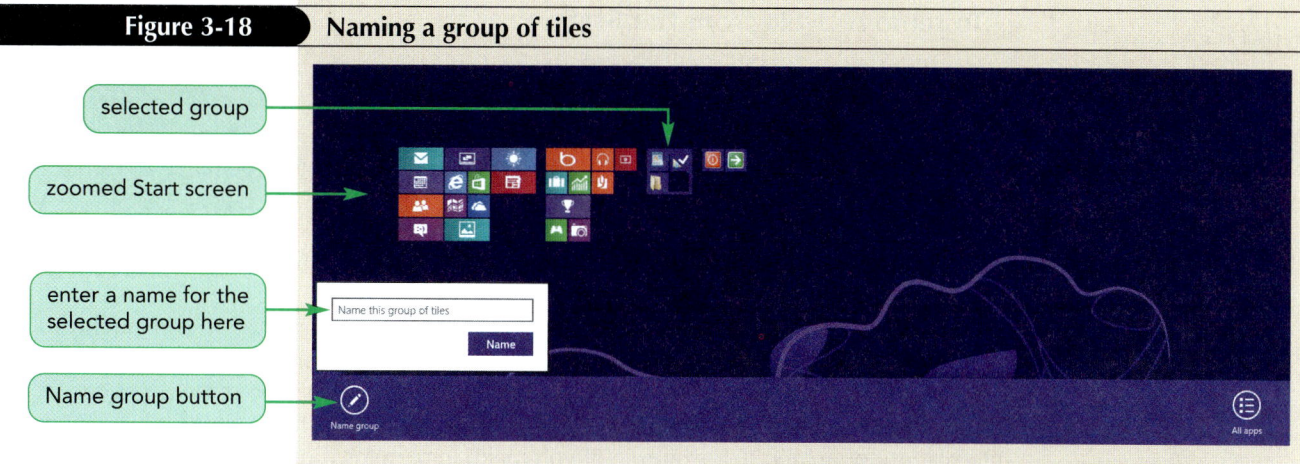

- selected group
- zoomed Start screen
- enter a name for the selected group here
- Name group button

4. Type **Daily Work** and then click the **Name** button to name the group.
5. Right-click the group containing the Shut down tile to select the group.
6. Click the **Name group** button on the Apps bar, type **Shut Down Options** in the text box, and then click the **Name** button to name the group.
7. Click a blank spot on the Start screen to zoom in and display the tiles at their original size. Scroll right to display the names of the groups, if necessary. See Figure 3-19.

Figure 3-19　Start screen with named groups

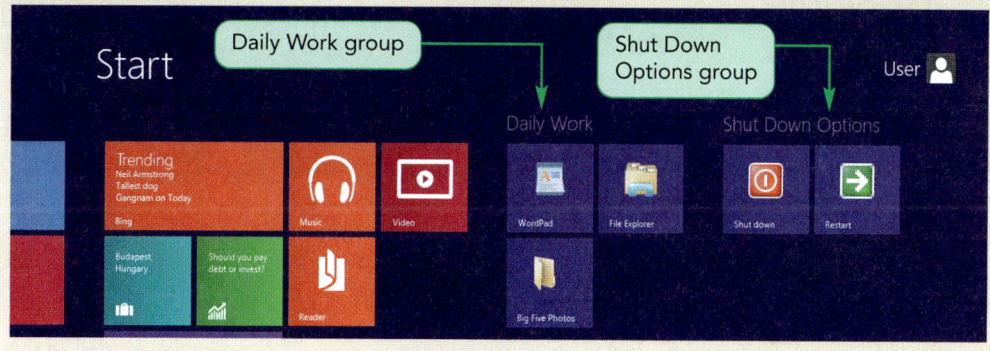

- Daily Work group
- Shut Down Options group

Arranging the tiles into groups organizes the Start screen so it's easier to find the tile you want.

Removing Tiles

To keep your Start screen clean and uncluttered, you can remove tiles to display only those you use often. If you discover that you want to add a tile to the Start screen again, you can use the Apps screen or desktop to pin the item to the Start screen. Keep in mind that when you remove a tile, you are only unpinning the item, not deleting an app or a folder.

Now that the Daily Work group contains tiles for File Explorer, WordPad, and the Big Five Photos folder, Jodi is reconsidering whether she needs a tile for File Explorer. She can easily open a File Explorer window by clicking the Desktop tile and then clicking the File Explorer button on the taskbar, or by clicking the Big Five Photos tile in the Daily Work group.

TIP

If you inadvertently select a tile that you want to keep, right-click the tile again to remove the check mark.

To remove a tile from the Start screen:

1. Right-click the **File Explorer** tile in the Daily Work group to display a check mark on the tile, indicating it is selected.

2. Click the **Unpin from Start** button on the Apps bar to remove the tile from the Start screen.

Modifying Tiles

Besides rearranging, grouping, and removing the tiles on the Start screen, you can also change their size. For example, if you need to scroll to display an entire group of tiles, you can reduce the size of large tiles to display more tiles on a single screen. You can modify tiles by making them live tiles, which change to display the contents or updated information for an app. For example, if you make the Photos tile a live tile, it displays a slide show of photos and other images.

INSIGHT

Turning on Live Tiles

As you know, many tiles on the Start screen are live tiles—they display the latest information from apps including Bing, Mail, Calendar, People, Photos, Weather, News, and Sports. When you open some apps such as News or Travel, you automatically turn on their live tile feature. For example, after you open the Travel app for the first time, its tile displays a slide show of popular travel destinations. To turn on live tiles for other apps, such as Mail and People, you need to set up an account or add information to the app. For example, after you use Mail to set up an email account, the Mail tile becomes a live tile and displays recent email messages. For the Weather app, you need to specify your location or let Windows use the location you entered during setup to have the Weather tile display up-to-date weather information for your location.

TIP

If a live tile becomes too distracting, right-click the tile and then click the Turn live tile off button on the Apps bar.

To display images in the live Photos tile, first make sure you have stored photos in a location the Photos app can access, such as the Pictures library, your SkyDrive, Facebook, or Flickr account, or a device containing photos, such as a camera, phone, or mobile computer. (*SkyDrive* is a location on a Microsoft server computer where you can store files and access them using a Web browser or other apps. Facebook is a social networking Web site you can join to share information with other members. Flickr is a photo-sharing Web site where you can post your own photos and view photos from other people.) If you store image files in a location the Photos app can access, you can make the Photos tile a live tile by right-clicking the tile and then clicking the Turn live tile on button on the Apps bar.

Jodi asks you to reduce the size of some tiles for Windows 8 apps so she can see how to display more tiles on the main part of the Start screen. She also wants to display the images in the Big Five Photos folder on the Photos tile.

To change the size of the Start screen tiles:

1. Scroll to the left to display the **People** tile on the Start screen, and then right-click it to select the tile and display the Apps bar.

2. Click the **Smaller** button on the Apps bar to reduce the size of the People tile. See Figure 3-20.

Figure 3-20 | Reducing the size of a tile

People tile is now smaller

3. Right-click the **Messaging** tile and then click the **Smaller** button on the Apps bar.

4. If necessary, drag the **Messaging** tile up to fill the space created by the smaller tiles.

Because you have already stored the five animal photos in a subfolder in the Pictures library, you can make the Photos tile a live tile by starting the app. First, you'll start the Photos app to make sure it detected the files in the Big Five Photos folder. Then, you'll turn on the live tile feature.

To make the Photos tile a live tile:

1. Click the **Photos** tile to start the Photos app, which displays five locations for storing photos. See Figure 3-21.

   Trouble? If you or someone else has already added photos to a Photos location, your screen will look different from Figure 3-21.

Figure 3-21 Photos app

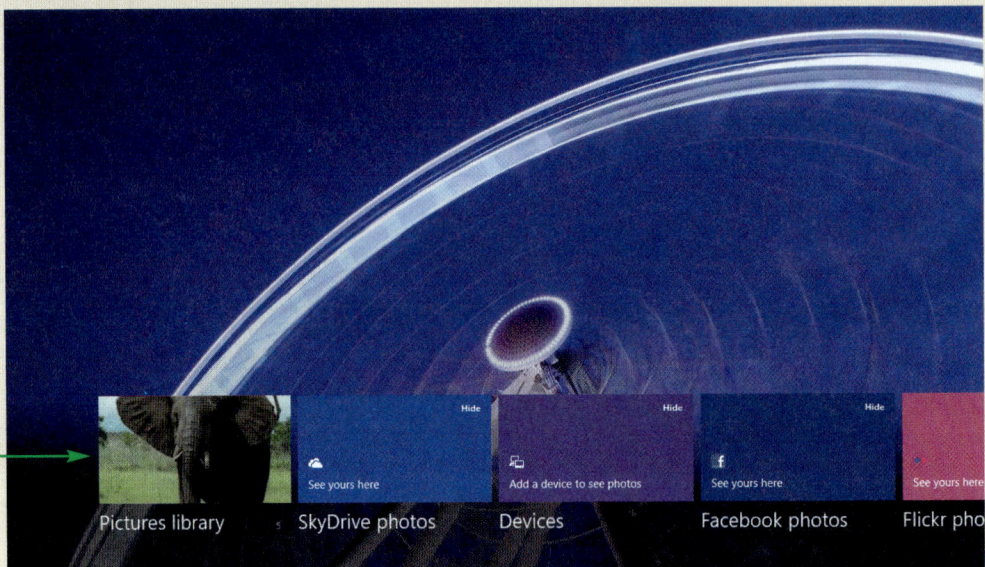

photos in the Big Five Photos folder in the Pictures library

Photo courtesy of Oliver Wright

2. Close the Photos app to return to the Start screen.

3. Right-click the **Photos** tile and then click the **Turn live tile on** button on the Apps bar. The Photos tile now displays the images in the Big Five Photos folder. See Figure 3-22.

   Trouble? If the Turn live tile off button appears on the Apps bar instead of the Turn live tile on button, the Photos tile is already a live tile. Skip Step 3.

Figure 3-22 Live Photos tile

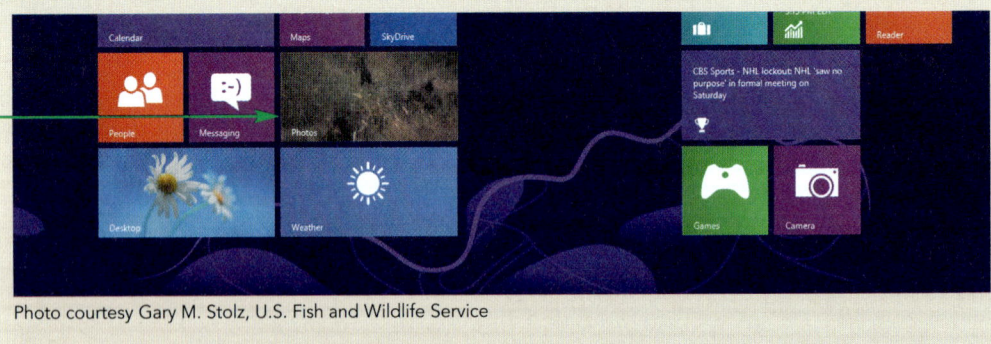

live Photos tile displays photos in the Pictures library

Photo courtesy Gary M. Stolz, U.S. Fish and Wildlife Service

Now the live Photos tile reflects the mission of the Preserve Africa organization.

Changing the Appearance of the Start Screen

Besides personalizing the Start screen to make it more useful and informative, you can change its appearance to suit your preferences. For example, you can change the background design or select a different color scheme, which is a set of colors including a background color and a coordinated accent color.

Windows displays a generic icon as the default user account picture, but you can change this picture to display a photo of yourself or anything else that identifies you. If your computer includes a built-in camera, you can use the camera to take a photo and display it as your user account picture. Otherwise, you can use any image file stored in a location your computer can access.

Changing the Start Screen Background

Windows provides a number of background patterns you can display on the Start screen—all of them designed in the Windows 8 style. You can select a background design different from the default to add your personal stamp to the Start screen. Many background designs include tattoos, which are colorful designs that can make the Start screen background distinctive and lively. In addition, you can select a color scheme for the background design.

REFERENCE

Changing the Start Screen Background

- Point to the upper-right corner of the screen to display the Charms bar.
- Click the Settings charm to open the Settings menu.
- Click the Change PC settings command to display the PC settings screen.
- Click the Personalize category in the left pane, if necessary.
- Click the Start screen link to display options for personalizing the Start screen.
- Click a background design to apply the design to the background of the Start screen.
- Drag the slider to select a color scheme for the background design.

Jodi asks you to show her the Start screen using a different background design and a brighter color scheme. You can make these changes using the PC settings screen, which you open from the Settings menu. You have used the Settings menu before to shut down the computer or put it to sleep.

To change the design and color of the Start screen background:

1. Display the Charms bar.
2. Click the **Settings** charm to display the Settings menu.
3. Click the **Change PC settings** command at the bottom of the menu to display the PC settings screen. See Figure 3-23.

   Trouble? If the Personalize category is not selected on your PC settings screen, as shown in the figure, click Personalize in the left pane to select the category.

TIP

Click the Lock screen link in the Personalize category to change the image displayed on the lock screen.

| Figure 3-23 | PC settings screen |

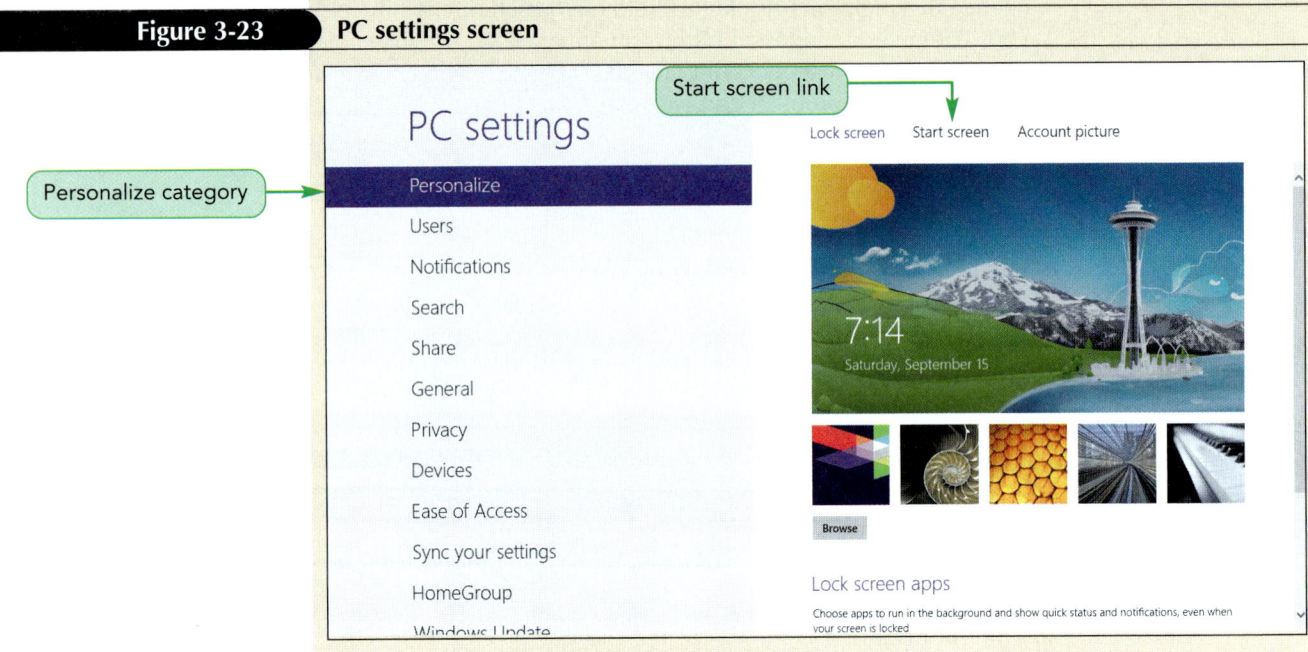

4. Click the **Start screen** link to display options for personalizing the Start screen. See Figure 3-24.

| Figure 3-24 | Start screen settings |

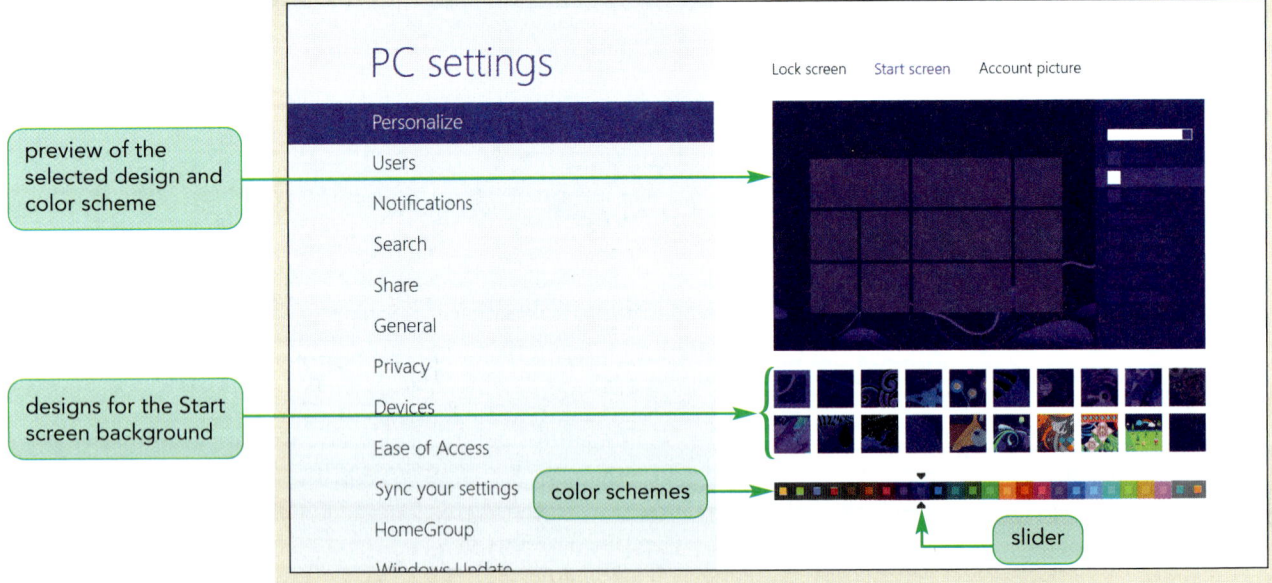

5. Click the fifth design from the left to select a new design.
6. Drag the slider two squares to the right to select a color scheme using shades of teal green.
7. Press the **Windows** key to display the Start screen, which now appears with a new design and different color scheme. See Figure 3-25.

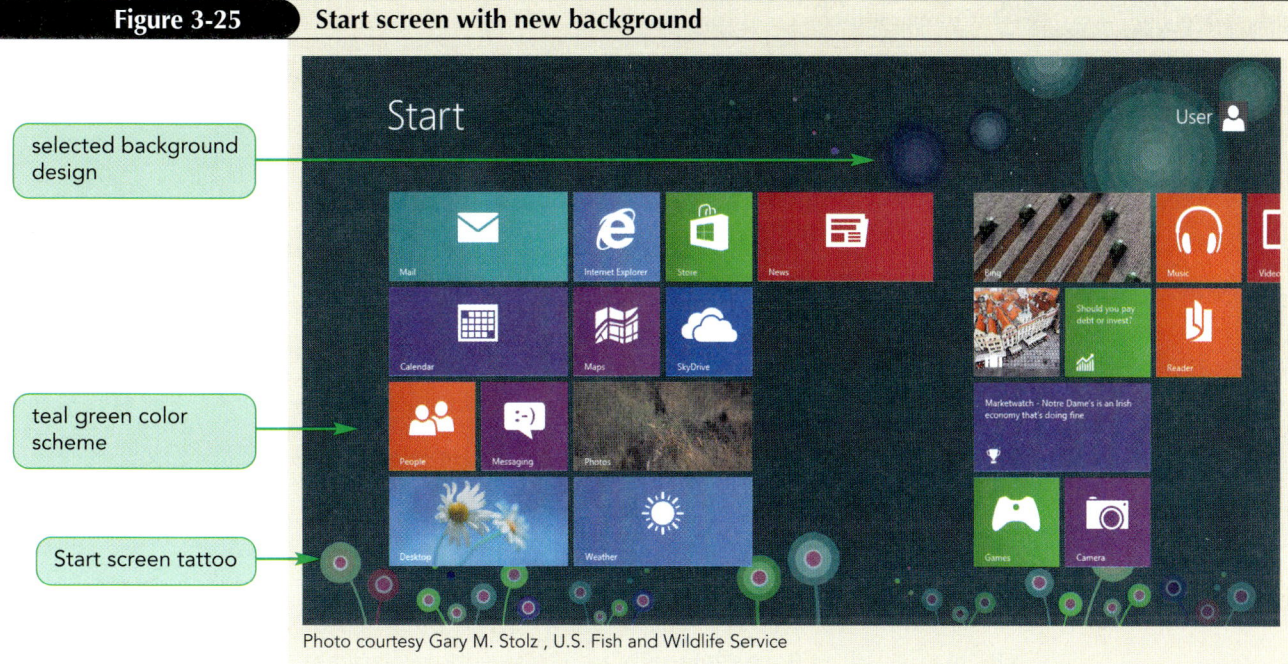

Figure 3-25 Start screen with new background

- selected background design
- teal green color scheme
- Start screen tattoo

Photo courtesy Gary M. Stolz, U.S. Fish and Wildlife Service

Jodi likes the new Start screen background and decides to use it for a while.

Changing the User Picture

Previous versions of Windows provided a collection of images from which you selected a user picture. Windows 8 lets you select any image file stored in a location your computer can access, such as the Pictures library. You can select a photo of yourself or another identifying place or object, an illustration you or someone else created using a graphics app, or any other image stored in a file. You can also use your computer's camera to take a photo and use it as your user picture. Your user picture represents your **user account**, which is a collection of information specifying how you can use the computer and its apps and includes appearance settings such as your Start screen background and color.

Jodi wants to use the photo of an elephant stored in the Big Five Photos folder as her user picture. You'll show her how to replace the generic user icon on the Start screen with a more meaningful photo.

To change the user account picture:

1. Right-click the **user icon** on the Start screen, and then click **Change account picture** on the shortcut menu to display the PC settings screen again with the Account picture link selected. See Figure 3-26.

Figure 3-26 Changing the account picture

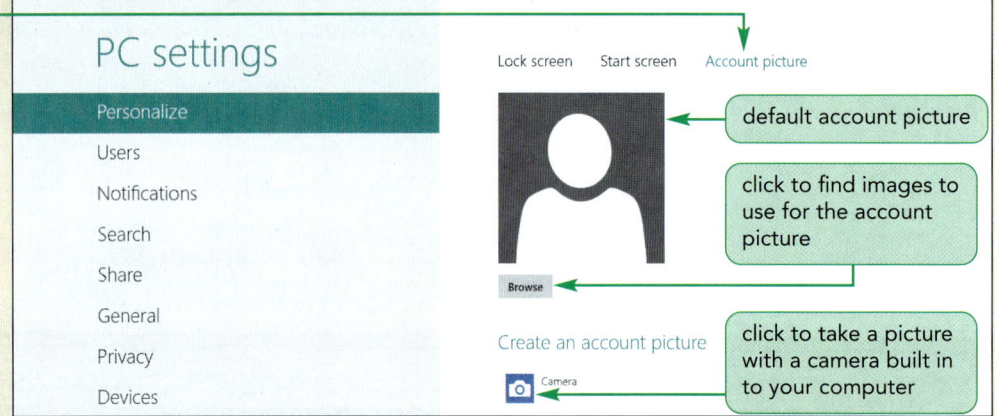

2. Click the **Browse** button to display the files and folders in the Pictures library.

3. If necessary, click the **Big Five Photos** folder to open it, and then click the **Elephant** file to select it.

4. Click the **Choose image** button to select the Elephant image as the account picture.

5. Press the **Windows** key to display the Start screen, which now includes the new account picture.

To create an image of the Start screen that displays many of the changes you made, you can take a screen shot of the Start screen. Jodi can use that image for reference as she customizes the other Preserve Africa computers.

To create a screen shot of the Start screen:

1. Press the **Print Screen** key to capture an image of the Start screen and save the image on the Clipboard. Depending on the type of computer you are using, the Print Screen key might be labeled differently (for example, PrtScn).

2. Click the **WordPad** tile on the Start screen to start WordPad on the desktop and open a new, blank document.

3. Type **Customized Start screen** and then press the **Enter** key.

4. Press the **Ctrl+V** keys to paste the Start screen image into the new WordPad document.

5. Click the **Save** button on the Quick Access toolbar, navigate to the **Public Documents** folder in the Documents library, type **Start screen** as the name of the file, and then click the **Save** button to save the file in the Public Documents folder.

   Trouble? If necessary, click the default name in the File name text box to select it before typing a new file name. WordPad will automatically add the file extension .rtf.

6. Close WordPad.

> **TIP**
> You can also press the Windows+Print Screen keys to create a screen shot named Screenshot (1), for example, which Windows stores in a folder named Screenshots in the Pictures library.

Jodi is satisfied with the changes you made and doesn't want to further personalize the Start screen.

In this session, you learned how to pin apps, folders, and custom shortcuts to the Start screen so they appear as tiles. You also learned how to customize Start screen tiles by grouping, removing, and modifying tiles. Finally, you personalized the appearance of the Start screen by changing the design and color of the background and selecting a new user picture.

Session 3.1 Quick Check

1. On the Start screen, a(n) _____ appears as a tile and is a shortcut you click to open a folder or an app.
2. Explain how to use the Apps screen to add a tile to the Start screen.
3. When you use the Create Shortcut wizard to create a custom shortcut, what command do you enter to perform a complete shutdown of your computer?
4. One way to organize the tiles on the Start screen is to _____ them so that similar tiles appear together.
5. Explain how to remove a tile from the Start screen.
6. Name two ways you can change the appearance of a tile on the Start screen.
7. What are properties?
8. Which screen do you use to change the Start screen background?

Session 3.2 Visual Overview:

The background image is part of the desktop **theme**, a collection of settings that determines the appearance of the desktop.

You can change the appearance of desktop icons.

Besides the Recycle Bin, you can display additional desktop icons.

The **Peek** feature displays previews of the open windows grouped on a taskbar button.

You can change the position of the buttons on the taskbar.

Photos courtesy of Garibgazi; Oliver Wright; Gary M. Stolz, U.S. Fish and Wildlife Service; Ken Stansell, U.S. Fish and Wildlife Service; Komencanto

Customized Desktop

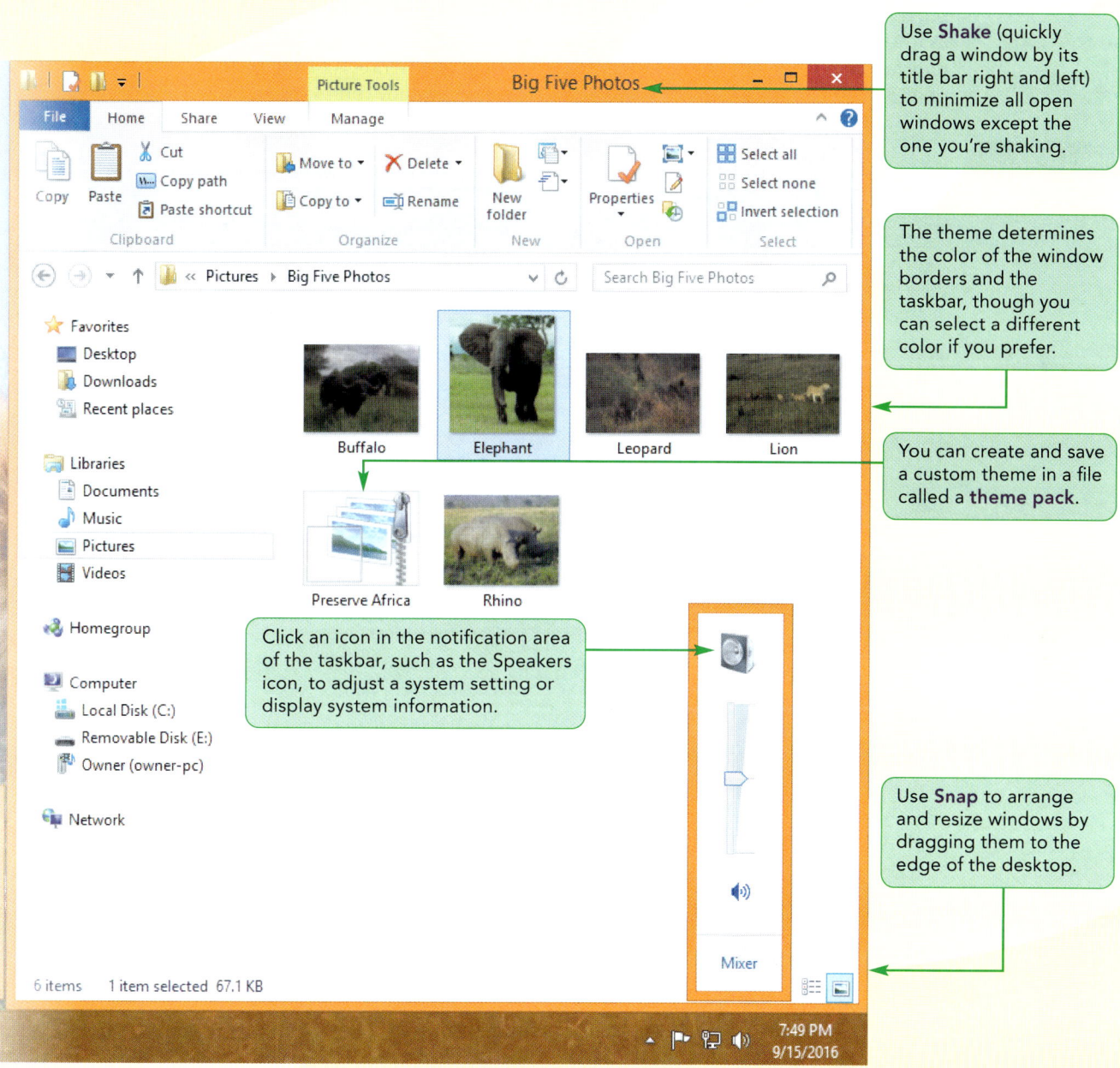

Personalizing the Desktop

When you click the Desktop tile on the Start screen, Windows displays the desktop, also called the classic desktop because of its similarity to the desktop in earlier versions of Windows. The desktop displays a background image, the Recycle Bin icon, and the taskbar by default.

You can place icons on the desktop that represent objects you want to access quickly or frequently when you are working on the desktop, such as Windows tools, drives, programs, and documents. Windows provides desktop icons for system tools, such as the Recycle Bin, the Computer window, and your personal folder. You can add or remove these icons according to your work preferences. Figure 3-27 shows the types of icons you can include on the desktop and the objects they represent.

Figure 3-27 Types of desktop icons

Icon	Description
	Computer icon
	Control Panel icon
	Document shortcut icon
	Drive shortcut icon
	Folder shortcut icon
	Network icon
	Program shortcut icon (such as Paint)
	Recycle Bin icon (full and empty)
	User's folder icon

© 2014 Cengage Learning

Besides these built-in desktop icons, you can use shortcuts to start a desktop program or access an object. Similar to clicking pinned items on the Start screen, double-clicking a shortcut on the desktop opens its associated file, folder, device, or program. When you delete a shortcut or desktop icon, you delete only the icon—the file or resource it represents remains in its original location. You typically create shortcuts on the desktop (or elsewhere, such as in a folder or on the taskbar) to locations, files, and devices that you use often.

Problem Solving: Simplifying Tasks with Shortcuts

If you work with many devices, programs, or folders, it might be difficult to access all of these resources efficiently. One way to solve this problem is to add shortcuts to the desktop. Shortcut icons can simplify tasks you perform regularly. For example, you can create a shortcut icon for a USB flash drive, and then drag files to the shortcut icon to copy them to the removable disk. You also can create a shortcut icon for a desktop program you use often, such as Calculator, and then double-click the icon to start the program. Some programs add a shortcut icon to the desktop when you install the program. If you work with a particular folder often, you can add a desktop shortcut to the folder. That way, you can double-click the folder shortcut to open the folder without navigating many folder windows.

While Amanda is in Kenya, you'll continue to work with Jodi to customize her computer, starting with adding icons to the desktop for system tools she uses often. Then you'll show her how to create a shortcut icon on the desktop to a USB flash drive.

Adding Icons to the Desktop

Windows provides five standard icons that you can display on the desktop. Besides the Recycle Bin, which appears on the desktop by default, you can display the Computer icon on the desktop to provide easy access to the Computer window and therefore the drives and devices connected to your computer. If you display the desktop icon for your personal folder (that is, the folder containing the current user's files), you can quickly find and open the folders containing your documents. Having the Network icon on the desktop gives you access to a window that lists the shared computers and other devices on your network. You can also add the Control Panel icon to the desktop. The Control Panel contains specialized tools you use to change the way Windows looks and behaves.

REFERENCE

Displaying Standard Desktop Icons

- Right-click an empty area of the desktop, and then click Personalize on the shortcut menu.
- In the left pane of the Personalization window, click Change desktop icons.
- In the Desktop Icon Settings dialog box, click to select a check box for each icon you want to add to the desktop.
- Click the OK button.

Jodi mentions that the Windows tools she uses most frequently are her personal folder, the Computer window, and the Control Panel. You'll add these icons to Jodi's desktop.

To display standard desktop icons:

1. If you took a break after the previous session, make sure the desktop is displayed. Close any open windows.

   Trouble? If the Start screen is displayed instead of the desktop, click the Desktop tile on the Start screen.

2. Right-click a blank area of the **desktop**, and then click **Personalize** on the shortcut menu. The Personalization window opens.

3. In the left pane, click **Change desktop icons**. The Desktop Icon Settings dialog box opens. See Figure 3-28. The Recycle Bin check box is already selected, indicating that Windows is displaying the Recycle Bin icon on the desktop.

   Trouble? If you are working in a computer lab, the Change desktop icons command might not appear in the left pane. In that case, read but do not perform the remaining steps in this section and the next section.

TIP

Note that the Recycle Bin icon has two appearances: one when it is empty, and another when it contains deleted items.

Figure 3-28 Desktop Icon Settings dialog box

- select the icons to display on the desktop
- default (or currently displayed) icons shown on the desktop
- click to select an icon to change the image it displays

Trouble? If the settings in your Desktop Icon Settings dialog box differ from those in the figure, note the current options so you can restore them later, and then change the options so only the Recycle Bin check box is selected.

4. Click the **Computer**, **User's Files**, and **Control Panel** check boxes. If necessary, click the **Allow themes to change desktop icons** check box to remove the check mark. You are going to make other changes to the desktop and you do not want these icons to reflect those changes.

5. Click the **OK** button. The icons for your personal folder, the Computer window, and the Control Panel appear on the desktop after Windows applies the new settings.

Now that you've added desktop icons for Jodi, you can customize their appearance according to her preferences.

Changing the Appearance of Desktop Icons

You can change the images displayed on the desktop icons using the same Change Icon dialog box you used earlier to customize the Shut down and Restart icons. Change the image to suit your preferences or to display a more accurate image. For example, the Computer icon shows an image of a desktop computer. If you work on a notebook or tablet computer, you might want to change this image to match your computer type.

Because she works on an all-in-one computer, with the computer and monitor built in to the same case, Jodi wants to change the image for the Computer icon on the desktop. To do so, you use the Personalization window again.

To change the image of the Computer icon:

1. In the left pane of the Personalization window, click **Change desktop icons**. The Desktop Icon Settings dialog box opens.

2. In the box displaying desktop icons, click the **Computer** icon, and then click the **Change Icon** button. The Change Icon dialog box opens and highlights the current image. Note the image currently used for the Computer icon so you can restore it later.

3. Click the icon of a computer monitor displaying a moon image (two icons to the left of the current icon), as shown in Figure 3-29.

Figure 3-29 Changing the default Computer icon

Trouble? If the computer monitor image shown in the figure does not appear in your Change Icon dialog box, click any other suitable image.

4. Click the **OK** button to close the Change Icon dialog box.

5. Click the **OK** button to close the Desktop Icon Settings dialog box, and then close the Personalization window. The Computer icon on the desktop now appears as a monitor displaying a moon image.

The standard Windows desktop icons provide quick access to common Windows tools. These are standard tools that Windows provides to simplify or enhance your computer work. However, other items you access often (such as documents, folders, and drives) might be different from the items other users access often. In addition, the folders you use frequently one week might differ from those you'll use frequently the next week. To personalize your desktop to provide quick access to these items, you can create and use shortcuts.

Creating Desktop Shortcuts

Many people use shortcuts on the Start screen and shortcuts on the desktop for different types of objects. They pin apps to the Start screen so they can quickly access and start an app. They create shortcuts on the desktop for other types of objects, typically folders and drives.

On the desktop, you can create shortcuts to access drives, documents, files, Web pages, programs, or other computer resources, such as a network folder. For example, you can easily open a document from the desktop by creating a shortcut icon for the document. A shortcut icon for a document works much the same way as a document icon does in a folder window—you can double-click the shortcut icon to open the document in the appropriate program. However, a shortcut icon is only a link to the actual document. If you move the icon, you move only the shortcut, not the document itself. One advantage of using shortcut icons is that if your desktop becomes cluttered, you can delete the shortcut icons without affecting the original documents.

You can also create shortcut icons for the folders, drives, and devices on your computer. This way, you can access your local hard disk, for example, directly from the desktop, instead of having to open a folder window and then navigate to the hard disk.

Windows provides several ways of creating shortcuts on the desktop. Figure 3-30 summarizes the techniques you can use to create shortcuts. The one you choose is a matter of personal preference.

Figure 3-30   Methods for creating shortcuts

Method	Description
Drag (for drives and devices only)	To create a drive shortcut on the desktop, use a folder window to locate the drive icon, and then drag the icon to the desktop.
Right-drag	Use a folder window to locate and select an icon, hold down the right mouse button, and then drag the icon to a new location. Release the mouse button and click Create shortcuts here on the shortcut menu.
Right-click, Create shortcut	Use a folder window to locate an icon, right-click the icon, click Create shortcut on the shortcut menu, and then drag the shortcut icon to a new location.
Right-click, Send to	To create a shortcut on the desktop, use a folder window to locate an icon, right-click the icon, point to Send to, and then click Desktop (create shortcut).

© 2014 Cengage Learning

Next, you'll create a shortcut to a USB flash drive on the desktop. You could use any technique for creating shortcuts, but you'll use the drag method because it involves the fewest steps.

Creating a Shortcut to a Drive

To create a shortcut to a drive, you can open the Computer window, and then drag the drive icon from the window to the desktop. Windows creates a shortcut icon that looks like a drive icon with a shortcut arrow and includes an appropriate label, such as Removable (E) – Shortcut. If you drag a document icon from a folder window to the desktop, you move the actual document from its original location to the desktop. However, you cannot move a drive, a program, or another computer resource—its location is fixed during installation. Therefore, when you drag a drive icon to the desktop, you automatically create a shortcut.

Tutorial 3 Personalizing Your Windows Environment | Windows   WIN 131

TIP

You can rename a shortcut icon the same way you rename a folder.

When you create a shortcut to a USB flash drive, you can insert the drive in a USB port and then double-click the shortcut to view your Data Files. You can move or copy documents to the drive without having to open a separate folder window.

Jodi regularly copies files from her computer to a USB flash drive and wants to use a shortcut to simplify the task. You'll show her how to create a shortcut to a USB flash drive on her desktop.

To create a shortcut to a USB flash drive:

1. If necessary, insert the USB flash drive containing your Data Files into a USB port on your computer.

2. Double-click the **Computer** icon on the desktop. If necessary, move or resize the Computer window so you can see the icons along the left side of the desktop. You need to see both the desktop icons and the Computer window to drag effectively.

3. Point to the **Removable Disk (E:)** icon in the Computer window, press and hold the left mouse button, and then drag the **Removable Disk (E:)** icon from the Computer window into an empty area of the desktop.

   Trouble? If your USB drive has a name other than Removable Disk (E:), substitute the appropriate name and drive on your system as you perform the steps. The steps in this tutorial assume that your Data Files are stored on Removable Disk (E:), a USB flash drive.

4. Release the mouse button. A shortcut labeled Removable Disk (E) – Shortcut now appears on the desktop. Click the desktop to deselect the shortcut icon. See Figure 3-31.

Figure 3-31   Shortcut to a removable disk

   Trouble? If you dragged with the right mouse button instead of the left, a shortcut menu appears when you release the mouse button. Click Create shortcuts here to add the Removable Disk (E) – Shortcut to the desktop.

5. Point to the **Removable Disk (E) – Shortcut** icon to view its ScreenTip, which indicates the permanent location of the drive on your computer.

Jodi wants to copy the Start screen document from the Public Documents folder to a folder on the USB flash drive so she can refer to the document while working on different computers. Use the shortcut on the desktop to copy the file to the Windows3\Tutorial folder on the USB flash drive.

To use the removable disk shortcut:

1. In the Navigation pane of the Computer window, click the **Documents** link to display the contents of the Documents library, which includes the Start screen document in the Public Documents folder.
2. Double-click the **Removable Disk (E) – Shortcut** icon on the desktop. A new window opens showing the contents of the USB flash drive.
3. Open the **Windows3** folder, and then open the **Tutorial** folder.
4. Drag the **Start screen** file from the Public Documents folder in the Navigation Pane to the Tutorial folder window. Because you are dragging a file on a hard drive to a removable disk, Windows copies the Start screen file rather than moving it to the Tutorial folder.
5. Close both open windows.

Using a shortcut to a drive saves a few steps when you want to make backup copies of files or transfer files from one computer to another.

Customizing the Desktop with the Control Panel

You've worked with the Start screen and with standard desktop and shortcut icons to personalize your desktop. You can also personalize Windows using the Control Panel, a window that contains specialized tools you use to change the way Windows looks and behaves. Some tools help you adjust settings that make your computer more fun to use. For example, use the Personalize tool to change the theme, which, as shown in the Session 3.2 Visual Overview, is a background plus a set of colors, sounds, and other elements. Other Control Panel tools help you set up Windows so that your computer is easier to use. For example, you can change display settings so that the desktop, icons, and windows are sharp and clear. All of the Control Panel tools provide access to dialog boxes that let you select or change the properties, or characteristics, of an object.

If you add the Control Panel icon to the desktop, as you did in a previous set of steps, you can open the Control Panel by double-clicking that icon. Otherwise, you can open the Control Panel from the Start screen as you would any other desktop app: Display the Apps bar, click the All Apps button, and then click Control Panel in the Windows System category. You can also open the Control Panel from the Settings menu on the Charms bar: Display the Charms bar, click Settings, and then click Control Panel.

TIP
You can click the View by button arrow and then click Large icons or Small icons to list each tool in alphabetical order.

To open the Control Panel:

1. Double-click the **Control Panel** icon on your desktop. The Control Panel window opens. See Figure 3-32.

| Figure 3-32 | Control Panel |

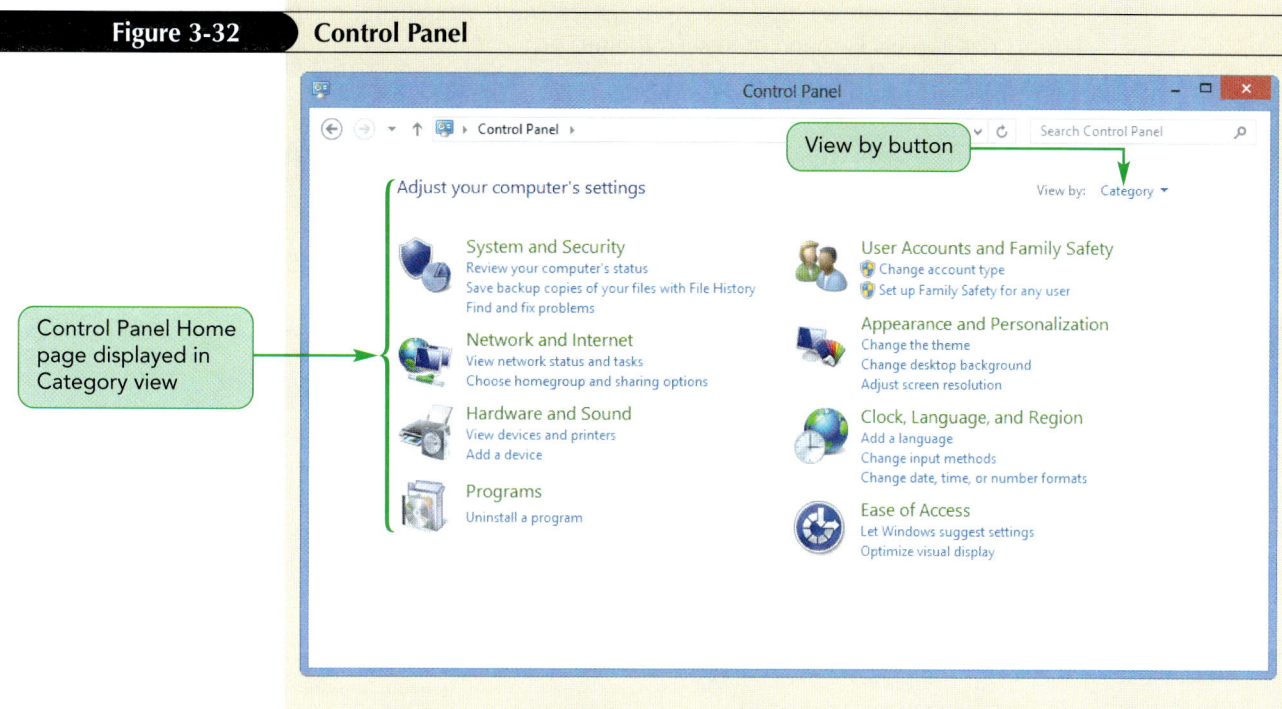

Control Panel Home page displayed in Category view

Trouble? If your screen doesn't look like the one in the figure, click the View by button, and then click Category.

The main window of the Control Panel is called the Control Panel Home page. By default, this page displays tools in Category view, which groups similar tools into categories. See Figure 3-33.

| Figure 3-33 | Control Panel categories |

Control Panel Category	Typical Tasks
System and Security	Schedule maintenance checks, increase the space on your hard disk, maintain Windows security settings, and keep Windows up to date.
Network and Internet	Set Internet options, view network status, and set up a home-group to share files and perform other network tasks.
Hardware and Sound	Change the sounds on your computer, and change the settings for your printer, keyboard, mouse, camera, and other hardware.
Programs	Install and uninstall programs and Windows features, set options for default settings and programs, and work with desktop gadgets.
Mobile PC	If you are using a mobile computer such as a laptop, use this category to change battery settings and adjust other common mobility settings.
User Accounts and Family Safety	Change user account settings, passwords, and associated pictures.
Appearance and Personalization	Change the appearance of desktop items, apply a theme or screen saver, and customize the Start screen and taskbar.
Clock, Language, and Region	Change the date, time, and time zone; the language you use on your computer; and the format for numbers, currencies, dates, and times.
Ease of Access	Change computer settings for vision, hearing, and mobility.

© 2014 Cengage Learning

To open a category and see its related tools, you click the appropriate link. For example, you can open the Appearance and Personalization window to change the desktop background or to set a theme.

To open the Appearance and Personalization window:

1. In the Control Panel window, click **Appearance and Personalization**. The Appearance and Personalization window opens, showing the tasks and tools related to personalizing your computer's appearance. See Figure 3-34.

Figure 3-34 Appearance and personalization options in the Control Panel

- Appearance and Personalization window
- options for customizing your work environment

The Appearance and Personalization window, like the other Control Panel category windows, lists tasks and tools in the right pane and links to the Control Panel Home page and other categories in the left pane. To change the desktop background, for example, you click the Change desktop background task in the right pane. The Desktop Background window opens so you can select a new desktop background and set other background options.

Jodi wants her office computers to reflect the image of Preserve Africa, and she'd like the desktop itself to be more appealing to her and her employees. You will work with the Control Panel to personalize Jodi's desktop.

Selecting Themes

The easiest way to personalize the desktop in Windows 8 is to select a theme. When you select a theme, you select one or more desktop background images; a color for window borders and the taskbar; a collection of sounds to play to signal system tasks, such as shutting down Windows; and a screen saver. Windows themes include collections of high-resolution images. You can select one of the images in a theme to display as the desktop background, or you can play a slide show of the images and switch from one image to another after a specified amount of time. Windows also provides a few high-contrast themes, which make the items on your screen easier to see.

Tutorial 3 Personalizing Your Windows Environment | Windows   WIN 135

REFERENCE

Selecting a Theme
- Open the Control Panel window and switch to Category view, if necessary.
- Click Appearance and Personalization.
- Click Personalization.
- Click a theme.

Jodi asks you to show her a few desktop themes to see if one would be suitable for Preserve Africa.

To change the theme:

1. In the Appearance and Personalization window, click **Change the theme** to open the Personalization window, which lists many types of themes. See Figure 3-35. Your Personalization window might differ. Note your current theme so you can restore it later.

Figure 3-35   Personalization window

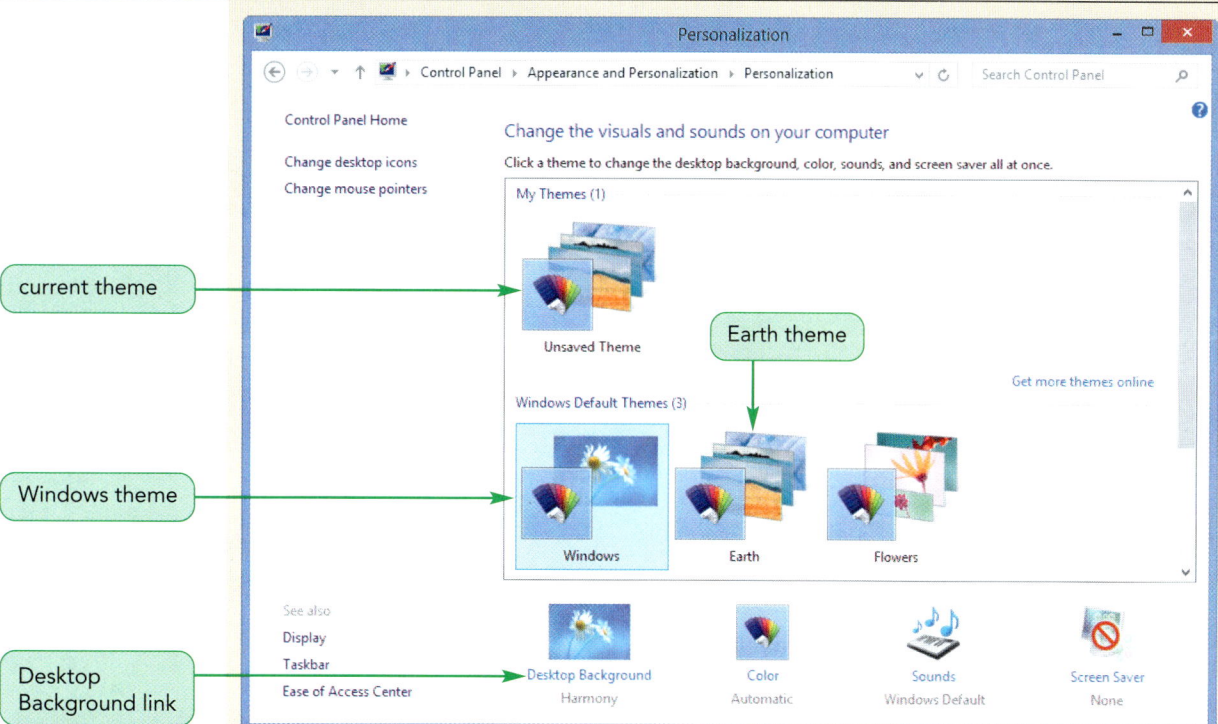

2. If necessary, scroll the themes, and then click **Earth**. The desktop background changes to an image of a glacier and its reflection, the taskbar and window borders change color, and a sound plays (if your speakers are turned on).

   Trouble? If the Earth theme does not appear in your Personalization window, select any other theme that displays photos.

3. Minimize the Personalization window.

Jodi thinks the Earth theme might work for her, but she wants to display a different image in the Earth theme collection. You'll show her how to do so by changing the desktop background.

Changing the Desktop Background

TIP

You can display any picture saved on your computer as your desktop background by right-clicking the picture, and then clicking Set as desktop background.

You can change the desktop background, or its **wallpaper**, to display one of the images that Windows provides, or you can select your own graphic to use as wallpaper. When you change the background, you are not placing a new object on the desktop; you are only changing its appearance. You can also determine how you want to position the picture—resized to fill the screen, resized to fit the screen, stretched across the screen (which might distort the image), tiled (repeated across the screen), or centered. If you center the wallpaper on the screen, you can select a color to frame the background image.

You and Jodi decide to examine the desktop backgrounds that Windows provides to find a suitable image.

To change the desktop background:

1. Click the **Control Panel** button on the taskbar to restore the Personalization window, and then, near the bottom of the window, click the **Desktop Background** link to open the Desktop Background window. See Figure 3-36. All six Earth images are selected because Windows uses all of the images for the desktop slide show. Your Desktop Background window might differ. Note your current desktop background so you can restore it later.

Figure 3-36   **Desktop Background window**

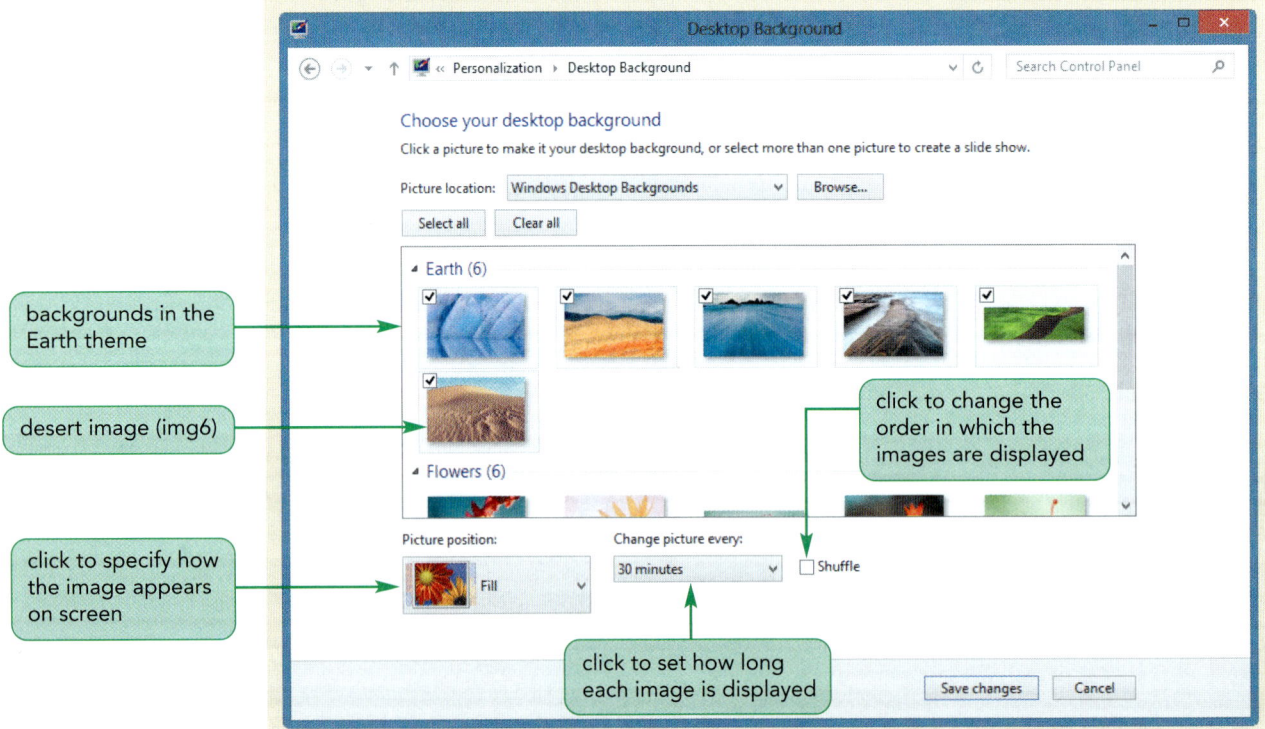

2. Click the **desert** image in the Nature category. (The ScreenTip indicates this image is named img6.) Windows displays the image you selected on the desktop. Now only the desert image is selected in the Earth category of themes.

3. Minimize the Desktop Background window to see the new background image.

After examining the desktop, Jodi doesn't think the desert image is right for her organization after all. However, she didn't notice other images in the Desktop Background window that would be more appropriate. You offer to show her how to find more desktop themes online.

To find a desktop theme online:

1. Click the **Control Panel** button on the taskbar to restore the Desktop Background window.
2. Click the **Back** button to display the Personalization window and the glacier image on the desktop.
3. Click the **Get more themes online** link to start the Internet Explorer Web browser and display a Web page on the Microsoft Web site where you can select and download desktop themes. Scroll down to display available themes. See Figure 3-37. Content on the Web changes frequently, so the themes displayed on your Web page might differ.

   Trouble? If your computer is not connected to the Internet, you cannot access the Web page with additional themes. Read but do not perform the remaining steps.

Figure 3-37   Online desktop themes

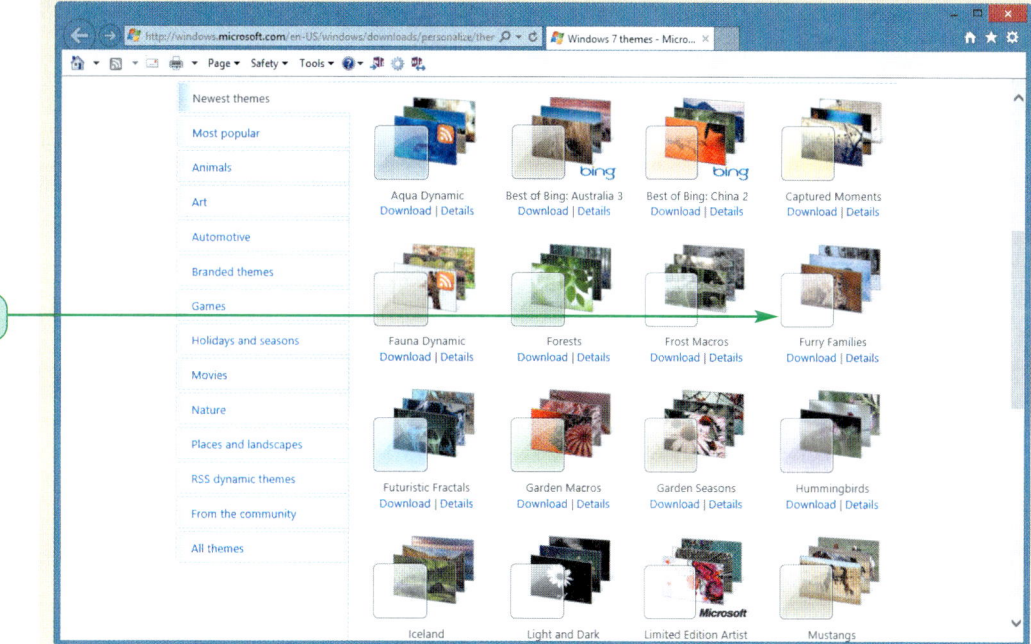

Furry Families theme

4. Locate the Furry Families theme, and then click its **Download** link to download the Furry Families theme to your computer.

   Trouble? If the Furry Families theme does not appear on the Web page, download any other theme.

5. When an information bar appears at the bottom of the window, asking if you want to open or save the theme, click the **Open** button. Windows displays the Furry Families theme in the Personalization window.
6. Click the **Desktop Background** link to select the images to display.

7. Click the **check boxes** for the two polar bear images and the penguin image to deselect them because these animals are not native to Africa.

8. Click the **Change picture every** button, and then click **15 minutes** to change the amount of time each picture is displayed in the theme slide show.

9. Click the **Save changes** button.

10. Minimize the Personalization window, and then close Internet Explorer to display the Furry Families theme on the desktop. Instead of displaying only one theme image, your desktop will play a slide show of the images in the Furry Families theme.

Jodi likes the new theme but comments that she would prefer a different color for the taskbar. You'll show her how to change the colors of the window borders and taskbar.

Changing Desktop Colors

Besides changing the desktop background, you can use the Color and Appearance window to set the color of windows and the taskbar. Each theme uses a particular color for window borders and the taskbar. For example, the Windows theme uses light blue by default for the window borders and taskbar, though you can change this to another color, such as orange.

To change the window colors:

1. Click the **Control Panel** button on the taskbar to restore the Personalization window.

2. Near the bottom of the window, click the **Color** link. The Color and Appearance window opens. See Figure 3-38. Note the current window color so you can restore it later.

TIP
The current color is set to Automatic by default, which means window borders and the taskbar use colors as specified in the current theme.

Figure 3-38 Color and Appearance window

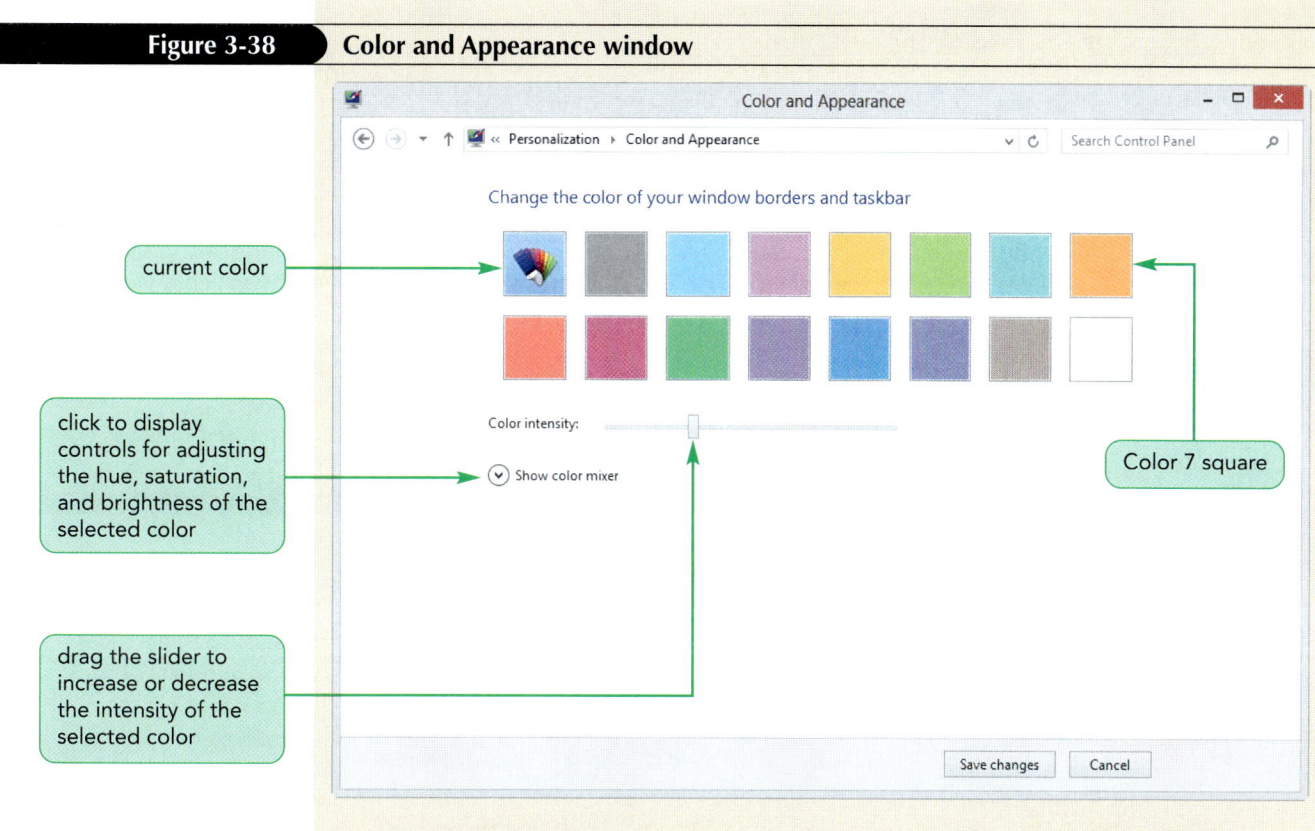

3. Click **Color 7**, which is the orange square in the first row. The title bar and border change to orange, which coordinates with the Furry Families wallpaper, and is easier to see than the original color.

4. Click the **Save changes** button to close the Color and Appearance window and apply your changes to the desktop, and then minimize the Personalization window. See Figure 3-39.

Figure 3-39 Personalized desktop

The desktop is now personalized for Jodi. It displays the Furry Families theme and taupe window elements.

Activating a Screen Saver

A **screen saver** is a program that blanks your computer screen or displays a moving design after the computer has been idle for a specified period of time. Screen savers can be entertaining and handy for hiding your data from the eyes of others if you step away from your computer. When a screen saver is on, you restore your desktop by moving your mouse or pressing a key. Windows 8 comes with several screen savers. Some show an animated design, while others play a slide show of pictures stored on your computer.

You can select how long you want the computer to sit idle before the screen saver starts. Most users find settings between 3 and 10 minutes to be the most convenient. You can change this setting using the options on the Screen Saver Settings dialog box.

INSIGHT

Using a Screen Saver for Security

To enhance the security of your computer and prevent unauthorized people from accessing your files, take advantage of a security setting available in the Screen Saver Settings dialog box. To have the screen saver request your user name and password before displaying your desktop, select the check box in this dialog box labeled On resume, display logon screen. This means that only you and other people who know your user name and password can work with your desktop and files.

Jodi wants to examine the screen savers that Windows provides and then choose the most appropriate one for her organization.

To activate a screen saver:

1. Click the **Control Panel** button on the taskbar to restore the Personalization window, and then, near the bottom of the Personalization window, click the **Screen Saver** link. The Screen Saver Settings dialog box opens. See Figure 3-40. Note the name of the current screen saver so you can restore it later.

Figure 3-40 Screen Saver Settings dialog box

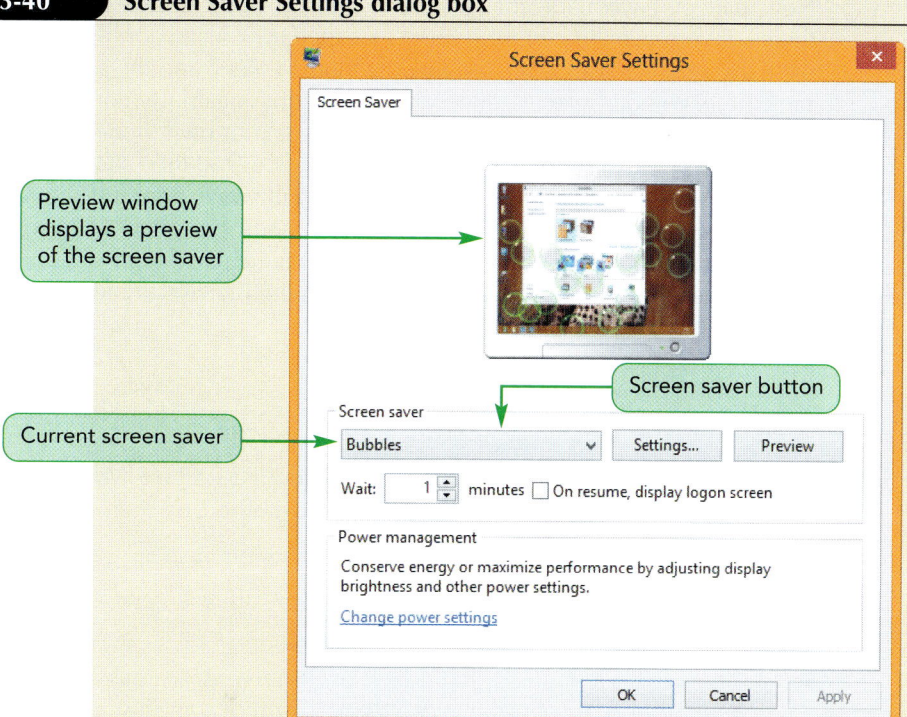

2. Click the **Screen saver** button to display the screen savers installed on your computer.

3. Click **Ribbons**. The animated screen saver plays in the Preview window. Jodi likes that screen saver, but it's not appropriate for her desktop theme. You suggest the Photos screen saver, which plays a slide show of the pictures and videos stored in the Pictures library by default.

4. Click the **Screen saver** button, and then click **Photos**. The preview window plays a slide show of the graphics files stored in the Pictures library, including those in the Big Five Photos folder.

5. To restrict the screen saver to display photos in the Big Five Photos folder only, click the **Settings** button to open the Photos Screen Saver Settings dialog box. You use this dialog box to specify which files to include in the slide show and other settings, such as the slide show speed.

6. Click the **Browse** button. The Browse For Folder dialog box opens.

7. Expand the **Pictures** library and the **Public Pictures** folder, if necessary, and then click the **Big Five Photos** folder. Click the **OK** button to indicate you want to include all the pictures in the Big Five Photos folder in the screen saver slide show.

8. Click the **Save** button to close the Photos Screen Saver Settings dialog box. Now only the pictures in the Big Five Photos folder appear in the Preview window.

9. Click the **OK** button to close the Screen Saver Settings dialog box.

10. Minimize the Personalization window.

After your computer is idle for a minute or so, the screen saver will start, playing a slide show of the photos.

Saving Themes

Now that you have made changes to the desktop, you can save these settings as a theme. If you save the current settings as a theme, you can apply all of the changes—the Furry Families wallpaper, the taupe window colors, and the screen saver—at the same time, without selecting the individual settings again. By default, Windows stores the theme files in a system folder. You can create your own theme file—called a theme pack—that you can store in a folder of your choice, and then share that theme with people on other Windows 8 computers. Although you cannot move or copy a theme from a system folder, you can move or copy a theme pack. You will save the desktop settings you created for Jodi as a theme and a theme pack, both called Preserve Africa. Jodi will use the theme pack and the photos in the Big Five Photos folder to apply the Preserve Africa theme to other office computers.

To save the desktop settings as a theme:

1. Restore the Personalization window, and then, in the My Themes section, click **Save theme**. The Save Theme As dialog box opens.

2. Type **Preserve Africa** as the name of this theme.

3. Click the **Save** button. The Preserve Africa theme now appears in the My Themes section.

4. To save the theme so that others at Preserve Africa can use it, right-click the **Preserve Africa** theme in the Personalization window, and then click **Save theme for sharing** on the shortcut menu.

5. In the Save Theme Pack As dialog box, open the **Big Five Photos** folder in the Public Pictures folder.

6. Click the **File name** text box, if necessary, and then type **Preserve Africa**. Note that the Save as type is Desktop Theme Pack (*.deskthemepack).

7. Click the **Save** button. Windows saves the Preserve Africa theme pack file in the Big Five Photos folder.

8. Close the Personalization window.

Managing the Desktop with Taskbar Tools

Windows 8 includes three taskbar tools you can use to manage the windows on your desktop: Snap, Peek, and Shake. With Snap you can drag the title bar of an open window to the top of the desktop to maximize the window. To restore the window to its original size, drag the title bar away from the top of the desktop. You can also use Snap to arrange windows side by side and expand windows vertically on the desktop.

Peek also helps you manage open windows. To quickly minimize all open windows, you click the Show desktop button on the far right side of the taskbar. To preview open windows without leaving your current window, you point to a taskbar button to display thumbnails of open files, and then point to a thumbnail. Any open windows fade to reveal the selected window, and then reappear when you move the pointer away from the thumbnail. To open the window you're previewing, you click the thumbnail.

Shake is another handy tool for managing windows. Use Shake to quickly minimize all open windows on the desktop except the one you want to focus on—you don't have to minimize the windows one by one. Click and hold the title bar of the window you want to keep open, and then shake it by quickly dragging the window to the right and left. When you do, you minimize all of the other open windows. To restore the minimized windows, shake the open window again.

Jodi sometimes needs to work with two windows open as she examines images and manages her files and folders. You offer to show her how to quickly arrange windows side by side using Snap.

To arrange windows side by side with Snap:

1. Click the **File Explorer** button on the taskbar to open File Explorer, open the **Pictures** library, and then open the **Big Five Photos** folder.

2. Right-click the **Lion** photo, point to **Open with** on the shortcut menu, and then click **Paint** to display the photo in Paint.

   Trouble? If the Paint window opens as maximized, click the Restore Down button to resize the window. If the window is still too large, use the resizing pointer to make it the same size as the Big Five Photos folder window.

3. Arrange the windows so that you can see parts of both windows.

4. Click the **title bar** of the Paint window to make it the active window, and then drag the **title bar** to the left of the desktop until an outline of the expanded window appears. See Figure 3-41.

   Trouble? If the outline does not appear, make sure most of the Paint window appears to the left of the screen. The window will snap to the desktop when you release the mouse button.

Figure 3-41 Arranging windows with Snap

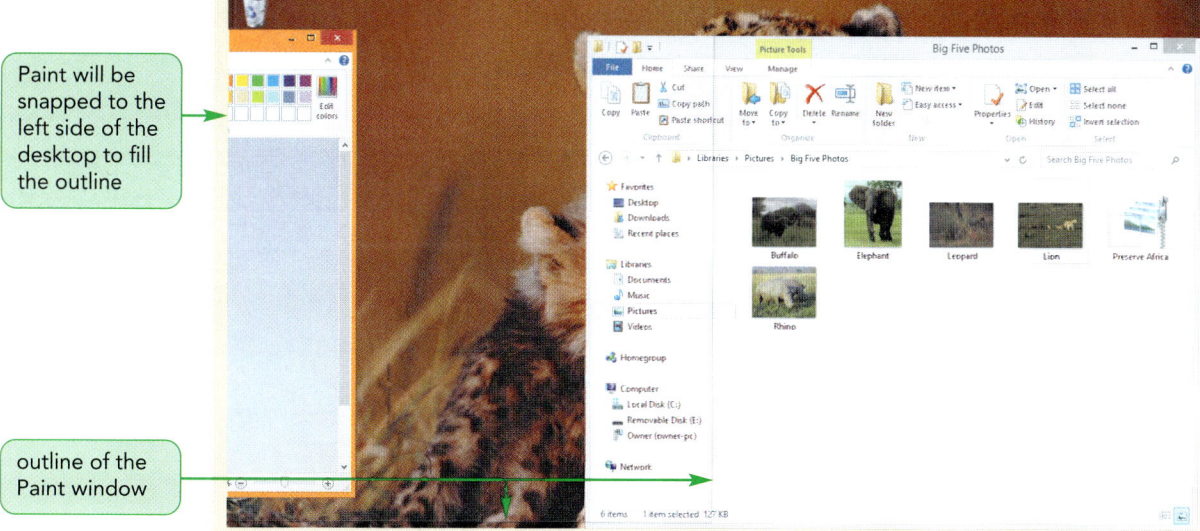

Paint will be snapped to the left side of the desktop to fill the outline

outline of the Paint window

Photos courtesy of Garibgazi; Oliver Wright; Gary M. Stolz, U.S. Fish and Wildlife Service; Ken Stansell, U.S. Fish and Wildlife Service; Komencanto

5. Release the mouse button to expand the Paint window to cover the left side of the desktop.

6. Drag the **title bar** of the File Explorer window to the right of the desktop until an outline of the expanded window appears.

   Trouble? If the File Explorer window is not visible on your screen, minimize the Paint window and then repeat Step 6.

7. Release the mouse button to expand the File Explorer window to cover the right side of the desktop.

Trouble? If you minimized the Paint window, click the Paint button on the taskbar to restore it.

Now each window covers half of the desktop, with Paint on the left and File Explorer on the right.

Jodi can use Snap when she needs to work with two windows side by side. However, she typically has many windows open, and often has to stop working with a document or an image to manage those windows. For example, she might open a few more image files and then decide to copy other files to a USB flash drive. She'd like to quickly view the desktop to verify that it contains a shortcut to the removable disk so she can copy the files using the shortcut icon. She also wants to know how to briefly display a particular window to view its contents. You'll show her how to use Peek to perform both tasks.

To use Peek:

1. Click the far right side of the taskbar (to the right of the date and time) to minimize all of the open windows. See Figure 3-42.

Figure 3-42 Displaying the desktop with Peek

far right side of the taskbar

2. Click the **File Explorer** button on the taskbar to display the Big Five Photos folder.

3. Right-click the **Buffalo** file, point to **Open with** on the shortcut menu, and then click **Paint** to open the Buffalo image file in Paint.

4. Minimize the new Paint window.

5. Right-click the **Elephant** file, point to **Open with** on the shortcut menu, and then click **Paint** to open the Elephant image file in Paint.

6. Minimize the new Paint window.

7. Point to the **Paint** button on the taskbar to display thumbnail previews of the three pictures open in Paint. See Figure 3-43.

Figure 3-43   Previewing windows with Peek

preview of Paint windows

Photos courtesy of Garibgazi; Oliver Wright; Gary M. Stolz, U.S. Fish and Wildlife Service; Ken Stansell, U.S. Fish and Wildlife Service; Komencanto

Trouble? If a list of filenames appears instead of thumbnails when you point to the Paint taskbar button, the thumbnails feature is probably disabled on your computer. Read but do not perform Steps 8 and 9.

TIP
To restore the desktop when you're previewing a window, move the pointer away from the thumbnail.

8. To preview the Elephant image, point to the **Elephant** thumbnail. The File Explorer window fades so that the Elephant window is the only one open on the desktop.

9. Click the **Elephant** thumbnail to display the Elephant image in Paint and make it the active window. The File Explorer window is also redisplayed, but it is not the active window.

Jodi mentions that when she needs to focus on the contents of a window, she likes to minimize all of the other open windows. You suggest she use Shake to do so.

To use Shake:

1. Point to the **Paint** button on the taskbar, and then click the **Buffalo** thumbnail to open the Buffalo image in Paint.

2. Point to the **Paint** button on the taskbar again, and then click the **Lion** thumbnail to open the Lion image in Paint.

3. Point to the **title bar** of the Lion window, hold down the mouse button, and then quickly drag the window about an inch to the right and left to shake it. The Lion window remains open while all of the other open windows are minimized.

4. To restore the minimized windows, shake the **Lion** window again.

5. Click the far right side of the taskbar to minimize all open windows.

Next, you can explore the display properties that affect the sharpness of the images on your desktop.

Changing Display Settings

After working with the properties for the desktop background, theme, and screen saver, you're ready to explore the display properties that affect the computer monitor itself. The Screen Resolution window lets you control the display settings for your monitor, such as the size of the desktop and whether to use more than one monitor. Windows chooses the best display settings, including screen resolution and orientation, based on your monitor. **Screen resolution** refers to the clarity of the text and images on your screen. At higher resolutions, items appear sharper and smaller, so more items fit on the screen. At lower resolutions, fewer items fit on the screen, but they are larger and easier to see. At very low resolutions, however, images might have jagged edges. Selecting the best display settings for your monitor enhances your Windows experience.

> **INSIGHT**
>
> ### Selecting the Best Display Settings for Your Monitor
>
> Notebook and desktop computers have either a standard or widescreen liquid crystal display (LCD) monitor. Display settings for standard LCD monitors typically differ from those for widescreen monitors. However, all LCD monitors display the sharpest images and clearest text at a particular resolution, which is called their **native resolution**. Screen resolution is measured horizontally and vertically in **pixels**, short for "picture elements," which are the tiny dots that make up a computer image. For example, most 19-inch standard LCD monitors have a native resolution of 1280 × 1024. A 22-inch widescreen LCD monitor usually has a native resolution of 1680 × 1050. You can change the resolution to a lower setting, such as 1024 × 768, to make the on-screen objects larger, though the text might not be as clear as text displayed at the native resolution. If you are using a standard monitor, be sure to select a resolution with an aspect ratio of 4:3, such as 1024 × 768. (An **aspect ratio** is the ratio of the width to the height.) If you are using a widescreen monitor, select a resolution with an aspect ratio of 16:9 or 16:10, such as 1366 × 768.

Changing the Screen Resolution

You use the Screen Resolution window to change the display settings. You click the Resolution button to display a list of available resolutions on your monitor and a slider bar. You can drag the slider bar to increase or decrease the resolution, or sharpness, of the image. You will change the screen resolution from its current setting to 1366 × 768, if that setting is not already selected.

> **To change the screen resolution:**
>
> ▶ 1. Right-click the **desktop**, and then click **Screen resolution** on the shortcut menu to open the Screen Resolution window. Note the original setting on the Resolution button so you can restore it later.
>
> ▶ 2. Click the **Resolution** button to display the options available on your computer, and then drag the slider to 1366 × 768, if necessary. The settings appear in the Resolution box as you drag the slider. The preview area shows the relative size of the new resolution. See Figure 3-44.

Figure 3-44 Changing the screen resolution

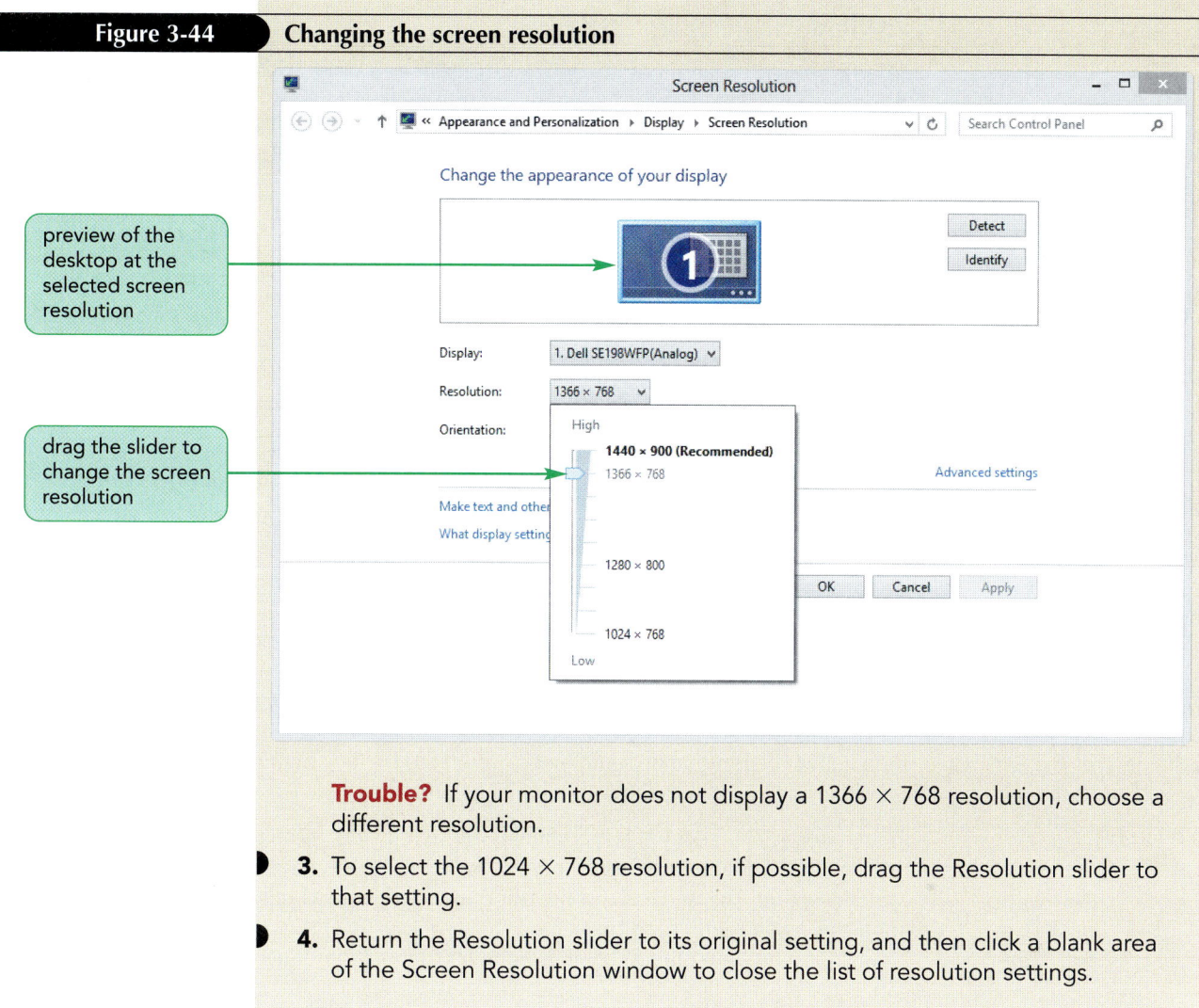

Trouble? If your monitor does not display a 1366 × 768 resolution, choose a different resolution.

3. To select the 1024 × 768 resolution, if possible, drag the Resolution slider to that setting.

4. Return the Resolution slider to its original setting, and then click a blank area of the Screen Resolution window to close the list of resolution settings.

If you select a screen resolution recommended for your monitor, but find the text and objects are now too large or small, you can adjust the size of the text and objects.

Changing the Size of Text and Objects

Without adjusting your screen resolution, you can change the size of the text and objects such as icons on your screen. This means you can increase or decrease the size of text and objects while maintaining the native resolution of your monitor. For example, if you use a low screen resolution, such as 1024 × 768, you can make text and objects smaller to display more information on the screen. Conversely, if you use a high resolution, you can make text and objects easier to see by making them larger while retaining the sharpness of the high resolution.

Jodi's computer uses the Smaller – 100% setting, which is the default for her monitor. You'll view the other settings to see if they would improve her desktop.

> **To view the display settings:**
>
> ▶ 1. In the Screen Resolution window, click **Make text and other items larger or smaller**. The Display window opens, showing the display settings: Smaller – 100%, Medium – 125%, and Larger – 150%. (Your window might not include the Larger – 150% setting.)
>
> ▶ 2. Click the **Medium – 125%** option button, and then note the image in the Preview area. This setting would not noticeably improve Jodi's desktop.
>
>   **Trouble?** If the Medium – 125% option button is already selected, click the Smaller – 100% option button.
>
> ▶ 3. If a Larger – 150% option button appears in the Screen Resolution window, click the **Larger – 150%** option button, and then note the image in the Preview area. The desktop objects are much larger and easy to see, but they take up too much space.
>
> ▶ 4. Click the original setting, such as the **Smaller – 100%** option button, and then close the Display window without applying any changes.

You have used the taskbar to manage open windows. Next, you'll learn how to modify the taskbar to work effectively on the desktop.

Modifying the Taskbar

As you know, the bar that appears by default at the bottom of the desktop is the taskbar. The taskbar is divided into the following three sections:

- Pinned items: This section, which begins at the left side of the taskbar, contains the Internet Explorer and File Explorer icons by default.
- Middle section: This section displays taskbar (or program) buttons for desktop applications currently running.
- Notification area: On the right side of the taskbar is the notification area, which shows the current time, icons for system tools, and system status information.

In the middle section of the taskbar, Windows displays buttons for each desktop application that is running. By default, each button is identified by an icon, not a text label, to conserve space. If you open another file in one of these applications, Windows groups the buttons for that app into a single button. A few windows might be grouped on the Paint button, for example. The Paint icon would appear on top, and the outlines of the open windows would be stacked behind it.

As you saw when working with Peek, when you point to a taskbar button, Windows displays a thumbnail preview of the corresponding window. The preview is designed to help you identify a window by more than the title alone. If a window is playing a video or an animation, the video or animation also plays in the preview. When you point to a grouped taskbar button, Windows arranges the thumbnail previews in a row above the taskbar. You can click a thumbnail to open a window. To close a window, you point to a thumbnail until a Close button appears in the upper-right corner of the thumbnail, and then you click the Close button.

You can personalize the taskbar to suit your preferences. For example, you can reorder the taskbar buttons by dragging them to a new location. You can also change the appearance of taskbar buttons by displaying button labels and specifying when buttons should be grouped together. To further customize the taskbar, you can change the size and position of the taskbar or hide it altogether.

PROSKILLS

Decision Making: Monitoring the Notification Area

The icons in the notification area of the taskbar let you access certain computer settings, such as the system time. The icons also communicate the status of programs running in the background. Background programs are those programs that Windows runs to provide a service, such as an Internet connection. By default, the notification area displays only a few icons, which are usually determined by your computer manufacturer and the programs installed on your computer. One of these icons (the flag) is for the Action Center, a window that displays notification messages about security and maintenance settings. Read these messages when they appear so you can make decisions about your computer. You can also point to the Action Center icon to display a summary of Action Center issues, and then click the flag icon to open the Action Center, which categorizes messages by color. Items highlighted by a red bar are important and need your immediate attention. For example, a message reminding you to update an antivirus program is flagged as important. Items highlighted by a yellow bar are suggestions you can address later, such as recommended maintenance tasks. To respond to Action Center messages, click the Action Center icon again.

In addition, you might receive notifications from other programs running in the background about a change in status, such as the addition of a new hardware device. Read the notification to find out whether you need to respond to or correct a problem. You can also point to any icon in the notification area to display its status or name. (You might need to click the Show hidden icons button (an arrow) on the taskbar to display all of the icons in the notification area.) For example, if you're having trouble hearing sounds on your computer, point to the Speakers icon to determine whether you need to turn up the volume.

Now you can personalize the taskbar on Jodi's computer. You'll start by showing her how to pin items to the taskbar.

Pinning Desktop Apps to the Taskbar

Internet Explorer and File Explorer are pinned to the left section of the taskbar by default. If you use another desktop app often, you can also pin that app to the taskbar. Pinning an app to the taskbar increases your efficiency because the pinned app is always visible as you work on the desktop, and you can start the app with a single click. (You need to double-click desktop shortcut icons for programs.) You can rearrange the buttons for pinned and running apps on the taskbar to suit your preferences.

REFERENCE

Pinning Desktop Apps to the Taskbar

- If the desktop app is already running, right-click the program button on the taskbar, and then click Pin this program to taskbar.

or

- If the desktop app is not running, display and then right-click the Start screen, click the All apps button on the Apps bar, locate and right-click the app on the Apps screen, and then click Pin to taskbar on the Apps bar.

Because Jodi frequently uses Paint, you suggest that she pin Paint to the taskbar. This task is particularly easy because Paint is already running and its button appears on the taskbar.

To pin Paint to the taskbar:

1. Right-click the **Paint** button on the taskbar, and then click **Pin this program to taskbar**.

2. To confirm that Paint is pinned to the taskbar, right-click the **Paint** button on the taskbar again, and then click **Close all windows**. All of the Paint windows close, but the Paint program button remains on the taskbar.

   Trouble? If a dialog box appears asking if you want to save changes to an image, click the Don't Save button.

TIP

To unpin a file, open the Jump List, point to the filename, and then click the Unpin from this list icon.

In addition to starting a desktop app from the taskbar, you can use a pinned item to open favorite and recent files from that program. To do so, you use a **Jump List**, a list of recently or frequently opened files, folders, or Web sites. When you right-clicked the Paint button in the previous steps, you displayed the Paint Jump List, which included the image files you opened for Jodi, such as Buffalo, Elephant, and Lion. If you want to make sure you can always access one of those files, you can pin it to the Jump List. To open a pinned file, you right-click the Paint button on the taskbar to display the Jump List, and then click the recent or favorite file you want to open in Paint.

Jodi plans to use the Lion image file often, so you'll show her how to pin the file to the Paint Jump List and then open the file from the taskbar.

To pin a file to the Paint Jump List:

1. Right-click the **Paint** button on the taskbar to display the Jump List.

2. Point to **Lion**, and then click the **Pin to this list** icon to pin Lion to the Jump List. See Figure 3-45. The items in your Paint Jump List might be different.

Figure 3-45   **File pinned to the Paint Jump List**

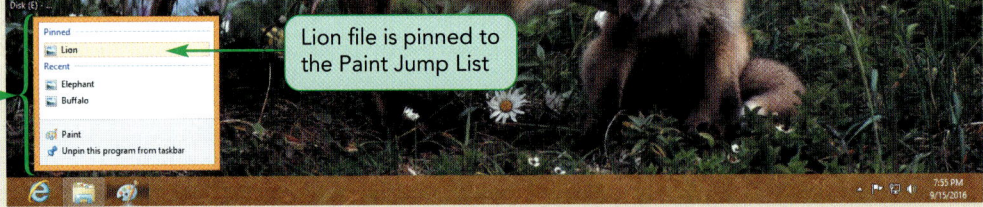

Paint Jump List

Lion file is pinned to the Paint Jump List

Trouble? If your Jump List does not include the Lion file, pin a different image file to the list.

3. To open the Lion file in Paint, click **Lion** on the Jump List. Paint starts and opens the Lion image file.

4. Close the Paint window.

Jodi says that the changes you made to the taskbar will help her work more efficiently. She'd also like to adjust the position of the taskbar buttons. She uses the File Explorer button more frequently than the Internet Explorer button, and she asks you to move the File Explorer button to the far left side of the taskbar for easy access.

Tutorial 3 Personalizing Your Windows Environment | Windows   WIN 151

To move a taskbar button:

1. Point to the **File Explorer** button 📁 on the taskbar, and then drag it to the left.
2. When the File Explorer button appears to the left of the Internet Explorer button, release the mouse button. See Figure 3-46.

Figure 3-46   Moving a taskbar button

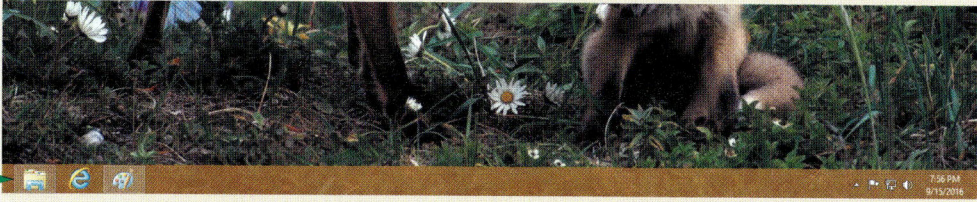

File Explorer is now on the left of the Internet Explorer button

You can move any taskbar button, even those for programs that are not pinned to the taskbar. When you do, you move the entire button group so the open files remain grouped on a program button.

Setting Taskbar Properties

You can set taskbar properties using the Taskbar Properties dialog box. Using this dialog box, you can increase the amount of screen space available for your desktop app windows by hiding the taskbar. In this case, the taskbar is not closed, removed, or minimized, but hidden under either the border of the desktop or the app windows open on the desktop. The taskbar still remains active and accessible—you can point to the area of your screen where the taskbar would be located to redisplay the taskbar when you need to use it.

You can also use the Taskbar Properties dialog box to determine whether to display small icons on the taskbar, group similar taskbar buttons, change the location of the taskbar to another position on the screen, and use Peek to preview the desktop.

You'll show Jodi how to increase the amount of screen space on the desktop by hiding the taskbar and using small icons.

To set taskbar properties:

1. Right-click a blank area on the taskbar, and then click **Properties** on the shortcut menu. The Taskbar Properties dialog box opens. See Figure 3-47.

| Figure 3-47 | Taskbar Properties dialog box |

Note the options currently selected in this dialog box so you can restore them later.

2. Click to select the **Auto-hide the taskbar** check box, and then click the **Apply** button. Windows hides the taskbar.

3. Point to the bottom of the desktop to redisplay the taskbar. Pointing away from the taskbar hides it again.

4. In the Taskbar Properties dialog box, click the **Auto-hide the taskbar** check box to remove the check mark, and then click the **Apply** button. The taskbar appears in its default position at the bottom of the desktop.

5. Click to select the **Use small taskbar buttons** check box, and then click the **Apply** button. The taskbar icons shrink and the height of the taskbar decreases accordingly.

6. Click the **Use small taskbar buttons** check box to remove the check mark, and then click the **Apply** button to display the taskbar icons at their default size.

7. Make sure the options in the Taskbar Properties dialog box are in their original state, and then click the **OK** button to close the dialog box.

You've finished personalizing the Windows 8 desktop on Jodi's computer, so you should restore your computer to its original settings.

Restoring Your Settings

Complete the steps in this section to restore the original settings on your computer.

To restore your settings:

1. Press the **Windows** key to display the Start screen, right-click the **Reader**, **WordPad**, **Big Five Photos**, **Shut down**, and **Restart** tiles to select them, and then click **Unpin from Start** on the Apps bar to unpin the apps from the Start screen.

2. Right-click the **People** tile on the Start screen and then click the **Larger** button on the Apps bar. Right-click the **Messaging** tile and then click the **Larger** button on the Apps bar.

3. Right-click the **Photos** tile on the Start screen and then click the **Turn live tile off** button on the Apps bar. The images of the animals are no longer displayed.

4. Open the PC settings screen via the Charms bar, click the **Start screen** link, click the first background design in the first row, and then drag the slider two color squares to the left to select the original violet color scheme.

5. Click the **Account picture** link on the PC settings screen, and then restore your original user icon image, if possible.

6. On the Start screen, click the **Desktop** tile to display the desktop. Right-click the **desktop**, and then click **Personalize** on the shortcut menu.

7. Click your original theme, such as **Windows**, to restore your original desktop background, window color, and screen saver (which might be "None").

8. Right-click the **Furry Families** theme, and then click **Delete theme** on the shortcut menu. Right-click the **Preserve Africa** theme, and then click **Delete theme** on the shortcut menu.

9. Click the **Screen saver** link, click the **Screen saver** button, click **Photos**, and then click the **Settings** button. Click the **Browse** button, click the **Pictures** library, click the **OK** button, and then click the **Save** button. Click the **Screen saver** button, and then click your original screen saver, if any, or click **(None)**. Click the **OK** button to close the Screen Saver Settings dialog box.

10. In the left pane of the Personalization window, click **Change desktop icons**. Click the **Computer** image in the box displaying desktop icons, and then click the **Restore Default** button. Click the check boxes to restore the original settings. By default, only the Recycle Bin appears on the desktop. Click the **OK** button to close the Desktop Icon Settings dialog box. Close the Personalization window.

11. Open the Public Pictures folder and then move the **Big Five Photos** folder in the Public Pictures folder to the **Windows3\Tutorial** folder provided with your Data Files. (*Hint*: Right-drag the Big Five Photos folder to the destination folder, release the mouse button, and then click Move here on the shortcut menu.) Delete the original **Buffalo**, **Elephant**, **Leopard**, **Lion**, and **Rhino** files from the Tutorial folder.

12. Navigate to the Public Documents folder, and then delete the **Start screen** document. Close all folder windows.

13. Click the desktop **shortcut icon** that you created in this tutorial, and then press the **Delete** key to delete the shortcuts.

▶ 14. Right-click the **Paint** button on the taskbar, point to **Lion**, and then click the **Unpin from this list** icon on the Jump List.

▶ 15. On the Paint button's Jump List, click the **Unpin this program from taskbar** icon.

▶ 16. Drag the **File Explorer** button on the taskbar to its original location to the right of the Internet Explorer button on the taskbar.

▶ 17. Close any open windows.

Session 3.2 Quick Check

REVIEW

1. When you delete a shortcut icon, what happens to the file or resource it represents?
2. What is a desktop theme?
3. Explain the difference between low- and high-screen resolutions.
4. What does a desktop app's Jump List contain?
5. The _____ is a window that contains specialized tools you use to change the way Windows looks and behaves.
6. What are two reasons for activating a screen saver on your computer?
7. What information does the notification area on the taskbar display?
8. Which taskbar property can you change to increase the amount of screen space displayed on your desktop?

Tutorial 3 Personalizing Your Windows Environment | Windows   WIN 155

Review Assignments

PRACTICE

See the Starting Data Files section at the beginning of this tutorial for a list of Data Files needed for the Review Assignments.

Preserve Africa keeps a computer in its conference area for any staff member to use when needed. Jodi asks you to customize that computer so it is appropriate for the organization. Jodi recently received photographs of wildlife in Kenyan game preserves and wants to make the photos available to staff members to use in promotional materials. As you perform the following steps, note the original settings of the desktop and other items so you can restore them later. Complete the following steps:

1. Insert the USB flash drive or other removable media containing your Data Files in the appropriate drive, and then create a shortcut to this drive on the desktop. Use **Review Removable Disk Shortcut** as the name of the shortcut.
2. Use the Review Removable Disk Shortcut on the desktop to copy the five image files in the Windows3\Review folder provided with your Data Files to a new folder in the Public Pictures folder. Use **Wildlife** as the name of the new folder.
3. Pin the Windows Reader app to the Start screen.
4. Pin the WordPad and Paint desktop apps to the Start screen.
5. Pin the Wildlife folder (which you created in Step 2) to the Start screen.
6. Complete the following tasks to create and pin a custom shortcut to the Start screen:
   - On the desktop, create a custom shortcut to the Restart command.
   - Name the shortcut **Restart**.
   - Change the icon to display an appropriate image.
   - Pin the Restart shortcut to the Start screen.
   - Delete the Restart shortcut icon from the desktop.
7. Add the Reader tile to a larger group of Windows 8 apps. Create an unnamed group for the Restart tile. Use **Promos** as the name of the group containing only the WordPad, Paint, and Wildlife tiles.
8. Apply a different design to the Start screen background. Change the color scheme to one that uses at least one shade of blue.
9. Change the user picture to display one of the images stored in the Wildlife folder.
10. Complete the following tasks to create a screen shot of your Start screen:
    - Display the Start screen, scroll to the right, and then press the Print Screen key to capture an image of the Start screen.
    - Start Paint, and then press the Ctrl+V keys to paste the image in the Paint file.
    - Save the file as **Review Start XY**, where XY are your initials, in the Windows3\Review folder provided with your Data Files.
11. Change the desktop icon settings on your computer to display the Computer and Control Panel icons in addition to the default Recycle Bin icon. Change the image for the Computer icon so that it displays any other appropriate image.
12. Change the desktop theme to any other theme that displays photographs.
13. Change the screen saver to play a slide show of the images in the Wildlife folder. Close all open windows.
14. Complete the following steps to open and work with Paint:
    - Use Paint to open the Impala image in the Wildlife folder, and then pin Paint to the taskbar.
    - Pin the Impala image file to the Paint Jump List.
15. Use Snap to align the Paint window on the right side of the desktop.
16. Press the Print Screen key to capture an image of the desktop. In Paint, press the Ctrl+V keys to paste the image in the Paint file. Save the file as **Review Desktop XY**, where XY are your initials, in the Windows3\Review folder provided with your Data Files.

17. Complete the following tasks to restore the settings on your computer:
    - Unpin the Windows Reader app from the Start screen.
    - Unpin the WordPad, Paint, Wildlife, and Restart tiles from the Start screen.
    - Apply the original design and color scheme to the Start screen background.
    - Restore the default image for the user picture.
    - On the desktop, restore the image of the Computer icon, and then display the original set of icons on the desktop.
    - Change the desktop theme to Windows and restore the original setting for the screen saver.
    - Unpin the Impala image file from the Paint Jump List, and then unpin Paint from the taskbar.
    - Delete the Wildlife folder in the Public Pictures folder.
    - Delete the Review Removable Disk Shortcut icon from the desktop.
18. Close any open windows.
19. Submit the results of the preceding steps to your instructor, either in printed or electronic form, as requested.

Case Problem 1

See the Starting Data Files section at the beginning of this tutorial for a list of Data Files needed for this Case Problem.

Santa Fe Productions   Roddy Hampton started Santa Fe Productions to provide multimedia shows and exhibits for area businesses so they can showcase their products and services at trade shows and conventions. His most effective presentations use vintage images. When he is not installing a multimedia project, Roddy manages 10 employees in an office on the outskirts of Santa Fe, New Mexico. He has hired you to help him run the office. Because he just installed Windows 8, he asks you to personalize the Start screen and desktop on his computer to focus on multimedia and business tools. As you perform the following steps, note the original settings of the Start screen and desktop so you can restore them later. Complete the following steps:

1. Insert the USB flash drive or other removable media containing your Data Files in the appropriate drive, and then create a shortcut to this drive on the desktop. Use **Case1 Removable Disk Shortcut** as the name of the shortcut.
2. Use the Case1 Removable Disk Shortcut on the desktop to copy the five image files in the Windows3\Case1 folder provided with your Data Files to a new folder in the Public Pictures folder. Use **Vintage** as the name of the new folder.
3. Unpin the News, Weather, Sports, and Games tiles from the Start screen.
4. Pin the Paint and Windows Media Player desktop apps to the Start screen. (*Hint*: The Windows Media Player is a desktop accessory.)
5. Pin the Vintage folder (which you created in Step 2) to the Start screen.
6. Complete the following tasks to create and pin a custom shortcut to the Start screen:
    - On the desktop, create a custom shortcut to the Shut down command.
    - Name the shortcut **Shut down**.
    - Change the icon to display an appropriate image.
    - Pin the Shut down shortcut to the Start screen.
    - Delete the Shut down shortcut icon from the desktop.
7. Create an unnamed group for the Shut down tile. Use the name **Multimedia** for the group containing the Paint, Windows Media Player, and Vintage tiles.
8. Apply a different design to the Start screen background, and then change the color scheme to one that uses at least one shade of gray.
9. Change the user picture to display one of the images stored in the Vintage folder.

10. Display the Start screen, scroll to the right, and then press the Print Screen key to capture an image of the Start screen. Start Paint and then press the Ctrl+V keys to paste the image in the Paint file. Save the file as **Case1 Start XY**, where *XY* are your initials, in the Windows3\Case1 folder provided with your Data Files.
11. Complete the following tasks to add desktop icons to the desktop:
    - Change the desktop icon settings on your computer to display the Computer, User's Files, and Control Panel icons in addition to the default Recycle Bin icon.
    - Change the image for the User's Files icon so that it displays any other appropriate image.
12. Change the desktop theme to any other theme (including an online theme) that seems appropriate for Santa Fe Productions. Close Internet Explorer, if necessary.
13. Change the color of the window borders and taskbar to Color 14.
14. Open the Screen Saver Settings dialog box and select the Bubbles screen saver, if necessary. Move the dialog box so that some or all of the desktop items are clearly visible. Use a taskbar tool to minimize other open windows.
15. Press the Print Screen key to capture an image of the desktop. Make Paint the active window, and then press the Ctrl+V keys to paste the image in the Paint file. Save the file as **Case1 Desktop XY**, where *XY* are your initials, in the Windows3\Case1 folder provided with your Data Files.
16. Complete the following tasks to restore the settings on your computer:
    - Pin the News, Sports, Weather, and Games apps to the Start screen, and then add them to the groups of Windows 8 tiles.
    - Unpin the Paint, Windows Media Player, Vintage, and Shut down tiles from the Start screen.
    - Apply the original design and color scheme to the Start screen background.
    - Restore the original user picture.
    - Display the original set of icons on the desktop and then restore the original image for the User's Files icon.
    - Change the desktop theme to Windows, and then delete any themes you downloaded.
    - Delete the Vintage folder in the Public Pictures folder.
    - Delete the Case1 Removable Disk Shortcut icon from the desktop.
17. Close any open windows.
18. Submit the results of the preceding steps to your instructor, either in printed or electronic form, as requested.

Case Problem 2

CHALLENGE

See the Starting Data Files section at the beginning of this tutorial for a list of Data Files needed for this Case Problem.

Sennett-Hayes Restoration Charlie Sennett and Lance Hayes own a furniture restoration company in New Haven, Connecticut. To promote their services, they provide computers in their showroom and invite people to browse their catalog, learn about furniture styles, and track the progress of their restoration project. You are the office manager for Sennett-Hayes Restoration and work with the staff and customers to help them use the company's resources. After installing Windows 8 on all of the office computers, Charlie asks you to personalize the desktop so it reflects the Sennett-Hayes company image. As you perform the following steps, note the original settings of the Start screen and desktop so you can restore them later. Complete the following steps:

1. Insert the USB flash drive or other removable media containing your Data Files in the appropriate drive, and then create a shortcut to this drive on the desktop. Use **Case2 Removable Disk Shortcut** as the name of the shortcut.
2. Use the Case2 Removable Disk Shortcut on the desktop to copy the five image files in the Windows3\Case2 folder provided with your Data Files to a new folder in the Public Pictures folder. Use **Furniture** as the name of the new folder.

3. Pin the following items to the Start screen: WordPad desktop app, Control Panel, and the Furniture folder.

⊕ **Explore** 4. Make the Weather tile a live tile. (*Hint:* If necessary, start the Weather app, and then specify a location.)

5. Change the Start screen color scheme to one that uses black.
6. Change the user picture to display one of the images stored in the Furniture folder.
7. Display the Start screen, scroll to the right, and then press the Print Screen key to capture an image of the Start screen. Start Paint, and then press the Ctrl+V keys to paste the image in the Paint file. Save the file as **Case2 Start XY**, where *XY* are your initials, in the Windows3\Case2 folder provided with your Data Files.
8. Change the desktop icon settings on your computer to display the Network and Control Panel icons in addition to the default Recycle Bin icon. Change the image for the Network icon so that it displays any other appropriate image.
9. Change the desktop theme to any other available theme besides Windows. Select one image other than the first one to display as wallpaper.
10. Change the color of the window borders and taskbar to Color 8.
11. Save the current desktop settings as a theme for sharing. Name the theme **Sennett-Hayes**, and store it in the Windows3\Case2 folder.
12. Change the screen saver to Mystify. Leave the Personalization window open, but close any other open windows.
13. Auto-hide the taskbar.
14. Hide the taskbar and then press the Print Screen key to capture an image of the desktop. Make Paint the active window, and then press the Ctrl+V keys to paste the image in the Paint file. Save the file as **Case2 Desktop XY**, where *XY* are your initials, in the Windows3\Case2 folder provided with your Data Files.

⊕ **Explore** 15. Complete the following tasks to restore the settings on your computer:
- Delete the Furniture folder from the Public Pictures folder on your hard disk.
- Unpin the WordPad, Control Panel, and Furniture tiles from the Start screen.
- Apply the default color scheme to the Start screen background.
- Restore the default image for the user picture.
- Turn off the live tile feature for the Weather tile.
- Display the original set of icons on the desktop and restore the default image for the Network icon.
- Change the desktop theme to Windows, and then delete the Sennett-Hayes theme.
- Restore the taskbar to its default state.
- Delete the Case2 Removable Disk Shortcut icon from the desktop.

16. Close any open windows.
17. Submit the results of the preceding steps to your instructor, either in printed or electronic form, as requested.

Case Problem 3

CHALLENGE

See the Starting Data Files section at the beginning of this tutorial for a list of Data Files needed for this Case Problem.

Skyway Balloons Brianna Sylvester is the manager of Skyway Balloons in Topeka, Kansas. Brianna provides piloted hot air balloons for people who enjoy the recreation of ballooning. Each balloon in the Skyway fleet is identified by color or design, and many have become attractions throughout the Topeka area. Brianna recently hired you as an assistant to provide customer service and general office support. She has a visual impairment and asks you to customize her computer so she can use it more effectively. As you perform the following steps, note the original settings of the desktop and other items so you can restore them later. Complete the following steps:

1. Insert the USB flash drive or other removable media containing your Data Files in the appropriate drive, and then create a shortcut to this drive on the desktop. Use **Case3 Removable Disk Shortcut** as the name of the shortcut.
2. Use the Removable Disk Shortcut on the desktop to copy the five image files in the Windows3\Case3 folder provided with your Data Files to a new folder in the Public Pictures library. Use **Balloons** as the name of the new folder.
3. Pin the following items to the Start screen: Paint desktop app, Magnifier desktop app, Narrator desktop app, and the Balloons folder.

Explore 4. Complete the following tasks to rearrange the tiles on the Start screen:
- Unpin four small tiles for Windows 8 apps from the Start screen. (Note which tiles you remove so you can pin them later.)
- Increase the size of two small tiles so that most Windows 8 apps have large tiles. (Note which tiles you expand so you can restore them to their original size later.)

Explore 5. Complete the following tasks to make the Start screen easier for Brianna to use:
- Use the PC settings screen to display the Ease of Access settings.
- Turn on high contrast.
- Increase the cursor thickness to 5.

6. Display the Start screen, scroll to the far right, and then press the Print Screen key to capture an image of the Start screen. Start Paint, and then press the Ctrl+V keys to paste the image in the Paint file. Save the file as **Case3 Start XY**, where *XY* are your initials, in the Windows3\Case3 folder provided with your Data Files.
7. Change the desktop icon settings on your computer to display all of the built-in desktop icons. Change the image for the Computer icon so that it displays any other appropriate image.

Explore 8. Use the desktop shortcut menu to change the view of the desktop so it displays large icons. (*Hint*: Right-click the desktop, point to View, and then click Large icons.)

9. Change the desktop theme to a High Contrast theme of your choice.
10. Make Paint the active window and then pin Paint to the taskbar.
11. Use Paint to open the five images in the Balloons folder. Pin each image to the Paint Jump List.

Explore 12. Start the Magnifier desktop app and then use it to magnify any part of the desktop.

13. Right-click the Paint program button on the taskbar to display its Jump List. Press the Print Screen key to capture an image of the desktop. Make Paint the active window, and then press the Ctrl+V keys to paste the image in the Paint file. Save the file as **Case3 Desktop XY**, where *XY* are your initials, in the Windows3\Case3 folder provided with your Data Files. Click the magnifying glass icon and then click the Close button to close Magnifier.
14. Complete the following tasks to restore the settings on your computer:
    - Delete the Case3 Removable Disk Shortcut icon from the desktop.
    - Unpin the Paint, Magnifier, Narrator, and Balloons tiles from the Start screen.
    - Restore the Ease of Access options to their original settings.
    - Restore the original size of the tiles you expanded.
    - Pin the tiles you removed from the Start screen.
    - Move the Windows 8 tiles so they appear in two groups.
    - Unpin Paint from the taskbar, and then unpin the five balloon pictures from the Paint Jump List.
    - Display the original set of icons on the desktop and change the Computer icon to its default image.
    - Change the theme to Windows.
    - Change the view of the desktop so it displays Medium icons.
    - Delete the Balloons folder in the Public Pictures folder.
15. Close all open windows.

16. Submit the results of the preceding steps to your instructor, either in printed or electronic form, as requested.

Case Problem 4

There are no Data Files needed for this Case Problem.

Singh Satellite After training to be a meteorologist, Dev Singh decided to start his own company providing satellite services to the airline industry in Houston, Texas. Dev recently upgraded all of the computers at Singh Satellite to Windows 8, and then hired you to manage the office. After working with a client in Dallas, Dev shows you a screen shot of that client's Start screen and another of his desktop. See Figure 3-48. He thinks the Start screen and desktop would be appropriate for the computers at Singh Satellite, and he asks you to re-create them on your computer.

Figure 3-48   Model Start screen and desktop for Singh Satellite

To create this Start screen, complete the following:

1. Select the following settings for the Start screen:
    - Blue background with blue highlights
    - Make sure Travel, Bing, Weather, and Sports are live tiles (start each app and then turn on live tiles, if necessary)
    - Windows Media Player tile pinned to the Start screen
2. Select the following settings for the desktop:
    - Theme featuring abstract designs
    - Bubbles screen saver
3. Capture an image of the Start screen, and then save the image in a Paint file named **Case4 Start XY**, where *XY* are your initials, in the Windows3\Case4 folder provided with your Data Files.
4. Capture an image of the desktop with the Screen Saver Settings dialog box open, and then save the image in a Paint file named **Case4 Desktop XY**, where *XY* are your initials, in the Windows3\Case4 folder provided with your Data Files.
5. Restore the original settings, and then close all open windows.
6. Resubmit the results from the previous steps to your instructor either in printed or electronic form, as requested.

TUTORIAL 4

Working with the Internet and Email

Communicating with Others

OBJECTIVES

Session 4.1
- Define the relationship between the Internet and the Web
- Open, view, and navigate Web pages in Internet Explorer
- Revisit recently opened Web pages
- Organize links to your favorite Web pages
- Use RSS feeds and Accelerators

Session 4.2
- Explain how email works
- Send, receive, reply to, and delete email with Mail
- Attach a file to an email message
- Add a contact using People
- Create appointments with Calendar

Case | San Antonio Historical Association

Jason Rowley is the director of the San Antonio Historical Association (SAHA) in San Antonio, Texas. SAHA works to preserve historic structures, provides guided walking tours of San Antonio, and offers workshops to residents and visitors about San Antonio history, culture, and architecture. One of the organization's most popular workshops is on genealogy, which teaches participants how to begin genealogical research, where to search, and how to find information on family histories. Recently, Jason hired you as a project assistant to help him run the historical association. He wants to learn about using online resources to research ancestries so he can conduct sessions of the genealogy workshop. You regularly use Microsoft Internet Explorer to gather information for SAHA on the World Wide Web. You also use the Windows 8 Mail app to exchange email with SAHA's members and visitors. Jason has asked you to get him up to speed on using these programs.

In this tutorial, you'll explore how the Internet and the Web work, and use Internet Explorer to visit and organize Web pages. You'll examine email technology and use Mail to send, receive, and reply to email messages. You'll also use two Windows 8 apps to manage your contacts and your schedule.

STARTING DATA FILES

WIN 161

Session 4.1 Visual Overview:

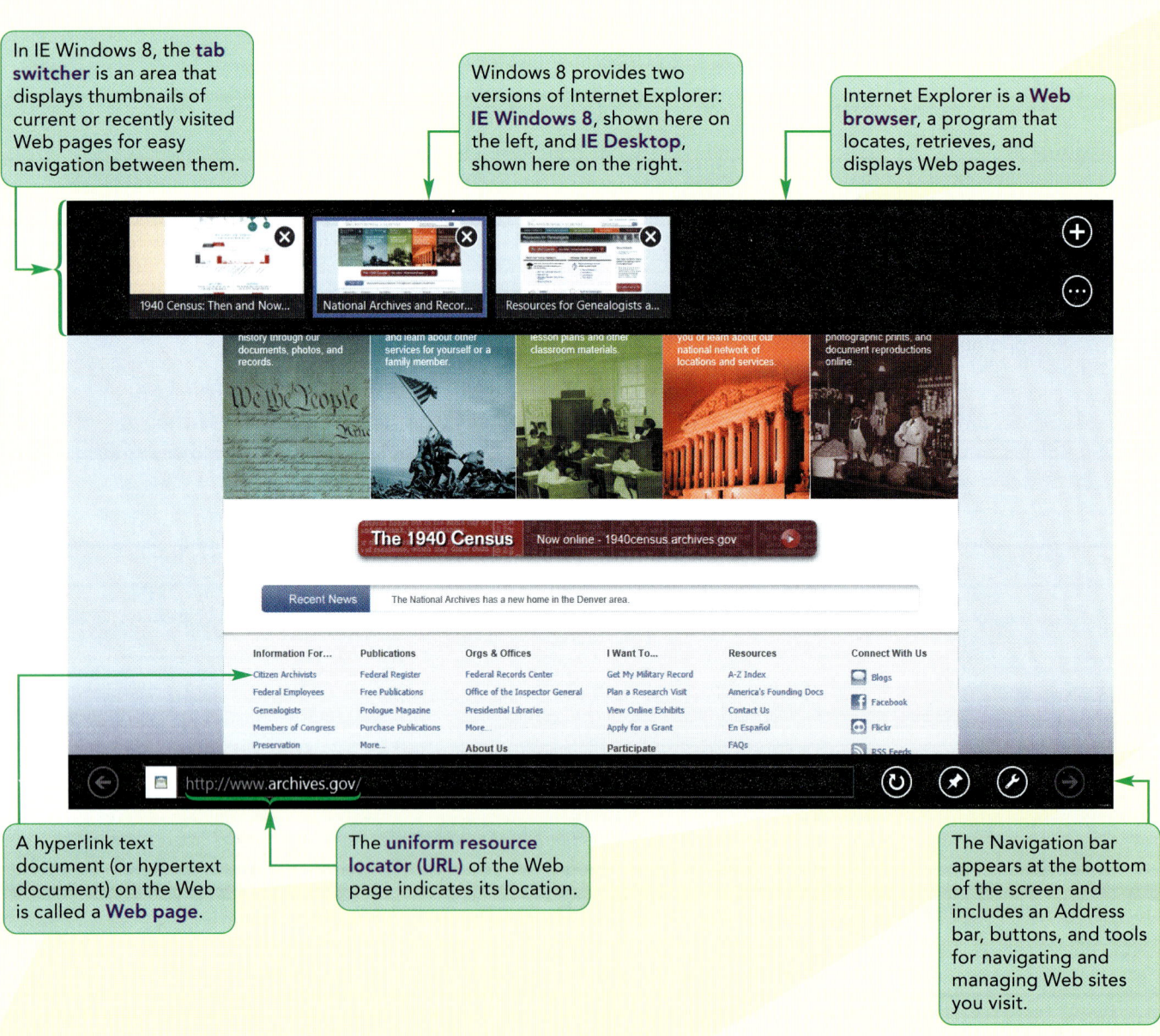

In IE Windows 8, the **tab switcher** is an area that displays thumbnails of current or recently visited Web pages for easy navigation between them.

Windows 8 provides two versions of Internet Explorer: **IE Windows 8**, shown here on the left, and **IE Desktop**, shown here on the right.

Internet Explorer is a **Web browser**, a program that locates, retrieves, and displays Web pages.

A hyperlink text document (or hypertext document) on the Web is called a **Web page**.

The **uniform resource locator (URL)** of the Web page indicates its location.

The Navigation bar appears at the bottom of the screen and includes an Address bar, buttons, and tools for navigating and managing Web sites you visit.

Courtesy of the National Archives and Records Administration; United States Census Bureau

Microsoft Internet Explorer

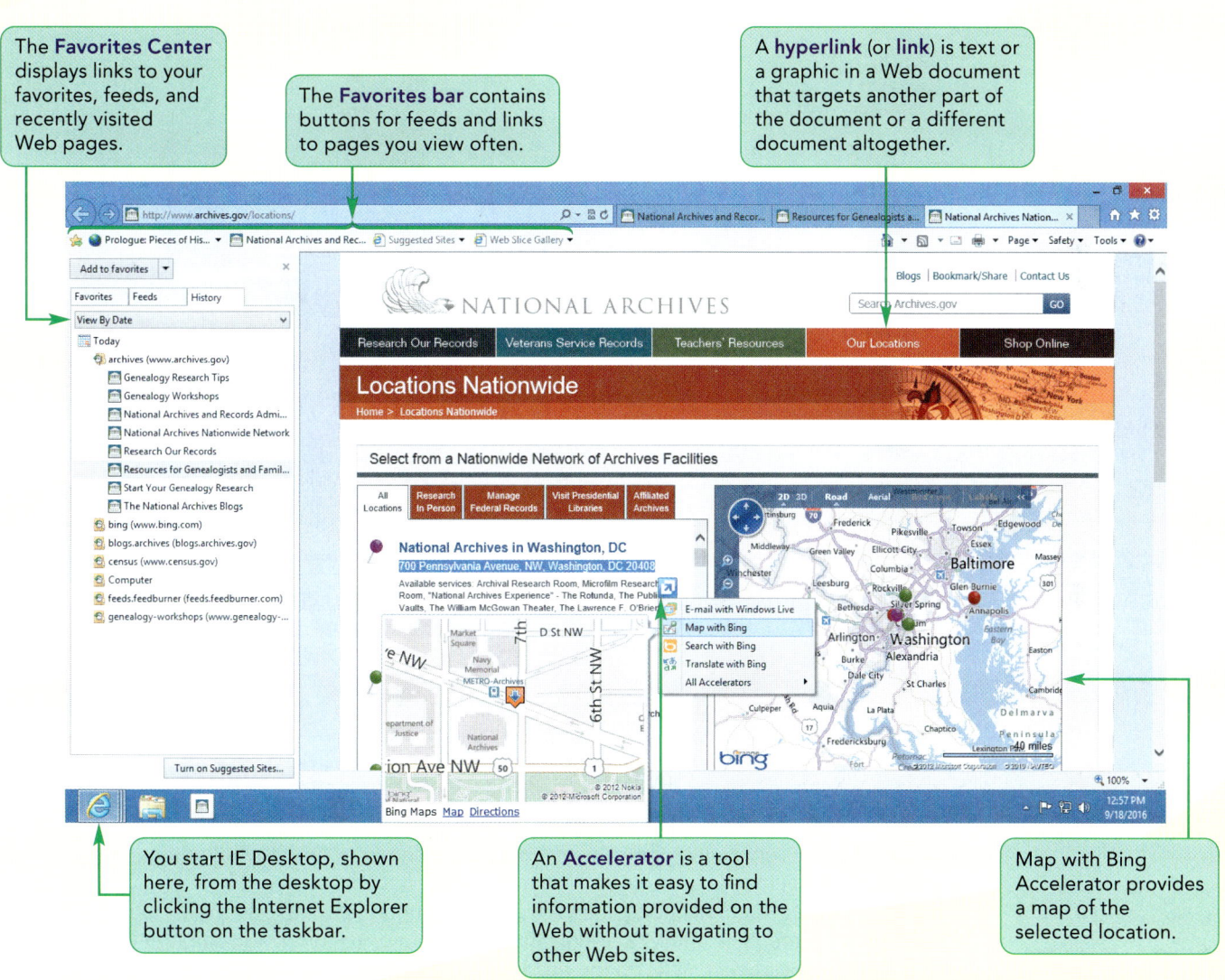

The **Favorites Center** displays links to your favorites, feeds, and recently visited Web pages.

The **Favorites bar** contains buttons for feeds and links to pages you view often.

A **hyperlink** (or **link**) is text or a graphic in a Web document that targets another part of the document or a different document altogether.

You start IE Desktop, shown here, from the desktop by clicking the Internet Explorer button on the taskbar.

An **Accelerator** is a tool that makes it easy to find information provided on the Web without navigating to other Web sites.

Map with Bing Accelerator provides a map of the selected location.

Exploring the Internet and the Web

When you connect two or more computers to exchange information and resources, they form a **network**. You can connect networks to each other to share information across a wide area. The worldwide, publicly accessible collection of networks is called the Internet, and it consists of millions of computers linked to networks all over the world. The Internet lets you access and exchange information via electronic mail (email), online newsgroups, file transfer, and the linked documents of the **World Wide Web**, better known as the **Web**. See Figure 4-1.

Figure 4-1   Connecting computers to the Internet

© 2014 Cengage Learning

The Web is a service that you can access via the Internet. While the Internet is a collection of networks connected by communication media such as fiber-optic cables and wireless connections, the Web is a collection of documents connected by hyperlinks. You click a link to display the targeted information. For example, in Figure 4-2, you can click links on the first Library of Congress Web document to display related documents.

| Figure 4-2 | Library of Congress Web page with links to other Web pages |

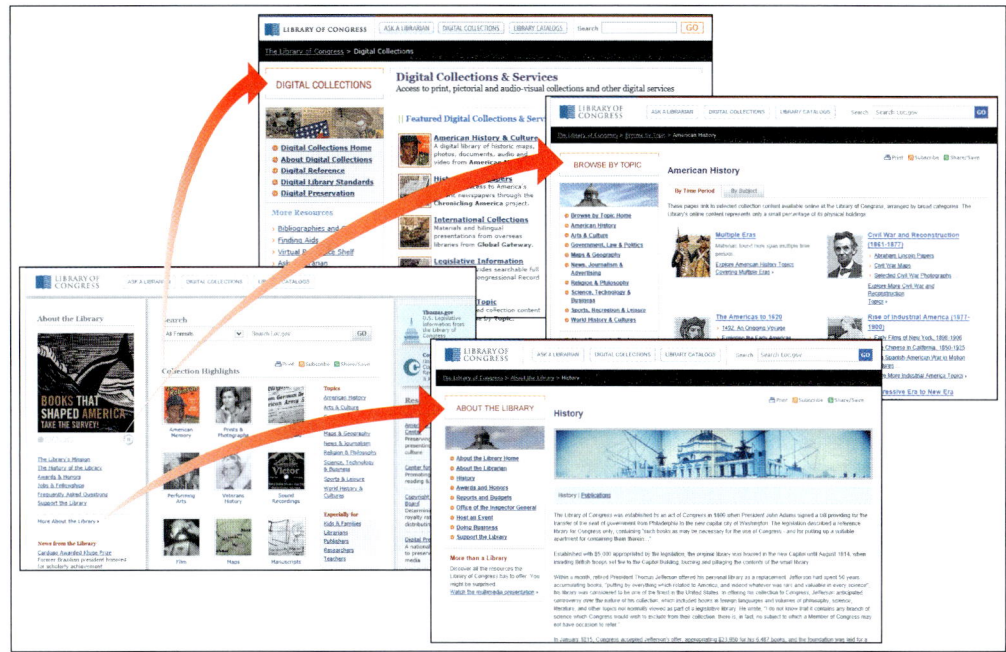

Courtesy of the Library of Congress

Web pages are stored on Internet computers called **Web servers**. A **Web site** is a collection of Web pages that have a common theme or focus, such as all pages containing information about the Library of Congress. The Web is appealing because it generally displays up-to-date information in a colorful, lively format that can use sound, video, and animation.

When you want to find information on the Web, you typically use a **search engine**, which is a program that conducts searches to retrieve Web pages. To work with a search engine, you enter a word or an expression as the search criteria. The search engine lists links to Web pages that fit your criteria. Popular general search engines include Google and Bing.

A recent innovation in Web technology is called **cloud computing**, which refers to providing and using computer tools, such as software, via the Internet (or the cloud). With cloud computing you can use your Web browser to access and work with software. You do not need to purchase and install a complete application. Instead, you use the software services you need for free or for a usage fee. For example, when you use a Web mapping service, such as MapQuest or Google Maps, to find directions from one location to another, you are using cloud computing. The software and data for the maps are not stored on your computer—they're on the cloud at the mapping service's Web site. This software is known as a **Web app**. For example, the Microsoft Office Web apps are provided on the cloud as simplified versions of the programs provided in Microsoft Office, such as Word and Excel.

Using Web Browsers

You use a Web browser, or browser, to visit Web sites around the world; interact with Web pages by clicking links; view multimedia documents; transfer files, images, videos, and sounds to and from your computer; conduct searches for specific topics; and run programs on other computers. The browser included with Windows 8 is called Internet Explorer.

When you attempt to view a Web page, your browser locates and retrieves the document from the Web server and displays its contents on your computer. The server stores the Web page in one location, and browsers anywhere in the world can display it.

For your browser to access the Web, you must have an Internet connection. In a university setting, your connection might come from your campus network. If you are working on a home computer, you have a few options for connecting to the Internet. Most likely, you are using a **broadband connection**, a high-capacity, high-speed medium for connecting to the Internet. Popular broadband technologies include a **digital subscriber line (DSL)**, which is a high-speed connection through your telephone line, and **digital cable**, which uses a cable modem attached to cable television lines. A **wireless connection** uses infrared light or radio-frequency signals to communicate with devices that are physically connected to a network or the Internet. Home connections also require an account with an **Internet service provider (ISP)**, a company that sells Internet access. The ISP provides instructions for connecting your computer to one of its servers, which is connected to the Internet. You can then use your browser to visit Web sites and access other Internet services.

Getting Started with Microsoft Internet Explorer

Microsoft Internet Explorer, the Web browser that comes with Windows 8, lets you communicate, access, and share information on the Web. Internet Explorer (IE) is available in two versions on your system: IE Windows 8 and IE Desktop. (See the Session 4.1 Visual Overview.) As its name suggests, IE Windows 8, which you open from the Start screen, uses the Windows 8 interface. Its clean design lets you focus on Web page content instead of browser controls. Large buttons, thumbnails, and horizontal scrolling make IE Windows 8 ideal if you are using a touchscreen device. IE Desktop, which you open from the desktop, includes toolbars, menus, and other controls designed for a pointing device such as a mouse. In general, you use IE Windows 8 when you are working with the Start screen or a Windows 8 app and want to quickly browse to a Web page or search for information. Choose IE Desktop when you are working on the desktop or with a desktop app and want to perform more extensive online tasks, such as saving a collection of sites as Favorites, viewing online media, or using Web apps.

When you start either version of Internet Explorer, it opens to a **home page**, which is the Web page a browser is set to open by default. The default home page for Internet Explorer is the Bing Web page, the Microsoft search engine. Your computer manufacturer or school might have set up a different home page.

Your first step in showing Jason how to research genealogy is to start Internet Explorer. Because your computer displays the Start screen after you sign in, you'll show Jason how to use IE Windows 8 first. You must be connected to the Internet to perform all of the steps in this session. Mute your speakers, if necessary, so the sounds that certain Web pages play do not disturb others.

To start IE Windows 8:

▶ 1. Click the **Internet Explorer** tile on the Start screen. IE Windows 8 opens to its home page. Figure 4-3 shows the Bing main page in IE Windows 8. You might have a different home page.

Trouble? If a Network Connection dialog box opens, enter your user name and password, and then click the Connect button. If you do not know your user name or password, ask your instructor or technical support person for help; you must have an Internet connection to complete the steps in this tutorial.

Figure 4-3   **IE Windows 8**

home page; yours might differ

Forward button

Page tools button

Pin site button

Refresh button

Address bar

Back button

When you start IE Windows 8, it displays your home page in the main part of the screen and a Navigation bar at the bottom. The Navigation bar includes the following tools:

- Address bar—View the address of the Web page; you can also type the address of a Web page you want to visit
- Back and Forward buttons—Browse to the previous or next Web page in a sequence of opened pages
- Page tools button—Download an app if the site provides one, find text on the page, or view the page in the desktop version of Internet Explorer
- Pin site button—Pin the current Web page to the Start screen
- Refresh button—Refresh the contents of the Web page

Now you're ready to use IE Windows 8 to open and view a Web page.

Opening a Page on the Web

To find a particular Web page among the billions stored on Web servers, your browser needs to know the uniform resource locator (URL) of the Web page. URLs are like addresses—they indicate the location of a Web page. As shown in Figure 4-4, a URL can consist of the following four parts:

- Protocol to use when transferring the Web page
- Address of the Web server storing the page
- Pathname of the folder containing the page
- Filename of the Web page

| Figure 4-4 | Parts of a URL |

© 2014 Cengage Learning

The URL for most Web pages starts with http, which stands for **Hypertext Transfer Protocol**, the most common way to transfer information around the Web. (A **protocol** is a standardized procedure computers use to exchange information.) When the URL for a Web page starts with http://, the Web browser uses Hypertext Transfer Protocol to retrieve the page.

The server address indicates the location of the Web server storing the Web page. In *www.loc.gov*, the *www* indicates that the server is a Web server, *loc* is the name the Library of Congress chose for this Web site, and *.gov* means that a government entity runs the Web server. Other common types of Web servers in the United States are .com (commercial), .net (network server providers or resources), .org (not-for-profit organizations), and .edu (educational institutions). The server address in a URL corresponds to an Internet Protocol (IP) address, which identifies every computer on the Internet. An **IP address** is a unique number that consists of four sets of numbers from 0 to 255 separated by periods, or dots, as in 216.35.148.4. Although computers can use IP addresses easily, they are difficult for people to remember, so domain names were created. A **domain name** identifies one or more IP addresses, such as loc.gov. URLs use the domain name in the server address part of the URL to identify a particular Web site.

In addition, each file stored on a Web server has a unique pathname, just like files stored on a disk. The pathname in a URL includes the names of the folders containing the file, the filename, and its extension. A common filename extension for Web pages is .html, or just .htm. For example, the pathname might be library/index.html, which specifies a file named index.html stored in a folder named library.

Not all URLs include a pathname. If you don't specify a pathname or filename in a URL, most Web browsers open a file named index.htm or index.html, which is the default name for a Web site's main page.

Opening a Web Page Using a URL

One way to open a Web page in Internet Explorer is to enter a URL, which you can often find in advertisements, in informational materials, and on the Web. You enter the URL in the Address bar of Internet Explorer.

In most cases, URLs are not case sensitive, so you can enter a URL using all lowercase or all uppercase text. However, if the Web server storing a Web page uses the UNIX operating system, the URL might be case sensitive. For mixed-case URLs, it's safer to enter them using the mixed case exactly as printed.

The first Web page you want to open for Jason is the home page of the U.S. Census Bureau, which has been providing statistics and information about the population and economy in the United States since 1790 and is a source of information for genealogists.

To open a page on the Web using a URL:

1. Click the **Address bar** to select its contents, which should be the URL for your home page. Anything you now type replaces the selected URL. When you click the Address bar, the Navigation bar expands to show tiles for Web pages you've visited frequently and for any Web pages you pinned to the Start screen. You'll use the expanded Navigation bar in another set of steps.

Trouble? If the contents of the Address bar are not selected, drag to select the entire address.

2. Type **www.census.gov** in the Address bar. As you type, Internet Explorer displays the names of other Web pages you've opened that have URLs starting with the same characters, a feature called AutoComplete.

3. Press the **Enter** key. Internet Explorer adds the http:// protocol to the URL for you, and then opens the main, or home, page for the U.S. Census Bureau Web site. See Figure 4-5.

Trouble? If you receive a Not Found error message, you might have typed the URL incorrectly. Repeat Steps 1–3, making sure that the URL in the Address bar matches the URL in Step 2. If you still receive an error message, ask your instructor or technical support person for help.

Trouble? If a window opens inviting you to download an app, click the Continue to Census.gov button.

Figure 4-5 Opening the U.S. Census Bureau home page

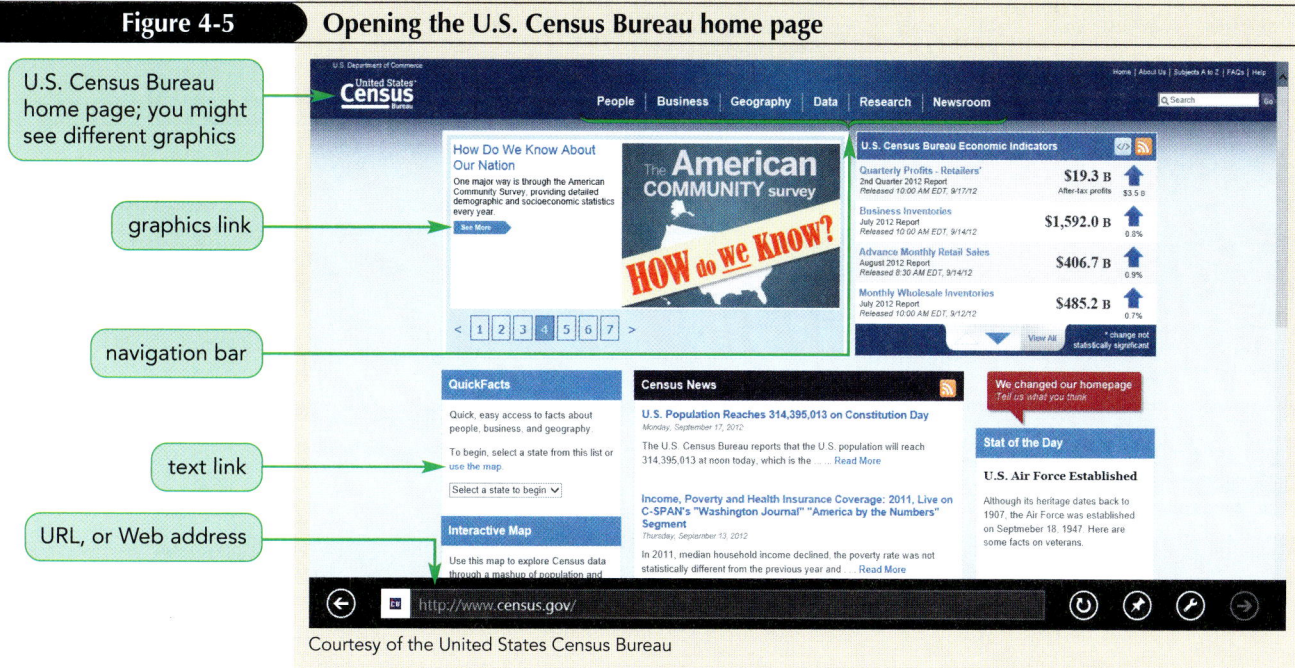

Courtesy of the United States Census Bureau

Because Web content changes frequently, the Web pages you open might differ from the figures in this tutorial.

A home page on the Web can have at least two meanings. It can be the Web page a browser is set to open by default. It can also be the main page for a Web site that provides links to other Web pages with related information.

Navigating with Links

The home page for a typical Web site includes plenty of links to help you navigate to its Web pages, and those pages also include links you can click to navigate from one page to another. Links can be text, images, or a combination of both. Text links are usually colored and underlined, though the exact style can vary from one Web site to another. To determine whether something on a Web page is a link, point to it. If the pointer changes to 🖑, the text or image is a link you can click to open a Web page. For some graphics links, a ScreenTip appears next to your pointer.

Jason's grandparents immigrated to the United States from northern England in 1940. You'll show Jason how to find information about the U.S. population in 1940 on the Census Bureau Web site.

To navigate a Web site using links:

1. Point to **People** on the site's Navigation bar. The pointer changes to 👆 and a menu of links in the People category appears below the Navigation bar. See Figure 4-6.

Figure 4-6 Pointing to a link

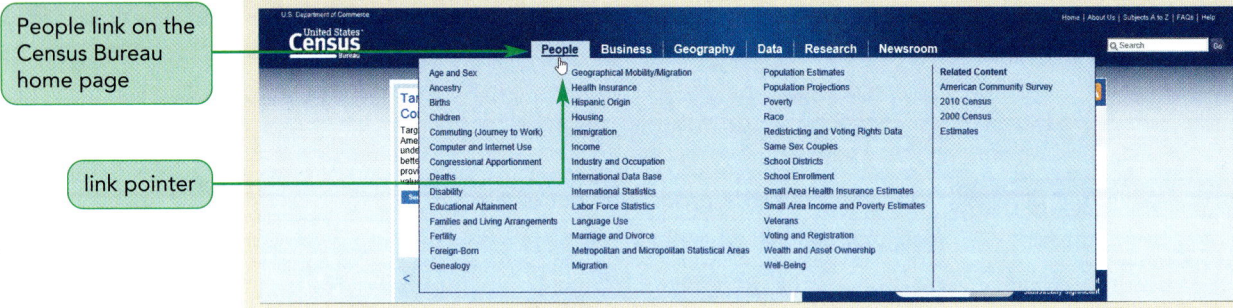

Courtesy of the United States Census Bureau

Trouble? If the current U.S Census Bureau home page does not include a People link, point to any other similar link and substitute that link when you perform Step 2.

2. Click **Genealogy** in the People menu to open the Genealogy Web page.

3. In the Quick Links list on the left, click **Historical Data** to open the Genealogy Data: Historical Data page, which includes a Census Then and Now link. See Figure 4-7. The Web page you open might look different.

Figure 4-7 Genealogy Data: Historical Data Web page

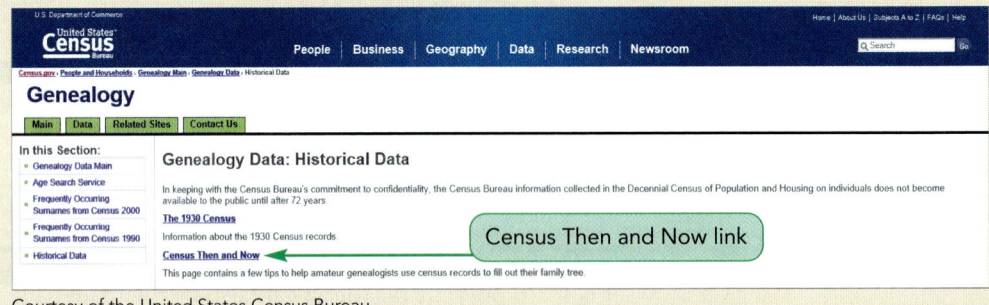

Courtesy of the United States Census Bureau

4. Click the **Census Then and Now** link to open the 1940 Census page, which illustrates how America has changed from 1940 to 2010.

Trouble? If the Census Then and Now link does not appear on the current Web page, click any other link on the page.

5. Scroll to the bottom of the Census Then and Now page to review the entire illustration.

Tutorial 4 Working with the Internet and Email | Windows   WIN 171

As you scroll the Census Then and Now page, Internet Explorer hides the tools on the Navigation bar so you can focus on the Web page content. You'll redisplay the Navigation bar and show other tools in IE Windows 8 shortly.

> **INSIGHT**
>
> ### Displaying Web Pages Designed for Earlier Versions of Internet Explorer
>
> IE Windows 8 and IE Desktop are versions of Internet Explorer 10. If you visit a Web site designed for earlier versions of Internet Explorer, the Web pages might not be formatted for Internet Explorer 10. For example, the Web page navigation bar, images, or text might appear out of place or the Web page might not scroll its full length. To improve the appearance of a Web site in your browser, you can turn on **Compatibility View**, which displays the page as it would appear in an earlier version of Internet Explorer. If Internet Explorer detects a Web page that might not appear correctly, the Compatibility View button appears on the Address bar. In IE Desktop, you can also click the Tools button on the Command bar and then click Compatibility View to reformat the current Web site. After turning on Compatibility View for a Web site, Internet Explorer displays the site in Compatibility View whenever you visit it unless the site is updated to appear correctly in Internet Explorer 10. In that case, Internet Explorer turns off Compatibility View and displays the site as designed.

Besides clicking links to navigate from one Web page to another, you can use tools that Internet Explorer provides.

Navigating with IE Windows 8 Tools

Recall that when you use File Explorer, you can click the Back and Forward buttons to navigate the devices and folders on your computer. IE Windows 8 includes similar buttons you can use to navigate from one Web page to another. IE Windows 8 keeps track of the pages you visited. To return to the previous page, you can click the left arrow button, which appears on your screen when you move the pointer to the left side of the screen. After you navigate to a previous page, you can click the right arrow button, which appears when you move the pointer to the right side of the screen, to continue to the next page in the sequence.

> **To return to previously viewed Web pages:**
>
> ▶ 1. Point to the left side of the screen, and then click the **left arrow button** to return to the Genealogy Data: Historical Data page.
>
> ▶ 2. Point to the right side of the screen, and then click the **right arrow button** to return to the Census Then and Now page.
>
> **Trouble?** If you opened different Web pages in the previous set of steps, substitute the names of the pages as appropriate in Steps 1 and 2.

Besides using the arrow buttons in the middle of the screen to navigate Web pages, you can display the Navigation bar and use its Back and Forward buttons to navigate from one page to another. To display the Navigation bar, you right-click the background of a Web page. When you do so, the Navigation bar appears at the bottom of the screen and the tab switcher appears at the top of the screen, displaying thumbnails of currently opened Web pages. The tab switcher also provides tools for using **tabbed browsing**, a feature that lets you have more than one Web page open at the same time.

To display and use the IE Windows 8 Navigation bar:

1. Right-click the background of the Web page to display the Navigation bar at the bottom of the screen and the tab switcher at the top of the screen. See Figure 4-8.

Figure 4-8	Navigation bar and tab switcher

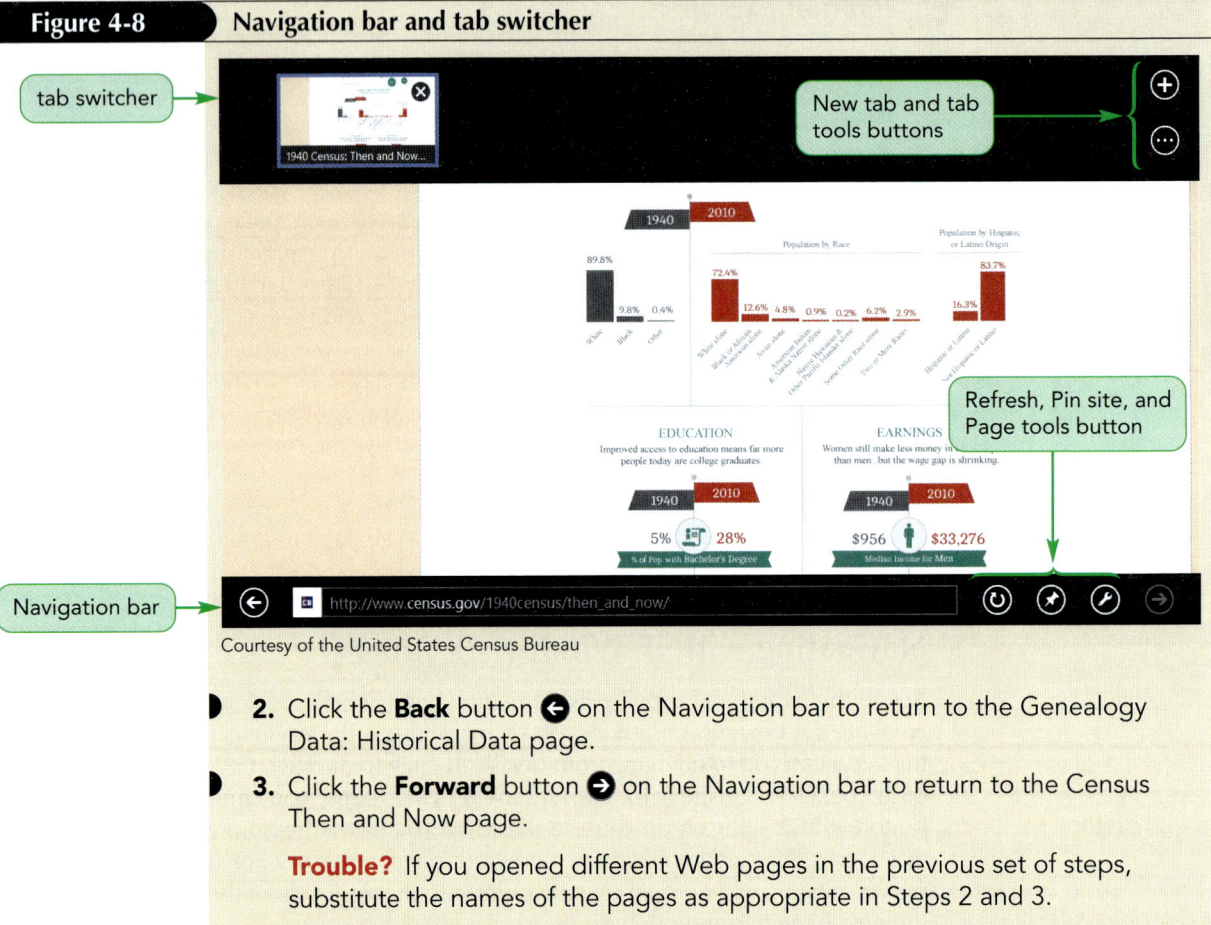

Courtesy of the United States Census Bureau

2. Click the **Back** button on the Navigation bar to return to the Genealogy Data: Historical Data page.

3. Click the **Forward** button on the Navigation bar to return to the Census Then and Now page.

Trouble? If you opened different Web pages in the previous set of steps, substitute the names of the pages as appropriate in Steps 2 and 3.

Next, you want to show Jason how to use tabs to open other Web pages without closing the Census Then and Now page.

Managing Web Pages in IE Windows 8

If you want to open a new Web page without closing the one you're currently viewing, you can use tabbed browsing to open more than one Web page at a time. To use tabbed browsing, you open a tab for each new page you want to view. To open a new tab, you can press the Ctrl key as you click a link on a Web page, or you can right-click the link and then click Open link in new tab on the shortcut menu. You can then switch from one Web page to another by clicking the tabs in the tab switcher. Each tab displays a thumbnail of its Web page so you can quickly identify the page you want to display. To close a tab, you click its Close Tab button in the Web page thumbnail on the tab switcher.

Now that you've explored a few pages on the Census Bureau Web site, you can compare that information to information on the National Archives Web site, which provides documents, photos, and records for people conducting family research. You'll show Jason how to open a new tab in IE Windows 8, and then use it to open the National Archives home page.

To open other Web pages on new tabs:

1. Right-click the background of the Web page to display the tab switcher, which includes a tab for the current Web page.
2. Click the **New Tab** button on the tab switcher to open a blank page and to expand the Navigation bar to display lists of frequently visited and pinned pages.
3. Click in the **Address bar**, if necessary, type **www.archives.gov**, and then press the **Enter** key. The National Archives home page opens on the new tab. See Figure 4-9. The Web page you open might look different.

Figure 4-9   National Archives home page

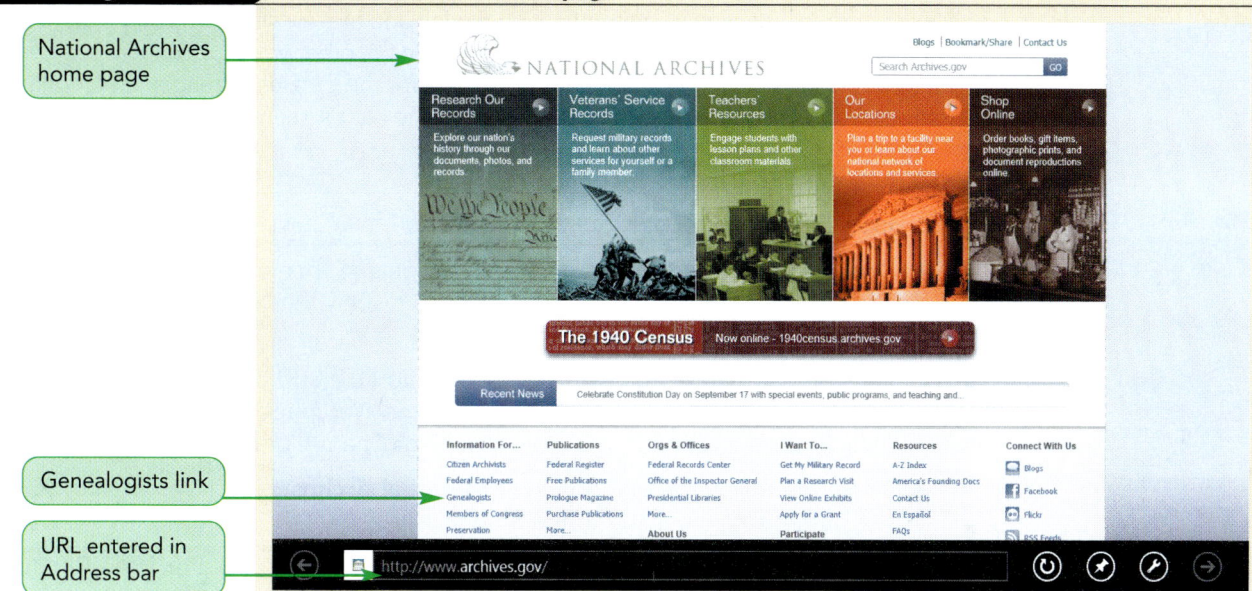

- National Archives home page
- Genealogists link
- URL entered in Address bar

Courtesy of the National Archives and Records Administration

4. Right-click the **Genealogists** link on the Web page, and then click **Open link in new tab** on the shortcut menu. The Resources for Genealogists Web page opens in a new tab, though the page is not visible yet. You need to display the tab switcher and then click the thumbnail for that page.

   Trouble? If the Genealogists link does not appear on the current Web page, right-click a different link on the page.

5. Right-click the background of the Web page to display the tab switcher, which includes thumbnails of each open Web page. See Figure 4-10.

Figure 4-10   Tabs for the open Web pages

- three tabs open in IE Windows 8

Courtesy of the National Archives and Records Administration; United States Census Bureau

6. Click the **Resources for Genealogists** thumbnail on the tab switcher to display that Web page.

Jason wants to be able to open the home pages for the Census Bureau and National Archives Web sites quickly, without entering the URL in the Address bar. You'll show him how to do so next.

Pinning Web Pages

When you find a Web site that you'll return to often, you can pin the site to the Start screen. Windows organizes all pinned sites into a group. However, you can further organize them into smaller groups if you pin many sites to the Start screen. To help you identify a pinned Web site at a glance, the tile for a pinned site reflects the site's color and icon. If you have an account on a Web site that displays messages or other account information, such as Twitter or Facebook, you can make the pinned site a live tile so it displays messages on the tile.

Pinning a site places a tile for the site on the Start screen and in the browser. When you click the Address bar, pinned sites appear on the left and tiles for sites you visit frequently appear on the right. In the browser, the tiles appear in the order you pinned them.

Because Jason wants to access the home pages for the Census Bureau and National Archives Web sites quickly, you'll pin the sites to the Start screen.

To pin Web sites to the Start screen:

1. Right-click the background of the Web page and then click the **National Archives** thumbnail on the tab switcher to display the National Archives home page.

2. Click the **Pin site** button ◉ on the Navigation bar and then click **Pin to Start**. A text box appears, showing the name of the Web page. You can accept the default name, change it to a more meaningful name, or in this case, shorten it.

3. Select the text in the text box, type **National Archives**, and then click the **Pin site** button to pin the site to the Start screen.

4. Right-click the background of the Web page, and then click the **1940 Census** thumbnail to display the 1940 Census Web page.

5. Click the **Address bar**, type **www.census.gov**, and then press the **Enter** key to display the home page for the Census Bureau Web site.

6. Click the **Pin site** button ◉ on the Navigation bar, click **Pin to Start**, delete **Homepage** in the text box to shorten the name to "Census Bureau", and then click the **Pin to Start** button to pin the page to the Start screen.

   Trouble? If the Navigation bar is no longer open, right-click the background of the Web page to display the Navigation bar.

7. Drag the top of the IE Windows 8 app down until it shrinks to a thumbnail, and then continue dragging it to the very bottom of the screen to close IE Windows 8.

8. On the Start screen, scroll to the right to display the two tiles for the pinned sites. See Figure 4-11.

> **TIP**
> You can also press the Backspace or Delete key to delete the text before typing a name for the pinned tile.

Figure 4-11 Pinned sites on the Start screen

9. Click the **National Archives** tile to open the site in IE Windows 8.
10. Click the **Address bar** to display tiles for frequently and recently visited Web pages and pinned sites. See Figure 4-12.

Figure 4-12 Pinned sites in the browser

Courtesy of the United States Census Bureau

11. Click the **Census Bureau** tile to open the home page for the Census Bureau Web site.

   Trouble? If a window opens inviting you to download an app, click Continue to Census.gov.

Now that Jason knows the basics of opening and navigating Web pages, he wants to learn how to search for a Web page and print it. He can do both using the Charms bar.

Using the Internet Explorer Charms Bar

You have already used the Charms bar to perform Windows tasks, such as searching for apps and accessing system settings. If you display the Charms bar while you are using IE Windows 8, you can perform Internet Explorer tasks, such as searching for Web sites, printing Web page content, and selecting IE Windows 8 settings. When you search the Web, IE Windows 8 uses the primary search engine, which is Bing by default. You can change the primary search engine if you prefer a different one.

Jason wants to find information about other genealogy workshops, so he asks you to search for Web pages that describe the workshops.

To search for and prepare to print a Web page:

1. Point to the upper-right corner of the screen to display the Charms bar.
2. Click the **Search** charm to display the Search Internet Explorer menu.

3. Type **genealogy workshops** in the Search box, and then press the **Enter** key. IE Windows 8 displays the results using your specified search engine. See Figure 4-13. Your results and search engine may differ.

Figure 4-13 Search Internet Explorer menu and search results

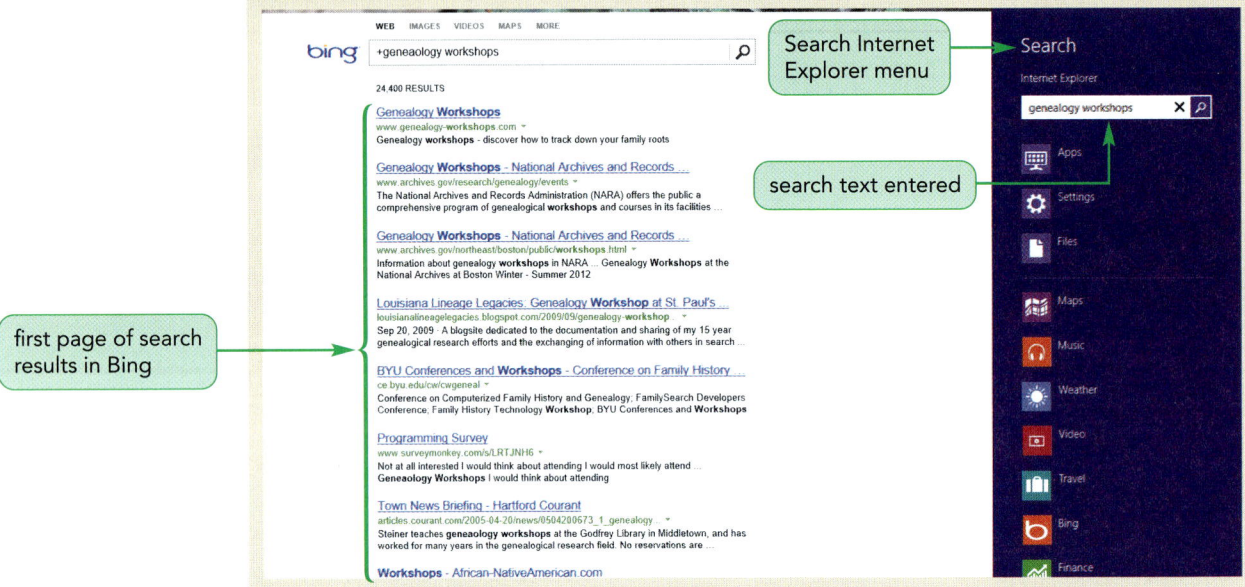

4. Click a link in the search results to display information about genealogy workshops.

5. Point to the upper-right corner of the screen to display the Charms bar again, and then click the **Devices** charm to display a list of devices Internet Explorer can use for printing. See Figure 4-14. Your list of devices will differ.

Figure 4-14 IE Windows 8 Devices list

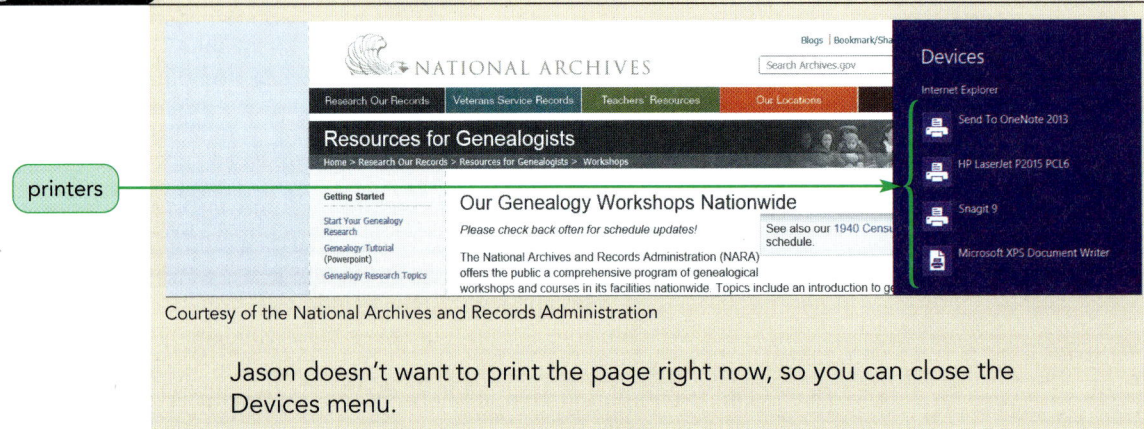

Courtesy of the National Archives and Records Administration

Jason doesn't want to print the page right now, so you can close the Devices menu.

6. Click a blank spot on the Web page to close the Devices menu.

You can also use the Charms bar to change IE Windows 8 settings and share a Web page via email.

Using Flip Ahead

If you find yourself visiting Web sites and then searching for a Next Page link to open the next page in a sequence, you can save time by using the **Flip ahead** feature. Flip ahead works with search results, articles printed on two or more Web pages, or any Web pages connected by Next Page buttons or links. For example, if you are browsing the results of a search in Google or Bing, you can use Flip ahead instead of scrolling to the bottom of the search results page and clicking a link to display the next page. You can also use Flip ahead if you are reading an online article, such as one published on a news Web site.

REFERENCE

Turning on Flip Ahead

- With IE Windows 8 open, display the Charms bar, and then click the Settings charm.
- Click Internet Options in the list of settings.
- Drag the Flip ahead slider from Off to On.

Flip ahead is turned off by default. To turn it on in IE Windows 8, you use the Internet Explorer Settings screen. When you view the first page of a multipage article, for example, or display the results of a Web search, the Forward button is activated in the Navigation bar. You can click the Forward button to display the next page of the article or search results.

Jason also wants to search for Web pages containing information about genealogy classes. You'll show him how to turn on Flip ahead and then use it to view search results.

To use Flip ahead:

1. Point to the upper-right corner of the screen to display the Charms bar, and then click the **Settings** charm to display a list of Internet Explorer settings.

2. Click **Internet Options** to display the Internet Explorer Settings screen. See Figure 4-15.

Figure 4-15   Internet Explorer Settings screen

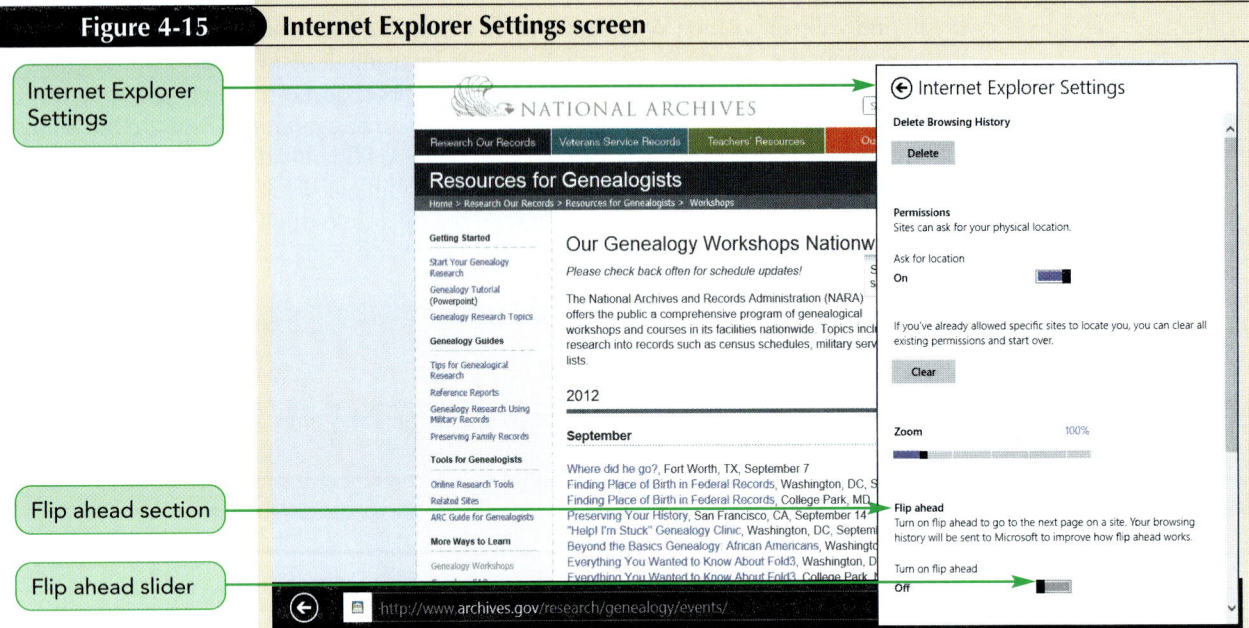

Courtesy of the National Archives and Records Administration

3. In the Flip ahead section, drag the slider from Off to **On** to activate the Flip ahead feature.

4. Click a blank spot on the Web page to close the Internet Explorer Settings screen.

5. Display the Charms bar again, and then click the **Search** charm to display the Search Internet Explorer menu.

6. Type **genealogy classes** and then press the **Enter** key. Click the **Address bar** to close the Search menu but not the Navigation bar. Using the default search engine (Bing, in this case), IE Windows 8 displays the first page of links to Web pages about genealogy classes. Because this is the first of many pages of search results, the Forward button is active in the Navigation bar. See Figure 4-16. Your results and search engine may differ.

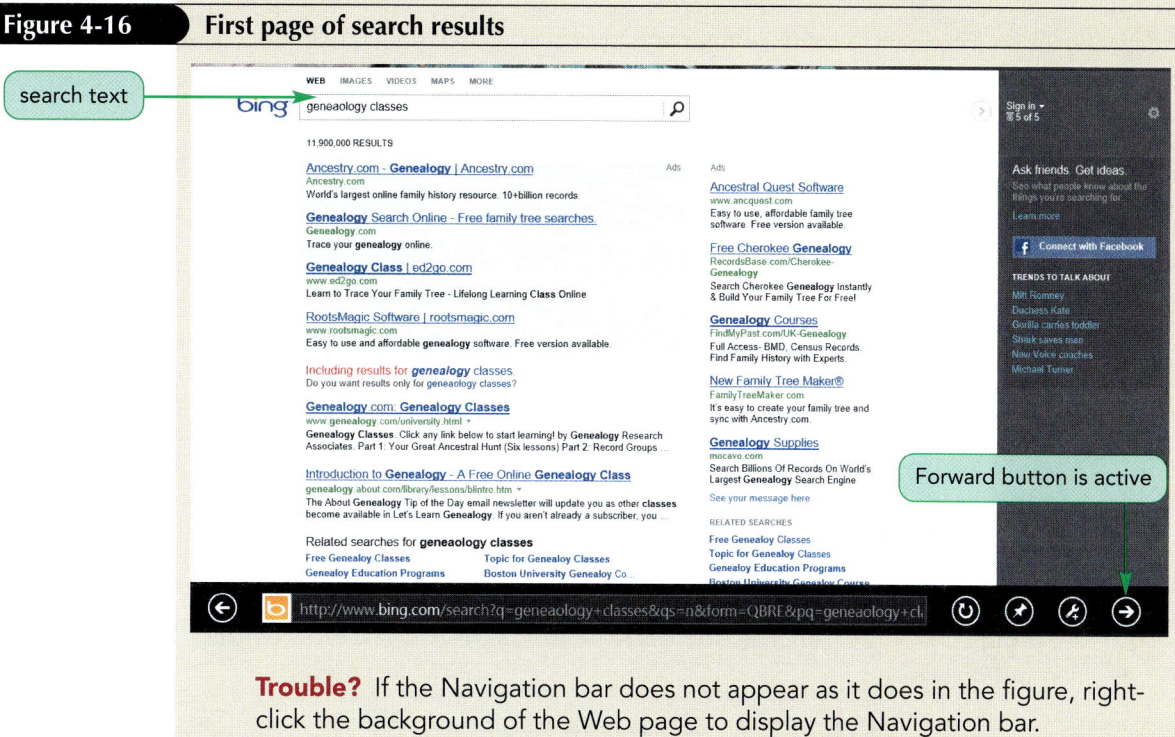

Figure 4-16 First page of search results

Trouble? If the Navigation bar does not appear as it does in the figure, right-click the background of the Web page to display the Navigation bar.

7. Click the **Forward** button ➡ to display the second page of search results.

8. Drag the top of the IE Windows 8 app down until it shrinks to a thumbnail, and then continue dragging it to the very bottom of the screen to close the app.

When you turn on the Flip ahead feature, you can still use the Back button on the Navigation bar as you usually do to navigate to the previous page you visited. To display the next page in a series of Web pages you visited during the current browser session, however, you use the right arrow button that appears in the middle of the screen when you move the mouse. The Forward button is reserved for navigating to the page a Web site designates as the next page in a sequence.

Next, you can switch to the desktop to use the other version of Internet Explorer 10—IE Desktop.

Using Internet Explorer on the Desktop

Using IE Desktop, you can perform all of the same tasks as you can with IE Windows 8, including opening Web pages, clicking links, navigating with Internet Explorer tools, and managing Web pages with tabbed browsing. The major difference between the two versions is the interface: IE Windows 8 is designed for touch browsing, while IE Desktop is designed for using a pointing device such as a mouse. IE Desktop features more controls and smaller buttons because you can make more precise selections with a pointer than you can with a fingertip. As mentioned earlier, the version you use depends on your current task. Usually, Windows starts the most appropriate version for you. For example, if you are working in a Windows 8 app and click a link to download a file or display information, Windows starts IE Windows 8. If you click a link while working in a desktop app, Windows starts IE Desktop.

IE Desktop provides more tools for Web browsing, especially if you are performing detailed work that requires precise control or lots of typing, such as using a Web app, completing forms, or conducting in-depth research. Jason asks you to start IE Desktop and give him a quick tour of its features.

To start Internet Explorer on the desktop:

1. Click the **Desktop** tile on the Start screen to display the desktop.
2. Click the **Internet Explorer** button on the taskbar.

   Trouble? If a Connection dialog box opens, enter your user name and password, and then click the Connect button. If you do not know your user name or password, ask your instructor or technical support person for help; you must have an Internet connection to complete the steps in this tutorial.

3. If necessary, click the **Maximize** button to maximize the Internet Explorer window. Figure 4-17 shows the Bing home page in the Internet Explorer window. You might have a different home page.

> **TIP**
> To change the home page displayed in IE Windows 8 or IE Desktop, start IE Desktop, navigate to the page you want to use, click the Tools button on the Command bar, click Internet options, and then click the Use current button on the General tab.

Figure 4-17   **IE Desktop window**

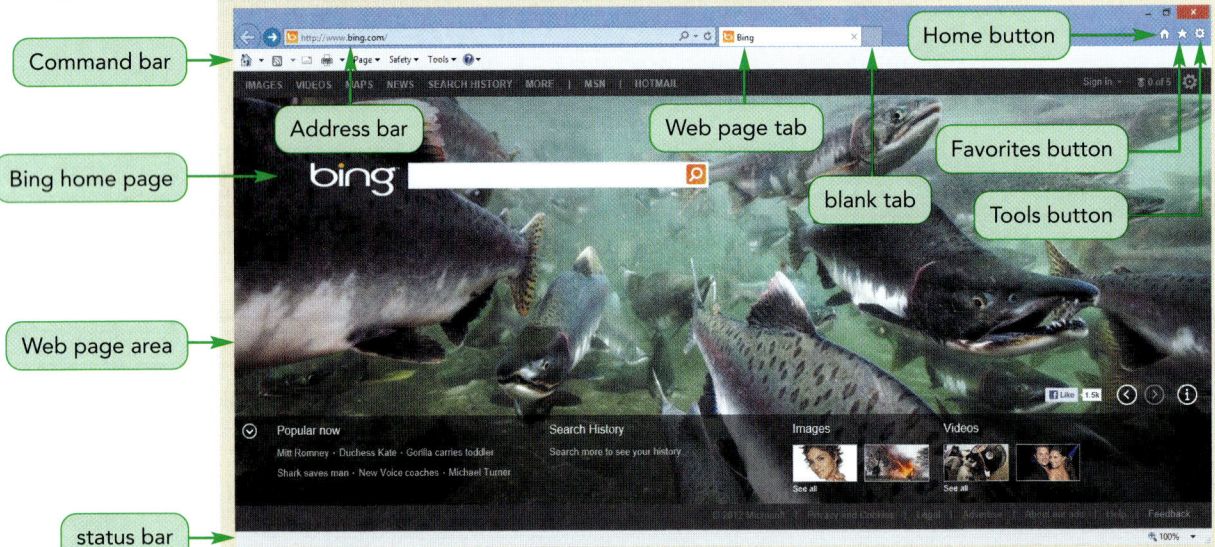

Trouble? If your IE Desktop window does not display the Command bar, right-click a blank area to the right of the tabs, and then click Command bar on the shortcut menu.

Trouble? If your Internet Explorer window does not display a status bar, click the Tools button on the Command bar, point to Toolbars, and then click Status bar.

The IE Desktop window includes the following elements:

- Address bar—Shows the address, or URL, of the Web page; you can also type an address here
- Command bar—Contains buttons you can click to perform common tasks, such as displaying the home page and printing a Web page

- Favorites button—Lets you open a pane displaying Web pages you've identified as favorites
- Home button—Lets you open the Web page specified as the home page for your browser
- Status bar— Shows information about the browser's actions; for example, indicates that a page is loading or is done loading
- Tab—Displays each Web page you open, letting you switch from one Web page to another
- Tools button—Lets you display a menu of options for working with IE Desktop
- Web page area—Shows the current Web page

Unlike IE Windows 8, IE Desktop includes a Command bar, a status bar, and a title bar, which are all typical elements in a window-based app. The Home and Tools buttons on the Command bar perform the same actions as the Home and Tools buttons on the right side of the Internet Explorer window.

Browsing Web Pages with IE Desktop

You browse Web pages using IE Desktop in the same way you do using IE Windows 8. Enter a URL or click a link to open a Web page and then use the browser tools to navigate from one page to another. Either version keeps track of the Web pages you visit so you can return to them quickly. The list of visited Web pages is called the **History list**. IE Desktop and IE Windows 8 share the same History list to make your Web browsing efficient no matter which version of Internet Explorer 10 you use. Instead of frequently entering the same URLs in the Address bar, you can begin to type an address and then let Internet Explorer's AutoComplete feature suggest the rest of the address, which it retrieves from the History list.

The National Archives Web site seemed to be the most promising resource for Jason as he prepares to teach workshops on researching family history. You'll show him how to explore that site using IE Desktop.

To browse Web pages and display them on separate tabs:

1. Click the **Address bar** to select the URL for your home page, and then type **www.arch**. After Internet Explorer fills in the rest of the URL for you (*ives.gov*), press the **Enter** key to display the home page for the National Archives Web site.

   Trouble? If Internet Explorer does not suggest the rest of the URL, type the complete address (www.archives.gov) and then press the Enter key.

2. Click the **Research Our Records** button to open the Research Our Records Web page.

3. Scroll down and then point to the **Research Your Ancestry** link to display the URL for the link in the status bar. See Figure 4-18. The Web page you open might look different. One way to tell if text or an image is a link in IE Desktop is to point to the item and then look in the status bar for the URL.

Figure 4-18 Research Our Records Web page

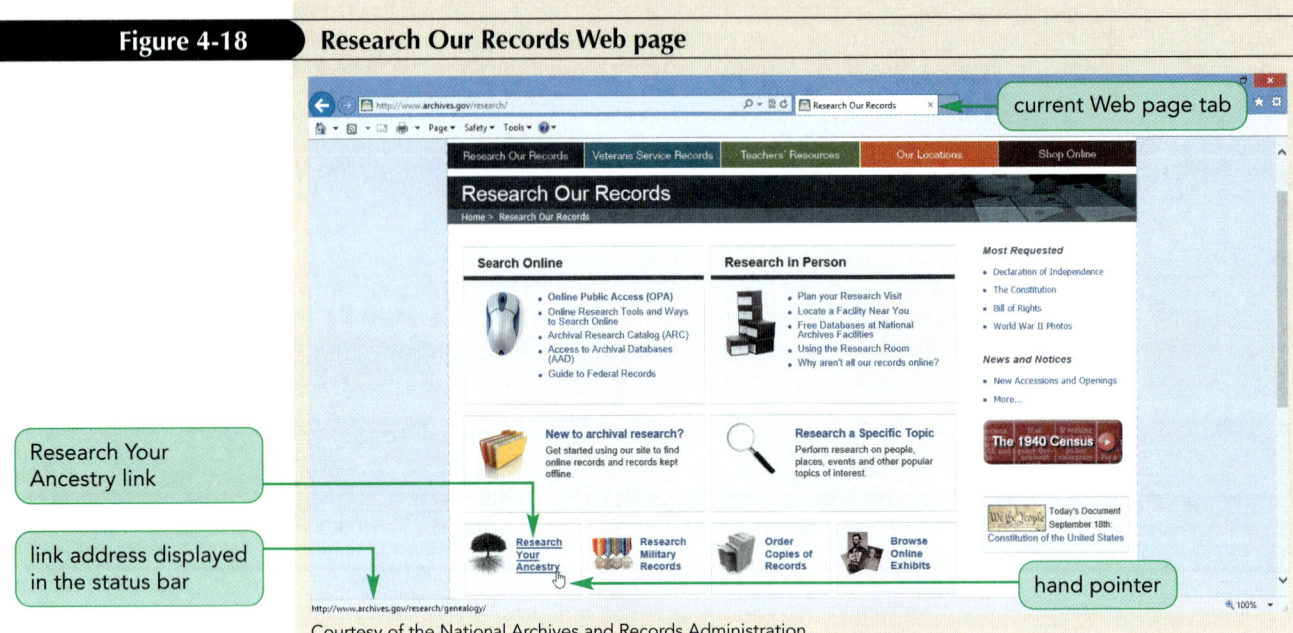

- Research Your Ancestry link
- link address displayed in the status bar
- current Web page tab
- hand pointer

Courtesy of the National Archives and Records Administration

▸ 4. Click the **Research Your Ancestry** link to open the Resources for Genealogists Web page.

   Trouble? If the Research Your Ancestry link does not appear on the current Web page, point to and then click any other link on the page.

▸ 5. Click the **Back** button ⬅ next to the Address bar to return to the Research Our Records Web page, and then click the **Forward** button ➡ next to the Address bar to return to the Resources for Genealogists page.

▸ 6. Press and hold the **Ctrl** key and then click the **Start Your Genealogy Research** link in the Start Your Family Research section. The Start Your Genealogy Research page opens on a new tab.

▸ 7. Press and hold the **Ctrl** key and then click the **Research Tips** link in the Start Your Family Research section. The Genealogy Research Tips page opens on a new tab. See Figure 4-19.

Figure 4-19 Three tabs open in IE Desktop

- tabs for the open pages
- New Tab button

Courtesy of the National Archives and Records Administration

▸ 8. Point to the **Genealogy Research Tips** tab and then click its **Close Tab** button ✕ to close the page. Use the same technique to close the **Start Your Genealogy Research** tab.

Tutorial 4 Working with the Internet and Email | Windows   WIN 183

9. Point to the **New Tab** button to display its icon, and then click the **New Tab** button to display a list of up to 10 Web sites you spend the most time using. This page is similar to the list of frequently visited sites displayed on the expanded Navigation bar in IE Windows 8. See Figure 4-20. The list of popular sites on your computer might differ.

Figure 4-20   New Tab page

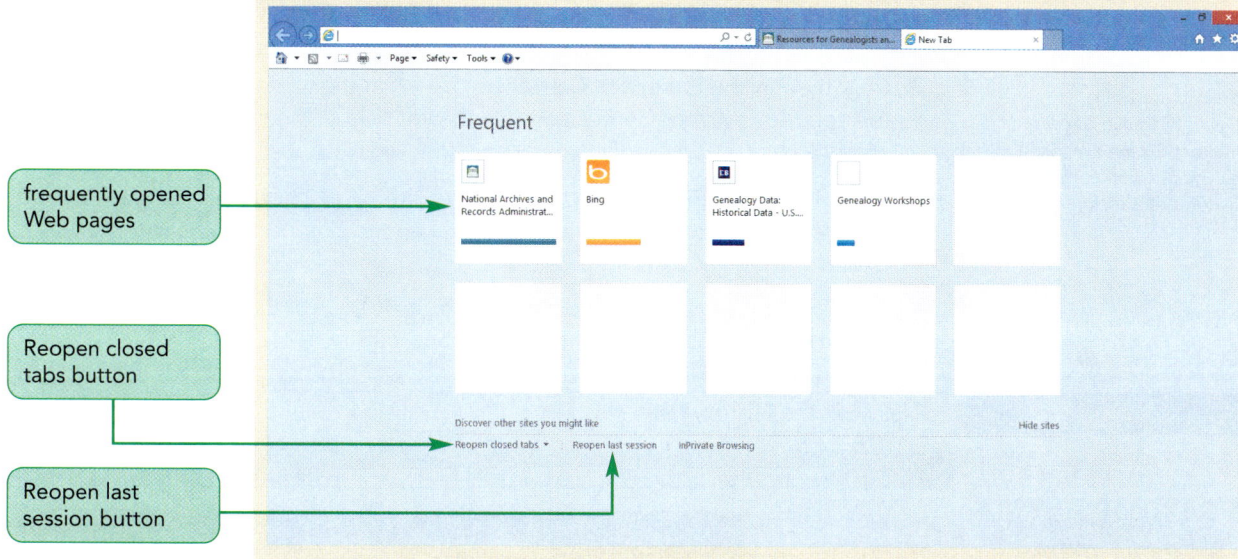

frequently opened Web pages

Reopen closed tabs button

Reopen last session button

TIP
To display all of the tabs you opened the last time you used IE Desktop, click the Reopen last session button.

10. Click the **Reopen closed tabs** button in the New Tab window, and then click **Open all closed tabs** to reopen the two tabs you closed.

11. Click the **Close** button on the Internet Explorer title bar to close IE Desktop. When a dialog box opens and asks if you want to close all tabs or the current tab, click the **Close all tabs** button.

   Trouble? If an Internet Explorer dialog box doesn't open, someone has already selected the Always close all tabs check box. All tabs will close automatically when you close Internet Explorer.

IE Desktop and IE Windows 8 share many of the same navigation features, including the Back and Forward buttons. One limitation of these buttons is that they apply only to your current session in the browser. If you close and then restart Internet Explorer, it starts keeping track of a fresh sequence of pages. To revisit Web pages you opened in previous sessions, you can use the History list.

Using the History List

To open any Web page you've recently visited, you can use the History list, which is available in the IE Desktop Favorites Center. The Favorites Center organizes Web page links and other information, including the History list. The History list includes the Web sites you visited today, last week, and up to three weeks ago by default. You can also click the View By Date button in the History list to change the default setup and view pages by date, by site, by the number of times visited, and in the order visited today. You can also search the pages in the History list to locate a specific Web site you've recently visited. Although both versions of Internet Explorer keep track of your browsing history, only IE Desktop lets you directly access the History list.

Jason wants to open the Web page on the National Archives Web site that provides tips for genealogy researchers. Because you already closed Internet Explorer, you can't use the Back button to return to that page. You'll use the History list to revisit the Genealogy Research Tips Web page.

To use the History list:

1. Start Internet Explorer on the desktop.

2. Click the **Favorites** button ⭐ to open the Favorites Center on the right side of the Internet Explorer window.

3. Click the **Pin the Favorites Center** button at the top of the Favorites Center to keep the Favorites Center open on the left side of the Internet Explorer window.

   > Be sure to pin the Favorites Center to the Internet Explorer window so you can work with its features efficiently.

   Trouble? If the Pin the Favorites Center button does not appear in your Favorites Center, the Favorites Center is already pinned to the Internet Explorer window. Skip Step 3.

4. If the History tab in the Favorites Center is not currently displayed, click the **History** tab to display the History list. See Figure 4-21.

Figure 4-21 Displaying the History list

- click a calendar icon to expand the list of Web sites visited
- your History list might include additional dates

Trouble? If your History list is not organized by date, click the View By button and then click View By Date.

5. Click **Today** in the History list. The list expands to show the Web sites you visited today.

6. Click **archives (www.archives.gov)** to expand the list to show the pages you visited on the National Archives Web site.

7. Click **Genealogy Research Tips**. The corresponding Web page opens in Internet Explorer. See Figure 4-22.

Figure 4-22 Revisiting a Web page

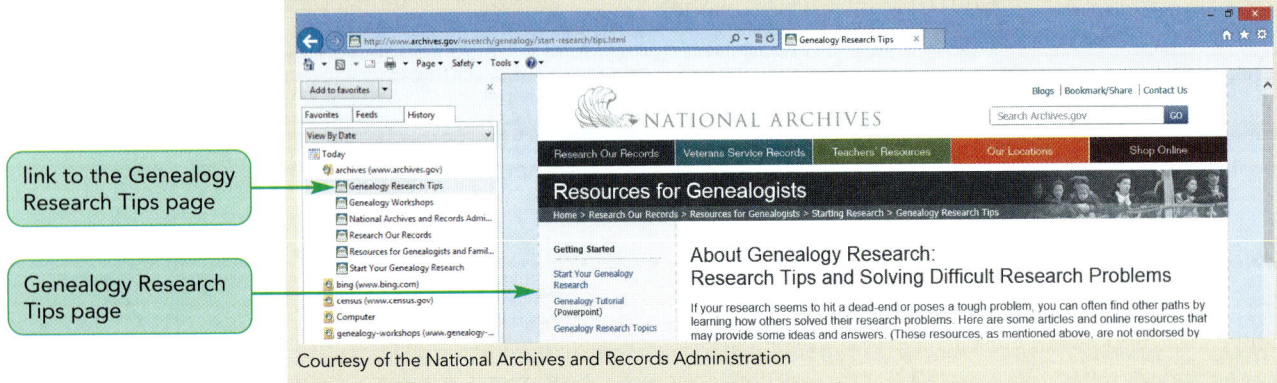

- link to the Genealogy Research Tips page
- Genealogy Research Tips page

Courtesy of the National Archives and Records Administration

Although the History list helps you access Web pages you opened recently, the Favorites Center helps you organize Web pages you open often, which you'll show Jason next.

Using Favorites

As you explore the Web, you'll find pages that are your favorites—those you visit frequently. When you use IE Desktop, you can save the location of your favorite Web pages in the Favorites list, a collection of links to the Web pages that you visit often. To display the Favorites list, you open the Favorites Center, where you can manage the Favorites list, Feeds, and the History list. The Favorites list initially includes a few folders of links, such as those to Microsoft Web sites. Your computer manufacturer might also include a few links in the Favorites list. If you find a Web page you want to visit often, you can add it to your Favorites list. When you want to retrieve one of your favorite Web pages, you can click its link in the Favorites list and display the page in your browser. As your list of favorite pages grows, you can organize the links into folders. For example, you could create a Favorites folder for travel Web sites and another for news Web sites.

To display the Favorites list:

1. Click the **Favorites** tab in the Favorites Center to display the Favorites list. See Figure 4-23. Your Favorites list might be different.

Figure 4-23 Displaying the Favorites list

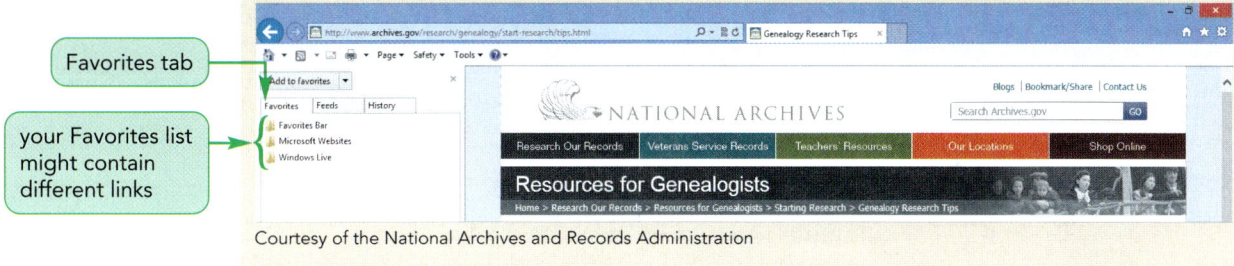

Courtesy of the National Archives and Records Administration

The Genealogy Research Tips Web page provides the kind of information Jason will refer to often when preparing workshops for the San Antonio Historical Association. You'll add that page to the Favorites list.

Adding an Item to the Favorites List

To add a Web page to the Favorites list, you access the page in IE Desktop, and then you use the Add to favorites command. By default, IE Desktop adds the new page to the end of the Favorites list. If you organize the Web pages into folders, you can add a Web page to one of the folders. You can store the page using the title of the Web page as its name, or you can change the name so it is more descriptive or meaningful to you.

REFERENCE

Adding a Web Page to the Favorites List

- Open the Web page in IE Desktop.
- Open the Favorites Center.
- Click the Add to favorites button in the Favorites Center.
- Enter a new name for the Web page and select a folder, if necessary.
- Click the Add button.

TIP

In IE Windows 8, right-click the Web page, click the Pin site button, and then click Add to favorites.

To add Web pages to your Favorites list:

1. With the Genealogy Research Tips page displayed in IE Desktop, click the **Add to favorites** button in the Favorites Center. The Add a Favorite dialog box opens, displaying the name of the Web page in the Name text box. You can change the name of the Web page, but the default name here makes the page easy to identify.

2. With Genealogy Research Tips displayed in the Name text box, click the **Add** button to add the Web page to the Favorites list.

Next, you can organize your favorite Web pages into folders.

Organizing the Favorites List

As you add more items to the Favorites list, you can organize its links by deleting some and moving others to new folders. Using folders is an excellent way to organize your favorite Web pages.

REFERENCE

Organizing the Favorites List

- Click the Add to favorites button arrow in the Favorites Center, and then click Organize favorites to open the Organize Favorites dialog box.
- To create a new folder, click the New Folder button, enter a folder name, and then press the Enter key.
- To move a link into a Favorites folder, drag the link to the folder, or select the item, click the Move button, select the new folder for the item, and then click the OK button.
- To remove an item from the Favorites list, select the item, and then click the Delete button.
- Click the Close button to close the Organize Favorites dialog box.

TIP

If you have many links and folders in the Favorites list, use the Move button in the Organize Favorites dialog box instead of dragging.

To organize your Favorites list:

1. Click the **Add to favorites button arrow** in the Favorites Center, and then click **Organize favorites**. The Organize Favorites dialog box opens.

   Trouble? If the Add a Favorite dialog box opens, you clicked the Add to favorites button instead of the arrow. Close the Add a Favorite dialog box, and then repeat Step 1.

2. Click the **New Folder** button, type **Ancestry Research** as the new folder name, and then press the **Enter** key.

3. In the Organize Favorites dialog box, drag the **Genealogy Research Tips** link to the Ancestry Research folder.

4. Click the **Close** button to close the Organize Favorites dialog box.

5. Click **Ancestry Research** in the Favorites list to display the contents of the folder. The new link you added is now stored in the Ancestry Research folder in the Favorites list.

Next, you want to show Jason another way to work with favorites—the Favorites bar.

Adding Pages and Feeds to the Favorites Bar

The Favorites bar provides another way to quickly access your favorite Web pages. The Favorites bar contains links to Web pages you view often and buttons for RSS feeds you subscribe to. An **RSS feed** (or **feed** for short) is frequently updated Web site content, such as news or commentary, delivered directly to your computing device when you are connected to the Internet. You can also use feeds to download audio content, such as a **podcast**, which is typically one of a series of audio files containing radio programs, comedy, or other information that you listen to on your computer or portable device.

When you visit a Web page that provides a feed or podcast, the Feeds button on the Favorites bar changes color to let you know that feeds are available. You can click the Feeds button and, if more than one feed is available, select one to subscribe to the feed. After you subscribe, you can add a feed to the Favorites bar so you can access the content quickly. When a feed publishes new information, Internet Explorer bolds the text in its button on the Favorites bar to alert you to the updated information.

First, you want to show Jason how to add the National Archives home page to the Favorites bar because you know he will use that page often. The Favorites bar is not open by default, so you need to open it before you can add links to it.

To display the Favorites bar and add a link to it:

1. Click the **Tools** button on the Command bar, point to **Toolbars**, and then click **Favorites bar**. The Favorites bar appears in the Internet Explorer window, shifting the Command bar to the right.

2. Click the **History** tab in the Favorites Center, and then click the **National Archives and Records Administration** link to display the National Archives home page.

3. Click the **Add to Favorites bar** button on the Favorites bar to add the National Archives home page to the Favorites bar. See Figure 4-24.

Figure 4-24   Adding a link to the Favorites bar

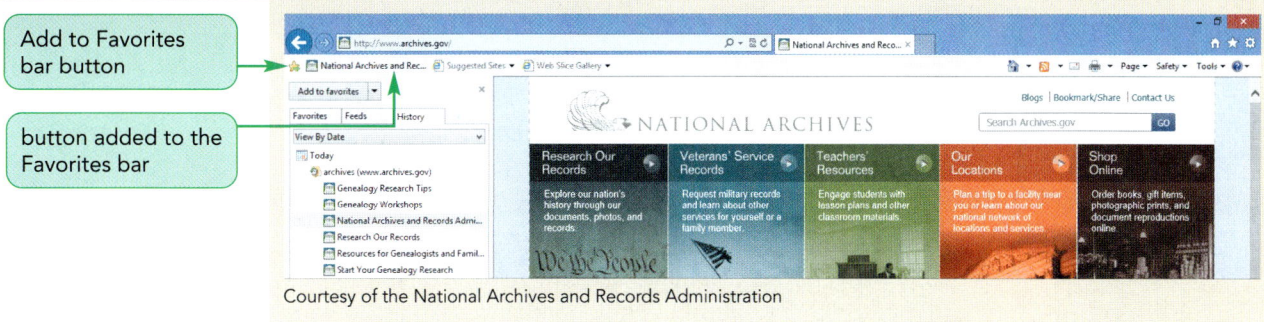

Courtesy of the National Archives and Records Administration

Jason wants to keep up with news and events at the National Archives. The Web site hosts a number of **blogs**, short for "Web logs," which are Web pages where an author or a group of authors post comments, articles, opinion, and other information on a regular basis. Each published piece of content is called a **blog post**. You can often subscribe to a blog as an RSS feed to access the changing information. You'll show Jason how to add a feed for a National Archives blog to the Favorites bar.

To add a feed to the Favorites bar:

1. Scroll to display the lower-right part of the National Archives home page, and then click the **Blogs** link in the Connect With Us list to display a list of blogs the National Archives hosts.
2. Scroll down the page and then click the **Prologue: Pieces of History** button to display the blog for Prologue, a magazine the National Archives publishes. The Feeds button on the Favorites bar is orange, indicating the page provides an RSS feed to which you can subscribe. See Figure 4-25.

Figure 4-25   RSS feed detected on the Web page

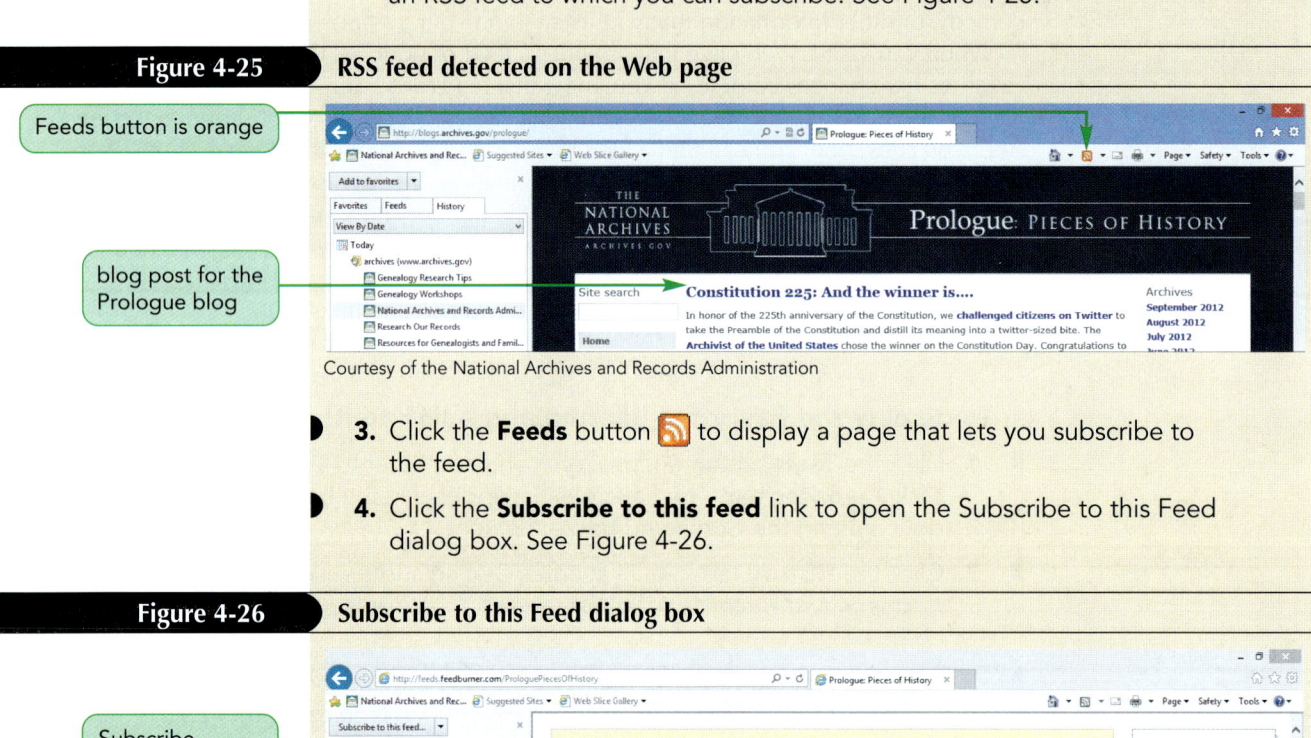

Courtesy of the National Archives and Records Administration

3. Click the **Feeds** button to display a page that lets you subscribe to the feed.
4. Click the **Subscribe to this feed** link to open the Subscribe to this Feed dialog box. See Figure 4-26.

Figure 4-26   Subscribe to this Feed dialog box

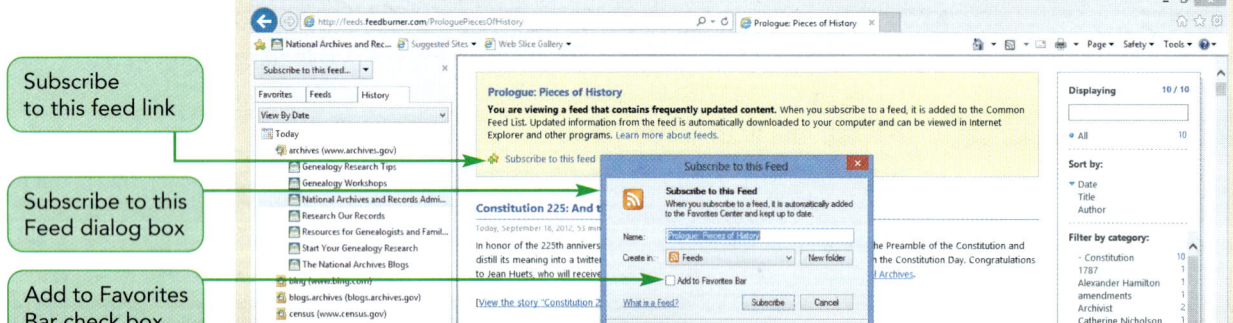

5. Click the **Add to Favorites Bar** check box and then click the **Subscribe** button to add a button for the Prologue: Pieces of History feed to the Favorites bar.

Another way to quickly access Web pages you open often is to pin them to the taskbar, which is similar to pinning them to the Start screen.

Pinning a Web Page to the Taskbar

If you want to open a Web page directly from the desktop without starting IE Desktop, you can pin the page to the taskbar. Doing so creates a shortcut to the Web page, which appears as a button on the taskbar. When you click the button for the pinned page, a streamlined IE Desktop window opens to display the page. Because you are probably using the pinned page for quick reference, this window contains fewer controls than the full version of IE Desktop. For example, it does not display the Command bar or Favorites bar.

Jason thinks he will often use the Resources for Genealogists page on the National Archives site. You'll pin this page to the taskbar and then show Jason how to open the page.

To pin a Web page to the taskbar:

1. On the History tab in the Favorites Center, click the **Resources for Genealogists and Family Historians** link to open the Web page.
2. Drag the **Resources for Genealogists and Family Historians** tab from the Internet Explorer window to the taskbar. When the Pin to Taskbar ScreenTip appears, release the mouse button to pin the page to the taskbar. See Figure 4-27.

Figure 4-27   Pinning a Web page to the taskbar

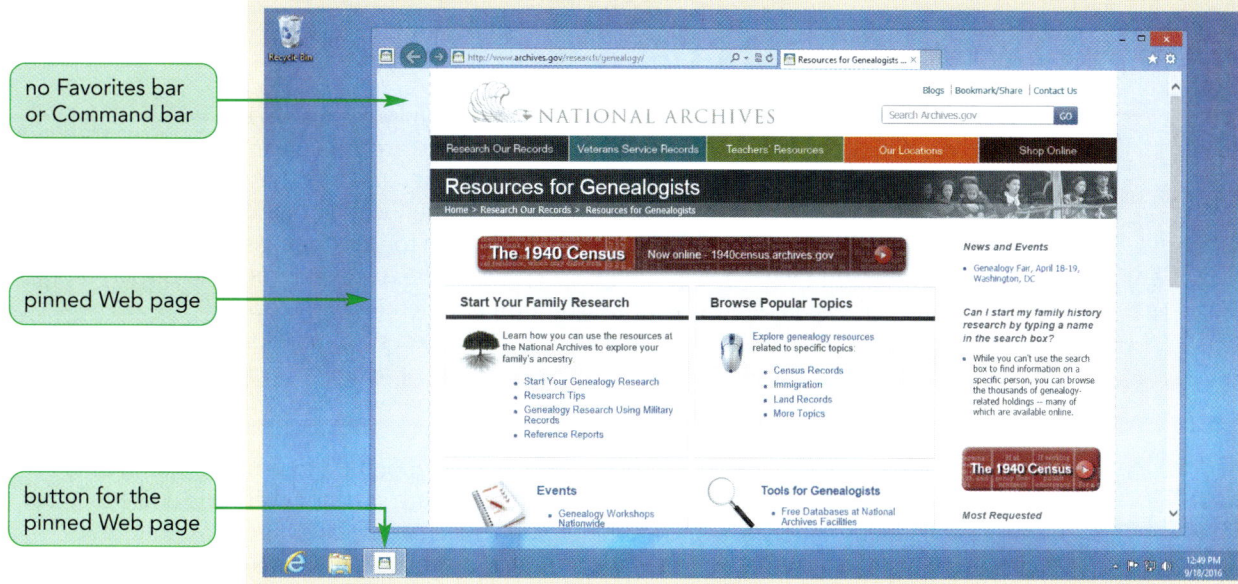

- no Favorites bar or Command bar
- pinned Web page
- button for the pinned Web page

Courtesy of the National Archives and Records Administration

3. Click the **Close** button on the Internet Explorer title bar to close Internet Explorer.
4. Click the **Resources for Genealogists and Family Historians** button on the taskbar to open the Web page in its own window.
5. Close Internet Explorer.

Now when Jason is working on the desktop, he can easily access the Web pages he needs in the Favorites list, on the Favorites bar, and on the taskbar.

> ### INSIGHT
>
> ### Letting Internet Explorer Suggest Sites
>
> To help you discover Web sites that might interest you, you can use the Suggested Sites feature. When you turn on Suggested Sites, Internet Explorer reviews the Web pages open in your browser and those stored in your browsing history. Based on that information, it suggests other Web sites related to the content of the sites you visit most often. To view these suggestions, you click the See Suggested Sites button on the Favorites bar. When you use Suggested Sites, Internet Explorer sends your browsing history to Microsoft for analysis. Suggested Sites is turned off by default to protect your privacy. To turn it on, you can click the Tools button on the Command bar, point to File, click Suggested Sites, and then click the Yes button. When selected, this option appears with a check mark on the File menu. If you want to prevent Internet Explorer from sending your browsing history to Microsoft, turn off Suggested Sites by clicking the Tools button on the Command bar, pointing to File, and then clicking Suggested Sites to remove the check mark.

Finding and Using Accelerators

Accelerators are tools that make it easier to find information on the Web without navigating to other Web sites. For example, if you are viewing a Web page about a hotel in a city you plan to visit, you can select the hotel's address, and then use an Accelerator to quickly display a map showing the location of the hotel. Instead of copying the address, navigating to the Web page for a mapping service, pasting the address, and then viewing a map, you point to the Accelerator icon to display a preview of the map. In this case, you perform one step instead of four.

Accelerators are services provided by Web sites, so some sites have them and others do not. Internet Explorer comes with a selection of default Accelerators, including Map with Bing and Translate with Bing. You can add or remove Accelerators as necessary using the Manage Add-ons dialog box.

Jason plans to visit Washington, DC, in a few months. He wants to spend time at the National Archives and possibly attend a lecture or other event. He'd like to know where the National Archives building is located as he plans his trip. A colleague recommended a hotel in Washington, near the intersection of North Capitol Street NW and New York Avenue NE, and Jason wants to determine if the hotel is near the National Archives. You can use a button on the Favorites bar to open the home page for the National Archives, and then use the Bing Maps Accelerator to find the building on a map.

To use the Bing Maps Accelerator:

1. Start Internet Explorer on the desktop, and then click the **Close the Favorites Center** button to close the Favorites Center. Maximize the window.

2. Click the **National Archives and Records Administration** button on the Favorites bar to open the National Archives home page.

3. Click the **Our Locations** button near the top of the page to display a list of National Archives locations.

   Trouble? If a Select a Location window opens, click its close link to close the window.

4. On the Locations Nationwide page, select the address of the National Archives in Washington, DC. A blue Accelerator icon appears next to the selected text. See Figure 4-28. Your Accelerator might appear in a different location.

| Figure 4-28 | Displaying an Accelerator |

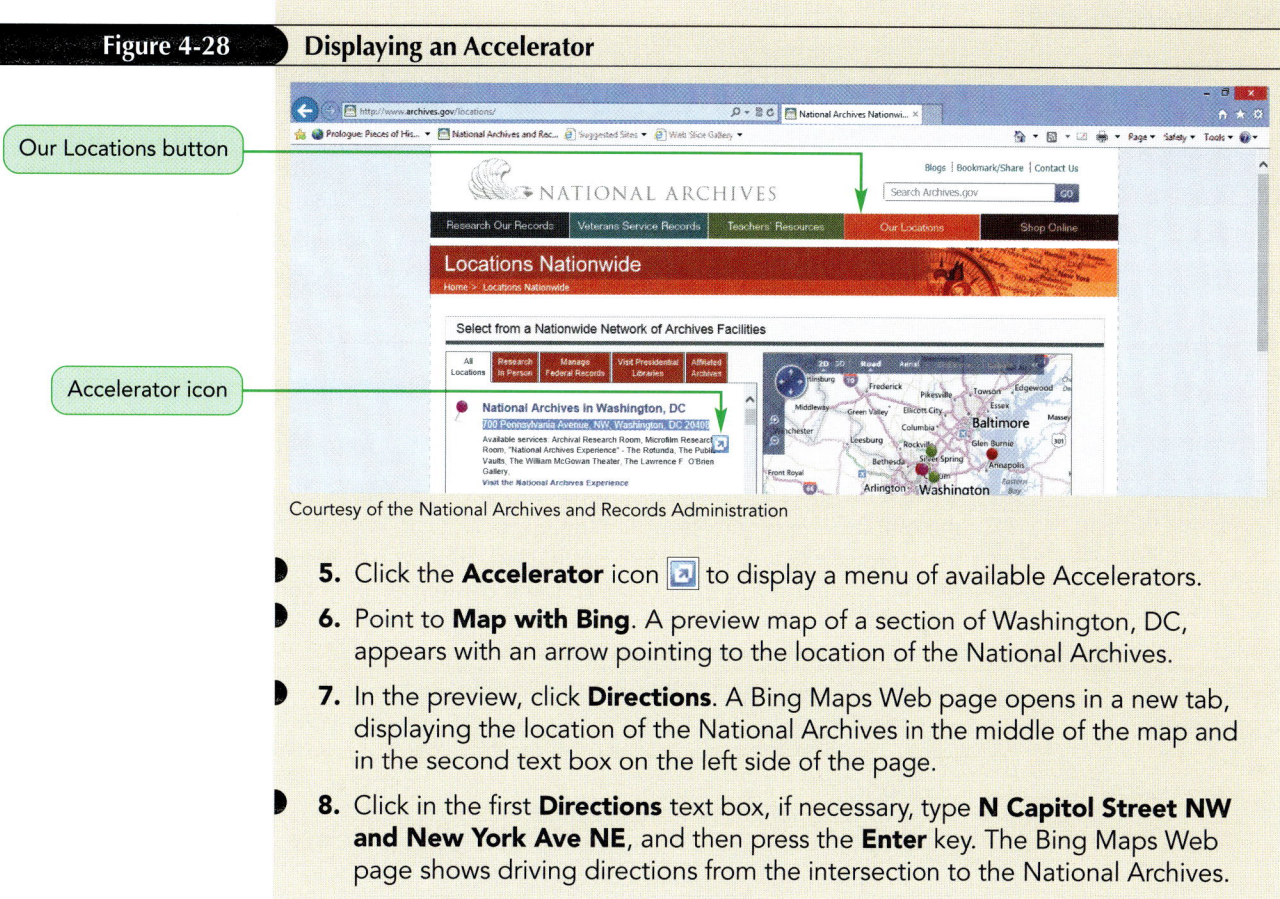

Courtesy of the National Archives and Records Administration

▶ 5. Click the **Accelerator** icon to display a menu of available Accelerators.

▶ 6. Point to **Map with Bing**. A preview map of a section of Washington, DC, appears with an arrow pointing to the location of the National Archives.

▶ 7. In the preview, click **Directions**. A Bing Maps Web page opens in a new tab, displaying the location of the National Archives in the middle of the map and in the second text box on the left side of the page.

▶ 8. Click in the first **Directions** text box, if necessary, type **N Capitol Street NW and New York Ave NE**, and then press the **Enter** key. The Bing Maps Web page shows driving directions from the intersection to the National Archives.

Printing and Saving Web Pages

If you find a page on the Web and want to refer to it when you don't have computer access, you can print the Web page. Sometimes, Web pages include a Printer-Friendly Format link or other similar link for printing a Web page, indicating that the Web site formats the page for a standard size sheet of paper before printing. However, not all Web pages provide such an option. Therefore, you should preview the page before you print it to see how it will look when printed. To preview a Web page, click the Print button arrow on the Command bar and then click Print preview. To print a page from Print preview, click the Print Document button on the Print Preview toolbar. To print a Web page without previewing it, you click the Print button on the Command bar.

You can also save Web pages and their content. To save a Web page as a file on your computer, click the Page button on the Command bar, and then click Save as. Enter a name for the file in the File name text box, and then select one of the four file types described in Figure 4-29 by clicking the Save as type button.

Figure 4-29 File types for Web pages

File Type	Description
Webpage, complete	Saves all files associated with the page, including graphics, frames, and style sheets in their original format
Web Archive, single file	Saves all information as a single file
Webpage, HTML only	Saves only the current page without graphics or other media files
Text File	Saves only the text on the current page

© 2014 Cengage Learning

PROSKILLS

Decision Making: Determining Whether to Save Web Page Content

Using a browser, you can easily save Web page content on your computer, including the graphic images displayed on the page, files the Web page provides, such as text or music files, and the Web page itself. However, doing so is not always legal or ethical. Before you save any Web page content on your computer, you need to determine whether you have the legal right to do so. This is especially important when you want to save and use images, video, and other media for work projects because commercial use of such content is often prohibited.

Web content such as software, video, music, and images is easy to copy in its digital form. However, if this material is protected by copyright, you usually are not allowed to copy or share it unless you receive permission from the owner. The term **copyright** refers to the originator's exclusive legal right to reproduce, publish, or sell works he or she creates. If you copy someone else's work without giving that person credit, you are committing plagiarism, and you may also be violating copyright laws.

Before you copy or save content from Web sites that you visit, you need to find out if and how you can use the materials. If you want to use material you find on a Web site, first get permission from the owner of the site. Often, Web sites include links to their copyright and permission-request information on their main pages. Even if you think that information or material you found is not copyrighted, you should always request permission to use it and give credit to any Web site that you use in your work or school projects.

Jason does not want to print or save any information you found for the National Archives because he can access it quickly using Internet Explorer tools. You can exit Internet Explorer.

To close tabs and exit Internet Explorer:

▶ 1. Click the **Close** button ☒ on the Internet Explorer title bar.
▶ 2. Click the **Close all tabs** button in the Internet Explorer dialog box to close all tabs.

So far, you have learned about the structure of the Internet and the Web, and how to use the Windows 8 and desktop versions of Internet Explorer to open, navigate, and organize Web pages. In the next session, you'll use another service the Internet provides—email.

REVIEW

Session 4.1 Quick Check

1. A(n) _____ is a collection of Web pages that have a common theme or focus.
2. Explain the difference between IE Windows 8 and IE Desktop.
3. What are two definitions for the term *home page*?
4. When you use tabbed browsing in IE Windows 8, what does each tab display?
5. You can display the _____ while you are using IE Windows 8 to perform Internet Explorer tasks such as searching for Web sites, printing Web page content, and selecting IE Windows 8 settings.
6. In IE Desktop, you can open the _____ to display a list of Web sites you visited today.
7. Explain why you would use an Accelerator in Internet Explorer.
8. What is an RSS feed?

Session 4.2 Visual Overview:

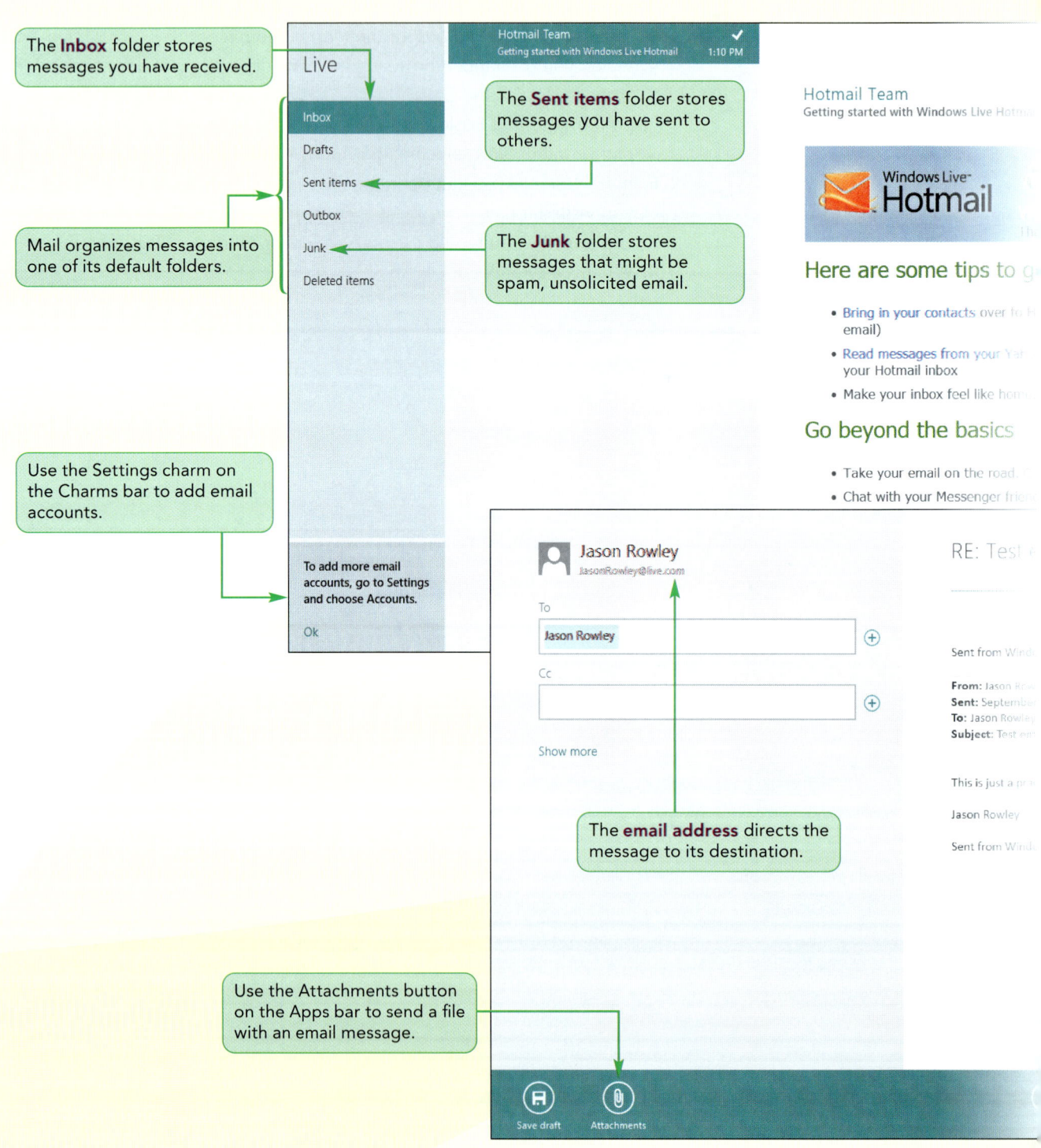

Tutorial 4 Working with the Internet and Email | Windows   WIN 195

Windows 8 Mail App

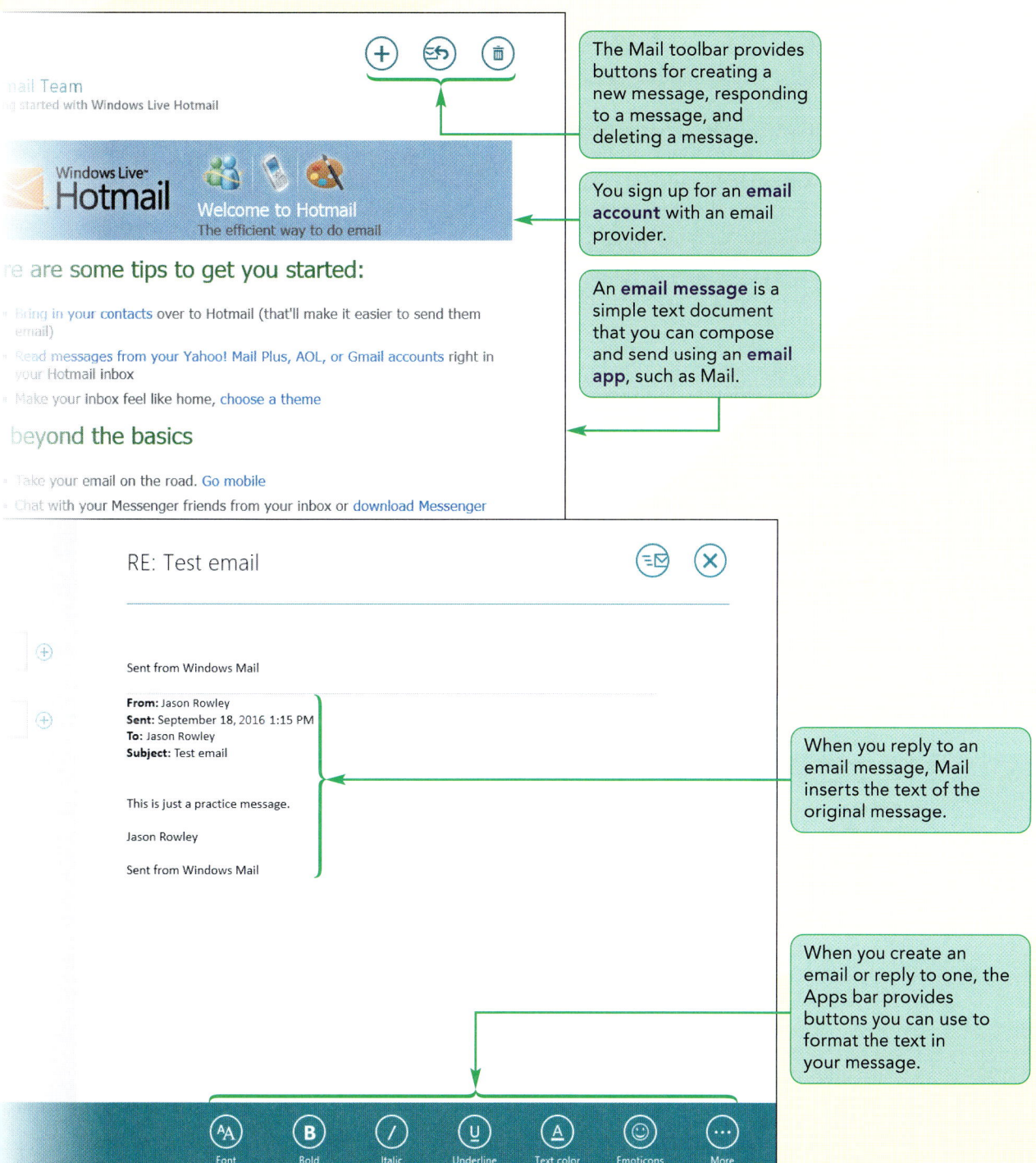

Getting Started with Mail

As you learned, the Web is a service that the Internet provides. Another service is electronic mail, or email. Just as you use a browser, such as Internet Explorer, to use the Web, you can use an email application to work with email. Windows 8 includes Mail, a Windows 8 app that you use to send, receive, and manage email. If you're like most computer users, you exchange many email messages every day with friends, family, colleagues, and other contacts. You probably also receive newsletters, coupons, offers, and other types of messages from companies and organizations. You might start your email app as soon as you turn on your computer and leave it running until you shut down at the end of the day. In short, email is a central part of your computing activities.

Using Mail, you can send email to and receive email from anyone in the world who has an email address, regardless of the operating system or type of computer the person is using. Although this tutorial provides steps for using the Mail app, the concepts and activities the tutorial covers apply to any email application, including Microsoft Outlook, Outlook.com, and Windows Live Mail.

> **TIP**
> You can also download and install Windows Live Mail, a Windows Essentials application that runs on the desktop. Visit the Microsoft Windows Web site at windows.microsoft.com, and then search for *Windows Essentials*.

Examining How Email Works

An email message is a simple text document that you can compose and send using an email program, such as the Windows 8 Mail app. When you send a message, it travels from your computer, through a network, and arrives at a computer called an **email server**. The email server stores the email messages until the recipients request them. Then the server forwards the messages to the appropriate computers. Typically, the system administrator of your network or ISP manages the email server.

Email uses **store-and-forward technology**, which means you can send messages to anyone on the Internet or a network, even if a recipient's computer isn't turned on. When it's convenient, your recipients log on to the Internet or network and use their email programs to receive and read their messages. Figure 4-30 illustrates the process of sending and receiving email messages.

Figure 4-30 Sending and receiving email

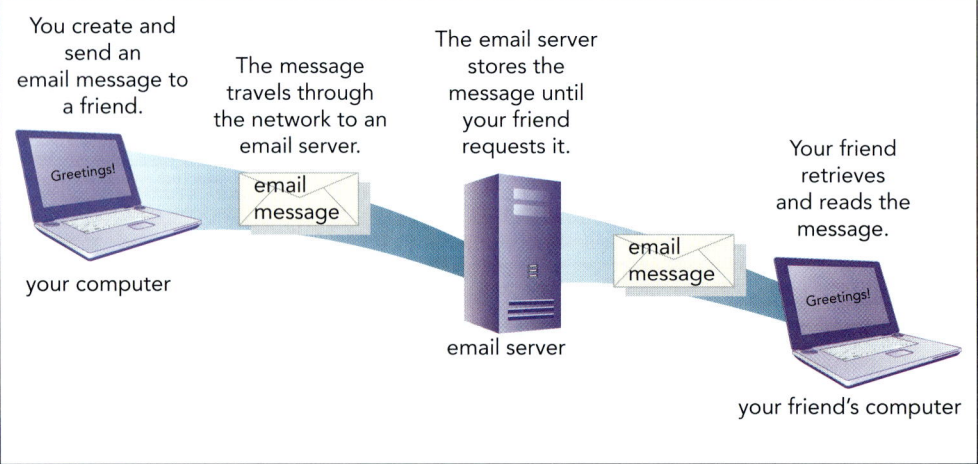

© 2014 Cengage Learning

To send and receive email, you must be able to access an email server on the network. If your computer is part of a network at a college or university, for example, you log on to the network to access its services. An email server provides mail services to faculty, staff, and students who have access to the network. When someone sends you a message, it is stored on your email server until you log on to the network and use an email program to check your mail. The email server then transfers new messages to your electronic mailbox. You use an email program to open, read, print, delete, reply to, forward, and save the mail.

If your computer is not part of a network, you can access an email server on the Internet. To do so, you open an email account with a service that provides Internet access. For example, email accounts are included as part of the subscription fee for most ISPs. Email accounts are also provided free of charge by advertiser-supported Web sites, such as Outlook.com and Google. After you establish an email account, you can connect to the Internet to send and receive your email messages.

Addressing Email

Just as you must address a piece of ordinary mail, you need to supply an address for an email message. The email address you enter directs the message to its destination. Your email address is included in the message as the return address, so your recipients can easily respond to your message. Anyone who has an email address can send and receive electronic mail. If you work for a company or attend a school that provides email, a system administrator probably assigns an email address for you. Other times, you create your own email address, though it must follow a particular format. See Figure 4-31.

Figure 4-31 Typical format of an email address

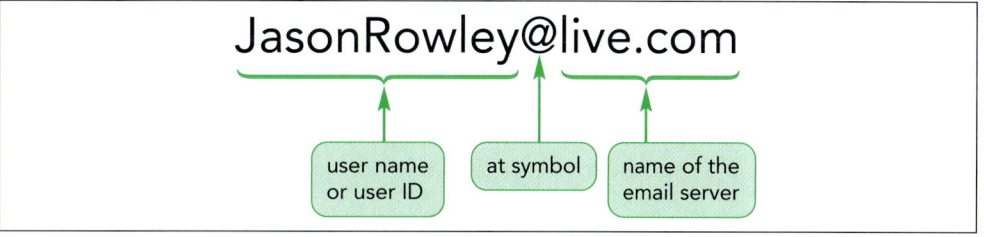

© 2014 Cengage Learning

The **user name**, or **user ID**, is the name entered when your email account is set up. The @ symbol signifies that the email server name is provided next. For example, "JasonRowley" is the user name and "live.com" is the email server.

The easiest way to learn a person's email address is to ask the person what it is. You can also look up an email address in a network or Internet directory. Most businesses and schools publish a directory listing email addresses of those who have email accounts on their network. Many Web sites also provide email directories for people with email accounts on the Internet, such as Yahoo! People Search at people.yahoo.com.

When you sign up for an email account, you can send your new email address to friends, colleagues, and clients. If your email address changes, such as when you change email services, you can subscribe to an email forwarding service so you don't miss any mail sent to your old address.

Setting Up Mail

To use email, you need an Internet connection, an email program, and an email address. Make sure you have an Internet connection and email address before performing the steps in this section. Having an email address means you have an email account, which is space on an email server reserved for your messages. You set up an account with an email service provider, which can be an ISP, an employer or school, or a Web service such as Outlook.com or Gmail.

You can set up the following types of email accounts in Mail:

- Hotmail—Microsoft offers Hotmail as a free Web-based email service.
- Outlook—This type of account can be an Exchange, Office 365, or Outlook.com account. Organizations such as a business or school typically offer Exchange accounts, which reside on an Exchange server. Home users usually do not have Exchange accounts.

- Google—Google provides Gmail, another free Web-based email service.
- Other—Account types other than Hotmail, Outlook, and Gmail, such as Internet Message Access Protocol (IMAP) accounts, which are often provided by ISPs.

If you already have one of these types of email accounts, you can set up Mail to send and receive email by starting Mail and then entering the user name and password you use for the account. If you use more than one of these email accounts, you can add them to Mail. For example, you might have an Exchange account at work or school and an Outlook.com account you use for personal email. Instead of switching from one email account to another, you can use Mail to receive email from your Exchange and Outlook.com accounts so you can manage all of your email from a single app.

If you do not have any of these types of email accounts, you can set up a free Outlook.com or Gmail account. To set up an Outlook.com account, use a browser to go to Outlook.com. Sign up for a Microsoft account by providing your name and other information and then selecting an account name (which is the same as a user name) and a password. If you start Mail before signing up for a Microsoft account, Mail lets you sign up as part of the email setup process. You can also set up a Gmail account in a similar way. Use a browser to go to mail.google.com, provide your name and other information, and then select a user name and password.

INSIGHT

Using a Microsoft Account

A Microsoft account provides access to online services such as SkyDrive for file storage and Outlook.com for email. You can sign in to a Microsoft account on any device connected to the Internet. When you do, you can read and respond to your Outlook.com email messages or access files stored on SkyDrive. If you access Outlook.com on a public computer, for example, and then return to your Windows 8 home computer, your email messages and responses also appear in Mail. Your Microsoft account synchronizes Outlook.com and Mail so your messages are up to date in either place.

Jason has an Outlook.com account, but he hasn't set up Mail to use it yet. Because this is the first time you're starting Mail on his Windows 8 computer, you'll show Jason how to set up Mail to use his Outlook.com account. The following steps assume that you have a Microsoft account.

To set up Mail:

1. If necessary, press the **Windows** key to display the Start screen.
2. Click the **Mail** tile to start the Mail app. If this is the first time you started Mail, the Sign in with a Microsoft account screen opens, requesting your Microsoft account information.

   Trouble? If you have already set up Mail, the main Mail screen opens instead of the Sign in with a Microsoft account screen. Read but do not perform the rest of the steps.

   Trouble? If you do not have a Microsoft account, click the Don't have a Microsoft account? Sign up now link, follow the instructions on the Microsoft Web site to create a Microsoft account, and then repeat Step 2.

   Trouble? If a dialog box opens asking if you want Mail to be your default mail program, click the Yes button only if you are using your own computer and want to use Mail as your mail program. If you are using a school or institutional computer, click the No button or ask your technical support person for assistance.

3. Enter the account name you use for your Hotmail or Outlook.com account, such as **JasonRowley@live.com**.
4. Click the **Password** text box, and then enter the password for the account.
5. Click the **Sign in** button. If this is the first time you are signing in to Mail, the app connects to your Hotmail account and displays messages received in that account.

Now you can show Jason how to send and receive email.

Sending and Receiving Email Using Mail

You can use the Mail app to compose, send, and receive email messages. After you set up an email account, you're ready to start using Mail to manage your email.

To start Mail:

1. Start Mail, if necessary (click the **Mail** tile on the Start screen). Figure 4-32 shows the Mail screen. The email account shown in the figures in this tutorial belongs to Jason Rowley. Your screens will look different from the figures.

Figure 4-32   Mail app

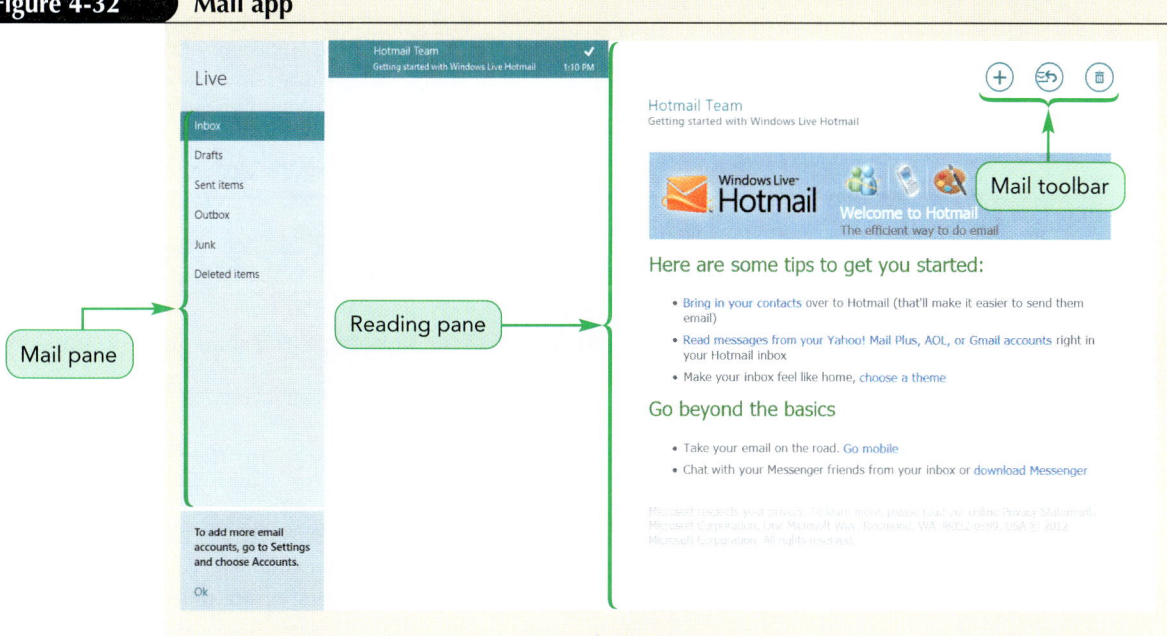

The Mail app includes the following tools and components:

- Mail pane—This part of the Mail screen lists your email accounts at the top followed by the default Mail folders, including the Inbox, Drafts, Sent items, Outbox, Junk, and Deleted items folders. Mail organizes your email into these folders automatically.
- Reading pane—This pane displays the contents of the selected message.
- Mail toolbar—The toolbar provides buttons for frequently performed commands, such as creating, replying to, and deleting email.

Creating and Sending Email Messages

An email message uses a format similar to a standard memo, which typically includes Date, To, and Subject lines, followed by the content of the message. The To line indicates who will receive the message. Windows 8 Mail automatically supplies the date you send the message (as set in your computer's clock). The Subject line, although optional, alerts the recipient to the topic of the message. You should always include a Subject line because people often delete messages without reading them if they do not contain subjects. Finally, the message area contains the content of your message. You can also include additional information, such as a Cc line, which indicates who will receive a copy of the message. The Mail screen separates this information into two panes, with the sender and receivers listed in the left pane and the subject and message content in the right pane.

> **INSIGHT**
>
> ### Using the Cc and Bcc Lines
>
> In the To line, restrict the email addresses to those of your primary recipients. Use the Cc (courtesy copy) line for secondary recipients who should receive a copy of the message. If you are sending an email message to a large group of people, you can also use the Bcc (blind courtesy copy) line. (Right-click a blank spot on the Mail screen, click the More button on the Apps bar, and then click Show Bcc.) Mail sends an individual message to each person listed in the Bcc line, though the only other email address that appears is the sender's.

To send an email message, you first compose the message and then click the Send button on the message window. Mail sends the message from your computer to your email server, which routes it to the recipient.

> **REFERENCE**
>
> ### Creating and Sending an Email Message
>
> - Click the New button on the Mail toolbar.
> - Enter the email address of the recipient in the To text box.
> - Click Add a subject at the top of the right pane and then type the subject of the message.
> - Click the message area and then type the content of the message.
> - Click the Send button.

Mail includes a built-in spelling dictionary. As you type the text of a message, Mail corrects any words it flags as misspelled according to its dictionary. If a red line appears under a word, that means it is not in Mail's spelling dictionary. You can right-click the word to display a shortcut menu of spelling suggestions and an option to add the word to the dictionary.

Now you can show Jason how to create and send an email message using Mail by sending a practice email to yourself.

To create and send an email message:

▶ 1. Click the **New** button ⊕ on the Mail toolbar. The screen for composing a new message opens. See Figure 4-33.

Figure 4-33   Composing a new message

- enter the recipient's email address in the To text box
- click to enter a subject
- click to enter a message
- Send button

TIP

To send this message to many people, you could type more than one email address in the To or Cc text boxes. Separate each address with a comma or semicolon.

2. Type your email address in the To text box.

   Trouble? If you're not sure what email address you should enter, check with your instructor or technical support person.

3. Click **Add a subject** in the right pane, and then type **Test email** as the subject.

4. Click **Add a message**, and then type **This is just a practice message**.

5. Press the **Enter** key twice, and then type your name.

6. Click the **Send** button on the toolbar. Mail places the message in the Outbox. After a second or two, Mail removes the message from the Outbox, sends the message to your email server, and then places a copy of the sent message in the Sent items folder.

   To make sure your message has been sent, you can open the Sent items folder to see all of the messages you have sent.

   Trouble? After several seconds have passed, if Mail still displays the number 1 to the right of the Outbox folder in the Mail pane, indicating it contains one unsent message, then Mail is not configured to send messages immediately. In that case, right-click the middle of the screen and then click the Sync button on the Apps bar to send your message.

7. Click **Sent items** in the Mail pane. Your message appears in the Message list in the left pane, and the content of the message appears in the Reading pane.

   Trouble? If the content of your message does not appear in the Reading pane, click your message in the Message list.

When you clicked in the message area while composing a message, you might have noticed that the Apps bar displayed buttons for formatting the text. The buttons include Font, Font color, Highlight, Bold, Italic, Underline, Bulleted list, Emoticons, and More. To bold a word, for example, select the word and then click the Bold button on the Apps bar. To insert an emoticon such as a happy face, click in the message area, click the Emoticons button on the Apps bar, click a category icon, such as People or Travel, at the top of the panel, and then click an emoticon. You use the More button to apply options such as a priority (high, normal, or low) to the message, add the Bcc box, and undo or redo the most recent command.

Receiving and Reading Email Messages

TIP
If your computer is using a screen resolution of 1366 × 768 or higher, you can snap the Mail app to the screen so that it stays open as you work with other apps.

Mail automatically checks to see if you've received email whenever you start the program and periodically after that. (Every 30 minutes is the default.) Mail also checks for received email when you click the Sync button on the Apps bar. Email you receive appears in your Inbox. By default, the Inbox shows the name of the sender, the subject, and the date you received the message. Mail you have received but have not read yet appears in bold. To read a message, you click the message in the list to display its contents in the Reading pane.

To receive and read the Test email message:

1. Click **Inbox** in the Mail pane to display the contents of the Inbox folder in the Message list.

2. If necessary, right-click a blank area of the screen to display the Apps bar, and then click the **Sync** button. Mail retrieves your messages from your email server, routes them to your Inbox, and displays them in the Message list. Your Inbox folder might contain additional email messages from other people.

   Trouble? If the message you sent doesn't appear in the Inbox, wait a few minutes, and then click the Sync button again.

3. If necessary, click the **Test email** message to display its contents in the Reading pane. See Figure 4-34.

Figure 4-34   Reading a message

- messages in the Inbox
- Message list
- content of the message in the Reading pane

Next, you'll show Jason how to perform another common email task—responding to the messages you receive.

Responding to Email Messages

Some of the email you receive may ask you to provide information, answer questions, or confirm decisions. Instead of creating a new email message, you can reply directly to a message that you receive. When you reply to a message, Mail inserts the email address of the sender and the subject into the proper places in the message screen, and includes the text of the original message.

You can respond to messages by using the Reply or Reply all command. If the original message was sent to more than one person, use the Reply command to respond to only the original sender. Use the Reply all command to respond to all other recipients as well. Use the Reply all command carefully so that the only messages people receive from you are those they need to read. You can also use the Forward command to create a message with the original message text, and then send the message to someone other than the original senders.

You will continue to show Jason the tools provided with Mail.

TIP

If you have added contacts to the People app, you can click the Add button (plus icon) next to the To text box, and then click a name to insert a contact's email address into the To text box.

To reply to the Test email message:

1. With the Test email message selected in the Message list, click the **Respond** button on the toolbar, and then click **Reply**. The screen displays the text of the original message, inserts the email address of the original recipient in the To text box, and displays RE: before the original subject text. See Figure 4-35.

Figure 4-35 Replying to a message

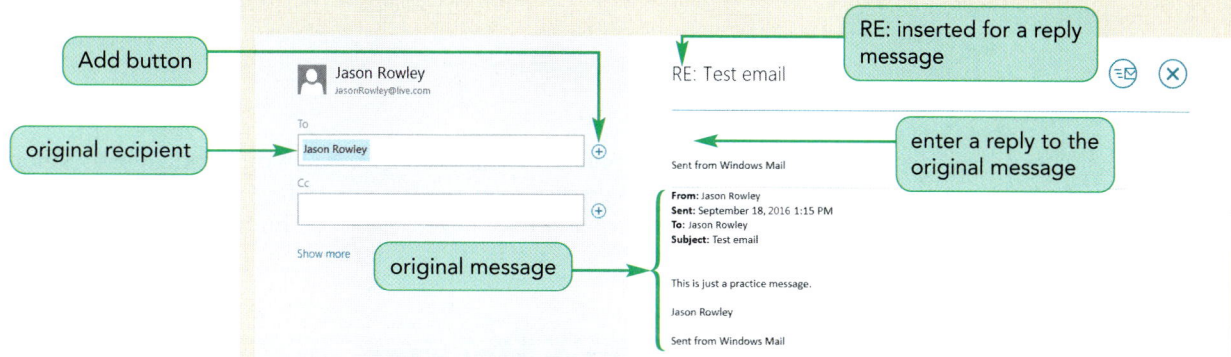

2. Type **This test was successful.** in the message area, and then click the **Send** button on the toolbar.

   Trouble? If the message doesn't appear in the Sent items folder, right-click the screen and then click the Sync button on the Apps bar to send the message.

3. When the RE: Test email message appears in your Inbox, click it to display its contents in the Reading pane.

Jason might want to delete the email messages he's read. You'll show him how to do so next.

Deleting Email Messages

After you read and respond to your messages, you can delete any message you no longer need. When you delete a message, it moves to the Deleted items folder. Messages remain in the Deleted items folder until you delete that folder's contents. This folder might be set up to permanently delete its contents when you close Mail. If not, you should delete them periodically by clicking the Deleted items folder in the Mail pane, selecting the messages, and then clicking the Delete button on the toolbar.

To delete the Test email messages:

1. With the RE: Test email message selected in the Message list, hold down the **Shift** key, click the **Test email** message, and then click the **Delete** button on the toolbar. The Inbox Message list no longer displays the Test messages.

> **INSIGHT**
>
> ### Dealing with Junk Email
>
> Junk email, or spam, is unsolicited email, often containing advertisements, fraudulent schemes, or legitimate offers. Mail includes a junk email filter that analyzes the content of the email messages you receive and moves suspicious messages to the Junk folder, where you can examine and manage them as necessary. To reduce the amount of junk email you receive, avoid posting your email address on Web sites or other public areas of the Internet. If a Web site requests your email address, read its privacy statement to make sure it doesn't disclose your email address to others. Finally, never respond to junk email—you're likely to receive even more spam. Be sure to open your Junk folder often to review the messages it contains, and then delete the spam messages, which are often from senders you don't recognize.

Jason mentions that visitors and members of the San Antonio Historical Association often request descriptions of upcoming events, which he stores in separate documents. You'll show him how to attach a file to an email message so he can reply to people and provide the documents they request.

Attaching a File to a Message

Besides sending email to others, you can also transfer files to them by attaching the files to messages. You can send any kind of file, including documents, pictures, music, or videos. Check the size of the files you attach before you send a message. If you attach a large file to an email message, it might take a long time for your recipient to download your message. Most email servers limit the size of the files you can attach; some allow files no larger than 3 MB. Check with your correspondents before sending large file attachments to find out about size restrictions and set up a convenient time to send the attachment.

You'll show Jason how to send and open an email message that includes an attachment. As before, you'll create a test message and send it to yourself.

> **To create and send a message with an attachment:**
>
> 1. Copy the **Events** file from the Windows4\Tutorial folder provided with your Data Files to the Public Documents folder in the Documents library, and then return to the Mail app.
> 2. Click the **New** button ⊕ on the toolbar.
> 3. Type your email address in the To box.
> 4. Click **Add a subject** in the right pane, and then type **Events list you requested** as the message subject.
> 5. Right-click a blank spot on the Mail screen, and then click the **Attachments** button on the Apps bar. The Files screen opens.
> 6. If necessary, click the **Go up** link, click **Documents**, click **Events**, and then click the **Attach** button. Mail attaches the file to the message and displays the filename and size next to the file icon.
> 7. Type **This is a test email message with a file attachment.** in the message area.
> 8. Click the **Send** button on the toolbar.
> 9. If necessary, right-click the screen and then click the **Sync** button on the Apps bar to send and receive the message.

When you receive a message that contains an attachment, you can choose to save or open the attached file. You should open files only after scanning them with antivirus software. Some people spread harmful software, called viruses, in email attachments. Before you open the file, you need to make sure the app used to create the attachment is installed on your computer. If it's not, you can sometimes use a text editor, such as WordPad or Notepad, to open and read the attached file.

To receive and open a message with an attachment:

1. When the Events list you requested message appears in your Inbox, click the message so the contents appear in the Reading pane.
2. Click the **Events.rtf** file icon in the Reading pane to display a shortcut menu, which lets you open, open with a specific program, or save the attachment.
3. Click **Open** on the shortcut menu. The file opens in a desktop word-processing program, such as Word or WordPad. You could save the document now if necessary.
4. Close the word-processing program.

PROSKILLS

Written Communication: Observing Email Etiquette

Because email is a widespread form of communication, you should follow standard guidelines and common sense when using it. For example, use language appropriate for the purpose of your message and your recipients. Following are a few guidelines to keep in mind when you are composing email messages so that you can communicate effectively, without offending or annoying your correspondents:

- Be concise and direct. People often read email messages while they are doing something else. As a courtesy to your correspondents and to make sure your message is read, get right to the point and keep your messages short.
- Include your response first. When you reply to an email, you can include text from the original message. If you do, make sure that your response is at the top of the message so your recipients can find it easily. If you respond to questions or insert comments in the original message, use a contrasting font color so your recipients can identify your additions.
- Don't email sensitive or confidential information. Email is not private, and your recipients can forward your message to others, either intentionally or accidentally. It's a good idea to be professional and careful about what you say to and about others.
- Avoid abbreviations. Although you should strive to be brief, don't overcompensate by using nonstandard abbreviations. Stick to the abbreviations that are common in business writing, such as FYI and ASAP.
- Don't use all capital letters. Using all capital letters, as in "SEND ME THE REPORT TODAY," can be difficult to read and makes it look like you're shouting.
- Pause and reread before sending. Be sure to reread the emails you write before you send them, and consider how they could be received. A message that you intend to be funny could be misinterpreted as rude. If you wrote an email in anger, calm down and revise your message before sending it. After you send an email message, you can't retrieve or stop it.

You're finished working with Mail for now, so you can close the app.

> **To close Mail:**
>
> 1. Press the **Windows** key to return to the Start screen, and then click the **Mail** tile.
> 2. Drag the top of the Mail app down until it shrinks to a thumbnail, and then continue dragging it to the very bottom of the screen to close the app.

If you were going to continue working on the desktop, you could use the Switch List to close the app: Point to the upper-left corner of the desktop, right-click the Mail window, and then click Close. However, you will continue using the Start screen to explore other new Windows 8 features with Jason.

Adding Information to the People App

Another communication app in Windows 8 is the People app, which you use to keep track of your contacts, including email correspondents. You can also use People on its own to save information about people and organizations. In addition to storing email addresses, you can store related information such as street addresses, home phone numbers, and personal information, such as anniversaries and birthdays. When you create an email message, you can click the Add button (a plus sign) next to the To text box to display a list of your contacts, and then click the name of the contact to insert the appropriate email address in the To text box.

You can add contact information to People by importing the information from social networking sites where you maintain contacts, such as Facebook, Google, LinkedIn, and Twitter. If you import the same contact information from two or more sources, the People app detects the duplicate contacts and combines them into a single entry called a linked contact. You can also create a new contact, and then enter as much information as you want about that contact on the New Contact screen.

If you import contact information from your accounts on social networking sites, People maintains a connection to those accounts so it can display updated contact information. If the People tile is a live tile on the Start screen, it also displays updated information as it becomes available.

REFERENCE

Adding a Contact in People

- Click the People tile on the Start screen.
- Click the New button on the Apps bar.
- Enter contact information on the New contact screen.
- Click the Save button.

Jason doesn't want to import his contacts from other services, so you'll show him how to use People to add a new contact.

To add a contact:

1. Click the **People** tile on the Start screen. The People app opens, listing any contacts added to the app. Your People window might not contain any contacts. If this is the first time you are starting People, the main screen lists contact sources, including Facebook friends, Twitter contacts, Outlook contacts, and LinkedIn contacts.

2. Right-click a blank spot on the screen, and then click the **New** button on the Apps bar to display the New contact screen. The type of online account you are using, such as Live, appears in the Account text box.

3. Click the **First name** text box, type **Jason**, press the **Tab** key, and then type **Rowley** in the Last name text box.

4. Press the **Tab** key, and then type **San Antonio Historical Association** in the Company text box.

5. Click the **Email** text box to specify Jason's personal email address, and then type **JasonRowley@live.com**.

   Trouble? If Personal does not appear under Email, click the option displayed (that is, Work or Other), click Personal, and then repeat Step 5.

6. Click the **Save** button on the Apps bar.

7. If the Jason Rowley contact information does not appear, click **Jason Rowley** on the People screen to display his contact information. See Figure 4-36.

> **TIP**
> You can click the Add button (plus icon) above a text box to enter additional names, email addresses, phone numbers, addresses, or other information for a contact.

Figure 4-36 New contact in People

Jason Rowley

Email
JasonRowley@live.com
Personal

Other info
San Antonio Historical Association
Company

Live

→ information entered for this contact

8. Close the People app.

When you select a contact, you can click the Send email link to send that person an email message without starting the Mail app first. You can also view the contact's profile on a social networking site such as Facebook. If you have a photo of the contact, you can add it to the contact information to quickly identify the contact.

Next, you want to help Jason manage his schedule with the Calendar app.

Managing Your Schedule with Calendar

Calendar is another app that works with Mail. You use it to schedule appointments, track tasks, and stay on top of deadlines. Calendar also lets you schedule recurring events, such as weekly staff meetings, and set reminders so you don't miss an important appointment. When you schedule an event, Calendar blocks out the time in your schedule, helping you avoid scheduling conflicts. If the event is a meeting, you can invite contacts stored in the People app to attend the meeting. You can also adjust the Calendar view to display scheduled events in the Day, Week, or Month format. The Day format shows you the events for today and tomorrow.

Calendar actually includes more than one calendar. The Main calendar displays your user name and is designed for scheduling all of your appointments and events. Other calendars include Birthday, Personal, Holidays, and Work. If you want to keep your personal appointments separate from work events, for example, you can maintain two calendars—Personal and Work. On the Birthday calendar, add birthdays of your contacts and other people. Calendar will remind you about the upcoming birthday in a notification message as you are working anywhere in Windows 8. The same is true for the Holidays calendar. If you list national and personal holidays in the calendar, Calendar will remind you about each one.

Because Jason works so often at his computer, he is ready to use an electronic calendar. You'll show him how to start Calendar, which you did earlier.

To start Calendar:

1. Click the **Calendar** tile on the Start screen. The Calendar screen opens, showing a calendar for the current day, week, or month.
2. If the calendar shows the day or week view, right-click the screen and then click **Month** on the Apps bar to display your schedule for the month.

Now that you've opened Calendar, you can use it to schedule appointments.

Scheduling Appointments

In Calendar, you can schedule appointments such as meetings that occur for part of a day. You can also schedule events that last 24 hours or longer. An appointment appears as a colored block in your calendar, while a day-long event appears in a banner at the beginning of a day. When you schedule appointments, you can specify that they are recurring, such as training that takes place once a week, sales meetings scheduled once a month, or birthdays and other annual events. If you set a reminder for an event, a notification appears as you're working on another task in Windows 8, such as browsing the Internet.

REFERENCE

Scheduling an Appointment in Calendar

- Click the Calendar tile on the Start screen.
- Click the New button on the Apps bar.
- In the right pane, click Add a title and then enter a description of the appointment.
- In the When text boxes, enter or select the date of the appointment.
- In the Start text boxes, enter or select the time the appointment starts.
- In the How long text box, enter or select the length of the appointment.
- In the Where text box, enter the location of the appointment.
- If you have more than one calendar, click the Calendar arrow, and then select the calendar you want to use to schedule the appointment.
- Click the Save this event button on the toolbar.

The first appointment Jason wants to schedule is for a staff meeting later today, which is usually 30 minutes long.

To schedule an appointment:

1. Double-click today's date. The Details pane opens on the left, displaying the details you can enter for the new appointment, such as the location and the start time.
2. In the right pane, type **Staff meeting** as the event title.

   Trouble? If the insertion point does not appear in the title area, click Add a title and then repeat Step 2.
3. Click **Add a message** and then type **Be prepared to summarize the status of your latest projects.**
4. Click each **Start** text box as necessary to select a time two hours from now.
5. Click the **How long** text box, and then click **30 minutes**.
6. Click the **Where** text box in the Details pane and then type **West conference room** as the location. You can accept the selection for the Calendar text box. See Figure 4-37.

Figure 4-37   Scheduling an appointment

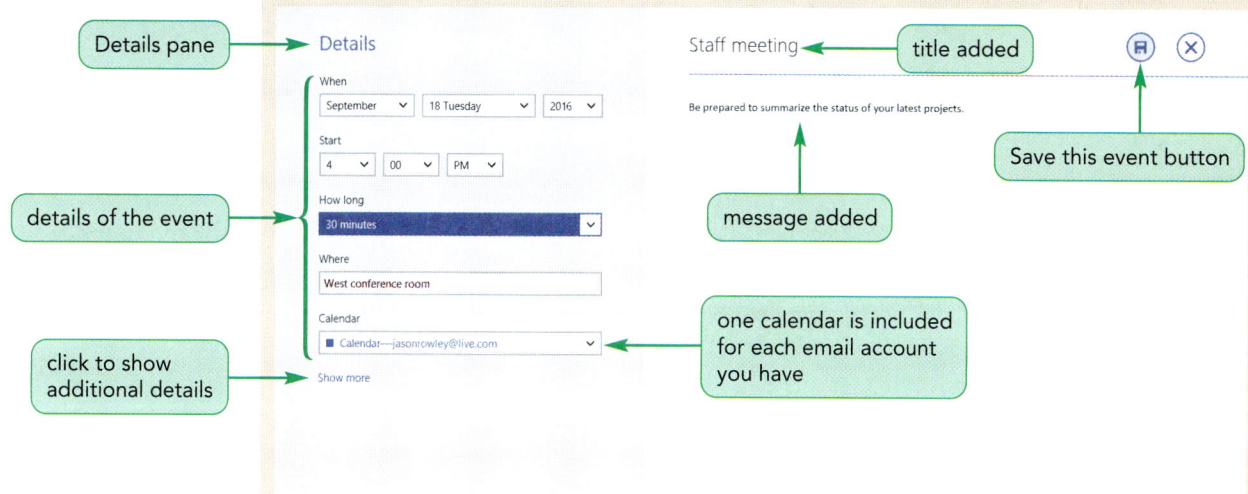

7. Click the **Save this event** button on the toolbar.
8. Close the Calendar app.

> **TIP**
> To edit an appointment already scheduled in the Calendar, double-click the appointment.

You've created an appointment for Jason's weekly staff meeting. Next, you can set appointment details to appear on your lock screen so you see them as soon as you turn on your computer or return to it after being away for awhile. You do so using the PC settings screen, which you've used in previous tutorials.

To display Calendar details on the lock screen:

1. Display the Charms bar, and then click the **Settings** charm to display the Settings menu.
2. Click the **Change PC settings** command to display the PC settings screen.

3. If necessary, click **Lock screen** to display the settings for the lock screen.

4. Scroll down to the Lock screen apps section. For the Choose an app to display detailed status setting, click the **Calendar** icon to display apps that can show detailed information on the lock screen. See Figure 4-38.

Figure 4-38 Selecting Calendar as a lock screen app

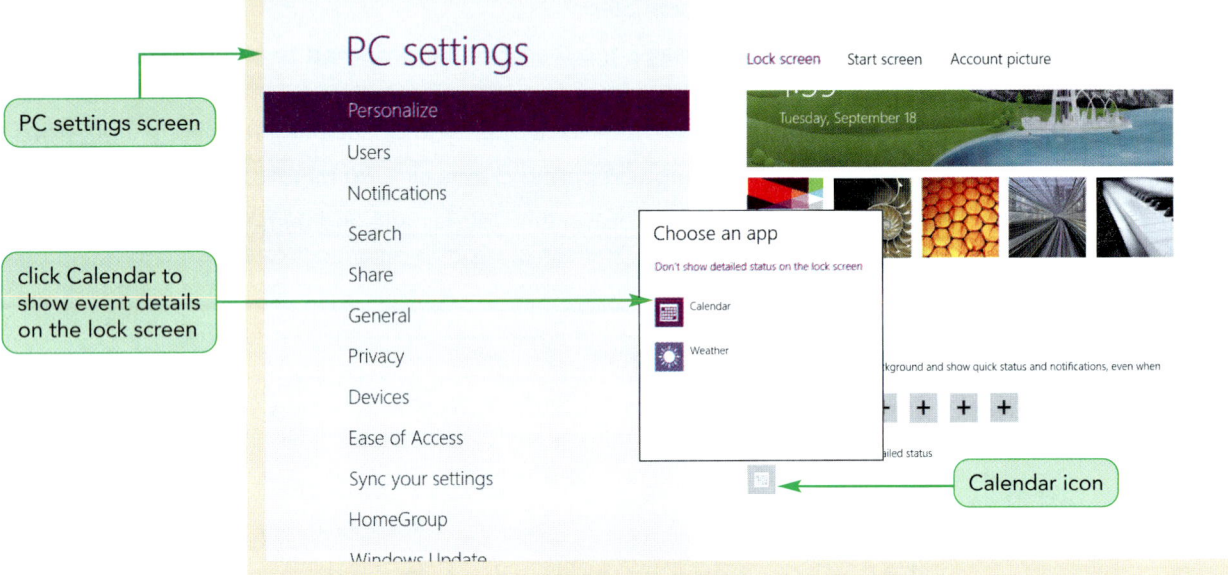

5. If Calendar is not selected, click **Calendar**, and then close the PC settings screen.

6. Press the **Windows+L** keys to display the lock screen, which now includes the appointment you entered in the Calendar app.

7. Clear the lock screen to display the Sign-in screen. Sign in as usual to display the Start screen.

Now that you've finished exploring the Internet and email on Jason's computer, you should restore the computer to its original settings.

Restoring Your Settings

If you are working in a computer lab or using a computer other than your own, complete the steps in this section to restore the original settings on the computer.

To restore your settings:

1. Click the **Desktop** tile to display the desktop.

2. Start Internet Explorer, click the **Safety** button on the Command bar, click **Delete browsing history**, click the **History** check box to select it (if necessary), deselect the other check boxes, and then click the **Delete** button. When a Notification bar appears at the bottom of the Internet Explorer window, click the **Close** button to close the Notification bar.

3. Open the Favorites Center, click the **Add to favorites button arrow**, and then click **Organize favorites**.

4. Click the **Ancestry Research** folder, and then click the **Delete** button. Click the **Close** button to close the Organize Favorites dialog box.

5. Right-click the **Prologue: Pieces of History** button on the Favorites bar, and then click **Delete** on the shortcut menu.

6. Use the same technique to delete the **National Archives and Records Administration** button on the Favorites bar.

7. Click the **Tools** button on the Command bar, point to **Toolbars**, and then click **Favorites bar** to remove the Favorites bar from the Internet Explorer window.

8. Close Internet Explorer.

9. Right-click the **Resources for Genealogists and Family Historians** button on the taskbar, and then click **Unpin this program from taskbar**.

10. Delete the **Events** file from the Public Documents folder in the Documents library.

11. Press the **Windows** key to return to the Start screen.

12. Scroll to the right, right-click the **National Archives** tile, and then click **Unpin from Start** on the Apps bar.

13. Right-click the **Census Bureau** tile and then click **Unpin from Start** on the Apps bar.

14. Click the **Internet Explorer** tile to start IE Windows 8.

15. Display the Charms bar, and then click the **Settings** button.

16. Click **Internet Options** and then drag the Flip ahead slider from On to **Off**.

17. Close the Settings screen and IE Windows 8.

18. Start Mail, click the **No** button if a message appears asking if you want to set Mail as your default email program, click the **Events list you requested** message in the Inbox, and then click the **Delete** button on the Mail toolbar.

19. Click the **Sent items** folder in the Mail pane; select the **Events list you requested**, **Re: Test email**, and **Test email** messages; and then click the **Delete** button on the Mail toolbar.

20. Click the **Deleted items** folder in the Mail pane, select all messages in the Deleted items folder, and then click the **Delete** button. Close the Mail app.

21. Click the **People** tile on the Start screen. Click **Jason Rowley** in the list of contacts, right-click his name, click the **Delete** button on the Apps bar, and then click the **Delete** button to confirm. Close the People app.

22. Click the **Calendar** tile on the Start screen. Click the appointment you added to the calendar, click the **Delete** button, and then click the **Delete** button to confirm. Close the Calendar app.

23. Display the Charms bar, click the **Settings** charm, click the **Change PC settings** command, click the **Calendar** icon in the Choose an app to display detailed status section, and then click **Don't show detailed status on the lock screen**.

24. Close all apps and windows.

REVIEW

Session 4.2 Quick Check

1. When you send an email message, it travels from your computer, through a network, and then arrives at a computer called a(n) _____, which stores the message until the recipient requests it.
2. Where does Mail display the contents of a selected message?
3. Identify the user name and the email server name in the following email address: RosaMing@mail.net.
4. What information does Mail automatically provide for you when you reply to an email message?
5. What is the purpose of the Deleted items folder in the Mail app?
6. Describe two ways to add contact information to the People app.
7. If you set a reminder for a scheduled event, how does Calendar remind you?

Tutorial 4 Working with the Internet and Email | Windows   WIN 213

PRACTICE

Review Assignments

Data File needed for the Review Assignments: Missions.rtf

You already showed Jason how to conduct research on genealogy to prepare for his genealogy workshops at the San Antonio Historical Association. He also needs information about the San Antonio Missions, national historical parks in San Antonio, Texas, for a presentation he is giving to SAHA. You'll use Internet Explorer to research information about the missions. Complete the following steps:

1. Start IE Windows 8 on the Start screen, and then go to **www.nps.gov/saan**, which is the home page for the San Antonio Missions in the National Park Service Web site.
2. Click a link on this page to open the Plan Your Visit Web page for the San Antonio Missions.
3. Click the Things To Do link on the left to display visitor information.
4. Click a link on this page to display information about Mission Espada.
5. Pin the Web page about Mission Espada to the Start screen.
6. Open the Photos & Multimedia link on a new tab, and then display the Photos & Multimedia page.
7. Click the Address bar and then press the Print Screen key to capture an image of the screen. Start Paint, paste the screen image in a new file, and then save the file as **IE Windows 8 Missions** in the Windows4\Review folder provided with your Data Files.
8. Close IE Windows 8.
9. Open Internet Explorer on the desktop, and then go to **www.tshaonline.org**, which is the home page for the Texas State Historical Association.
10. Click The Handbook of Texas Online link, and then search for information about missions in Texas. Open two Web pages about the San Antonio missions on new tabs.
11. Open the Favorites Center and pin it to the Internet Explorer window. Use the History list or other Internet Explorer tools to navigate to a Web page you think will be especially useful to the San Antonio Historical Association, and then add it to your Favorites list.
12. Open the Favorites bar, go to **www.nps.gov/saan**, and then add a button for this Web page to the Favorites bar.
13. On any open Web page displaying information about a San Antonio mission, select the name of a location, and then use the Map with Bing Accelerator to preview a map of the location.
14. Press the Print Screen key to capture an image of the Internet Explorer window. In Paint, paste the screen image in a new file, and then save the file as **IE Desktop Missions** in the Windows4\Review folder provided with your Data Files.
15. Close Internet Explorer. Copy the **Missions** file from the Windows4\Review folder to the Public Documents folder in the Documents library.
16. Start Mail and create an email message. Enter your email address and your instructor's email address in the To text box and use **San Antonio mission** as the subject of the message.
17. In the message area, write a message describing one mission Jason should be sure to include in his presentation, based on your research.
18. Attach the **Missions** file to the message.
19. Send the message, and then add your email address and your instructor's email address to the People app.
20. Add an appointment to the Calendar for a 30-minute meeting with Jason at the San Antonio Historical Association today.

21. Complete the following tasks to restore your computer to its original settings:
    - In IE Desktop, clear the History list, delete the Web page you added to the Favorites list, delete the button you added to the Favorites bar, close the Favorites bar, and then close the Favorites Center.
    - Close Internet Explorer.
    - Delete the Missions document from the Public Documents folder.
    - On the Start screen, delete the tile for the pinned Web page.
    - In Mail, delete the emails you sent and received, and then empty the Deleted items folder.
    - In People, delete yourself and your instructor from the contacts list.
    - In Calendar, delete the appointment you created.
22. Close all open windows and apps.
23. Submit the results of the preceding steps to your instructor, either in printed or electronic form, as requested.

Case Problem 1

APPLY

There are no Data Files needed for this Case Problem.

Geology Central Chad Marcus runs Geology Central, a nonprofit organization in Wichita, Kansas, that promotes geology education for students in grades 1 through 12. Chad runs a summer program on volcanoes, which is especially popular with students in all grades. He wants to take advantage of the volcano information posted on the Web by national geology organizations and use it in his program. Recently, Chad hired you to help administer the program. He asks you to find online information about volcanoes, especially information involving students. Complete the following steps:

1. Start Internet Explorer on the Start screen, and then go to the U.S. Geological Survey Education Web page at **education.usgs.gov**.
2. Using the tools on this page, look for information about volcanoes. (*Hint*: You might need to search for this information.) Open one of the pages you found.
3. On new tabs, open three other geology Web pages:
   - NASA Science: **kids.earth.nasa.gov**
   - The Dynamic Earth: **www.mnh.si.edu/earth**
   - Geology.com: **geology.com/volcanoes**
4. Click links on these Web pages and use the Charms bar to search for three other Web pages that provide information about volcanoes in the United States.
5. Pin the three Web pages you found to the Start screen.
6. Click the Address bar and then press the Print Screen key to capture an image of the screen. Start Paint, paste the screen image in a new file, and then save the file as **IE Windows 8 Volcanoes** in the Windows4\Case1 folder provided with your Data Files.
7. Close IE Windows 8.
8. Open Internet Explorer on the desktop, and then open The Dynamic Earth Web page at **www.mnh.si.edu/earth**, which is part of the Smithsonian National Museum of Natural History Web site. Turn down the volume on your speakers or use headphones before you click the Multimedia Version link, and then watch the Plate Tectonics and Volcanoes part of the multimedia presentation.

9. Pin The Dynamic Earth page to the taskbar. Close IE Desktop and then start it again.
10. Use Internet Explorer tools to explore the Smithsonian National Museum of Natural History Web site at **www.mnh.si.edu**, looking for pages on volcanoes. Save three Web pages about volcanoes in your Favorites list in a folder named **Volcanoes**.
11. Find a blog on the Smithsonian National Museum of Natural History home page, and then subscribe to its RSS feed. Add the feed to the Favorites bar, and then display the Favorites bar in the Internet Explorer window. Display the main page of the Natural History blog.
12. Pin the Favorites Center to the Internet Explorer window, if necessary, so that the Favorites list stays open. Open the Volcanoes folder in the Favorites list to display the Web pages you found.
13. Press the Print Screen key to capture an image of the desktop. In Paint, paste the screen image in a new file, and then save the file as **IE Desktop Volcanoes** in the Public Documents folder in the Documents library.
14. Close Internet Explorer.
15. Start Mail and create an email message. Enter your email address and your instructor's email address in the To text box and enter **Ideas for volcano program** as the subject of the message.
16. In the message area, write a message describing the volcano information provided on one of the Web pages you found.
17. Attach the **IE Desktop Volcanoes** file to the message, and then send it.
18. Restore your computer by completing the following tasks:
    - In IE Desktop, clear the History list, delete the folder you added to the Favorites list, delete the RSS feed you added to the Favorites bar, and then close the Favorites bar and the Favorites Center. Close IE Desktop.
    - Unpin the Web page from the taskbar.
    - Move the **IE Desktop Volcanoes** file to the Windows4\Case1 folder provided with your Data Files.
    - On the Start screen, delete the tiles for the pinned Web pages.
    - In Mail, delete the email you sent, and then delete the messages from the Deleted items folder.
19. Close all open windows and apps.
20. Submit the results of the preceding steps to your instructor, either in printed or electronic form, as requested.

Case Problem 2

There are no Data Files needed for this Case Problem.

Folk Art Reproductions Lorraine Rojas owns a company called Folk Art Reproductions in Bowling Green, Ohio. Lorraine's company acquires reproduction rights from museums and artists so it can create replicas of paintings, sculpture, quilts, and other decorative objects. Lorraine recently hired you as a research assistant. Your main responsibility is to learn about the folk art collections at American museums, which you can do by using Internet Explorer. Complete the following steps:

1. Start Internet Explorer on the Start screen, and then go to the American Folk Art Museum Web site at **folkartmuseum.org**.
2. On additional tabs, open the home pages for the following Web sites:
    - Museum of Craft and Folk Art: **www.mocfa.org**
    - Craft and Folk Art Museum: **www.cafam.org**

3. Click links and use the Internet Explorer tools to find a description of a current exhibition on each Web site.
4. Pin the three exhibition Web pages to the Start screen.
5. Click the Address bar and then press the Print Screen key to capture an image of the screen. Start Paint, paste the screen image in a new file, and then save the file as **IE Windows 8 Folk Art** in the Windows4\Case2 folder provided with your Data Files.
6. Close IE Windows 8.
7. Open Internet Explorer on the desktop, and then open the home page for the American Folk Art Museum.
8. Click links and use the Internet Explorer tools to find information about location and hours at the museum.
9. Pin the page you found to the taskbar. Close the Internet Explorer window and then start IE Desktop again.
10. Return to the American Folk Art Museum home page. (*Hint*: Use the History list.) On separate tabs, open three pages that show images of furniture, pottery, and quilts. Save these Web pages in your Favorites list in a folder named **Folk Art**.
11. Pin the Favorites Center to the Internet Explorer window, if necessary, so that the Favorites list stays open. Open the Folk Art folder in the Favorites list to display the Web pages you found.
12. Open the Web page pinned to the taskbar, and then select an address on the page. Use the Bing Maps Accelerator to preview a map of the location.
13. Press the Print Screen key to capture an image of the desktop. In Paint, paste the screen image in a new file, and then save the file as **IE Desktop Folk Art** in the Windows4\Case2 folder provided with your Data Files.
14. Close Internet Explorer.
15. Start Mail and create an email message addressed to you and your instructor. Enter **Folk Art Exhibition** as the subject.
16. In the message area, write a message describing the types of folk art objects collected by the museums you researched. Send the message to yourself and your instructor.
17. Restore your computer by completing the following tasks:
    - In IE Desktop, clear the History list, delete the folder you added to the Favorites list, and then close the Favorites Center.
    - Unpin the Web page from the taskbar.
    - Close Internet Explorer.
    - On the Start screen, delete the tiles for the pinned Web pages.
    - In Mail, delete the email you sent, and then empty the Deleted items folder.
18. Close all open windows and apps.
19. Submit the results of the preceding steps to your instructor, either in printed or electronic form, as requested.

CHALLENGE

Case Problem 3

There are no Data Files needed for this Case Problem.

Pro-Fit Chefs Nicholas DeMars started Pro-Fit Chefs in Miami, Florida, to train chefs in preparing vegetarian dishes that are healthy and appealing. He also works in Miami public schools to create school lunches that feature produce from Florida farmers. Nicholas hired you as his project assistant, and asked you to find Web sites providing basic nutritional information for the chefs he trains. Complete the following steps:

1. Start Internet Explorer on the Start screen, and then go to the Choose My Plate Web site at **www.choosemyplate.gov**.
2. On additional tabs, open the following Web pages:
    - Nutrition.gov: **www.nutrition.gov**
    - Dietary Guidelines for Americans: **health.gov/dietaryguidelines**
3. Click links and use Internet Explorer tools to find at least one Web page from each site that provides lists of recommended foods to include in shopping and meal-planning lists or recipes.
4. Pin the three Web pages you found to the Start screen.
5. **Explore** Use the Charms bar to send one of the Web pages you found to yourself and your instructor via email.
6. In IE Windows 8, click the Address bar and then press the Print Screen key to capture an image of the screen. Start Paint, paste the screen image in a new file, and then save the file as **IE Windows 8 Nutrition** in the Windows4\Case3 folder provided with your Data Files.
7. Close IE Windows 8.
8. Start Internet Explorer on the desktop. Open the home page for the Nutrition.gov Web site. (*Hint*: Use the History list.)
9. **Explore** On separate tabs, open three Web pages that would be helpful to Pro-Fit Chefs. Save the group of open tabs in your Favorites list in a folder named **Nutrition**. (*Hint*: Open the Favorites Center, click the Add to favorites button arrow, click Add current tabs to favorites on the shortcut menu, name the folder **Nutrition**, and then click the Add button.)
10. **Explore** Turn on Suggested Sites to allow Internet Explorer to discover Web sites you might like based on the Web sites you've visited. Display the Favorites bar, and then click the Suggested Sites button to display a list of Suggested Sites. Open two suggested sites on separate tabs.
11. Pin one of the suggested sites to the taskbar.
12. **Explore** On the Nutrition.gov home page, click the En Español link on the navigation bar. Select the first paragraph on the page, click the Accelerator icon, and then point to Translate with Bing. Press the Print Screen key to capture an image of the desktop. In Paint, paste the screen image in a new file, and then save the file as **IE Desktop Nutrition** in the Windows4\Case3 folder provided with your Data Files.
13. **Explore** Open the Dietary Guidelines for Americans Web page at **health.gov/dietaryguidelines**, and then click the links on the Web page to find a file you can download that provides nutritional guidelines. For example, look for a PDF link next to the name of an article. (Recall that PDFs, or Portable Document Format files, contain text and images that you can often download from a Web site and read with Windows Reader.) Right-click the link to a nutrition file, click Save target as, and then save the file as **Guidelines** in the Public Documents folder in the Documents library.

14. Start Mail and create an email message addressed to you and your instructor. Enter **Nutritional Guidelines** as the subject.
15. In the message area, write a message listing two guidelines for preparing nutritional meals.
16. Attach the **Guidelines** file to the message, and then send the message.
17. Restore your computer by completing the following tasks:
    - In IE Desktop, clear the History list, delete the folder you added to the Favorites list, and then turn off Suggested Sites. Close the Favorites bar and the Favorites Center.
    - Unpin the Web page from the taskbar.
    - Move the **Guidelines** file from the Public Documents folder to the Windows4\Case3 folder provided with your Data Files.
    - On the Start screen, delete the tiles for the pinned Web pages.
    - In Mail, delete the email you sent, and then empty the Deleted items folder.
18. Close all open windows and apps.
19. Submit the results of the preceding steps to your instructor, either in printed or electronic form, as requested.

Case Problem 4

CHALLENGE

There are no Data Files needed for this Case Problem.

American Crew Club The American Crew Club is a group of rowers in Bethesda, Maryland, that supports and promotes women's crew teams at colleges and universities in the United States. Maureen Upton, the club president, recently hired you as a part-time assistant. You help Maureen write the club newsletter and organize promotional events. Maureen wants you to visit college Web sites periodically to make sure they are promoting their women's crew teams. Complete the following steps:

1. Start Internet Explorer on the Start screen, and go to the women's crew page at the Wesleyan University Web site at **www.wesleyan.edu/athletics/wcrew**.
2. On additional tabs, open the following Web pages:
    - Williams College Women's Crew page: **athletics.williams.edu/sports/wcrew**
    - Sacramento State Women's Rowing page: **www.hornetsports.com/sports/wcrew**
3. Click links and use Internet Explorer tools to find at least one Web page from each site that shows the schedule for the current or upcoming season.
4. Pin the three Web pages you found to the Start screen.

Explore 5. Use the Charms bar to print one of the schedules you found.

6. In IE Windows 8, click the Address bar and then press the Print Screen key to capture an image of the screen. Start Paint, paste the screen image in a new file, and then save the file as **IE Windows 8 Crew** in the Windows4\Case4 folder provided with your Data Files.
7. Close IE Windows 8.
8. Open Internet Explorer on the desktop, and then on separate tabs, open the same three pages you opened in Steps 1 and 2.

Explore 9. Save all of the open tabs in your Favorites list in a folder named **Crew**. (*Hint*: Open the Favorites Center, click the Add to favorites button arrow, click Add current tabs to favorites, name the folder **Crew**, and then click the Add button.)

Explore 10. On the Web site for any of the three colleges, find a Web page showing the results of a recent season. Click the Page button on the Command bar, click Save as to open the Save Webpage dialog box, navigate to the Windows4\Case4 folder provided with your Data Files, click the Save as type button, click Web Archive, single file (*.mht), and then type **Results** as the filename. Click the Save button.

Explore 11. Turn on Suggested Sites to allow Internet Explorer to discover Web sites you might like based on the Web sites you've visited. Display the Favorites bar, and then click the Suggested Sites button to display a list of Suggested Sites.

12. Pin one of the suggested sites to the taskbar, and then close the window for the suggested site.

13. Press the Print Screen key to capture an image of the desktop. In Paint, paste the screen image in a new file, and then save the file as **IE Desktop Crew** in the Windows4\Case4 folder provided with your Data Files.

14. Restore your computer by completing the following tasks:
    - In IE Desktop, clear the History list, delete the folder you added to the Favorites list, turn off Suggested Sites, and then close the Favorites bar and the Favorites Center. Close IE Desktop.
    - Unpin the Web page from the taskbar.
    - On the Start screen, delete the tiles for the pinned Web pages.

15. Close all open windows and apps.

16. Submit the results of the preceding steps to your instructor, either in printed or electronic form, as requested.

TUTORIAL 5

Protecting Your Computer

Managing Computer Security

OBJECTIVES

Session 5.1
- Use the Action Center
- Set up Windows Firewall and Windows Update
- Protect your computer from viruses and other malicious software
- Use Windows Defender to protect against spyware
- Examine Mail security

Session 5.2
- Manage Microsoft Internet Explorer security
- Protect privacy with InPrivate Browsing and Tracking Protection
- Set up user accounts
- Control access to your computer
- Examine other built-in security features

Case | Catapult Product Design

A few years ago, Duane Ellison founded Catapult Product Design in Edison, New Jersey. Catapult designs, creates, and tests new products, ranging from industrial tools to consumer goods for corporate clients around the world. Recently, Duane has become concerned with the security of Catapult's computers. Many of Duane's product designers work at client offices using portable computers running Windows 8. Although these designers can access the Internet with their computers, they can't usually connect to the Catapult network, where an administrator oversees security. Instead, they must take advantage of the security tools in Windows 8 to prevent problems stemming from viruses, spyware, and other types of harmful software. Duane recently hired you to support the design staff. One of your first duties is to investigate the security features in Windows 8 and show Duane how to use them to address security threats.

In this tutorial, you'll explore the tools in the Action Center, including Windows Firewall and Windows Update. You'll learn how to set up Windows 8 to work with antivirus software and how to implement other security measures, including setting up user accounts. You will also examine Internet Explorer security settings so that you can use the Internet safely.

STARTING DATA FILES

There are no starting Data Files needed for this tutorial.

Session 5.1 Visual Overview:

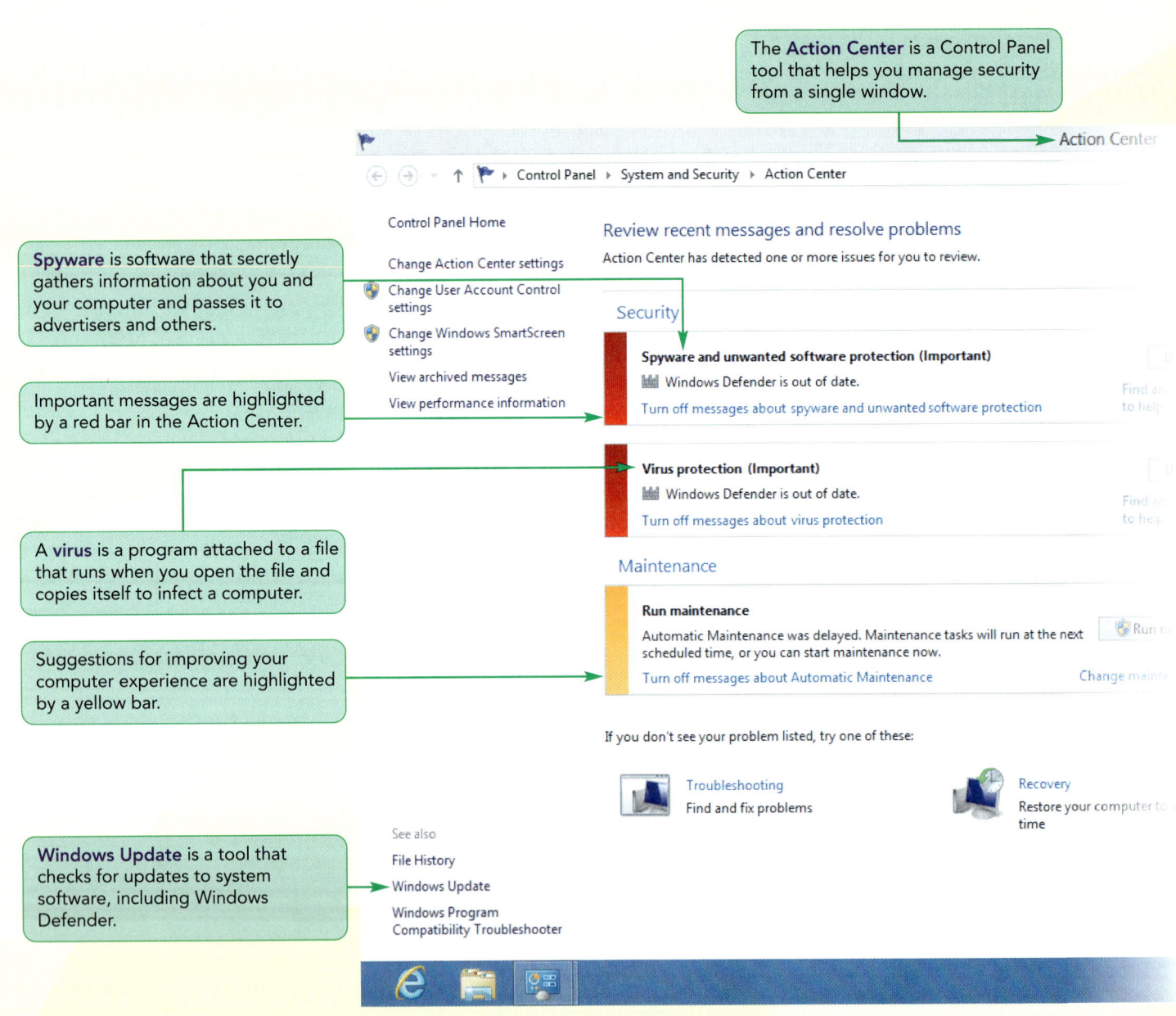

The **Action Center** is a Control Panel tool that helps you manage security from a single window.

Spyware is software that secretly gathers information about you and your computer and passes it to advertisers and others.

Important messages are highlighted by a red bar in the Action Center.

A **virus** is a program attached to a file that runs when you open the file and copies itself to infect a computer.

Suggestions for improving your computer experience are highlighted by a yellow bar.

Windows Update is a tool that checks for updates to system software, including Windows Defender.

The Action Center

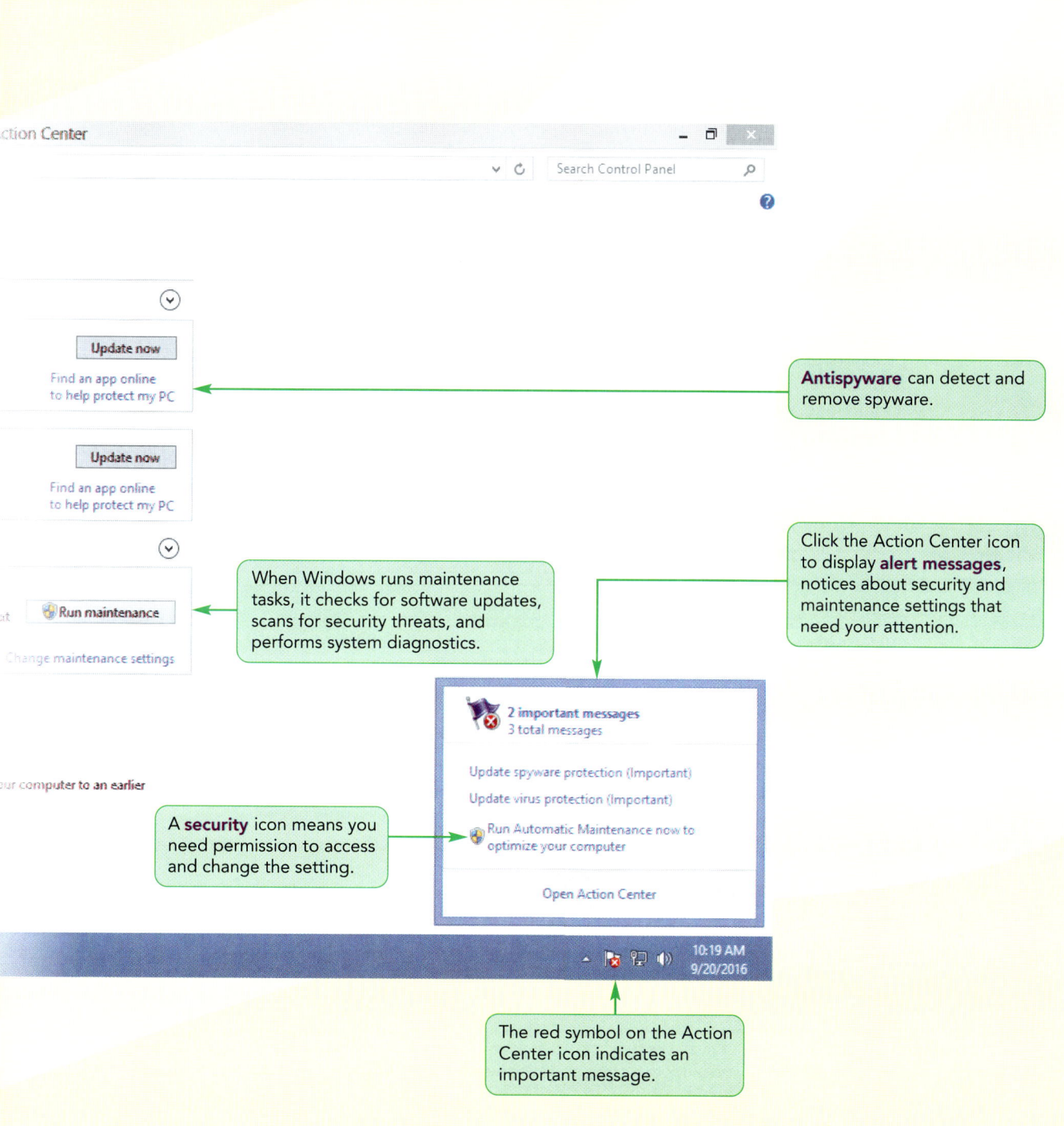

Using the Action Center

Windows 8 provides many tools that help you keep your computer safe from threats such as harmful software, unsolicited email, and invasions of your privacy. When you connect to the Internet, send and receive email, or share your computer or files with others, your computer is vulnerable to harm from people who might attempt to steal your personal information, damage your files, or interrupt your work. You should use the Windows 8 security tools and other techniques to defend against these threats.

Harmful software (referred to as **malicious software**, or **malware**) includes viruses. By copying itself and triggering computer code, a virus can infect your computer. The damage a virus causes can range from changing your desktop settings to deleting or corrupting files on your hard disk. Viruses are often spread by email and run when you open an email attachment or the email message itself. Files you download from Web sites can also contain viruses that run when you save the files on your computer.

People who create and send malware are called **hackers**, a generic term that refers to anyone who intends to access a computer system without permission. (Hackers with criminal intent are sometimes called **crackers**, or black hat hackers.) Hackers can also invade your privacy by accessing your computer via the Internet to find information such as passwords and financial account numbers. Hackers sometimes access your computer using spyware, software that secretly gathers information about you and your computer actions, including sensitive information.

If you are working on a computer connected to a network, a network administrator probably defends the network against security threats such as viruses, worms, spyware, and hackers. Otherwise, if you are working on a home computer, for example, you should take advantage of the security features that Windows 8 provides.

The first place to go to secure your computer is the Action Center, a Control Panel tool that helps you manage security from a single window. Some of the security settings you can manage in the Action Center are listed in Figure 5-1.

Figure 5-1 Action Center features

Security Feature	Description
Network Firewall	This feature uses Windows Firewall by default to monitor and restrict communication with the Internet, which helps protect your computer from hackers. Before an app can send or receive information via the Internet, Windows Firewall must allow it to do so.
Windows Update	This feature checks for the latest Windows updates on the Microsoft Web site, and then downloads and installs the updates for you. Because Windows updates often include security enhancements, using this feature helps to make sure that your computer is secure against most current threats.
Virus protection	Antivirus software is your best protection against viruses, worms, and other types of harmful software. If you have antivirus software, Windows reminds you to use it regularly to scan your computer for virus infections and to monitor email. If you do not have antivirus software, Windows Defender runs automatically to defend your computer against malware.
Spyware and unwanted software protection	Antispyware software, such as Windows Defender, prevents some types of malware from infecting your system.
Internet security settings	Action Center checks that your Web browser is using appropriate security settings to block malware from being installed on your system when you visit Web sites.
User Account Control (UAC)	This service displays a dialog box requesting your permission to install software or open programs that could harm your computer.
Windows SmartScreen	This tool protects your computer from unrecognized apps and files you download from the Internet.

© 2014 Cengage Learning

Most of the features listed in Figure 5-1 are considered essential—you should turn on all of these Action Center features to keep your computer secure. If Windows detects a problem with one of these essential security features, such as when your firewall is turned off, Windows displays an alert message. If you're working on the Start screen or in a Windows 8 app, the message appears and fades as you're working. If you're working on the desktop, the message appears near the Action Center icon in the notification area of your taskbar. For example, you might see the following alert message, "Solve PC issues: 1 message." You can click the alert message or click the Action Center icon and then click Open Action Center to open the Action Center on the desktop and find out how to address the problem. You can also see if the Action Center lists any new messages by pointing to the Action Center icon.

You'll start showing Duane how to use the security features in Windows 8 by opening the Action Center.

To open the Action Center:

1. Click the **Desktop** tile on the Start screen to display the desktop.

2. Click the **Action Center** icon in the notification area of the taskbar. A message window opens.

   Trouble? If the Action Center icon does not appear in the notification area of the taskbar, display the Charms bar, click the Settings charm, click PC info, and then click Action Center in the System window.

3. In the message window, click **Open Action Center** to open the Action Center.

4. If necessary, click the **expand** button to expand the Security section. See Figure 5-2.

Figure 5-2 Action Center

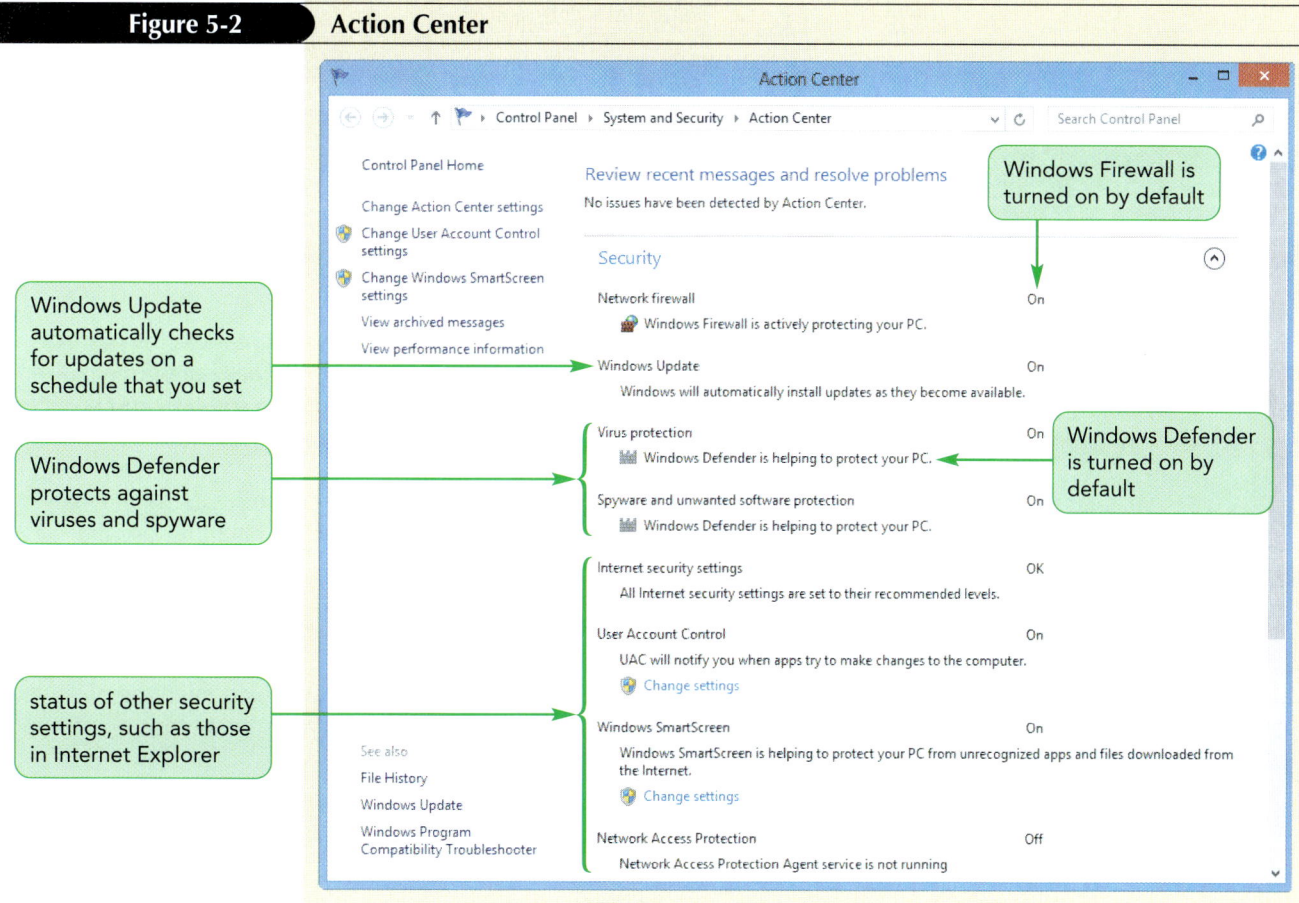

When you click the Action Center icon on the taskbar, the message window might list links to alert messages. If a security icon appears next to a link, you might need permission to access and change the setting. You usually indicate that you have permission by entering an administrator password. Requiring a user to enter a password to change system settings is another way to protect your computer.

Leave the Action Center window open to perform the tasks described in the following sections.

Managing Windows Firewall

Windows Firewall is software that serves as a barrier between your computer and a network or the Internet. As shown in Figure 5-3, Windows Firewall checks information coming from the network or the Internet and either blocks it from your computer or allows it to pass, depending on your settings. In this way, Windows Firewall prevents unauthorized users from accessing your computer and is the first line of defense against malware. Many antivirus programs include a firewall that works in a similar way.

Figure 5-3 How Windows Firewall protects your computer

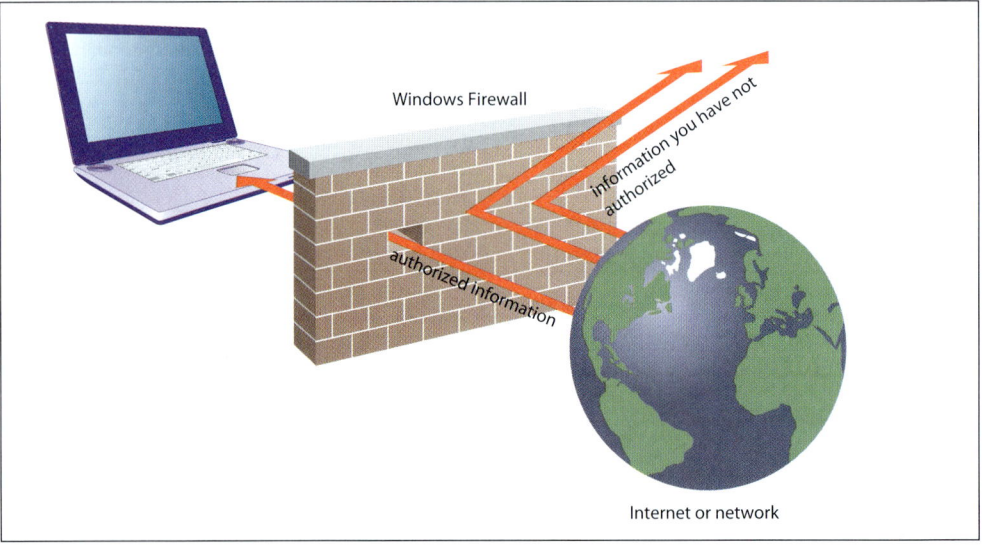

© 2014 Cengage Learning

A firewall defends against malware trying to gain access to your computer by monitoring your network and Internet connections. However, a firewall does not scan email, so it cannot detect viruses sent in email messages (a common way to spread viruses). Neither can a firewall detect viruses in files you download from the Web. Furthermore, a firewall can't protect you from email scams, called phishing, that try to deceive you into revealing private information such as passwords. To protect against viruses in email and downloaded files, use antivirus software. To minimize phishing attempts, use the Windows SmartScreen filter. (Both topics are covered later in this tutorial.)

Windows Firewall is turned on by default, so it doesn't allow communications with most programs via the Internet or a network. However, your computer manufacturer or someone else might turn off Windows Firewall, so you should verify that it is running. Typically, Windows Firewall is turned off only if another firewall, which might be provided by other security software or your network, is protecting your computer.

Tutorial 5 Protecting Your Computer | Windows **WIN 227**

To turn on Windows Firewall:

1. In the Action Center window, click **System and Security** in the Address bar to display the System and Security window.
2. Click **Windows Firewall** to open the Windows Firewall window. See Figure 5-4.

| Figure 5-4 | Windows Firewall window |

- click to add or remove apps from the allowed apps list
- click to turn Windows Firewall on or off
- status of Windows Firewall settings

Trouble? If a different firewall is installed on your computer and is managing the firewall settings, your Windows Firewall window will look different from the figure, and you might not be able to change the settings. In that case, read but do not perform Steps 3–5.

3. Click **Turn Windows Firewall on or off** in the left pane.

   Trouble? If a User Account Control dialog box opens requesting an administrator password or your permission to continue, make sure you have permission to change Windows Firewall settings (check with your instructor, if necessary), and then enter the password or click the Yes button.

4. In the Customize Settings window, click the first **Turn on Windows Firewall** option button (the one for Private network settings). See Figure 5-5.

Figure 5-5 Customize Settings window

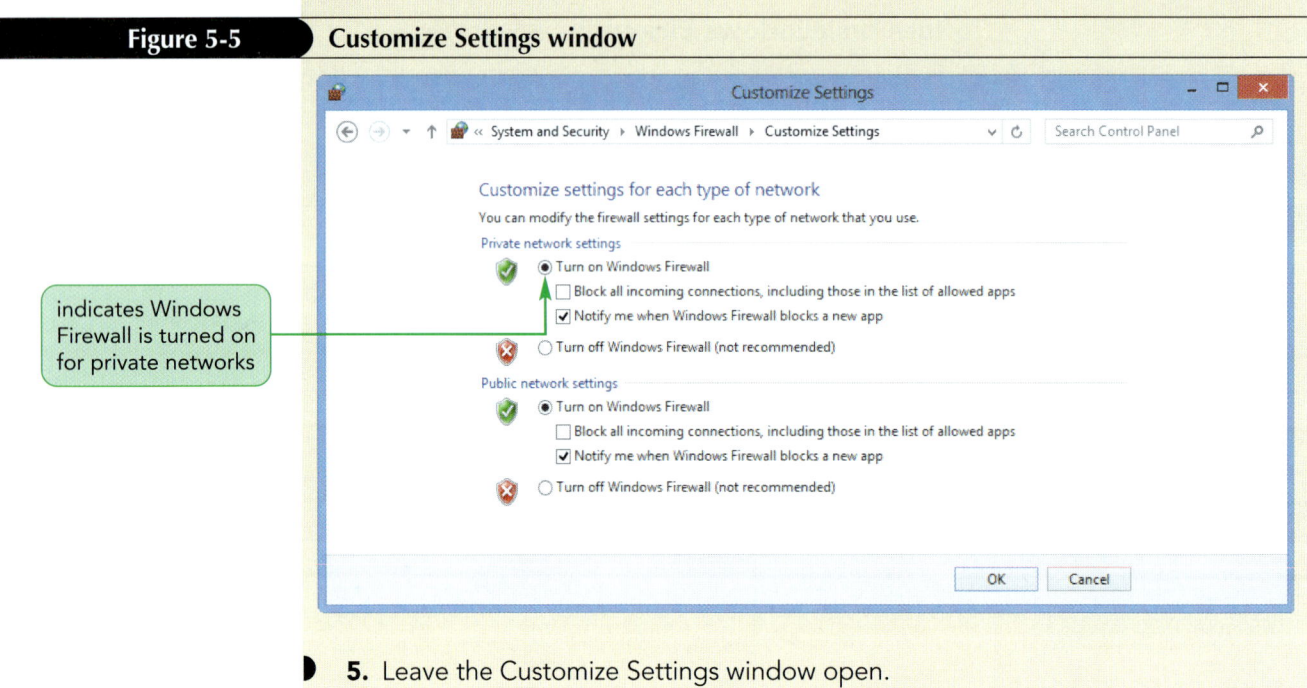

indicates Windows Firewall is turned on for private networks

> 5. Leave the Customize Settings window open.

When Windows Firewall is turned on and someone tries to connect to your computer from the Internet, Windows Firewall blocks the connection. Instead of turning off Windows Firewall every time you want to use a blocked program, you can customize the firewall by adding programs to its allowed list so that it maintains a level of security that's right for you.

In the Customize Settings window, you can specify firewall settings for each type of network location that you use. For example, you might use a private network at home or work and a public network in other locations. For each network location, you can select one of the following settings:

Turn on Windows Firewall—This setting is selected by default, meaning that most apps are blocked from communicating through the firewall.

Block all incoming connections, including those in the list of allowed apps—When you connect to a public network, such as in a hotel or an airport, you might want to select this setting. Windows blocks all apps, even those in the allowed list.

Notify me when Windows Firewall blocks a new app—When you select this check box, Windows Firewall informs you when it blocks a new app, giving you the option of adding the app to the allowed apps list.

- Turn off Windows Firewall (not recommended)—The only time you should select this setting is when another firewall is running on your computer.

Duane often uses network projectors to give presentations to potential clients in other locations. (A network projector is a video projector connected to a wireless or wired network, and it lets you give presentations using a network connection.) Before a network projector can communicate with a computer to indicate it is turned on and ready for the presentation, Windows Firewall must allow incoming connections from the network projector. You'll show Duane how to add the Connect to a Network Projector program to the allowed programs list so he can give network presentations without any problems.

If you are performing the following steps in a computer lab, you might not be allowed to change allowed programs. Check with your instructor or technical support person to determine whether you can specify Connect to a Network Projector as an allowed program in Windows Firewall. If you cannot, read but do not perform the following steps.

Tutorial 5 Protecting Your Computer | Windows **WIN 229**

To add a program to the allowed programs list:

1. Click the **Back** button to return to the Windows Firewall window.

2. In the left pane, click **Allow an app or feature through Windows Firewall** to open the Allowed apps window. See Figure 5-6.

   Trouble? If the Allow an app or feature through Windows Firewall link is inactive in the Windows Firewall window, click the Back button ⬅ to return to the System and Security window, and then click Allow an app or feature through Windows Firewall.

   Trouble? If a dialog box opens requesting an administrator password or your permission to continue, make sure you have permission to change the Windows Firewall settings (check with your instructor, if necessary), and then enter the password or click the Yes button.

Figure 5-6   Allowed apps window

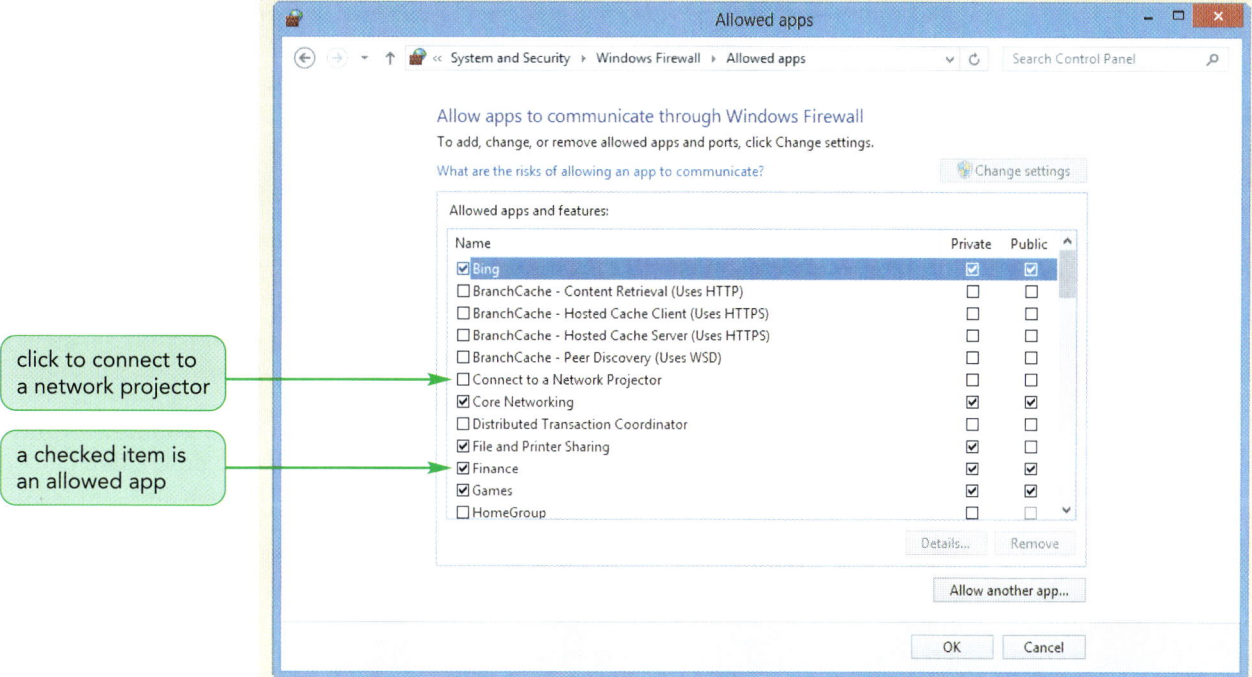

click to connect to a network projector

a checked item is an allowed app

3. Click the **Connect to a Network Projector** check box, if necessary, to select it. A check mark automatically appears in the Private column, indicating that Duane will be able to connect to the device within the company network.

   Trouble? If you cannot select an app in the list, click the Change settings button, and then repeat Step 3.

   Trouble? If you are not allowed to change the allowed apps in Windows Firewall, click the Cancel button in the Allowed apps window, and then skip Step 4.

4. Click the **OK** button to add Connect to a Network Projector to the allowed apps list and to return to the Windows Firewall window.

5. Click **System and Security** in the Address bar to return to the System and Security window.

Keep in mind that when you add an app to the Windows Firewall allowed apps list, you are making your computer easier for apps to access and therefore more vulnerable to malware infection. You should allow an app only when you really need it, and never allow an app that you don't recognize—it could be a virus or a worm. Finally, be sure to remove an app from the allowed apps list when you no longer need it.

Setting Up Windows Update

An **update** is a change to software that can prevent or repair problems, enhance the security of a computer, or improve a computer's performance. Microsoft regularly releases updates to Windows 8 and provides them for download from its Web site. You can look for, download, and install these updates any time you visit the Microsoft Web site. However, because updates often include critical security repairs and enhancements, Microsoft also makes them available to you through the Windows Update feature. Windows Update makes sure your operating system and its tools have the most recent software improvements and security enhancements.

When you use the Windows Update feature, Windows periodically checks for updates to the operating system from Microsoft, including security updates, critical updates, and service packs. (When Microsoft combines many updates in one package, the collection of updates is called a **service pack** and is often abbreviated as **SP**.) If an update is available, Windows Update can download the software and install it for you. Windows downloads the updates in the background according to a schedule you set, as long as you're connected to the Internet. If you are disconnected from the Internet before Windows finishes downloading, Windows continues downloading the next time you connect to the Internet.

You can specify whether Windows automatically downloads only important updates, downloads both important and recommended updates, or does not download automatically at all. Important updates are those you should install to maintain the security and reliability of Windows. Recommended updates usually enhance your computing experience and repair problems that are not considered critical. Microsoft also provides optional updates that don't apply to all Windows users. For example, if you use a particular piece of hardware, such as a digital music player, Windows might provide an optional update for the player's driver. Be sure to read the description of each optional update in the Windows Update window to determine whether you need to download and install the update.

In addition to the types of updates you want Windows to download, you can specify when Windows should install the updates. To notify you that updates are available or that Windows is ready to download or install updates, a notification appears on the Sign in screen. If you've set up automatic updating, Windows will download and install the update as you work on your computer. If restarting your computer is necessary to complete the update, Windows waits until you save data before restarting your computer. If your computer task takes up the entire screen, such as when you're watching a movie, Windows waits until you are finished with that task. You can also choose to have updates downloaded automatically but install them yourself: Click an update option on the Sign in screen or the Shutdown screen to install the updates.

To view your current update status and settings for Windows Update, you open the Windows Update window from the System and Security category of the Control Panel. You can also use this window to review your update history.

You recommend that Duane turn on automatic updating for important and recommended updates so he doesn't miss any of these updates for Windows 8. He wants to check for updates every morning at 8:00 while he is typically meeting with his staff. That way, Windows will not interrupt his work if it needs to install updates. Although he is not using his computer then, it is turned on and connected to the Internet.

As you perform the following steps, note your original settings so you can restore them later.

Tutorial 5 Protecting Your Computer | Windows   WIN 231

To set up Windows Update:

1. In the System and Security window, click **Windows Update**. The Windows Update window opens. See Figure 5-7. Your settings might differ.

Figure 5-7   Windows Update window

2. In the left pane, click **Change settings**. The Change settings window opens. See Figure 5-8.

Figure 5-8   Changing Windows Update settings

3. Make sure "Install updates automatically (recommended)" appears on the first button in the Important updates section. If it does not, click the button and then click **Install updates automatically (recommended)** in the list. Selecting this option means that Windows checks for updates according to a schedule, and then downloads and installs them for you when they are available.

TIP

To check for updates manually, click Check for updates in the left pane of the Windows Update window.

4. Click the **Updates will be automatically installed during the maintenance window**. link to open the Automatic Maintenance window so you can schedule the update check.

5. Click the **Run maintenance tasks daily at** button (which appears as 3:00 AM by default), and then click **8:00 AM**.

6. If necessary, click the **Allow scheduled maintenance to wake up my computer at the scheduled time** check box to select it. This option allows Windows to wake your computer for scheduled updates.

7. Click the **OK** button to close the Automatic Maintenance window.

   Trouble? If a dialog box opens requesting an administrator password or your permission to continue, enter the password or click the Yes button.

8. Click the **OK** button to accept the new Windows Update setting.

9. Click **System and Security** in the Address bar to return to the System and Security window.

Now that you know Duane's copy of Windows 8 is up to date, you can turn to protecting his computer from viruses and other types of malware.

Protecting Your Computer from Malware

Your best protection against malware is to use the current version of your antivirus software to scan email messages, attachments, and other files on your computer for viruses, worms, and other types of malware. Antivirus software locates a virus by comparing identifying characteristics of the files on your computer to the characteristics of a list of known viruses, which are called **virus definitions**. When it finds a virus, or any type of malware, the antivirus software notifies you about the virus.

INSIGHT

Recognizing Types of Malware

Recall that a virus is a program that replicates itself and attaches to files or programs, usually affects your computer's performance and stability, and sometimes damages or removes files. Viruses are often transmitted through email attachments or downloaded files, but they don't spread until you open the infected attachment or file. In contrast, a **worm** is harmful computer code that spreads without your interaction. A worm slips from one network connection to another, replicating itself on network computers. As it does, a worm consumes network resources, overwhelming computers until they become slow or unresponsive. Another type of malware is a **Trojan horse**, which is malware that hides inside another program, such as a photo-viewing program you download from the Web. When you install the program, the Trojan horse infects the operating system, allowing a hacker to access your computer. Trojan horses can't spread on their own; they depend on programs, including viruses and worms, to proliferate. If attackers access your system through a Trojan horse, they might install a **rootkit**, malware that gains administrator-level, or root-level, access to a computer or network without the system or users detecting its presence. Attackers use rootkits to monitor keystrokes (to learn passwords, for example), modify files, disable or alter tools that might detect the rootkit, and attack other devices on the network. Common symptoms of malware are when your computer runs much slower than normal, messages appear unexpectedly, programs start or close on their own, or Windows shuts down suddenly.

When you buy a new computer, most likely it comes with antivirus software already installed as a trial version so you can test it for a limited time. (Look for the antivirus software on the Apps screen.) Windows Defender is also installed on any Windows 8 computer to make sure the computer is protected from malware. To determine whether you should continue running the preinstalled antivirus software or Windows Defender, you should compare their features and read reviews from security experts to learn how well each app protects against viruses, spyware, Trojan horses, rootkits, and other malware.

Windows 8 can detect whether you have antivirus software installed on your computer. If you do not, Windows runs Windows Defender to protect your computer from malware. If you have antivirus software installed on your computer but the subscription has expired, Windows reminds you to renew the subscription, activate Windows Defender, or select another antivirus program from the Windows Store. If you have antivirus software installed and it's up to date, do not also run Windows Defender to scan for viruses because only one antivirus app should be running on your computer at any time.

Most vendors of antivirus software offer fee-based subscription services that provide regular updates for current virus definitions. You can refer to the antivirus software's help system to learn how to run the software and receive regular updates, or you can use the Action Center to check for updates. Besides Windows Defender, Windows recognizes most types of antivirus software and displays their status in the Action Center window. In most cases, you can use the Action Center to determine whether your antivirus software needs to be updated and then run the updating program. Windows Update keeps Windows Defender and its virus definitions up to date. Keeping the virus definition list current helps to protect your computer from new attacks. If your list of viruses is out of date, your computer is vulnerable to new threats.

Although Duane is certain that antivirus software is installed on his computer, he asks you to make sure it is up to date and that virus scanning is turned on.

To check for virus protection on your computer:

▶ 1. In the System and Security window, click **Action Center** to return to the Action Center window. If necessary, click **Security** to expand the Security section.

▶ 2. Examine the settings in the Virus protection section, which should report if an installed antivirus program is up to date and is protecting your computer. In Figure 5-9, the Action Center window reports that the antivirus program is out of date.

Trouble? If the Action Center window reports that your virus protection is up to date and is protecting your computer, skip Step 3.

Figure 5-9 Antivirus software needs to be updated

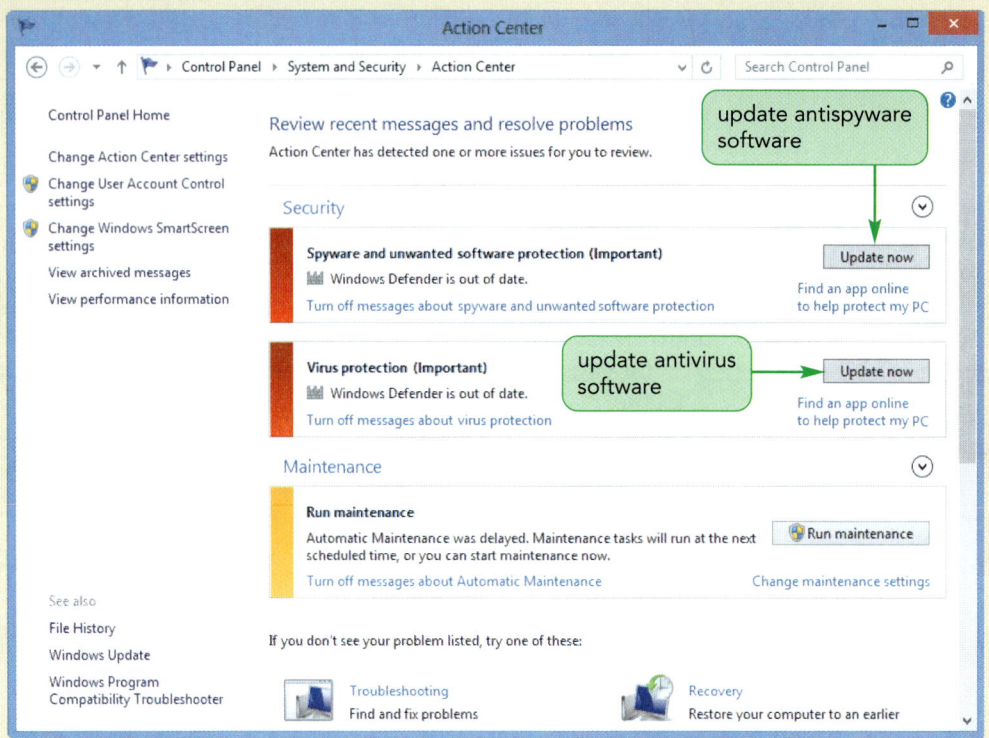

3. If necessary, click the **Update now** button. Your antivirus software starts and checks for updates on its manufacturer's Web site. When it is finished updating, close the antivirus software window, if necessary.

4. Close the Action Center.

Problem Solving: Avoiding and Removing Viruses

One of the most difficult computer problems to solve is removing a virus from your system. To avoid this problem, you can defend against viruses in the following ways so that they do not infect your computer:

- Do not open unexpected email attachments. If the message containing the attachment is from a trusted source, send an email to that person asking about the file and what it contains.
- Regularly scan your hard drive with an antivirus program. Most antivirus software includes an option to schedule a complete system scan. You only need to make sure your computer is turned on to perform the scan.
- Set your antivirus program to scan all *incoming email*.
- Keep your antivirus software up to date. New viruses are introduced frequently, and your antivirus software needs to use the latest virus definitions to protect your computer.
- Create backups of your work files periodically. Viruses can corrupt or destroy data files, which are the most valuable files on your computer.

When you notice symptoms such as your computer running slowly or turning off on its own, suspect a virus. You can try to remove a virus in the following ways:

- Update your antivirus software. Look for an update feature that connects with the Web site of your antivirus software developer to download the latest virus definitions.
- Use the antivirus software to scan your entire computer. The software might be able to remove the virus for you or identify the virus by name.
- Use an online scanner. If your antivirus software does not find or report a virus, visit the Microsoft Web site (www.microsoft.com) and search for "Windows security software providers". Look for vendors in the search results that provide free online virus scanners to help you find and remove the virus.
- Search for instructions on removing the virus. If your antivirus software or online scanner identifies but does not remove the virus, search an antivirus vendor's Web site to find information about removing the virus.

Another security concern is spyware, which can also affect your computing experience.

Defending Against Spyware

TIP

Before installing any software from a Web site, read the license agreement. Do not install software that requires you to accept pop-up ads and to let the program send data about you to the software publisher.

Spyware can install itself or run on your computer without your consent or control. It's called spyware because it monitors your computing actions, usually while you are online, to collect information about you. Spyware can change system settings, interrupt programs, and slow your computer's performance. Spyware may infect your computer when you visit a certain Web site or download a free program, such as a screen saver or search toolbar. Less frequently, spyware is distributed along with other programs on a CD, DVD, or other type of removable media. Sometimes, spyware passes information about your Web browsing habits to advertisers, who use it to improve their products or Web sites. Other times, a special type of spyware called **adware** changes your browser settings to open **pop-up ads**, which are windows that appear while you are viewing a Web page and advertise a product or service. Pop-up ads interrupt your online activities and can be difficult to close; they can also be vehicles for additional spyware or other types of malware.

Because spyware can download, install, and run on your computer without your knowledge or consent, it's often difficult to know if spyware is infecting your computer. If you are experiencing any of the following symptoms, they are most likely due to spyware:

New toolbars, links, or favorites appear in your Web browser unexpectedly.
Your home page, mouse pointer, or search program changes without your consent.

When you enter a URL for a Web site, such as a search engine, you go to a different Web site without notice.

Pop-up ads interrupt you, even when you're not on the Internet.
- Your computer suddenly restarts or runs slowly.

Be sure to scan your computer with a program, such as Windows Defender, to detect and remove any spyware on your computer.

Scanning Your Computer with Windows Defender

To protect your computer against spyware, you can run up-to-date antispyware software or antimalware software, such as Windows Defender, to check for both spyware and viruses. Windows Defender helps prevent malware from installing itself and running on your computer, and it periodically scans your computer to detect and remove malware.

REFERENCE

Performing a Quick Scan with Windows Defender
- On the Start screen, type *Windows Defender*.
- Click Windows Defender in the search results.
- Click the Quick option button on the Home tab.
- Click the Scan now button.

You need to keep the malware definitions in the antimalware up to date. Windows Defender refers to the definitions to determine if software it detects is a virus or spyware. When you update your computer, Windows Update installs any new virus and spyware definitions. You can also set Windows Defender to check for updated definitions before scanning your computer.

You'll show Duane how to start Windows Defender and scan for malware. You can run a quick scan, a full system scan, or a custom scan. A quick scan checks the locations on your computer that spyware is most likely to infect. A full scan checks all your files and programs, but takes longer and can make your computer run slowly. With a custom scan, you select the locations you want Windows Defender to check.

To start Windows Defender and perform a quick scan:

TIP

You can find Windows Defender in the Windows System category on the Apps screen.

1. Press the **Windows** key to display the Start screen, type **Windows Defender**, and then click **Windows Defender** on the Apps screen. The Windows Defender window opens on the desktop. See Figure 5-10, which shows that Windows Defender is up to date. Your settings might differ.

   Trouble? If a dialog box opens indicating that Windows Defender is turned off, click the click here to turn it on link.

Figure 5-10 Windows Defender

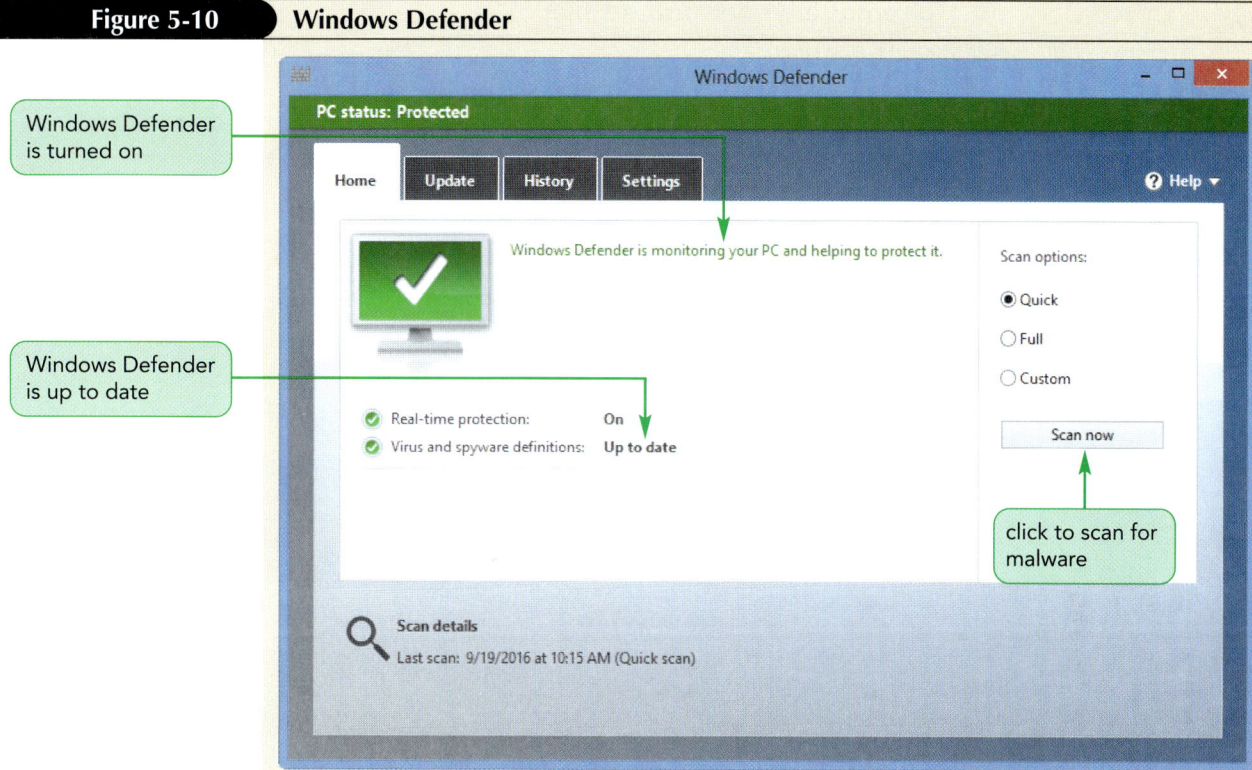

2. If Windows Defender is not up to date, click the **Update** tab, and then click the **Update** button. Windows Defender checks for program and malware definition updates, downloads and installs any updates, and then reports the update status.

3. If necessary, click the **Home** tab, click the **Quick** option button (if necessary), and then click the **Scan now** button. Windows Defender scans your computer, displaying first its progress and then the results of the scan. Depending on the number of programs on your computer, your scan might take a few minutes. Wait for the scan to finish and for Windows Defender to display the results before continuing.

If Windows Defender finds suspicious files, it alerts you that these files have been **quarantined**, which means Windows Defender moved them to another location on your computer to safely segregate them from other files. Quarantined files cannot run, so they cannot harm your computer. You can review all quarantined files to determine what to do with them. Open the History page in Windows Defender, click the Quarantined items option button, and then click the View details button to display a list of quarantined files. The file list includes the filename, alert level, and date of quarantine. The alert level can help you decide whether to remove or restore a file. Remove files with a Severe or High alert level. If you do not recognize or trust the publisher of files with Medium or Low alert levels, search the Web for information on those files to determine whether it is safe to restore them.

TIP
Most antivirus programs quarantine suspicious files so you can choose to restore or delete them.

Windows Defender occasionally identifies a file as potential malware when the computer actually needs the file. If your computer has experienced problems since quarantining those files, start Windows Help and Support, and then click Microsoft Answers website on the Help home page to contact a Microsoft support person and determine what to do with the files. If you haven't had any computer problems since Windows Defender quarantined the files, you can remove the files or leave them in the quarantine location.

To remove a quarantined file:

1. In the Windows Defender window, click the **History** tab to display the History page, click the **Quarantined items** option button, if necessary, and then click the **View details** button to display details about quarantined items. See Figure 5-11.

   Trouble? If a dialog box opens requesting an administrator password or your permission to continue, enter the password and then click the Yes button.

   Trouble? If Windows Defender did not quarantine any items after its quick scan, or if you do not have permission to work with quarantined items, read but do not perform Step 2.

Figure 5-11   Quarantined items in Windows Defender

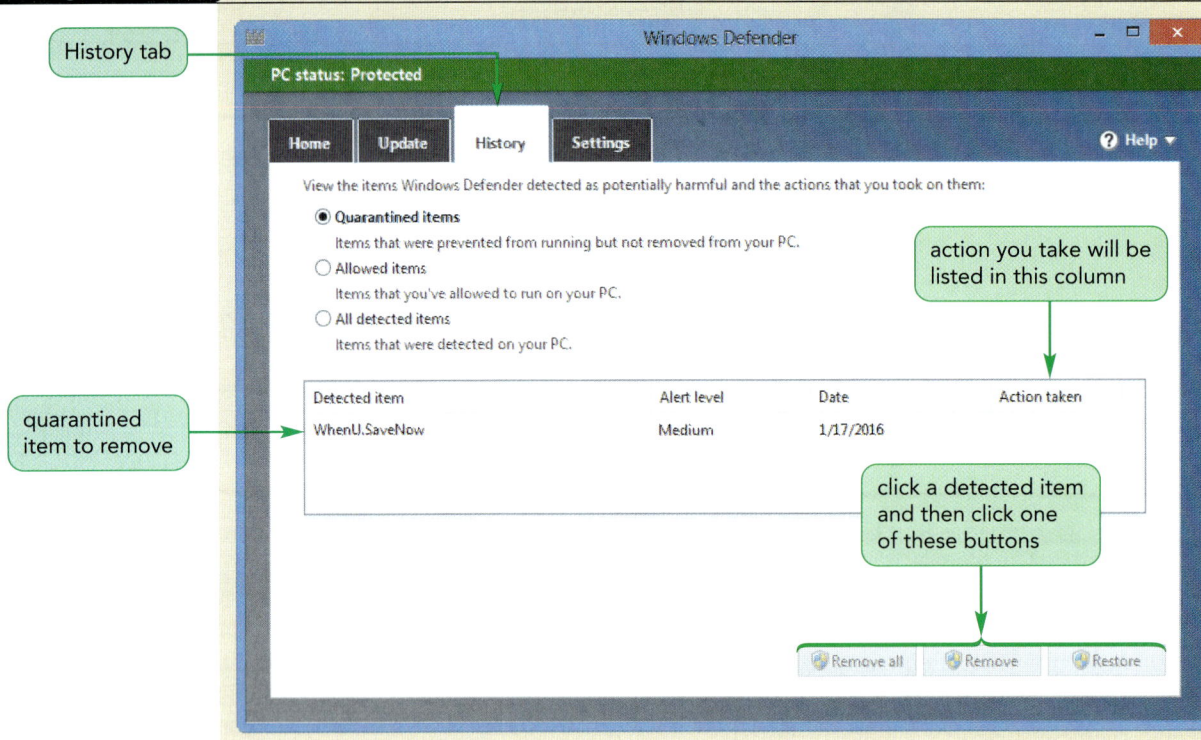

The quarantined item, WhenU.SaveNow, has a Medium alert level. Duane does not recognize the publisher of this program, so you will remove it.

2. In the Quarantined items list, click **WhenU.SaveNow** (or another item with a Severe, High, or Medium alert level and a publisher you do not recognize), and then click the **Remove** button.

   Trouble? If a dialog box opens requesting an administrator password or your permission to continue, enter the password or click the Yes button.

Now that you've scanned Duane's computer and handled the items Windows Defender found, you can set an option to make sure Windows Defender runs effectively and then learn how to turn Windows Defender on and off.

Setting Windows Defender Options

To turn Windows Defender on or off, you use an option on the Settings page. If you have been using Windows Defender and then install a different antimalware app, you should turn Windows Defender off so it doesn't interfere with the other antivirus or antispyware program. If you remove other antimalware software or do not renew an antimalware subscription, Windows Defender runs automatically. To make sure your computer is being protected, you can verify Windows Defender's status on the Settings page.

Another option you can set for Windows Defender is whether to use Real-time protection. This setting is selected by default, which means Windows Defender is set to constantly monitor your computer for virus and spyware activity. Windows Defender then alerts you when suspicious software attempts to install itself or to run on your computer, and notifies you when programs try to change important Windows settings. As with quarantined items, when Windows Defender detects suspicious software, it assigns an alert level to the software and then displays a dialog box where you can choose one of the following actions:

Quarantine—Quarantine the software. Windows Defender prevents the software from running and allows you to restore it or remove it from your computer.
Remove—Permanently delete the software from your computer.
- Allow—Add the software to a list of allowed items so the software can run on your computer. Windows Defender does not alert you to risks that the software might pose to your privacy or your computer unless you remove the program from the Allowed items list.

You'll show Duane how to make sure Windows Defender is turned on and using real-time protection.

To verify Windows Defender options:

1. In the Windows Defender window, click the **Settings** tab to display the Settings page. See Figure 5-12.

Figure 5-12   Windows Defender Settings page

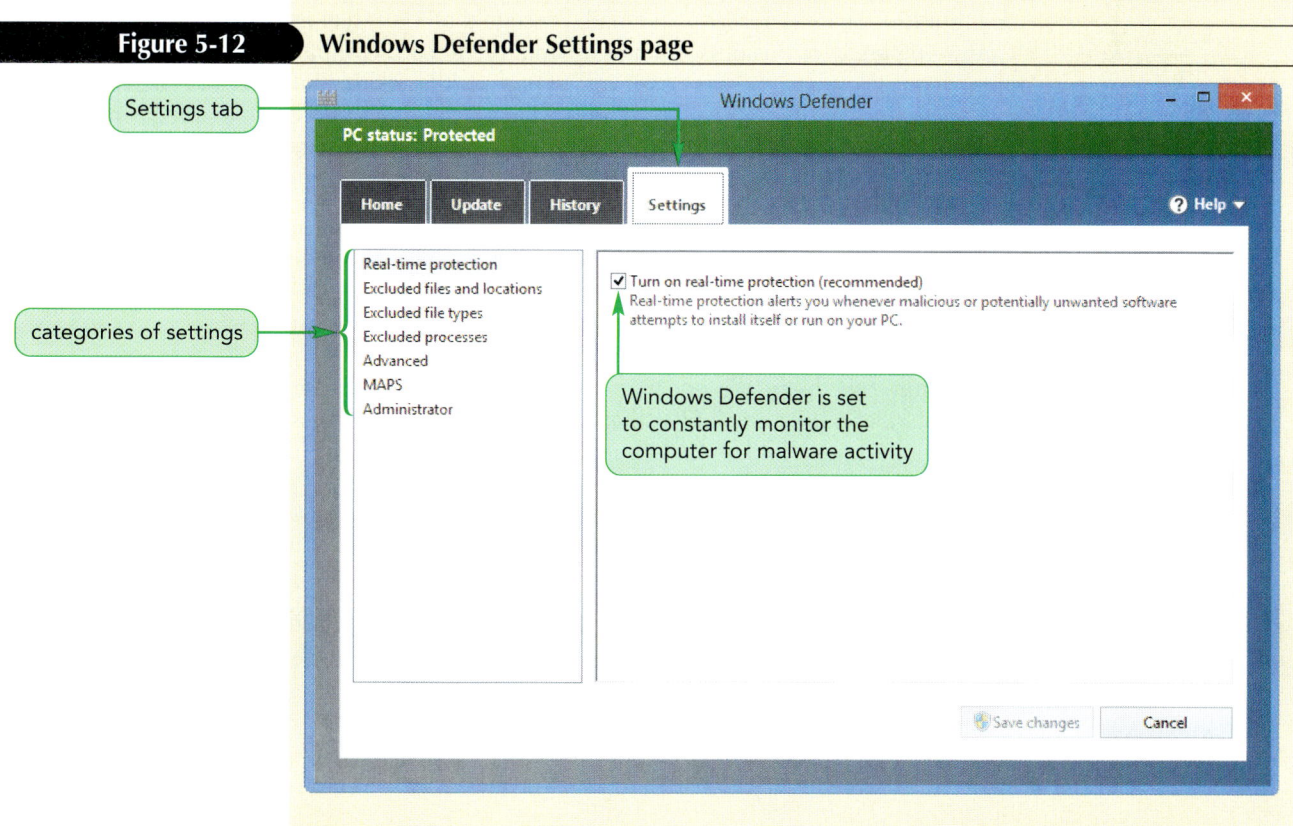

2. If necessary, click the **Turn on real-time protection (recommended)** check box to select it.

3. In the left pane, click **Administrator** to view the Administrator options. Make sure the Turn on Windows Defender check box is selected.

4. Click the **Save changes** button.

   Trouble? If you don't make any changes, the Save changes button is not available. Skip Step 4.

5. Close the Windows Defender window.

Defending Against Email Viruses

An annoying and potentially dangerous type of privacy invasion is **spam**, or junk email, messages offering products and services that are sometimes fake or misleading. Some users receive thousands of spam messages a day; the volume alone makes spam a nuisance. In addition, spam can be a vehicle for malware. Communicating via email is one of the most popular activities on the Internet, and email is the most common way for computer viruses to spread. Viruses and other security threats are often contained in email attachments, especially files with filename extensions such as .exe, .bat, and .js.

To help prevent spam and potentially offensive material, Mail does not download graphics with messages sent in HTML format. People sending spam (called spammers) often use graphics to access your email address. Spammers can also take advantage of vulnerabilities in your computer to use it to send spam to other computers without your permission, a practice known as an **email relay**. This lets spammers work without being detected and can seriously downgrade the performance of your computer.

Phishing (pronounced *fishing*) is an attempt to deceive you into revealing personal or financial information when you respond to an email message or visit a Web site. A typical phishing scam starts with an email message that looks like an official notice from a trusted person or business, such as a bank, credit card company, or reputable online merchant. The email message asks you to reply with sensitive information, such as an account number or password, or directs you to a fraudulent Web site that requests this information. Phishers often use the information for identity theft.

To combat these threats, Mail provides the following built-in security settings:

- Mail automatically blocks email attachments that might be harmful, such as files with .exe, .bat, and .js filename extensions. When Mail blocks an attachment, it displays a notification explaining that it did so.
- Mail displays a notification when it blocks graphics. If you trust the sender, you can click an option on the notification to download and display the pictures.
- By default, Mail helps prevent spammers from using your computer for email relays.
- Mail includes a junk email filter that catches obvious spam messages and moves them to a built-in Junk folder. You can then examine the messages in the Junk folder and delete them, open them, or move them back to your Inbox, if necessary.
- If Mail detects links to Web sites in the email messages you receive, and if the links seem fraudulent, Mail blocks access to the links and displays a notification explaining its actions. If you are certain the message contains legitimate links, you can click an option on the notification to turn on the links in the message.

In the next session, you'll also work with Internet Explorer settings to protect against phishing attempts.

TIP

Viewing a picture in a junk email message might validate your email address and result in your receiving more junk email.

REVIEW

Session 5.1 Quick Check

1. What is malware?
2. The _____ is a Control Panel tool that helps you manage security from a single window.
3. _____ checks communication coming from the Internet and either blocks it from your computer or allows it to pass.
4. What is Windows Update?
5. What does Windows 8 do if you do not have antivirus software installed on your computer?
6. If pop-up ads interrupt your computer work, even when you're not on the Internet, what should you suspect?
7. If Windows Defender finds files that might be spyware, it _____ the files, which means it moves them to another location on your computer and prevents them from running until you remove or restore the files.
8. _____ is a form of electronic direct mail, and can be a vehicle for malware.

Session 5.2 Visual Overview:

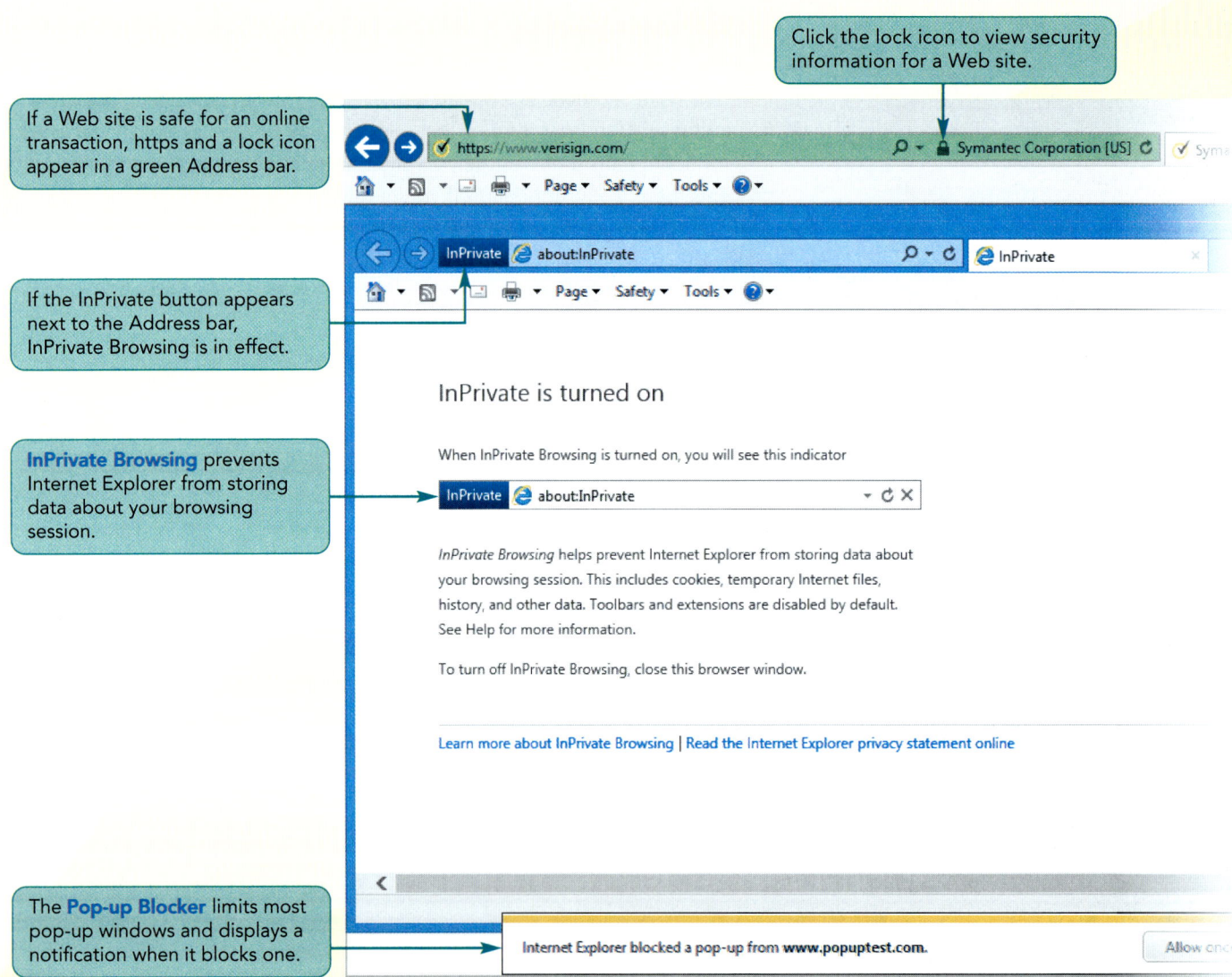

Click the lock icon to view security information for a Web site.

If a Web site is safe for an online transaction, https and a lock icon appear in a green Address bar.

If the InPrivate button appears next to the Address bar, InPrivate Browsing is in effect.

InPrivate Browsing prevents Internet Explorer from storing data about your browsing session.

The **Pop-up Blocker** limits most pop-up windows and displays a notification when it blocks one.

Internet Explorer Security Features

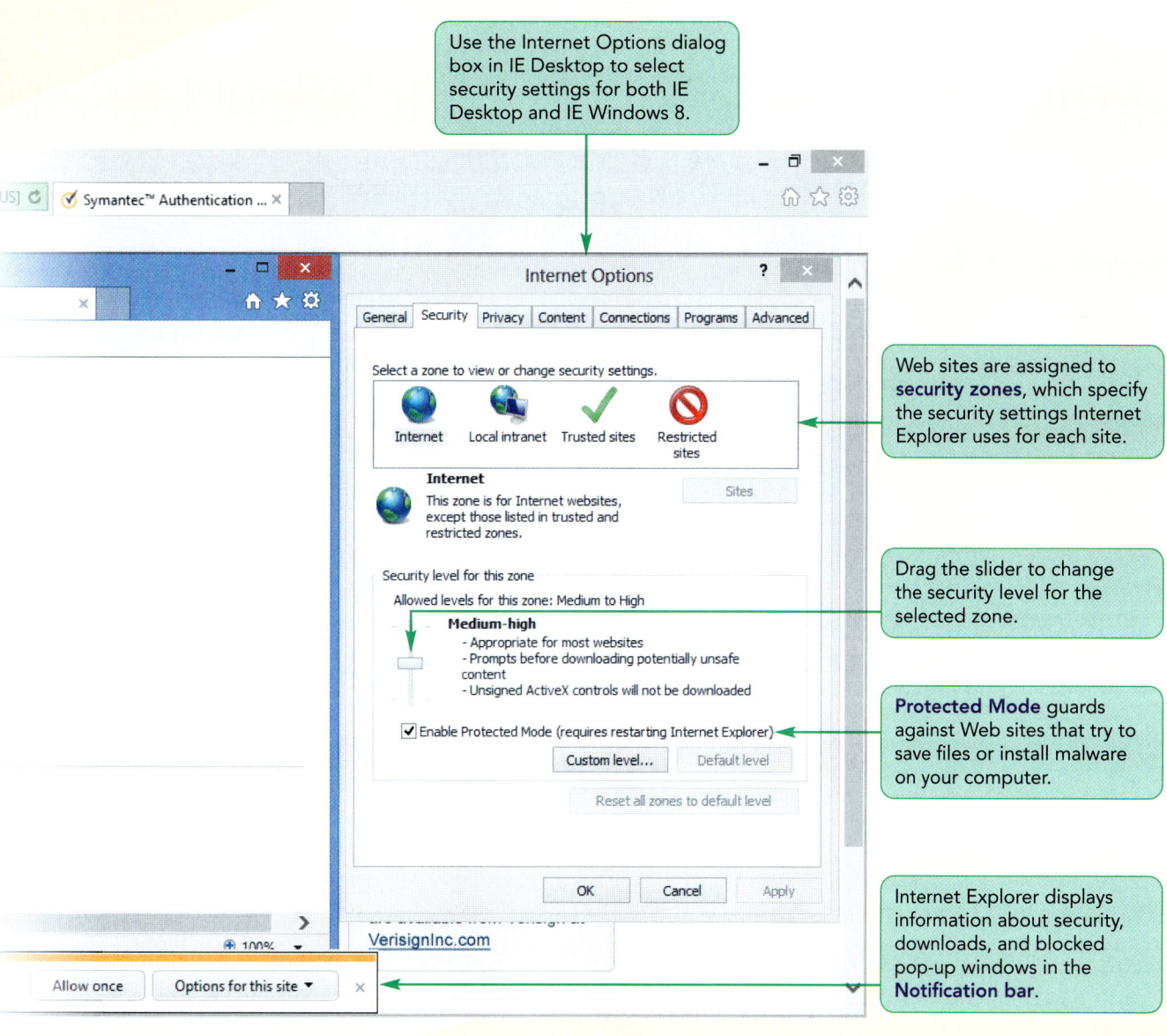

Managing Microsoft Internet Explorer Security

Your computer is most vulnerable to security threats when you are connected to the Internet. You should therefore take advantage of the security settings in Internet Explorer to help protect your computer by identifying viruses and other security threats that are circulated over the Internet, making your computer and personal information more secure. Internet Explorer uses the security features provided in the following list. In general, you set options for these features using IE Desktop. When you do, they apply to IE Windows 8 as well.

- SmartScreen Filter—This feature helps detect online scams, such as Web sites that try to trick you into revealing financial account information. The SmartScreen Filter also helps detect and block unknown and potentially malicious programs in files that you download from Web sites.
- Protected Mode—This feature guards against Web sites that try to save files or install malware on your computer.
- Digital signatures—Internet Explorer can detect and display **digital signatures**, which are electronic security marks added to files to verify their authenticity.
- Pop-up Blocker—This tool allows you to limit or block most pop-up windows.
- Add-on Manager—This tool lets you disable or allow programs or controls that extend your browser's features.

Checking Web Sites with the SmartScreen Filter

> **TIP**
> The SmartScreen filter is part of Windows, so it works with Internet Explorer and other browsers such as Firefox and Chrome.

Recall that phishing is an attempt to deceive you into revealing personal or financial information when you respond to an email message or visit a Web site. Internet Explorer can protect you from online scams by detecting possible phishing Web sites. The SmartScreen Filter helps to protect you from phishing attacks, online fraud, and spoofed Web sites. (A **spoofed Web site** is a fraudulent site posing as a legitimate one.) The SmartScreen Filter operates in the background to analyze a Web site you visit by comparing its address to a list of reported phishing and malicious software Web sites. If the SmartScreen Filter finds that the Web site you're visiting is on the list of known malware or phishing sites, Internet Explorer does not display the suspicious Web site. Instead, it shows a blocking Web page where you can choose to bypass the blocked Web site and go to your home page instead. If you are certain the blocked Web site is safe, you can continue to the site, though Microsoft does not recommend it.

If a spoofed site has not been reported as possibly malicious, the SmartScreen Filter will not detect it as a site to avoid. Commonly spoofed Web sites are those where you perform financial transactions, such as online banking or shopping sites. They often use phony Web addresses to mislead you into thinking you are visiting a legitimate site. When you visit a site that requests personal or financial information, look in the Address bar for the Web address. Internet Explorer displays the true domain you are visiting. For example, you might do your online banking at an Accounts Web page with the address *www.bank.com/accounts*. If you visit the Accounts Web page but notice that the Address bar displays the address *www.phony.com/accounts*, you are visiting a spoofed site and should close the Web page and report it as a possible phishing site. The Microsoft support team will investigate the site and add it to the list of known phishing sites as appropriate.

INSIGHT

Protecting Yourself from Phishing Attempts

In addition to using the SmartScreen Filter, use the following guidelines to protect yourself from online phishing:
- Never provide personal information in an email, an instant message, or a pop-up window.
- Do not click links in email and instant messages from senders you do not know or trust. Even messages that seem to be from friends and family can be faked. Therefore, check with the sender to make sure he or she actually sent the message (especially if the message contains only a link to a Web site).
- Only use Web sites that provide privacy statements or indicate how they use your personal information.

You can turn on the SmartScreen Filter to check Web sites and files automatically in both IE Desktop and IE Windows 8, or you can check them manually in IE Desktop by using the Tools button.

To turn on the SmartScreen Filter and check a Web site:

1. If necessary, click the **Desktop** tile on the Start screen to display the desktop.
2. Click the **Internet Explorer** button on the taskbar to start the browser.
3. Click the **Tools** button on the right side of the Internet Explorer window, point to **Safety**, and then click **Check this website**. Internet Explorer sends the URL of the page to Microsoft for verification.

   Trouble? If a dialog box opens explaining how the SmartScreen Filter works, click the OK button.

4. When the SmartScreen Filter dialog box opens to indicate it checked the Web site and does not report any threats, click the **OK** button.
5. Click the **Tools** button, point to **Safety**, and then click **Turn on SmartScreen Filter**. The Microsoft SmartScreen Filter dialog box opens. See Figure 5-13. Internet Explorer selects the Turn on SmartScreen Filter (recommended) option button for you.

   Trouble? If Turn off SmartScreen Filter appears when you point to Safety, the SmartScreen Filter is already turned on. Skip Steps 5 and 6.

Figure 5-13 Microsoft SmartScreen Filter dialog box

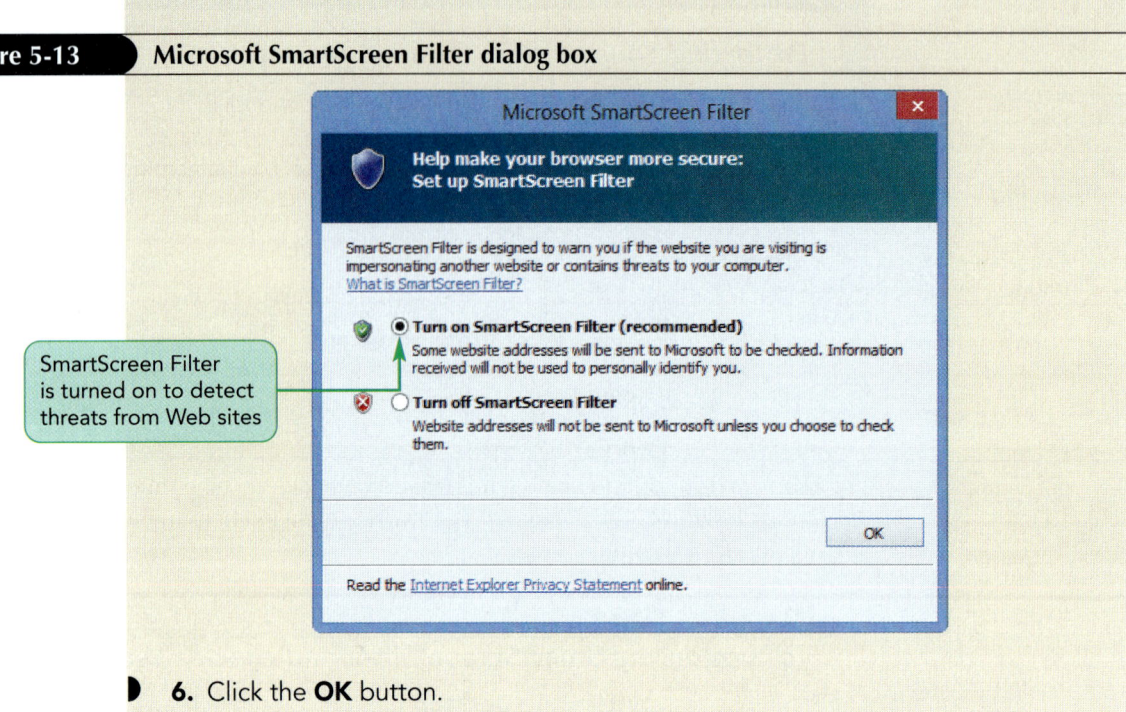

SmartScreen Filter is turned on to detect threats from Web sites

6. Click the **OK** button.

7. To see how to report a possible phishing site, click the **Tools** button, point to **Safety**, and then click **Report unsafe website**. The Microsoft SmartScreen Filter Web page opens so you can report information about the Web site. See Figure 5-14.

Figure 5-14 Microsoft SmartScreen Filter Web page

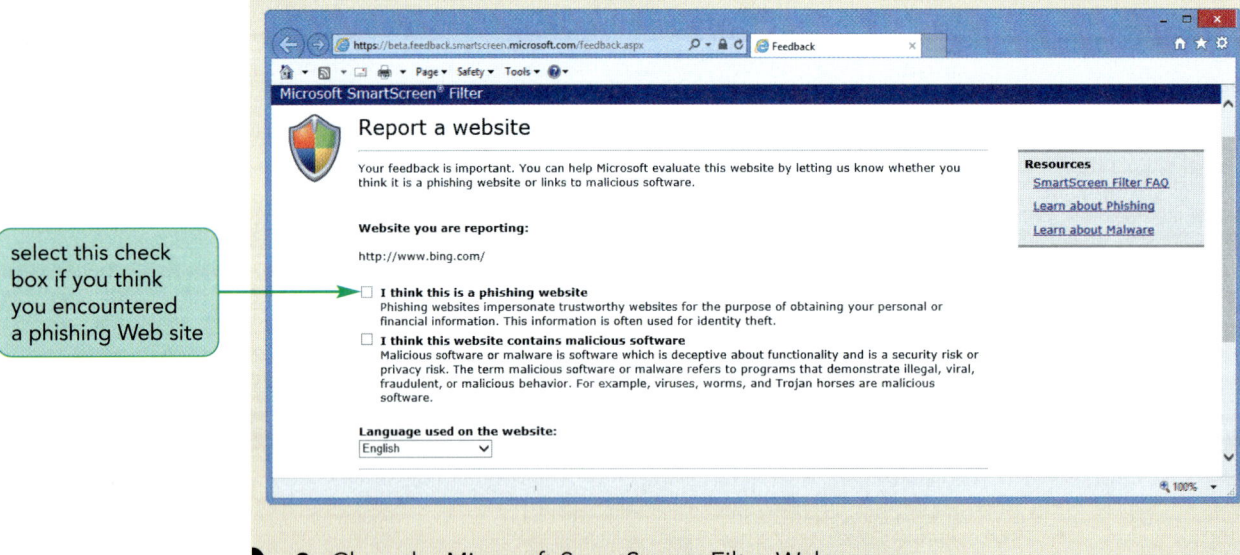

select this check box if you think you encountered a phishing Web site

8. Close the Microsoft SmartScreen Filter Web page.

As you visit Web sites, Internet Explorer checks their certificates. A **certificate** is a digital document (similar to a digital signature) that verifies the security of a Web site you visit. Internet Explorer can detect certificate errors, which are signs that you are visiting a phishing site or one that uses spyware or other malware. If Internet Explorer detects a certificate error or other security problem, it identifies the problem type in the Address bar. For example, a certificate error message might appear in the Address bar. You can click the error message to learn about the problem. See Figure 5-15.

Figure 5-15   Security message in the Address bar

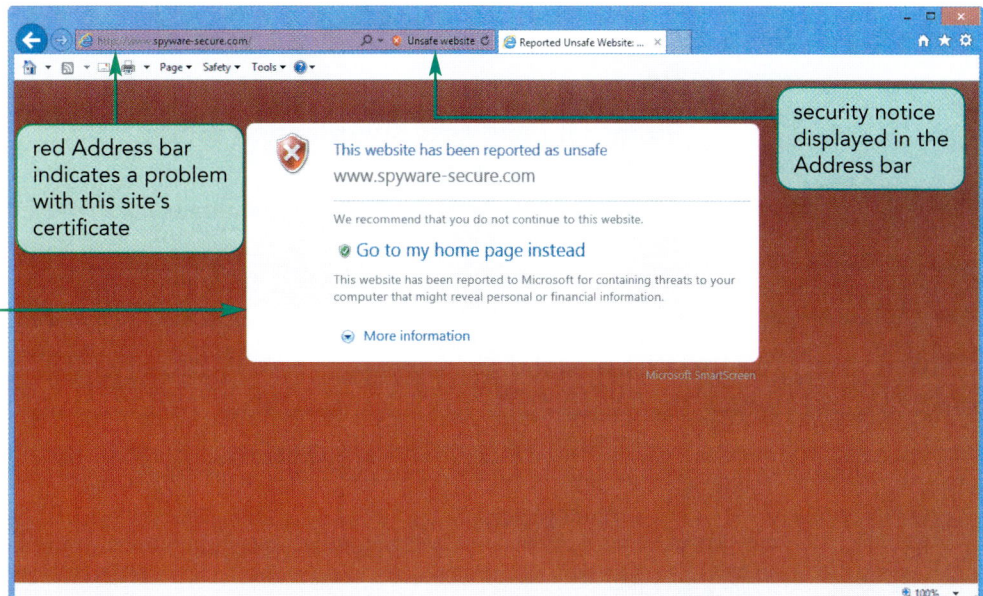

The color of the Address bar also indicates the type of error or problem. Red means the certificate is out of date, is invalid, or has an error. Yellow signals that the certificate cannot be verified, which sometimes happens with a suspected phishing site. White means the certificate is normal, and green indicates sites that have high security, such as those for financial transactions.

Downloading Files Safely

The SmartScreen Filter also works with Internet Explorer's Download Manager to manage downloaded files. Download Manager lists the files you download from the Internet, keeps track of where they're stored on your computer, and lets you pause, open, run, delete, or save the downloaded files. The SmartScreen Filter analyzes files you want to download in a way similar to how it analyzes Web sites. When you select a file to download from a Web site, the SmartScreen filter refers to a list of files known to be malicious. If the file you want to download is on that list, the SmartScreen Filter blocks the download and explains the file is unsafe. If the file is not on the list of malicious files, the SmartScreen Filter refers to a list of programs downloaded by a significant number of other Internet Explorer users. The SmartScreen Filter notifies you if the file is not on the list of commonly downloaded files. In that case, you should not open or install the file unless you trust its publisher and the Web site that provided the file. You can use Download Manager to delete the program or run it if you know the file is safe.

WIN 248 Windows | Tutorial 5 Protecting Your Computer

If you download a file and later suspect it might be harmful, you can use Download Manager to run a set of security checks, including the SmartScreen Filter, before you open the file. The SmartScreen Filter checks to see if the file is on its updated list of malicious files. If you learn from another source that a downloaded file is unsafe, you can use Download Manager to report the file, which adds the file to the SmartScreen Filter list of malicious files.

You'll show Duane how to use Internet Explorer to display a list of downloaded files. Duane also wants to know where Download Manager stores downloaded files on his computer. If he suspects a downloaded file contains malicious software, he can quickly find the file and delete it using File Explorer. He can also use Download Manager to test, delete, and report suspicious files.

To display and test downloaded files:

▸ 1. Click the **Tools** button ⚙ on the right side of the Internet Explorer window, and then click **View downloads** to display Download Manager. See Figure 5-16. The list of downloaded files on your computer will differ.

Trouble? If Download Manager on your computer does not list any files, read but do not perform the remaining steps.

Figure 5-16 Download Manager

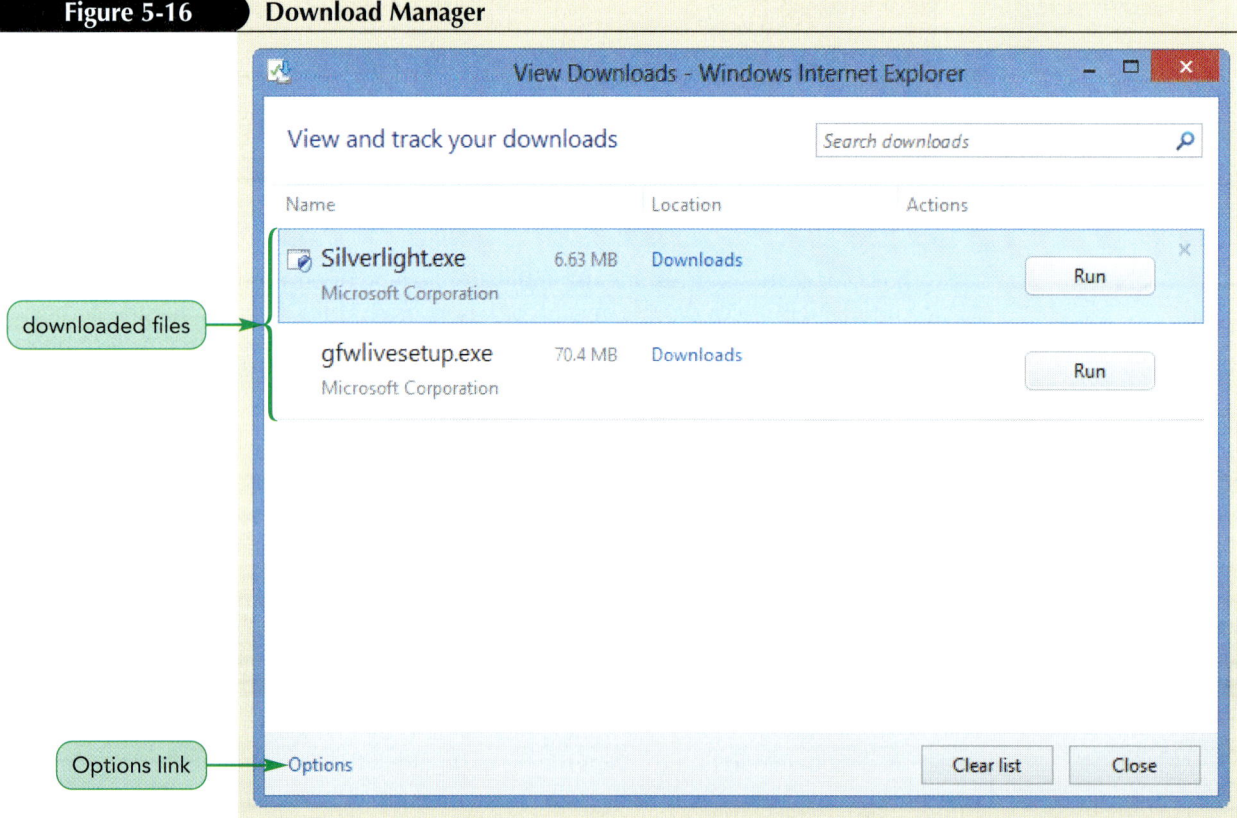

▸ 2. Click the **Options** link to open the Download Options dialog box, which indicates the default location for downloaded files. By default, Windows 8 uses the Downloads folder for downloaded files. (If you wanted to change this location, you could click the Browse button in the Download Options dialog box.)

▸ 3. Click the **OK** button to close the Download Options dialog box.

TIP

If you right-click a program file, the command on the shortcut menu is "Rerun security checks on this program."

4. Right-click the first file listed in Download Manager, and then click **Rerun security checks on this file** on the shortcut menu. The SmartScreen Filter scans the file. If the file is safe, Download Manager displays only an Open button or a Run button. If the file is unsafe, Download Manager also displays a Delete button and indicates that the file could harm your computer.

5. Close the View Downloads window.

Windows stores downloaded files in the Downloads folder on your hard disk by default. Therefore, if you use Download Manager to delete a downloaded file, Windows moves the file to the Recycle Bin. If you change the location to a removable disk that does not use a Recycle Bin, the file is permanently removed when you delete it.

Blocking Malware with Protected Mode and Security Zones

To install or run programs on your computer, hackers often take advantage of Web programming tools, such as scripts and ActiveX controls, that are designed to enhance your online experience. A **script** is programming code that performs a series of commands and can be embedded in a Web page. For example, a Web site designer might use a script to verify that you've completed all the necessary fields in an online form. In contrast, hackers use scripts on a Web page to automatically download programs to your computer that can collect and transmit information about you without your knowledge or authorization.

A common way for hackers to distribute adware and spyware is to download **ActiveX controls**, which are small, self-contained programs, from a Web page to your computer. Some ActiveX controls make it easier to perform tasks, such as submitting information to a Web site. Other ActiveX controls can harm your computer and files, especially those controls that lack digital signatures, meaning they are unverified. Recall that a digital signature is an electronic security mark that can be added to files, similar to a certificate added to Web sites. A digital signature identifies the publisher of a file and verifies that the file has not changed since it was signed. Internet Explorer offers a few ways to protect against malicious scripts and ActiveX controls, including Protected Mode and security zones. You can also specifically block a Web site from using ActiveX controls, which you do later in the tutorial.

INSIGHT

Digital Signatures

Internet Explorer (and other programs, including Windows 8) detects whether a file has a digital signature. A file without a valid digital signature might not be from the stated source or might have been tampered with (possibly by a virus) since it was published. Avoid opening an unsigned file unless you know for certain who created it and whether the contents are safe to open. However, even a valid digital signature does not guarantee that the contents of the file are harmless. When you download a file, determine whether to trust its contents based on the identity of the publisher and the site providing the file.

Internet Explorer runs in Protected Mode by default, making it difficult for hackers to install malware on your computer. If a Web page tries to install any type of software or run a script, Internet Explorer displays a message in the Notification bar warning you about the attempt. If you trust the program, you can allow it to run once or always. If you are not familiar with the program or don't want to run it, you can deny it once or always.

In addition to Protected Mode, Internet Explorer uses security zones so you can tailor your security settings to the kind of online computing you do. Internet Explorer classifies all Web sites in one of four security zones: Internet, Local intranet, Trusted sites, and Restricted sites. Each zone uses a certain level of security setting ranging from Low to High. When you visit a Web site that has been assigned to a security zone, the appropriate icon appears in the Internet Explorer status bar. Figure 5-17 summarizes the four security zones.

Figure 5-17   Internet Explorer security zones

Security Zone	Description
Internet	Internet Explorer assigns all Internet Web sites to this zone by default and applies a Medium-high security level, which is appropriate for most sites. You can change the security level to Medium or High.
Local intranet	Internet Explorer assigns Web sites on your intranet (a corporate or business network) to this zone and applies a Medium-low security level. You can change this to any other level.
Trusted sites	You can assign Web sites to this zone that you trust not to damage your computer or files. This zone has a Medium level of security by default, but you can change it to any other level.
Restricted sites	You assign Web sites to this zone that might damage your computer or files. Adding sites to this zone does not block them, but it does prevent them from using scripts or active content. This zone has a High level of security by default and cannot be changed.

© 2014 Cengage Learning

You'll show Duane how to check the security level of his home page.

To check the security level of your home page:

1. With Internet Explorer open to your home page, click the **Tools** button on the right side of the Internet Explorer window, and then click **Internet options** to open the Internet Options dialog box.

2. Click the **Security** tab to display the security settings. See Figure 5-18. Leave the dialog box open for now.

Figure 5-18 Security tab in the Internet Options dialog box

Duane's home page is assigned to the Internet zone, which uses a Medium-high security level and Protected Mode by default. At this level, Internet Explorer does not download unsigned ActiveX controls and requests permission before downloading content that might be unsafe.

Next, you'll show Duane how to use the Pop-up Blocker to limit or block most pop-up windows when he visits Web sites. You use the Internet Options dialog box to select settings for the Pop-up Blocker.

Blocking Pop-Up Windows

A pop-up ad is a small Web browser window that appears when you visit a Web site and advertises a product or service. Many legitimate advertisers use pop-up ads because they effectively get your attention and provide information or services that might interest you. However, some pop-up ads are annoying because they repeatedly interrupt your online activities, are difficult to close, or display objectionable content. Other pop-up ads are dangerous because they can download spyware or **hijack** your browser—meaning they seize control of the browser, opening many more new windows each time you close one pop-up window until you have to close your browser or restart your computer.

To avoid the nuisance and danger of pop-up ads, Internet Explorer includes the Pop-up Blocker, which warns you about or blocks pop-up ads. The Pop-up Blocker is turned on by default, meaning that Internet Explorer blocks most pop-up windows. Not all pop-up windows are ads. If a pop-up window opens as soon as you visit a Web site, it probably contains an ad. However, many Web sites use pop-up windows to display tools such as calendars. For example, if you visit a travel Web site to make flight or hotel reservations, the site might provide a calendar in a pop-up window so you can select your travel dates. If you click a link or button to open the pop-up window,

Internet Explorer does not block it by default. However, it does block pop-up windows that appear automatically if you have not clicked a link or button.

To display a blocked pop-up window, you can use the Notification bar shown in the Session 5.2 Visual Overview. When you visit a Web site with pop-up windows and the Pop-up Blocker is turned on, the Notification bar opens to display a message informing you that it blocked a pop-up window. You can click the Options for this site button on the Notification bar to display a menu of settings, such as Temporarily Allow Pop-ups. To select long-term settings, you use the Pop-up Blocker Settings dialog box to block all pop-up ads, allow more pop-up ads, or specify which Web sites can display pop-up ads in your browser.

Duane has had problems with pop-up ads before, so he wants to block all pop-ups in Internet Explorer. You'll show him how to change the Pop-up Blocker settings to do so. As you perform the following steps, note your original settings so you can restore them later.

To change the Pop-up Blocker settings in Internet Explorer:

1. In the Internet Options dialog box, click the **Privacy** tab, and then click the **Settings** button. The Pop-up Blocker Settings dialog box opens. See Figure 5-19.

Figure 5-19 | Pop-up Blocker Settings dialog box

2. Click the **Blocking level** button, and then click **High: Block all pop-ups (Ctrl+Alt to override)**.

   Trouble? If you are working in a computer lab, you might not have permission to change the Pop-up Blocker settings. In that case, skip Step 2.

3. Click the **Close** button to close the Pop-up Blocker Settings dialog box.

4. Click the **OK** button to close the Internet Options dialog box.

Next, you'll learn how to find out which add-on programs are installed to work with Internet Explorer.

Managing Add-On Programs

A browser **add-on** is a program offered by any software vendor that provides enhancements such as a toolbar or an improved search feature. For example, Microsoft Silverlight is a popular add-on that enhances the multimedia, animation, and other effects displayed in Internet Explorer. Some add-ons are safe and make your browser more effective; other add-ons, especially those that are installed without your permission, can affect the performance of Internet Explorer and even make it stop working. Internet Explorer provides an Add-on Manager so you can review, disable, update, or report add-ons to Microsoft. Other security features, such as Protected Mode, security levels, and the Notification bar, warn you when a Web site is trying to download add-on software to your computer.

You can usually install and use browser add-ons without any problems, but some cause Internet Explorer to shut down unexpectedly. If this happens, you can disable the add-on.

Internet Explorer usually asks for permission before running an add-on for the first time. If you don't recognize the program or its publisher, you can deny permission. Internet Explorer also maintains a list of preapproved add-ons that have been checked and digitally signed. It runs add-ons in this list without requesting your permission. You can view the list of preapproved add-ons in the Manage Add-ons dialog box.

Duane isn't aware of any add-ons his browser uses, so he wants to view the preapproved add-ons and any others that Internet Explorer is running.

To examine and manage add-ons:

1. Click the **Tools** button on the right side of the Internet Explorer window, and then click **Manage add-ons**. The Manage Add-ons dialog box opens. By default, this dialog box displays the toolbar and extension add-ons that are currently loaded in Internet Explorer.

2. Click the **Currently loaded add-ons** button, and then click **Run without permission**. The preapproved add-ons appear in the list.

3. Click the first add-on in the list to display details about it. See Figure 5-20.

Figure 5-20 Manage Add-ons window

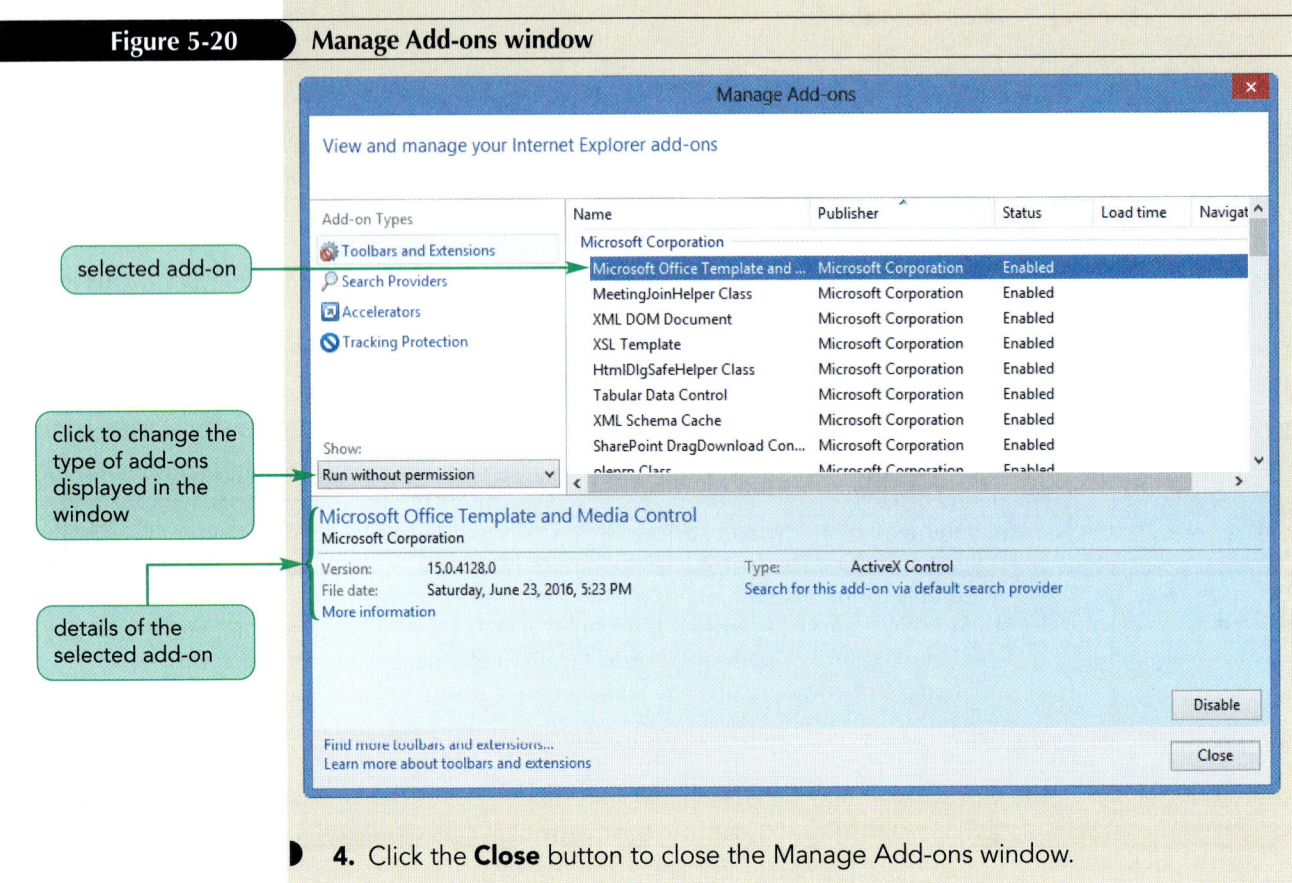

4. Click the **Close** button to close the Manage Add-ons window.

Now that you have explored the security settings in Internet Explorer, you can turn your attention to its privacy settings.

Selecting Internet Explorer Privacy Settings

In addition to security protection, Internet Explorer also includes the following tools and features to protect your privacy:

Privacy settings and alerts—These settings specify how to handle identifying information when you're online, and alert you when a Web site you're visiting doesn't meet your criteria.

InPrivate Browsing—This feature helps prevent Internet Explorer from storing data about your browsing session by opening a separate InPrivate Browsing Internet Explorer window to keep your browsing actions private.

Tracking Protection—This feature helps prevent Web site content providers from collecting information about sites you visit.

- Secure connections—Internet Explorer informs you when it is using a secure connection to communicate with Web sites that handle sensitive personal information.

REFERENCE

Selecting Privacy Settings

- Click the Tools button, and then click Internet options.
- Click the Privacy tab in the Internet Options dialog box.
- Drag the slider to select a privacy setting ranging from Block All Cookies to Accept All Cookies.
- Click the OK button.

One privacy concern is cookies, which many Web sites store on your computer when you visit them. A **cookie** is a small file that records information about you, such as the type of browser you are using, your email address, and your preferences for using a Web site. Like other Web tools, cookies can enhance your online experience by helping trusted Web sites customize their service to you. However, they can also pose a security risk—hackers can retrieve cookies to search for private information such as passwords, or use cookies to track the Web sites you visit. In Internet Explorer, you can specify privacy settings to either allow Web sites to save cookies on your computer or prevent them from doing so.

One way to protect your privacy with Internet Explorer is to block cookies on some or all of the Web sites you visit. You should be selective about which Web sites you allow to store cookies on your computer. Blocking all cookies keeps your Web site visits private, but might also limit your experience or prove annoying. Allowing all cookies might compromise your privacy. Most users find that the default Medium-high privacy setting provides a good balance because it allows most **first-party cookies**, which are generated from the Web sites you visit and contain information the Web site reuses when you return. For example, to keep track of products you add to an electronic shopping cart or wish list, a Web site saves a first-party cookie on your computer. In contrast, the Medium-high privacy setting blocks most **third-party cookies**, which are generated from Web site advertisers, who might use them to track your Web use for marketing purposes.

Duane often visits his clients' Web sites for research as he prepares to develop products. He wants to protect the privacy of Catapult Product Design and his clients by blocking all cookies and then allowing only those issued by sites he trusts.

As you perform the following steps, note your original settings so you can restore them later.

To change privacy settings for saving cookies:

1. Click the **Tools** button on the right side of the Internet Explorer window, and then click **Internet options**. The Internet Options dialog box opens.

2. Click the **Privacy** tab to view the privacy settings. See Figure 5-21. The Settings section describes how cookies are treated based on the security zone selected and the level of risk set.

Figure 5-21 Privacy tab in the Internet Options dialog box

Trouble? If you are working in a computer lab, you might not have permission to change the privacy settings. In that case, read but do not perform Steps 3–6.

3. Drag the slider up to the **Block All Cookies** setting. When you select this setting, Internet Explorer will not let a Web site store any cookies on your computer unless you explicitly allow it to do so.

4. Drag the slider back to **Medium**. This setting blocks cookies except for some first-party cookies and those created by Web sites you identify.

5. Click the **Sites** button to open the Per Site Privacy Actions dialog box. You use this dialog box to specify the Web sites you want to allow to store cookies on your computer. (If you had selected a lower privacy setting, you could also use this dialog box to block certain Web sites from storing cookies.)

6. Click the **OK** button to close the Per Site Privacy Actions dialog box. Leave the Internet Options dialog box open for the next set of steps.

TIP
To view temporary files before deleting them, click the Tools button, click Internet options, click the General tab, click the Settings button in the Browsing history section, and then click View files.

Internet Explorer will block most cookies on Duane's computer from now on. However, if Web sites stored cookies on his computer before you changed the privacy setting, they will remain there until you delete them. You can delete cookies by clearing your browsing history. In addition to cookies, Internet Explorer stores temporary Internet files, a history of the Web sites you've visited, information you've entered in the Address bar, and Web passwords you've saved. (A temporary Internet file is a copy of a Web page you viewed. Internet Explorer stores this file for a specified number of days, such as 20, so it can display the page quickly if you open it again.) Usually, maintaining this history information improves your Web browsing because it can fill in information that you would otherwise have to retype. If you have particular privacy concerns, however, such as when you are using a public computer, you can clear some or all of your browsing history to delete this information. Duane wants to delete all of the cookies and the list of Web sites he has visited.

To clear your browsing history:

1. Click the **General** tab in the Internet Options dialog box, and then click the **Delete** button in the Browsing history section. The Delete Browsing History dialog box opens. See Figure 5-22.

Figure 5-22 Delete Browsing History dialog box

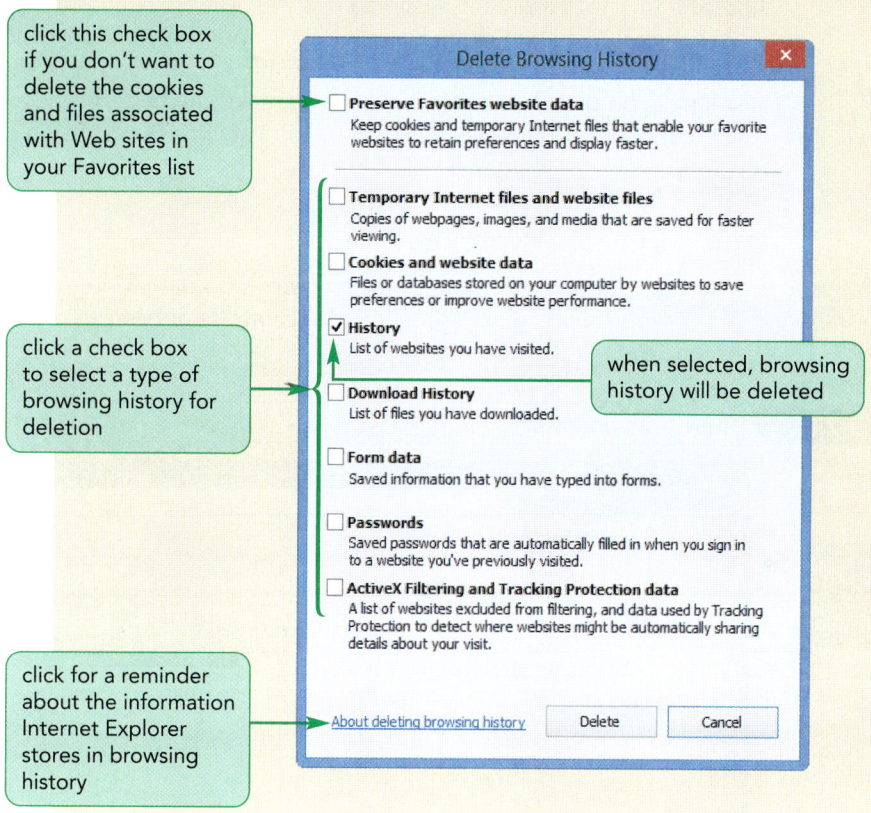

click this check box if you don't want to delete the cookies and files associated with Web sites in your Favorites list

click a check box to select a type of browsing history for deletion

when selected, browsing history will be deleted

click for a reminder about the information Internet Explorer stores in browsing history

Trouble? If you are working in a computer lab, you might not have permission to clear your browsing history. In that case, read but do not perform Steps 2–6.

TIP

When you delete all of your browsing history, you do not delete your list of favorites or subscribed feeds.

2. If necessary, click the **Cookies and website data** check box to insert a check mark and indicate you want to delete all of the cookies stored on your computer.

3. If necessary, click the **History** check box to insert a check mark and indicate you want to delete the list of Web sites you have visited.

4. Click the **Delete** button to delete cookies and your browsing history.

5. Click the **OK** button to close the Internet Options dialog box. A Notification bar appears on the bottom of the Internet Explorer window confirming that Internet Explorer deleted the selected browsing history.

6. Click the **Close** button to close the Notification bar.

Another privacy feature of Internet Explorer is InPrivate Browsing, which you'll explore next.

Protecting Your Privacy with InPrivate Browsing

TIP

To open an InPrivate window in IE Windows 8, right-click a blank spot on a Web page, click the Tab tools button, and then click New InPrivate tab.

If you want to keep information about your Web browsing private, you can use InPrivate Browsing. This feature prevents Internet Explorer from storing data about your browsing session. If you are searching online for a gift, for example, or want to prevent another user from retracing your steps to a Web site containing your financial information, use InPrivate Browsing to hide the history of the Web pages you visited. When you do, Internet Explorer opens a new window and displays InPrivate in the Address bar. As you work in the InPrivate window, Internet Explorer protects your privacy. To end your InPrivate Browsing session, close the browser window.

Keep in mind that InPrivate Browsing does not make you anonymous on the Internet. Web sites might still be able to identify you through your Web address, and any forms you complete and selections you make can be recorded and saved by those Web sites. You will show Duane how an InPrivate Browsing session works.

To turn on InPrivate Browsing:

▶ 1. Click the **Tools** button on the right side of the Internet Explorer window, point to **Safety**, and then click **InPrivate Browsing** to open the InPrivate window. See Figure 5-23.

Figure 5-23   InPrivate window

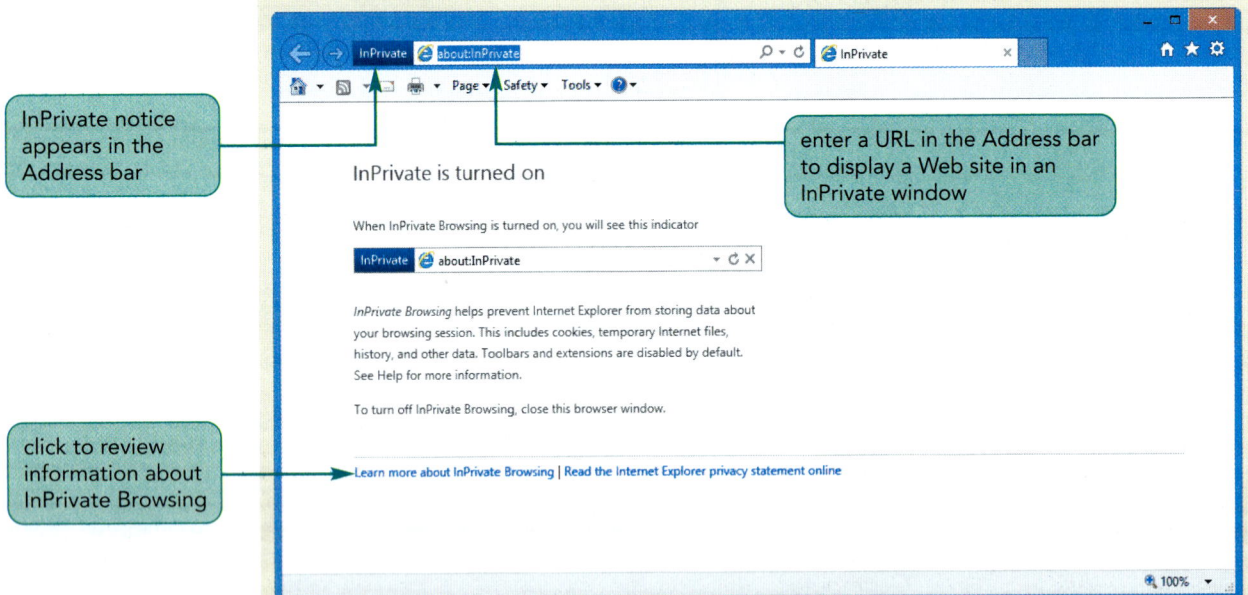

▶ 2. In the Address bar, type **www.whitehouse.gov** and then press the **Enter** key. The home page for the White House Web site appears in the InPrivate browser window. Maximize the window.

    Trouble? If a window opens other than the one for the White House home page, close the window or click a link to continue to the Web site.

▶ 3. Point to the **Briefing Room** link near the top of the page, and then click the **Your Weekly Address** link.

> **Trouble?** If the Your Weekly Address link does not appear on the Web page you are viewing, click any other link.

- 4. Click the **Show Address bar Autocomplete** button on the Address bar to display a list of recently visited Web sites and your favorite Web pages. Note that the White House Web pages you visited during your InPrivate Browsing session are not listed under History. When you close the InPrivate window, the list of recent Web pages in the regular Internet Explorer window will not include any of the White House pages either.

- 5. Close the InPrivate window.

- 6. In the regular Internet Explorer window, click the **Show Address bar Autocomplete** button on the Address bar to display a list of pages you visited recently except for those you visited during your InPrivate Browsing session.

Internet Explorer includes another privacy feature—Tracking Protection—which you'll learn about next.

Using Tracking Protection

Many Web pages use content such as ads, maps, or Web analysis tools that count the number of visitors to the Web site. This content is typically supplied by other Web sites called content providers or third-party Web sites. When you visit a Web site with third-party content, information that identifies your computer is sent to the content provider. For example, the content provider can learn your browser type, operating system, Web address, and screen resolution. If you visit many Web sites that the same content provider uses, the content provider can create a profile of your browsing preferences. The profile can be used to target ads that are likely to appeal to you, for example.

Web tracking tools, such as visitor counters, sometimes appear as visible content, but not always. For example, **Web beacons** are transparent images that invisibly track Web site usage. Web analysis tools often contain scripts that can track information such as the pages you visit and the selections you make. To control the information sent to content providers, you can use Tracking Protection.

Tracking Protection analyzes the content of Web pages you visit. If it finds content that is used on other Web sites, Tracking Protection blocks the content from Web sites that appear on Tracking Protection lists. Internet Explorer generates a personal Tracking Protection list based on sites you visit. You can also download Tracking Protection Lists created by software developers and have Internet Explorer block content from the providers on those lists.

By blocking content, Tracking Protection can protect your privacy on the Web. However, content providers often pay for Web site content that you can view or use for free. Blocking all third-party content can make Web pages load slowly and prevent Web sites you like from earning income they need. Instead of blocking all third-party content, you can use Tracking Protection to examine which content providers supply content to Web sites you've visited. The Web address of the content provider collecting information on a Web page is often displayed in the Internet Explorer status bar as the Web page opens. If you notice that you have trouble displaying Web pages when a content provider's address appears in the status bar, you can block that content provider to improve performance. Content providers who supply content to 30 or more Web pages might be collecting too much information about you, so you can block them as well.

Duane notices that when Web pages are slow to open, a Web address such as ads.doubleclick.net appears in the status bar. You suggest he block this content provider to see if that improves his browsing experience.

To block a content provider:

1. Click the **Tools** button on the right side of the Internet Explorer window, point to **Safety**, and then click **Tracking Protection**. The Manage Add-ons dialog box opens with Tracking Protection selected in the Add-on Types pane.

2. Click **Your Personalized List** in the right pane. If the status for this list is "Disabled," click the **Enable** button to turn on Tracking Protection. Note the original setting so you can restore it later.

3. With Your Personalized List still selected, click the **Settings** button to open the Personalized Tracking Protection List dialog box. See Figure 5-24. The content providers in your dialog box will differ.

Figure 5-24 Personalized Tracking Protection List dialog box

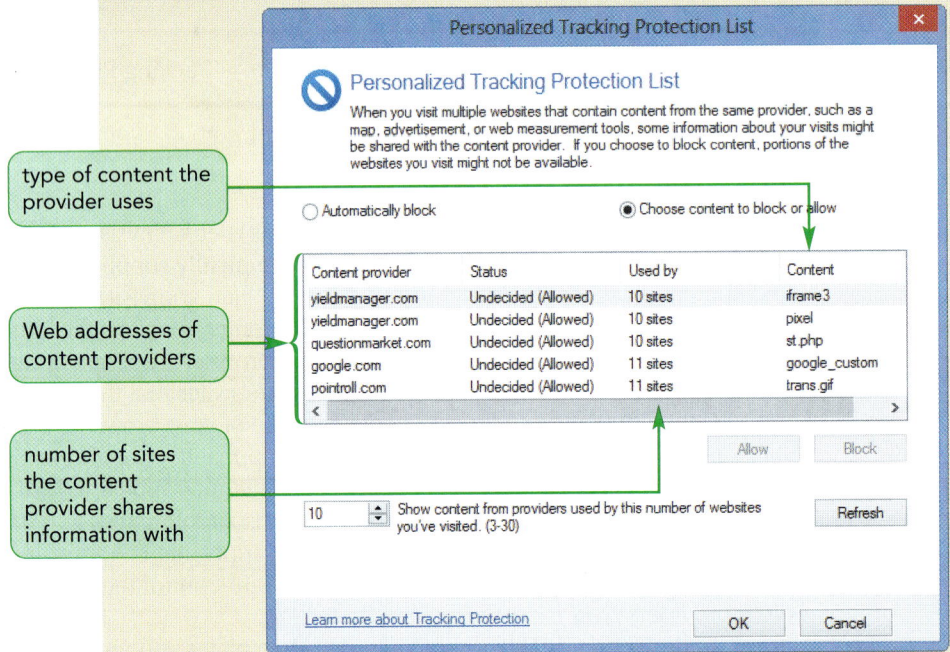

4. Click the **Used by** column heading to sort the list in descending order by the number of sites that use each content provider. The providers that are used by the most sites appear at the top of the list.

   Trouble? If no content providers appear in the list, skip Steps 4–6.

5. If necessary, scroll the list and then click **doubleclick.net** where "test_domain.js" appears in the Content column. The .js file in this column indicates that this Web site provides a script file to other Web sites. Because the content is used by many sites, you can block the content to improve performance.

   Trouble? If *doubleclick.net* does not appear in your Personalized Tracking Protection List dialog box, select any other content provider with content used by 20 or more sites.

6. Click the **Block** button to block this content.

7. Click the **OK** button to close the Personalized Tracking Protection List dialog box.

8. Click the **Close** button to close the Manage Add-ons dialog box.

If Duane is having trouble displaying Web pages, he can return to the Personalized Tracking Protection List dialog box and allow content from *doubleclick.net*.

Blocking ActiveX Controls

Recall that ActiveX controls are small programs that allow Web sites to provide content such as videos. Hackers can also use ActiveX controls to collect information from your computer without your consent, damage applications and data, install software on your computer without your knowledge, or control your computer remotely. To prevent Web sites from installing and using ActiveX controls, you can turn on ActiveX Filtering in Internet Explorer. Because many Web sites provide ActiveX controls to extend the capabilities of the browser, you can turn on ActiveX Filtering for specific Web sites.

You'll show Duane how to turn on ActiveX Filtering and then turn it off for a trusted Web site.

To use ActiveX Filtering:

1. Click the **Tools** button on the right side of the Internet Explorer window, point to **Safety**, and then click **ActiveX Filtering** to turn on ActiveX Filtering.

   Trouble? If ActiveX Filtering appears on the Safety list with a check mark, skip Step 1.

2. Click the **Tools** button again, and then point to **Safety** to verify that ActiveX Filtering appears with a check mark on the Safety list.

3. Navigate to the Microsoft Web site at **www.microsoft.com**.

4. Click the **filter** icon in the Address bar to display a dialog box notifying you that some content is filtered on this site. See Figure 5-25.

Figure 5-25 Filtering options for a Web site

5. Click the **Turn off ActiveX Filtering** button. Now the Microsoft Web site can use ActiveX controls to provide content such as videos.

Although you have turned off ActiveX Filtering for the Microsoft Web site, this safety option is still enabled for other Web sites. To turn off ActiveX Filtering for all Web sites, use the Tools button on the right side of the Internet Explorer window.

PROSKILLS

Decision Making: Deciding Whether to Trust a Web Site

Your decision about whether to trust a Web site should be based on who publishes the Web site, what information the publisher wants from you, and what you want from the site. To make your Web browsing more efficient and productive, consider the following guidelines when deciding whether to trust a Web site with confidential information:

- Ensure you have a secure connection to the Web site. Look in the Address bar for a Web site address that begins with "https" rather than "http." Also, look for a security icon such as a padlock in the Address bar or status bar, which indicates that the Web site is secure.
- Confirm that you are familiar with the organization that sponsors the Web site. If you are a satisfied customer of a business that provides products in a physical location, you can probably trust its Web site. Read the Web site's privacy or terms of use statement to make sure you are comfortable with the terms. Avoid Web sites that require you to accept email offers or advertising from the Web site.
- Check to see if the Web site is certified by an Internet trust organization. An Internet trust organization verifies that a Web site has a privacy statement and gives you a choice about how it uses your information. Approved Web sites display one or more privacy certification seals, usually on their home page or order forms. However, unscrupulous Web sites sometimes fraudulently display these trust logos. You can contact the trust organization to see if the Web site is registered with it. Reputable trust organizations include TRUSTe (www.truste.com), the Better Business Bureau or BBBOnLine (www.bbb.org/online), and WebTrust (www.webtrust.org). On the Web site of each trust organization, you can display a list of certified Web sites.
- Stay away from sites that unnecessarily request confidential personal information. Provide personal or confidential information such as credit card numbers only when necessary and only on a secure form. Make sure you are using a secure connection when completing the form. Also, look for a message explaining that your information will be encrypted for security.
- Avoid sites that use untrustworthy ways to contact you. Untrustworthy Web sites are often referred to you through an email message from someone you don't know. Stay away from Web sites making offers that seem too good to be true.

Now that you have thoroughly explored the privacy and security settings in Internet Explorer, you can show Duane another way to protect his company's computers—by using user accounts.

Setting Up User Accounts

In Windows, a **user account** is a collection of information that indicates the files and folders you can access, the types of changes you can make to the computer, and your preferred appearance settings (such as your desktop background or color scheme). If you have a user account on a computer that you share with other people, you can maintain your own files and settings separate from the other users.

REFERENCE

Setting Up a User Account

- Display the Charms bar, click the Settings charms, and then click Change PC settings.
- Click Users in the left pane of the PC settings screen.
- Click the Add a user button.
- Enter your email address.
- Enter a user name and password, and then click the Next button.
- Click the Finish button.

You can create two types of accounts in Windows 8:

- **Microsoft account**—This type of account provides access to Microsoft cloud computing services, such as Outlook.com for email, SkyDrive for file storage, and Xbox Live for games. With this type of user account, you can use Windows 8 and some Windows 8 apps to access files and other data stored in your online Microsoft account. For example, if you keep albums of photos on your SkyDrive, you can use the Photos app to display those photos on your PC. If you run Windows 8 on more than one PC, you can also **synchronize**, or **sync**, (that is, to make sure data on the two devices match) your settings, preferences, and some apps so that all your PCs are set up the same way. The advantage of a Microsoft account is that you provide one user name and one password to connect to the cloud and to sync settings.
- **Local-only user account**—This type of account accesses only resources on your computer.

In addition, a Microsoft account or a local-only user account is a Standard account or an Administrator account, which determines how much control the user has over the computer:

- **Standard account**—A Standard account is designed for everyday computing and can protect your computer and data by preventing users from changing settings that affect all users. To make changes such as installing software or changing security settings, Windows requests permission or a password for an Administrator account. Microsoft recommends that every regular user on a computer have a Standard account.
- **Administrator account**—An Administrator account is created when Windows 8 is installed and provides full access to the computer. The administrator can access the files of any user, install software, and change any settings. The intention is that when you install Windows 8, you first sign in to the computer as the administrator, and then create a Standard user account for yourself and for each person who will use the computer.

If someone needs temporary access to a computer, the administrator can turn on the **Guest account**, which is a built-in account that is inactive by default. The Guest account user cannot make any changes to settings or software.

When you install Windows 8, the setup program guides you through the steps of creating an Administrator account. During that process, you select whether you want to use your Microsoft account or a local-only user account as the Administrator account. If you don't have a Microsoft account, you can create one as you install Windows. After completing the installation, you can set up Standard accounts from the Start screen or the desktop. (You can turn on a Guest account or turn it off only from the desktop.) Any accounts you create after the initial Administrator account are Standard accounts by default. Standard accounts can be Microsoft or local-only user accounts.

Selecting a User Name and Password

When you create an Administrator account or a Standard account, Windows asks for your user credentials, which are a user name and a password. If you have a Microsoft account, you can provide the user name and password you use for that account. If you don't have a Microsoft account, you can create one as you set up a new Administrator or Standard account. To use a Microsoft account, you provide your email address and a password as your user credentials.

INSIGHT

Synchronizing Accounts

If you use your Microsoft account credentials for your user account on a Windows 8 laptop, for example, you can synchronize settings, preferences, and some apps that you use on other computers, such as a Windows 8 tablet. No matter which computer you use, the Start screen and desktop will look the same, and you'll have access to the same apps.

Before you can synchronize accounts, you need to trust each computer you use. (**Trusting** a computer means you verify that you have an account on that computer.) To trust a computer, open the PC settings screen and then select Users. If a message appears below your user name and picture indicating that your saved passwords for apps, Web sites, and networks won't sync until you trust the PC, click the Trust this PC link. Internet Explorer starts and opens a Manage your security info Web page on the Windows Live Web site to confirm you are adding the PC to your Microsoft account. The Web site sends you an email message with a confirmation link. When you receive the email message, open it and click the link to make the PC a trusted PC for your Microsoft account. The PC will then sync settings and data automatically.

If you set up a new Administrator or Standard account as a local-only user account, you must provide a user name, but the password is optional. However, Microsoft strongly recommends that you use a password for all accounts, which is one of the most effective ways you can keep your computer secure. When your computer is protected with a password, only someone who knows the password can sign in to Windows.

A **text password** is a series of letters, numbers, spaces, and symbols that you provide to access your files, applications, and other resources on the computer. Windows passwords are case sensitive, so *DnEllson18* is different from *dnellson18*. Passwords strengthen computer security because they help to make sure that no one can access the computer unless he or she is authorized to do so. Therefore, you should not give your passwords to others or write them in a place where others can see them.

When creating a text password, make sure you devise a strong password—one that is difficult to guess but easy for you to remember. Strong text passwords have the following characteristics:

Contain at least eight characters
Do not include your user name, real name, or company name
Are not words you can find in the dictionary
Are significantly different from your previous passwords
- Contain characters from each of the following categories: uppercase letters, lowercase letters, numbers, and symbols (not including spaces)

For any account that has a text password, you can also set up a four-digit **personal information number (PIN)** and a picture password to protect the account. Similar to a PIN you use for banking transactions, you can use a PIN for a Windows account as a fast way to sign in. (Keep in mind, however, that a PIN does not meet the requirements for a strong password.) A **picture password** involves an image and gestures, and is easiest to provide on a touchscreen device. You select a photo or another graphic stored in a location your computer can access, and then draw three gestures (that is, circles, lines, and taps or clicks) on the picture to create a password. You must remember the size, position, and direction of the gestures and the order you make them so you can repeat the gestures to gain access to your account. At times, Windows requests your text password, such as when you want to change system settings. At other times, you can use a PIN or picture password, such as to sign in to your account.

Creating a Microsoft Account

Duane is concerned that he and his staff at Catapult Product Design are all using the Administrator accounts that Windows created when it was installed. He wants to make sure that everyone creates a Standard user account with a password. Some part-time employees share a single computer, and Duane wants those employees to create separate Standard accounts on the same computer. To take advantage of cloud services and synchronization, he also wants the new accounts to be Microsoft accounts.

Duane wants to start by creating a Standard Microsoft user account on his computer. To do so, you provide his user name, which is the email address for his Microsoft account, and use the password for that account. Duane will also set up a PIN so he can sign in quickly and create a picture password as an alternate method for signing in to Windows.

Before you use a Microsoft account on your computer, you can create one at the Windows Live Web site to streamline the process. If you already have a Microsoft or Windows Live account, skip the following steps. You must be signed in using an Administrator account to perform the following steps. If you do not have access to an Administrator account, read but do not perform the following steps.

To set up a Microsoft account:

1. In IE Desktop, click the **Address bar**, type **https://signup.live.com**, and then press the **Enter** key. The Microsoft account Web page opens. Because you included "https" in the Web address, you can be confident this is a secure page.

2. Enter your name, birth date, and other requested information. For the Microsoft account name, you must provide an email address. Note your account name and password so you can use it with Windows 8.

3. Click the **I accept** button (or a similar button) to display the home page for your new Microsoft account.

4. Close Internet Explorer.

Next, you can create a Standard account using your Microsoft account credentials. You must be signed in using an Administrator account to perform the following steps. If you do not have access to an Administrator account, read but do not perform the following steps.

To create a Standard Microsoft user account:

1. Display the Charms bar, click the **Settings** charm, and then click **Change PC settings** to display the PC settings screen.

2. Click the **Users** category in the left pane to display a screen with your account information. See Figure 5-26. Your screen will differ.

Figure 5-26   Your account screen

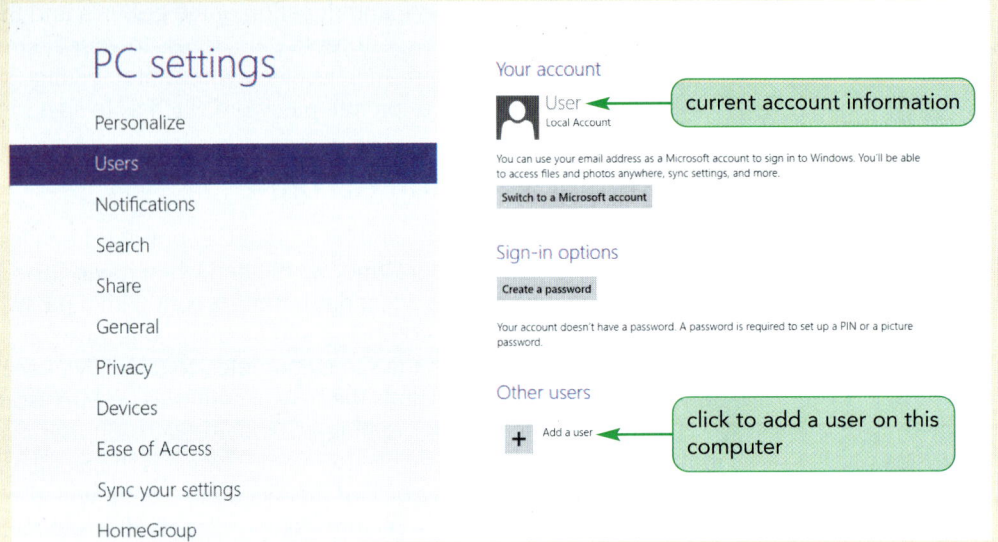

Trouble? If a message appears on your account screen about trusting the PC, disregard the message. You don't need to sync settings now.

3. Click the **Add a user** button to display the Add a user screen.

4. Enter the email address you use for your Microsoft account, and then click the **Next** button to display a screen confirming the email address.

Trouble? If you do not have a Microsoft account, enter information for the new account, click the Next button, and then complete the setup steps.

5. Click the **Finish** button to create the account.

After you create an account, you can switch to that account and then change your text password, create a picture password, and create a PIN. You'll switch to the Standard account and then change its password. You'll use cPult!10 as the password, a combination of the name of Duane's company and the year it was founded.

To switch accounts and change a password:

1. Press the **Windows** key to return to the Start screen.

2. Click the user icon in the upper-right corner of the screen, and then click **Sign out**. Windows signs out of your account and displays the lock screen.

3. Clear the lock screen, and then click the icon for the new account you just created.

4. Enter the password for your Microsoft account, and then press the **Enter** key. Windows takes a few minutes to set up the new account.

5. When the Start screen appears, display the Charms bar, click the **Settings** charm, click **Change PC settings**, and then click **Users** in the left pane.

6. In the Sign-in options section, click the **Change your password** button. The Change your Microsoft account password screen appears. See Figure 5-27.

Figure 5-27 Change your Microsoft account password screen

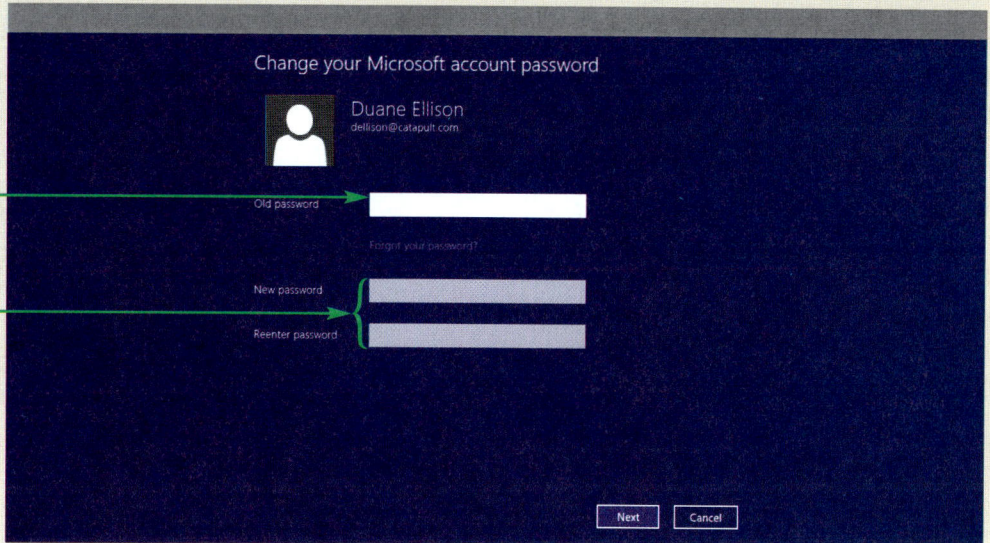

enter the password for your email account

enter and confirm the new password

TIP

If you forgot your password, click the Forgot your password link, and then go online to reset the password.

7. In the Old password text box, type your email password.

8. In the New password text box, type **cPult!10**. You must type the password again to confirm it.

9. Click the **Reenter password** text box, and then type **cPult!10**.

10. Click the **Next** button to confirm that you changed your password, and then click the **Finish** button.

If you forget your password and you're using a Microsoft account, you can reset your password online (go to https://signup.live.com and search for *reset password*). If you forget your password and you're using a local account, use your password hint as a reminder. You can also ask someone with an administrator account on your computer to change the password for you.

Next, you can create a PIN and a picture password. Duane wants to use 5410 as the PIN, the date he founded the company.

To create a PIN:

1. On the PC settings screen for Users, click the **Create a PIN** button to display a screen where you enter your account password.

2. Enter **cPult!10** as the password, and then click the **OK** button to display the Create a PIN screen. See Figure 5-28.

Figure 5-28 Create a PIN

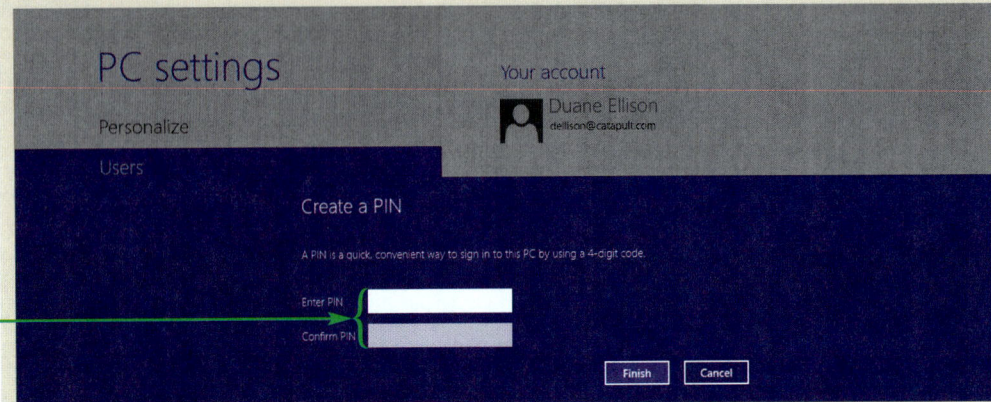

enter and confirm a four-digit PIN

> 3. Enter **5410** in the Enter PIN text box.
> 4. Click the **Confirm PIN** text box, type **5410**, and then click the **Finish** button to create the PIN. Note that a Remove button now appears next to the Change PIN button so you can delete the PIN if necessary.
> 5. Close the PC settings screen.

Next, you can create a picture password for Duane's account. First, you'll take a screen shot of the White House home page and then use that image for the picture password.

To create a picture password:

> 1. Start Internet Explorer, navigate to the White House Web site at **www.whitehouse.gov**, and then find a Web page you want to use for the picture password image.
> 2. Press the **Print Screen** key to capture an image of the screen, and then close Internet Explorer.
> 3. Right-click a blank spot on the Start screen to display the Apps bar, and then click the **All Apps** button to display the Apps screen.
> 4. Click **Paint** under Windows Accessories to start Paint on the desktop, and then press the **Ctrl+V** keys to paste the screen image in a new Paint file.
> 5. Click the **Save** button on the Quick Access toolbar, and then save the screen image as a PNG file named **White House** in the Pictures library. Close Paint.
> 6. Return to the PC settings screen for Users, and then click the **Create a picture password** button.
> 7. Enter **cPult!10** as the password, and then click the **OK** button to display the Welcome to picture password screen. See Figure 5-29.

Figure 5-29 Welcome to picture password screen

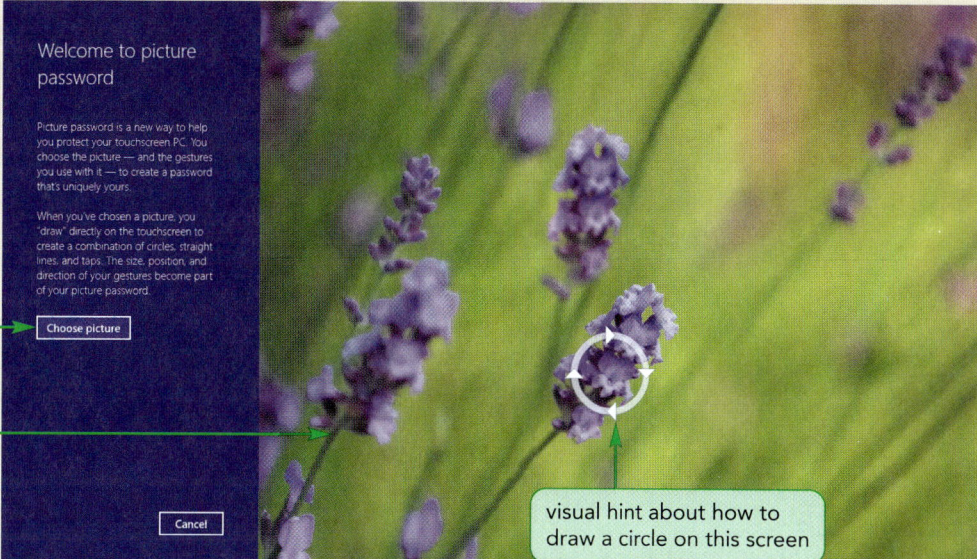

8. Click the **Choose picture** button, click the screen shot you saved in the Pictures library, and then click the **Open** button to select the picture.

9. Click the **Use this picture** button. The Set up your gestures screen appears.

10. Draw three gestures on the picture as described in the left pane of the screen. Select objects on the picture and use gestures you can remember easily.

11. When the Confirm your gestures screen appears, repeat the gestures in the same order you used in Step 10.

    Trouble? If the "Something's not right" message appears, click the Try again button and repeat Step 11, carefully redrawing the gestures you created. If you are still having trouble, click the Start over button and repeat Steps 10 and 11, but make sure you use simple gestures (for example, draw a line under a word or picture) and note their placement on the screen.

12. Click the **Finish** button, and then close the PC settings screen.

To perform the remaining steps in the tutorial, you need to sign out of the Standard account and sign in with your original (that is, Administrator) account.

To switch accounts:

1. On the Start screen, click the user icon, and then click **Sign out**. Windows signs out of your account and displays the lock screen.

2. Clear the lock screen, and then click the icon for your Administrator account.

3. If necessary, enter your password, and then press the **Enter** key.

Now you and Duane can show all of the Catapult Product Design employees how to create accounts and passwords on their computers.

Controlling Access to Your Computer

One way to manage access to your computer is to take advantage of **User Account Control (UAC)**, a feature that is turned on by default and can help prevent unauthorized changes to your computer. As you performed the previous steps, you might have seen UAC at work, asking for permission by providing an administrator password before performing actions that could affect your computer's settings. A UAC dialog box usually opens when a program or an action is about to start. The dialog box requests an administrator password as permission to start the program. By notifying you, UAC can help prevent malware from installing itself on or changing your computer without permission. Make sure the name of the action or program in the UAC dialog box is one that you intended to start. The dialog box indicates whether the program or action is part of Windows, is not part of Windows, is unidentified, or is blocked by the administrator. The dialog box also indicates whether the program has a digital certificate. If you are working on a computer on which you've set up an Administrator account and one or more Standard accounts, the UAC dialog box asks for an administrator password so that software can't be installed without the administrator's knowledge or permission.

The UAC feature is turned on by default and should not be turned off. You'll show Duane how to make sure UAC is turned on for all of the Catapult computers.

To verify that User Account Control is turned on:

1. On the Start screen, type **Control Panel** and then click **Control Panel** in the list of apps to open the Control Panel.

2. Click **User Accounts and Family Safety** to display the User Accounts and Family Safety window, and then click **User Accounts** to display the User Accounts window.

3. Click **Change User Account Control settings**. The User Account Control Settings window opens. See Figure 5-30.

Figure 5-30   User Account Control Settings window

> **4.** Drag the slider up and down to examine each setting, drag the slider to the **Notify me only when apps try to make changes to my computer (default)** setting, and then click the **OK** button.
>
> **Trouble?** If a User Account Control dialog box opens asking if you want to allow the program to make changes to this computer, click the Yes button.

Besides controlling access to your computer with passwords and UAC, you should be aware of security features that Windows provides at startup when installing apps.

Startup and App Security Features

Besides the tools and features covered so far in this tutorial, Windows provides behind-the-scenes security protections that don't require your intervention. One of these is a new boot method called **Unified Extensible Firmware Interface (UEFI)**. When you turn on the power to a computer, it performs a series of steps and checks as it loads the operating system and prepares for you to use it. This startup process is called **booting** the computer. UEFI boots a computer faster and in a more secure way than previous methods. Some malware is designed to start as the operating system loads. The computer is vulnerable at this point because antivirus software hasn't started yet. Rootkits in particular can interfere with operating system files and start before antivirus software can detect them. The Secure Boot feature in UEFI makes Windows 8 resistant to this type of malware. **Secure Boot** can detect when a file has interfered with the operating system and prevent that file from loading so it doesn't interfere with the operating system again.

After the operating system loads, the next application that starts is antivirus software. Malware sometimes tampers with antivirus software as it loads so it appears to be running but is in fact disabled. Windows 8 detects any tampering with the antivirus software and restores the unmodified version so it protects against malware.

Computers are also vulnerable to attack when you install new software. Malware can attach itself to legitimate files posted for download on Web sites, for example. When you download a new app, you might also be downloading a virus or worm. This scenario is very unlikely with apps you download from the Windows Store. Microsoft rigorously screens apps posted for download on the Windows Store to make sure they are free from malware. Microsoft provides a digital signature to verify the app is safe, and Windows tools such as the SmartScreen Filter and Windows Defender read the digital signature to make sure the file was not intercepted and changed during the download. Windows 8 also runs apps so they have only limited access to other resources on your computer, which minimizes the damage any malware could cause.

Restoring Your Settings

If you are working in a computer lab or on a computer other than your own, complete the steps in this section to restore the original settings on the computer. If a User Account Control dialog box opens requesting an Administrator password or confirmation after you perform any of the following steps, enter the password or click the Yes button.

> **To restore your settings:**
>
> **1.** On the desktop, display the Control Panel Home page in Category view, click **System and Security**, and then click **Windows Firewall**.

2. In the left pane of the Windows Firewall window, click **Allow an app or feature through Windows Firewall**, and then click the **Change settings** button.

3. Click the **Connect to a Network Projector** check box to remove the check mark, and then click the **OK** button.

4. Click **System and Security** in the Address bar, click **Windows Update**, and then click **Change settings** in the left pane. Click the **Updates will be automatically installed during the maintenance window** link, click the **Automatic Maintenance** button, click the original time set for installing updates, and then click the **OK** button. Minimize the Control Panel window.

5. Start Internet Explorer on the desktop, click the **Tools** button on the right side of the screen, and then click **Internet options**. Click the **Privacy** tab, and then click the **Settings** button. Click the **Blocking level** button, and then click your original setting. Click the **Close** button to close the Pop-up Blocker Settings dialog box.

6. On the Privacy tab, drag the **Internet zone slider** to its original setting.

7. Click the **General** tab in the Internet Options dialog box, and then click the **Delete** button in the Browsing history section. Click the **Cookies and website data** check box and the **History** check box to remove the check marks. Click **Cancel** in the Delete Browsing History dialog box. Click the **OK** button to close the Internet Options dialog box.

8. Click the **Tools** button, point to **Safety**, and then click **Tracking Protection**. Click **Your Personalized List**, and then click the **Settings** button. Click **doubleclick.net** (or the name of the content provider you selected earlier) in the content provider list, click the **Allow** button, and then click the **OK** button. If Tracking Protection was disabled at the beginning of the tutorial, click the **Disable** button with Your Personalized List selected to turn off Tracking Protection. Close the Manage Add-ons window and Internet Explorer.

9. Display the Control Panel window, return to the Control Panel home page, click **User Accounts and Family Safety**, and then click **Remove user accounts**. Click the icon for the Standard account you created, click **Delete the account**, click the **Delete Files** button, and then click the **Delete Account** button. Close the Control Panel window.

10. Close all open windows.

REVIEW

Session 5.2 Quick Check

1. The _____ helps detect online scams, such as Web sites that try to trick you into revealing financial account information.
2. What is the purpose of Protected Mode?
3. What is a Web site certificate?
4. Explain how you can use Download Manager to run a security check on a downloaded file.
5. By default, what types of pop-up windows does Internet Explorer block?
6. If you don't want anyone to track the Web pages you visited, you can use _____.
7. What is the advantage of having a Microsoft account?
8. Name the three types of passwords you can use with Windows 8 and describe the purpose of each type.

Review Assignments

There are no Data Files needed for the Review Assignments.

Duane Ellison, owner of Catapult Product Design, recently bought a new Windows 8 computer for you to share with Serena Olivera, one of his project managers. To market products, Serena specializes in using multimedia, which she plays using Windows Media Player. She is preparing to visit a client in Rockville, Maryland, and is concerned about the security of her computer during the visit. You'll show Serena how to keep the new computer secure. Complete the following steps, noting your original settings so you can restore them later:

1. Open the Action Center, and then perform the following tasks:
    Choose to allow an app through Windows Firewall.
    Change the settings to add Windows Media Player Network Sharing Service (Internet) to the allowed programs list.
    If the Allowed apps window is maximized, click the Restore Down button to resize it.
2. Open another Control Panel window and then change the settings in Windows Update to automatically check for and install updates every day at 7:00 AM. (*Hint*: Make sure you note the original time so you can restore the setting at the end of the exercise.) If the Automatic Maintenance window is maximized, click the Restore Down button to resize it.
3. Arrange the Allowed apps window and the Automatic Maintenance window to display the settings you changed. Press the Print Screen key to capture an image of the screen. Open Paint or WordPad, and then press the Ctrl+V keys to paste the image in a new file. Save the file as **Updated Settings** in the Windows5\Review folder provided with your Data Files.
4. Start Windows Defender, and then use it to perform a quick scan on your computer.
5. With the Windows Defender window open on your desktop and displaying the scan results, press the Print Screen key to capture an image of the window. Open Paint or WordPad, and then press the Ctrl+V keys to paste the image in a new file. Save the file as **Defender** in the Windows5\Review folder provided with your Data Files. Close all open windows.
6. In IE Desktop, open a Web page in your Favorites list or go to the home page of a popular search engine, such as Google (**www.google.com**) or Bing (**www.bing.com**). Use the SmartScreen Filter to verify this Web site is not a phishing Web site.
7. Make sure the Pop-up Blocker in Internet Explorer is turned on, and then visit a Web site that uses pop-up windows such as **www.merriam-webster.com** or **www.movies.com**. Enter a search term (for example, **dabble** or **The King's Speech**) to display a Notification bar explaining that Internet Explorer blocked a pop-up. Press the Print Screen key to capture an image of the desktop. Open Paint or WordPad, and then press the Ctrl+V keys to paste the image in a new file. Save the file as **Blocked** in the Windows5\Review folder provided with your Data Files.
8. Turn on InPrivate Browsing in Internet Explorer and then perform the following tasks:
    Visit the Maryland state Web site at **www.maryland.gov**.
    Click the VISITING tab.
    Click the Maryland Film Office link in the Arts & Culture section.

9. In the original Internet Explorer window you opened in Step 7 (that is, the dictionary or movie Web site), pin the Favorites Center to the window, click the History tab, if necessary, and then click the Today link to display Web sites you visited today except for those visited during your InPrivate Browsing session. (*Hint*: You can also click the Show Address bar Autocomplete button to display your browsing history.)
10. Perform the following tasks to capture an image of the windows:

    Arrange the InPrivate Browsing window so it appears on top of the dictionary or movie Web site window.

    Resize the windows so that the Favorites Center in the original Internet window is visible.

    Click the Show Address bar Autocomplete button in the Address bar of the InPrivate Browsing window to display a list of Web sites visited during this browsing session.

    Press the Print Screen key to capture an image of the desktop.

    Open Paint or WordPad, and then press the Ctrl+V keys to paste the image in a new file.

    Save the file as **InPrivate** in the Windows5\Review folder provided with your Data Files.

    Close all open windows.
11. Create a PIN for your user account using **6695** as the number.
12. With the Create a PIN (or Change your PIN) screen open, press the Print Screen key to capture an image of the screen. Open Paint or WordPad, and then press the Ctrl+V keys to paste the image in a new file. Save the file as **Pin** in the Windows5\Review folder provided with your Data Files. Return to the Start screen and then switch to your original account.
13. Restore the settings on your computer, including restoring the Pop-up Blocking level to its original setting. Remove Windows Media Player Network Sharing Service (Internet) from the Windows Firewall allowed programs list. Restore the settings in Windows Update and Windows Defender to install updates and scan at their original times. Close the Favorites Center in Internet Explorer and delete your browsing history. Remove the PIN you created for your user account.
14. Close all open windows.
15. Submit the results of the preceding steps to your instructor, either in printed or electronic form, as requested.

Case Problem 1

There are no Data Files needed for this Case Problem.

Mulcahy Sports Medicine Deanne Mulcahy runs a small business in Libertyville, Illinois, called Mulcahy Sports Medicine, which helps to train sports teams at small colleges and universities so the athletes avoid injury and work toward peak physical fitness. Deanne uses a laptop computer running Windows 8 to create most of her training plans, which she develops while visiting schools. She is concerned about maintaining security as she researches the latest in physical therapy and training programs on the Internet. In particular, she has experienced problems with pop-up ads and spyware and wants to know how to block pop-ups in Internet Explorer. You'll help her use the Windows 8 security settings to protect her computer. Complete the following steps, noting your original settings so you can restore them later:

1. Open the Action Center, and then add Wireless Portable Devices to the Windows Firewall allowed apps list. Leave the Allowed apps window open.
2. Change the settings in Windows Update to automatically check for and install updates every day at 5:00 AM. Leave the Automatic Maintenance window open.
3. Start Windows Defender, and then use it to perform a quick scan on your computer.
4. Arrange all windows to show the settings you changed, and then press the Print Screen key to capture an image of the desktop. Open Paint or WordPad, and then press the Ctrl+V keys to paste the image in a new file. Save the file as **Security** in the Windows5\Case1 folder provided with your Data Files. Close all open windows.
5. In IE Desktop, open the Internet Options dialog box to the Privacy tab. Open the Pop-up Blocker Settings dialog box. Set Internet Explorer to block all pop-ups. Press the Print Screen key to capture an image of the dialog box. Open Paint or WordPad, and then press the Ctrl+V keys to paste the image in a new file. Save the file as **Popups** in the Windows5\Case1 folder provided with your Data Files. Close the Pop-up Blocker Settings dialog box.
6. Change the security level for the Trusted sites zone to Low. Press the Print Screen key to capture an image of the window. Open Paint or WordPad, and then press the Ctrl+V keys to paste the image in a new file. Save the file as **SecurityZone** in the Windows5\Case1 folder provided with your Data Files. Close the Internet Options dialog box.
7. In the Manage Add-ons dialog box, display a list of the currently loaded add-ons for toolbars and extensions. Press the Print Screen key to capture an image of the window. Open Paint or WordPad, and then press the Ctrl+V keys to paste the image in a new file. Save the file as **AddOns** in the Windows5\Case1 folder provided with your Data Files. (*Hint*: If there are no add-ons listed, display the list of add-ons that run without permission.)
8. Enable Tracking Protection, if necessary, and then open the Personalized Tracking Protection List dialog box. Block a content provider, such as one that provides content with a .js extension. Press the Print Screen key to capture an image of the dialog box. Open Paint or WordPad, and then press the Ctrl+V keys to paste the image in a new file. Save the file as **Tracking** in the Windows5\Case1 folder provided with your Data Files.
9. Start a Windows 8 app and then capture the screen. Save the image as a file named **Windows 8 App** in the Pictures library. Close the Windows 8 app.
10. Create a picture password for your user account using the Windows 8 App picture. Enter the required three gestures.
11. Before you confirm the three gestures, press the Print Screen key to capture an image of the screen. Open Paint or WordPad, and then press the Ctrl+V keys to paste the image in a new file. Save the file as **PicPassword** in the Windows5\Case1 folder provided with your Data Files. Confirm the gestures and then close the PC settings screen. Switch to your original user account.

12. Restore the settings on your computer. Remove Wireless Portable Devices from the Windows Firewall allowed programs list. Restore the settings in Windows Update and Windows Defender to install updates and scan at their original times. Change the Pop-up Blocker setting to its default setting. Restore the security level for the Trusted sites zone to its original setting. Delete your browsing history. Remove the picture password from your user account, and then delete the Windows 8 App file from the Pictures library.
13. Close all open windows.
14. Submit the results of the preceding steps to your instructor, either in printed or electronic form, as requested.

Case Problem 2

There are no Data Files needed for this Case Problem.

St. Joseph City Center Brenda Gargano is the director of the St. Joseph City Center, a performing arts center in St. Joseph, Michigan. The City Center hosts a children's theater, and schedules theatrical and musical performances throughout the year. Because the City Center computers are not part of the municipal network, Brenda uses Remote Desktop to connect to other computers in the city, and regularly uses Mail and Internet Explorer to run the organization. She has experienced problems with spyware and viruses, and wants to know when to trust Web sites she visits. You'll help her use the Windows 8 security settings to protect her computer. Complete the following steps, noting your original settings so you can restore them later:

1. Change the settings to add Remote Desktop to the Windows Firewall allowed programs list. Capture an image of the Allowed apps window, and then save it in a Paint file named **Firewall** in the Windows5\Case2 folder provided with your Data Files.

Explore 2. In Windows Update, view your update history. (*Hint*: In the Windows Update window, click View update history in the left pane.) Capture an image of the View update history window, and save it as a Paint file named **Update History** in the Windows5\Case2 folder provided with your Data Files. Close all open windows.

3. In IE Desktop, open a Web page in your Favorites list or go to the home page of a popular search engine, such as Google (**www.google.com**) or Bing (**www.bing.com**). Use the SmartScreen Filter to verify this Web site is not a phishing Web site. Capture an image of the Internet Explorer window and SmartScreen Filter dialog box, and then save it in a Paint file named **Phishing** in the Windows5\Case2 folder provided with your Data Files.

4. In IE Desktop, change the security level for the Internet sites zone to High. Capture an image of the dialog box, and then save the image as a Paint file named **HighSecurity** in the Windows5\Case2 folder provided with your Data Files. Close all open windows.

Explore 5. Activate a guest account on the computer. (*Hint*: Open the Control Panel, click User Accounts and Family Safety, click User Accounts, and then click Manage another account. In the Manage Accounts window, click the Guest account, and then click the Turn On button.)

6. With the Manage Accounts window open on the desktop, capture an image of the window, and then save the image as a Paint file named **Guest** in the Windows5\Case2 folder provided with your Data Files.

7. Restore the settings on your computer. Remove Remote Desktop from the Windows Firewall allowed programs list. Restore the security level for the Internet sites zone to its original setting. Turn off the Guest account.

8. Close all open windows.

9. Submit the results of the preceding steps to your instructor, either in printed or electronic form, as requested.

Case Problem 3

There are no Data Files needed for this Case Problem.

Andiamo Caffé Michael Monti owns the Andiamo Caffé in Providence, Rhode Island, and has designed the restaurant as a casual gathering place for the neighborhood. Besides Italian coffee and baked goods, Michael offers books, Internet connections, and computers to customers who want to use them. Michael is particularly concerned about the security of these computers. You'll help him use the Windows 8 security settings to protect a public computer. Complete the following steps, noting your original settings so you can restore them later:

⊕ **Explore** 1. In Windows Firewall, block all incoming connections. (*Hint*: Select an option in the Customize Settings window.)

⊕ **Explore** 2. Set Windows Defender to perform a custom scan of your removable disk.

3. Arrange the Windows Defender Options window and the Windows Firewall window to display the settings you changed, and then capture an image of the screen. Save the image as a Paint file named **Scan** in the Windows5\Case3 folder provided with your Data Files. Close all open windows.

4. In Internet Explorer, change the privacy level for the Internet zone to High. Capture an image of the dialog box, and then save it as a Paint file named **HighPrivacy** in the Windows5\Case3 folder provided with your Data Files.

5. Delete all temporary files and cookies in Internet Explorer.

⊕ **Explore** 6. Set IE Desktop so that it does not store the browsing history. (*Hint*: On the General tab of the Internet Options dialog box, click the Delete browsing history on exit check box.) Capture an image of the dialog box, and then save it in a Paint file named **NoHistory** in the Windows5\Case3 folder provided with your Data Files.

⊕ **Explore** 7. Activate a guest account on the computer. (*Hint*: Open the Control Panel, click User Accounts and Family Safety, click User Accounts, and then click Manage another account. In the Manage Accounts window, click the Guest account, and then click the Turn On button.)

8. With the Manage Accounts window open on the desktop, capture an image of the window, and then save it as a Paint file named **Account** in the Windows5\Case3 folder provided with your Data Files.

9. Restore the settings on your computer. Restore the original general settings in Windows Firewall. Restore the settings for a Windows Defender scan to their original settings. In Internet Explorer, restore the privacy level for the Internet zone to its original setting, and then restore the original setting of the Delete browsing history on exit check box. Turn off the Guest account.

10. Close all open windows.

11. Submit the results of the preceding steps to your instructor, either in printed or electronic form, as requested.

Case Problem 4

RESEARCH

There are no Data Files needed for this Case Problem.

Kapur Research Martin Kapur is the president of Kapur Research, a firm in Des Moines, Iowa, that conducts plant and seed research for agricultural companies. Martin wants to protect the computers his researchers use against security threats. To do so, he first wants to understand who typically attacks computers and their data. He also wants to learn more about the types of attacks people use to access computers, and how much damage such attacks have caused. He asks you to research these topics and report your findings. Complete the following steps:

1. Use your favorite search engine to find information about the types of people behind attacks on desktop computers. (Attacks on networks are in a separate category.) Search for information about the following types of attackers:
    White hat hackers
    Black hat hackers
    Script kiddies
    Hacktivists
2. Use your favorite search engine to find information about the techniques attackers use to exploit a computer. Search for information about the following types of techniques:
    Key loggers
    Password cracking
    Social engineering
    Spoofing or phishing attacks
    Vulnerability scanners
3. Use a word processor to summarize your findings in one or two pages. Be sure to define any new terms and cite the Web sites where you found your information. Save the document as an RTF file named **Security**.
4. Submit the results of the preceding steps to your instructor, either in printed or electronic form, as requested.

TUTORIAL 6

Searching for Information

Finding Apps, Settings, Files, and Information

OBJECTIVES

Session 6.1
- Develop search strategies
- Search for apps and settings
- Find files by name, type, and category
- Filter the search results
- Add tags to files

Session 6.2
- Use Boolean filters in advanced searches
- Search within Windows 8 apps
- Search the Internet
- Narrow searches using advanced search features
- Select search providers in Internet Explorer

Case | *Columbia Collectibles*

A few years ago, Jay Park opened Columbia Collectibles, a shop in Columbia, Missouri, that buys and sells collectible items, especially baseball cards, postcards, and posters. Jay wants to develop a Web site to showcase his collectibles and plans to feature valuable items for sale each week. He recently hired you to help him organize materials and keep the Web site up to date. Along with assisting Jay at the shop, your duties include taking digital photos of the collectible items, organizing them logically, and finding items for the Weekly Features Web page and the customer newsletter.

In this tutorial, you'll learn how to develop strategies for finding information, and then use the Windows 8 search tools to find files. You'll refine your searches by using advanced techniques such as Boolean filters and multiple criteria. You'll also learn how to apply these search strategies in Windows 8 apps and when using Internet Explorer to find information on the Web.

STARTING DATA FILES

Microsoft product screenshots used with permission from Microsoft Corporation.

WIN 282 | Windows | Tutorial 6 Searching for Information

Session 6.1 Visual Overview:

Use the Search tab in a folder window to work with search results.

A **search filter** narrows a search to files that share a specified detail.

Select a condition when you use a search filter.

Saved searches are displayed in the Favorites list in the Navigation pane.

Click the Save search button to save the search criteria.

Search results are the files that meet your search conditions.

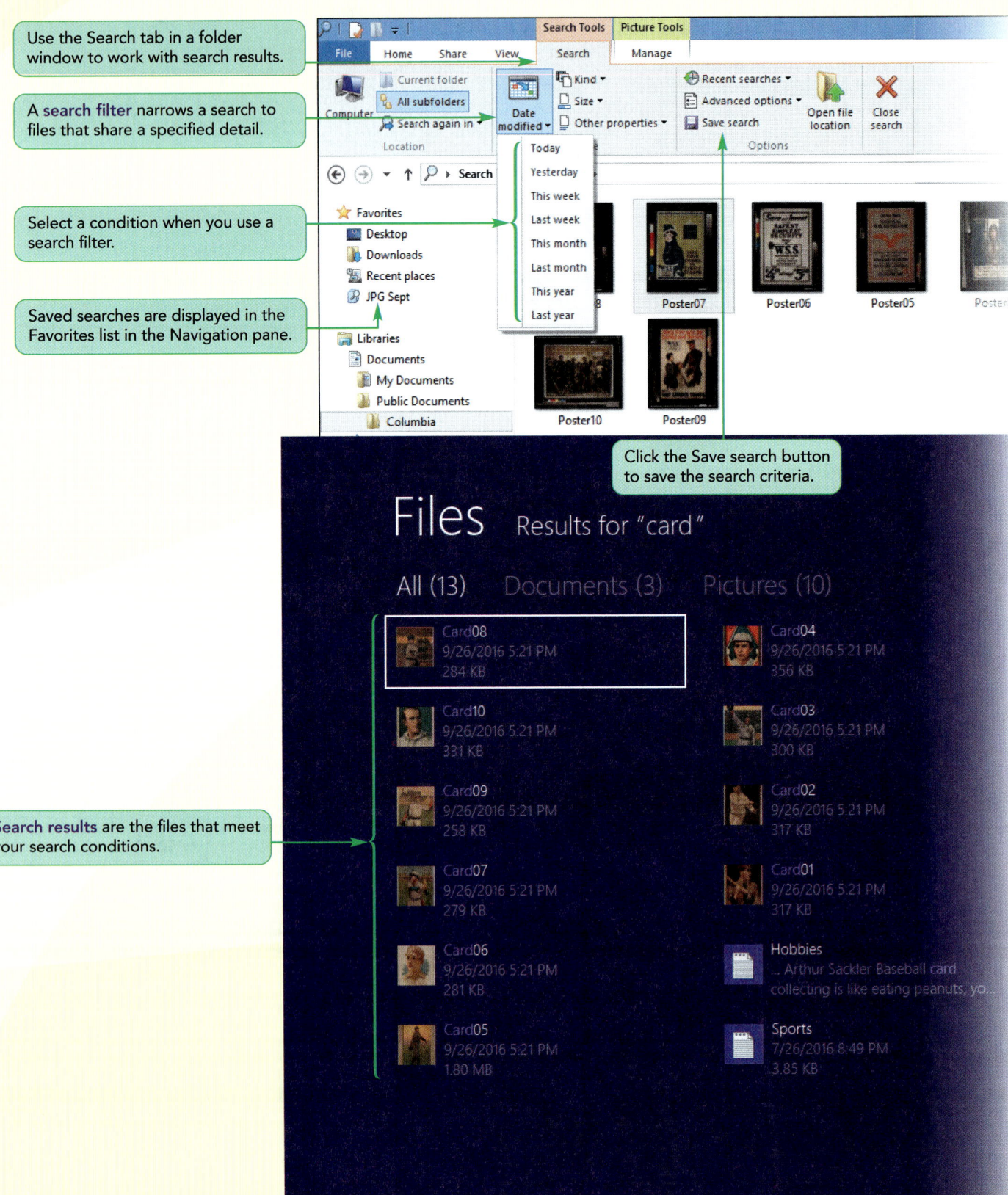

Courtesy of the Library of Congress, Prints and Photographs Division

Tutorial 6 Searching for Information | Windows   WIN 283

Searching for Files

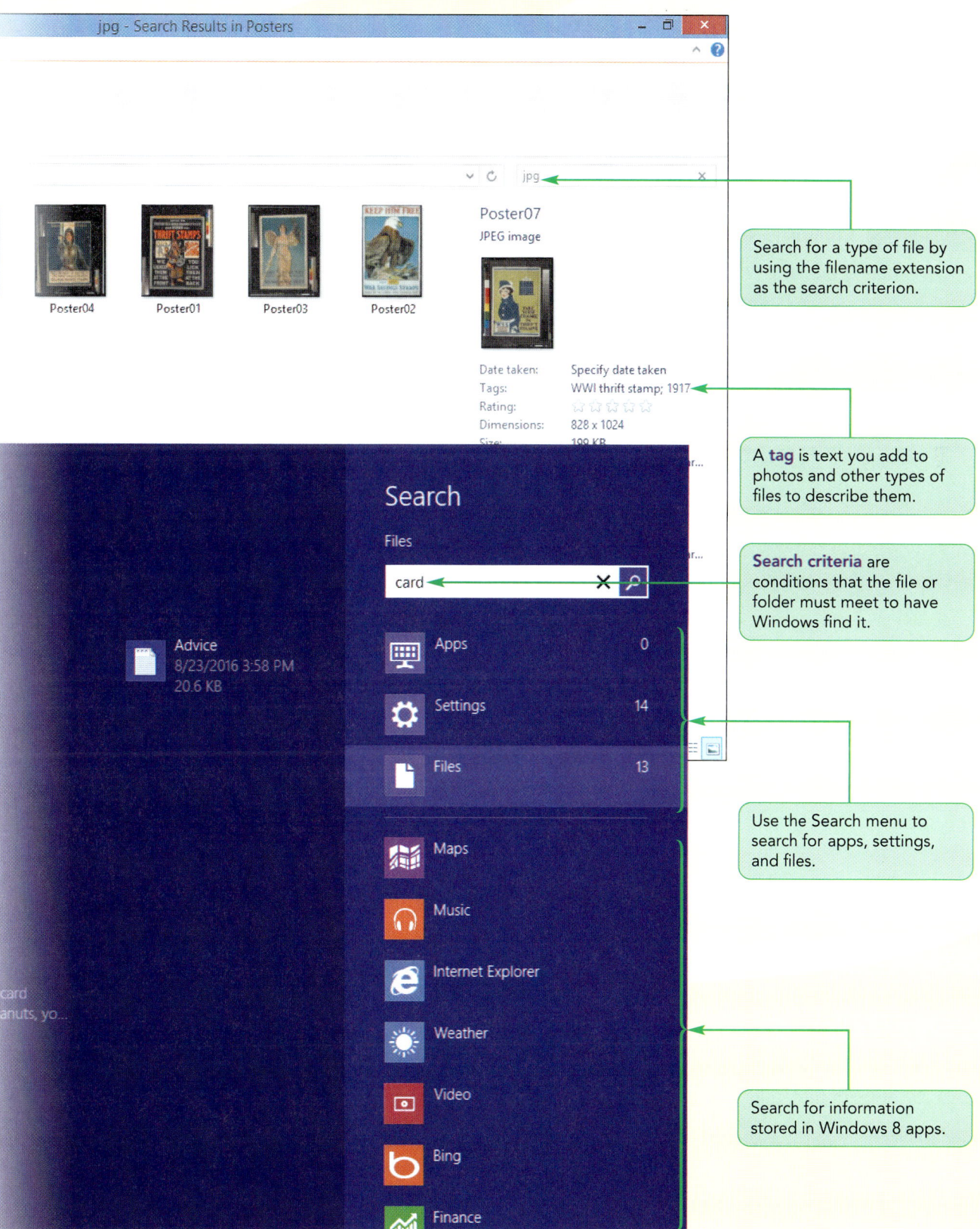

Search for a type of file by using the filename extension as the search criterion.

A **tag** is text you add to photos and other types of files to describe them.

Search criteria are conditions that the file or folder must meet to have Windows find it.

Use the Search menu to search for apps, settings, and files.

Search for information stored in Windows 8 apps.

Developing Search Strategies

As you install programs and store data on your computer, the number of files and folders you have grows, and it becomes harder to locate a particular item. Using an efficient organization scheme helps you find files and folders when you need them. Knowing your way around the Start screen and the desktop makes it easier to find apps and settings. However, if pinpointing an item means browsing dozens or hundreds of files and folders, or if you don't know where to look, you can use a Windows 8 search tool. You have already used the Search menu to find apps and the Search text box in a folder window to find files. Figure 6-1 offers recommendations on when to choose one search tool over another.

Figure 6-1   Choosing a search tool

Search Tool	What to Find	What You Know	Technique to Use
Search menu (also called Start Search)	App	Some or all of the app name	Enter some or all of the app name
	Setting	Some or all of the setting name, description, or keyword	Enter some or all of the setting name, description, or keyword
	File anywhere on the computer, including system files	Some or all of the filename or a file detail	Enter some or all of the filename or enter a detail, an operator, and a filter
	Information in an app	Word or phrase appropriate for the app	Enter some or all of the word or phrase
Search text box in a folder window	File in the current folder or its subfolders	Some or all of the filename	Enter some or all of the filename
		Word or phrase in the file	Enter some or all of the word or phrase
		Details listed below the Search text box	Select a detail, such as size, and then select a filter, such as Large
		Details not listed below the Search text box	Enter a detail, an operator, and a filter
	File anywhere on the computer	Name, contents, or details	Expand the search, such as to libraries or the entire computer
Search text box in a Control Panel window	Control Panel tool	Some or all of the tool name, description, or keyword	Enter some or all of the tool name, description, or keyword

© 2014 Cengage Learning

To develop a search strategy, you need to know what you are looking for and you need to have some information about the item. Start by identifying what you want to find or what task you want to perform. The Search menu groups searches into three categories: Apps, Settings, and Files. Apps is selected by default. To search for settings or files, select the appropriate category on the Search menu. Folder windows also include a Search text box that makes it easy to find files. Likewise, Control Panel windows include a Search text box for finding Control Panel tools. For example, if you want to start Notepad, a text-editing application, to open a text file named Stamps.txt, you use the Apps category on the Search menu. If you want to find the Stamps.txt file and you're working on the Start screen, you can use the Files category on the Search menu. If you're working on the desktop, you can use the Search text box in a folder window.

Next, identify what you already know about the item you want to find. This information becomes your search criteria, which are conditions that the app, setting, or file must meet to have Windows find it. These conditions help you define and narrow your search so you can quickly find the item you want. For example, if you are searching for an app and using *explore* as the search condition, Windows locates and displays every app that matches that condition—in other words, all apps whose name contains a word starting with "explore," such as Internet Explorer and File Explorer. Note that case doesn't matter—you could type *explore*, *Explore*, or even *EXPLORE* to include Internet Explorer and File Explorer in the search results.

When you know what you want to find and what information you have about the item, you can choose the search tool that best fits your needs, and then use search criteria that are most likely to find the item. For example, suppose you want to find a photo that you took last New Year's Eve and stored somewhere in the Pictures library. Because you know the location of the photo, you can use the Search text box in the Pictures library window. You also know when you took the photo, so you can search for files created on 12/31/2015.

Searching for Apps

You have already used the Search menu to find apps installed on your computer. On the Start screen, you start typing a word that appears in the app's name. As you type, Windows displays the search results on the left and the Search menu on the right. Windows searches for apps by default, so the results include Windows 8 and desktop apps whose names contain a word starting with the text you typed. Because you start the search from the Start screen, this search method is also called Start Search.

When you use Start Search, Windows keeps track of the search text you use. As you enter text on the Search menu, Windows displays **search hints**, suggested words and phrases that begin with the letters you typed and have used previously as search text. You can click a search hint to search using that word or phrase again.

Jay often works with a stamp dealer in Berlin, Germany, to buy and sell stamps. He needs a quick way to convert the price of a stamp from U.S. dollars to euros when he's selling the stamp, and to convert from euros to U.S. dollars when he's buying the stamp. He asks you to find tools on his Windows 8 computer that let him perform these tasks.

You know that one app Jay can use to convert currencies is the Calculator app. You'll show him how to use Start Search to find the Calculator app.

To search for an app:

▶ 1. On the Start screen, type **cal** to display the Apps screen and Search menu. See Figure 6-2.

   Trouble? If the Start screen is not displayed on your computer, press the Windows key and then repeat Step 1.

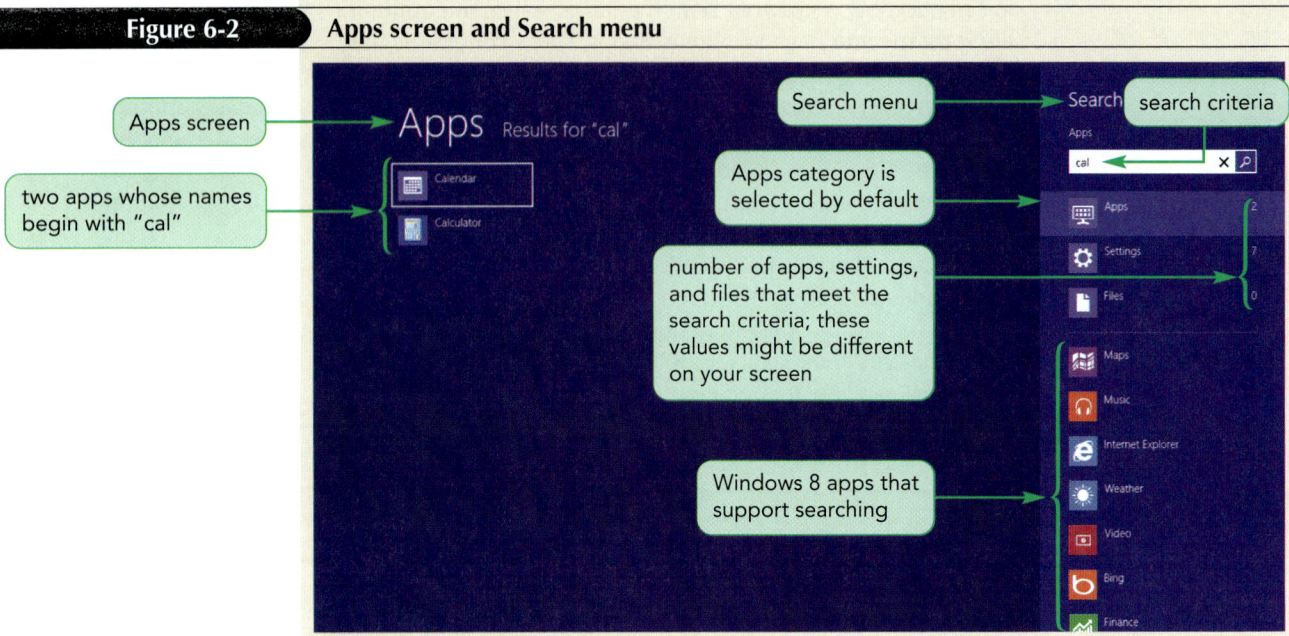

Figure 6-2 Apps screen and Search menu

2. In the search results, click **Calculator** to start the Calculator program.

When you use Start Search, the Search menu lists the number of apps, settings, and files that match your search criteria. Recall that you can display settings or files instead of apps by clicking Settings or Files on the Search menu. Below the Apps, Settings, and Files categories, the Search menu lists the Windows 8 apps that support searching. For example, you can search the Mail app to find email messages that match your search criteria. You'll search within an app later in this tutorial.

Jay has a stamp that he usually sells for $12. He knows that $1 currently equals 0.805 euros. You'll use the Calculator to determine the cost in euros of the $12 stamp.

To use the Calculator to convert dollars to euros:

1. With Calculator as the active program, type **12 * .805** and then press the **Enter** key to display the results: 9.66.
2. Click the **Close** button to close the Calculator app.
3. Press the **Windows** key to return to the Start screen.

TIP: Instead of typing the equation, you can also use the Calculator keypad.

Besides converting between euros and dollars, Jay wants to display a clock that shows the current time in Germany. You'll use Start Search to look for such a tool on Jay's computer.

Searching for Settings

Windows settings include Control Panel tools, such as the Personalization tool, and items on the PC settings screen, such as your account picture. The Settings search results screen lists each PC settings item with a Settings icon and each Control Panel tool with an icon identifying the tool, such as the Personalization icon.

To make searching more effective, each setting has a name, a description, and one or more keywords. For example, the Personalization tool on the Control Panel uses

"Personalization" as the name, "Change desktop background" as the description, and keywords such as "personalize" and "customize."

When you search for apps, Windows matches your search text to a word in the app name. For example, using *cal* as the search text produced two apps in the search results—Calendar and Calculator—because the names of both apps start with "cal." However, when you search for settings, Windows matches your search text to the setting name, description, and keywords. For example, when you search settings using "background" as the search text, the results include the Change desktop background setting, which you can click to open the Personalization tool in the Control Panel.

To find a tool that displays a clock in a different time zone, you can use the Settings category on the Search menu. (If you were already working in the Control Panel, you could use the Search text box in the Control Panel window.) You will use "clock" as the search text.

To search for a setting:

1. On the Start screen, type **clock** to display the Apps screen and Search menu. Although no apps are displayed in the search results, a number of items appear in the Settings category. You can display the found items in the Settings category to see if one contains a tool you can use.

2. Click **Settings** on the Search menu to display the settings and tools on your computer that include a word beginning with "clock" in their name, description, or keywords. See Figure 6-3. Your results might differ.

TIP

You can also press the Windows+W keys to search settings from the Start screen, Windows 8 app, or desktop.

Figure 6-3   Settings search results

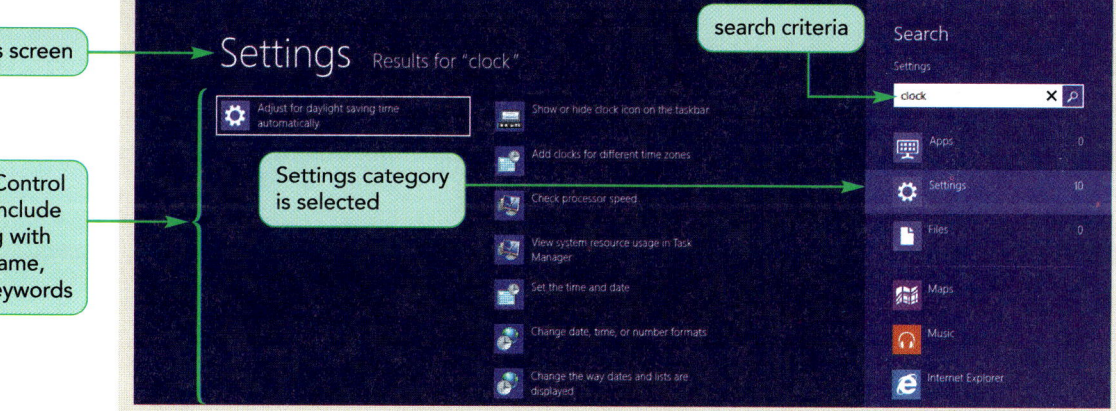

- Settings screen
- PC settings and Control Panel tools that include a word beginning with "clock" in their name, description, or keywords
- Settings category is selected
- search criteria

The results include one PC setting and nine Control Panel settings, as identified by the icon that appears next to each setting. How do you know if any of these settings will display a clock in another time zone? You can analyze the results by examining each item more carefully. The setting, "Add clocks for different time zones," sounds promising. To learn more about a setting, you can point to an item in the search results to display a ScreenTip that identifies the category of the setting and its description. To select a setting, you click it in the search results.

To examine and select a setting:

1. Click a blank spot in the search results to close the Settings menu, and then point to **Add clocks for different time zones**. The ScreenTip indicates that this setting is in the Date and Time category of the Control Panel and repeats the setting description.

2. Click **Add clocks for different time zones** to display the Date and Time dialog box, which is open to the Additional Clocks tab. See Figure 6-4.

Figure 6-4   Date and Time dialog box

click the Show this clock check box to add the first additional clock

Select time zone button

enter a name for the additional clock

3. Click the first **Show this clock** check box to select it. The current time zone is selected for the additional clock, so you need to change it to show the time zone in Germany.

4. Click the **Select time zone** button, and then click **(UTC + 01:00) Amsterdam, Berlin, Bern, Rome, Stockholm, Vienna** to select the time zone for Germany.

5. Select the text in the Enter display name text box, and then type **Germany** to name the clock.

6. Click the **OK** button to close the Date and Time dialog box.

7. Point to the date and time control in the notification area of the taskbar to display the local time and the current time in Germany.

Jay is confident he will use the additional clock frequently when communicating with the German stamp dealer.

Searching for Files

You can search for files using Start Search or the Search text box in a folder window. Start Search looks for files stored anywhere on your computer, including system files stored in a system folder. The Search text box looks for files contained in the current folder or one of its subfolders. The tool you choose depends on your current task. If you just signed in to Windows or are working on the Start screen, use Start Search. If you are working on the desktop or in a folder window, use the Search text box.

When you search for files using either tool, you can conduct a basic search or an advanced search. If you use text from the filename or the file contents as search criteria, you are conducting a basic search. If you use other properties such as tags or file size as search criteria, you are conducting an advanced search. The other properties you can use as search criteria include any detail you can display as a column in a folder window. (Recall that you can display additional columns in a folder window by right-clicking any column heading, and then clicking a detail on the shortcut menu. If the detail you want to display does not appear on the shortcut menu, click More to open the Choose Details dialog box.) Figure 6-5 describes common criteria you can use when you conduct basic and advanced searches to find a file.

Figure 6-5 Typical search criteria

File Property	Description	What to Find	Search Criterion
Basic Searches			
Filename	All or part of the filename	File named April sales.docx	Apr or sales
File type	Filename extension	All of your photos	jpg
Contents	Text the file contains	File that uses "Baseball Card Sets" as a heading	Baseball Card Sets
Advanced Searches			
Date	Date the file was modified, created, or accessed	Document edited on May 15, 2016	datemodified:5/15/2016
Size	Size of the file	Files larger than 3 MB	size>3 MB
Tag	Word or phrase in the file properties	Photo with "winter," "vacation," and "ski" as tags	tag:winter vacation ski
Author	Name of the person who created the file	Document that Jay created	author:Jay

© 2014 Cengage Learning

When you combine criteria, such as to find a file named Agenda that you created last Monday, you are also conducting an advanced search. You'll learn how to combine search criteria later in the tutorial.

Finding Files by Name and Contents

Suppose you want to start working with a spreadsheet file named Poster Collection as soon as you sign in to Windows. On the Start screen, start typing a word in the filename, for example "poster," to display the Apps screen and the Search menu. Click Files on the Search menu to display all the files on your hard disk with filenames or contents that include a word beginning with the letters you typed. Performing this type of basic search using Start Search or a folder window is the most common way to find files on a Windows 8 computer.

A sales clerk for Columbia Collectibles created a short video that showcases the World War I posters in the shop's collection. Jay knows this video is stored somewhere on his computer, but isn't sure of the exact location or the complete filename. He does know that the filename includes the word "poster." You'll show him how to use Start Search to find the file.

First, however, you'll copy the Data Files for this tutorial to the Public Documents folder on your hard disk. The Windows6\Tutorial folder includes three subfolders: Cards, Posters, and Quotations. The Cards folder includes images of baseball cards and the Posters folder contains files related to the shop's poster collection. The Quotations folder contains text documents of quotations from authors, comedians, and other people on various subjects. Jay likes to include at least one quotation on the shop's Weekly Features Web page.

To search for files by name:

1. Open File Explorer on the desktop, open the **Public Documents** folder in the Documents library, and then create a folder named **Columbia** in the Public Documents folder.
2. If necessary, insert the USB flash drive containing your Data Files into a USB port on your computer.
3. Right-click the **File Explorer** button on the taskbar, and then click **File Explorer** to open a second folder window. Display the contents of the Windows6\Tutorial folder provided with your Data Files. Copy the **Cards**, **Posters**, and **Quotations** folders from the Tutorial folder to the Columbia folder.
4. Close the Tutorial folder window (the second window displaying the USB flash drive), but leave the Columbia folder window open on the desktop.
5. Press the **Windows** key to display the Start screen.
6. Type **poster** to display the Search menu and the Apps screen.
7. Click **Files** on the Search menu to display the files on the hard disk that meet the search criteria. See Figure 6-6.

Figure 6-6 — Using Start Search to find files

- number of files found by type
- number of total files found
- files whose name or contents include a word starting with "poster"

Courtesy of Library of Congress, Prints and Photographs Division

TIP
You can also press the Windows+F keys to search for a file from the Start screen, Windows 8 app, or desktop.

8. In the search results, click **Videos (1)** to display the video file Windows found: WWI Posters.
9. Click the **WWI Posters** file to display a list of apps that can play this file, and then, if necessary, click **Video** to begin playing the file in the Video app.

   Trouble? If a message appears advising you to create an account, close all open windows and screens and then press the Windows key to return to the Start screen.

10. When the video stops playing, close the Video app to return to the Start screen.

Tutorial 6 Searching for Information | Windows

The search results for the previous steps included 11 files with names containing a word that starts with "poster." The results also included three text files named Advice, Hobbies, and Humor. To find out why, perform the same basic search again.

To search for files by contents:

1. Type **poster** to display the Search menu and the Apps screen.

2. Click **Files** on the Search menu to display the files and folders on the hard disk that meet the search criteria.

3. Click a blank spot in the search results, and then point to the **Advice** text file to display its location in a ScreenTip. Next, point to the **Hobbies** and **Humor** files to display their ScreenTips.

4. Click the **Advice** text file to open it in Notepad. This file contains quotations that provide advice from authors, comedians, and other people.

5. Press the **Ctrl+F** keys to open the Find dialog box, type **poster** in the Find what text box, and then click the **Find Next** button. Notepad selects the first instance of "poster" in the Advice file.

6. Close the Find dialog box and then close Notepad. The Columbia folder window is displayed on the desktop.

7. In the Columbia folder window, double-click the **Quotations** folder, and then double-click the **Hobbies** text file to open it in Notepad.

8. Repeat Step 5 to find the first instance of "poster" in the Hobbies file, and then close the Find dialog box and close Notepad. The Quotations folder window is still displayed.

9. Open the **Humor** text file, find the first instance of "poster" in the file, and then close the Find dialog box and close Notepad.

Although the Advice, Hobbies, and Humor filenames do not include a word starting with *poster*, the file contents do. When you conduct a basic search to find files stored on a hard disk, Windows includes the file contents in the search. However, if you search files stored on a removable disk, such as a USB drive, Windows searches only the filenames, not the contents, by default.

Searching by File Type

Using the Search text box in a folder window to find files based on their filenames and contents is similar to using Start Search. You type text in the Search text box, and Windows displays only those files in the current folder or its subfolders that match the criterion: files whose contents or filename include a word starting with the text you typed.

You can also use a filename extension as the search criterion to find files by type. For example, you could enter *jpg* to find files with a JPG extension (also called JPGs), which are usually photo files. When you search for files by type, you can enter the filename extension on its own (*jpg*) or use an asterisk and a dot before the filename extension (*.jpg*). In this case, the asterisk is a **wildcard**, a symbol that stands for one or more unspecified characters in the search criterion.

Using a wildcard is a good idea if you want to search for certain types of files, such as those with a DOC extension. Suppose some of your filenames include words that start with the extension text, such as "Doctor Visit," "June Docket," or "Jay Docs." In this case, using a wildcard and a dot makes it clear that you are searching by filename extension only, and produces more accurate search results.

Jay is creating Web pages and printed marketing materials that feature notable baseball cards and posters in the shop's collection. He has been photographing these items and saving the photos on his computer. First, he wants to know how many card and poster photos he has saved. Because all of these photos are stored in two subfolders, you can provide the information Jay wants by conducting a basic search in a folder window using the filename extension .jpg as the search criterion.

To search for files by type:

1. In the folder window open on the desktop, display the contents of the Columbia folder in the Public Documents folder. If necessary, click the **Expand the Ribbon** button to display the controls on the ribbon.

2. Click the **Search** text box, and then type **jpg**. Windows displays only the files with a .jpg extension in the folder window.

3. If necessary, click the **Large Icons** button in the status bar to display the contents of the files. See Figure 6-7. Maximize the window, if necessary, to see all of the items, as shown in the figure.

Figure 6-7 Searching for files with a .jpg filename extension

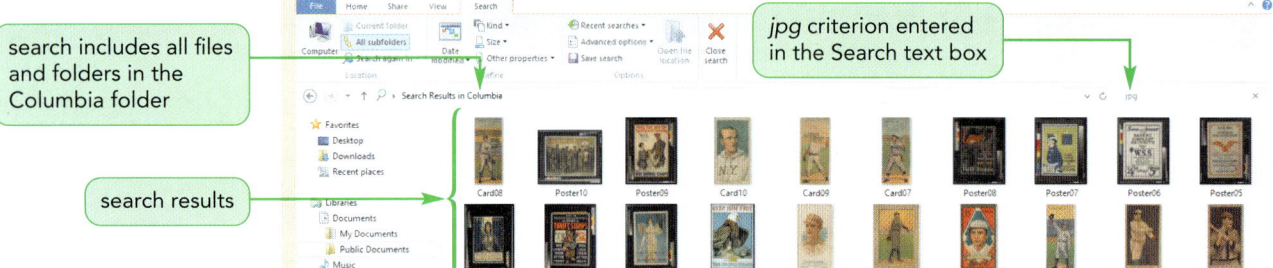

- search includes all files and folders in the Columbia folder
- jpg criterion entered in the Search text box
- search results

Courtesy of the Library of Congress, Prints and Photographs Division

Decision Making: Searching vs. Sorting, Filtering, or Grouping

Recall that instead of using the Search text box, you can often quickly find files by sorting, filtering, or grouping files using the column headings or View menu in a folder window. The method you choose depends on the number of files you want to search, the location of the files, and their names. For example, suppose you need to find JPG files. If you want to search the current folder *and* its subfolders, use the Search text box—the other options find files only in the current folder.

If you're searching a single folder, the Search text box is also preferable if the folder contains similar filenames (because sorting would list many files that start with the same text) or many types of files (because grouping would produce many groups). If you want to find a particular file in a very large folder, it is often easier to use the Search text box rather than dealing with a long file list; however, if the folder doesn't contain too many files, then sorting, grouping, or filtering is usually a more efficient method.

Now that you found the photos of baseball cards and posters, Jay wants you to research the items so he can provide accurate information in the Web pages and printed brochure. Some of the JPG files you found have filenames starting with "Card" followed by a number, such as Card01 and Card02. The other JPG files have filenames starting with "Poster" followed by a number. Jay set his digital camera to assign these names so he could take the photos quickly. The camera used Card01 for the first photo Jay took of a baseball card and then automatically added 1 to the number each time he took another photo until he finished photographing the baseball cards. The camera used the same process to name the poster photos. Although this filenaming scheme worked well to save the photo files quickly, it poses challenges for your research because the filenames do not reveal anything about the content except that they show baseball cards or posters.

Filtering the Search Results by Size

Besides simply typing a few letters in the Search text box, you can also conduct more advanced searches using Start Search or a folder window. To search for files modified on a certain date or files of a certain size, for example, you can add a filter to narrow a search to files that share a specified detail. (Recall that a filter displays only files with a certain characteristic you specify.)

When you enter text in the Search text box of a folder window, Windows displays the results in the right pane and opens the Search tab on the ribbon. You use the buttons in the Refine group on the Search tab to narrow the results. For example, if you are searching the Pictures library for photos you took last week, you can click the Search text box in the Pictures library and then type *jpg* to display all the photos stored in the Pictures library. To narrow the results to display only the photos you took last week, click the Date modified button in the Refine group on the Search tab, and then click Last week. Windows displays only the files in the Pictures library that meet your criteria.

> **REFERENCE**
>
> ### Filtering Search Results
>
> - Open the folder, library, or drive you want to search.
> - Enter text in the Search text box.
> - To specify a filter, click a button in the Refine group on the Search tab, and then click a criterion.
>
> or
>
> - On the Start screen, type a file property name, a colon, and the criterion.
> - Click Files on the Search menu.

When you select a search filter, Windows automatically adds a file property name, a colon, and the criterion to the Search text box. The file property name is shorthand for the detail you want to use to narrow the search. The criterion determines how to narrow the search. For example, when you click the Date modified button on the Search tab and then click Last week, Windows inserts "datemodified:last week" in the Search text box.

To conduct an advanced search using Start Search, you enter the file property name, a colon, and the criterion directly in the text box on the Search menu.

Jay photographed one of the collectible items using a high resolution, which makes the image sharp and clear even when printed. He wants to use this photo in a printed brochure. However, he can't recall which photo has the high resolution. He mentions that high-resolution images are usually large files, often more than 1 MB in storage size. You can use this information to find the file Jay wants. Conducting a basic search using the jpg extension as the search text finds all the JPG files in the Cards and Posters folders. To narrow the search to large files only, you'll refine the results.

To narrow a search using a search filter:

1. In the folder window displaying the results of the previous search, click the **Search Tools Search** tab, if necessary, and then click the **Size** button in the Refine group to display a list of size options. See Figure 6-8.

   Trouble? If the folder window open on the desktop does not display the results of the previous search, type jpg in the Search text box.

Figure 6-8   Selecting a search filter

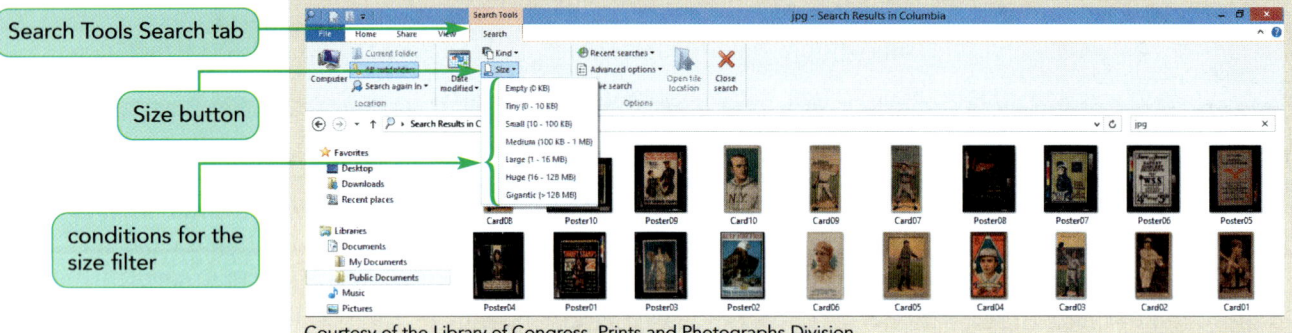

Courtesy of the Library of Congress, Prints and Photographs Division

2. Click **Large (1–16 MB)** in the Size options list. Windows reduces the search results to files that meet both criteria—large JPG files.

Only one file meets the search criteria: Card05, which is a high-resolution photo of a Cy Young baseball card.

Filtering Search Results by Date Modified

Jay usually photographs a collectible item as soon as he receives it. On the shop's Weekly Features Web page, Jay wants you to display photos of collectible items he acquired recently, which are those photos taken after August 31, 2016. To find these files, you can start with the same criterion you used to find all the JPG files, and then narrow the results by specifying the date condition. When you use the Date modified button in the Refine group on the Search tab, you can select only predefined options such as Today, This week, or Last year. To use a specific date, you select one of these criteria and then click the Search text box to display a calendar where you can select a date or date range.

To find JPG files taken after August 31, 2016:

1. In the folder window, click the **Back** button ⬅ until you return to the Columbia window.

2. Click the **Search** text box, if necessary, and then type **jpg**. Windows displays all the JPG files in the search results.

3. Click the **Date modified** button in the Refine group on the Search tab, and then click **Today** to select a date option. No results appear, so you need to modify the date further.

4. Click in the text "today" in the Search text box to display a calendar control. See Figure 6-9.

TIP

Click the Search text box to display a list of recently used search text.

Tutorial 6 Searching for Information | Windows   WIN 295

| Figure 6-9 | Using a date modified search condition |

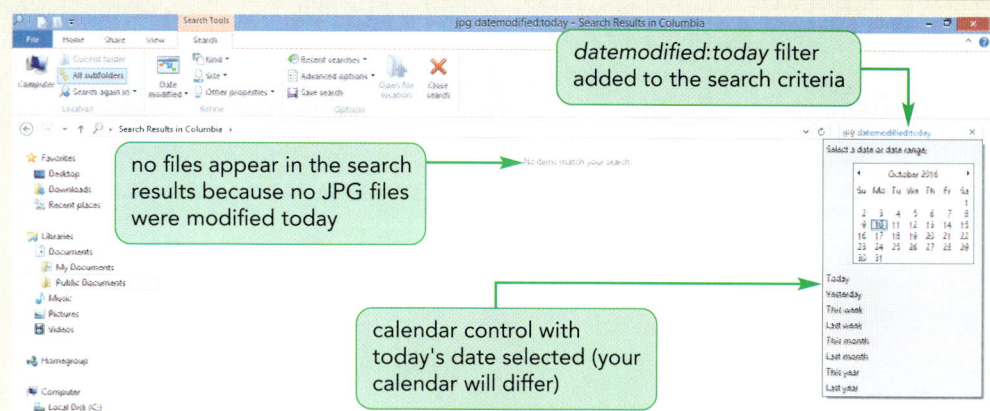

5. Use the calendar controls to display the **August 2016** page. To change the month, click the **left arrow** ◀ and **right arrow** ▶ buttons. When the calendar page for August 2016 appears, click **31**. See Figure 6-10.

| Figure 6-10 | Setting date criteria |

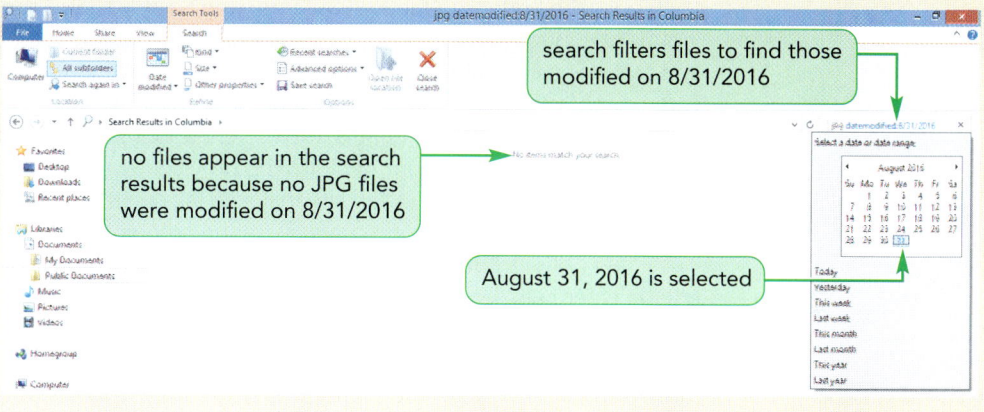

No files appear in the search results because no files in the Columbia folder were modified on August 31, 2016. You want to find files that were modified after that date. To do so, you use the greater than (>) operator. You can use the greater than operator with any property in the Search text box or the Search menu. For example, to find files that are larger than 500 KB, enter *size:>500KB*. (You can include a space after the colon or omit it—the space does not affect the search results.) You can also use the less than (<) operator in the same way. To find files less than 500 KB, enter *size:<500KB*. To find files modified after August 31, 2016, you use the greater than operator to enter *datemodified:>8/31/2016* in the Search text box.

To modify the search criteria:

1. Click the **Search** text box.
2. Move the insertion point after the colon (:) in datemodified, and then type **>**. Six files appear in the search results.

To make sure you find the files you need or to expand a search, you should examine the search results.

Examining the Search Results

After you enter search criteria using the Search text box, Windows filters the view of the folder window to display files that meet your criteria. These are your search results. Figure 6-11 shows the results of the search performed in the preceding set of steps: JPG files modified after August 31, 2016.

Figure 6-11 Search results

Courtesy of the Library of Congress, Prints and Photographs Division

Search results windows provide extra tools and information to help you work with the files you found. The title bar displays the search criteria. In Details view, the search results display the name, location, date modified, size, and other available properties of each file. If the results include text files, they preview their first two lines of text to help you identify the file contents.

Besides the buttons in the Refine group, the Search Tools Search tab contains other groups of controls to help you find the files or information you need. The Location group and Options group provide other search tools that you can use to broaden or narrow your search. Using the buttons in the Location group, you can change the default search location on your computer (that is, the current folder and all of its subfolders) or even search the Internet using your default Web browser (such as Internet Explorer) and **search provider**, which is a Web site that specializes in searching the Internet, such as Bing. The Options group stores a history of the criteria for your last eight searches. The Advanced options button in this group allows you to change how Windows uses the criteria entered to search for files using an exact match setting, for example. To speed up a search, you can set Windows to search an indexed location, such as the Documents library or Pictures library on your hard disk, so Windows searches the file contents. (An **indexed location** is one or more folders that Windows indexes so it can search them quickly. Libraries and other locations that contain your personal files—not system files—are indexed locations.) The Options group provides tools for saving the criteria and folder location of a search.

Jay occasionally works with files stored on a removable disk, so you want to show him how to search filenames and contents in that location.

To search for files on a removable disk:

1. If necessary, insert the USB flash drive containing your Data Files into a USB port on your computer.

2. In the folder window open on the desktop, display the contents of the Windows6\Tutorial folder on the USB flash drive.

3. Type **poster** in the Search text box to display files with filenames that contain a word beginning with *poster*.

4. Click the **Advanced options** button in the Options group on the Search Tools Search tab, and then click **File contents** under the In the non-indexed locations section (which includes the USB flash drive). Windows adds the three text files that contain a word beginning with "poster" to the search results.

Trouble? If File contents is already selected, the text files are already displayed in the results for Step 3. Do not click File contents; this will deselect the option. Press the Esc key to close the list of advanced options.

In addition to the extra tools provided in a search results window, you can use the standard folder window tools to open, move, copy, rename, or delete a file.

Saving a Search

If you conduct a successful search that you are likely to conduct again, especially one that uses two or more criteria, you might want to save the search. Saving a search preserves your original criteria and folder location so you can perform the search again without reconstructing the criteria. By default, Windows saves the search in the Searches folder, which you can open from the Favorites list of any folder window's Navigation pane. You can double-click a saved search to use the same criteria in a new search. The search results display the most current files that match the original conditions, so the results might differ from other times when you conducted the same search.

To save a search and perform it again:

TIP
Click the Search text box to display the recent searches, and then click jpg datemodified:>8/31/2016.

1. In the search results window, click the **Back** button ⓐ to navigate back to the results of the jpg datemodified:>8/31/2016 search.

2. Click the **Save search** button in the Options group on the Search Tools Search tab. The Save As dialog box opens, providing jpg datemodified8-31-2016 as the filename. (Windows doesn't include the colon and greater than symbol because they are not allowed in filenames; Windows also replaces the forward slashes with dashes for the same reason.) See Figure 6-12.

Figure 6-12 Saving a search

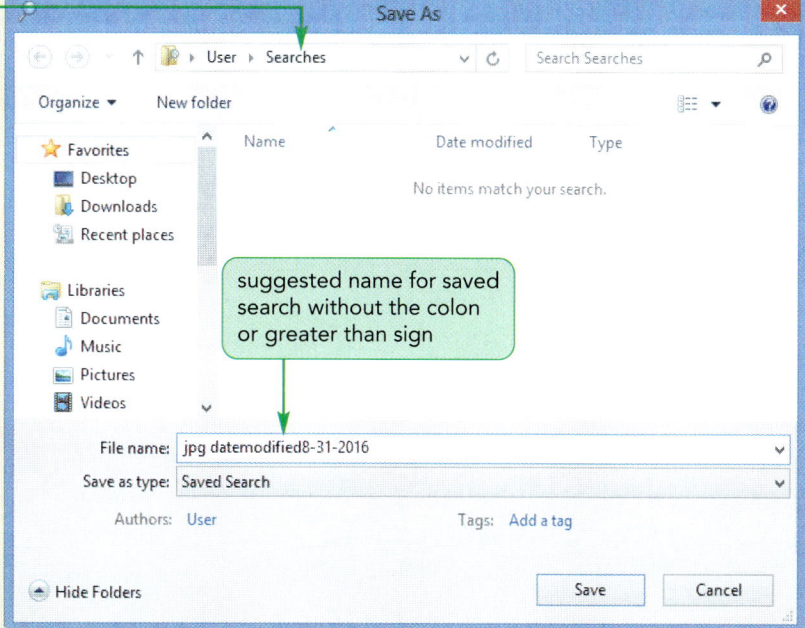

by default, Windows saves your searches in the Searches folder in your personal folder

suggested name for saved search without the colon or greater than sign

Be sure to save the search so you can use it again.

3. Change the filename to **JPG Sept**, and then click the **Save** button to save the search in the Searches folder.

4. To view the saved search, display the Favorites list in the Navigation pane, if necessary. The JPG Sept search appears in the Favorites list.

5. To test the search, click **Libraries** in the Navigation pane to change your current location, and then click **JPG Sept** in the Favorites list. Windows conducts the search again and finds the JPG files modified after August 31, 2016. See Figure 6-13.

Figure 6-13   Performing a saved search

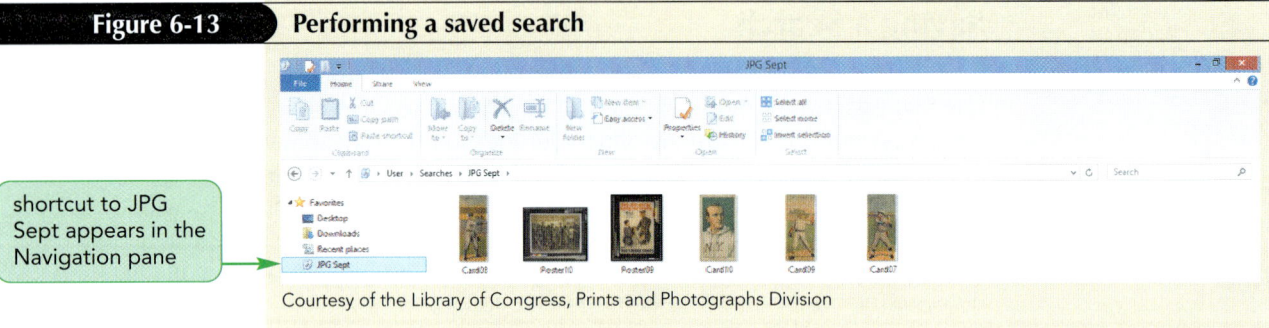

shortcut to JPG Sept appears in the Navigation pane

Courtesy of the Library of Congress, Prints and Photographs Division

Jay asks if using tags would help him find and identify files. In fact, one of the most useful properties when searching for files is a file tag, which is one or more descriptive words you store with a file to help identify its purpose or contents. You are sure that adding tags to the photo files would save you and Jay a lot of time when searching for photos. You'll show him how to do so next.

Using Tags and Other Properties

As you know, properties are characteristics of files, such as names and sizes. When you create or modify a file, you automatically set some file properties, including the filename, location, and date created or modified. You can add other properties later, including tags, ratings, titles, and authors. Tags are often the most useful because they make finding similar files easier.

To add properties to a file, you can use the Details pane in a folder window or the file's Properties dialog box. (You can use the Details pane to add or modify the properties of only some types of files, such as Microsoft Office documents, but not TXT or RTF files.) To open the Details pane in a folder window, you click the Details pane button in the Panes group on the View tab. Figure 6-14 shows the Details pane when the Card05 file is selected in the Cards folder.

Figure 6-14   File properties in the Details pane

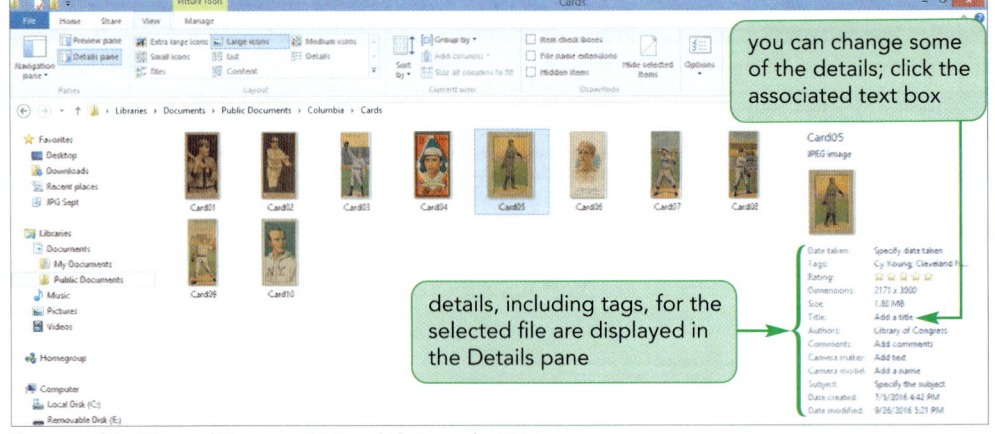

you can change some of the details; click the associated text box

details, including tags, for the selected file are displayed in the Details pane

Courtesy of the Library of Congress, Prints and Photographs Division

Properties you can add using the Details pane vary by file type. For photos, you can specify date taken, tags, and other properties by using the appropriate text box in the Details pane. You can also rate photos by clicking a star in a series of five stars. If you click the first star, you apply a one-star rating. If you click the fourth star, you apply a four-star rating.

If you want to specify file properties other than the ones that appear in the Details pane by default, you can open the Properties dialog box for a file. To do so, you right-click the file and then click Properties on the shortcut menu. On the Details tab, you can add or modify dozens of properties. Figure 6-15 shows the Properties dialog box for the Card05 file.

Figure 6-15   **File details in the Properties dialog box**

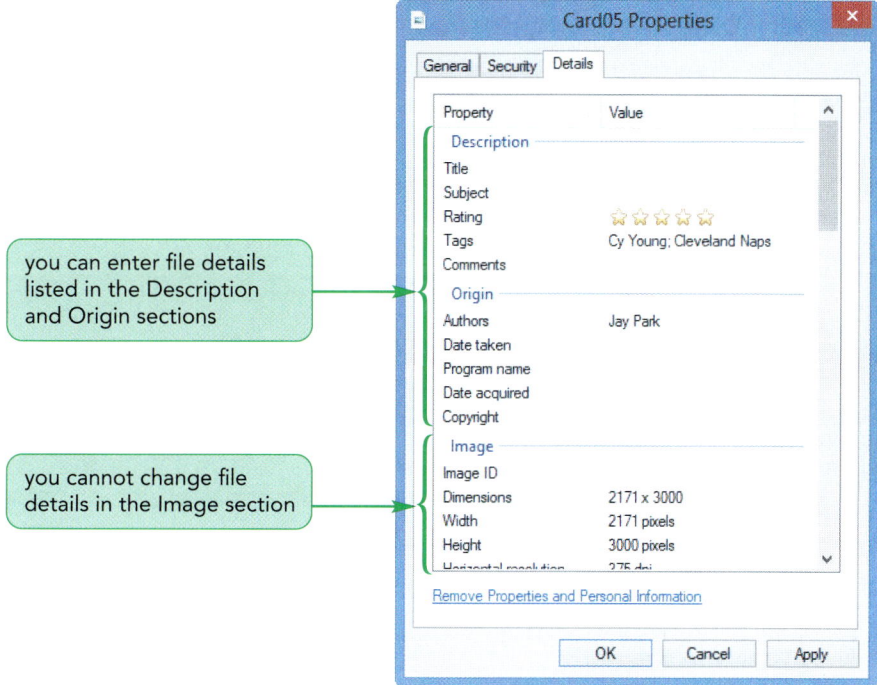

you can enter file details listed in the Description and Origin sections

you cannot change file details in the Image section

Adding Tags to Files

You can add a tag to a file by using the Save As dialog box when you save the file, or by using the Details pane or the file's Properties dialog box after you save the file. To use the Details pane, you select the file, click the Tags text box in the Details pane, and then type a word or phrase that will help you find the file later. To add more than one tag, separate each word or phrase with a semicolon (;). For example, if you have a photo of yourself on the peak of the Blackrock Mountain in Virginia, you could use *Blackrock; mountain; Virginia* as tags.

REFERENCE

Adding Tags to Files

- In a folder window, click the file to which you want to add a tag.
- Click the Details pane button in the Panes group on the View tab to display the Details pane.
- Click the Tags text box in the Details pane, and then type a tag. To enter another tag, type a semicolon (;) and then type the next tag.
- Click the Save button on the Details pane.

Jay has already added tags to most of the photo files in the Cards and Posters folders, but two recent files still need tags. Jay asks you to add descriptive tags to these files.

To add tags to files:

1. Open the **Posters** folder in the Public Documents\Columbia folder on your hard disk, and then switch to Details view. Maximize the window, if necessary.
2. Click the **Details pane** button in the Panes group on the View tab to display the Details pane.
3. Display the Tags column, if necessary, by right-clicking any column heading and then clicking **Tags** on the shortcut menu.
4. If necessary, click the **Size all columns to fit** button in the Current view group to display all of the columns in the window.
5. Click each file in the file list to examine its properties in the Details pane. Note that WWI Posters, Poster09, and Poster10 do not have any tags. WWI Posters is a video, so it's easy to identify that file without tags.
6. Click **Poster09** to display its image and text boxes for file details such as tags in the Details pane. Jay knows that this poster advertises World War I savings stamps and was printed in 1918.
7. Click the **Tags** text box in the Details pane, and then type **1918** as the first tag. Windows inserts an ending semicolon for you. Click after the ; (a semicolon), and then type **WWI savings stamps** as the second tag. See Figure 6-16.

Figure 6-16	Adding tags to a file

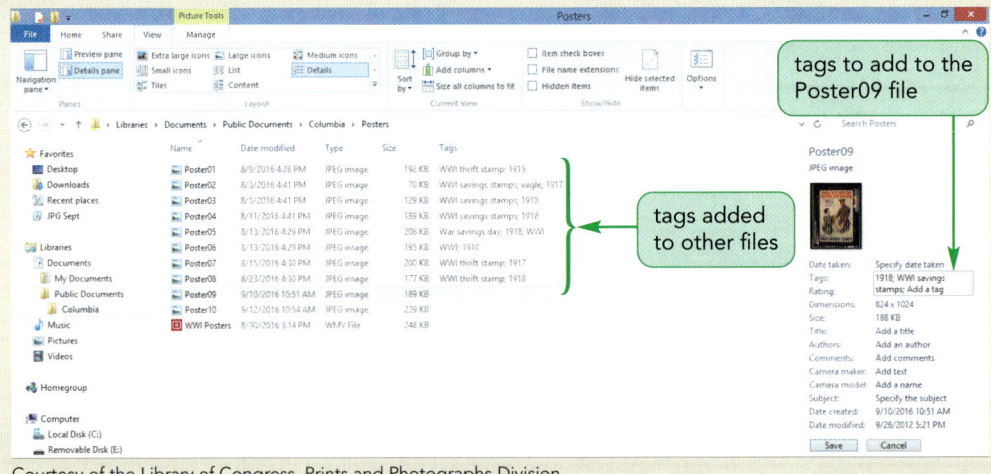

Courtesy of the Library of Congress, Prints and Photographs Division

8. Click the **Save** button in the Details pane. Windows saves the tags you added.
9. Add the tags **1917; WWI savings stamps; U.S. Treasury** to the Poster10 file, and then click the **Save** button. Note that after you save a tag in one file, that tag appears in the list of suggested tags for other files.

TIP
If Windows suggests tags as you begin to type, click the tag you want.

INSIGHT

Selecting Tags for Files

To create tags that will help you find files later, keep the following guidelines in mind:
- Include the obvious. Use words or phrases that describe the overall purpose or content of the file. For photo files, use tags that list the people in the picture, the location of the photo, and the occasion. For documents, describe the type of document, such as a proposal or report, and its subject.
- Consider the sample tags. If you are working with files on a hard drive, you can find typical tags by typing a letter in the Tags text box in the Details pane. For example, type *p* to find sample tags that start with the letter *p*, such as people, pet owners, pets, and photography.
- Use complete words and phrases. Avoid abbreviations and codes because you might not remember them later. Assign complete words or use phrases to be as clear as possible. Feel free to use text that appears in the filename; doing so might help you find other related files with the same tag but a different filename.

You've already explored many ways to search for files on your computer. You conducted basic searches by searching filenames and contents. You also conducted advanced searches by using properties to filter the search results. In the next session, you'll build on these techniques by searching tags and combining criteria using shorthand notation and Boolean filters. You'll apply these new skills to search for information in Windows 8 apps and on the Internet.

REVIEW

Session 6.1 Quick Check

1. How do you search for an app from the Start screen?
2. When you search for settings, what two groups of items does Windows search?
3. Explain when you typically use Start Search to search for files, and when you use the Search text box in a folder window.
4. When you conduct a basic search for files stored on a removable disk, what does Windows search by default? How does this differ from a basic search for files stored on a hard disk?
5. Explain how to search for TXT files in a folder window.
6. After searching for JPG files in the Pictures library, you can click the _____ button in the Refine group on the Search tab to narrow the results to display only the photos you took last week.
7. When you save a search, what exactly are you saving?

Session 6.2 Visual Overview:

Searching the Internet

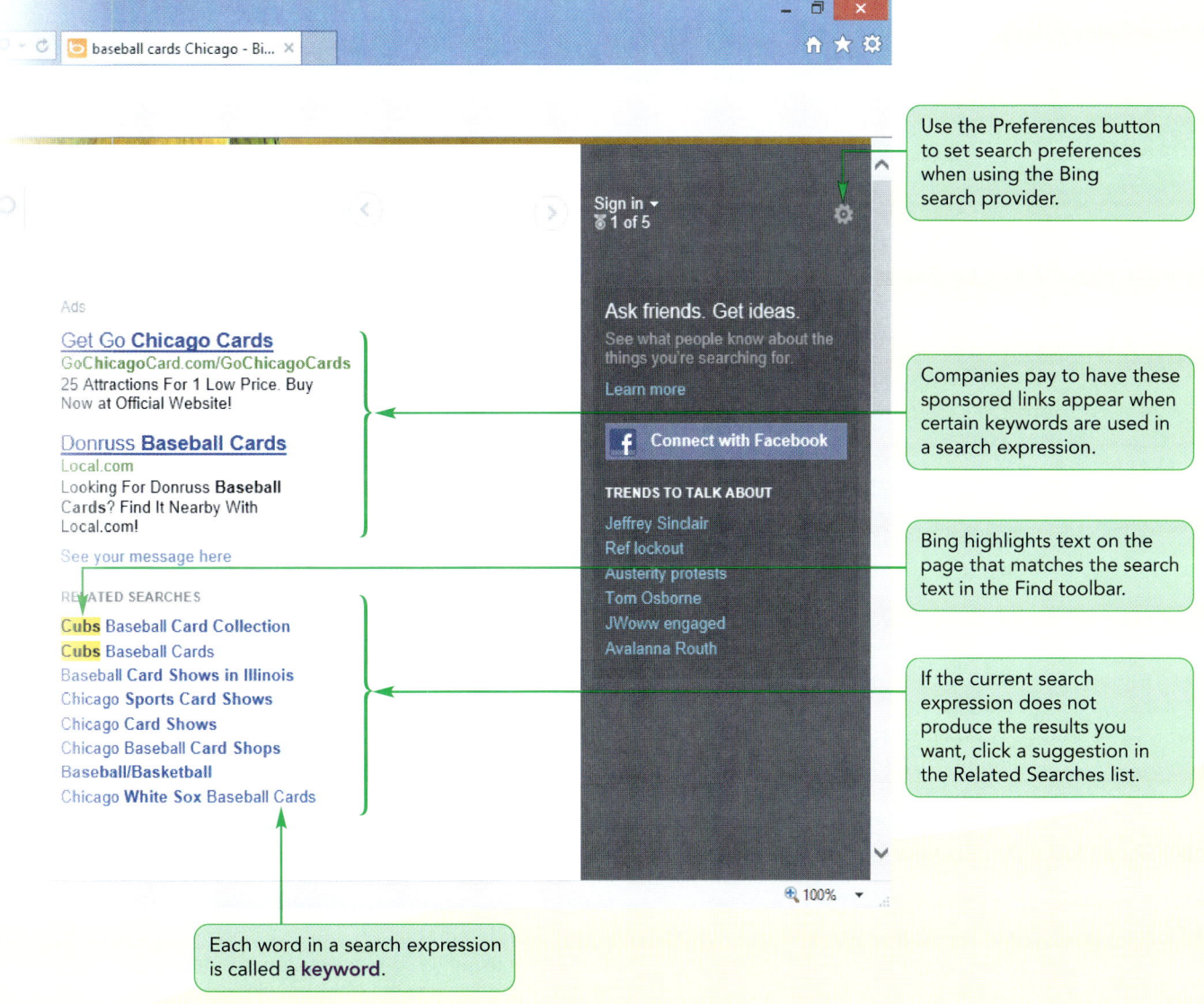

Using Advanced Search Criteria

In addition to searching for files using common properties such as file type or size, you can use the Search text box or the Search menu to search for other properties, including tags, title, and subject. To use any property as a criterion, you specify the property using the following shorthand notation: *property name:criterion*. (You can include or omit the space after the colon.) For example, if you want to search for files that include the word "Chicago" as a tag, you could enter *tag:chicago*. (The properties are not case sensitive, so you could also enter *Tag:Chicago*.) The properties you can use as search criteria include any detail you can display as a column in a folder window. Figure 6-17 provides examples of the shorthand notation you can use to specify file properties as search criteria.

Figure 6-17 Examples of using file properties as search criteria

Property	Example	Finds
Name	Name:city	Files and folders with names that contain a word beginning with "city"
Date modified	DateModified:10/28/2016	Files and folders modified on October 28, 2016
	DateModified:<10/28/2016	Files and folders modified before October 28, 2016
Date created	DateCreated:>10/28/2016	Files and folders created after October 28, 2016
	DateCreated:2016	Files and folders created during the year 2016
Size	Size:200KB	Files with a size of 200 KB
	Size:>1MB	Files larger than 1 MB
Type	Type:docx	Files with a .docx filename extension
Tags	Tag:Chicago	Files that include "Chicago" as a tag
Authors	Author:Jay	Files that specify "Jay" as the author
Artists	Artist:Elvis	Files that specify artists with "Elvis" in their names, such as Elvis Presley and Elvis Costello
Rating	Rating:4 stars	Files with a rating of four stars

© 2014 Cengage Learning

Being able to include any file detail as a search criterion is especially useful when you are working with photos, music, and videos because they have special properties for their file types that are useful when searching, such as Artists, Album, Rating, and Length.

When searching in a folder window, you can use the Other properties button in the Refine group on the Search Tools Search tab to display a list of properties you can use in a search, such as authors, tags, and title. In each case, when you click a property on the Other properties list, Windows inserts the property name and a colon in the Search text box. Click the Search text box to display a list of suggested criteria. You can then click one of the suggestions or type the criterion directly in the Search text box. Using the Other properties button helps you create advanced criteria that use the proper shorthand notation. If you do know the correct shorthand notation, however, entering it directly in the Search text box is usually faster than using the Other properties button.

For the upcoming Weekly Features Web page, Jay wants to show baseball cards of players who were members of a St. Louis baseball team. Jay inserted the team name as a tag for each photo in the Cards folder. You can search the tags of the files in the Cards folder to find baseball card photos Jay can use.

To find files by specifying a property in the Search text box:

1. Open the **Cards** folder in the Public Documents\Columbia folder on your hard disk.

2. Click the **Search** text box, and then type **tag:St. Louis**. As you type, Windows filters the view of the files in the folder window, and then displays two files that contain the text "St. Louis" in their Tags property: Card06 and Card09.

3. Click **Card06** and examine the information in the Details pane. This is a photo of a baseball card from 1887, showing Charles Comiskey when he played for the St. Louis Browns.

4. Click **Card09** and examine its details. This is a photo of Ernest Lush, a member of the St. Louis Cardinals in 1911.

By searching for text in the Tags property, you found two photos to display on the Weekly Features Web page.

Combining Criteria When Searching File Contents

TIP

When you use two or more words as a search condition, Windows searches as if the condition includes the AND Boolean filter.

To perform a precise search, you can combine criteria in the Search text box or on the Search menu. For example, suppose you store your financial documents on your computer and need to find a list of charitable donations you made in 2016. You don't recall where you've stored this information, and scanning the filenames in your Financial folder doesn't reveal the file. If you search the contents of the files using *donation* as the search criterion, you'll find lists of donations for many years as well as other documents, including those with text such as "Thanks for your support! Every donation helps." If you search the contents of files using *2016* as the search criterion, you'll find dozens of documents that mention that year. To pinpoint your search, you can combine the criteria to find files that contain the word "donations" and the year "2016." When you search file contents, you can use **Boolean filters**, which are filters that let you search for specific information using the words AND, OR, and NOT to combine search criteria. You can use quotation marks and parentheses to refine the search conditions further. Figure 6-18 describes how to use AND, OR, and NOT along with quotation marks and parentheses when combining search criteria.

Figure 6-18 Combining search criteria

Word or Punctuation	Examples	When to Use
AND	donations AND 2016 donations 2016	To narrow the search to files that contain "donations" and "2016" even if the words are not next to each other
OR	donations OR 2016	To broaden the search to files that contain "donations" or "2016"
NOT	donations NOT 2016	To restrict the search to files that contain "donations" but not "2016"
" " (quotation marks)	"donations 2016"	To pinpoint the search to files that contain the exact phrase "donations 2016"
( ) (parentheses)	(donations 2016)	To open the search to files that contain both items next to each other in any order

© 2014 Cengage Learning

Note that when you use the words AND, OR, and NOT, you must enter them using all uppercase letters.

One of your ongoing projects for Columbia Collectibles is maintaining an archive of quotations, which Jay uses on the shop's Web pages and in the monthly customer newsletter. Jay, employees, and customers provide these quotations in various ways, such as in a word-processing document or an email message. You store the quotations in TXT documents to make sure anyone at the shop can use the documents. However, this means that you cannot add tags or other properties to the files—you can add these details only to Microsoft Office documents.

Next week's Weekly Features Web page will showcase a few baseball cards from the shop's collection. To accompany photos of the cards, Jay wants to include at least one quotation about baseball card collecting. You can use Boolean logic to combine search criteria and search the contents of the Quotations folder to find suitable quotations.

INSIGHT

Preparing to Combine Search Criteria

Before you combine search criteria, select the search text, select the filter you plan to use, if any, and then select the condition. For example, choose *.txt as the search text to find text files. If you want to find text files modified after a certain date, use the datemodified: filter, and then select the appropriate date, such as >8/31/2016. Next, determine whether you should use AND, OR, or NOT to combine the criteria, and whether you need quotation marks or parentheses to find the files you want. For example, if you want to find files that use "Chicago" as a tag and have "Jay" as the author, you use the AND filter, whether you insert AND or not. In other words, *tag:Chicago AND author:Jay* is the same as *tag:Chicago author:Jay*.

If you want to find either text files or Word documents, you need to insert OR, as in *.txt OR *.doc*. (The search condition *.doc* finds Word documents that have a .doc or a .docx filename extension.) To determine the best criteria, test each method in order starting with AND. Keep in mind that AND narrows the search results, while OR broadens the results. For example, if you search for files that are photos and use "Chicago" as a tag, you find fewer files than searching for files that are photos or use "Chicago" as a tag.

Although you want to find quotations about baseball card collecting, using *baseball card* and *collecting* as search criteria won't find quotations that include "collection" or "collector" or even "collect," which might be appropriate quotations. A good rule of thumb when specifying search text is to use the root of the word; for example, use *collect* to find documents containing "collecting," "collection," "collector," and "collect". Using the root of a word is also called **stemming**. You can shorten the search text further by using "baseball" and "collect" as search criteria because cards are the most common items collected in baseball.

Next, determine the best way to combine the criteria, as shown in the following list:

- *Baseball collect* (or *baseball AND collect*) finds documents that include both words.
- *Baseball OR collect* finds documents that include at least one of the words.
- *Baseball NOT collect* finds documents that include "*baseball*" but not those that include "*collect.*"
- *"Baseball collect"* finds documents that include the exact phrase *"baseball collect."*
- *(Baseball collect)* finds documents that include the exact words "baseball" and "collect" consecutively in either order.

Because the phrase *baseball collect* will produce the results you want, you'll use that as your search criteria to find quotations about baseball card collections.

To find files using AND criteria:

1. Open the **Quotations** folder in the Public Documents\Columbia folder on your hard disk.
2. Click the **Search** text box, and then type **baseball collect**. As you type, Windows searches filenames and file contents that meet your criteria and finds one file. See Figure 6-19.

Figure 6-19   Finding files that contain *baseball* AND *collect*

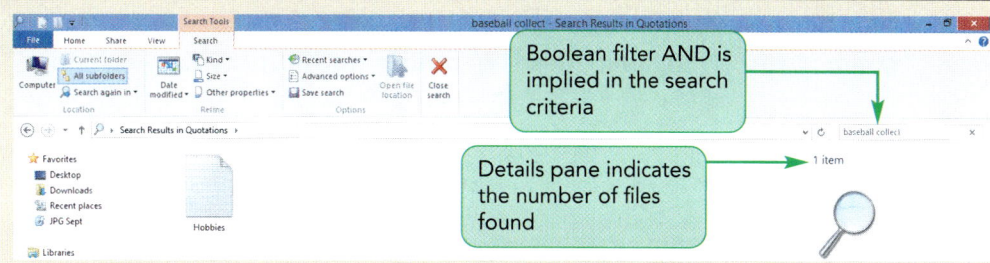

3. To verify this file contains a quotation you can use, double-click **Hobbies** to open it in a text-editing program such as Notepad.
4. Press the **Ctrl+F** keys to open the Find dialog box, type **baseball** in the Find what text box, click the **Find Next** button until you find a quotation Jay can use, such as "Baseball card collecting is like eating peanuts, you just can't stop," and then close the Find dialog box and Notepad.

Jay plans to use that quotation, but says that he could also use quotations that mention baseball or mention collecting—he can work either type into the Web page. You can try your search again, this time using the Boolean filter OR to find files that contain either "baseball" or "collect."

To find files using OR criteria:

1. Display the contents of the Quotations folder again.
2. Click the **Search** text box, and then type **baseball OR collect**. Now Windows finds two files that contain the word "baseball" or "collect." See Figure 6-20.

Figure 6-20   Finding files that contain *baseball* OR *collect*

To pinpoint what you want to find and to refine your search criteria, you can combine Boolean filters and file properties.

Combining Boolean Filters and File Properties

When you search files by file property, you can use Boolean filters to combine criteria. For example, suppose Jay is working on the baseball card Web page and requests a photo of a baseball card showing a Chicago baseball player in 1912. You can search the tags of the photo files to find those that contain this text. To search efficiently, you can use the Boolean filter AND to combine the criteria and search for photos that include the tags "Chicago" and "1912." (If you used the Boolean filter OR, you would find photos of baseball cards for Chicago players, but not necessarily those who played in 1912, and photos of baseball cards issued in 1912 that are not necessarily of Chicago players.) If you use *tag: Chicago 1912*, Windows searches for files that include "Chicago" as a tag and "1912" in any property. To restrict the search to tags only, enclose the criteria in parentheses.

To find files by combining file property criteria:

1. Display the contents of the Public Documents\Columbia folder on your hard disk.
2. Click the **Search** text box, and then type **tag: (Chicago 1912)**. Windows finds one file that meets your criteria. See Figure 6-21.

Figure 6-21 Combining Boolean filters with file properties

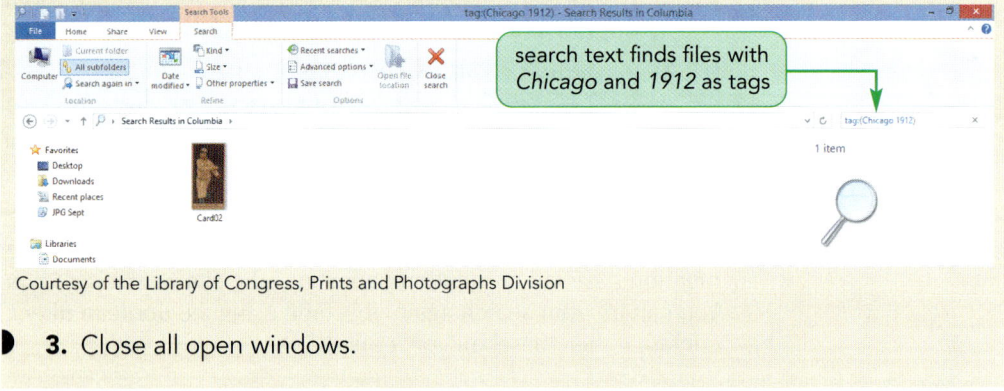

Courtesy of the Library of Congress, Prints and Photographs Division

3. Close all open windows.

You now know many expert techniques to search for files. One other type of search you can conduct is new to Windows 8: searching for information in Windows 8 apps.

Searching Within Windows 8 Apps

As you've learned, you can use Start Search to find apps installed on your computer by typing search text on the Search menu. Sometimes, however, the information you want to find is contained within an app. For example, suppose you are planning a trip to Chicago and want to find information that might be helpful for your trip. On the Start screen, you can type search text such as *Chicago* to display the Search menu. To display destination information about Chicago, click Travel in the list of Windows 8 apps on the Search menu. Windows starts the Travel app, which presents an overview of Chicago, lists recommended restaurants and hotels, displays photos of Chicago locations, and provides a tool you can use to find flights to Chicago. If you click Maps on the Search menu, Windows displays a detailed map of Chicago. If you click News on the Search menu, Windows displays previews of recent news stories about Chicago. You can click a preview to read the entire article.

REFERENCE

Searching for Information in Windows 8 Apps

- On the Start screen, begin typing search text.
- Click a Windows 8 app on the Search menu.

TIP
You can right-click a Windows 8 app on the Search menu, and then click Pin on the shortcut menu to keep an app at the top of the list.

Just as Windows keeps track of search text to display search hints, it keeps track of the Windows 8 apps you search. Windows rearranges the list of Windows 8 apps on the Search menu so that the apps you search the most often are near the top of the list.

The Search menu does not list all of the Windows 8 apps installed on your system—only those that are compatible with the Start Search feature. Figure 6-22 lists popular Windows 8 apps you can search and describes the types of information you can find.

Figure 6-22 Popular Windows 8 apps for searching

Windows 8 App	Information to Find	Search Text
Bing	Information on the Web	Keywords for a Web page
Finance	Financial news and stock performance about a particular company	Company name or stock symbol
Internet Explorer	Information on the Web	Keywords for a Web page
Mail	Information in the subject line or body of an email message, sender name, and email address	Text in any part of an email message
Maps	Location or local business	Location or business name
News	Recent news stories	Text in a news story, source name, or author name
People	Contact name and other information such as email address	Any contact information, such as name, phone number, or email address
Photos	Photos on your computer or a service your computer can access, such as your Flickr account	Filename or tag
Sports	Sports scores and other information	Sport, team, or player name
Store	Windows 8 and desktop apps	App name or description
Travel	Information about a destination	Destination name
Weather	Weather in a specified location	Location name
Xbox apps	Videos, games, music, TV shows, and movies	Media name

© 2014 Cengage Learning

Next week, Jay is planning to travel to Chicago, Illinois, to meet with other baseball card dealers to exchange information and to buy and sell baseball cards. He asks you to find information about Chicago of general interest to travelers, including attractions, hotels, and restaurants. He also wants to know what kind of weather to expect in Chicago next week. You can find all of this information by searching Windows 8 apps.

TIP

You can use this same technique to search the Internet by clicking Internet Explorer or Bing on the Search menu.

To search for information in Windows 8 apps:

1. Press the **Windows** key to display the Start screen.

2. Type **Chicago** to display the Apps screen and the Search menu with "Chicago" entered in the Search menu text box.

3. Click **Travel** in the list of Windows 8 apps on the Search menu, scrolling down the menu if necessary. The Travel app starts and displays a photo of a Chicago location. See Figure 6-23. The Chicago photo in your Travel app might differ.

Figure 6-23 Searching for information in the Travel app

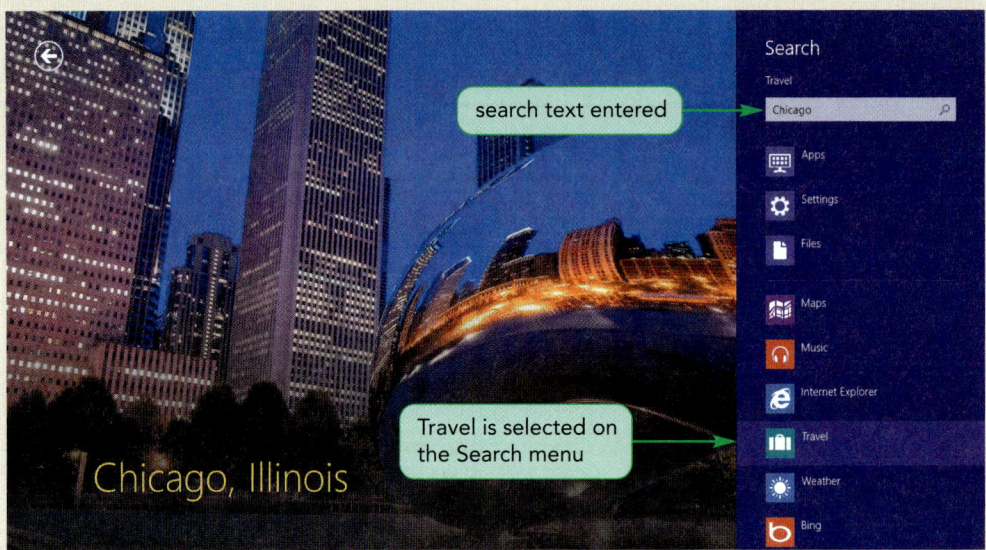

4. Move the pointer to display a horizontal scroll bar, and then drag the scroll bar to the right to display an overview of Chicago. Continue dragging the scroll bar to the right to display lists of attractions and hotels. Click **Art Institute of Chicago** in the Attractions list to display detailed information about the museum.

5. Display the Charms bar and then click the **Search** charm on the Charms bar. The Search menu opens with "Chicago" still entered in the text box.

6. Click **Weather** in the list of Windows 8 apps on the Search menu, scrolling as necessary. A Search Results screen appears listing locations that contain a word beginning with "Chicago." See Figure 6-24. Your search results might differ, but should include Chicago, Illinois.

Figure 6-24 Selecting a location in the search results

- click to display weather information about Chicago, Illinois
- Weather app is being searched
- Weather app is selected; you might need to scroll the Search menu to display the app

▶ 7. Click **Chicago Illinois, United States** in the search results to display the weather conditions in Chicago for today and forecasts for the next few days.

▶ 8. Click the background of the Weather app, and then click the **right arrow** button to scroll the screen and show weather forecasts for next week.

▶ 9. Close the Weather app. You return to the Start screen.

Now that you've found general travel information about Chicago, Jay wants to find more specific information. He plans to visit a few baseball card shops so he can learn about their collections and any other goods or services they offer. This information is not available in any of the files on your computer or stored in a Windows 8 app. Instead, you can use Internet Explorer to search the Internet for the information.

Searching the Internet

The Internet provides access to a wealth of information; the challenge is to find the information you need or want. You have already learned how to develop search strategies and specific criteria to find files on your computer. You can use many of the same search strategies to find information on the Internet. Instead of using Windows tools such as the Search text box and Search menu, you use the search tools provided in Internet Explorer. Figure 6-25 summarizes the search tools you can use in IE Windows 8 and IE Desktop.

Figure 6-25 Internet Explorer search tools

Search Tool	Description
Address bar	Enter search text in the Address bar to have your default search provider such as Google or Bing display the search results
Find on page	Search for text on the current Web page
Search provider	Add a search provider or select one to use its tools to search the Internet

© 2014 Cengage Learning.

The terminology that you use when searching the Internet is slightly different from the terminology you use to search for files on your computer. As shown in the Session 6.2 Visual Overview, the word or phrase you use to search the Internet is typically called a search expression. Each word in the search expression is called a keyword. After you enter a search expression using one of Internet Explorer's search tools, Internet Explorer displays the results, which are links to Web pages that meet your criteria. You can click these links, or hits, to access Web pages that contain the keywords in your search expression.

When you provide a search expression to Internet Explorer, it uses a search provider, which is a search engine such as Bing or Google or a reference Web site such as Wikipedia. Because searching all of the Web pages on the Internet to find those that contain your search expression would take a prohibitive amount of time, search providers typically search a database of indexed Web pages. These databases are updated periodically, though not often enough to keep all of the indexed Web pages up to date. This is why a page of search results might include inactive or broken links.

Web site designers and owners can make their Web pages easier for search providers to find by **optimizing** the site. In its Web page headings, an optimized site lists keywords and phrases that you and other Web users are likely to use to find the information on the Web page. Conversely, you are more likely to find the Web pages you want if you are aware of the types of keywords Web designers often use.

PROSKILLS

Problem Solving: Searching the Internet Effectively

Because the Internet provides access to a vast amount of information, finding the information you need can be a problem. Conducting a search that finds millions of results is inefficient, even if search providers list the Web pages most relevant to your search first. To work effectively, you need to use search techniques that provide a few high-quality results. Keep the following guidelines in mind to search the Internet efficiently:

- Be specific. If you search for general categories, you'll find an overwhelming number of pages. Searching for specific terms or details is more likely to provide results you can use. For example, instead of searching for "desserts," search for "pear cake recipe."
- Form a question. Think of your search expression as a question you want answered, such as "Are there restaurants in the Denver area that serve vegetarian food?" Eliminate the articles and common words to form a workable search expression, such as "restaurants Denver vegetarian."
- Search the results. Most search providers let you reduce the number of pages to review by searching your results. For example, suppose you search for "pear cake recipe" and find many thousands of results. If you want a recipe similar to the one your Swedish grandmother made, you can search the results using "Swedish" as your search expression.

Jay wants to know about the baseball card shops in Chicago, and you offer to search the Internet to find the information. You could use IE Windows 8 or IE Desktop to search for this information. (You could also use the Bing app to display search results in a tiled format; you click a tile to display the Web page in IE Windows 8.) In the following steps, you use IE Windows 8 because you are currently working on the Start screen. You'll start the search by using *Chicago baseball card shop* as the search expression to find Web pages describing baseball card shops in Chicago.

Because Web pages and search indexes change frequently, the search results you find when you perform the steps in this section will differ from those shown in the figures. The following steps use Bing as the search provider. If you are using a different search provider, your results will differ.

To search using a search expression:

1. On the Start screen, click the **Internet Explorer** tile to start IE Windows 8.
2. Click the **Address bar**, type **Chicago baseball card shop**, and then press the **Enter** key. Bing looks for Web pages containing the search expression you entered, and then displays the results. See Figure 6-26.

Figure 6-26 Search results for the search expression *Chicago baseball card shop*

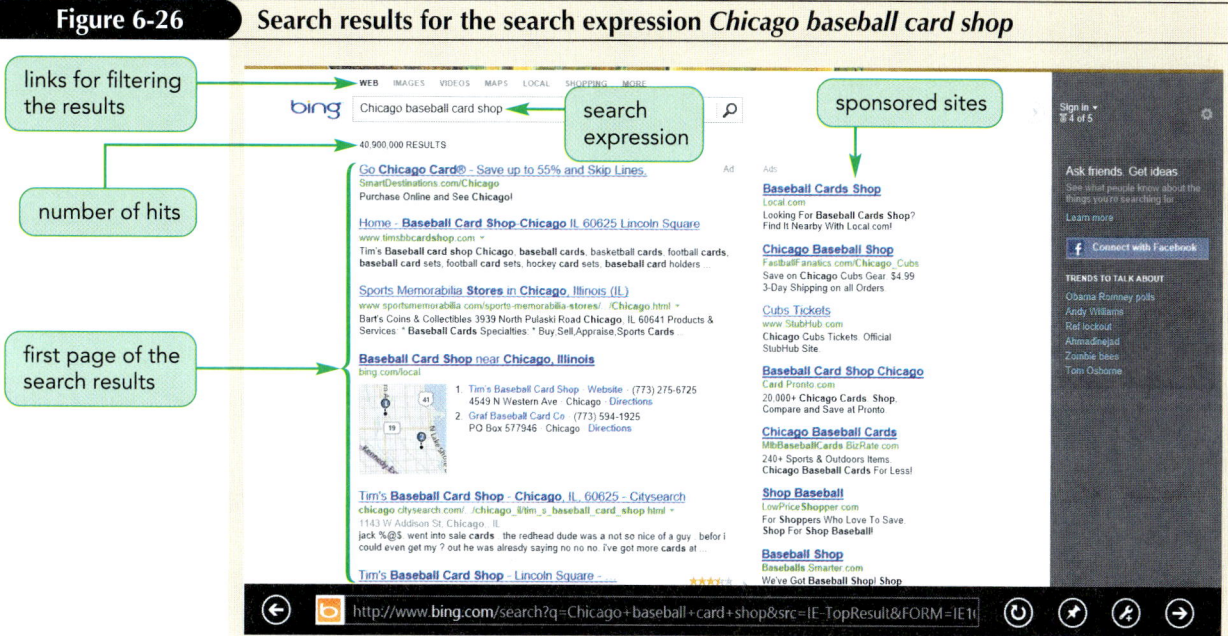

Using *Chicago baseball card shop* as the search expression produced more than 37 million results, which is not unusual and can change daily. Although the first few Web pages listed might provide the information you seek, you need to narrow your search to find more useful Web pages.

Narrowing Your Search

You can narrow your Internet search by modifying your search expression or by limiting the kinds of Web pages you want in your results. One way to modify your search expression is to use quotation marks to search for specific phrases. If you enclose a phrase in quotation marks, you restrict the results to Web pages that contain that exact phrase. For example, using a search expression such as *Stanford University Library* finds Web pages that include those three words anywhere on the page. If you enclose the search expression in quotation marks, as in *"Stanford University Library"*, you find only Web pages that include the exact text in the specified order.

Another way to modify your search expression is to use the advanced search features that search providers typically offer. Figure 6-27 shows the Advanced Search page from Google, a popular search provider.

| Figure 6-27 | Google Advanced Search page |

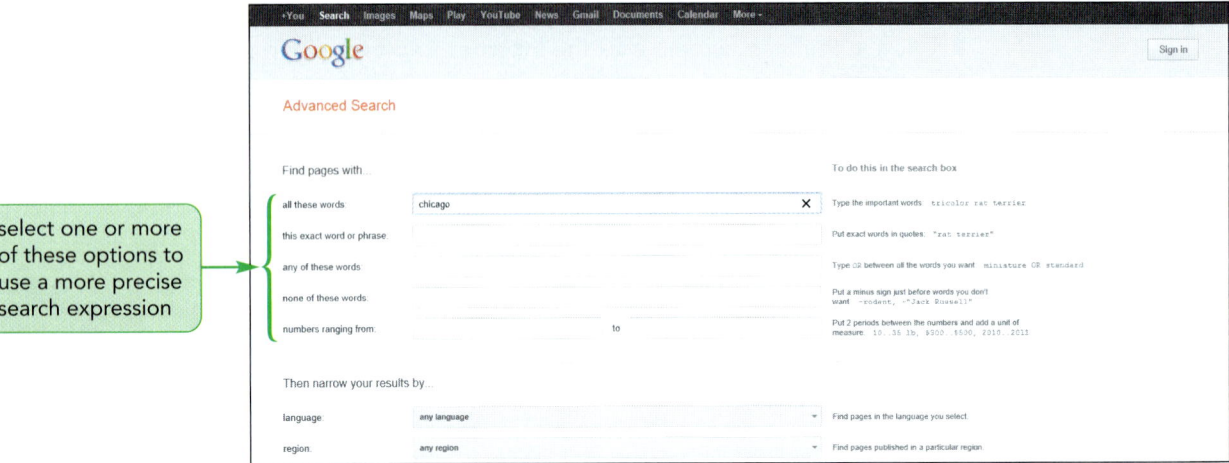

select one or more of these options to use a more precise search expression

© Google 2012.

An advanced search page lets you specify and combine search conditions. Most advanced search pages provide the following types of options:

- Find pages that include all of the words. This is the default for most search providers.
- Limit the results to pages that match the exact phrase. This is the same as using quotation marks to enclose an expression.
- Find pages that include at least one of the words in the search expression.
- Specify keywords that you do not want included on the Web page.

Search engines often provide extensive help information. For example, enter a search term in Google, click the Options button, and then click Search Help to display the Google Inside Search Web page, which provides links to basic search information and more advanced tips for searching. In Bing, click the Help link at the bottom of the Bing home page to display the Bing Help page.

Besides providing an advanced search page for narrowing your search expression, most search providers include tabs or links that specify the kind of results you want. For example, the Bing results page shown earlier includes a navigation bar at the top of the page with links such as Web, Images, Videos, and Maps. By default, Bing displays Web pages in the results. If you are searching for images, such as photos and drawings, you can click the Images link before or after you enter a search expression to restrict the results to pages including images that meet your criteria.

Some of the Web pages you found when you used *Chicago baseball card shop* as a search expression described Chicago baseball, but didn't necessarily focus on baseball card shops. You can try narrowing your search by enclosing part of the expression in quotation marks to see if the results are more useful. You don't want to enclose the entire phrase in quotation marks because that would find only Web pages that contain that exact text in the same order, but not pages for Buck's Baseball Card Shop in Chicago, for example.

To narrow a search to an exact match:

1. On the search results page, click in the search text box at the top of the page.

    Trouble? If a message regarding the Flip Ahead feature appears at the bottom of the screen, click the Close button (unless your instructor requests that you click the Turn on flip ahead button).

2. Edit the text so it appears as **Chicago "baseball card shop"** and then press the **Enter** key. This time, you find fewer results because the search is restricted to only those Web pages that use *Chicago* as a keyword and include the exact phrase you entered in quotation marks. See Figure 6-28.

Figure 6-28 **Search results for an exact phrase search expression**

using quotation marks for an exact match narrows the search

results are significantly reduced

results can vary every time you perform a search

Including an exact phrase produced a list of baseball card shops in Chicago that is useful to you and Jay. Now he wonders if other places in Illinois have baseball card shops that he should know about. These are any baseball card shops that are not located in Chicago. To specify this kind of search condition, you can use a search provider's advanced search page. You can try this search using Google instead of Bing. You'll use Google's Advanced Search page to specify that you want to search for baseball card shops in Illinois, but not those in Chicago.

To narrow a search by excluding keywords:

1. Click the **Address bar**, type **www.google.com**, and then press the **Enter** key to open the main page on the Google Web site.

2. In the text box, type **Illinois** and then press the **Enter** key to display the results, which total millions of hits.

3. Click the **Options** button on the right side of the page, and then click **Advanced search** to open the Advanced Search page with "Illinois" already entered in the first text box.

4. Click the **this exact word or phrase** text box, type **baseball card shop**, and then press the **Enter** key. The search results list several thousand Web pages, including many for baseball shops in Chicago, Illinois. Next, you'll exclude the keyword "Chicago" from the search.

   Trouble? If a message appears, asking whether you want AutoComplete to remember web form entries, click the No button.

5. Click the **Options** button in the upper-right corner of the window, click **Advanced search** to open the Advanced Search page again, click the **none of these words** text box, type **Chicago**, and then press the **Enter** key. The search results page includes more hits with the best matches on the first page, which helps Jay identify baseball card shops he might want to visit outside of Chicago.

INSIGHT

Evaluating Web Pages in the Search Results

Although a Web page might be listed at the top of the search results, that doesn't guarantee the page provides reliable and up-to-date information that will meet your needs. On a search engine's Web page, the search results are usually organized into sections. At the top or in another prominent location on the page are sponsored links; companies pay to have these links appear when certain keywords are used in a search expression. The companies pay an additional fee when you click one of their sponsored links. Using sponsored links helps search engines offer their services free to the public. However, that doesn't mean a sponsored link will lead to the information you want. Before using a Web page or citing it as a source, review the content with a critical eye. At the bottom of the Web page, look for the author's name and evidence of the author's credentials. Look for links to the original source of quoted information, which tends to validate the information on a Web page. Also look for signs of bias, such as unsubstantiated claims or extreme points of view.

Jay wonders if you can quickly show where the shops are located outside of Chicago. To fulfill his request, you can use the Maps button on the Google toolbar. Recall that Bing and other search providers include a similar tool.

To display a map of shops in the search results:

TIP

The *-Chicago* in the search expression is a shorthand way of excluding "Chicago" from the search.

1. In the Google search results page, click the **Maps** button on the toolbar near the top of the page. Google lists the results on the left and shows a map on the right with markers for each location in the search results. See Figure 6-29.

Figure 6-29 Displaying locations in the search results

search expression modified to apply to a location search

marker shows the location of the first shop in the search results

marker for each Web page in the search results

© Google 2012.

Because you are now searching locations, Google modified the expression to specify shops near Illinois. Using *near* in the expression means Google is searching for locations near or in Illinois, not locations named Illinois.

Jay notes that one shop is right outside of Chicago, close enough that he could drop in during his visit next week.

Choosing Search Providers

In Internet Explorer, you can choose which provider you want to use when you search for information on the Internet. You can change the search provider for a specific search, and you can specify which search provider you prefer to use by default. When you first install Internet Explorer, only one provider might be available; however, you can add search providers to increase your searching options. You can only add a search provider in IE Desktop.

Keep in mind that you can use a search provider's Web site, such as google.com, to perform a search even if it is not selected as your search provider.

Adding a Search Provider

REFERENCE

- In IE Desktop, click the Show Address bar Autocomplete button on the Address bar, and then click Add.
- On the Internet Explorer Gallery Web page, click a search provider to select it, and then click the Add to Internet Explorer button.
- In the Add Search Provider dialog box, click the Add button.

You and Jay often use Wikipedia, an online encyclopedia, to search for information. Internet Explorer lets you use Wikipedia as a search provider, which is handy if you want to look up factual information about a topic. You'll add Wikipedia Visual Search to the provider list, which you can access by clicking the Show Address bar Autocomplete button on the Address bar. You can also choose to make a new search provider the default one to use when you search from the Address bar.

To add a search provider to the provider list:

1. Click the **Back** button on the Navigation bar to return to the Google search results, click the **Page tools** button on the Apps bar, and then click **View on the desktop** to open IE Desktop and display the same page.

2. Click the **Show Address bar Autocomplete** button on the Address bar, and then click **Add** to open the Internet Explorer Gallery Web site, which lists possible search providers. See Figure 6-30.

   Trouble? If you can't find the Show Address bar Autocomplete button, point to the icons in the Address bar and view the ScreenTips to find the right one. Then repeat Step 2.

Figure 6-30   Adding search providers

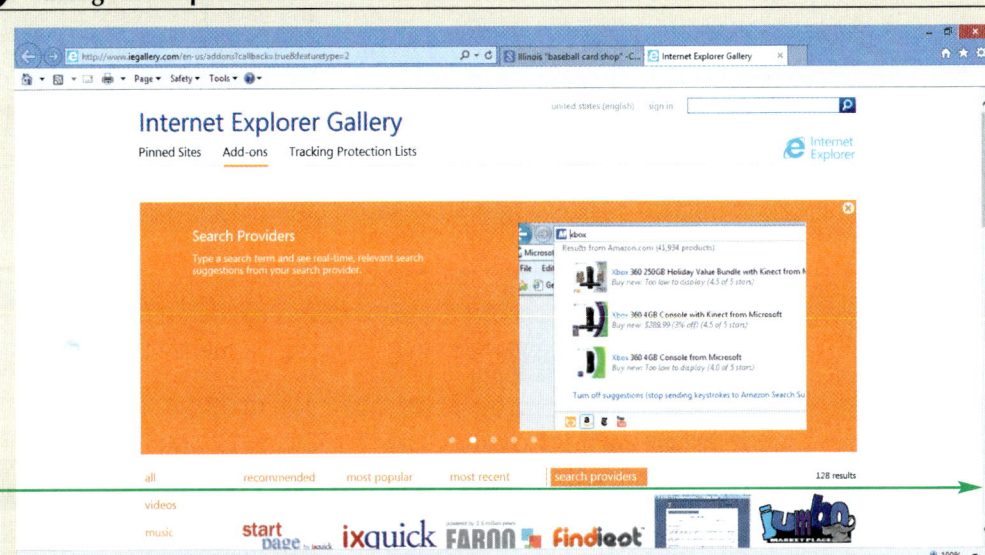

scroll to display additional search providers

3. Scroll the page, looking for the Wikipedia Visual Search provider. If that search provider does not appear on the first Web page, click the **right arrow** button to display another page of search providers.

TIP

To set the new search provider as the default, click the Make this my default search provider check box in the Add Search Provider dialog box.

4. Click **Wikipedia Visual Search** to select it as a search provider, and then click the **Add to Internet Explorer** button to open the Add Search Provider dialog box.

5. Click the **Add** button.

6. Click the **Show Address bar Autocomplete** button on the Address bar to verify that Internet Explorer added Wikipedia to the list of search providers.

One of Columbia Collectibles' most valuable baseball cards shows Johnny Evers, who was part of a famous double-play combination with Joe Tinker and Frank Chance known as Tinker-to-Evers-to-Chance. Jay is familiar with Evers' career as a player, but wants to review his career as a coach. You can use Wikipedia as the search provider to find a summary of Johnny Evers' coaching career.

To use Wikipedia as the search provider:

1. If necessary, click the **Show Address bar Autocomplete** button on the Address bar to display the list of search providers, and then click **Wikipedia** to make Wikipedia the current search provider.
2. On the Wikipedia Web page, select the text in the Search text box, type **Johnny Evers**, and then press the **Enter** key. Wikipedia displays a page of search results, with an entry for Johnny Evers at the top.
3. Click **Johnny Evers** to display his page in Wikipedia.

When you are displaying a Web page, you can use the Find toolbar in IE Windows 8 or IE Desktop to find specific information on the page. To open the Find toolbar in IE Windows 8, display the Apps bar, click the Page tools button, and then click Find on page. To open the Find toolbar in IE Desktop, press the Ctrl+F keys. You'll show Jay how to search for information about Johnny Evers' coaching career using the Find toolbar in IE Desktop.

To find information on a Web page:

1. Press the **Ctrl+F** keys to display the Find toolbar at the top of the Internet Explorer window.
2. In the Find text box, type **coach**. Internet Explorer highlights all instances of "coach," selects the first instance, and displays the number of matches on the page. See Figure 6-31.

Figure 6-31   Using the Find toolbar

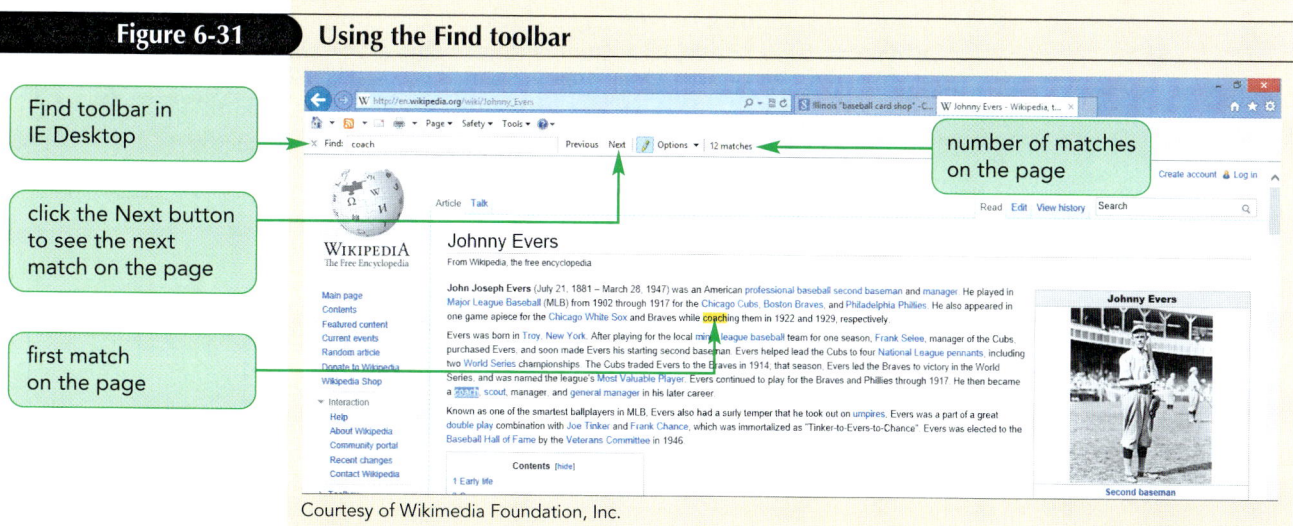

- Find toolbar in IE Desktop
- number of matches on the page
- click the Next button to see the next match on the page
- first match on the page

Courtesy of Wikimedia Foundation, Inc.

3. Click the **Next** button as many times as necessary to display the section titled "Coaching and managing career," which summarizes the positions Johnny Evers held as a baseball coach.
4. Click the **Close the Find bar** button to close the Find toolbar.
5. Close Internet Explorer.

If you use a particular search provider often, you can make it the default search provider. You use IE Desktop to set the default search provider. When you do, you automatically set the default search provider for IE Windows 8 as well. To change the default search provider, click the Tools button on the right side of the IE Desktop window, and then click Manage add-ons. In the Add-on Types list, click Search Providers. Click the search provider you want to use, and then click the Set as default button.

Restoring Your Settings

If you are working in a computer lab or on a computer other than your own, complete the steps in this section to restore the original settings on the computer.

To restore your settings:

1. Open File Explorer, and then click **JPG Sept** in the Favorites list on the Navigation pane to conduct the saved search.

2. Click the **Search** text box to display the Search Tools Search tab, click the **Advanced options** button in the Options group, and then click **File contents** under the In the non-indexed locations section to remove the check mark.

3. Cut the **JPG Sept** search file from the Navigation pane, and then paste it in the **Columbia** folder in the Public Documents folder.

4. Move the **Columbia** folder to the **Windows6\Tutorial** folder provided with your Data Files.

5. Close the Details pane in the folder window, and then close File Explorer.

6. Start IE Desktop, click the **Tools** button on the right side of the window, and then click **Manage add-ons**. In the Add-on Types list, click **Search Providers**, click **Wikipedia (en)**, and then click the **Remove** button.

7. Press the **Windows** key, type **clock**, click **Settings**, click **Add clocks for different time zones**, click the first **Show this clock** check box to remove the check mark, and then click the **OK** button to close the Date and Time dialog box.

8. Close all open windows.

Session 6.2 Quick Check

1. What shorthand notation would you use to find files that include the word "stamp" in the Title property?
2. If you use *tag: Chicago OR 1912* as search criteria, what files would you find?
3. Explain how you would use the Search menu to find news stories about Columbia, Missouri.
4. When you enter a search expression to search the Internet, each word in the search expression is called a(n) _____.
5. How can you narrow a Web search to search for a specific phrase?
6. After using a search expression to search the Web, how can you specify that you want to display only images in the results?
7. Explain how to find search providers to add to Internet Explorer.

Review Assignments

Data Files needed for the Review Assignments: American Postcards.wmv, European Postcards.wmv, Postcard01.jpg–Postcard10.jpg

You are now working with Jay Park on developing and showcasing the postcard collection at Columbia Collectibles. You have taken photographs of his most recently acquired postcards and created two videos featuring American and European postcards. Jay wants to post the videos and some photos on the shop's Web site. Jay wants you to help him search for apps that can play videos and find postcards for specific Web pages. Complete the following steps:

1. In the Public Documents folder on your hard disk, create a folder named **Postcards**. Copy all of the files in the Windows6\Review folder provided with your Data Files to the Postcards folder.
2. Display the Start screen. Search for a file that contains the word "European" in its filename. Play the file in the Video app.
3. Press the Print Screen key to capture an image of the screen, and then paste the image in a new Paint or WordPad file. Save the file as **Video App** in the Windows6\Review folder provided with your Data Files. Minimize Paint or WordPad, and then close the Video app.
4. Search for an app you can use to play media files, and then start the app. (*Hint*: If a dialog box opens where you can select initial settings, click the Recommended settings option button, and then click the Finish button.) Click Videos in the left pane of the app window, drag the American Postcards video stored in the Postcards folder to the app's window, and then play the video.
5. Press the Print Screen key to capture an image of the screen, and then paste the image in a new Paint or WordPad file. Save the file as **Media App** in the Windows6\Review folder provided with your Data Files. Close the media app.
6. Search for a setting on your computer related to media files. Display a setting for using AutoPlay with all media and devices. Press the Print Screen key to capture an image of the window, and then paste the image in a new Paint or WordPad file. Save the file as **Media Setting** in the Windows6\Review folder provided with your Data Files. Close the AutoPlay window. Minimize the Paint or WordPad window.
7. Search for all of the **JPG** files in the Postcards folder.
8. Add the following tags to Postcard02: **Statue of Liberty; 1905**. Change the filename to **Statue of Liberty**.
9. Add the following tags to Postcard09: **Eiffel Tower; Paris; France; 1900**. Change the filename to **Eiffel Tower**.
10. In the Postcards folder, search for photos that have **France** as a tag. Move the files you found to a new subfolder named **French Postcards** in the Postcards folder.
11. In the Postcards folder, find a photo that has **New York** and **1904** as tags. Change the name of this file to **1904**. Close File Explorer. Minimize the Paint or WordPad window, and then close all other open windows.
12. Start IE Desktop and use Bing to find Web pages providing information about postcard collections. Narrow the search to find Web pages about vintage postcard collections. Narrow the search again by finding only images of vintage postcard collections. (*Hint*: Click the Images link on the results page.) Press the Print Screen key to capture an image of the first screen of search results, and then paste the image in a new Paint or WordPad file. Save the file as **Vintage1** in the Windows6\Review folder provided with your Data Files.
13. Add a new search provider to Internet Explorer, and then use it to search for vintage postcard collections. (*Hint*: Add a search provider not used in the tutorial.) With the search results displayed, press the Print Screen key to capture an image of the first screen of search results, and then paste the image in a new Paint or WordPad file. Save the file as **Vintage2** in the Windows6\Review folder provided with your Data Files.

14. Using the new search provider, display Web pages for postcards from the 1960s. Open one of the Web pages on the first page of search results, and then find a postcard on the page associated with the Kennedy family. (*Hint*: If you are having difficulty finding a Web page associated with the Kennedy family, go to www.zazzle.com/1960s.) Press the Print Screen key to capture an image of the Web page, and then paste the image in a new Paint or WordPad file. Save the file as **1960s** in the Windows6\Review folder provided with your Data Files.

15. Restore your computer by removing the new search provider from Internet Explorer. Move the Postcards folder from the Public Documents folder on your hard disk to the Windows6\Review folder provided with your Data Files. Close the Details pane in the folder window, and then close all open windows.

16. Submit the results of the preceding steps to your instructor, either in printed or electronic form, as requested.

Case Problem 1

Data Files needed for this Case Problem: Pic01.jpg–Pic10.jpg

Farm to Table Bernie and Sarah Underwood started a Web site called Farm to Table, which is devoted to providing information about farmer's markets, farm stands, and community supported agriculture (CSA) services in the Hudson River Valley in New York. They primarily serve as content editors, selecting articles, reviews, and photos from contributors in the area. You work as an all-around assistant to Bernie and Sarah. Currently, they want you to help them find photos from contributors for their Web pages on summer fruits and vegetables. They also want to back up their files online, and ask you to find information about programs they can use to do so. Complete the following steps:

1. Search for an app you can use to read news stories. Start the app and then scroll to the far right to display news on health or technology.
2. Press the Print Screen key to capture an image of the app, and then paste the image in a new Paint or WordPad file. Save the file as **News App** in the Windows6\Case1 folder provided with your Data Files. Close the app.
3. Search for a setting on your computer related to backups. Display the setting or tool for saving backup copies of files.
4. Press the Print Screen key to capture an image of the tool, and then paste the image in a new Paint or WordPad file. Save the file as **Backups** in the Windows6\Case1 folder provided with your Data Files. Close the window or screen.
5. On the Start screen, search for information about Hudson, New York, and then display the information in the Maps app. Zoom in to display the city. Press the Print Screen key to capture an image of the tool, and then paste the image in a new Paint or WordPad file. Save the file as **Hudson** in the Windows6\Case1 folder provided with your Data Files.
6. Open File Explorer and then review the tags and other properties already assigned to the files in the Windows6\Case1 folder. Add the tag **fruit** or **vegetable** to files as appropriate.
7. Using the Details pane, add **Lori Scott** as the author of the following photos: Pic01, Pic06, and Pic07.
8. Use the Search text box to find a photo that includes the tag **grapes** and has **Sharon Nikas** as the author. Rename the file **Summer Fruit**.
9. Start IE Desktop and use Bing to find Web pages providing information on farms in the Hudson River Valley. Narrow the search to find Web pages on organic farms in the Hudson River Valley. Display images of the farms. (*Hint*: Click the Images link on the results page.) Press the Print Screen key to capture an image of the screen, and then paste the image in a new Paint or WordPad file. Save the file as **Organic Farms** in the Windows6\Case1 folder provided with your Data Files.

10. If necessary, add Google as a search provider in Internet Explorer, and then use Google to show a map of organic farms near Hudson, New York. Modify the search to show information about organic farms in the state of New York in the Hudson River Valley. Press the Print Screen key to capture an image of the screen, and then paste the image in a new Paint or WordPad file. Save the file as **Organic Map** in the Windows6\Case1 folder provided with your Data Files.
11. Restore your computer by removing the new search provider from Internet Explorer. Close all open windows.
12. Submit the results of the preceding steps to your instructor, either in printed or electronic form, as requested.

Case Problem 2

Data Files needed for this Case Problem: Site01.jpg–Site10.jpg

Salem Architectural Society Tiffany Garrity is the director of the Salem Architectural Society (SAS) in Salem, Oregon. She is developing a presentation to give to local groups about the services and activities the society offers, such as architectural tours and walks, workshops on historical preservation, and information about architectural styles and periods. As an intern at the SAS, you help Tiffany prepare for presentations and workshops. She asks you to help her organize the pictures she has of sites in Salem and to research general information about architectural styles and terms. Tiffany would like to play appropriate music during her presentations, so she wants information about music-playing apps. She also wants to minimize the file size of the presentation so she can email it on request. Complete the following steps:

1. Search for an app you can use to play music. Start the app and then display the my music screen. (*Hint*: Scroll the music app screen to the left.)
2. Press the Print Screen key to capture an image of the app, and then paste the image in a new Paint or WordPad file. Save the file as **Music App** in the Windows6\Case2 folder provided with your Data Files. Close the music app.
3. Search for a setting that lets you adjust the system volume. Open the setting window, and then press the Print Screen key to capture an image of the window. Paste the image in a new Paint or WordPad file. Save the file as **Volume** in the Windows6\Case2 folder provided with your Data Files. Close the volume setting window.
4. Add a tag to each JPG file in the Windows6\Case2 folder to identify the type of site shown in the photo. Use **bridge**, **building**, **church**, **fountain**, **gargoyle**, and **window** as tags. Add more than one tag as appropriate to fully describe the site.
5. Using the Details pane, add **Historic site** as a comment in the following photos: Site01, Site02, Site07, Site09, and Site10.

Explore 6. Search for historic sites that have gargoyles. (*Hint*: Start your search using **comment** as the property name in the Search text box.) Move the files you found to a new subfolder named **Gargoyles** in the Windows6\Case2 folder.

Explore 7. Using **dimensions** as the property name in the Search text box, find files in the Windows6\Case2 folder that have 484 pixels as one of their dimensions. Press the Print Screen key to capture an image of the search results showing the files you found. Paste the image in a new Paint or WordPad file, and save the file as **Dim 484** in the Windows6\Case2 folder provided with your Data Files.

8. In the Windows6\Case2 folder, search for files that are less than 100 KB in size. (*Hint*: Add **KB** to the search text.) Press the Print Screen key to capture an image of the search results showing the files you found. Paste the image in a new Paint or WordPad file, and save the file as **100 KB** in the Windows6\Case2 folder provided with your Data Files.

9. Start IE Desktop, and use Bing to find Web pages providing information on architectural styles. Narrow the search to Web pages that provide this information only about Salem, Oregon. Press the Print Screen key to capture an image of the screen, and then paste the image in a new Paint or WordPad file. Save the file as **Salem** in the Windows6\Case2 folder provided with your Data Files.
10. Use any other search provider to conduct a search for information about architectural styles. Open a page displaying information about this topic. Use the Find toolbar to find information on the page about architectural styles in the Victorian era. Press the Print Screen key to capture an image of the screen showing the Find toolbar, and then paste the image in a new Paint or WordPad file. Save the file as **Victorian** in the Windows6\Case2 folder provided with your Data Files. Close all open windows.
11. Submit the results of the preceding steps to your instructor, either in printed or electronic form, as requested.

CREATE

Case Problem 3

Data Files needed for this Case Problem: Climb01.jpg–Climb10.jpg

Peak Performers Derek Cruz started a club called Peak Performers in Salt Lake City, Utah, for mountain-climbing enthusiasts. The club has grown in popularity and now has hundreds of active members around the country. In his online newsletter, Derek is starting a feature called Top Ten Climbs. He wants to kick off the feature by posting photos and writing descriptions of his 10 favorite climbs. He also wants to follow current sports news to learn about climbers around the world. As his editorial assistant, you offer to help him find this information and produce the description text. Complete the following steps:

1. Search for an app you can use to follow sports events. Start the app and then display sports news.
2. Press the Print Screen key to capture an image of the app, and then paste the image in a new Paint or WordPad file. Save the file as **Sports App** in the Windows6\Case3 folder provided with your Data Files.
3. Search within any Windows 8 app for information about Yosemite National Park. With information that clearly identifies Yosemite National Park displayed, press the Print Screen key to capture an image of the opening window. Paste the image in a new Paint or WordPad file. Save the file as **Yosemite** in the Windows6\Case3 folder provided with your Data Files. Close the app.
4. Working in the Windows6\Case3 folder, add **El Capitan; Yosemite** as tags to the Climb08 file. Add the tag **Hoffman Peak** to the Climb09 file.
5. Conduct a search in the Case3 folder to find photo files with **glacier** as a tag or **Derek** as an author.
6. Press the Print Screen key to capture an image of the search results, and then paste the image in a new Paint or WordPad file. Save the file as **Search1** in the Windows6\Case3 folder provided with your Data Files.
7. Conduct another search in the Case3 folder to find files with **glacier** as a tag and **Derek** as an author.
8. Press the Print Screen key to capture an image of the search results, and then paste the image in a new Paint or WordPad file. Save the file as **Search2** in the Windows6\Case3 folder provided with your Data Files.
9. Conduct another search in the Case3 folder to find files with **park** or **mountain** as a tag.
10. Press the Print Screen key to capture an image of the search results, and then paste the image in a new Paint or WordPad file. Save the file as **Search3** in the Windows6\Case3 folder provided with your Data Files.
11. Start IE Desktop and conduct a search to produce the results shown in Figure 6-32.

Figure 6-32 Bing search results

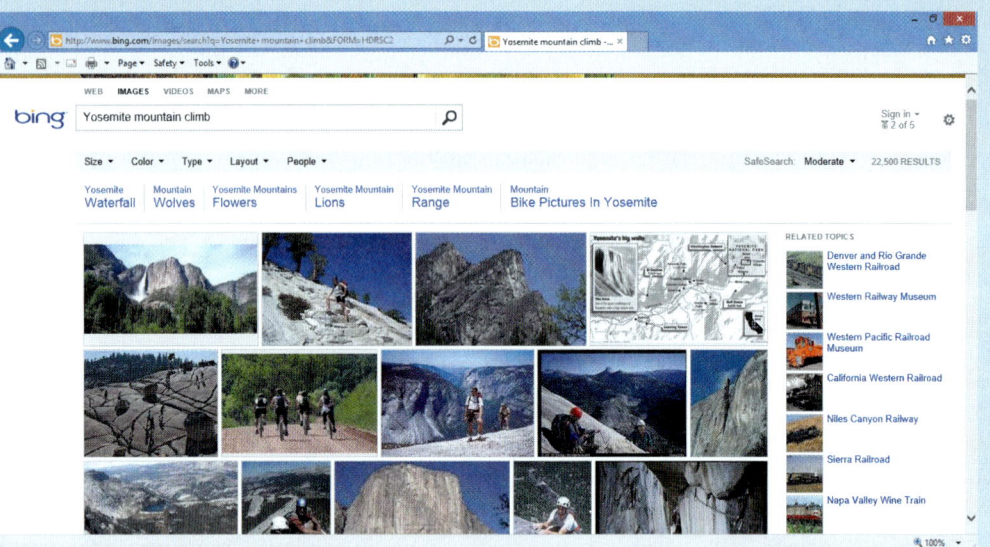

12. Press the Print Screen key to capture an image of the first screen of search results, and then paste the image in a new Paint or WordPad file. Save the file as **Search4** in the Windows6\Case3 folder provided with your Data Files. Close all open windows.
13. Submit the results of the preceding steps to your instructor, either in printed or electronic form, as requested.

Case Problem 4

There are no Data Files needed for this Case Problem.

Thornton Research Lindsey and Sam Thornton are starting a company called Thornton Research. They plan to provide research services for businesses and others, especially those who need marketing and demographic information. They learned their research techniques using print materials and through casual Internet use. They hired you as an assistant to help them learn how to take full advantage of the Internet. Complete the following steps:

1. Start Internet Explorer and use any search provider to research the following terms:
   Web 2.0
   Web 3.0
   Deep Web
   Metasearch engine
   Subject directory
2. Use WordPad or another word-processing program to create a document that lists these terms and provides a definition for each one. Save the document as **Research** in the Windows6\Case4 folder.
3. Search providers such as Google and Bing offer many tools for online research. For example, Bing has a social search tool that lets you collaborate with others to find information. After you enter a search term, Google displays a list of search tools to the left of the search results including Sites with images, Related searches, and Dictionary. Learn how to use one of these specialty search tools.
4. In the Research document, describe the search tool you selected and then explain how to use it. Be sure to mention the purpose of the tool and the steps for using it. Save the document.
5. Submit the results of the preceding steps to your instructor, either in printed or electronic form, as requested.

Problem Solving

Selecting the Best Settings for Efficient Computer Work

When you solve problems, you work through a series of stages to gather information about the problem and its possible solutions. Problem solving in general involves the following tasks:

1. Recognize and define the problem.
2. Determine possible courses of action.
3. Collect information needed to evaluate alternative courses of action.
4. Evaluate each alternative's merits and drawbacks.
5. Select an alternative.
6. Implement the decision.
7. Monitor and evaluate performance to provide feedback and take corrective action.

If you are involved in solving a complex problem with many possible causes, you perform all seven steps in the process. If you are solving a simpler problem or have limited time to explore solutions, you can condense the steps. For example, you might recognize the problem in one step; determine possible actions, and evaluate and select an alternative in the next step; and then implement and evaluate your decision in another step.

Recognize and Define the Problem

A problem is an obstacle that prevents you from reaching a goal. This definition is especially fitting for work with a computer. For example, suppose your goal is to create a report containing text and graphics, but you don't know which program to use. In this case, your lack of familiarity with the programs on your computer is an obstacle preventing you from reaching your goal of efficiently creating a report with text and graphics.

After identifying a simple problem, such as which computer program to use, you can focus on solutions. Start by considering any possible solution. For example, start each program on your computer related to text and graphics and examine its features. Next, compare and evaluate those alternatives. Which programs help you meet your goal most effectively? Select the best solution and then try it, observing the results to make sure it actually solves the problem. Can you efficiently create the report with the program you selected? If not, try a different program until you find the best possible solution.

Set Up Your Computer to Work Efficiently

The way you set up your computer can help you avoid problems and work with efficiency. Two common problems for Windows users are not being familiar with the programs installed on their computers, and not being able to quickly access folders, files, devices, and information they use often. You can avoid or solve these problems by personalizing your computer and using a few Windows programs that let you work efficiently and securely. As you select settings, capture and save images of your computer so you can document what you've done. Complete the following tasks:

1. Start Windows 8 and sign in, if necessary.
2. Change the Start screen, account picture, lock screen, desktop icons, and taskbar to suit your preferences.
3. Use IE Windows 8 or IE Desktop to research themes you can use on your computer. If you find a theme you like, download and install it on your computer.
4. Pin tiles to the Start screen for the apps you use often. Pin apps you use often to the taskbar. Add files you use often to the Jump Lists for these programs.
5. Set up shortcuts on your desktop to the folders and devices you use often. Capture an image of the desktop and of the Start screen.
6. In IE Windows 8, pin Web pages you visit often to the Apps bar. In IE Desktop, add the Web pages that you visit often to your Favorites list. Open the Favorites Center, and then capture an image of the Internet Explorer window.
7. Using the People app, create contacts for your correspondents. Capture an image of the contact list in the People app.
8. Using the Calendar app, set up your appointments and tasks for the upcoming week. Capture an image of the event calendar.
9. Open the Windows 8 Action Center, and make sure you are using all of the recommended security settings. In particular, make sure you are using an up-to-date antivirus program and that Windows Update is set to check for updates regularly. Both settings help you avoid the problems of security threats to your computer. Capture an image of the Action Center window.
10. Submit the images you captured to your instructor, either in printed or electronic form, as requested.

APPENDIX A

Using Windows 8 with a Touchscreen Device

OBJECTIVES
- Use touch gestures
- Navigate the Start screen
- Use Windows 8 and desktop applications
- Enter text on a touch keyboard
- Adjust touchscreen settings

Mastering Touch Features in Microsoft Windows 8

If you use a computing device with a touchscreen, you can take advantage of the touch features in Windows 8 to perform all of your computing tasks. For example, you can start apps, switch from one app to another, and organize the Start screen using your finger as a pointing device. With the built-in touch keyboard, you can enter text anywhere you need to, such as in search boxes, email messages, and documents.

Windows 8 is designed to let you use any type of computer to interact with the operating system and applications. For example, you can use a mouse and keyboard connected to a desktop PC, a touchpad on a laptop, a pen or stylus on a slate, or a touchscreen on a tablet. This appendix is designed for people with touchscreen devices. It explains how to use touch gestures to select objects, navigate the computer, and start apps. It also provides step-by-step instructions for using a touch keyboard, interacting with the Start screen and desktop, and using Windows 8 apps and desktop programs. Finally, the appendix describes how to adjust touchscreen settings.

STARTING DATA FILES

There are no starting Data Files needed for this appendix.

Microsoft product screenshots used with permission from Microsoft Corporation.

Appendix A Visual Overview:

Drag a Windows 8 app to the left or right of the screen to make it a **snapped app**.

Enter text by tapping keys on the **touch keyboard**, an on-screen keyboard for users with touchscreen devices.

Tap the &123 key to display symbols and numbers; tap it again to redisplay letters.

Tap the smiley face key to display **emoticons**, symbols that represent facial expressions.

Using Touch Features

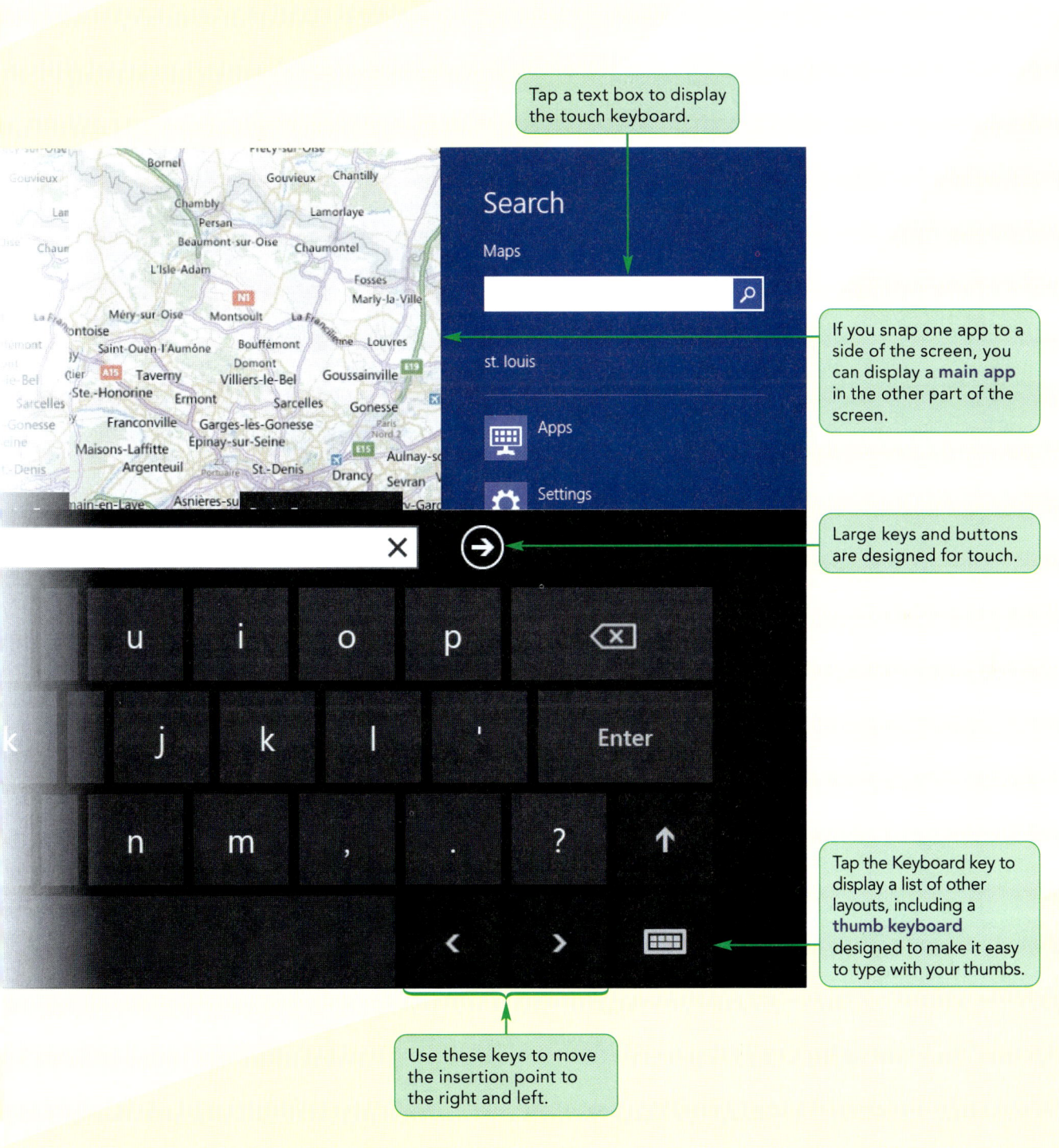

Using Touch Gestures

If you have a computer with a touchscreen, such as a tablet or laptop with a multitouch monitor, you can touch the screen directly to interact with Windows 8. The movements you make as you touch the screen with your fingertips are called **touch gestures**. You use the same touch gesture to perform a particular task in Windows 8 as you do in its applications. For example, to select an item on the Start screen or in a Windows 8 app, you tap the item, which means you use your fingertip to touch the item briefly. The six basic touch gestures are tap, press, swipe, slide or drag, pinch, and rotate. Figure A-1 illustrates these six touch gestures.

Figure A-1 — Touch gestures and mouse equivalents

Touch Gesture	Description	Illustration
Tap	Touch an item with a fingertip	Tap for primary Action
Press	Touch and hold an item	Press and hold to learn
Swipe	Drag a fingertip across the screen and then release	Swipe to select
Slide or drag	Drag a fingertip across the screen without releasing	Slide to pan
Pinch	Touch the screen with two fingers and then drag your fingertips toward each other	Pinch and stretch to zoom
Rotate	Touch the screen with two fingers and then drag either clockwise or counterclockwise	Turn to rotate

© 2014 Cengage Learning

Appendix A Using Windows 8 with a Touchscreen Device | Windows   WIN A5

In the following steps, you use touch gestures to start the Calendar app, select a date and use other features, and then close the app. To perform these steps, make sure your Windows 8 touchscreen device is turned on and displays the Start screen.

To start and close an app:

1. Tap the **Calendar** tile on the Start screen to open the Calendar app.
2. Tap a date on the calendar to select the date and display its details. See Figure A-2. Your details might differ.

Figure A-2 Details of the selected date

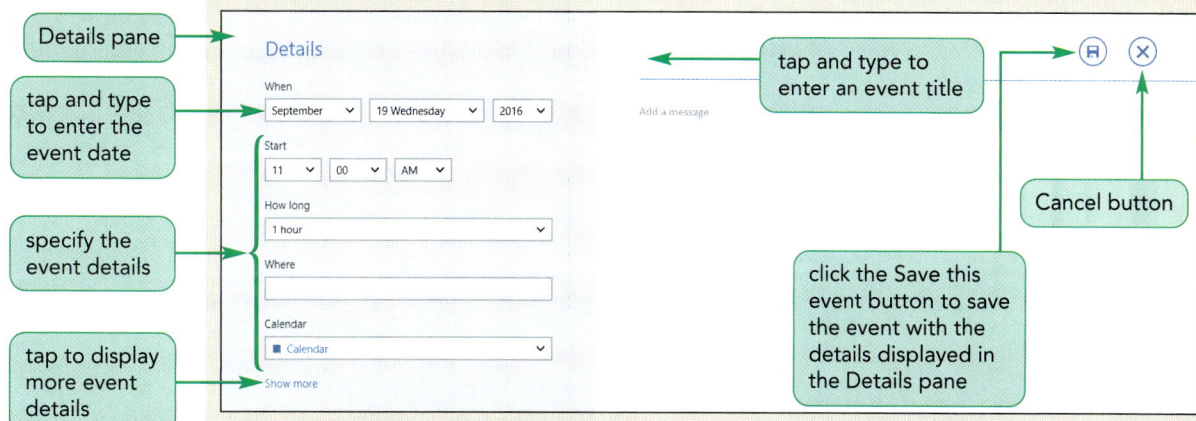

3. Press the **Cancel** button ⓧ to display its name in a ScreenTip.

   Trouble? If the Details screen closes, you tapped the Cancel button instead of pressing it. To press the Cancel button, continue touching the button until the ScreenTip appears, and then repeat Steps 2 and 3.

4. Tap the **Cancel** button ⓧ to close the Details screen.
5. Swipe from the bottom edge of the screen toward the center to display the Calendar Apps bar. See Figure A-3.

Figure A-3 Calendar Apps bar

6. Tap the **Week** button on the Apps bar to display the Calendar in Week view.

7. Drag the top of the Calendar app to the bottom of the screen to close the app.

   Trouble? If the Calendar app shrinks instead of closes, press the top edge of the app, drag it down until the app shrinks, continue dragging it to the very bottom of the screen, and then release your finger.

Touch gestures are often more comfortable than mouse actions, but mouse actions are more familiar for most computer users. In general, if you are using a mouse, you locate on-screen items by pointing to the screen corners. If you are using a touchscreen, you swipe from the screen edges. You can use your forefinger and thumb when you need two fingers to gesture. To help you make the transition from mouse to touch, Figure A-4 lists common Windows 8 tasks and their touch and mouse equivalents.

Figure A-4: Performing tasks with touch or mouse

Task	Touch Gesture	Mouse Action
Display a ScreenTip	Press an object such as a button	Point to an object such as a button
Display an Apps bar	Swipe from the top or bottom of the screen toward the center	Right-click the bottom edge of the screen
Display the Charms bar	Swipe from the right edge of the screen toward the center	Point to the upper-right or lower-right corner of the screen
Display thumbnails of open apps (the Switch List)	Swipe from the left edge of the screen toward the center	Point to the upper-left corner of the screen
Drag an object	Touch, hold, and then drag	Click, hold, and then drag
Scroll the Start screen	Swipe from the right edge of the screen to the left	Click the scroll arrows, or drag the scroll bar
Select an object or perform an action such as starting an app	Tap the object	Click the object
Zoom	Pinch two fingers to zoom in or move the fingers apart to zoom out	Click the Zoom button

© 2014 Cengage Learning

Navigating the Start Screen

The Start screen is where you begin your work in Windows 8. The Start screen is designed to be especially easy to use on touchscreen devices. To start apps, use Windows 8 tools, and navigate from one app to another, you use the touch gestures described in the previous section of this appendix. In the following sets of steps, you perform some of the same tasks using touch gestures that you have already performed with a mouse: scroll and zoom the Start screen, switch between two apps, and snap an app to a side of the screen. When you use two or more fingers to manipulate objects, you are using the **multitouch** feature of Windows 8.

To navigate the Start screen:

1. Touch the right side of the screen and then swipe your finger to the left side of the screen. The Start screen scrolls to show additional tiles not displayed on the main Start screen.

   Trouble? If the screen does not scroll, your Start screen does not contain additional tiles.

2. Touch the left side of the screen and then swipe to the right to scroll back to the main Start screen.

3. Touch a blank part of the Start screen with your forefinger and thumb, and then pinch them together to zoom out and reduce the size of the tiles. See Figure A-5.

Figure A-5   Zoomed Start screen

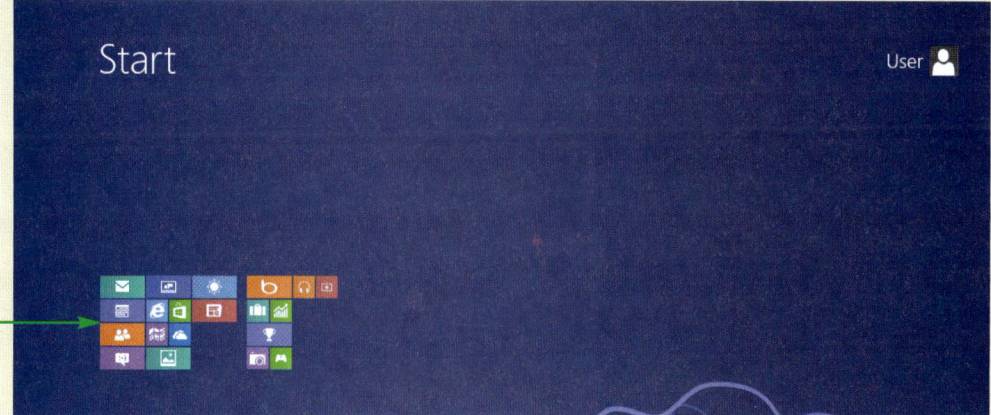

tiles are reduced in size

4. Touch a blank part of the Start screen with your forefinger and thumb again, and then move them apart to zoom in and increase the size of the tiles.

Next, you start two apps, use the Charms bar to return to the Start screen, and then switch from one app to another.

To switch between apps:

1. On the Start screen, tap the **Weather** tile to start the Weather app, which displays the current weather conditions in a specified location and provides a five-day forecast.

   Trouble? If a message appears asking whether you want to turn on location services and allow Weather to use your location, tap the Block button.

2. Swipe from the right side of the screen toward the center to display the Charms bar. See Figure A-6. The information displayed in your Weather app will differ from Figure A-6.

   Trouble? If your Charms bar is active, status information such as the current date and time appear on the left side of the screen.

Figure A-6 Charms bar and Weather app

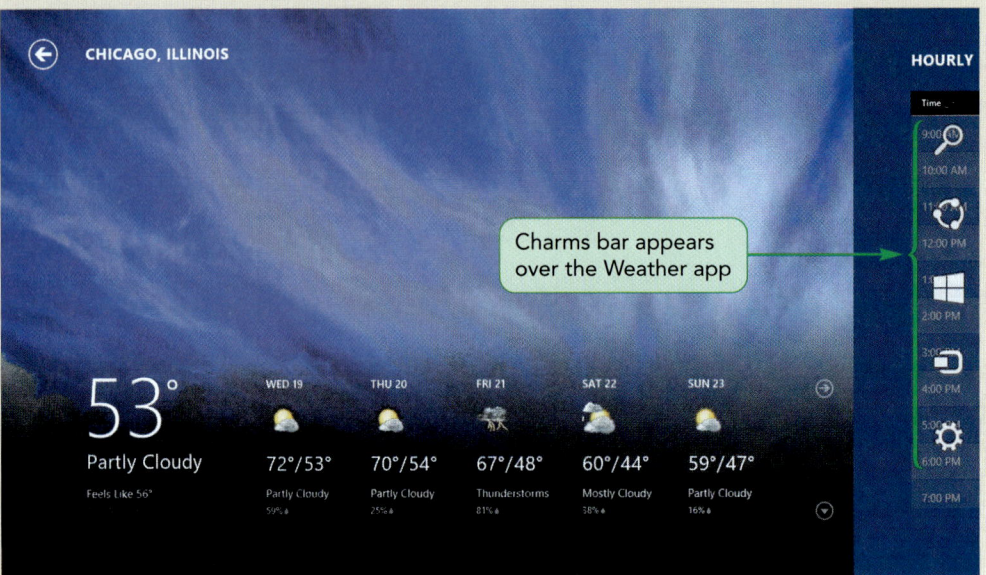

- **3.** Tap the **Start** button on the Charms bar to return to the Start screen.
- **4.** Tap the **Maps** tile to start the Maps app, which displays a map of a specified location.

    Trouble? If a message appears asking whether you want to turn on location services and allow Maps to use your location, tap the Block button.

- **5.** Swipe from the left side of the screen toward the center to switch to the Weather app.
- **6.** Slide a finger from the left side of the screen and then swipe back to the left (quickly tracing a ">" with your finger) to display the Switch List, which includes thumbnails of the other open application and the Start screen. See Figure A-7.

Figure A-7 Switch List

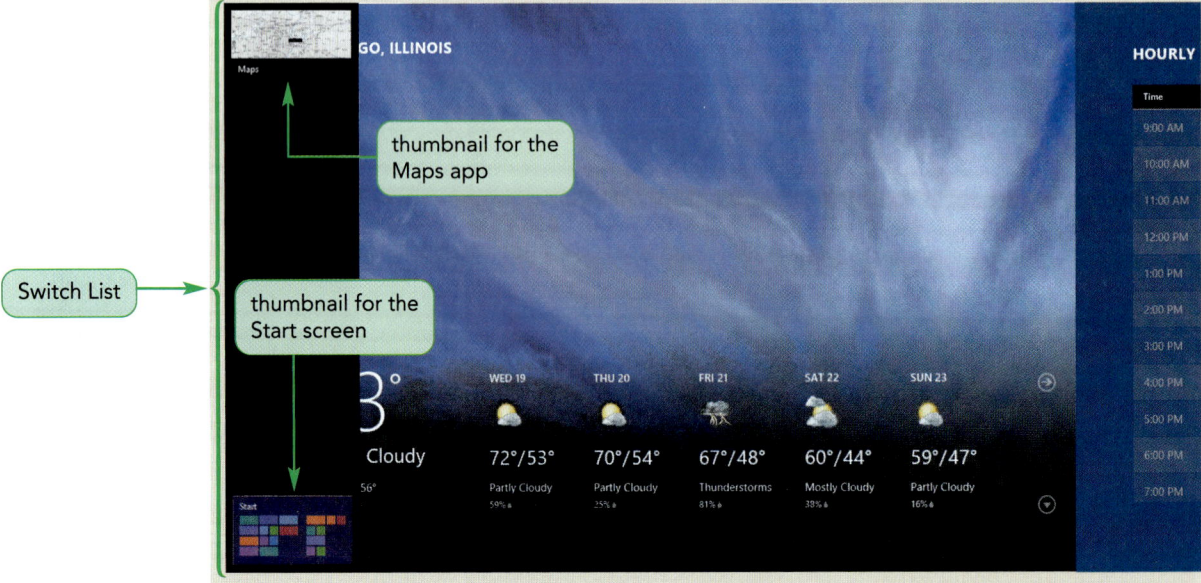

Appendix A Using Windows 8 with a Touchscreen Device | Windows **WIN A9**

▶ **7.** Tap the **Maps** thumbnail to switch to the Maps app.

Finally, you can snap an app to the screen. When you snap an app, you reduce it to a pane on the left or right side of the screen. If another app is open, it appears in the rest of the screen and is called the main app. You can drag the separator bar between the snapped app and the main app to change the amount of screen each app occupies. Your touchscreen device must be using a screen resolution of at least 1366 × 768 to snap apps.

The easiest way to snap an app is to display it on the screen and then drag it to the right or left, which is the technique you use in the following steps.

To snap an app:

▶ **1.** Swipe from the left side of the screen toward the center to switch to the Weather app.

▶ **2.** Drag the **Weather** app from the top of the screen down until the app appears as a large thumbnail, and then drag the thumbnail to the left until it expands and snaps to the left side of the screen.

Trouble? If the Weather app did not snap to the left side of the screen, your screen resolution is probably not high enough to snap apps.

▶ **3.** Swipe from the left and then back to display the Switch List, and then tap the Maps app to display it as the main app. See Figure A-8.

| Figure A-8 | Weather app snapped to the left side of the screen |

Maps is the main app

Weather is the snapped app

According to Microsoft, Windows 8 apps running in the background don't slow down your computer the way desktop applications do. You can open Windows 8 apps and leave them running without affecting the performance of your computer. If you don't use an open Windows 8 app for a period of time, Windows eventually closes it. However, if the Switch List becomes crowded or you have to swipe many times to find the open app you want to work with, it's a good idea to close apps. In the following steps, you close the snapped Weather app and the main Maps app.

> **To close Windows 8 apps:**
>
> ▶ 1. Drag the top of the **Maps** app down to the bottom of the screen to close it.
>
> ▶ 2. Drag the top of the **Weather** app down to the bottom of the screen to close it and display the Start screen.

Using Windows 8 Apps

Windows 8 provides a number of apps when you install the operating system. These apps use the streamlined Modern design, which features large, clear text and an uncluttered workspace. Windows 8 apps do not run in windows the way desktop applications do; instead, they expand to cover the entire screen unless you snap them. For example, Figure A-9 shows the Windows 8 version of Internet Explorer with its clean interface and touch-friendly controls.

| Figure A-9 | Windows 8 Internet Explorer |

In addition to the built-in Windows 8 apps, you can purchase and download Windows 8 apps from the **Windows Store**, a Web site where Microsoft developers and independent programmers showcase Windows 8 apps they designed and posted. If you are connected to the Internet, you can visit the Windows Store by selecting the Store tile on the Start screen. Because Microsoft wants to protect Windows 8 apps from security threats by restricting them to a central distribution site, the Windows Store is the only place to purchase Windows 8 apps.

Using a Touch Keyboard

If you do not have a physical keyboard attached to your touchscreen device, you can use the touch keyboard, which is a keyboard that appears on the screen when you need to enter text. For example, you can use the touch keyboard to enter a search term on the Search menu and type text in any Windows 8 or desktop application. As you type, Windows suggests complete words that begin with the letters you typed, a feature called **AutoComplete**.

Appendix A Using Windows 8 with a Touchscreen Device | Windows   WIN A11

In addition to typing letters and common punctuation symbols such as the question mark (?) and period (.), you can tap the Symbols and numbers key (marked as &123) to display symbols such as an ampersand (&) and numbers from 0 to 9. If you are writing an email or a chat message, for example, you can tap the Smiley key to display smiley face symbols and emoticons, combinations of keyboard symbols that represent facial expressions. In informal messages, you can insert smiley face symbols and emoticons to express your mood or to help readers interpret the text.

To display the touch keyboard, tap a text box or another location where you want to enter text. In the following steps, you use the touch keyboard to search for a location in the Maps app.

To use the touch keyboard with the Search menu:

1. On the Start screen, swipe from the right to the center of the screen to display the Charms bar.
2. Tap the **Search** button to display the Search menu.
3. Tap the **Search** box to display a full-size touch keyboard. See Figure A-10.

Figure A-10   Full-size touch keyboard

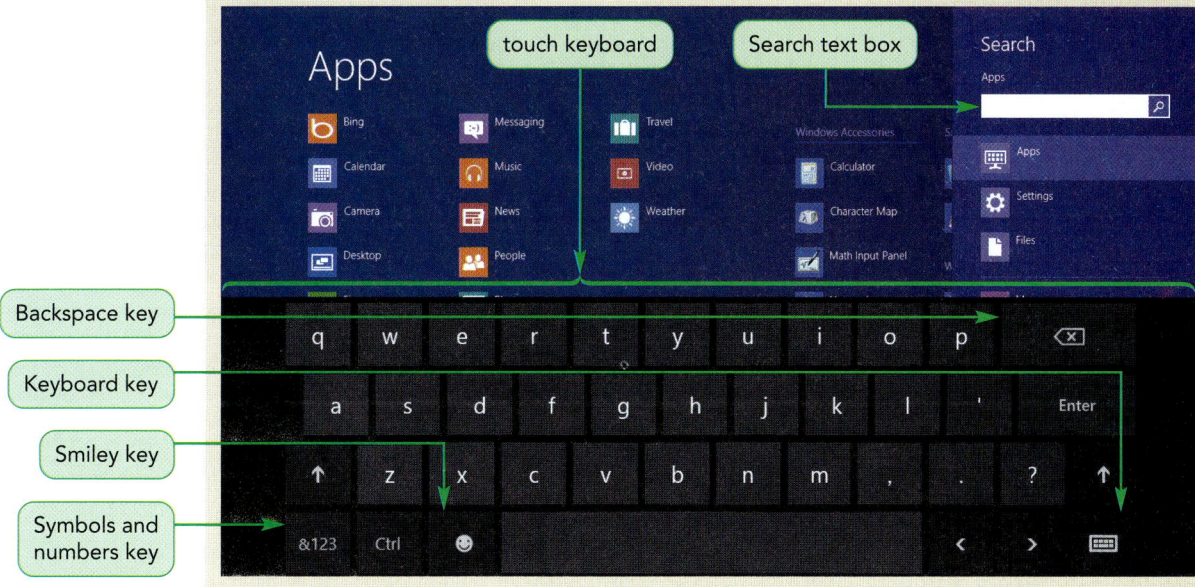

4. Tap the keys on the touch keyboard to enter **paris, france** in the Search box.

   Trouble? If you make a typing error, tap the Backspace key in the upper-right corner of the keyboard to delete the error and then retype.

5. Tap **Maps** on the Search menu to display Paris, France, in the Maps app. See Figure A-11.

TIP

Use the left and right arrow keys (< and >) to move the insertion point through the text you typed.

| Figure A-11 | Searching for Paris, France, in the Maps app |

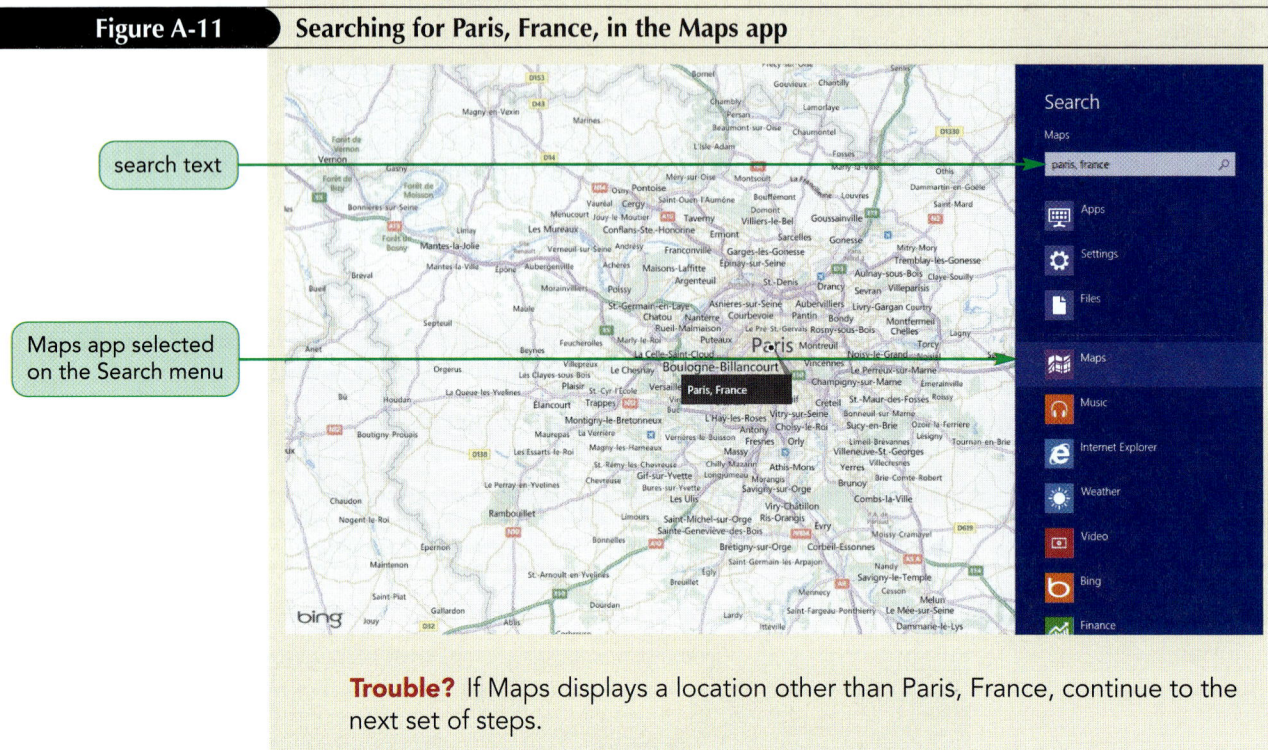

- search text
- Maps app selected on the Search menu

Trouble? If Maps displays a location other than Paris, France, continue to the next set of steps.

The touch keyboard has two layouts: the full-size keyboard with large buttons and a split thumb keyboard. The full-size keyboard is designed for typing when your touchscreen device is on a surface such as a table or desk. The thumb keyboard, which splits the keyboard into three sections, is ideal when you are holding your touchscreen device with both hands and want to type with your thumbs.

To use the thumb keyboard:

1. Swipe from the right to display the Charms bar, and then tap the **Search** button to display the Search menu.
2. Tap the **Search** box to display the full-size touch keyboard.
3. Tap the **Keyboard** key in the lower-right corner of the touch keyboard to display a list of layouts.
4. Tap the **Split keyboard** button to display the thumb keyboard. See Figure A-12.

TIP

When you're working on the desktop, tap where you want to enter text, and then tap the keyboard icon on the taskbar to display the touch keyboard.

Figure A-12 Thumb keyboard

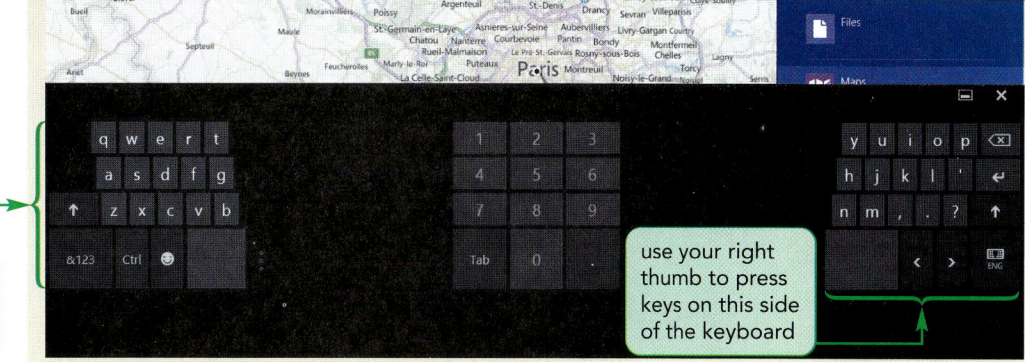

use your left thumb to press keys on this side of the keyboard

use your right thumb to press keys on this side of the keyboard

5. Tap the keys on the thumb keyboard to type **helsi** in the Search box. As you type, Windows suggests complete words that begin with those letters.

6. Tap **helsinki** in the list of suggestions to display a map of Finland with Helsinki identified.

   Trouble? If a list of suggestions does not appear, type *helsinki* and then tap the Search button.

7. Swipe from the right to display the Charms bar, and then tap the **Start** button to return to the Start screen.

Adjusting Touch Keyboard Settings

When you use a touch keyboard, Windows 8 applies the following settings by default:

- Shows text suggestions as you type
- Adds a space after you choose a text suggestion
- Adds a period after you double-tap the Spacebar
- Capitalizes the first letter of each sentence
- Uses all uppercase letters when you double-tap the Shift key
- Plays key sounds as you type
- Makes the standard keyboard layout available

To change a touch keyboard setting, you use the PC settings screen, which you can access on the Settings menu.

To display the touch keyboard settings:

1. Swipe from the right to the center of the screen to display the Charms bar.
2. Tap the **Settings** button to display the Settings menu.
3. Tap **Change PC settings** to display the PC settings screen.
4. In the left pane, tap **General** to display General settings on the right.
5. Slide down to scroll the General settings and display the Touch keyboard section. See Figure A-13.

Figure A-13 Touch keyboard settings

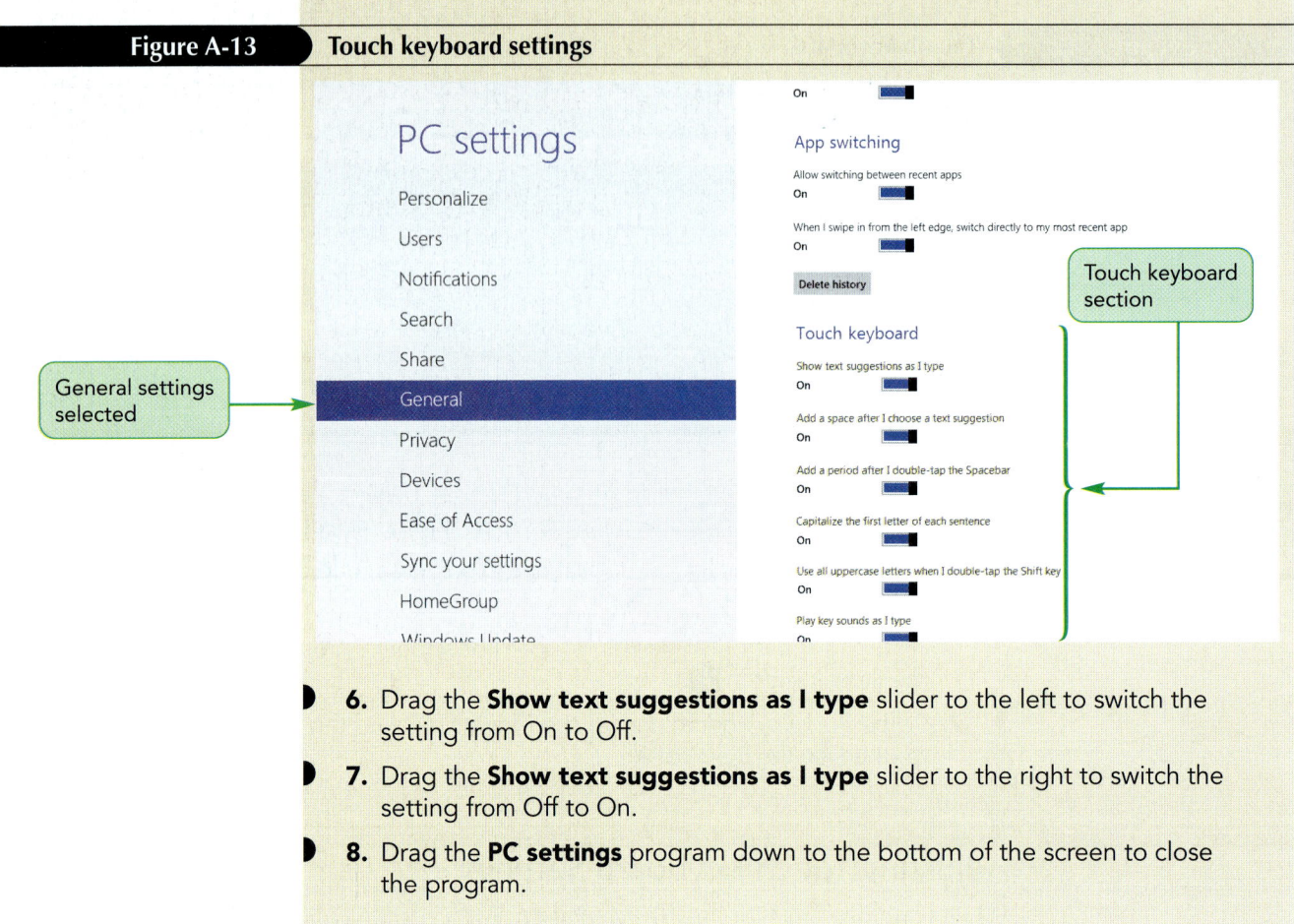

> 6. Drag the **Show text suggestions as I type** slider to the left to switch the setting from On to Off.
>
> 7. Drag the **Show text suggestions as I type** slider to the right to switch the setting from Off to On.
>
> 8. Drag the **PC settings** program down to the bottom of the screen to close the program.

You change other PC settings the same way: by dragging the slider from right to left to enable a setting, and from left to right to disable a setting.

Interacting with the Desktop

Touch gestures work on the desktop just as they do on the Start screen. You tap the File Explorer button on the taskbar to display a folder window, tap an icon in the Navigation pane, and then double-tap (tap twice quickly) to open a file or folder in the right pane. You also tap a button on the ribbon to change the view, select a setting, and perform other File Explorer tasks.

One feature unique to touchscreen devices is the technique you use to select files. By default on a touchscreen device, files and folders are displayed in File Explorer with a check box to their left. You tap a check box to select the corresponding file or folder. This feature is especially useful if you are selecting more than one file or folder. For example, if you want to copy a few files, tap the check box next to each file, tap the Home tab (if necessary), and then tap the Copy button in the Clipboard group.

In the following sets of steps, you use touch gestures to explore the desktop. You display the desktop, open a shortcut menu, start File Explorer, navigate to a folder, and change the view of the icons in a folder window.

Appendix A Using Windows 8 with a Touchscreen Device | Windows   WIN A15

To display the desktop and open a shortcut menu:

1. On the Start screen, tap the **Desktop** tile to display the desktop.
2. Press the **Recycle Bin** icon on the desktop (that is, touch the icon and keep your finger pressed down).
3. When a box appears around the icon, lift your finger to display the shortcut menu, which lists all the actions you can take with the Recycle Bin icon. See Figure A-14. For example, you can open the Recycle Bin, empty it, or display its properties.

Figure A-14   **Recycle Bin shortcut menu**

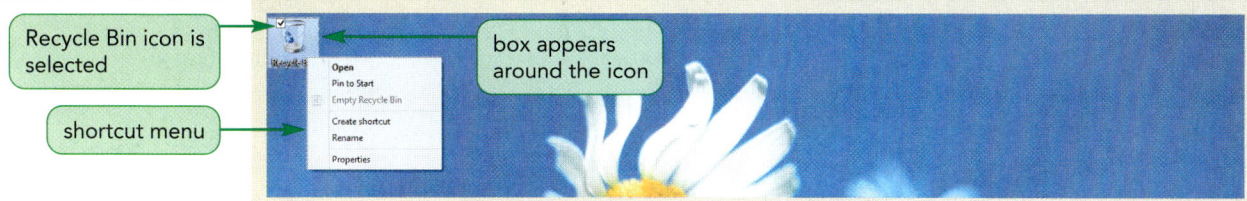

Recycle Bin icon is selected

box appears around the icon

shortcut menu

4. Tap a blank spot on the desktop to close the shortcut menu.

Next, you can start File Explorer, navigate to the Computer folder, and then change the view of the icons in that folder window.

To use File Explorer:

1. Tap the **File Explorer** button on the taskbar to start File Explorer and display the standard libraries.
2. In the Navigation pane, tap the **Desktop** icon to display the resources available from the desktop.
3. In the right pane, double-tap the **Computer** icon to display the drives and devices on the computer.
4. Tap the **Expand the Ribbon** button to expand the ribbon.
5. Tap the **View** tab on the ribbon, and then tap **Medium icons** in the Layout group to display the drive icons in Medium icons view. See Figure A-15. The icons on your screen might differ.

   Trouble? If the Details pane or Preview pane is open in the Computer window, your screen will look different from the figure, though the size of the icons should be the same.

Figure A-15: Drive icons in Medium icons view

6. Tap **Tiles** in the Layout group on the View tab to return to the default view for this window.

7. Tap the **Close** button to close File Explorer.

In this appendix, you learned how to use touch gestures to interact with Windows 8 on a touchscreen device, such as a tablet computer. You navigated the Start screen, started Windows 8 apps, switched from one app to another, and used two types of touch keyboards. You also used touch gestures while working with the classic desktop and File Explorer.

Microsoft Windows 8, Introductory REF 1

GLOSSARY/INDEX

Note: Boldface entries include definitions.

SPECIAL CHARACTERS
() (parentheses), WIN 305–306
"" (quotation marks), WIN 305–306, WIN 314–315

A

Accelerator A tool that makes it easier to find information on the Web without navigating away from your current Web site. WIN 163, WIN 190–191

Action Center A Control Panel tool that helps you manage security from a single window. WIN 222–240
    defending against email viruses, WIN 240
    defending against spyware, WIN 235–240
    features, WIN 224–225
    opening, WIN 225
    protection against malware, WIN 232–235
    Windows Firewall, WIN 226–230
    Windows Update, WIN 230–232

active object A selected object with which you can interact. WIN 8

active window The window you are currently working with. WIN 19

ActiveX control A small, self-contained program you can run in other programs, especially Internet Explorer. WIN 249
    blocking, WIN 261

add-on A program offered by any software vendor that provides enhancements. such as a toolbar or an improved search feature. WIN 253–254

Address bar The bar at the top of a folder window that shows the location of the current window in the Windows hierarchy. WIN 28
    navigating to folders, WIN 53
    navigating with, WIN 58–60
    searching the Internet, WIN 311

Administrator account A type of user account created when Windows 8 is installed that provides full access to the computer. The administrator can access the files of any user, install software, and change any settings. WIN 263

adware A type of spyware that changes your browser settings to display advertisements. WIN 235

alert message A notice about security and maintenance settings that need your attention. WIN 223

All apps button A button that appears on the Start screen's Apps bar to provide access to the Apps screen, which lists all the applications installed on your computer. WIN 99

AND Boolean filter, WIN 305–307

antispyware program A program that can detect and remove spyware. WIN 223

app A small Windows 8 application created for a specific purpose. WIN 3
    adding, WIN 100
    categories, WIN 103
    pinning to Start screen, WIN 101–106
    searching for, WIN 285–286

Appearance and Personalization category, Control Panel, WIN 133, WIN 134

application Software that a computer uses to complete tasks; also called a program. WIN 14
    closing, WIN 22, WIN 26–27, WIN A6
    multiple, running, WIN 18–20
    snapping, WIN 20–21, WIN A9
    starting, WIN 14–17, WIN A5
    switching between, WIN 19–20, WIN A7–A9

appointment, scheduling, WIN 208–210

Apps bar A bar that appears at the bottom of Windows 8 apps and includes buttons that change depending on your current task. WIN 99, WIN 105
    security features, WIN 271

aspect ratio The ratio of the width to the height. WIN 146

attaching a file to an email message, WIN 204–206

AutoComplete A feature that suggests complete words beginning with the letters you type on an onscreen keyboard. WIN A10

B

Back A button that takes you back to your previous location in your sequence of opened locations; appears next to the Address bar in a folder window. WIN 46, WIN 53

background
    desktop, changing using Control Panel, WIN 136–138
    Start screen, changing, WIN 119–121

background Where an application runs when it is open but not visible on the screen. WIN 19

backup A duplicate copy of a file. WIN 68

BBBOnLine, WIN 262

Bcc line, email messages, WIN 200

Better Business Bureau, WIN 262

Bing, searching, WIN 309

blog Short for "Web log," a Web page where an author or a group of authors posts comments, articles, opinion, and other information on a regular basis. WIN 191

blog post A published piece of content to which you can subscribe via an RSS feed so you can have access to the changing information. WIN 191

Boolean filter A word such as AND, OR, or NOT that lets you combine search criteria. WIN 305–307
    combining Boolean filters and file properties, WIN 308

boot To turn on the power to a computer and trigger a series of steps and checks as the computer loads the operating system and prepares for use. WIN 271

broadband connection A high-capacity, high-speed medium for connecting to the Internet. WIN 166

Browse help list, WIN 36

browsing a Web page, WIN 181–183

browsing history, clearing, WIN 257

C

Calendar, WIN 207–210

categories, Control Panel, WIN 133

Cc line, email messages, WIN 200

certificate A digital document that verifies the security of a Web site you visit. WIN 247

Change Icon dialog box, WIN 110

charm A button that appears on the Charms bar. WIN 8

Charms bar A bar of buttons that appears on the right edge of the Start screen and provides access to several options, including the Settings menu and the Start screen. WIN 8, WIN 175–176

clearing the browsing history, WIN 257

click To press a mouse button and immediately release it. WIN 7

Clipboard A temporary storage area for files and information that you have copied or moved from one place and plan to use somewhere else. WIN 64–65
    adding icons, WIN 127–128
    changing appearance, WIN 128–129
    personalizing, WIN 126–129

Clock, Language, and Region category, Control Panel, WIN 133

closing
    applications, WIN 21, WIN 22, WIN 26–27, WIN A6
    Mail app, WIN 206

cloud computing Providing and using computer tools, such as software, via the Internet (or the cloud). WIN 165

collapse icon An icon that you click to hides the contents of an object in the Navigation pane. WIN 28

color, desktop, changing using Control Panel, WIN 138–140

Color and Appearance window, WIN 139

color scheme A set of colors including a background color and a coordinated accent color. WIN 98

column heading A title for a column in a folder window that can be clicked to sort a list of files and folders. WIN 77–79

Compatibility View An option in Internet Explorer that displays Web pages as if you were using an earlier version of the browser. WIN 171

compressed file, WIN 86–88

compressed folder A zipped folder that reduces the size of the files it contains so they take up less disk space. WIN 68

Computer icon An icon in the Navigation pane of a folder window that shows the drives on your computer. WIN 46

computer setting, restoring, WIN 153–154, WIN 210–211, WIN 271–272, WIN 320

contents, searching for files by, WIN 289–291

contextual tab A tab that appears at the top of the window just above any standard Window tabs and contains options related to your current task. WIN 31

control A graphical or textual object used for manipulating a window and for using a program. WIN 24–26

Control Panel, WIN 132–142
    activating screen savers, WIN 140–141

categories, WIN 133
changing desktop background, WIN 136–138
changing desktop colors, WIN 138–140
opening, WIN 132–133
saving themes, WIN 142
selecting themes, WIN 134–136

cookie A small file that records information about you when you visit a Web site. WIN 255
    blocking, WIN 255–256
    first-party, WIN 255
    third-party, WIN 255

copy To place a file or folder in a new location that you specify without removing it from its current location. WIN 63–65

copyright The originator's exclusive legal right to reproduce, publish, or sell intellectual property. WIN 192

cracker A hacker with criminal intent. WIN 224

Create Shortcut wizard A series of dialog boxes that guides you through the steps of creating a shortcut. WIN 108–109

custom shortcut A shortcut you create on the Start screen for items you cannot pin directly, such as commands. WIN 99

customizing
    desktop, with Control Panel, WIN 132–142
    Navigation pane, WIN 85–86
    Start screen, WIN 100–112

D

date modified, filtering files by, WIN 294–295

default setting A set of standard settings that control how the screen is set up and how a document looks when you first start typing. WIN 6

Delete Browsing History dialog box, WIN 257

deleting
    email messages, WIN 203
    files or folders, WIN 71–72

desktop Your work area for using applications designed to run in previous versions of Windows. WIN 2, WIN 10–14
    adding shortcuts, WIN 130–132
    customizing with Control Panel. See Control Panel
    displaying, WIN 10
    features, WIN 11
    Internet Explorer on, WIN 179–185
    taskbar tools, WIN 142–145
    touch gestures, WIN A14–A16

desktop application A program developed for previous versions of Windows. WIN 14
    controls, WIN 24–26
    pinning to taskbar, WIN 149–151

Desktop Background window, WIN 136

Desktop Icon Settings dialog box, WIN 128

Details pane The pane at the bottom of a folder window that displays the characteristics of the folder or selected object. WIN 69

Details view A view of a folder window that displays details about a file or folder, such as Name, Date modified, Type, and Size. WIN 28

dialog box A special kind of window in which you enter or choose settings for how you want to perform a task. WIN 25–26

digital cable A broadband technology that creates a high-speed connection to the Internet using a cable modem attached to cable television lines. WIN 166

digital signature An electronic security mark added to a file to verify its authenticity. WIN 244, WIN 249

digital subscriber line (DSL) A broadband technology that creates a high-speed connection to the Internet through standard telephone lines. WIN 166

disk A computer device for storing data. WIN 48

display setting, selecting, WIN 146–148

displaying. See also viewing
    Accelerators, WIN 191
    desktop, WIN 10
    downloaded files, WIN 248
    History list, WIN 184
    Recycle bin contents, WIN 11–12
    shortcut menus, WIN 12–13
    standard icons, WIN 127–128
    touch keyboard settings, WIN A13–A14
    Web pages on separate tabs, WIN 181–183
    Web sites designed for earlier version of Internet Explorer, WIN 171
    windows, WIN 22

domain name An identifier on the Internet that includes one or more IP addresses. WIN 168

double-click To click the left mouse button twice in quick succession. WIN 11

downloading a file safely, WIN 247–249

drag To click an object and then press and hold down the mouse button while moving the mouse. WIN 23, WIN 67
    windows, WIN 23

drag touch gesture, WIN A4

drive A computer device that can retrieve and sometimes record data on a disk. WIN 48
    creating shortcuts to, WIN 130–132

DSL. See digital subscriber line

E

Ease of Access category, Control Panel, WIN 133

email. *See* Mail app

email account Space on an email server reserved for your incoming and outgoing email messages. WIN 194

email address A notation that directs an email message to its destination. WIN 194, WIN 197

email app An application you use to exchange email messages. WIN 195. *See also* Mail app

email message A simple text document that you can compose and send using an email app. WIN 195
- Bcc line, WIN 200
- Cc line, WIN 200
- creating and sending, WIN 200–201
- deleting, WIN 203
- etiquette, WIN 205
- junk email, WIN 204
- receiving and reading, WIN 202
- responding to, WIN 202–203

email relay A practice spammers use to take advantage of vulnerabilities in your computer to send spam to other computers without your permission. WIN 240

email server A computer that stores the email messages until the recipients request them, and then the server forwards the messages to the appropriate computers. WIN 196

emoticon A combination of keyboard symbols that represents facial expressions. WIN A2

etiquette, email, WIN 205

expand icon An icon that you click to displays the contents of an object in the Navigation pane. WIN 28

extract To create an uncompressed copy of a compressed file in a folder you specify. WIN 86, WIN 87–88

F

Favorites bar A toolbar that contains buttons for feeds and links to Web pages you view often. WIN 163
- adding link to, WIN 187

Favorites Center A pane in IE Desktop that displays links to your favorites, feeds, and recently visited Web pages. WIN 163

Favorites list, WIN 185–189
- adding items, WIN 185–186
- adding pages and feeds, WIN 187–188
- organizing, WIN 186

feed. *See* RSS feed

file A collection of related information; typical types of files include text documents, spreadsheets, photos, and songs. WIN 10
- adding tags, WIN 299–301
- compressed, WIN 86–88
- copying, WIN 66–67
- creating, WIN 72–73
- deciding where to store, WIN 51
- deleting, WIN 71–72
- finding with Search text box, WIN 60–61
- grouping, WIN 80
- hidden, WIN 83
- loss, preventing, WIN 77
- managing, WIN 61–67
- moving, WIN 63–65
- naming, WIN 70–71
- navigating to, WIN 52–53, WIN 56–58
- need to organize, WIN 49
- opening, WIN 75–77
- renaming, WIN 70–71
- saving, WIN 73–75
- searching for. *See* searching for files
- selecting, WIN 66
- sorting and filtering, WIN 77–79
- strategies for organizing, WIN 50–51

File Explorer A Windows 8 tool that displays the contents of your computer and uses icons to represent drives, folders, and files. WIN 30, WIN 46
- navigating using, WIN 30–31

file icon An icon in a folder window that indicates the file type. WIN 47

file path A notation that indicates a file's location. WIN 47

file system An operating system's hierarchy of folders and files, which ensures system stability and enables Windows to find files quickly. WIN 49

file type, searching for files by, WIN 291–293

filename The name of a file; provides important information about the file, including its contents and purpose. WIN 47

filename extension Three or more characters following a dot in a filename to identify the file's type. WIN 69

filter To display in a folder window only files and folders with a certain characteristic you specify. WIN 77–79
- Boolean filters, WIN 305–307
- filtering files by date modified, WIN 294–295
- filtering files by size, WIN 293–294
- searching, sorting, or grouping vs. WIN 292

Finance app, searching, WIN 309

Find toolbar An Internet Explorer toolbar that helps you find specific information on a Web page. WIN 302

finding. *See also* searching
- files, WIN 60–61

first-party cookie A cookie generated from a Web site you visit; contains information the Web site reuses when you return. WIN 255

Flip ahead Windows feature that works with search results, articles printed on two or more Web pages, or any Web pages connected by Next Page buttons or links. Turning on this feature allows you to use "flip ahead" to a Web page instead of scrolling to the bottom of the search results page and clicking a link to display the next page. You can also use Flip Ahead if you are reading an online article, such as one published on a news Web site. WIN 177–179

folder A container that helps to organize the contents of your computer. WIN 10
- copying, WIN 66
- creating, WIN 62–63
- deleting, WIN 71–72
- managing, WIN 61–67
- moving, WIN 63–64
- navigating to, WIN 53–56
- need to organize, WIN 49
- pinning to Start screen, WIN 106–107
- selecting, WIN 66
- strategies for organizing, WIN 50–51
- viewing contents, WIN 53

Folder Options dialog box, WIN 84

folder window A window that displays the contents of your computer. WIN 51
- changing, right pane layout, WIN 82
- customizing, WIN 81–86

Forward A button that takes you to the next location in your sequence of opened locations; appears next to the Address bar in a folder window. WIN 46, WIN 53

G

GB. *See* gigabyte

Get help A button that opens the Windows Help and Support window from any folder window. WIN 29

Get started topic, WIN 36

gigabyte (GB) 1 billion bytes of data. WIN 48

group A collection of controls for related actions on a ribbon tab. WIN 24

group A collection of tiles on the Start screen that you can name and separate from other groups. WIN 99

group A sequential list of files in a folder window that share a particular detail, such as file type or size. WIN 68, WIN 80

grouping
searching, sorting, or filtering vs. WIN 292
tiles on Start screen, WIN 112–115

Guest account A built-in user account that is inactive by default. The Guest account user cannot make any changes to settings or software. WIN 263

H

hacker A person that intends to access a computer system without permission. WIN 224

hard disk A storage device permanently housed inside the computer case. WIN 48

Hardware and Sound category, Control Panel, WIN 133

Help and Support A window that provides articles, video demonstrations, and steps for performing tasks in Windows 8. WIN 34

hidden file A file not listed in a folder window, though it is actually stored in that folder. WIN 83

hijack To seize control of a browser. WIN 251

History list The list of Web pages you have visited recently. WIN 181, WIN 183–185

hit A link in the list of Internet search results. WIN 302

home page The Web page a browser is set to open by default. WIN 166

Home tab A ribbon tab that provides access to commands you perform frequently. WIN 28

hot corners The four corners of the Start screen; you point to one to display objects for interacting with Windows. WIN 2

HTTP. *See* Hypertext Transfer Protocol

hyperlink (or link) Text or a graphic in a Web document that targets another part of the document or a different document altogether. WIN 163
to Favorites bar, WIN 187

Hypertext Transfer Protocol (HTTP) The most common way to transfer information around the Web. WIN 168

I

icon A small picture that represents an object available on your computer. WIN 5
adding to desktop, WIN 127–128
changing appearance, WIN 128–129
standard, displaying, WIN 127–128
types, WIN 126

IE Desktop The version of Internet Explorer provided with Windows 8 that runs on the desktop. WIN 162
Suggested Sites feature, WIN 190

IE privacy setting, WIN 254–262. *See also* IE Windows 8
blocking ActiveX controls, WIN 261
blocking cookies, WIN 255–256
clearing browsing history, WIN 257
deciding whether to trust a Web site, WIN 262
InPrivate Browsing, WIN 258–259
Tracking Protection, WIN 259–261

IE security, WIN 242–272
add-on programs, WIN 253–254
blocking malware, WIN 249–251
blocking pop-up windows, WIN 251–52
checking Web sites, WIN 242–247
downloading files safely, WIN 247–249

IE Windows 8 The version of Internet Explorer provided with Windows 8 that runs on the Start screen. WIN 162
Accelerators, WIN 190–191
browsing Web pages, WIN 181–183
Charms bar, WIN 175–176
Favorites list, WIN 185–189
Flip ahead feature, WIN 177–179
History list, WIN 183–185
managing Web pages, WIN 172–179
opening Web pages, WIN 167–172
pinning Web pages, WIN 174–175
printing Web pages, WIN 191
privacy settings. *See* IE privacy setting
saving Web pages, WIN 191–192
security. *See* IE security
starting, WIN 166–167
using on desktop, WIN 179–185

Inbox A folder in the Mail app that stores messages you have received. WIN 194

indexed location One or more folders that Windows indexes so it can search them quickly. WIN 296

InPrivate Browsing A feature that prevents Internet Explorer from storing data about your browsing session. WIN 242, WIN 258–259

Internet, WIN 164–166
searching. *See* searching the Internet

Internet Explorer. *See also* IE Desktop; IE privacy setting; IE security
searching, WIN 309

Internet Options dialog box, WIN 251, WIN 256

Internet security zone, WIN 250

Internet service provider (ISP) A company that sells Internet access. WIN 166

IP address A unique number that identifies every computer on the Internet; consists of four sets of numbers from 0 to 255 separated by periods, or dots, as in 216.35.148.4. WIN 168

ISP. *See* Internet service provider

J

Jump List A list of recently or frequently opened files, folders, or Web sites. WIN 150

Junk A folder in the Mail app that stores unsolicited email. WIN 194

K

keyboard shortcut A key or combination of keys that perform a command. WIN 13

keyword Each word in a search expression. WIN 303
narrowing a search by excluding, WIN 315–316

L

Large icons view A view of a folder window that displays an image representing the contents of an object. WIN 29

library A central place to view and organize files and folders stored anywhere that your computer can access, such as your hard disk, removable drives, and network. WIN 30, WIN 53–54

link. *See* hyperlink

live tile A tile on the Start screen that displays frequently changing content. WIN 3
turning on, WIN 116

Local intranet security zone, WIN 250

local-only user account A user account that accesses only resources on your computer. WIN 263

lock screen A screen that appears before you log onto Windows or after your computer has been idle for a certain amount of time; the lock screen displays the date and time and other information such as network and battery status. WIN 4
displaying Calendar details, WIN 209–210

lost file problems, preventing, WIN 77

M

Mail app, WIN 194–206. *See also* email *entries*
addressing email, WIN 197
attaching files to messages, WIN 204–206
closing, WIN 206
email operation, WIN 196–197
searching, WIN 309
sending and receiving mail, WIN 199–204
setting up, WIN 197–199

main app The app that appears next to a snapped app. WIN A3

malicious software (or malware) Harmful software such as viruses that can damage your files or disrupt the operation of your computer. WIN 224. *See also* virus
    blocking, WIN 249–251
    protecting against, WIN 232–235
    types, WIN 232

Maps app, searching, WIN 309

maximizing a window, WIN 22

menu A group or list of commands. WIN 8

menu command Text on a menu that you click to perform a task. WIN 8

Microsoft account A type of user account that provides access to Microsoft cloud computing services; also called a Windows Live account. WIN 198, WIN 263
    creating, WIN 263–269

Microsoft Windows 8 A recent version of the Windows operating system. WIN 4
    apps. *See* Windows 8 app
    starting, WIN 4–5
    turning off, WIN 38–39
    user interface, WIN 6

minimizing a window, WIN 22

Mobile PC category, Control Panel, WIN 133

monitor, selecting display settings, WIN 146–148

mouse The most common type of pointing device. WIN 6

move To remove a file or folder from its current location and places it in a new location. WIN 63–64

multitask To work on more than one task at a time and to switch quickly between projects. WIN 18

multitouch A feature in Windows 8 that lets you use two or more fingers to manipulate objects on a touchscreen. WIN A6

N

name, searching for files by, WIN 289–291

naming a file, WIN 70–71

native resolution The resolution a monitor is designed to display best, based on its size. WIN 146

navigate To move from one location to another on a computer, such as from one file or folder to another. WIN 30
    with Address bar, WIN 58–60
    to data files, WIN 56–58
    navigating IE Windows 8 tools, WIN 171–172
    navigating with links, WIN 169–171
    using File Explorer, WIN 30–31

Navigation pane The left pane of a folder window that provides access to resources and locations on your computer. WIN 28, WIN 33–34
    customizing, WIN 85–86
    displaying icons and links to locations on your computer, WIN 51–53

network Two or more computers connected to exchange information and resources. WIN 164

Network and Internet category, Control Panel, WIN 133

Network Firewall, WIN 224

News app, searching, WIN 309

NOT Boolean filter, WIN 305–306

notification area of taskbar, monitoring, WIN 149

Notification bar A bar in Internet Explorer that displays information about security, downloads, and blocked pop-up windows. WIN 242

O

object, changing size, WIN 147–148

opening
    Action Center, WIN 225
    Control Panel, WIN 132–133
    files, WIN 75–77

operating system Software that manages and coordinates activities on the computer and helps the computer perform essential tasks such as displaying information on the computer screen and saving data on disks. WIN 4

optimize To add keywords and phrases to a Web page that users are likely to use to find the information on the Web page. WIN 312

OR Boolean filter, WIN 305–306, WIN 307

P

pane A separate area of a menu or window. WIN 30

parentheses (()), Boolean filter, WIN 305–306

password A confidential series of characters that you must enter before you can work with Windows. WIN 4
    changing, WIN 266–267
    picture, WIN 264–265, WIN 268–269
    text, WIN 264

PDF file A Portable Document Format (PDF) file, a file in a format developed by Adobe Corporation that typically includes text and graphics and can be opened on any type of computer. WIN 101

Peek A feature that helps you manage desktop windows, such as by displaying previews of the open windows grouped on a taskbar button. WIN 124, WIN 144–145

People app
    adding information, WIN 206–207
    searching, WIN 309

personal information number (PIN) A four-digit number you use to sign in to a Windows account. WIN 264
    creating, WIN 267–268

Personalized Tracking Protection List dialog box, WIN 260

phishing An attempt to deceive you into revealing personal or financial information when you respond to an email message or visit a Web site. WIN 240
    protecting against, WIN 244–247

Photos app, searching, WIN 309

picture password A combination of a picture and three gestures (circles, lines, and taps or clicks) drawn on the picture to identify a user. WIN 264–265
    creating, WIN 268–269

PIN. *See* personal information number

pin To add a shortcut that appears as a tile on the Start screen. WIN 100
    pinning apps to Start screen, WIN 101–106
    pinning desktop apps to taskbar, WIN 149–151
    pinning folders to Start screen, WIN 106–107
    pinning Web pages, WIN 174–175
    pinning Web pages to taskbar, WIN 188–189

pinch touch gesture, WIN A4

pinned item A shortcut that appears as a tile on the Start screen; you click the tile to open an app or folder or to run a command. WIN 98

pixel Short for "picture elements." The measurement used to determine a screen resolution, which is made up of the tiny dots in horizontal and vertical rows on a computer screen. WIN 146

podcast One or more audio files containing content that you subscribe to and then download to your computer or portable device. WIN 187

point To move the mouse pointer over an object on the screen using a pointing device. WIN 6

pointer A small object, such as an arrow, that moves on the screen when you move your mouse. WIN 6

pointing device A piece of hardware connected to a computer that helps you interact with objects on the desktop. WIN 6

pop-up ad A window that appears while you are viewing a Web page and advertises a product or service. WIN 235
    blocking, WIN 251–252

Pop-up Blocker An Internet Explorer tool that limits or blocks pop-up windows. WIN 242

press touch gesture, WIN A4

Preview pane The pane in a folder window that displays the contents of a selected file. WIN 82

printing a Web page, WIN 191

Programs category, Control Panel, WIN 133

Properties dialog box, WIN 299

property A characteristic of an object such as a file or shortcut. WIN 109
    combining Boolean filters and file properties, WIN 308
    searching using, WIN 298–301

Protected Mode A feature in Internet Explorer that guards against Web sites trying to save files or install malware on your computer. WIN 242, WIN 244

protocol A standardized procedure used by computers to exchange information. WIN 168

Q

quarantine To move a file to another location on your computer and prevent it from running until you remove or restore the file. WIN 237

Quick Access toolbar A row of buttons on a program's title bar that give you one-click access to frequently used commands. WIN 46

quotation marks (""), Boolean filter, WIN 305–306, WIN 314–315

R

reading email messages, WIN 202

receiving email messages, WIN 202

Recent locations A button that displays a list of locations you've visited recently; appears next to the Address bar in a folder window. WIN 46, WIN 53

Recycle bin, viewing contents, WIN 11–12

redisplaying a window, WIN 22

resizing a window, WIN 23–24

resolution, screen, changing, WIN 146–147

responding to email, WIN 202–203

restoring
    settings, WIN 153–154, WIN 210–211, WIN 271–272, WIN 320
    windows, WIN 23

Restricted sites security zone, WIN 250

ribbon The area at the top of a program window that provides access to a main set of commands, which are organized by task into tabs and groups. WIN 24–25

right pane The pane on the right side of a folder window that shows the contents of the object that is selected in the Navigation pane. WIN 29, WIN 30

right-click To click an object with the right mouse button and display the object's shortcut menu. WIN 12

right-drag To point to an object with the mouse, hold down the right mouse button, and then drag the object. WIN 47

root directory The location at the top of the file system hierarchy where Windows stores folders and important files that it needs when you turn on the computer. WIN 49

rootkit Malware that gains administrator-level, or root-level, access to a computer or network without the system or users detecting its presence. WIN 232

rotate touch gesture, WIN A4

RSS feed Frequently updated Web site content, such as news or blogs, delivered directly to your desktop when you are connected to the Internet. Also called a feed. WIN 187

S

saving
    files, WIN 73–75
    searches, WIN 297–298
    themes, WIN 142
    Web pages, WIN 191–192

scanning computer, Windows Defender, WIN 236–238

schedule, managing with Calendar, WIN 207–210

screen resolution A term that refers to the clarity of the text and images on your screen. The higher the resolution, the more items that can fit on-screen because they are sharper and smaller. The lower the resolution, fewer items fit on the screen, but they are larger and easier to see. At very low resolutions, however, images might have jagged edges. WIN 146

screen saver A program that causes your computer screen to go blank or displays an animated design after the computer has been idle for a specified period of time. WIN 5, WIN 140
    activating, WIN 140–141
    security, WIN 140

Screen Saver Settings dialog box, WIN 141

ScreenTip On-screen text that appears when you point to certain objects; tells you the purpose or function of the object to which you are pointing. WIN 24

script Programming code that performs a series of commands and can be embedded in a Web page. WIN 249

Search box A text box at the bottom of the Search menu that helps you quickly find anything stored on your computer, including programs, documents, pictures, music, videos, and settings. WIN 16

search criteria Conditions that the file or folder must meet to have Windows find it. WIN 283, WIN 289
    advanced, WIN 304–308
    combining Boolean filters and file properties, WIN 308
    combining when searching file contents, WIN 305–307

search engine A program that conducts searches to retrieve Web pages. WIN 165, WIN 302

search expression The word or phrase that best describes the information you want to find. WIN 302, WIN 313

search filter A condition that narrows a search to files that share a specified detail. WIN 282

search hint When you use Start Search, a word or phrase Windows suggests that begins with the letters you typed and has been used previously as search text. WIN 285

Search menu A menu that provides access to applications, documents, settings, and much more. WIN 8, WIN 283, WIN 284

search provider A Web site that specializes in searching the Internet. WIN 296
    choosing, WIN 317–320
    searching the Internet, WIN 311

search results The files that meet the conditions of your search conditions. WIN 282

Search text box A text box next to the Address bar in a folder window that lets you find a file in the current folder or any of its subfolders. WIN 47, WIN 53, WIN 284
 finding files, WIN 60–61

searching, WIN 281–321. *See also* finding
 advanced search criteria, WIN 304–308
 for apps, WIN 285–286
 for files. *See* searching for files
 Help pages, WIN 37
 Internet. *See* searching the Internet
 for settings, WIN 286–288
 sorting, filtering, or grouping vs. WIN 292
 strategies, WIN 284–285
 using tags and other properties, WIN 298–301
 within Windows 8 apps, WIN 308–311

searching for files, WIN 288–298
 combining search criteria when searching file contents, WIN 305–307
 examining search results, WIN 296–297
 by file type, WIN 291–293
 filtering by date modified, WIN 294–295
 filtering by size, WIN 293–294
 by name and contents, WIN 289–291
 saving searches, WIN 297–298

searching the Internet, WIN 311–320
 choosing search providers, WIN 317–320
 effective searches, WIN 312
 evaluating Web pages in search results, WIN 316
 narrowing searches, WIN 313–317

Secure Boot A feature that makes 8 resistant to malware that starts before the operating system is loaded. WIN 271

security
 Action Center. *See* Action Center
 apps, WIN 271
 Internet Explorer. *See* IE security
 screen saver for, WIN 140
 startup, WIN 271

security icon An icon that indicates you need permission to access and change a setting. WIN 222

security zone A collection of security settings Internet Explorer uses for a site. WIN 242, WIN 250–251

select To point to or click an object in order to work with it. WIN 11

sending email, WIN 200–201

Sent items A folder in the Mail app that stores messages you have send to others. WIN 194

service pack (SP) A collection of software updates combined in one package. WIN 230

setting
 restoring, WIN 153–154, WIN 210–211, WIN 271–272, WIN 320
 searching for, WIN 286–289

Shake A desktop feature that lets you quickly minimizes all open windows on the desktop by shaking the title bar of the window you want to focus on. WIN 125, WIN 145

shortcut A quick way to perform an action, such as starting an app. WIN 100
 creating, WIN 130–132
 custom, adding to Start screen, WIN 107–112
 simplifying tasks, WIN 126

shortcut menu A list of commands associated with an object that you right-click. WIN 12–13

signing out, WIN 38

size, filtering files by, WIN 293–294

SkyDrive, WIN 74

sleep A low-power state in which Windows saves your work and then turns down the power to your monitor and computer. WIN 38

slide touch gesture, WIN A4

SmartScreen Filter, WIN 244–247

Snap A desktop feature that lets you arrange and resize windows by dragging them to the edge of the desktop. WIN 125, WIN 143–144

snap To display an app on the left or right side of the screen (displayed at a resolution of at least 1366 x 768) and leave it open as you work in other apps. WIN 20–21, WIN A9

snapped app A Windows 8 app dragged to the left or right of the screen where it appears until you close it. WIN A2

sort To list files and folders in a particular order, such as alphabetically by name or type or chronologically by their modification date. WIN 77–79
 searching, filtering, or grouping vs. WIN 292

SP. *See* service pack

spam Junk email. WIN 204, WIN 240

spoofed Web site A fraudulent site posing as a legitimate one. WIN 244

Sports app, searching, WIN 309

spyware Software that secretly gathers information about you and your computer actions and passes it to advertisers and others. WIN 222
 defending against, WIN 235–240

Standard account A user account designed for everyday computing that does not allow changes to the computer that affect all users. WIN 263

Start screen The screen that appears after you sign into Windows 8 and use to begin working on your computer and start apps. WIN 2, WIN 5, WIN 6–10
 changing background, WIN 119–121
 changing user picture, WIN 121–123
 custom shortcuts, WIN 107–112
 grouping tiles, WIN 112–115
 modifying tiles, WIN 116–118
 navigating, WIN A6–A10
 personalizing, WIN 100–112
 pinning apps to, WIN 101–106
 pinning folders to, WIN 106–107
 removing tiles, WIN 115–116
 returning to, WIN 13–14
 scrolling, WIN 6–7
 zooming, WIN 7–8

starting
 applications, WIN 14–17, WIN A5
 Windows, WIN 4–5

status bar A strip at the bottom of a window that provides information about the selected object or window. WIN 28

stemming Using the root of a word in a search expression. WIN 306

storage device, identifying, WIN 33

Store app, searching, WIN 309

store-and-forward technology The practice of an email server storing email messages until the recipients request them and then forwarding the messages to the appropriate computers. WIN 196

subfolder A folder contained in another folder. WIN 33, WIN 46

Suggested Sites feature, WIN 190

swipe touch gesture, WIN A4

Switch List A list that appears on the left side of the screen and displays thumbnails of open apps. WIN 15, WIN 19–20

switching between apps, WIN 19, WIN A7–A9

synchronize (or sync) To make sure data on two devices match. WIN 263

System and Security category, Control Panel, WIN 133

system software The software that runs a computer, including the operating system. WIN 14

T

tab A collection of commands that perform a variety of related tasks on a program's ribbon. WIN 24

tab switcher In IE Windows 8, an area that displays thumbnails of current or recently visited Web pages. WIN 162

tabbed browsing A feature of Internet Explorer that lets you open more than one Web page in a single browser session. WIN 171–172

tag A descriptive word or phrase you add to a file's properties to identify or describe the file. WIN 53,

WIN 283
    adding to files, WIN 299–301
    searching using, WIN 298–301
    selecting, WIN 301

tap touch gesture, WIN A4

taskbar A strip that gives you quick access to common tools and running desktop applications; appears by default at the bottom of the desktop. WIN 17
    modifying, WIN 148–152
    monitoring notification area, WIN 149
    pinning desktop apps to, WIN 149–151
    setting properties, WIN 151–152

taskbar button A button on the taskbar that you can click to open a program, make a program active, or minimize a program. WIN 17

Taskbar Properties dialog box, WIN 152

taskbar tool, WIN 142–145

tattoo A design element you can add to the Start screen to personalize the screen. WIN 99

text, changing size, WIN 147–148

text password A series of letters, numbers, spaces, and symbols that you provide to access your files, applications, and other resources on a computer. WIN 264

theme A collection of settings that determines the appearance of the desktop. WIN 124
    finding online, WIN 137–138
    saving, WIN 142
    selecting, WIN 134–136

theme pack A file (with a .deskthemepack file extension) that contains settings you have specified for the appearance of your desktop. WIN 125

third-party cookie A cookie generated from Web site advertisers, who might use them to track your Web use for marketing purposes. WIN 255

thumb keyboard An onscreen keyboard designed to make it easy to type with your thumbs, such as when you are standing or walking. WIN A3

thumbnail A miniature version of a larger image. WIN 13

tile A rectangle on the Start screen that represents an application or other resource, such as a Web page. WIN 2, WIN 15
    grouping, WIN 112–115
    live. *See* live tile
    modifying, WIN 116–118
    naming groups, WIN 114–115
    removing from Start screen, WIN 115–116

touch gesture A movement you make as you touch the computer screen with your fingers. WIN A4

touch keyboard A keyboard that appears onscreen when you need to enter text. WIN A2, WIN A10–A14

touchscreen A display that lets you touch areas of the screen to interact with software. WIN 4, WIN A4

Tracking Protection, WIN 259–261

Travel app, searching, WIN 309

Trojan horse Malware that hides inside another program, often one downloaded from the Web. WIN 232

TRUSTe, WIN 262

Trusted sites security zone, WIN 250

trusting A term that applies to a computer you want to synchronize with another computer, having verified your Microsoft account on each of them. WIN 264

U

UAC. *See* User Account Control

UEFI. *See* Unified Extensible Firmware Interface

UI. *See* user interface

Unified Extensible Firmware Interface (UEFI) A boot method that starts a computer faster and in a more secure way than previous methods. WIN 271

uniform resource locator (URL) The address of a Web page. WIN 162
    opening Web pages, WIN 168–169

update A change to software that can prevent or repair problems, enhance the security of a computer, or improve a computer's performance. WIN 230–232

URL. *See* uniform resource locator

USB flash drive A removable disk you can plug into your computer and use to store files. WIN 48

user account A collection of information that indicates the files and folders a user can access, the types of changes the user can make to the computer, and the user's preferred appearance settings. WIN 121
    changing user picture, WIN 121–123
    setting up, WIN 262–269
    switching, WIN 269

User Account Control (UAC) A feature that displays warnings and asks for confirmation to help prevent unauthorized changes to your computer. WIN 224, WIN 270–271

User Account Control settings window, WIN 270–271

User Accounts and Family Safety category, Control Panel, WIN 133

user icon An icon that identifies the current user and represents the user access account settings. WIN 3

user interface (UI) The part of the operating system you use when you work with a computer, including the layout of the screen and the controls, such as icons and buttons, so you can make selections and change settings. WIN 6

user name A unique name that identifies you to Windows. WIN 4

user name (or user ID) The name entered when your email account is set up. The @ symbol signifies that the email server name is provided next. WIN 197
    selecting, WIN 264

V

view
    changing, WIN 31–32
    selecting, WIN 32

view button Button that appears in the lower-right corner of most windows and let you switch between Details view and Large icons view. WIN 29

View tab A ribbon tab that provides controls for changing the view of the folder window and its contents. WIN 29, WIN 68
    options, WIN 81

viewing. *See also* displaying
    folder contents, WIN 53

virus A program attached to a file that runs when you open the file and copies itself to infect a computer. WIN 222
    avoiding, WIN 235

email, defending against, WIN 20
protection against, WIN 233–234
removing, WIN 235

virus definition Characteristics of a known virus. WIN 232

W

wallpaper An image you can select as the background displayed onscreen to replace the default background image. WIN 136

Weather app, searching, WIN 309

Web (or World Wide Web) A service on the Internet that lets you access linked documents. WIN 164

Web app Software stored on a Web site, which you use a browser to access. WIN 165

Web beacon On a Web page, a transparent image that invisibly tracks Web site usage. WIN 259

Web browser (browser) A program that locates, retrieves, and displays Web pages. WIN 162, WIN 165–166

Web page A hypertext document on the Web. WIN 162
adding to Favorites list, WIN 185–186
evaluating, WIN 316

opening, WIN 167–172
pinning, WIN 174–175, WIN 188–189

Web server An Internet computer that stores Web pages. WIN 165

Web site A collection of Web pages that have a common theme or focus. WIN 165
deciding whether to trust, WIN 262
designed for earlier version of Internet Explorer, displaying, WIN 171
navigating with links, WIN 169–171
spoofed, WIN 244

WebTrust, WIN 262

wildcard A symbol that stands for one or more unspecified characters in the search criterion. WIN 291

window A rectangular work area on the screen that contains a program, text, graphics, or data. WIN 17
displaying, WIN 22
dragging, WIN 23
minimizing and maximizing, WIN 22
resizing, WIN 23–24
restoring, WIN 23

Windows 8 app Application designed to use the Windows 8 interface and work with touch-screen devices. WIN 2, WIN A10

searching within, WIN 308–311

Windows Defender, WIN 224
scanning computer with, WIN 236–237
setting options, WIN 239–240

Windows Firewall, WIN 226–230

Windows SmartScreen, WIN 224

Windows Store A Web site that provides Windows 8 apps for purchase and download. WIN A10

Windows Update An operating system tool that checks for updates to system software. WIN 222, WIN 224, WIN 230–232

wireless connection A broadband technology that uses infrared light or radio-frequency signals to communicate with devices that are physically connected to a network or the Internet. WIN 166

wizard A series of dialog boxes that guide you through the steps of performing a task. WIN 108

worm Harmful computer code that spreads without your interaction. WIN 232

X

Xbox app, searching, WIN 309

TASK REFERENCE

TASK	PAGE #	RECOMMENDED METHOD
Accelerator, use	WIN 190–191	Display Web page with accelerator, click [icon], click the Accelerator you want to use
Action Center, open	WIN 225	Display the desktop, click [icon], click Open Action Center
Application, start	WIN 14	See Reference box: Starting an Application
App, search for	WIN 285	Display Start screen, type the name of the app
Calculator, use	WIN 285–286	Display Start screen, type *cal*, click Calculator
Calendar, set appointment in	WIN 208	See Reference box: Scheduling an Appointment in Calendar
Calendar, start	WIN 208	Click the Calendar tile on the Start screen
Charms bar, display	WIN 8	Point to upper-right corner of Start screen (or press [icon]+C)
Compressed folder, create	WIN 86–87	In a folder window, select files and folders to be compressed, click Share tab, click Zip button in the Send group, type a folder name, press Enter
Compressed folder, extract all files and folders from	WIN 87–88	In a folder window, click Extract tab, click Extract all to start wizard, navigation to a location, click Extract
Contact, add to People app	WIN 206	See Reference box: Adding a Contact to People
Control Panel, open	WIN 132	Display the Charms bar from the desktop, click Settings, click Control Panel
Desktop application, close	WIN 26	See Reference box: Closing an Application
Desktop application, switch to another open	WIN 19	Click the program button on the taskbar
Desktop application, switch to Windows 8 app	WIN 19	Point to upper-left corner of the desktop, click the thumbnail of the app in Switch List
Desktop apps, pin to Start screen	WIN 101	See Reference box: Pinning an App to the Start Screen
Desktop apps, pin to taskbar	WIN 149	See Reference box: Pinning Desktop Apps to the Taskbar
Desktop background, change	WIN 136–138	Open the Personalization window in the Control Panel, click the Desktop Background link, click the image in the category you want to use, click Save changes
Desktop colors, change	WIN 138–139	Open the Personalization window in the Control Panel, click the Color link, click color you want to use, Click Save changes
Desktop, display	WIN 10	Click Desktop tile on Start screen
Desktop icon, change image of	WIN 129	Right-click the desktop, click Personalization, click Change desktop icons, click the desktop icon you want to change, click Change Icon, click the icon you want to use, click OK, click OK
Desktop icon, display standard	WIN 127	See Reference box: Displaying Standard Desktop Icons
Desktop shortcut, create to drive	WIN 131	Insert the USB flash drive, click [icon] on the taskbar, click the Computer icon in the Navigation pane, point to the Removable Disk icon, press and hold the left mouse button and drag the Removable Disk icon from the Computer window into an empty area of the desk-top, release the mouse button
Desktop shortcut, create to file or folder	WIN 130	Navigate to the folder window to locate the file or folder icon, right-click the icon, point to Send to, click Desktop

TASK	PAGE #	RECOMMENDED METHOD
Desktop shortcut, delete	WIN 112	Right-click the shortcut icon on the desktop, click Delete
Desktop theme, save	WIN 142	Open Personalization window in the Control Panel, click Save theme, type a name for the theme you want to save, click Save
Desktop theme, select	WIN 135	*See* Reference box: Selecting a Theme
Email message, attach file to	WIN 204	Right-click a blank spot on the Mail screen, click Attachments on the Apps bar, navigate to and click the file you want to attach, click Attach
Email message, create	WIN 200	*See* Reference box: Creating and Sending an Email Message
Email message, delete	WIN 203	Click the email message in the Message list, click 🗑
Email message, reply	WIN 203	Select email message in the Message list, click ↩, click Reply, type message, click Send
Email message, send	WIN 200	*See* Reference box: Creating and Sending an Email Message
Favorites bar, display	WIN 187	Click Tools on the Command bar, point to Toolbars, click Favorites bar
Favorites Center, open in Internet Explorer Desktop	WIN 184	Start Internet Explorer Desktop, click ⭐
Favorites list, add Web page to	WIN 185	*See* Reference box: Adding a Web Page to the Favorites List
Favorites list, open	WIN 185	Open Favorites Center, click Favorites tab
Favorites list, organize	WIN 186	*See* Reference box: Organizing the Favorites List
Feed, subscribe to	WIN 188	Click 📶, click Subscribe to this feed, click Subscribe
File, copy	WIN 66	*See* Reference box: Copying a File or Folder in a Folder Window
File, create	WIN 72	Start application and enter data
File Explorer, open	WIN 30	Click 📁 on the taskbar
File, delete	WIN 71	*See* Reference box: Deleting a File or Folder
File, move	WIN 63	*See* Reference box: Moving a File or Folder in a Folder Window
File, open from folder window	WIN 76	Navigate to the file, double-click the file
File, rename	WIN 71	Right-click the file, click Rename on shortcut menu, type new filename, press Enter
File, save	WIN 74	Click File menu, click Save As, navigate to a location, type the filename, click Save
File, search for by name, content, or file type from the Start screen	WIN 290–292	Type search text, click Files
File, search for by name, content, or file type on the desktop	WIN 290–292	Open a folder window, type search criteria in the Search text box, press Enter
File, search for within a folder window	WIN 60	In a folder window, click the Search text box, enter text associated with the file (including filename, tags, or other file properties), press Enter
File, search for using AND or OR	WIN 307	Open a folder window, click the Search text box, type search text AND (or OR) search text
File, search for using Boolean filter and file properties	WIN 308	Open a folder window, click the Search text box, type property: search text
File, search for using property	WIN 305	Open a folder window, click the Search text box, type a property

TASK	PAGE #	RECOMMENDED METHOD
File, test for viruses with Download Manager	WIN 248–249	Click ⚙, click View downloads, right-click a file, click Rerun security checks on this file, click Close
Filename extension, show or hide	WIN 83	Click View tab, click the File name extensions check box in the Show/hide group
Files, select multiple	WIN 66	Hold down Ctrl key and click the files
Files, sort files in	WIN 78	In a folder window, click a column heading
Flip ahead, turn on in Internet Explorer Windows 8	WIN 177	See Reference box: Turning on Flip Ahead
Folder, copy	WIN 66	See Reference box: Copying a File or Folder in a Folder Window
Folder, create	WIN 62	See Reference box: Creating a Folder in a Folder Window
Folder, delete	WIN 71	See Reference box: Deleting a File or Folder
Folder, expand	WIN 33	In a folder window, click ▷ in the Navigation pane
Folder, filter files In	WIN 78	In a folder window, point to a column heading, click ▼, click filtering option
Folder, group files in	WIN 80	Click View tab, click ▣ in Current view group, click group by option
Folder, move	WIN 63	See Reference box: Moving a File or Folder in a Folder Window
Folder, pin to Start screen	WIN 106–107	Click the File Explorer tile on the Start screen, navigate to and right-click the folder you want to pin, click Pin to Start on the shortcut menu
Folder window, return to previously visited location	WIN 34	Click ⬅
Help and Support, find topic	WIN 36	Click Browse help link, click Files, folders, and search
Help and Support, search	WIN 37	Click Help home link, type search text in the Search box
Help and Support, start	WIN 34–35	On the Start screen, type help, click Help and Support
Internet Explorer Desktop, turn on InPrivate Browsing	WIN 258	Click ⚙, point to Safety, click InPrivate Browsing, type URL in the Address bar, press Enter
Internet Explorer WIndows 8, turn on InPrivate Browsing	WIN 258	Right-click a blank spot on a Web page, click Tab tools, click New InPrivate tab
Internet Explorer, block ActiveX controls	WIN 261	Click ⚙, point to Safety, click ActiveX Filtering to turn on
Internet Explorer, block content using Tracking Protection	WIN 260	Click ⚙, point to Safety, click Tracking Protection, click Your Personalized List, click Settings, click content provider, click Block, click OK, click Close
Internet Explorer, change settings using Pop-up Blocker	WIN 254	Display Web page, click ⚙, click Internet options, click Privacy tab, click Turn on Pop-up Blocker check box, click Settings, select Blocking level, click Close, click OK
Internet Explorer, delete browsing history in	WIN 257	Click ⚙, click Internet options, click General tab, click Delete in the Browsing history section, select options, click Delete, click OK
Internet Explorer, manage add-ons in	WIN 253	Click ⚙, click Manage add-ons

TASK	PAGE #	RECOMMENDED METHOD
Internet Explorer, select privacy settings in	WIN 255	*See* Reference box: Selecting Privacy Settings
Internet Explorer, start from desktop	WIN 180	Display the desktop, click
Internet Explorer, start from Start screen	WIN 166	Click the Internet Explorer tile on the Start screen
Internet Explorer, turn on SmartScreen Filter	WIN 245–246	Click , point to Safety, click Turn off SmartScreen Filter, click Turn on SmartScreen Filter, click OK
Internet search provider, add	WIN 317	*See* Reference box: Adding a Search Provider
Internet, search using search expression	WIN 313	Type search expression in the Address bar, press Enter
Jump list, pin file to	WIN 150	Right-click the taskbar button, point to file, click
Library, expand	WIN 33	In File Explorer, click
Library, open	WIN 31	In File Explorer, click a library In the Navigation pane
Lock screen, clear	WIN 4	Press any key
Mail, start	WIN 198	Click the Mail tile on the Start screen
Microsoft account, set up	WIN 265	Start Internet Explorer Desktop, type https://signup.live.com in the Address bar, press Enter, enter your email address and other required information, click I accept
Navigation bar, display in Internet Explorer Windows 8	WIN 172	Right-click the background of the Web page
Password, change	WIN 266–267	Display the Charms bar, click Settings button, click Change PC settings, click Users, click Change your password, enter old password, enter new password, reenter new password, click Next, click Finish
Password, create picture password	WIN 268–269	Display the Charms bar, click Settings button, click Change PC settings, click Users, click Create a picture password, enter your password, click OK, click Choose picture, navigate to and click a picture file, click Open, click Use this Picture, draw three gestures, repeat the gestures, click Finish
Password, create PIN	WIN 267–268	Display the Charms bar, click Settings button, click Change PC settings, click Users, click Create a PIN, enter password, click OK, enter PIN, reenter to confirm, click Finish
Peek, use	WIN 144–145	Click the far right side of the taskbar to minimize all of the open windows, point to the taskbar button to display thumbnails of opened files
Recycle Bin, view	WIN 11	Double-click Recycle Bin icon
Screen resolution, change	WIN 146–147	Right-click the desktop, click Screen resolution, click Resolution, drag the slider to the settings you want to use, click OK
Screen saver, activate	WIN 140–141	Open the Personalization window in the Control Panel, click the Screen Saver link, click Screen saver, click the screen saver you want to activate, click OK
Screen, capture	WIN 122	Display the screen you want to capture, press Print Screen
ScreenTip, display	WIN 24	Point to the object

TASK	PAGE #	RECOMMENDED METHOD
Search menu, display	WIN 9	Click Search charm on Charms bar
Search results, filter	WIN 293	See Reference box: Filtering Search Results
Search, save	WIN 297	Click Save search, enter a name for the search, click Save
Settings, search for	WIN 287	Display Start screen, type the name of the setting, click Settings
Shake, use	WIN 145	Open several windows on the desktop, point to the title bar of the window you want to keep open, hold down the mouse button and quickly drag the window about an inch to the right and left to shake it, minimizing all other open windows
Shortcut, change icon	WIN 110	Right-click the shortcut icon on the desktop, click Properties, click the Shortcut tab, click Change Icon, click the image you want for the shortcut icon, click OK, click OK
Shortcut, create custom	WIN 108–109	Right-click a blank area of the desktop, point to New, click Shortcut, type a command, click Next, type a name for the shortcut, click Finish
Shortcut menu, display	WIN 13	Right-click object
Shortcut, pin to Start screen	WIN 111	Right-click the shortcut icon on the desktop, click Pin to Start
Start screen, change background	WIN 119	See Reference box: Changing the Start Screen Background
Start screen, display	WIN 13	Press ⊞
Start screen, group tiles on	WIN 112	See Reference box: Grouping Tiles on the Start Screen
Start screen, scroll	WIN 7	Point to right or left edge, click right or left scroll arrow
Start screen, zoom in	WIN 7–8	Click ▬
Start screen, zoom out	WIN 8	Click zoomed Start screen
Tab switcher, display in Internet Explorer Windows 8	WIN 172	Right-click the background of the Web page
Tag, add to file	WIN 299	See Reference box: Adding Tags to Files
Taskbar button, move	WIN 151	Point to the taskbar button, drag it to the left or right, release the mouse button
Taskbar, set properties	WIN 151–152	Right-click a blank area on the taskbar, click Properties, select the check boxes for the properties you want to set, click OK
Text and objects, change size of	WIN 148	Open the Screen Resolution window, click Make text and other items larger or smaller, click the option button for the size you want, click Apply
Tile, remove from Start screen	WIN 116	Right-click the tile on the Start screen, click Unpin from Start
Tile, resize on Start screen	WIN 117	Right-click the tile on the Start screen you want to resize, click Smaller or Larger
Tile, turn on live	WIN 117–118	Click the app tile on the Start screen, drag to close the app, right-click same app tile, click Turn live tile on
Tiles, name group on Start screen	WIN 114–115	Display the Start screen, click ▬, right-click the group of tiles, click Name group, type a name for the group, click Name
Touch keyboard, adjust settings	WIN 13	Swipe to display Charms bar, click Settings charm, to Change PC settings, adjust settings
Touch keyboard, display	WIN A11	Tap a text box or another location where you want to enter text
Touchscreen, use gestures on	WIN A4	Tap, swipe, slide (or drag), pinch, rotate

TASK	PAGE #	RECOMMENDED METHOD
User account, change picture	WIN 121–122	Right-click the user icon on the Start screen, click Change account picture, click Browse, navigate to the location of the file, click the file to select it, click Choose image
User account, control access to	WIN 270	Open Control Panel, click User Accounts and Family Safety, click User Accounts, click Change User Account Control settings, drag slider to a setting, click OK
User account, create	WIN 263	See Reference box: Setting Up a User Account
View, change in a folder window	WIN 31	See Reference box: Changing the Icon View
Virus protection, update	WIN 233–234	Open Action Center, click Security, click Update now
Web page link, open on new tab in Internet Explorer Windows 8	WIN 182	Press and hold the Ctrl key and click the link on the Web page
Web page, check security level	WIN 250	Display Web page in Internet Explorer Desktop, click ⚙, click Internet options, click Security tab
Web page, go to next	WIN 172	Click ➡
Web page, open on new tab	WIN 173	Display the tab switcher, click New Tab, type URL in the Address bar, press Enter
Web page, open using URL	WIN 168	Type the URL in the Address bar, press Enter
Web page, pin to taskbar	WIN 189	Drag the Web page tab from Internet Explorer window to the taskbar
Web page, print	WIN 191	Click Print on the Command bar
Web page, return to previously viewed	WIN 171	Click ◀ or ▶
Web page, return to recent	WIN 172	Click ⬅
Web page, return using History list in Internet Explorer Desktop	WIN 184	Open Favorites Center, click History tab, click the day of the week, click the Web site link you want to return to
Web page, save	WIN 191	Click Page on the Command bar, click Save as, enter a name for the file in the File name text box, click Save as type and select a file type, click Save
Web site, pin to Start screen	WIN 174	Display tab switcher, click thumbnail, click ⊙, click Pin to Start, type the new of the web site, click Pin to Start
Windows 8 app, close	WIN 26	See Reference box: Closing an Application
Windows 8 app Information, search using Search menu	WIN 309	See Reference box: Searching for Information in Windows 8 Apps
Windows 8 app, pin to Start screen	WIN 101	See Reference box: Pinning an App to the Start Screen
Windows 8 app, snap	WIN 20	Right-click the app in Switch List, click Snap left (or Snap right)
Windows 8, log in	WIN 4	Click or type your user name, type password, press Enter
Windows 8, start	WIN 4	Turn on the computer
Windows 8, turn off	WIN 38–39	Display Charms bar, click Settings charms, click Power, click Shut down
Window, close	WIN 12	Click ✕
Windows Defender, perform a quick scan with	WIN 236	See Reference box: Performing a Quick Scan with Windows Defender

TASK	PAGE #	RECOMMENDED METHOD
Windows Defender, set up	WIN 239–240	Start Windows Defender, click Settings tab, select options, click Save changes
Windows Defender, start	WIN 236	Display Start screen, type Windows Defender, click Windows Defender
Windows Firewall, add app to allowed list	WIN 229	Open Action Center, click System and Security in the Address bar, click Windows Firewall, click Allow an app or feature through Windows Firewall, click Change settings, click apps and features you want to allow, click OK
Windows Firewall, turn on	WIN 229	Open Action Center, click System and Security in the Address bar, click Windows Firewall, click Turn Windows Firewall on or off, click Turn on Windows Firewall for private or public network, click OK
Window, maximize	WIN 22	Click ☐
Window, minimize	WIN 22	Click ▬
Window, move	WIN 23	Drag the title bar
Window, resize	WIN 23–24	Drag an edge or corner of the window
Window, restore down	WIN 18	Click ❐
Windows Update, set up	WIN 231–232	Open the Control Panel, click System and Security, click Windows Update, click Change settings, click Install updates automatically (recommended), click Updates will be automatically installed during the maintenance window, select time, click the Allow scheduled maintenance to wake up my computer at the scheduled time check box, click OK, click OK
Windows, arrange with Snap	WIN 143	Open and arrange two windows so that you can see parts of each, drag the title bar of one of the windows to the left of the desktop and release the mouse button, drag the title bar of the other window to the right of the desktop and release the mouse button